RANCH VACATIONS

Gene Kilgore's RANCH VACATIONS

THIRD EDITION

The Complete Guide to Guest and Resort, Fly-Fishing, and Cross-Country Skiing Ranches

John Muir Publications
Santa Fe, New Mexico

The information in this book is subject to change without notice. We strongly recommend that you call ahead to verify the information presented here before making final plans or reservations. The author and publisher make no representation that this book is absolutely accurate or complete. Errors and omissions, whether tyopgraphical, clerical, or otherwise, may sometimes occur herein. All ranches are included without charge to them. The ranches that have photographs have paid a fee to help defray the cost of publication.

John Muir Publications, P.O. Box 613, Santa Fe, New Mexico 87504

Printed in the United States of America

Third edition. First printing March 1994

Library of Congress Cataloging-in-Publication Data
Kilgore, Eugene, 1953-
Ranch vacations : the complete guide to guest and resort, fly-fishing, and cross-country skiing ranches / by Gene Kilgore. — 3rd ed.
p. cm.
Includes index.
ISBN 1-56261-143-7 : $19.95
1. Resorts—United States—Guidebooks. 2. Resorts—Canada, Western—Guidebooks. 3. Dude ranches—United States—Guidebooks. 4. Dude ranches—Canada, Western—Guidebooks. 5. Fly fishing—United States—Guidebooks. 6. Fly fishing—Canada, Western—Guidebooks. 7. Cross-country skiing—United States—Guidebooks. 8. Cross-country skiing—Canada, Western—Guidebooks. I. Title.
TX907.2.K55 1994
9796.5'0973—dc20 93-32359
CIP

Typeface: Berkeley Oldstyle
Typesetter: Copygraphics
Printer: Quebecor Printing Semline Inc.

Cover photo of Lost Creek Ranch by Latham Jenkins, First Light Photography
Back cover photo by Jim Elder

Distributed to the book trade by
W. W. Norton & Co., Inc.
New York, New York

Dedicated to my parents,
Eugene and Mimi, my sister, Bee, and
my one and only Regina, with all my love

"You can get in a car to see what man has created, but you have to get on a horse to see what God has made."

—C. M. Russell

"Thousands of tired, nerve-shaken, over-civilized people are beginning to find out that going to the mountains is going home; that wilderness is a necessity; and that mountain parks and reservations are useful, not only as fountains of lumber and irrigation rivers but as fountains of life."

—John Muir

"From the forest and wilderness come the tonics and barks which brace mankind."

—Henry David Thoreau

"All America lies at the end of the wilderness road, and our past is not a dead past, but still lives in us. Our forefathers had civilization inside themselves, the wild outside. We live in the civilization they created, but within us the wilderness still lingers. What they dreamed, we live, and what they lived, we dream."

—T. K. Whipple

"Our world in steel and speed is sometimes a trap in which we become enslaved as we chase after the materialism of life. Thus, we have a tendency to forget that which we too often take for granted—Nature's wondrous beauty."

—Bruce Harvey,
Queenstown, New Zealand

"Of all the teachings we receive this one is the most important. Nothing belongs to you. Of what there is, of what you take, you must share."

—Sioux Teaching

"The Earth does not belong to man, man belongs to the Earth. All things are connected like blood which unites us all. Man did not weave the web of life, he is merely a strand in it. Whatever he does to the web, he does to himself."

—Chief Sealth (Seattle),
Suquamish Indian Tribe

WHAT RANCHERS ARE SAYING

"I want to express my overwhelming appreciation for all your efforts. Keep up the good work. You are the authority in this field." K.J., Colorado

"We stand in awe! You're like having all the railroads rolled into one and then accomplishing even more. You have worked marvels. Your book is done with such care, such insight, and with the knack, it would seem, of leading potential guests to the ranch that will be right. You've managed to lift awareness of dude ranching in the midst of all sorts of other vacation opportunities right to the top. And once that awareness takes hold, your book leads each person in the right direction. It's as if a friend were advising each person as to the place that would suit him best. We appreciate you very, very much." J.M., Arizona

"I can only try and explain the degree to which your involvement and dedication to the Ways of the West and to those of us who share our hospitality has furthered our commitment to our purpose. Thank you." R.S., Wyoming

"You and Ranch Vacations *provide the key—the connecting link to the Western experience which people are seeking."* W.S., Wyoming

"Thank you for all you are doing for the ranching industry." D.T., New York

"I appreciate your sincere, professional approach to marketing an industry you enjoy. Your love of dude ranching is reflected in your productions." D.A., Montana

WHAT READERS ARE SAYING

"I love your book! I am so glad that you've taken the time to write such a comprehensive book about what I love so much—dude ranches!" H.W., California

"An excellent publication." M.B., Australia

"If you are a fan of ranch life, Gene Kilgore's woven tapestries of discerning descriptions and available services form an indispensable guidebook on this thrilling subject of Americana." J.N., California

"Ranch Vacations *arrived today. It's just terrific! I loved the foreword and find its organization so helpful. Congratulations on a great job."* D.O., California

"I recently purchased your book on ranch vacations and have read it cover to cover. Excellent!!" D.S., New Jersey

"I have enjoyed your publication and only wish that more families would experience the pleasures of guest ranching." R.G., Georgia

"I have recently purchased your book and am captivated by it!" L.G., Maryland

"I was asked to choose a location for a small working meeting (50-60 participants). . . . A friend gave me your guest ranch guide, and it was indeed a boon! We are now in the process of making a final decision, and I wanted to write and thank you for the help your guide provided." L.D., California

Contents

Forewords

> *While it may be comforting to imagine a life free of stresses and strains in a carefree world, this will remain an idle dream. . . . Man could escape danger only by renouncing adventure, by abandoning that which has given to the human condition its unique character and genius among the rest of living things. Since the days of the cave man, the earth has never been a Garden of Eden, but a Valley of Decision where resilience is essential to survival.* ***The earth is not a resting place.*** *Man has elected to fight, not necessarily for himself, but for a process of emotional, intellectual, and ethical growth that goes on forever. To grow in the midst of dangers is the fate of the human race, because it is the law of the spirit.*
>
> —René Dubos

I started this on Sunday, half an hour past noon, beside a mountain stream on the first day of August. To the north, the Wyoming Range with late patches of snow on its peaks and ridges, which even now with our cold, wet spring and summer turn the stream roiling and fast. There are no cars, no overhead planes, no crowds of people, and none of the man-made noises we associate with progress. The only sounds are the rustle of a breeze in the willow and the gurgling of the stream.

Since your last edition, Russia has collapsed, Eastern Europe struggles in blood of survival, and Africa and parts of Asia fight to rid themselves of dictators molded to serve our interests during the cold war.

In our own country, the high living on the backs of future generations is coming to some sort of an end. Many politicians struggle to preserve their vested interests while calling on those they represent to sacrifice. Instant solutions are sought for chronic problems in the nation's economy as well as in medicine.

The end of the cold war and giant strides in communications have combined to fill our TV screens with the signs and symptoms of massive national and cultural shake-outs throughout the world. News is downloaded from myriad databases fed by thousands of reporters hungry for high drama, analysts, experts whose past experience may not be all that relevant to present crises, and pseudo-experts who, in their ignorance of history, want to throw it out and remake the world in their own narrow, superficial image.

Is it any wonder that anxiety and depression are pandemic in our country? Yet, the adventure of living, so aptly defined by Dubos, remains true—even truer today than a few years ago when big power hegemony exerted its control over states. Today, politicians are losing credibility around the world, and individual responsibility and initiatives become more important than ever. If politicians, banks, the Feds, the FBI, and many of our schools are seen as lacking in wisdom to deal with today's challenges, individuals can still make a difference if they have time to think, to read, and above all to reflect.

As you know, we are lucky to live in a place where nature's majesty is at our door. Where "to get away" is a ten-minute walk or a twenty-minute drive to an isolated trout stream or a stand of spruce and aspen. We are lucky enough to live in a mountain valley at 7,000 feet where the sky reflects the weather and not pollutants.

Today, more than ever, the greatest need for thinking men and women is time for re-creation and reflection. I have often written a prescription, "Get dog and walk him in the hills." And yet, the most difficult acquisitions today are time and place to reflect, to review the goals of life, and, as we get older, to review what we will leave behind.

Your new edition is a prescription to "get away," to renew in beautiful settings, among people who care, the real values of life. Among the vacation ranches in your book are those that serve gourmet food and specialize in exciting and varied recreational activities. There are others where isolation encourages reflection among the wildflowers and mountain brooks where the sand-hill cranes dance and the sun sets to the yip-yippings of a coyote mother and her pups. For me, the ranches in your book are special places. They can help preserve our sanity and become the seed beds of creative reflection and positive thinking so often hammered out of life by the cacophony that surrounds us and the frantic speed of modern living.

Congratulations on the third edition. I am sure that because it meets a real need, it will be as successful as your previous editions.

Big Piney, Wyoming — William T. Close, M.D.

Out where the hand clasp's a little stronger
Out where the smile dwells a little longer
That's where the West begins;

Where there's more of singing and less of sighing;
Where there's more of giving and less of buying,
And a man makes friends without half trying—
That's where the West begins.

—Arthur Chapman (1915)

To stipple through the sage on a fine mount in May, with a bank of rocky mountains at your side, is to remember that the land is not just where we live but how we gain perspective on the outside world we came from. All the better if it's raining, as the scent of thirsty herbs can overwhelm. This is where the West begins.

As a painter, I have the opportunity to visit the great cattle ranches. I am often invited to ride out at dawn and make a circle. It allows me to view ranch life and the working cowboy with scrutiny and admiration. This culture of the West is enjoying real revival. With the advent of the Cowboy Poetry Gathering in Elko, Nevada, there has been a great deal of attention both here and abroad. As Americans, we can take enormous pride in the depth and originality of our cowboy culture.

As the world is closing in around us and electronic gadgets intercept the spoken word, we yearn to be reminded of the big sky and wide-open space. For those who have never ridden through timber in Montana, the West is an attainable dream. And it's a state of mind.

Since 1879, when Howard Eaton accepted "a little money each week" from an Eastern friend for the privilege of bunking down at headquarters, guest ranches have hosted many of the uninitiated. They have ridden and fished, hiked and dined, and enjoyed the best the West has to offer. Thousands return each year and wouldn't consider their summers complete without time spent around a campfire.

The cornerstone of most of these ranches is the stable and their string of horses. Great pride is taken in outfitting each rider with the appropriate pony to fit his or her ability. There are organized activities and time to be alone, trail rides and bike rides, cookouts and dances. Some have swimming pools, tennis courts, and even a golf course or two.

You are holding the bible of ranch vacation guides. I applaud Mr. Kilgore and his undying effort to update and honestly assess the changing landscape of these ranches. Peruse this volume, dream about the future, and enjoy our West. You will always return with a clearer vision of life back home.

Evergreen, Colorado — William Matthews

Preface

This guide will open your eyes to a world of unforgettable pleasure, wholesome fun, and natural beauty. It will put you in touch with beautiful properties in North America as well as the top western museums around the country and annual western events in the United States and Canada. After you have taken this guide home and wandered through it, I guarantee that you will pause, wondering how something so unbelievably special has been kept such a secret. Ranch vacations today offer more than horseback riding and cattle drives. In fact, you don't even have to like horses or horseback riding. On a ranch vacation today, you can even indulge in gourmet dining, tennis, swimming, white-water rafting, natural history seminars, helicopter fishing, massage, and more. Although, quite simply, what makes ranch vacations so special is their simplicity and wholesome, unforgettable pleasures in nature. And everyone from grandparents to children to singles to the handicapped can find a ranch vacation to suit them. Ranches offer facilities to professional groups, corporations, schools, and churches for seminars, retreats, and workshops. And they can provide beautiful settings for family reunions, weddings, and honeymoons.

I began researching this guidebook in 1979, while I was working as a cowboy for one of the largest cattle operations in the country, Miller Land and Livestock, which is about 75 miles south of Jackson Hole, Wyoming. I undertook this exciting project to share with people around the world a truly magnificent way of life.

Today, more than ever, people are seeking relief from the ever-increasing stresses of our fast-paced world. There is no better way for families and individuals to unwind, recharge batteries, gain perspective, reconfirm values, spend time with family members, meet interesting people from around the world, and, most of all, experience the natural beauty and tranquillity of the outdoors than on a ranch vacation. As we approach the year 2000, I believe there will continue to be a reawakening to our great North American wilderness heritage.

John Naisbitt, author of the best-selling book *Megatrends*, puts it this way: "To counter a world going mad with technology, man will seek high touch environments to counter the hard edges of technology." What he seems to be saying is that the more advanced we become technologically, the more we crave the simpler pleasures of life. Nature, home-cooked meals, kindness, and hospitality are just a few things that we and our loved ones want, for ourselves and for each other. The vacations described in this book offer all of the above and so much more. This guide is not the last word, nor is it a history of ranch vacations. It is merely a friendly vehicle to put you in touch with a wonderful, unique group of people who offer an incredible experience. Some call it a way of life; all say it is a vacation filled with pleasure, to be enjoyed by both the young and the young at heart.

Ranch vacations offer the greatest year-round vacation opportunity in the world today. Welcome to Kilgore's ranch country. Ride on, pardner!

Third Edition Thoughts

Welcome to the new and exciting third edition of *Ranch Vacations*. It has been completely revised and updated. There are more ranches and beautiful photographs. Better than ever, it will put you in touch with the best in ranch country.

In this third edition, we have the contributions of two brilliant gentlemen, William T. Close and William Matthews. Both have written a foreword. Both know and cherish ranch country. I'd like you to know something about them.

William Close is one of the most distinguished physicians and thinkers in the world. Today, he and his wife live just outside the little town of Big Piney, Wyoming. It is here that he practices medicine, writes, and reflects. Dr. Close has traveled the world. Many years ago he trained with my father in surgery at Roosevelt Hospital in New York City. A cherished friend and adviser, he helped me get my first job cowboying on one of the largest cattle ranches in the country. Dr. Close offers words of wisdom.

William Matthews is recognized as one of America's leading painters. In his rural Colorado studio, he brings to life the world of cowboys and ranches like no other artist alive today. As Matthews says, "I want my paintings to weather longer than the obvious stories." Mark my words, they will. It is his sensitivity to life, people, and culture that makes this man so great. An old family friend, yet a new friend of mine, I am delighted that he has shared his artistic perspective on ranch country. If you would like to see his magnificent paintings, contact the William Matthews Gallery in Denver, Colorado.

Since the second edition was released in 1991, I have been traveling across the United States and abroad. I have had the opportunity to be a guest on numerous television and radio shows, including CNN's "Living in the 90s," "Live with Regis and Kathy Lee," and "Voice of America Radio." I was asked to speak for the Department of Commerce-United States Travel and Tourism Administration in Paris, France, and at the World Congress for the American Society of Travel Agents. In the years to come, I look forward to more opportunities to speak and share the ranch country story around the world.

Here's wishing you and yours many happy trails. May your campfire burn bright and your coffee always be hot.

Ride on, pardner!

Acknowledgments

There are so many special folks who have helped me to make this book and my work the success it is. It is impossible to mention everyone.

To all of you, family, friends, ranchers, television and radio producers, newspaper and magazine writers, business associates, state and government agencies, along with my wonderful associates here in Tahoe and around the world who continue to assist me and keep me on the trail, I say thank you! Without your help, support, and enthusiasm, none of this would be possible. My extra special thanks to Sharon Peterson who has typed all three manuscripts with a smile, most of the time, Janice Hans, who oversees all my office and publishing activities with a smile, all of the time, and my publisher, John Muir Publications.

With all of you, I share this special message from one of my ranchers:

Kindness in words
Creates confidence

Kindness in thinking
Creates profoundness

Kindness in giving
Creates love

—Rankin Ranch,
California

The Kilgore Ranch Real Estate Network and Consulting

A Division of the Kilgore Ranch Company

The Kilgore Ranch Company specializes exclusively in ranch and wilderness lodge properties.

In recognition of the challenges qualified buyers face locating suitable ranch and wilderness lodge properties, the Kilgore Ranch Real Estate Network was established. This exclusive network selectively refers buyers to ranch and wilderness lodge owners and/or the brokers who represent them.

In addition, we offer consulting services in the areas of guest ranch development, public relations, and marketing. Because of our knowledge of the industry we are able to put buyers and new owners in touch with industry experts in the areas of brochure development, ranch management, and key media and travel people as well as individuals who develop top fly-fishing streams or leading log construction experts, just to name a few. This saves buyers and new ranch owners time and costly mistakes.

If you are seriously interested in the guest ranch/wilderness lodge business and would like information about our services, please call 916-583-6926 or fax 916-583-6900, or drop us a letter with your name, address, and telephone and fax numbers. Please indicate your interests.

Kilgore Ranch Real Estate Network
P.O. Box 1919
Tahoe City, CA 96145
Ranch Country, U.S.A.

Kilgore Ranch Travel Company

The Most Specialized Ranch Travel Service in the World

Ranch Vacations provides detailed information to put you directly in touch with ranches throughout North America. I encourage you to read and study the book. If after doing so, you still would like our assistance, please call us.

Since 1990, our office has been contacted by people (singles, families, groups, and corporations) who have read *Ranch Vacations* but still want help. They either cannot make up their minds or want someone else to make all their travel arrangements to ranch country.

To continue to provide the very best service to those of you who wish assistance, we have established the Kilgore Ranch Travel Service, which offers custom travel and consulting to ranch country. If you would like information about this service, please telephone:

U.S. only: 1-800-4-RANCHS (1-800-472-6247)
International calls: (916) 939-1009, ask for Operator 74
To send a fax inquiry: (916) 939-1010, Attention: Kilgore Ranch Travel

When you call or fax, please provide the following information:

Name

Address

Telephone number

Fax number

Where you wish to travel (state/province)

Month you wish to travel

Type of ranch vacation desired

Resort ranch

Guest/Dude ranch

Fly-fishing ranch

Cross-country skiing ranch

Working cattle ranch

Cattle drives

After you have provided this information, one of our associates will contact you.

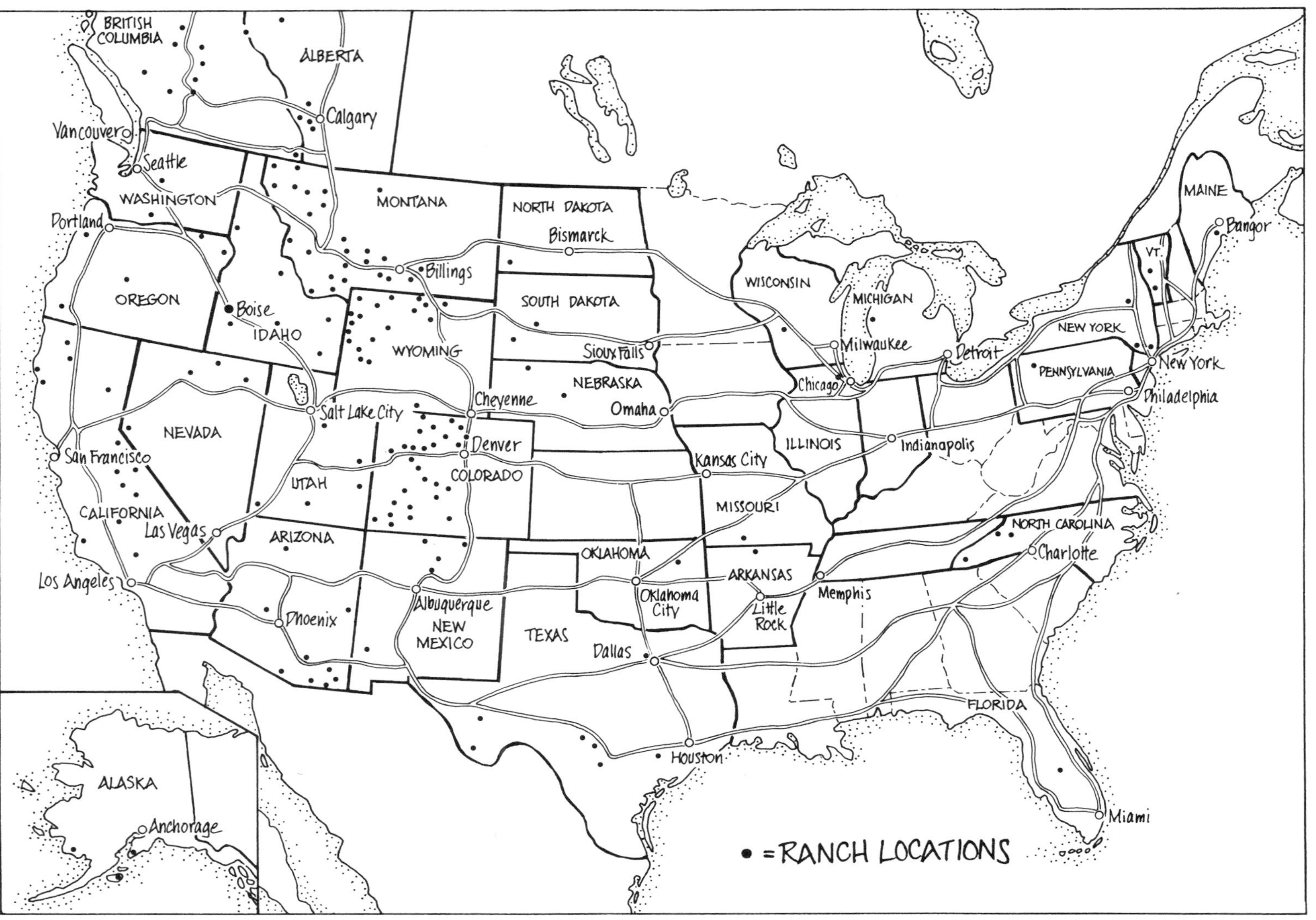
BRITISH COLUMBIA
ALBERTA
Calgary
Vancouver
Seattle
WASHINGTON
Portland
OREGON
Boise
IDAHO
MONTANA
Billings
NORTH DAKOTA
Bismarck
SOUTH DAKOTA
WYOMING
Sioux Falls
NEBRASKA
Omaha
Cheyenne
Salt Lake City
NEVADA
San Francisco
CALIFORNIA
Las Vegas
Los Angeles
UTAH
Denver
COLORADO
ARIZONA
Phoenix
Albuquerque
NEW MEXICO
TEXAS
Dallas
Houston
OKLAHOMA
Oklahoma City
Kansas City
MISSOURI
ARKANSAS
Little Rock
Memphis
ILLINOIS
Indianapolis
WISCONSIN
MICHIGAN
Milwaukee
Chicago
Detroit
NEW YORK
PENNSYLVANIA
New York
Philadelphia
VT.
MAINE
Bangor
NORTH CAROLINA
Charlotte
FLORIDA
Miami
ALASKA
Anchorage
• = RANCH LOCATIONS

Introduction

The Wild West, cowboys, Indians, horses, and cattle have been in my blood since I was about five years old. The cowboy's rugged independence, his rough-and-tumble lifestyle, and the wide open spaces of the West still capture our imaginations and conjure up images that hold a special place in all our hearts. "Cowboy" is hot, and ranches are in. Every year, millions of Americans, Canadians, Europeans, and visitors from around the world trade in their city shoes for a pair of cowboy boots to experience this unique way of life.

One of the most remarkable things about a ranch vacation is the lasting impression it makes, especially on children. One of the things I say is, "Take your children to the beach for a week and ask them ten years later the name of it; they will have forgotten. Take them to a ranch, and they will remember its name and maybe even the names of their horses for the rest of their lives." And that's the truth!

The history of ranch vacations can be traced to the days of Theodore Roosevelt's Rough Riders in the late nineteenth century. As the story goes, the Eaton Brothers—Howard, Willis, and Alden—established a hay and horse ranch near Medora, North Dakota, in 1879. Soon, friends from the East headed West by train to be a part of the Eatons' new and exciting life. Before they knew it, the Eatons were baby-sitting these big-city dudes, taking them out to help with the chores and cattle. The more the dudes did and the dirtier they became, the happier they were.

Word spread to more of the three-piece-suited, high-heeled tenderfeet, who came out and fell in love with the rugged simplicity of the West and all it gave them. In those days, visitors came by train, not for a week but for months at a time. One guest was so at home on the range that he asked Howard Eaton if he could pay room and board in order to stay on. This exchange of money gave birth to an industry.

The Eaton brothers realized the potential in dude ranching and hosting visitors with varying backgrounds and interests. In 1904, they moved their operation from the flatlands of North Dakota to the mountains of Wolf, Wyoming. Today, the Eaton Ranch is run by third and fourth generations of the family.

Soon, other ranchers got into the act. In 1926, the Dude Ranchers' Association held its first meeting. This association is more active today than ever. In 1934, a group of Colorado ranches formed their own Colorado Dude & Guest Ranch Association. In 1989, ranches in British Columbia, Canada, started the British Columbia Guest Ranch Association. All three groups (not to mention all the first-rate fly-fishing, cross-country skiing, hunting, and outfitting organizations) are dedicated to preserving and maintaining high standards in the guest ranching industry.

In general, the underlying theme of today's ranch vacation is the horse. Most of the properties included in this guide provide a variety of riding opportunities—from beginners to advanced riders. Every ranch property is different, however, expressing the personality of the terrain as well as that of the host or owner. Riders and nonriders alike enjoy these vacations.

Today, while most of the properties are preserving the old West, many are keeping up with the present by offering modern amenities and services. Besides horseback riding programs, many offer swimming, mountain biking, fishing, hiking, rodeos, tennis, skeet shooting, hayrides, and even ballooning. Many realize the importance and enjoyment of learning and have incorporated naturalist talks and art and photography workshops.

A ranch vacation also enables parents to vacation with their children. Both learn an appreciation for animals and nature. In addition, on a ranch vacation, people from all walks of life and of all ages can interact socially, intellectually, and artistically in a marvelously wholesome, intimate, and unique atmosphere.

Accommodations range from very rustic cabins (even sleeping under the stars) to plush, modern suites. Some have natural hot-spring pools, golf, and tennis; others feature whirlpool spas, saunas, exercise equipment, and even massage.

Ranches that take guests include guest ranches, resort ranches, working cattle ranches, fly-fishing ranches, hunting ranches, and cross-country skiing ranches. They can be found throughout the United States and Canada. Most are in the western United States (Colorado, Wyoming, Montana, Idaho, California, and Oregon), the Southwest (Arizona and New Mexico), the South (Florida and North Carolina), Texas, and New York State. In Canada, the majority are in the provinces of British Columbia and Alberta.

Ranches in the Southwest and Southeast will have different weather and landscapes from those in the Northwest. Native ranch customs, architecture, equipment, and clothes will vary, too. If you want to see adobe buildings and mesquite and enjoy arid, warm temperatures, there is a property in this guide for you. If the sawtoothed Rocky Mountains are more to your liking, you can experience that, too. Each region offers different attractions and activities. While the location and climate vary, one thing remains the same—down-home hospitality.

On Being a Good Dude

The term "dude" goes way back. Lawrence B. Smith, in his book *Dude Ranches and Ponies*, wrote, "Dude was applied to an outsider, city person, or tenderfoot; one who came from another element of society and locality; in short, a stranger as far as the West and its ways were concerned. As dude was applied to a male, so the word dudeen later was made to fit the female, and the business of catering to them was called dude ranching."

If you feel uncomfortable being referred to as a "dude," you might like to know that President Theodore Roosevelt was one of the first men to receive this name. It could be said that everyone is a dude when traveling in unfamiliar territory. Most ranchers and guests would agree that the key ingredients to being a great dude are a love and respect for nature, a willingness to listen and learn, patience, and understanding. One rancher summed it up by saying, "The perfect dude is one who sees beauty, savors nature's peace and quiet, has compassion for his or her fellowman, and has an understanding for what the host of the ranch must contend with each day to make the ranch holiday seem effortless."

The perfect dude takes it easy the first two days at the ranch and works slowly into the program. "Relax, unwind, don't push too hard too fast," said one rancher to a young options broker from Wall Street. He added, "Remember, you will be able to come back year after year for the rest of your life." Most of all, the ability to relax and have fun is essential to being the perfect dude.

Selecting a Ranch

The ranches included in this guide offer a wide range of choices. The most challenging part of your vacation will be selecting where you want to go and what ranch to choose. As rates are in constant fluctuation, we have chosen to use the following daily rate code:

$=$0-$100 per person per day
$$=$100-$150
$$$=$150-$250
$$$$=$250-$300
$$$$$=$300 and up

For the most part, rates listed are American Plan with meals, lodging, and activities included. There are ranches that offer Modified American Plan and European Plan rates, and they have been noted. When you are confirming your reservation, it is recommended that you verify what the rates are and what exactly they include. The symbol • preceding the rate code indicates that the ranch offers travel agent commissions.

I recommend that you first turn to the color photographs at the center of the guide. Here you will quickly get a feel for some of the beautiful properties listed. After you have looked these over carefully, making notes along the way, mosey through the rest of the guide. If you have special interests, turn to the back to find a listing of special activities. After you have selected a few ranches, write or telephone those you are interested in. I suggest you telephone the ranches and lodges and speak personally with the owners or managers. You can get a pretty good feel for things on the telephone. Ask for a brochure and for the names of several past guests who you might be able to telephone. Call them and ask what sort of time they had, if they have children too, if they have any special considerations like yours. Perhaps the most important thing of all in ranch travel is chemistry between owner/manager/staff and you, their guest. If you still can't decide after all this, or if you want someone else to handle this anyway, call the Kilgore Ranch Travel Service at (800) 4-RANCHS (472-6247) or (916) 939-1009 (domestic and international calls) or send a fax to (916) 939-1010. An operator will ask you several important questions and take this information over the telephone. Then one of our associates will contact you personally.

Regardless of what you decide to do, below are some questions you might like to look over before you call the ranch or lodge.

Kilgore's Questions to Ask

- *What are your rates?*
- *Are your rates all-inclusive?*
- *Are there special rates for families, children, seniors, and corporations?*
- *Are there off-season rates?*
- *Besides state and local taxes, what do your rates not include? What is the tipping policy?* (Rates do not always include gratuities or all activities.)
- *If you are traveling with children, you might like to know the following: Children must be what age to ride?* (Today's insurance regulations may not allow very young children to ride alone.) *Is child care provided, and to what extent? Is this a child-oriented ranch?*
- *Is there a minimum length of stay?* (At some ranches you may stay just overnight; others have minimum stay requirements.)
- *Will the ranch cater to special diets?* (Some will do vegetarian, low salt, and low cholesterol menus.)
- *Will the ranch provide guest references?* (Usually never a problem. Most guests would love to share their experiences with you.)
- *Will you send a clothing/equipment list?* (Usually standard procedure.)
- *Does the ranch provide equipment?* (Fishing rods, tennis rackets, etc.)
- *Should we buy a fishing license before we arrive?*
- *What will the weather be like?*
- *Can we buy sundry items at the ranch?* (Not all ranches have stores on the premises.)
- *Do you provide airport, train, or bus pickup?* (Many ranches are happy to pick you up. There is often a nominal charge, however.)
- *Do you recommend rental cars?* (In most instances, once you arrive, you will not want to leave the ranch you have selected. However, you may decide you want flexibility and independence.)
- *Are laundry facilities available?* (Many ranches have laundry facilities; some will even do your laundry.)
- *Is liquor provided?* (Many ranches would like you to bring your own wine or liquor. If desired, you can pick these up on your way, or the ranch will pick them up for you with advance notice. Some ranches offer wine and beer, and a number have fully licensed bars and extensive wine lists.)
- *Are any foreign languages spoken?*
- *Are pets allowed?*
- *Are riding lessons available?*
- *What kind of a riding program does the ranch have? Is it meadow riding, or head to tail mountain trail riding? Is the program best suited for beginners, or are there opportunities for advanced riders too?*
- *Do you need your own cowboy boots, or is there a cowboy boot rental program?*
- *Do you get the same horse all week?*

- *Can you brush and saddle your own horse?*
- *Do the owners/managers take part in the riding program?*
- *How long are typical rides? If you are a medium or advanced rider, can you trot or lope? How many wranglers and guests go out on rides at a time?*
- *What is the altitude of the ranch?*
- *Are there wheelchair facilities?*
- *Is smoking permitted?*

Getting There

Whatever method of transportation you choose, it is a good idea to check with the ranch or lodge you have selected before you make travel plans. Your hosts will advise you about roads, major commercial airports, and private airstrips. Should you fly or take the train? They will also tell you whether they will pick you up.

Your vacation will be greatly enhanced if you make travel plans early. Give yourself plenty of time driving or between flights. A missed plane, lost baggage, or driving all night is not a good way to begin your ranch experience.

What to Wear

Clothing is an essential part of the ranch vacation experience. It is important to pack right and bring those clothes that will enable you to enjoy your western experience. One rule of thumb is to pack one-third of what you think you need.

One of the nice things about a ranch vacation is that you do not need a lot of clothes. A pair of boots, several pairs of jeans, a good cowboy belt with buckle, a cowboy hat, several shirts, and a warm jacket are just about all you will really need. Over the years, after hundreds of miles on horseback and thousands of miles in automobiles and airplanes, I know quality clothing is better than quantity. Well, I guess that goes for most everything in life.

Here are a few Kilgore clothing tips. Along with quality, think comfort. Invest in a good pair of boots and a cowboy hat. Make sure your boots are well worn before you arrive. You don't want blisters. Buy at least three pair of jeans and wash them at least four times using softener. This will make them much more comfortable and help to fade them a bit so you don't look quite so "fresh." Take along a warm jacket, a sweater, and even a vest. Early mornings and evenings can be cool.

Finally, when you are making your reservation, ask the ranch or lodge to send you a clothing list, which will help you when you are packing. And pardner, one last thing, don't forget a flashlight, some lip protection, and mosquito repellent.

If you feel overwhelmed, relax. The ranch or lodge you have selected will be more than happy to give you advice. Otherwise, you may write the Kilgore Ranch Company Store, P.O. Box 1919, Tahoe City, CA 96145. Or, you may call 1-800-4-RANCHS (472-6247) or (916) 939-1009 (international calls), or send a fax to (916) 939-1010. For a couple of dollars, we'll send you a catalog with first-rate cowboy gear (the real thing and the right stuff). You'll enjoy it, the clothing, and the products.

Definitions

British Columbia Guest Ranch Association (BCGRA): An association of Canadian ranches in the province of British Columbia, formed in 1989 to market ranch vacations throughout Canada and the United States. The association works closely with the British Columbia Department of Tourism.

Colorado Dude and Guest Ranch Association (CDGRA): An association founded in 1934, made up solely of Colorado ranch and ranch resort properties and dedicated to marketing and maintaining excellence in the Colorado guest ranch industry. Members meet annually.

Cross-Country Skiing Ranch: A ranch that offers cross-country skiing opportunities. Trails are normally groomed with specialized, professional equipment. Instruction, guide service, and equipment are usually available.

Day Ranch: A ranch or ranch setting (maybe even a western town) that offers travelers the opportunity to visit and enjoy the spirit of the Old West without providing overnight accommodations. Often there are horseback rides and full meal service available.

Dude: Any individual who is not in his or her natural environment. A business or pleasure traveler who is in another state or even a foreign country. Basically, a dude = you and me. We are all dudes in one way or another!

Dude/Guest Ranch: Usually a family owned and operated ranch with the primary objective of offering its guests a Western experience. Horseback riding is usually the main activity; hiking, fishing, and swimming are often included.

The Dude Ranchers' Association (DRA): An association of Western dude ranches, founded in 1926, dedicated to maintaining the quality and high standards of Western hospitality established by early ranches. Elected board members meet regularly with an annual general session. Each DRA ranch included in this guide has been designated as such.

Fly-Fishing Ranch: A facility offering an extensive fly-fishing program with instruction and guides. Some ranches/lodges have an on-premises tackle shop.

Hideaway Report: A privately published newsletter dedicated to the discovery of peaceful vacations and executive retreats for the sophisticated traveler. Author's Note: This monthly newsletter is highly esteemed by experts in the travel industry. All those properties that have been featured in the Hideaway Report are so noted under "Awards."

Gymkhana: A series of games or events on horseback.

Hunting Lodge: A facility that specializes in seasonal big game or bird hunting. Many of these lodges offer activities for nonhunting family members. Some provide full-service hunting and support facilities. Many have father-son programs.

Orvis Endorsed: Orvis, the internationally known fly-fishing company, realized there was a need to check out and endorse top-notch fishing lodges with first-rate guides. Today, Orvis-endorsed lodges are monitored by Orvis personnel. These lodges provide full and complete fly-fishing guide service. Each has its own fly-fishing tackle shop. Each Orvis-endorsed lodge in this book has been designated as such.

Pack Trip: An overnight, multiple day, week-long, or month-long trip on horseback. All supplies, including food, tents, and equipment, are carried by horses, mules, or sometimes even by llamas. Usually a magnificent wilderness experience.

Professional Rodeo Cowboys Association (PRCA): An association dedicated to promoting and setting the standards of the professional rodeo industry.

Resort Ranch: A facility that may or may not have a Western theme but does offer horseback riding. Usually the amenities are very upscale, with a range of activities offered. Some offer facilities with massage.

Rodeo: A cowboys' tournament or competition in which men and women compete in an arena involving livestock such as horses, steers, Brahma bulls, and barrel racing.

Wagon Trains: Original or restored covered wagons that transport participants on day or overnight trips so that they can experience the life of pioneers, explorers, and mountain men. (See Appendix for list of companies.)

Wilderness Lodge: In the heart of wilderness areas, these facilities offer a retreat from civilization. Generally, all supplies arrive by plane, boat, horse, or sometimes four-wheel-drive vehicle.

Wrangler: Originally a cowboy who was hired on at a guest ranch to wrangle horses and take dudes out on day and overnight rides. Today, a wrangler may be male or female, a college student or a cowboy. There is no telling what a wrangler's background might be. The important ingredient is that the wrangler is experienced with horses and patient and understanding with dudes.

WANTED

A Few Good Guests

You are about to begin one of your most exciting adventures: selecting the right ranch or lodge for you, your family, friends, your company, or your clients. This is not easy and so to begin I ask you first to sit back and relax. Maybe even put your feet up on your desk or sit down in your favorite chair in front of a blazing fire. My goal is to help you by putting you in touch with a wide variety of properties across North America. After you have looked at all the beautiful color and black and white photos, read about the ranches and lodges, and contact those that interest you. Unlike any other holiday experience that I know of, the secret to this one is chemistry. Just like a marriage, if the chemistry is good, the marriage is golden. If not, as an old cowboy told me, "Better saddle up and ride on."

So mosey through this guide, look at the beautiful color photographs, make a few notes, make some calls, ask questions, and—this is so important—*ask for references* (former guests who have enjoyed the ranch or lodge and whom you may call). You may have to do a little work, but just like a horseback ride, once you get in the saddle, all kinds of exciting things can happen.

ONE OF KILGORE'S FAVORITE RANCH SAYINGS

We have gentle horses for gentle people,
Spirited horses for spirited people,
And for people who don't like to ride,
we have horses that don't like to be ridden.

—Lake Mancos Ranch,
Colorado

Guest and Resort Ranches

Kachemak Bay Wilderness Lodge
China Poot Bay, Homer, Alaska

Mike and Diane McBride call on their special talents to enrich your vacation in North America's last great frontier—Alaska. Mike is a member of the prestigious Explorers Club and has more than twenty years of experience in Alaska's wilderness. He is a master guide, naturalist, licensed skipper, and former bush pilot. His wife and partner, Diane, has a background in biology and will help you understand the natural history of the region. Kachemak Bay Wilderness Lodge is a hideaway in Alaska's wilderness. It is a place for nature lovers, fishermen, photographers, and those seeking the quiet solitude of lush forests and untracked beaches. The lodge is nestled among the towering spruce of China Poot Bay. It commands a spectacular view of the surrounding mountain peaks, sea, seabird rookeries, and seal herds on sand bars. Kachemak Bay lies at the end of the famous Kenai Peninsula, one hundred air miles southwest of Anchorage, and is accessible only by seaplane or boat. You will see why so many world photographers come. Here the sea is at your feet and the forest at your back.

Address: P.O. Box 956 K, China Poot Bay, Homer, Alaska 99603
Telephone: (907) 235-8910; fax: (907) 235-8911
Airport: Homer
Location: 7 air miles east of Homer
Memberships: Explorers Club, Interpretive Naturalists, Audubon Society
Awards: Listed in *America's Best 100* as "America's best wilderness lodge," *Hideaway Report* Hideaway of the Year 1981
Medical: Homer South Peninsula Hospital, 15 miles; emergency helicopter service
Conference: 12
Guest Capacity: 12
Accommodations: Each of the four log cabins has its own wood-burning stove, electricity, homemade quilts, full modern bathrooms, and porch. The main lodge has a wonderful stone fireplace. Private outdoor hot tub and sod-roofed Finnish sauna are about fifty feet from the lodge.
Rates: $$$$. American Plan. Half-price for children; rates may vary for Chenik Camp (bear-viewing camp) and Mountain Lake Loon Song Camp for canoeing and hiking. Rates include floatplane transportation.
Credit Cards: None. Personal checks accepted.
Season: May to mid-November
Activities: The lodge is a naturalist's and fisherman's haven. Observe and photograph marine mammals, seabirds, nesting bald eagles, moose, bears, sea otters, and whales. Tide-pooling (29-foot tidal range), clams and mussels, fishing for trout, salmon, char, flounder, and halibut. Kayaking, canoeing, rowboating.
Children's Programs: Individualized program. Baby-sitting available.
Dining: Master chef; fresh seafood from the bay including Dungeness crab daily. Fine wine and beer served. Bring your own liquor.
Entertainment: Weekly natural history slide program, piano, guitar, accordion-playing host.
Summary: Without question, Mike and Diane McBride run one of the premiere wilderness lodges in the world. Besides a tremendous emphasis on personal service, both, along with their staff (all of whom have a special interest in and knowledge of the environment), offer a superb naturalist program. Mike is a member of the Explorers Club and is a master guide. Interpretive naturalists, photography workshop. Outreach Chenik Camp is an adjunct for observing brown bears near McNeil River Brown Bear Sanctuary.

See color photos, page 178

Northland Ranch Resort
Kodiak, Alaska

Northland Ranch is a low-key 31,000-acre working cattle ranch with spectacular horseback riding and tremendous fishing opportunities. It is located in the beautiful emerald green Kalsin Valley with the blue Pacific Ocean on one side and rugged mountains on the other sides. Omar Stratmar, along with his young son, Cody, and his small staff, share their ranch with people from all walks of life. The diversity of riding and fishing opportunities and the ranch's proximity to the Pacific Ocean are the drawing cards. Omar grew up in Colorado and is a teacher and rancher by profession. As a boy he dreamed of Alaska. Like many, his came true. As Omar says, "What we offer is scenery, wildlife, and friendly folks. If you are looking for fancy accommodations and high cuisine, this is definitely not for you. Our accommodations are very modest, but our Alaskan wilderness is a sportsman's/nature lover's paradise." Wait until you see the brilliant Alaskan sunsets.

Address: P.O. Box 2376K, Kodiak, Alaska 99615
Telephone: (907) 486-5578
Airport: Kodiak Airport, 24 miles
Location: 30 miles south of Kodiak at Chiniak-Pasagshak Y. (Both of these go through the ranch.)
Memberships: National Buffalo Association, Alaska Farmers and Stock Growers, Scotch Highland Breeders Association, Kodiak Chamber of Commerce, Kodiak Island Convention and Visitors Bureau, Alaska Visitors Association, Kodiak Soil and Water Conservation Service
Medical: Kodiak Island Hospital, 31 miles
Guest Capacity: 20
Accommodations: In 1992, Omar experienced a disastrous fire that took the main lodge and accommodations. Since then, with a triumphant effort, he has rebuilt and added attractive modular units. They are new, clean, and comfortable. Some have individual baths and carpeting. As Omar says, "There's more to come!"
Rates: • $-$$$. There are five different packages to choose from. All American Plan. Call for details. Ask about the ranch's package and week-long package with the eighth day free.
Credit Cards: Visa, MasterCard, American Express
Season: Year-round. Open by reservation in the winter.
Activities: The incredible Alaskan scenery, grasslands, mountains, and views of the Pacific make riding and fishing opportunities at Northland extra special! Riding is tailored to guests' abilities. One-hour to eight-hour rides. Rides tailored to least experienced rider in the group. Ask about Summit Lake, Cow Camp, Portage, and the Beach rides. Fishing for five species of salmon and two species of trout is a very big activity. Bring your own gear. Lots of wildlife, including eagles, birds, deer, fox, and occasional whale sightings. There is an active eagle nest 100 yards from the lodge each summer.
Children's Programs: None. Children welcome. Ages five and over ride on trails.
Dining: The ranch serves its own beef and buffalo and will cook your fresh catch. Hearty ranch meals and desserts. Everything is fresh. There is a full bar, and the restaurant is open to the public.
Entertainment: Team hay wagon rides, monthly rodeos (Omar is the stock contractor). The art of conversation thrives. Omar has a few bear stories.
Summary: This is a 31,000-acre cattle and horse ranch with spectacular Alaskan scenery and wonderful riding and fishing. The views, wildlife, and hospitality make up for modest accommodations. Lots to see and do. Best for independent travelers who do not like schedules but enjoy nature and a country atmosphere. Most guests stay four to seven nights.

See color photos, page 179

Circle Z Ranch
Patagonia, Arizona

The Circle Z Ranch nestles in a mountain valley at 4,000 feet surrounded by steep canyons, desert cactus, and dramatic hills. Unique to the ranch, and most unusual in southern Arizona, is a wonderful creek they call "Sonoita" which runs year-round and is bordered by century-old cottonwood trees. This was Apache country in the early days, and relics of the Spanish conquistadors are still found. Hollywood has been here, too, filming *Tom Horn* and *Young Riders*, to name a few. The Circle Z is romantic with its adobe buildings reflecting the Spanish influence and early West simplicity. Circle Z is run by delightful resident managers and has been owned since 1974 by Lucia Nash, who fell in love with it when brought here by her family as a child. Excellent horses and a great variety of trails coupled with delicious food and warm hospitality bring guests back year after year. Bird-watchers flock to the Circle Z to see some of the rarest species in the United States, such as the rose-throated becard and the thick-billed kingbird. Horses, birds, the comfortable pleasures of dude ranch life—you'll find them all at the Circle Z.

Address: P.O. Box 194, Dept. K, Patagonia, Arizona 85624
Telephone: (602) 287-2091; fax: (602) 394-2010 at Patagonia Library
Airport: Tucson. Private planes at Nogales International, 8 miles away.
Train: Amtrak in Tucson
Location: 60 miles south of Tucson, directly off Highway 82, 15 miles north of Mexican border
Memberships: Dude Ranchers' Association
Medical: Carondelet Holy Cross Hospital, 15 miles
Guest Capacity: 40
Accommodations: The accommodations are comfortable and attractive. There are seven adobe cottages containing 27 rooms with private baths and showers, many with Mexican tile, a variety of bed sizes, and colorful rugs on wooden floors. Electric blankets are available. All rooms, suites, and cottages have individually controlled heat and outside entrances onto porches or patios. Laundry facilities available.
Rates: $-$$. American Plan. Weekend and off-season rates available. Three-day minimum stay.
Credit Cards: None. Personal checks accepted.
Season: November to mid-May
Activities: Riding is the main activity, with twice-daily and many all-day rides on numerous trails such as Skyline, Squaw Gulch, and Bathtub Canyon across 6,000 acres of deeded ranchland, plus the contiguous Coronado National Forest. The emphasis is on maintaining the atmosphere of an old-time family ranch: riding instruction, hiking, swimming in an outdoor heated pool, an all-weather tennis court. Fishing and 18-hole championship golf courses nearby.
Children's Programs: Kids are the responsibility of their parents. Most children under 5 do not ride.
Dining: Meals are served in the dining room or on the patio of the main lodge. Varied fine-quality cuisine. Ranch specialties include mesquite-grilled steaks and mild Southwest dishes, home-baked breads, and desserts. Adobe cantina for adults has piano, game table, and large wooden deck for relaxing. BYOB. Children dine earlier in their own dining room.
Entertainment: Mostly rest and relaxation but occasional country music. Ranch has player piano with 100 tunes.
Summary: Riding is the main thing here. Great for people who enjoy nature and will not miss television and in-room telephones. Unstructured other than riding and meals. Most guests enjoy the "do what you like" spirit. Bird-watcher's paradise at ranch and at adjacent Nature Conservancy preserve. Nearby attractions also include mining and ghost towns, an artisan village, Spanish mission, and Mexican border town shopping. Spanish spoken.

See color photo, page 180

Elkhorn Ranch
Tucson, Arizona

The Miller's Elkhorn Ranch is old-time dude ranching at its best! At 3,700 feet, the ranch sits in a secluded mesquite-covered valley, surrounded by the picturesque Baboquivari Mountain Range, with canyons, rolling hills, and the open desert to the east. The ranch is small and informal, well out of the city, and with activities centering on the outdoors. It's a lovely part of the Southwest in all its variety. This is a riding ranch, and the Miller family has been operating it since 1945. Run now by third-generation family, the Elkhorn offers unexcelled riding and relaxed living for 32 guests. The ranch spirit encourages family group fun but offers lots of time to be alone if so desired. The cabins and ranch buildings are designed in the Southwestern architectural style. With 10,000 acres and over 100 horses, unlimited riding and hiking are assured. The less adventurous can relax by the pool or outside each cabin. Bring your camera and binoculars as the birds of Arizona are numerous.

Address: Sasabe Star Route 97 K, Tucson, Arizona 85736
Telephone: (602) 822-1040
Airport: Tucson
Location: 50 miles southwest of Tucson, off Route 286 between Mile Posts 25 and 26
Memberships: Dude Ranchers' Association
Medical: St. Mary's Hospital in Tucson, 50 miles
Guest Capacity: 32
Accommodations: Guests enjoy southwestern-style cabins that vary from one to two bedrooms, some with sitting rooms, all with private baths, electric heat, and open fireplaces. Cabins have tiled and cement floors with Mexican throw rugs, some original art. Daily maid service and nightly bed turn-down service.
Rates: $$. American Plan. Special rates for stays of three weeks or longer. One-week minimum stay in high season, four-day minimum stay in low season.
Credit Cards: None. Personal checks or traveler's checks accepted.
Season: Mid-November through April
Activities: Some of the best riding in the country. Each morning at breakfast, Charlie Miller meets with guests to discuss riding interests and options. As Charlie says, "If someone really wants to ride, we sure try and accommodate them." And he does! With more than 100 horses, all levels of guided riding are provided on desert or mountain trails. Lions' Hotel, Sycamore Canyon, and Mine Canyon are just a few of the favorites. Moonlight rides offered. Surfaced tennis court and kidney-shaped 50-foot heated swimming pool. Shuffleboard, table tennis, horseshoe pitching, and a pistol/rifle range (bring your own guns) are offered, as well as bird-watching and hiking.
Children's Programs: Kiddie wrangler. No special program. No baby-sitting, but nannies are welcome. Prefer children old enough to ride.
Dining: Delicious home-cooked meals served buffet-style in the long house or on the patio. Cookouts on the trail, picnics in the desert, and dinners cooked on the barbecue. BYOB in cabins only.
Entertainment: Rest and relaxation. Stargazing, bridge. You are pretty much on your own.
Summary: One of the nicest families in the business. Many repeat families, couples and singles. Newcomers always feel a part of the family. Superb desert and mountain riding program. Excellent ranch-raised horses and one of the best dude ranch riding programs in the country. Beginners can learn here, and the advanced rider can be challenged. Nearby: Arizona-Sonora Living Desert Museum, Kitt Peak Observatory, the Papago Reservation, and old Spanish missions of San Xavier and Tumacacori.

See color photos, page 181

Flying E Ranch
Wickenburg, Arizona

As one guest noted, "At the Flying E the stars wink shimmering in the night, pursuading me to stay where my heart feels right," and that's just the way it is. George and Vi Wellik discovered the Flying E Ranch from their private plane in April 1949. By 1952, they had become its absentee owners with a resident manager. In 1958, they moved to Wickenburg to manage the ranch themselves. Being guests over those years provided great insights into ranch management and how to keep guests happy. The ranch's guest capacity has increased from sixteen to thirty-two. Today, Vi and her staff get to know all the guests; special service is a trademark of the Flying E. The ranch sits on a mesa at 2,400 feet looking out to Vulture Peak. It is surrounded by 21,000 acres of rolling desert hills with endless trails to ride or roam and beautiful scenery in every direction. The days are warm, dry, and dust-free, averaging in the mid-70s, and the nights are brisk and starlit. The Flying E is one of the most beautifully kept (the grounds are immaculate) private ranches I have ever seen, serving registered guests only.

Mailing Address: Box EEE-Dept. K, Wickenburg, Arizona 85358
Telephone: (602) 684-2690; fax: (602) 684-5304
Airport: Phoenix
Location: 4 miles west of Wickenburg, off Wickenburg Way, 60 miles northwest of Phoenix
Memberships: Dude Ranchers' Association
Medical: Wickenburg Community Hospital, 5 miles
Guest Capacity: 32
Accommodations: Rooms are immaculate, comfortable, electrically heated, and delightfully western. All rooms have TV, private bath, air-conditioning, and electric blankets. All have refrigerators and bars. Ask about the family wigwam and private poolside units. The Ocotillo is really special!
Rates: • $$. American Plan. Children's rates available. Horseback riding is an extra charge. Two-night minimum stay. Four-night minimum stay during holidays.
Credit Cards: None. Cash or personal checks accepted.
Season: November to May
Activities: Very relaxed; do as much or as little as you wish. You will not be programmed every minute. Two-hour morning and two-hour afternoon horseback riding to places like Mt. Everett, Robbers Roost, and Yucca Flats. Beginner, intermediate, and advanced rides. Guests ride out among cattle from time to time. Instruction available. Breakfast cookouts, lunch rides, and chuck wagon feeds. Shuffleboard, basketball/volleyball, horseshoe pitching, rock hounding, and a lighted tennis court. Beautiful heated pool, hot spa, exercise room, and sauna. While many come to horseback ride, some prefer to experience the desert scenery on foot. Nearby: Eighteen-hole championship golf course at the Los Caballeros Golf Club, three miles away.
Children's Programs: Children are the responsibility of parents; no children's program.
Dining: Hearty and genuinely good food served family-style. Cocktail hour with hors d'oeuvres, BYOB.
Entertainment: Occasional "inner ranch" square dancing and "dudeos" (a dudes' rodeo), hay rides, TV, video, and piano in the spacious lounge with fireplace.
Summary: As Vi says, "The Flying E is a spirit." And so it is. All the ranch staff are dedicated to sincere, friendly service. Because of this, most of the families, couples, and singles who come are repeat guests or friends of former guests. Very relaxed atmosphere: you are not programmed every minute. The Flying E is a riding ranch. Ask about the New Year's Eve Flying E rendezvous. Nearby: the charming western town of Wickenburg with its outstanding museum, art galleries, and western stores; excellent golf at championship course.

See color photos, page 182

Grand Canyon Bar Ten Ranch
near St. George, Utah, in Arizona

The main lodge at the Bar Ten Ranch is eight miles from the rim of the Grand Canyon. From the modern sandstone brick lodge, one can see in the distance the grandeur of these fabled red cliffs. Since the late 1970s, the Bar Ten has been the launching and returning point for visitors to one of the wonders of the world. The history and excitement of the Grand Canyon and the Colorado River are yours at the Bar Ten Ranch, a 6,000-acre spread with 250 head of cattle. There are no telephones; urgent messages are delivered by two-way radio from town. Tony and Ruby Heaton's guests come from around the world to experience the Colorado River raft trips and helicopter tours of the canyon and three-day cattle drives. The Bar Ten is a wonderful weekend escape offering a unique combination of remoteness and modern comforts. One guest wrote, "You have created an experience that enriches the lives of your guests! The Bar Ten Ranch is an unforgettable experience!"

Address: P.O. Box 1465 K, St. George, Utah 84771
Telephone: (801) 628-4010/(800) 582-4139; fax: (801) 628-5124
Airport: McCarren, Las Vegas; direct charter flights available; dirt airstrip on ranch
Location: 80 miles south of St. George, Utah, 100 miles east of Las Vegas (4-hour drive, 1-hour flight; most guests fly)
Medical: Dixie Medical Center, St. George, Utah; Life Flight helicopter available
Conference: 60
Guest Capacity: 60
Accommodations: For the adventurous, there are several comfortable covered wagons on the hillside behind the main lodge with bathroom facilities nearby. Great for couples. Surrounded by manicured lawns and desert landscape, the two-story Bar Ten lodge has comfortable dormitory-style rooms with bunk beds. The ground level has a gift shop with T-shirts and souvenirs.
Rates: • $-$$. American Plan. Includes everything except airfare and raft trips. Call for package rates.
Credit Cards: Visa, MasterCard
Season: March through October
Activities: The Bar Ten Ranch is a wonderful base camp for a variety of activities and tour packages including three- and six-day Colorado River trips, three-day cattle drives, Grand Canyon scenic helicopter flights, and one or more days at the ranch, including horseback riding. Skeet shooting, horseshoes, hiking, basketball, volleyball, and other group activities.
Children's Programs: No specific programs. Children under 10 not advised. Children under 8 do not go on river trips.
Dining: Country breakfast, chuck wagon sandwich bar, Dutch oven dinners with potatoes, steaks, chicken, biscuits, and corn. BYOB.
Entertainment: The Bar Ten gang puts on a terrific patriotic show with singing, clogging, and fiddle playing, country songs with wranglers, and slide shows depicting the evolution of the Bar Ten. Usually the show ends with watermelon and mingling.
Summary: Remote ranch 8 miles from the rim of the Grand Canyon offering a great variety of outdoor adventures including scenic Grand Canyon helicopter tours, Colorado River rafting, and three-day cattle drives. Ranch airstrip.

Grapevine Canyon Ranch
Pearce, Arizona

Grapevine Canyon Ranch, a working cattle ranch as well as a guest ranch, lies in the heart of Apache country at a 5,000-foot elevation. The ranch buildings, nestled in groves of Arizona oak, manzanita, and mesquite trees, are almost invisible in this wooded canyon, with mountains forming a dramatic, three-sided backdrop. The ranch is owned and operated by Eve and Gerry Searle. Their philosophy can be summed up in two words: personal attention. Gerry, a longtime rancher, also spent many years in the movie industry, doubling stars in stunt riding, including every episode of "High Chaparral." Eve came to the United States from Melbourne, Australia, where she worked as a flight instructor. She has a cosmopolitan background, having lived in Europe, India, Australia, and Mexico before settling in Arizona. Grapevine is famous for its riding program of trail rides, seasonal cattle work, riding lessons, horseback games, and all-day adventure rides, for which riders and horses are transported to the trail head in the forest wilderness. Also history rides to abandoned ghost towns, Fort Bowie, and the Chiricahua National Monument. One European couple summed the ranch up best: "As children we dreamed it, as adults we have lived it at Grapevine Canyon Ranch."

Address: P.O. Box 302 K, Pearce, Arizona 85625
Telephone: (800) 245-9202; fax: (602) 826-3636
Airport: Tucson International
Location: 85 miles southeast of Tucson, off Interstate 10
Memberships: Dude Ranchers' Association
Medical: Benson Hospital, 40 miles
Conference: 25
Guest Capacity: 25
Accommodations: Six-hundred-square-foot casitas or pleasant single-room cabins. Each is air-cooled; all are quiet and individually decorated in delightful country style with a southwestern touch. Most are secluded in groves of Arizona oak. All are fully carpeted, equipped with full baths, coffee pots, stocked refrigerator, sun deck, and porch.
Rates: • $$$. American Plan. Group and off-season rates available. Four-night minimum stay during high season, two-night minimum stay during low season.
Credit Cards: Visa, MasterCard, Discover, American Express. Personal checks accepted.
Season: Year-round including Christmas, Thanksgiving, and Easter
Activities: Horseback riding is the most popular. Rides are small so riders with similar ability can ride together. Long and short rides, catering both to novice and experienced riders. For safety, a check-out ride to prove that you can handle a horse at speed is required before you can join the fast rides. Occasional cattle work. Beautifully curved swimming pool (heated April to October), Jacuzzi, dummy steer roping, darts, recreation room with pool table and Ping-Pong, interesting sightseeing, including Mexico and legendary Tombstone. Miles of hiking trails, over 90 species of birds, and a lake stocked with bass and catfish—the ranch will provide necessary equipment. Golf nearby (7 miles).
Children's Programs: No children under 12. The over 12s are treated as responsible adults and, provided they qualify, may help the wranglers with horses and ranch chores.
Dining: Hearty ranch breakfasts cooked to individual order. Lunch and dinner are served buffet-style in the Cook Shack dining room. Roast Cornish game hens, chimichangas, barbecued pork and beef ribs, steak and roast beef, rich homemade desserts and ice creams. Beer and wine available.
Entertainment: Video/TV room with film library, books, and magazines, occasional live country music.
Summary: Intimate family and corporate ranch retreat, with an international clientele. Emphasis is on quiet, personalized service, small group rides, some cattle work depending on riding ability, ghost town excursions, and just plain relaxation in the beautiful Arizona high country.

See color photos, pages 184-185

Kay El Bar
Wickenburg, Arizona

Operated by two sisters and their husbands, the Kay El Bar is mostly a riding ranch with lots of friendly Arizona country hospitality. Jan and Jane bought the ranch in 1980 after a lifetime love affair with dude ranches, starting when they were kids in Washington, D.C. This lovely old guest ranch is listed in the National Register of Historic Places. Its warm and friendly adobe buildings are situated on 60 acres, shaded by eucalyptus and salt cedar trees. Since the ranch was established in 1926, there has been an open door policy. Guests don't have to worry about losing room keys; there are none. One word of caution: when you arrive you may be greeted by Trouble, Biscuit, and Bear, three fiercely friendly golden retrievers, the unofficial greeters of Kay El Bar. The atmosphere here is very casual, and that is just what brings people back year after year.

Address: P.O. Box 2480 K, Wickenburg, Arizona 85358
Telephone: (602) 684-7593
Airport: Phoenix Sky Harbor, 60 miles; private planes, Wickenburg Airport, with a 5,050-foot airstrip, 5 miles
Location: 60 miles northwest of Phoenix off Route 89
Memberships: Dude Ranchers' Association
Medical: Hospital, 5 minutes away
Guest Capacity: 20
Accommodations: The main lodge consists of eight rooms with private baths, each room with hand-painted Monterey furniture, a large living room with 13-foot ceilings, comfortable furniture, a bar, books, and a huge stone fireplace. Homestead House, a two-bedroom, two-bath cottage with living room and fireplace completes the accommodations.
Rates: • $-$$. American Plan. Children's, monthly, and special group rates are available. Two-day stay minimum until mid-February, then 4-day minimum stay until beginning of May.
Credit Cards: Visa, MasterCard
Season: Mid-October through April
Activities: Scenic horseback riding through the Bradshaw Mountains with half-day (2 hours) and all-day rides. Heated swimming pool, hiking, bird-watching (over 150 species have been seen), and plenty of wildlife watching, including roadrunners, deer, javelinas, coyotes, and big jackrabbits. Golf at two fine golf courses and tennis nearby.
Children's Programs: Children are the responsibility of parents. Kids under 7 can ride only in the corral. Young children are not encouraged.
Dining: Announced by the dinner bell, excellent family-style meals provide a time to swap stories of the day. American, Mexican, and Chinese cuisine, unscheduled cookouts. Food is always good. Honor system at a fully stocked bar.
Entertainment: Card table, board games, lots of western movies on videotape, large library in main lodge. Most guests do their own thing in the evening.
Summary: Very cozy, casual atmosphere in a desert environment. Singles, couples, and families will feel at home. Very casual and not structured at all. Only scheduled activities are meals and riding. Historic Registry Ranch. Nearby: Desert Caballeros Museum, Joshua tree forest, old gold mines, Gold Rush Days each February, Blue Grass Festival in November, Cowboy Poetry gathering in December.

Lazy K Bar Guest Ranch
Tucson, Arizona

Just sixteen miles northwest of Tucson, the Lazy K Bar Guest Ranch nestles against the Tucson Mountains overlooking the Santa Cruz Valley. Owned by Rosemary Blowitz and son, Bill Scott, and managed by Carol Moore, the ranch is run on the "Arizona plan." That is, all facilities and entertainment are included in one nightly rate with a three-night minimum stay. The Lazy K Bar is a well-rounded vacation destination offering riding, swimming, tennis, hiking or relaxing—something for everyone in the family. Guests also enjoy the ranch's spacious library with numerous books and can meet before dinner at the ranch's Long Horn Bar for a cocktail. While there are no televisions or telephones in the rooms, there is a large-screen television in the main lodge. At the Lazy K Bar you will enjoy home cooking, a family atmosphere, and Arizona desert beauty.

Address: 8401 N. Scenic Drive, Dept. K, Tucson, Arizona 85743
Telephone: (602) 744-3050, (800) 321-7018
Airport: Tucson International, private airstrip nearby
Location: 16 miles northwest of Tucson off Silverbell Road. Call ranch for directions.
Memberships: Dude Ranchers' Association
Awards: AAA 2 Diamond
Medical: Northwest Hospital, 10 miles
Conference: 50
Guest Capacity: 65
Accommodations: The main lodge is the center for all social activities. Guests can stroll comfortably down the gravel paths from the lodge to single rooms and suites located in the nine adobe buildings. Each of the 23 rooms has individually controlled heat and air-conditioning, private baths, carpeting, and king, queen, or extra-long twin beds. Large family rooms are equipped with day beds or sofa beds. Southwestern motif. Laundry facilities available.
Rates: • $-$$. American Plan. Rates depend on season and size of cottage. Children's rates. Minimum three-night stay. Trap shooting, tennis lessons, riding lessons, and massage available at additional charge. Riding excursions off-premises may be booked at additional charge.
Credit Cards: Visa, MasterCard, American Express, Discover. Personal checks accepted.
Season: September through mid-June
Activities: Horseback riding through mountain and desert country. Two rides (slow and fast) twice a day. Weekly breakfast or lunch rides go into Saguaro National Monument West. Small groups may make private arrangements to van out to surrounding mountain ranges for riding excursions. No riding on Sundays. Heated pool, two lighted tennis courts, Jacuzzi, volleyball, horseshoe pitching, trap shooting, shuffleboard, and basketball. Recreation room with billiards, Ping-Pong, and shuffleboard table. Excellent golf in Tucson, 20 minutes away.
Children's Programs: No special program. Kids under 6 ride with supervision in arena. Babysitting can be arranged at an hourly rate. Kids are the responsibility of their parents.
Dining: Hearty ranch-style meals served in lodge dining area. On Saturday night T-bone steaks are mesquite broiled and served under the stars next to the ranch's 10-foot waterfall. Breakfast cooked to order, luncheon buffets, many great Mexican dishes. BYOB.
Entertainment: Nature talks, team-drawn hayrides, square dancing, western music, country/western dance lessons, TV room for viewing special programs, rodeos in town. Team roping, calf roping, and barrel racing exhibitions. Tucson evening entertainment within a 20-minute drive.
Summary: Casual, relaxed ranch. Riding program geared to individual ability with opportunities to increase your horse knowledge. Ranch is great for those who enjoy outdoor activities or just relaxing in the fresh Arizona sunshine. A haven for bird-watchers. Sunday excursions to the Sonoran Desert Museum or Old Tucson Movie Studio. Other points of interest include San Xavier Mission, Colossal Cave, and the Biosphere.

See color photos, page 183

Muleshoe Ranch
Willcox, Arizona

Amidst 49,000 acres of cooperatively managed land, Muleshoe Ranch is a wildlife oasis in the desert. Diversity is evident, not only in the plant and animal life but also in the topography. Situated in the foothills of the Galiuro Mountains, the elevation rises from 4,000 to 7,600 feet, encompassing scenic vistas of the desert uplands contrasted with several lush canyons with year-round streams. Muleshoe is home to 190 bird species, as well as javelinas, coatimundis (cousins of raccoons), bobcats, mountain lions, white-tailed and mule deer, and bighorn sheep. Muleshoe is cooperatively managed by the U.S. Forest Service, the Bureau of Land Management, and the Nature Conservancy. The headquarters, which is owned and operated by the Nature Conservancy, offers overnight lodgings, camping, visitors' center, hiking trails, and special events. Located at the end of 30 miles of dirt road, there is nothing to disturb the quiet or block the view of the stars at night. This is a ranch for those who enjoy peaceful solitude, hiking, wildflowers, and all that nature has to offer.

Address: Muleshoe Ranch, RR1, Box 1542 K, Willcox, Arizona 85643
Telephone: (602) 586-7072; call for fax number
Airport: Commercial to Tucson, 110 miles; private to Willcox, 30 miles
Location: 110 miles east of Tucson in the foothills of the Galiuro Mountains, 30 miles northwest of Willcox off Airport Road
Memberships: Nature Conservancy, Willcox Chamber of Commerce and Agriculture
Medical: Northern Cochise County Hospital, 30 miles
Conference: 20
Guest Capacity: 20
Accommodations: Four housekeeping casitas arranged hacienda-style around the courtyard ranging from a two-person efficiency to an apartment suitable for six people and a stone cabin. Private baths and kitchens in all units.
Rates: $. Two-night minimum stay part of the year
Credit Cards: None. Personal checks and cash accepted.
Season: Year-round (closed Thanksgiving and Christmas days)
Activities: You are pretty much on your own to explore. Most guests who visit love to hike and be independent. There are a number of hiking trails. The friendly and knowledgeable staff will orient guests accordingly. A backcountry ranger is based at Muleshoe, and the staff members are all naturalists at heart. Horseback riding and jeep tours can be arranged throughout the year with a local outfitter. In April and October, the ranch organizes a four-day naturalist-guided trip into the backcountry, where guests return each night to the ranch. November and March include planned hiking and jeep tours into remote canyons. Guests can relax and soak in the soothing hot springs waters that are pumped into a large livestock tub. A large commons area for guests doubles as a meeting hall and dining area for groups.
Children's Programs: None. Children of all ages are welcome. Nannies encouraged.
Dining: Guests are responsible for preparing their own meals in the kitchens available with each room. You must bring your own food. Spring water is plentiful! Several special weekends are completely catered by the ranch staff.
Entertainment: Only the twinkling stars and the avian symphony each evening.
Summary: This is a remote Nature Conservancy outpost for those who appreciate nature and/or those who wish to relax completely. Cook your own meals. You may bring your own horse. Naturalists on staff. Hot springs waters and sweet spring drinking water. A wonderful, peaceful getaway at the end of 30 miles of dirt road. Special activities throughout the year provide natural history interpretation programs. Staff available to provide insight and answer questions. Inquire about calendar of events.

Phantom Ranch
Grand Canyon, Arizona

If you don't mind a thrilling all-day excursion by mule or on foot down a narrow switchback trail, keep reading. In the early 1920s, Phantom Ranch served as a retreat for the rich and famous. Over the years, the guest book has logged hundreds of entries that sum up the abundant joy experienced at Phantom. Words like "peace," "quiet," and "isolation" are found in entry after entry. Eventually, middle-income Americans discovered the ranch, and now visitors from around the world come on foot or by mule. Phantom offers a glimpse of yesteryear, steeped in stillness and the natural beauty of the Grand Canyon. Phantom Ranch lies at the base of Granite Gorge and is surrounded by high, spring-fed cottonwood trees. The ranch is a welcoming sight after descending the steep 10-mile trail that winds down to it. As in the 1920s, mules pack people, food, supplies, and mail to the ranch. Yes, the mules take everything back out, too. At Phantom you can practice the almost lost art of communication. You may listen and commune with the Lord's greatest creation—nature.

Address: Reservations: Grand Canyon National Park Lodges, P.O. Box 699 K, Grand Canyon, Arizona 86023
Telephone: (602) 638-2401 for reservations; fax: (602) 638-9247; no telephone at ranch
Airport: Phoenix or Las Vegas with connections to Grand Canyon
Location: 80 miles north of Flagstaff
Medical: Clinic on South Rim, EMT-trained rangers on staff
Guest Capacity: 92
Accommodations: Four dormitories with ten bunk beds each, heated or water evaporation cooled, showers and bathrooms. Beds are made with crisp white sheets, blankets, and pillows. Towels and soap provided. Dorms are segregated by sex. There are eleven private cabins for mule riders, each with a sink, toilet, and separate shower house.
Rates: $$$$. Includes mule ride plus three meals and overnight accommodations. Call for hiker's rates.
Credit Cards: Visa, MasterCard, American Express
Season: Year-round
Activities: Six-hour mule ride to ranch on Bright Angel Trail, four-hour ride to rim on the Kaibab Trail. Hiking, fishing (no equipment or boat provided). Colorado River rafting trips available with local rafting companies. Camping available with National Park Service permit.
Children's Program: None. Not recommended for children under age 12. The hike out is really tough!
Dining: There are two meal plans: hikers' plan, which is á la carte, and the mule trip plan. All meals are served family-style at set times in the Phantom Ranch dining hall. Breakfasts, sack lunches, and New York steak and stew dinners. Call reservations for details.
Entertainment: Seasonal ranger programs each day discussing the Grand Canyon, geology, wildlife, plants, and history. Because of the strenuous hike or mule ride in, most of the entertainment consists of relaxing, resting, or snoozing under the cottonwood trees.
Summary: Secluded park ranch at the bottom of the Grand Canyon, accessible only by a long mule ride or hike. Seasonal ranger nature talks. Author's note: While this is a beautiful and tremendous opportunity, people should be in reasonably good physical shape, like the outdoors, be willing to endure the elements, that is, the heat, and not be afraid of heights. Bring a wide-brimmed hat, lots of water, and sunscreen.

Price Canyon Ranch
Douglas, Arizona

On the northeastern slope of the Chiricahua Mountains (that's "big mountain" in Apache) at 5,600 feet is the headquarters for Price Canyon Ranch. These Arizona mountains, which attract visitors and scientists from around the world for their wealth of wildlife and natural history, rise to over 9,000 feet and are located in the Coronado National Forest. Since the late 1960s, Scotty and Alice Anderson have been mixing ranching and hospitality on their 19,000-acre working cattle spread just 40 miles from the Mexican border. "We've had guests from around the world except Russia and China," says Scotty. Don't expect anything fancy, though; this is a working ranch. As Scotty explains, "We are not a dude ranch but a working cattle ranch that takes a few paying guests at times." Guests participate in cattle roundups, work with livestock depending on the time of year, and, of course, enjoy plenty of horseback riding. The Andersons raise over 300 head of Texas longhorns and Brangus, both of which adapt well to this high desert climate. The terrain is desert mesa, with rolling grasslands, high mountain meadows, and bluffs. Summer temperatures can reach the 90s; winter temperatures can drop into the 30s at night. Alice sums it up best: "Our guests are those who appreciate our low-key but sincere hospitality and, most of all, a chance to be a part of our family, sharing our daily cattle ranching chores and our love for Mother Nature and the great outdoors."

Address: P.O. Box 1065 K, Douglas, Arizona 85608
Telephone: (602) 558-2383
Airport: Tucson
Location: 150 miles southeast of Tucson, 42 miles northeast of Douglas
Memberships: Conchise-Graham Cattlemen's Association, People for the West, Stewards of the Range
Medical: Hospital in Douglas, 42 miles
Guest Capacity: 15
Accommodations: Guests are put up in the family bunkhouse, a loft room in the main house, an apartment with kitchen with an adjoining singles' bunkhouse, or the large, cozy people's barn with pool table. Ten RV and trailer hookups available in the live oak grove. All bedding provided.
Rates: • \$-\$\$. American Plan. Children's and group rates available. Special hunting and pack trip rates.
Credit Cards: None. Personal checks and traveler's checks accepted.
Season: Year-round including Christmas, Thanksgiving, and Easter
Activities: This is a working cattle ranch. Depending on the season, various types of work need to be done. Daily horseback riding and ranch activities like branding and roundups. Fishing for bass and catfish in pond, solar-heated swimming pool open in summer, pack trips (only if you wish), hiking, cookouts, small jet tub in private room for aching muscles.
Children's Programs: Children are welcome, but children under 5 are not advised.
Dining: Good home-style ranch cooking. BYOB.
Entertainment: The main house is always open for guests to watch TV, read, or play board games. Rodeos in town at certain times of the year. Pretty much do your own thing after supper.
Summary: This is a very low-key, easygoing ranch for people who want to experience cattle ranching and all that goes along with it. As Scotty says, "Here carrying on a tradition of the West is one we hope will not be lost." You may bring your own horse if you wish, and many people do. English riding on request. Ten RV hookups available. Historical sites, Indian lore, natural well formation, and Mexico just across the border. Pets allowed under supervision.

Rancho de la Osa Guest Ranch
Sasabe, Arizona

This is a place where the gracious way of life of the old Southwest is captured and treasured. Established by Franciscan monks in the early 1700s on the border of Mexico, the ranch is one of the last great Spanish haciendas still standing today. Bill Davis, Sr., a retired United Airlines captain, bought and refurbished the ranch in the early 1980s. Today it is run by his son, Bill, and wife, Cheri. The Spanish settlers called it "Ranch of the She-Bear," and while the ranch offers modern amenities, it has retained its history and its tradition of hospitality. Guests may enjoy a fine string of horses, all bred and trained at the ranch. In addition, visitors may see deer, javelinas, coyotes, jackrabbits, and more than 200 species of birds. Rancho de la Osa is adjacent to the 130,000-acre Buenos Aires Wildlife Refuge. Rooms and suites are built of adobe. Guests can visit before dinner in the 260-year-old cantina, originally a Spanish/Indian mission. The ranch can accommodate up to 60 people for a sit-down dinner in the 100-year-old hacienda. This lovely old Spanish hacienda is remote, small, and quiet. There are those who come to ride and others who simply come to take in the desert scenery, watch birds, and relax.

Address: P.O. Box 1 K, Sasabe, Arizona 85633
Telephone: (602) 823-4257, (800) 872-6240; fax: (602) 823-4238
Airport: Tucson International
Location: 66 miles southwest of Tucson off Hwy 286
Memberships: Nature Conservancy, Audubon Society
Medical: Tucson Medical Center, 66 miles
Conference: 36
Guest Capacity: 36
Accommodations: There are 18 guest rooms in adobe buildings arranged in a quadrangle. This includes four family units. All rooms have fireplaces or wood-burning stoves, modern baths, electric blankets, coffee makers, and ceiling fans. Some have air-conditioning.
Rates: • $-$$. American Plan. Special rates for children. Nonriding packages available. Two-night minimum stay. Summer discounts and group rates available.
Credit Cards: Visa, MasterCard, American Express
Season: Year-round
Activities: The main activities here are riding, bird/nature watching, and walking and resting. Riders sign up each day for morning and afternoon rides or a weekly all-day ride to Presumide ghost town. Mostly walk and trot rides due to rocky terrain. Ask about the Rockhouse, Refuge, and Sasabe rides. Heated pool, whirlpool.
Children's Programs: Children welcome, but no kiddie wrangler and no children's programs. Children under 6 cannot go on trail rides.
Dining: Meals are served in the beautiful 1890s hacienda. Traditional ranch-style recipes, spare ribs, steaks, chicken, and homemade apple pie. Weekly Mexican fare, too. Wine served with dinner once a week. Happy hour in the fully stocked cantina.
Entertainment: Tractor hay-wagon rides, cookouts, and country-western singing.
Summary: Lovely old private historic Spanish hacienda run as a ranch by the Davis family. Very casual and low-key. There are two groups of guests—riders and relaxers (bird and nature watchers). The 118,000-acre Buenos Aires National Wildlife Refuge borders the ranch property. Nearby: Old Tucson, Sonora Desert Museum, San Xavier Mission. Nogales, Mexico, is almost a stone's throw away. Spanish spoken.

Rancho de los Caballeros
Wickenburg, Arizona

Rancho de los Caballeros is one of the premiere ranch resorts in North America. Set amid 20,000 acres of beautiful desert scenery, the ranch has maintained a long tradition of excellence and continues to attract families and individuals who enjoy a host of recreational activities, first-rate personal service, and comfort. In recent years, Los Caballeros has become well known for its 18-hole championship golf course. *Golf Digest* rated it one of the top 75 resort courses in the country. Many do come just to play golf. Others come to play tennis, ride horseback in the open desert country, sit by the pool, or just enjoy the relaxing atmosphere and camaraderie. The ranch recently built a superb conference center called Palo Verde. This center is ideal for small and large groups up to 150 people. Rancho de los Caballeros means "Ranch of the Gentlemen on Horseback." Perhaps what it should really stand for is "excellence": great people, great resort amenities, great golf, and great western fun.

Address: 1551 South Vulture Mine Road, Drawer K, Wickenburg, Arizona 85390
Telephone: (602) 684-5484; fax: (602) 684-2267
Airport: Phoenix; private planes at Wickenburg Municipal Airport on a 5,050-foot paved runway, fuel available. Call ranch for details.
Location: 4 miles southwest of Wickenburg, 56 miles northwest of Phoenix
Memberships: Arizona Hotel and Motel Association, American Cattlemen's Association, Desert Sun Ranchers' Association
Awards: AAA 4 Diamond
Medical: Wickenburg Community Hospital, 4 miles
Conference: 150, 275 (day meetings only); excellent 4,500-square-foot conference center. Ask for conference brochure.
Guest Capacity: 150
Accommodations: Guests enjoy 20 two- and four-room air-conditioned southwestern adobe casitas with private baths, sun patios, and separate entrances. Each room is tastefully decorated in the southwest style, including handcrafted furnishings and Indian rugs.
Rates: • $$-$$$. American Plan. Special family, children's, and group rates. Golf and riding packages available. Rates vary depending on season and type of accommodations.
Credit Cards: None
Season: October through May
Activities: The ranch offers slow, medium, and fast riding. Riding instruction on request. Breakfast, lunch, and dinner cookout rides. Four tennis courts with resident tennis pro, swimming, and guided nature walks with information on flora and fauna. Trap and skeet shooting is extra (guns provided). Los Caballeros Golf Club with 18-hole course includes a head pro and several assistants, a driving range, pro shop, locker rooms, golf carts, and rental equipment. Food and beverages available at club grill.
Children's Programs: Optional children's programs for kids ages 5 through 12—riding, swimming, hiking during the day and games in the evening. Baby-sitting is available for younger children (extra). Christmas, Thanksgiving, and holiday programs are popular.
Dining: Reserved individual tables. Menu features four entrées plus daily specials. Luncheon buffets served poolside. Full-service bar. Children may eat together or with parents.
Entertainment: Cookouts twice a week, songfests, card and table games, billiards, square dancing, and movies. Bingo games, putting, and card tournaments. Occasional cowboy poetry and sing-alongs.
Summary: One of the great ranch resorts in the country. Championship 18-hole golf course, rated by *Golf Digest* as one of the top 75 resort courses in the country. Golf and tennis pros on staff. Daily horseback riding. Excellent conference facilities for up to 150. Nearby: the town of Wickenburg for shopping, Wickenburg Museum, Vulture Mine, Hassayampa River Preserve (a natural preserve), and the scenic Southwest desert.

Tanque Verde Ranch
Tucson, Arizona

The Carrillo family founded the Tanque Verde Ranch on a Spanish land grant in the 1880s. In 1928, cattleman James Converse bought the ranch and transformed it from a working cattle ranch to a dude ranch, with massive adobe walls, beamed ceilings, pine log frames, fireplaces, and mesquite wood corrals—all in the Sonoran style. In 1957, the Cote family bought the ranch. In honor of southwestern tradition and of preserving the desert land and life-style, Bob Cote along with his fine staff provide guests with authentic Western hospitality year-round. They run a first-class operation and continue to receive the prestigious Mobil 4 Star award, as well as being written up in countless magazines and newspapers from around the world. In 1992, Bob purchased the grazing rights to the national forest adjoining the ranch and is currently running 300 head of cattle on 22,000 acres. The Cote family's philosophy is simple—provide the very best in friendly professional service in an exciting environment for the entire family. Tanque Verde Ranch is a luxurious oasis and without question one of the country's leading resort/guest ranches.

Address: 14301 E. Speedway—Dept. K, Tucson, Arizona 85748
Telephone: (602) 296-6275, (800) 234-DUDE (3833); fax: (602) 721-9426
Airport: Tucson International
Location: 15 miles east of Tucson at the end of East Speedway
Awards: Mobil 4 Star, *Family Circle* magazine Family Resort of the Year Award
Medical: Tucson Medical Center, 15 miles
Conference: 100; 1,000-square-foot conference room, conference director on-site, conference packet available
Guest Capacity: 125
Accommodations: 60 spacious casitas and patio lodges feature western decor, private baths, and individually controlled heat and air-conditioning. Each room is decorated with original southwestern artwork and antiques, down pillows, and southwestern comforters. Most have adobe-style fireplaces, private patios, and telephones. Laundry facilities available.
Rates: • $$$-$$$$. American Plan. Children's rates available. Rates vary depending on season. All activities included.
Credit Cards: Visa, MasterCard, Discover, American Express
Season: Year-round
Activities: Over 115 horses with daily guided rides going out twice in the morning for up to two hours. Riding instruction available, including slow scenic rides and loping for the advanced rider. Breakfast, all-day, and lunch rides. Pack trips for beginner and advanced riders. Five professional tennis courts with tennis pro, outdoor heated pool, indoor health spa with pool, saunas, whirlpool, and exercise room. Fishing for bass in spring-fed ranch lake, hiking, full-time naturalist with guided hikes. Nature museum, weekly bird banding by licensed professionals. The ranch has banded more than 70,000 birds and 171 species. Golf at two nearby clubs.
Children's Programs: Counselor-supervised programs from November to May includes kids' dining room, riding program, and wading pool. Baby-sitting available.
Dining: The Doghouse Saloon for happy hour. Hostess seats you at dinner. Continental and American cuisine featuring Cabrilla Creole and duck á l'orange. Three choices every day or buffet. Enormous salad bar. Weekly cookouts in Cottonwood Grove. Wine and beer available at all meals (extra).
Entertainment: Nightly programs include lectures by historians/naturalists. Country/western dancing.
Summary: Internationally known resort ranch with guests of all ages. Lots of Southwest historical charm and active guest participation. Resident naturalist at ranch and evening lectures on desert wildlife. Delightful ranch gift shop. Nearby: Old Tucson and Arizona-Sonora Desert Museum.

See color photos, page 186

Sprucedale Ranch
Eagar, Arizona

This is a small working cattle and horse ranch located high in the White Mountains of eastern Arizona. At 7,800 feet, the ranch is surrounded by forests of ponderosa pine, spruce, and aspen. The average summertime temperature is 76°. Owned by the Wiltbank family since 1941, the ranch offers an opportunity to experience life on a cattle ranch and enjoy mountain living in a wholesome, relaxed atmosphere. The morning horseback rides will take you on relaxing, yet exhilarating rides along Mint Creek, Beaver Creek, and Black River. On many of the rides you will enjoy a great view of Mt. Baldy while riding through fields of wildflowers. Chances are good that you will see elk or deer in the nearby trees. Milking the cows takes place every morning and cattle branding every week. This ranch is rustic but very cozy and clean. Plenty of warm hospitality is provided by Emer and Esther and their seven children. Their goal is to give guests a fun and safe ranch vacation and a feeling for the peace and beauty that can only be experienced in the great wide-open spaces of the Old West.

Address: P.O. Box 880 K, Eagar, Arizona 85925
Telephone: (602) 333-4984 winter (answering service in summer months). Emergency radio telephone at ranch.
Airport: Phoenix, Arizona; Albuquerque, New Mexico; El Paso, Texas
Location: 230 miles northeast of Phoenix, 50 miles south of Springerville, 25 miles south of Alpine, Arizona
Memberships: Arizona Cattle Growers Association
Medical: Springerville Hospital, 45 miles
Guest Capacity: 55
Accommodations: There are 15 one-, two-, and three-bedroom rustic cabins. Each is clean and comfortable, with a wood-burning stove for the cool mountain nights. Twin and double beds with quilts made by the family and full bathrooms. All electricity is generated at the ranch, so bring only essential electrical items. Lights out at 10:30 p.m.
Rates: $. American Plan. Children's and off-season rates available. Riding extra. Six-day minimum stay.
Credit Cards: None. Personal checks, traveler's checks, and cash accepted.
Season: June to September
Activities: Two-hour rides each morning except Thursdays, when an all-day ride is offered. Branding each week. Guests can work with young horses in the corral. Fishing for rainbows and German browns, hiking, watching for elk and deer.
Children's Programs: Children 6 and over can participate in trail rides. Children under 6 can participate in pony cart rides and other supervised horse-related activities but may not go on the organized trail rides.
Dining: Three hearty ranch-style meals including ranch-raised beef, soups, salads, casseroles, Esther's famous homemade breads and strawberry, raspberry, and peach jams, and desserts. An evening of Dutch oven cooking. BYOB.
Entertainment: Big Emer is very entertaining and always has a good story or joke to tell. Weekly gymkhanas, bonfires, square dancing, and weekly slide show of wildflowers. Horse-drawn hayrides.
Summary: Small, family-run cattle/horse ranch. When the Wiltbanks say remote, they mean it. It is a good six-hour drive by car from Phoenix but well worth it! No neighbors, just surrounded by national forest. Kids can roam and parents can relax knowing they are completely safe and having a great time. High percentage of return families. Make your reservation early. Ranch may be filled a year in advance. Kids can milk the cows. Nearby: Apache Indian reservation, Sitgreaves National Forest.

The Wickenburg Inn Tennis and Guest Ranch
Wickenburg, Arizona

If you can picture yourself riding high in the saddle or perfecting your topspin serve, the Wickenburg Inn is for you. This unique resort combines the informality and spirit of the Old West with the comfort and amenities of today's luxury resorts. This is an activity-oriented resort, where horseback riding, tennis, nature study, and arts and crafts are enjoyed in a magnificent 4,700-acre ranch and desert wildlife setting. A friendly staff and sincere western hospitality are at their best here. The tennis facilities and programs are outstanding. Riding is also superb, with expert wranglers and vibrant desert scenery. As a desert preserve, the inn has a resident naturalist and an abundance of things to see and observe. Of special interest is the arts and crafts center, where parents and children can sketch, paint, macramé, and do beadwork.

Address: P.O. Box P, Drawer K, Wickenburg, Arizona 85358
Telephone: (602) 684-7811 / (800) 528-4227; fax: (602) 684-2981
Airport: Phoenix Sky Harbor, or Wickenburg Airport for private planes, with 5,050-foot paved, lighted runway
Location: 70 miles northwest of Phoenix, 8 miles north of Wickenburg off Highway 93. Ranch will send map.
Memberships: American Hotel and Motel Association, Meeting Planners International
Awards: AAA 3 Diamond, Mobil 3 Star, selected by *Tennis Magazine* as one of the top 50 tennis resorts in the U.S.
Medical: Wickenburg Community Hospital, 9 miles
Conference: 30-125; executive meeting facilities, two meeting rooms with AV equipment. Ask for the conference packet.
Guest Capacity: 160
Accommodations: *Travel & Leisure* summed it up this way: "The casitas may be the best housing arrangement on any Arizona ranch." Each casita has its own charm and personality. Each comes with a wet bar and a fireplace. Some have private sun decks. Whirlpool spa nearby overlooking ranch. Rooms in the ranch lodge are adjacent to the tennis courts and swimming pool. All rooms have color television and telephone. Free laundry facility.
Rates: • $$-$$$$. American Plan. Rates vary depending on season. Special rates for children and teens. Group rates available. Tennis clinics available for extra charge. No minimum stay except during holidays.
Credit Cards: Visa, MasterCard, Discover, and American Express. Personal checks accepted.
Season: Year-round, all holidays
Activities: Riding includes breakfast, moonlight, and sunset rides. Hourly rides are scheduled each day, 10-15 per ride, beginner, intermediate and advanced. Riding instruction and gaited horses (Tennessee walkers and Paso Finos) available in season. Tennis on eleven acrylic courts. Clinic with certified instructors and complete pro shop. Daily lessons available. Heated swimming pool, spa. Golf is available nearby; transportation can be arranged. Arts and crafts and nature center.
Children's Programs: Special program with counselors and baby-sitting available during holidays—Christmas, Thanksgiving, and Easter—for an extra charge. Call for details.
Dining: Continental and southwestern cuisine from a menu. Licensed bar in lounge.
Entertainment: Holiday "dudeos" in which guests participate. Saturday night cookouts; guests can ride to cookout or take the hay-wagon truck. Western sing-alongs around the campfire.
Summary: One of Arizona's premiere tennis and guest ranch experiences. Excellent tennis and horseback riding. Ask about the special brochure on gaited horses. Good for executive retreats. The ranch is on a 4,700-acre wildlife preserve with animals, birds, flowers, trees, and cacti. Full-time naturalist on staff. Nearby: Lots of sightseeing, golf, Desert Caballeros Western Museum, February Gold Rush Days, Sedona and Arizona ghost towns.

White Stallion Ranch
Tucson, Arizona

Just 17 miles from downtown Tucson, surrounded by rugged desert mountains, is White Stallion Ranch. The True family bought this quiet, peaceful, 3,000-acre ranch in the 1960s, which looks out to Safford and Panther peaks and the Tucson Mountain Range. "The only sounds you will hear are those of the desert and the ranch," says Cynthia True, who oversees this lovely high desert ranch, along with her sons Russell and Michael and their families. One is impressed with the warmth and beauty of the land and the Trues' hospitality. The ranch features a herd of purebred Texas longhorn cattle and a rodeo each week with team roping, a cutting horse exhibition, steer wrestling, and barrel racing. Many scenes from the television series "High Chaparral" were filmed here. Children will enjoy the petting zoo with all the animals. Peacocks run free on the ranch, as do roadrunners. White Stallion Ranch is close to civilization and yet so far.

Address: 9251 W. Twin Peaks Road, Dept. K, Tucson, Arizona 85743
Telephone: (602) 297-0252/(800) 782-5546; fax: (602) 744-2786
Airport: Tucson International
Location: 17 miles northwest of Tucson
Memberships: Dude Ranchers' Association
Awards: Mobil 3 Star
Medical: Northwest Hospital, 11 miles
Conference: 30-75; 1,200 square feet
Guest Capacity: 50-75
Accommodations: White Spanish-style bungalows with adobe exteriors with single rooms and deluxe suites and a few suites and cabins. Each has a private bath, air-conditioning, and most have double or king-size beds and private patios with views through the cactus garden to the mountains. There are no televisions or telephones. Two deluxe suites have high exposed beam ceilings, antique Mexican furniture, whirlpool tub, and fireplaces. Laundry facilities.
Rates: • $-$$. American Plan. Nightly, weekly, off-season, and children's rates available.
Credit Cards: None. Traveler's checks or personal checks accepted.
Season: October through April. Open Thanksgiving, Christmas, and Easter.
Activities: Riding schedule is posted each day except Sunday. Children and adults may, if they wish, brush and saddle their own horse. Four rides a day, usually two fast and two slow, and seasonal all-day rides into the Saguaro National Monument. If you think you are a fast rider, the ranch has a riding test for you. Breakfast and mountain rides. Nature walks along foothills of the Tucson Mountain Range, swimming in key-shaped heated pool, shuffleboard, volleyball, basketball, two professional tennis courts, and indoor redwood hot tub. Golf nearby.
Children's Programs: Children of all ages are very much a part of the ranch programs and participate fully. Children are the responsibility of parents. Baby-sitting available at extra charge. Children under 5 ride with parents.
Dining: Breakfast menu-style, lunch buffet, dinner family-style. Wednesday hayrides, desert cookouts, and the outdoor Indian oven. Happy hour with hors d'oeuvres precedes dinner, when Cynthia introduces guests and bids farewell to those leaving in the morning. No smoking in dining room.
Entertainment: Weekly bonfire with cowboy singer and square dancing. Seasonal stargazing with visiting astronomer.
Summary: White Stallion Ranch and the True family offer one of the most relaxing, yet active environments, for the young and the young at heart. The Trues' brand of hospitality and warmth is very special! Lovely Spanish-style ranch close to Tucson but isolated. Part of 100,000-acre game preserve adjacent to Saguaro National Monument. Singles and families welcome. Ranch rodeo, "T-Bone" the longhorn steer. Nearby: Madera Canyon (bird-watcher's paradise), Living Desert Museum in Tucson, Old Tucson.

See color photos, page 187

Scott Valley Resort and Guest Ranch
Mountain Home, Arkansas

In the serenity of the Ozarks, amid 375 acres of beautiful meadows, woodlands, rocky cliffs, and spring-fed streams, is the Coopers' white, clean-cut, red-trimmed Scott Valley Guest Ranch. Scott Valley began operation in 1953. Tom and Kathleen Cooper have shared the joys of their ranch and their down-home hospitality with people from around the country since 1985. Rated as one of the most popular vacation spots in the Ozarks, Scott Valley offers a variety of activities for its guests, including excellent riding for the experienced as well as the novice. Fishermen will enjoy some of the best fishing on the White (ranked fourth in the world for trout fishing) and North Fork rivers. Both are famous for rainbow and brown trout. You will feel the warm and friendly hospitality that is the secret of the Coopers' success. Children, too, will experience all the treasures of the great outdoors. Guests have been known to say, "It's just like home and being with family."

Address: Box 1447 K, Mountain Home, Arkansas 72653
Telephone: (501) 425-5136; fax: (501) 424-5800
Airport: Springfield, Missouri; Little Rock, Arkansas; Memphis, Tennessee; Mountain Home, Arkansas (via St. Louis, Missouri, or Dallas, Texas)
Location: 6 miles south of Mountain Home off Highway 5; 156 miles north of Little Rock; 196 miles west of Memphis
Awards: *Family Circle*'s Family Resort of the Year 1990, 1991, and 1992
Memberships: Dude Ranchers' Association
Medical: Baxter County Regional Hospital, 6 miles
Conference: 125; two rooms (1,200 square feet), off-season only
Guest Capacity: 65
Accommodations: Each of the 28 one- or two-bedroom, motel-type guest rooms has a full bathroom with tub and shower, air-conditioning, electric heat, and maid service.
Rates: • $. American Plan. Children under 3 free. Prefer one-week stay. Weekly family, group, seniors, and military rates. Rates include horseback riding (canoes and boats on stays of three days or more).
Credit Cards: Visa, MasterCard. Traveler's checks or personal checks accepted.
Season: March through November, including Thanksgiving and Easter
Activities: Horseback riding on an hourly basis. Experienced riders should inquire about the spring and fall rides. The Coopers have Tennessee walkers, Missouri fox trotters, quarter horses, Appaloosas, and thoroughbreds. Hiking; swimming in a heated pool spa that is enclosed during cooler months or in nearby lakes and streams. Ten minutes from world-class fishing on the White River, as well as boating and canoeing. Jet skiing, sailing, and scuba diving available at nearby Lake Norfolk (extra). Table tennis, badminton, tennis, volleyball, and nature and fitness trails. Shuffleboard and nearby 18-hole golf.
Children's Program: Fully equipped playground. Ranch encourages families to interact with their children. Baby-sitting available; pony rides for children under 7. Petting zoo with lots of animals.
Dining: Down-home, good cooking including biscuits and gravy, ham, great Mexican fare, cornbread, and chicken and dumplings. There are salads for lighter appetites. Weekly dinner cruise on Lake Norfolk during summer season.
Entertainment: Summer: every evening there is some type of scheduled activity. Be sure to ask the Coopers about the famous Western entertainment in Branson, Missouri. Summer entertainment is geared for families.
Summary: A haven for families to spend time together in a low-key, relaxing atmosphere. Spring and fall months best for adults, singles, couples, and experienced riders. Great for off-season bus tours. Arkansas is one of the best values you can find for your vacation dollar and is one of the United States' great hidden treasures. Nearby: Blanchard Springs Caverns and the Ozark Folk Center.

See color photos, page 188

Alisal Guest Ranch
Solvang, California

This secluded, 10,000-acre ranch is 40 miles northwest of Santa Barbara, in the Santa Ynez Valley, near the Danish community of Solvang. Resort elegance in a ranch country setting is what the Alisal offers, with 30 miles of riding trails, a par 72 championship golf course, a 100-acre lake, and seven tennis courts. It is also a working cattle ranch with 2,000 head of cattle. Guest rooms are lovely, whitewashed bungalows and garden rooms with fireplaces. Seclusion, sports, excellent food, and pampering are paramount here. This year-round ranch has it all. Today, guests come from around the United States and Europe. Deer graze the sycamore- and oak-studded landscape, while guests partake of the many activities or just relax, soaking up California sunshine.

Address: 1054 Alisal Road, Dept. K, Solvang, California 93463
Telephone: (805) 688-6411; reservations: (800) 4-ALISAL (800-424-4725); fax: (805) 688-2510
Airport: Santa Barbara Airport with commercial jet service, 35 miles; Santa Ynez Airport for private planes, 5 miles
Location: 40 miles northwest of Santa Barbara
Awards: *Family Circle*, Family Resort of the Year
Medical: Santa Ynez Hospital, 3 miles
Conference: 200; 5,500-square-foot corporate meeting space
Guest Capacity: 150-200, 73 suites
Accommodations: 73 cottages and garden rooms scattered around the estate grounds, which feature century-old sycamores. They range from studios with sitting rooms to executive suites, all with fireplaces. All are modern with high ceilings, fireplaces, and carpeting. There are no televisions or telephones in the rooms, but pay phones are available. Laundry service is available.
Rates: • $$$-$$$$. Modified American Plan (including breakfast and dinner). A wide variety of seasonal activity packages are available. Ask about the Roundup Vacation Package. Two-night minimum stay requirement.
Credit Cards: Visa, MasterCard, American Express
Season: Year-round
Activities: The Alisal's 10,000-acre spread includes 30 miles of riding trails, a 100-acre lake, seven professional tennis courts, an 18-hole championship par 72 golf course, and golf and tennis pro shops. Two-hour trail rides go out twice each day separated into walking, trotting or loping rides. Private rides and riding instruction available. Also offered are semiweekly breakfast rides. Lake activities include fishing, boating, and wind surfing. The Alisal also has a heated pool and a 10-person whirlpool. There is an area for volleyball and shuffleboard, as well as a game room with table tennis and billiards.
Children's Programs: Daily arts and crafts program. Summertime and holiday evenings are filled with bingo, storytellers, and talent shows. Special events include the Giant Easter Bunny and egg hunt at Easter, Santa's visit with caroling and gifts, and the Fourth of July pageant.
Dining: Dinner attire required. Served in the Ranch Room, the menu varies daily and features contemporary regional cuisine. Excellent wine selection. Summer lunches served poolside. Lunches in the winter served in the main dining room or at the golf clubhouse. Limited room service available.
Entertainment: The southwestern-decorated Oak Room, with a large stone fireplace and cathedral ceiling, provides nightly dancing, cocktails, and relaxation with live music. There is a large adults-only library for quiet reading. The recreation room has a pool table, table tennis, and a large-screen television.
Summary: Superb resort ranch ideal for families during the summer and holidays. It is also an excellent meeting environment for groups of up to 150 people from September to June. Nearby: Solvang Danish community, 22 local wineries, and a large artist community. Video available upon request.

See color photos, page 190-191

Circle Bar B Guest Ranch
Goleta, California

About 20 miles north of Santa Barbara hidden in the Refugio Canyon in the foothills of the Santa Ynez Mountains is the Brown family's Circle Bar B Ranch. Cooled by ocean breezes from Refugio State Beach, 3 miles away, this nearly 1,000-acre ranch has played host to guests since 1939. The atmosphere at the ranch is always casual and relaxed, and guests are made to feel at home by the personable staff. Guests come for the friendly, casual atmosphere, the proximity of the ocean, Santa Barbara, and Los Angeles, and the scenic riding program. The trails head out the back gate up through Indian Canyon, crossing streams, passing by seasonal waterfalls, through the lush ferns, sycamore trees, and vegetation at the bottom of the canyon. After a short rest at Sweetwater, the trail climbs out of the canyon bottom and breaks out over a ridge where guests can take in magnificent views of the Santa Ynez coastal mountains, the Pacific Ocean, and the Santa Barbara Channel Islands. Farther along the trail at Look Out Point, guests can look 1,000 feet down onto the main ranch buildings in the canyon. The ranch offers a half-day lunch ride that climbs to the summit of Refugio Pass where the ranch borders former President Reagan's ranch. At the Circle Bar B Guest Ranch, you'll find a relaxed, friendly atmosphere.

Address: 1800 Refugio Canyon Road, Dept. K, Goleta, California 93117
Telephone: (805) 968-1113
Airport: Santa Barbara Airport in Goleta
Location: 22 miles north of Santa Barbara at the Refugio State Beach exit off Highway 101, 110 miles northwest of Los Angeles
Medical: Goleta Hospital, 18 miles
Guest Capacity: 30; Dinner Theater 100
Accommodations: Guests are housed in eight delightful, private cabins individually decorated, each with a fireplace, porch, and down comforters on the beds. Some have small sleeping lofts. There are also five older ranch rooms with private baths. (Plans are currently under way to completely replace these with a deluxe fiveplex.)
Rates: • \$\$-\$\$\$. American Plan. Children's rates available. Riding not included. Call for theater rates. Two-night minimum on weekends. Three-night minimum on holiday weekends.
Credit Cards: Visa, MasterCard. Personal checks accepted.
Season: Year-round, closed Christmas day
Activities: Trail rides take you over the 1,000 acres surrounding the ranch, offering views of the ocean as well as the Channel Islands. Horseback rides are a minimum 1½-hours, with 2½-hour rides and 4-hour, half-day picnic rides offered as well. Enjoy hiking, ocean fishing, unheated swimming pool, and hot tub. Nearby activities include golf and wine tasting.
Children's Programs: None. Children are welcome. Children have a good time and make their own fun.
Dining: Over the years the ranch has hired trained chefs. Hearty ranch cooking, served buffet-style. Tri-tip beef barbecues, chicken, and fish. Special diets catered to with advance notice. BYOB.
Entertainment: Dinner Theater Friday and Saturday nights, May through December
Summary: A great family-owned and operated year-round guest ranch with horseback riding to high California scenic bluffs overlooking the Pacific Ocean. Only two hours from Los Angeles. The ranch is very accommodating to families, children, and couples. Groups, corporate retreats, and family reunions are always welcome. Comfortable, new accommodations and a rustic fourplex, home-cooking, and an atmosphere that is informal, friendly, and sincere. Ask about the Dinner Theater and nearby Santa Barbara and the Santa Ynez wineries.

See color photos, page 189

IF YOU ENJOYED YOUR
RIDE, PAT YOUR

Coffee Creek Ranch
Trinity Center, California

In the mid-1970s, Ruth and Mark Hartman sold their house in the San Francisco Bay area and bought their riverside ranch in northern California. Coffee Creek Ranch, named after the creek that flows through the property, covers 127 acres at the base of the majestic Trinity Alps Wilderness Area. At 3,100 feet, Coffee Creek is in a river canyon, surrounded by a mountain wilderness area full of wildlife. The ranch is not far from Trinity Lake and 13 miles from the Trinity Center Airport.

Address: HC 2, Box 4940 K, Trinity Center, California 96091
Telephone: (916) 266-3343/(800) 624-4480; fax: call for number
Airport: Redding, or Trinity Center Airport (3,300-foot runway) for small planes only
Train: Amtrak to Redding. Contact ranch concerning Greyhound bus.
Location: 278 miles north of San Francisco, 72 miles northwest of Redding, 45 miles north of Weaverville off Highway 3
Memberships: Dude Ranchers' Association
Medical: Weaverville Hospital (Clinic), 45 miles
Conference: 50
Guest Capacity: 50
Awards: Honorable mention *Family Circle* 1990, 1991
Accommodations: All 14 cabins have porches. Handicap cabin or ranch house room with front porch is available. Most two-bedroom cabins have one or two baths and wood-burning stoves. The one-bedroom, one-bath cabins have potbelly stoves to keep you warm and cozy. All cabins have showers, some with bathtub/shower combinations. Daily maid service and laundry facilities are available.
Rates: • $$. American Plan. Horseback riding extra by the ride or weekly. Special rates for spring and fall. Children's, teen, and senior rates available. One-week minimum stay during summer, Saturday to Friday. Two-day minimum stay in spring, fall, and winter.
Credit Cards: Visa, Mastercard, American Express, Discover. Personal checks, cash, or traveler's checks accepted.
Season: Year-round, closed periodically between seasons
Activities: Coffee Creek offers scheduled riding in the summer, including breakfast and twilight rides. Ask about their riding program in the spring and fall. Picnic and all-day rides and overnight pack trips. No riding on Fridays in summer. Guided hiking; fishing in stocked pond, Coffee Creek, Trinity Lake, and alpine lakes. Archery, badminton, shuffleboard, volleyball, trap shooting, and rifle range (guns provided). Swimming in heated pool or in Coffee Creek and canoeing on the pond. Health club. Seasonal hunting of deer and bear. In winter, wilderness cross-country skiing, snowmobiling, inner-tubing, ice fishing, and ice skating, weather permitting.
Children's Program: Excellent children's program for ages 3 to 12 includes pony rides, crafts (jewelry making, painting), nature hikes. Wonderful international counselors. Baby-sitting during rides for children under 3.
Dining: Three nutritious meals a day, all you can eat, family-style; fresh fruit, vegetables, and family recipes. Barbecues and steak fries. Ask about the "crazy cake." Beer and wine bar. BYOB, but it must be kept in the cabins (check with office).
Entertainment: Truck-drawn hayrides, bonfires, bingo, talent shows, gymkhanas, live music several times a week by the Coffee Creek band, "The Rattlesnakes," square dancing. Rec room, pool table, table tennis, horseshoes, shuffleboard, and basketball. Satellite TV.
Summary: Family owned and operated with strong emphasis on families. Serious riders should consider early summer and fall. June and July have the best weather and lots of wildflowers. National Scenic Byway. Adults/singles-only weeks. Video available on request. Spanish, Dutch, German spoken. Handicapped facilities. Nearby: Trinity Center Western Museum, historical town of Weaverville, and Chinese "Joss House" temple.

See color photos, page 192

Drakesbad Guest Ranch
Chester, California

Tucked away in the southeast corner of Lassen Volcanic National Park is a century-old guest ranch that is peaceful and quiet, the way it has always been. Forty-seven miles from the park's southwest entrance, Drakesbad is secluded in one of California's most scenic mountain valleys. Surrounded by thousands of acres of forest and oodles of lakes, this rustic ranch—knotty pine lodge rooms with sinks, toilets, and kerosene lanterns—is known for its hot springs that fill the ranch's warm baths and pool. This ranch is for those who like fresh mountain air and quiet surroundings and don't mind not having electricity. Here the only schedule is when the meals are served. One guest commented, "We don't want too many people to know about Drakesbad because we enjoy it so much." There is only one major drawback to this old ranch—its popularity. It gets booked many months in advance. Great scenery, great staff, and lots of rest and relaxation. Drakesbad is very, very special!

Address: Drakesbad Guest Ranch, Lassen Volcanic National Park, Drawer K, end of Warner Valley Road, Chester, California 96020 (summer); 2150 Main Street, Dept. K, Suite 5, Red Bluff, California 96080 (year-round)
Telephone: Summer: Dial operator and ask for Susanville operator, area code 916, then ask for Drakesbad 2. Be patient; this may take a little while. Winter: (916) 529-1512.
Airport: Redding, Reno, or Sacramento; private planes into Chester Airport, 17 miles
Location: 117 miles southeast of Redding off Highway 36 in Chester; 125 miles northwest of Reno
Medical: Seneca Hospital, Chester, 40 minutes
Guest Capacity: 75
Accommodations: Thirteen cabins and six lodge rooms. All are delightful with wood floors, sinks, and toilets, some with showers. Kerosene lamps give an old-time ranch flavor; no electricity; daily housekeeping is provided; bathhouse for cabins without showers.
Rates: $-$$. American Plan. Discount for stays over seven nights. Horseback riding extra.
Credit Cards: Visa, MasterCard. Personal checks accepted.
Season: Early June to early October
Activities: This is not the place for someone who needs something to do every moment of the day. It is leisure oriented and best suited for those who enjoy communing with nature and relaxing. Fishing, riding, hiking, swimming in modern pool heated by thermal volcanic heat. Daily horseback riding is available by reservation the night before. One-hour to all-day rides. Insurance and terrain require walking only. Helmets offered to those who wish them.
Children's Programs: Supervised children's program for ages 6 to 12 is available three afternoons each week. Parents are responsible for children.
Dining: Unique and very special! Wonderful cuisine. Breakfast and dinner served in dining room; buffet or sack lunch. Menu is varied and features delightful nutritious food. Special diets can be accommodated with advance notice. Weekly cookouts of ribs and steaks, with hamburgers and hot dogs for the kids. Beer and wine service at lunch and dinner (extra).
Entertainment: Star-studded skies and marvelous fireside ranger chats.
Summary: A diamond in the rough! A remote, charmingly rustic ranch with hot springs pool and hydrothermal area. Great for families, couples, and singles who want an unhurried environment in scenic and remote northern California. Hot springs swimming, hiking, relaxing, and horseback riding are the main activities here. Excellent food and staff. Nearby: Drakes Lake, Boiling Springs Lake, Devil's Kitchen, Pacific Crest Trail.

Highland Ranch
Philo, California

Highland Ranch is located in the beautiful Redwood Country of Mendocino County amid sky-reaching redwoods. Secluded and very private, the ranch sits above the Anderson Valley, known for fine wines and friendly vineyards. Highland Ranch is owned and operated by George Gaines, who has had a fascinating international legal and business career. George bought the ranch in the late 1980s and has transformed it into a relaxing, rustic paradise. Here you will find deer and other local wildlife, tall redwood trees, fruit trees, and meadows divided by split rail fences. The wonderful old yellow and white ranch house is the meeting spot where guests relax by a crackling fire and savor subtle aromas from the kitchen. Highland Ranch specializes in catering to couples, small corporate/business groups, holiday celebrations, and family reunions. With its proximity to the Mendocino Coast and some of California's finest wineries and towering Redwoods, Highland Ranch is, indeed, a slice of heaven and a piece of paradise.

Address: P.O. Box 150 K, Philo, California 95466
Telephone: (707) 895-3600; fax: (707) 895-3702
Airport: San Francisco, 135 miles, and Santa Rosa, 50 miles, for commercial flights; Ukiah, 24 miles, for private jets and small planes; Boonville, 11 miles, for small planes only
Location: 125 miles (2½ hours) north of San Francisco, 6 miles northwest of Philo off Highway 128
Medical: Ukiah Community Hospital, 24 miles
Conference: 12-20. Very quiet 250-square-foot conference room. Audiovisual equipment available.
Guest Capacity: 24
Accommodations: There are several cabins and duplexes with various sleeping arrangements. Most have fireplaces and sitting areas (a wonderful place to read or write); all have telephones, private baths, porches, electric blankets, good towels, very comfortable mattresses and pillows.
Rates: • $$$. American Plan. Discounts for children under 12.
Credit Cards: None. Personal and traveler's checks accepted. Master billing preferred for groups.
Season: Year-round, except December 24-26
Activities: Do as much or as little as you wish, from wine tasting or whale watching to reading your favorite book. Very individualized program. If you are looking for set schedules and planned activities, this may not be the place for you. Wonderful riding on over 100 miles of trails through the towering Redwoods, open meadows, along the ridges overlooking the Anderson Valley or along the Navarro River. Rides are tailored to the individual group with English saddles available. Tennis on two well-surfaced courts, swimming in ranch pool or several ponds, hiking, fishing, shooting, or simply relaxing in four hammocks just outside the ranch house.
Children's Programs: Children are welcome with a family gathering. No formal programs.
Dining: Delicious food featuring local produce and fresh fish in season is served in the charming country dining room, family-style. Each evening George offers complimentary cocktails and Anderson Valley and international wines with dinner. Special menus can be planned. The food is scrumptious!
Entertainment: Many enjoy relaxing in a hammock heaven while reading their favorite book. Some enjoy the extensive library and music collection or tune into the ranch's satellite television. Great local Anderson Valley entertainment.
Summary: Wonderful, small, very private ranch near Anderson Valley wineries and Mendocino Coast. Superb food and fine wine, along with delightful and stimulating conversation. Spectacular redwood groves. Excellent for small corporate/business groups and family gatherings. Lazy Creek, Pepperwood Springs, Obester, Roederer, Husch, Navarro, Scharffenberger, and other vineyards. Be sure to stop by the Apple Farm for fresh apple cider. French and Italian spoken. Video available.

See color photos, page 193

Howard Creek Ranch
Westport, California

In 1867, Howard Creek Ranch covered thousands of acres along California's northern coast. The homesteaders ran sheep and cattle and operated a sawmill, a blacksmith shop, and a dairy. All the buildings were made of virgin redwood milled right on the property. Today, this charming ranch inn is surrounded by bright green lawns and vibrant flowers, offering a simple, wholesome getaway just off the highway. People come to unwind and enjoy the wilderness, the rustic setting, and the dramatic ocean and mountain views. Howard Creek is cheerful, friendly, and countrylike and just 300 yards from the ocean. Charlie and Sally are in the process of restoring the old ranch barn. As in years gone by, the ranch is a cozy nest, close to the sea and mountains with an abundance of wildlife and all the little homey touches that show someone cares. One guest summed it up: "It's beautiful, quiet, peaceful, and rustic."

Address: P.O. Box 121 K, 40501 North Highway One, Westport, California 95488
Telephone: (707) 964-6725
Airport: San Francisco International
Location: 3 miles north of Westport, 124 miles south of Eureka, 150 miles north of San Francisco
Memberships: Mendocino Coast Innkeepers Association, California Association of Bed and Breakfast Inns
Awards: Frommer's *The 100 Best Bed and Breakfast Homes in North America*
Medical: Fort Bragg, 18 miles
Conference: 25
Guest Capacity: 18
Accommodations: There are two small cabins (which are by Howard Creek and a meadow) and the Beach Cabin with a view of the ocean. There are four rooms in the New England-style white-sided ranch house: two open out onto the second story balcony through French doors (ask Sally about the Lucy Howard etching story), and two rooms are in the back. All accommodations reflect early California character with antiques and fresh flowers. Many have intricate handcrafted redwood detailing. You may listen to the pounding surf or gaze at the stars from skylights and picture windows. Inquire about the boathouse cabin. Some cabins have refrigerators and microwave ovens. All have wood stoves with glass doors.
Rates: $-$$. European Plan. Winter rates available.
Credit Cards: Visa, MasterCard
Season: Year-round
Activities: Guests enjoy the ambience, the flowers, the hot tub overlooking the ranch, and, most of all, the coastal enchantment, including whale watching, birding, and tidal pools. There is also a cold plunge pool, a long sandy beach (a short walk under the overpass), hiking, and nearby horseback riding. Many enjoy the proximity to the nearby redwood groves, Nature Conservancy, and 60 miles of wilderness trails. To top it off, massage is available on the mountaintop.
Children's Programs: By prior arrangement only. Infants welcome.
Dining: Only breakfast is served: omelets and Sally's famous fresh blackberry-banana buttermilk hotcakes. Chickens produce fresh ranch eggs. Sally will help you with local restaurant selections.
Entertainment: You may sit by the fireplace, read in the library, play a piano, or stroll over the 75-foot swinging bridge.
Summary: Ranch bed and breakfast 300 yards from the beach and ocean, making it a great place for whale watching. Massage available. Italian, Dutch, and German spoken. Pets allowed by prior arrangement. Nearby: Skunk Train through the redwoods, Mendocino shops, and Fort Bragg.

Hunewill Circle H Ranch
Bridgeport, California

With Lake Tahoe and Yosemite nearby, this old-time family cattle ranch has been taking guests since 1930. The ranch is situated in the lovely, wide-open lush green cattle-ranching Bridgeport Valley in the heart of the Sierras, back-dropped by the Sawtooth Ridge that marks the northeastern boundary of Yosemite National Park. It was founded by the great-great-grand-parents of the present owners, the Hunewill family. The ranch runs about 2,000 head of cattle over 5,000 acres. While horseback riding is the main activity, hikers will find miles of trails, and fishermen enjoy nearby streams and lakes. The Hunewills say, "We love this old ranch and our way of life." Families have been returning here for years. The ranch offers a beautiful setting, great hosts, and a low-key western atmosphere.

Address: P.O. Box 368 K, Bridgeport, California 93517 (summer); 200 K Hunewill Lane, Wellington, Nevada 89444 (winter)
Telephone: (619) 932-7710 (summer); (702) 465-2201 (winter); or (702) 465-2325 (Stan and Jan)
Airport: Reno, Nevada; private airplanes, Bridgeport
Location: 115 miles south of Reno on Highway 395, 50 miles north of Mammoth, 5 miles southwest of Bridgeport on Twin Lakes Road
Memberships: Dude Ranchers' Association
Medical: Mono Medical Clinic, 5 miles
Guest Capacity: 40-45
Accommodations: As Bridgeport was one of the early gold mining areas, the ranch buildings have a Victorian flavor. There are twenty-four white cottages in the ranch quadrangle, each with private bath, electric and gas heat, carpeting, and porches. The ranch house is a lovely two-story Victorian, built in 1880 and surrounded by tall poplars. Laundry facilities available.
Rates: • $-$$. American Plan. Rates vary depending on accommodation and month. Children's rates available late June to early September. One-week minimum stay, Saturday to Saturday.
Credit Cards: None. Personal checks accepted.
Season: May to late September
Activities: Riding is the main thing. Three rides go out mornings and afternoons for the beginner, intermediate, and advanced rider. Beginner riders (both children and adults) appreciate special rides designed to build confidence and skills with instruction-oriented wranglers and gentle horses. Beautiful wide-open meadow rides. Ask about the rides to Eagle Peak, Buckeye Canyon, and Tamarack Lake. Riding helmets provided for those who wish. Breakfast and lunch rides. Anytime the ranch does cattle work, guests are welcome to join in. Fishing in nearby streams and lakes (bring your own gear), nature walks, volleyball, and horseshoes. Tennis five miles away. Ask about Buckeye Hot Springs.
Children's Programs: Children are included in all ranch activities and have an enjoyable experience in a healthy, outdoor environment. During adult riding times, youngsters 6 and under are watched by a "Buckaroo" counselor and may be led on a gentle horse. Kids 6 to 11 go on beginning rides with adults.
Dining: Ranch-style, everyone eats together. Two barbecues each week. Wonderful ranch food. Don't miss the Hunewill's own mountain spring well water. BYOB.
Entertainment: The Hunewill "Summer House" plays host to square dancing, skit night, impromptu singing, and music.
Summary: One of California's most renowned dude/cattle ranches. Great old California family. Riding is the main activity here. Very casual and low-key. Very western. Two-day cattle roundup in mid-September. Watercolor workshops and fall color rides (advanced riders only) if enough people sign up. Five-day November cattle drive for advanced riders only. Nearby: ghost towns of Bodie, Aurora, Lundy, and Buckeye Hot Springs, courthouse in Bridgeport.

See color photos, page 194

Muir Trail Ranch
Lakeshore, California

Since the turn of the century, Muir Trail Ranch has been one of those best-kept secrets. At 7,665 feet, the ranch is the only outpost on the 180-mile John Muir Trail between Mount Whitney and Devil's Postpile National Monument. The ranch experience begins and ends with horseback riding or a hike. After a boat ride across Florence Lake, those who wish to ride will be met by a wrangler for the beautiful 1½-hour to 2-hour ride to the ranch. In 1990, the ranch began the decade with a new weekly groups-only (15-20) policy. That's not to say an individual or couple could not book the entire ranch for a week. Along with this, guests must supply all their own food, do their own cooking, and bring their own sleeping bags. On departure, guests must leave the ranch as they found it—spotless. Limited ranch staff are on hand to ensure that all your gear is safely packed in and out, to help you get acquainted, and to maintain the hot springs baths. They are also available for horseback rides/pack trips and to answer questions. This 200-acre ranch is a rustic hideaway in nature's paradise with its own clear mineral-rich and odor-free, two-temperature hot springs (110°F and 99°F).

Address: P.O. Box 176 K, Lakeshore, California 93634 (summer); P.O. Box 269 K, Ahwahnee, California 93602 (winter)
Telephone: No telephones in summer; (209) 966-3195 winter
Airport: Fresno
Location: 100 miles northeast of Fresno off Highway 168
Memberships: National Forest Recreation Association, High Sierra Packers Association-Western Unit
Medical: Fresno hospitals; emergency helicopters available
Guest Capacity: Up to 20
Accommodations: Shelter is in eight log cabins with toilets, wash basins (with cold running water), outdoor fire pits, and electric lights (ranch has a hydroelectric generator). Tent cabins are also available. Many guests like the latter because they are almost on the south fork of the San Joaquin River. Bring your own sleeping bags or bedding and towels. Hand soap, toilet paper, and cleaning supplies will be provided.
Rates: Weekly minimum ranch rate. Call Adeline Smith (owner) for details. Riding and pack trips extra.
Credit Cards: None. Personal checks accepted.
Season: Mid-June through September
Activities: Beautiful, clear rock pools, hot spring baths with constant running water, nature hikes with some of the best hiking in California, fishing (fly-fishing only on the ranch). Guided horseback rides and overnight pack trips. Fish in glacial lakes, river, and creeks for golden, rainbow, German brown, and brook trout.
Children's Programs: Children should be old enough to enjoy this wilderness experience and the trip into the ranch. They should also be old enough to ride a horse. Those under 6 do not ride.
Dining: You are the chef and are responsible for bringing all your food and beverages. Some groups and families have arranged for their own chefs or caterers who will take care of everything. The kitchen and dining room are fully equipped. Beautiful terrace with wood-burning barbecue, table benches, and buffet-style serving tables. Large walk-in refrigerator and freezer. Automatic ice machine.
Entertainment: Whatever you wish. It's your ranch for the week.
Summary: Rustic wilderness ranch retreat to be rented on a weekly basis by one or more families, groups, or a couple. Accessible by horse or by foot. The Muir Trail Ranch "green sheet" will explain everything, as will owner Adeline Smith when you telephone her. Muir Trail Ranch is very special.

Rankin Ranch
Caliente, California

The Rankin Ranch is one of California's old ranching traditions. It is here in a secluded valley in southern California that Bill and Glenda, along with Bill's mother, Helen Rankin, the matriarch of the ranch, share their love for people and the West. The Rankin family has been in the cattle business since 1863. On 30,000 acres in northern Kern County, things are pretty much as they always have been. Slow and easy is the pace. Warm and friendly are the folks. Over the years lots of people have driven up over the winding, slow-going road and down into this beautiful grassy valley to spend time at the ranch. Those who return yearly have a real appreciation for country living and are able to leave their businesses and professions behind. Here it is quality family time.

Address: P.O. Box 36 K, Caliente, California 93518
Telephone: (805) 867-2511. Call for fax.
Airport: Bakersfield
Location: 42 miles northeast of Bakersfield off Highway 58 via Caliente-Bodfish Road
Memberships: National Cattlemen's Association, California Historical Society
Awards: California 100 Year Club
Medical: Lake Isabella Hospital, 25 miles
Conference: 36; 1,500-square-foot meeting/rec room
Guest Capacity: 36
Accommodations: There are many wonderful family antiques in the twelve comfortable, wood-paneled duplex cabins named after sites on the ranch like Lightner Flat, Ruby Mine, and Rankin Hill. Each cottage has a bath, carpeting, and picture windows. Daily maid service and cribs available.
Rates: • $-$$. American Plan. Children's rates. Rates vary depending on time of year. No minimum stay policy.
Credit Cards: Visa, MasterCard, American Express. Personal checks accepted.
Season: Late March through September
Activities: Daily, one hour, morning and afternoon guided horseback rides are available for all guests (4 years and older). This is scenic mountain country, so most riding is done at a walk. There are areas in the meadow where some loping can be done. When there are cattle to be moved in the meadow, guests are invited to help the cowboys. FYI, this is not a weekly activity. Julia Lake and Walker Basin Creek are stocked with rainbow trout (bring your own fishing pole). There is tennis, archery, and hiking. The ranch has a lovely shaded swimming pool area where many guests enjoy swimming in the heated pool, reading, or just plain relaxing. Shuffleboard, table tennis, horseshoes, and volleyball are also available.
Children's Programs: Supervised seasonal children's programs. Trail rides, excellent crafts program, talent shows, swim meets, picnics, and games. Ask about the kids' favorite afternoon picnic Indian hike and bottle-feeding the baby calves. Baby-sitting available with advance notice.
Dining: Amid Rankin Ranch cowboy photos, guests enjoy three hearty ranch-style meals in the spacious high-ceilinged dining room, the Garden Room. Don't come here to lose weight. Breakfast is served from 7:30 to 9:00. BYOB for adult patio party at 5:30 p.m. daily featuring the Rankin Ranch's famous guacamole dip and chips. Vegetarians will not be disappointed. Evening hay wagon ride, meadow barbecue, and horseshoe tournament.
Entertainment: There is something planned each evening: square dancing, pool tournaments, hayrides, talent show, and indoor horse races. Rec room for all ages.
Summary: A great family running an old-time family cattle ranch. Come here to relax, recharge, and enjoy wonderful easygoing western hospitality and kindness. Lots of space, peace, and quiet. Excellent for celebrating special birthdays, anniversaries, and family reunions. Spanish spoken. Nearby: The gold rush town of Havilah.

See color photos, page 195

Spanish Springs Ranch
Ravendale, California

Spanish Springs is an authentic working cattle ranch with 5,000 mother cows and 200 head of horses. Located on 70,000 acres of deeded property surrounded by a million acres of public land, Spanish Springs is comprised of a series of ranches and homesteads scattered over northern California's rugged high desert country and Nevada's spectacular Black Rock Desert. Guests may choose from a wide range of outdoor adventure vacations and authentic western ranch activities suitable for families and singles, beginners and experienced riders.

Address: P.O. Box 70 K, Ravendale, California 96123 (reservations)
Telephone: (800) 272-8282 (California)/(800) 228-0279 (out of state)/(415) 456-8600 (general office); fax: (415) 456-4073 (general office); ranch phone: (916) 234-2050; fax: (916) 234-2041
Airport: Reno; Lassen County Airport in Susanville; public airstrip in Ravendale, 6 miles from ranch
Location: 125 miles northwest of Reno on Highway 395, 45 miles northeast of Susanville
Medical: Susanville Hospital, 45 minutes
Conference: 100 overnight, 250 corporate/group day cookouts
Guest Capacity: 110; 50 including all outlying ranches
Accommodations: Accommodations vary depending on the ranch you choose to visit. Spanish Springs headquarters is the most modern of all the ranches and is still growing. Guests stay in one of the newly built log cabins or the deluxe bunkhouse with private rooms and a large bunk room. Great for large families or groups. There are also comfortable wood-sided duplex units and Western suites. For the experienced rider/adventurer, the old, refurbished outlying ranches —The Marr, Evans, Horne, Cold Springs Camp, Roberts Ranch, and historic Soldier Meadows—all provide a private, remote western setting.
Rates: • $$. American Plan. Children's rates and special package/group rates available.
Credit Cards: Visa, MasterCard, American Express, Discover. Personal checks accepted.
Season: Year-round, including Thanksgiving, Christmas, and Easter
Activities: Summer offers tremendous riding potential, from half-hour lessons and barrel racing in the professional rodeo arena to all-day trail rides. The terrain is varied, as is the riding. Three- to ten-day pack trips. Excellent fishing in ranch-stocked trout ponds. Outdoor heated swimming pool. Skeet shooting and sporting clays (guns provided), archery, horseshoes, tennis, volleyball, shuffleboard. Seasonal hunting for deer, antelope, pheasant, dove, chukker, duck, geese, and buffalo. In winter, weather permitting, guests enjoy cross-country skiing, horse-drawn sleigh rides, sledding, and ice skating. Working ranch vacations include authentic spring and fall roundups, brandings, and cattle and horse drives. Special annual events include wild horse viewings in the spring, Buckaroo Camp, and 4th of July Junior Rodeo.
Children's Programs: Flexible children's programs. Baby-sitting available with advance notice.
Dining: Western-style meals are served family-style in the intimate, comfortable dining room. Large outdoor barbecue area will accommodate over 250. Sunday champagne brunch served. Bill of fare includes famous Harris Ranch beef.
Entertainment: Beer and wine bar in the main lodge. Cowboy sing-alongs, campfires, hay wagon rides, ranch rodeos in professional arena with bucking stock, roping, penning, cutting horse, and gymkhana competitions.
Summary: This is a 70,000-acre ranch that encompasses a series of new and older outlying ranches. A wide variety of accommodations and western activities are available. Excellent for family reunions and conferences. Well-stocked western apparel ranch store. Spring horse drives. Authentic spring and fall cattle drives and roundups. You may see wild horses, antelope, and buffalo. Nearby airstrip. Newsletter and video available on request.

See color photos, page 196

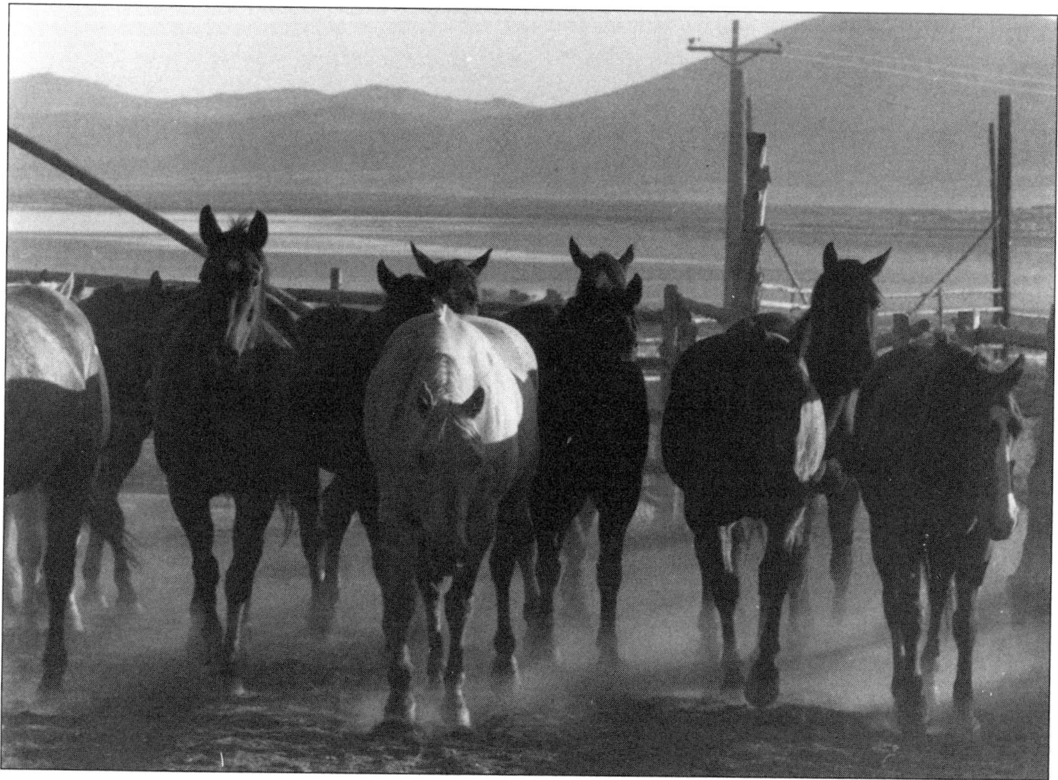

Trinity Mountain Meadow Ranch
Trinity Center, California

This lovely mountain lodge is in the Trinity Alps Wilderness Area, at 5,072 feet. It is a long and dusty 18-mile drive in, but what a delightful surprise it is when you finally arrive. The ranch is owned by ten California families who have operated it since 1976 with a common dedication and love for the wilderness. Surrounded by spectacular distant jagged peaks, the lodge looks out to Caribou Peak and the site was once a trading post for packers and miners in this historic gold mine district. Today, the lodge offers families a host of activities in a mountain paradise. Each day begins and ends with good food and hospitality. It's a great, rustic family vacation, and you don't have to sleep in a tent or cook.

Address: Coffee Creek Road, Star Route 2, Box 5700 K, Trinity Center, California 96091 (summer); 24225 K Summit Woods Drive, Los Gatos, California 95030 (winter)
Telephone: (916) 462-4677 (summer); (408) 353-1663 (winter)
Airport: Redding Municipal Airport, 90 miles; Trinity Center Airport, 29 miles from ranch, where private planes will be met
Location: A map will be sent. Six hours north of San Francisco off I-5, two hours northwest of Redding off Highway 299.
Medical: Memorial Hospital in Redding, 90 miles; California Highway Patrol emergency helicopter available
Conference: 40
Guest Capacity: 40
Accommodations: Ten rustic one-room family cabins with baths and heaters, double and king-size beds, and bunk beds for kids. Everyone sleeps in one room. Each cabin is situated with its own view out toward the meadow. Many sit on their front porches before they turn in and call it a day. All linens provided. Laundry facilities with washing machines and scenic clothes lines. Four very small lodge rooms above the dining room, with a bath at the end of the hall, each with beautiful mountain views. The ranch generates all its own power, so when lights are out at night, they really are out. The generator is off from 11:00 p.m. to 6:30 a.m. No smoking allowed in buildings.
Rates: $. American Plan. Children's and teenagers' rates available.
Credit Cards: None. Personal checks or cash accepted.
Season: Late June through August
Activities: The beauty of this area can be enjoyed by everyone from the rugged hiker to the sportsman or sportswoman who enjoys a day in the wilderness followed by a dip in the heated pool. Spinning and fly-fishing at headwaters of the Salmon River, an hour hike away. The farther you go, the better it gets. For the historian who wants to relive the days of the gold miners, there are trails with many relics. There are endless subjects for the photographer's lens. Bring your own horse; mountain bikes available.
Children's Programs: Full program, early supervised dinner hour, crafts, hikes, 9:00 a.m. to 5:00 p.m. child care available at minimal rates. Children are supervised while mom and dad are eating.
Dining: Family-style in the main dining room of the lodge on long tables seating 10. Nothing fancy, just wholesome, plentiful, and delicious. Weekly Mexican dinners and turkey buffet with all the trimmings. Beer and wine available.
Entertainment: Campfires, sing-alongs, conversation. People like to talk to each other here. Volleyball, badminton, horseshoes.
Summary: An excellent family place. In fact, almost everyone who comes has children. Very compatible families gather here. Lots of hiking, fishing. Photography seminars offered. You may bring your own horse. Great for family reunions. Nearby: Dorleska and Yellow Rose gold mines.

Aspen Canyon Ranch
Parshall, Colorado

In 1987, the Mitchell family bought a beautiful ranch that straddles the Williams Fork River in Grand County. The family has transformed this lovely old ranch into the Aspen Canyon Ranch, a new guest facility with Colorado mountain flavor. It is in the heart of some of Colorado's best fishing and hunting, with miles of mountain trails for horseback riding and hiking. Local history includes many fascinating tales of the early settlers, giving the ranch a real connection with the Old West. While the ranch offers lots of activities, one of the favorites is savoring the magical lullaby of the Williams Fork River as it runs by the guest cabins. As Ron says, "It will either put you into deep sleep or keep you awake at night, depending on your temperament."

Address: 13206 County Road 3, Drawer K, Parshall, Colorado 80468
Telephone: (800) 321-1357, (303) 725-3518 (ranch), fax: (303) 724-3559; (812) 421-2109 (business office), fax: (812) 421-2115
Airport: Denver; private aircraft to Kremmling Airfield
Train: Amtrak to Granby
Location: 25 miles north of Silverthorne, 90 miles west of Denver. Ranch will send detailed map.
Memberships: Dude Ranchers' Association, Colorado Dude and Guest Ranch Association, Colorado Guides and Outfitters
Medical: Kremmling Hospital, 26 miles
Conference: 24
Guest Capacity: 24
Accommodations: Guests stay in three fourplex log cabins, named Deer, Elk, and Trout Lodge. Each is on the banks of the Williams Fork River. All have comfortable accommodations, natural gas fireplaces, flannel comforters, carpeting, refrigerators and coffee makers, porches, and old-fashioned swings. You will find a large jar of freshly baked cookies each day in your room. The main lodge, with a wonderful porch, houses both the dining and living rooms and two cozy fireplaces. Be sure to ask about the hot tub and deck by the river.
Rates: • $$-$$$. American Plan. Children's, off-season, group, and hunting rates available. Children under 3 free. Baby-sitting available.
Credit Cards: Visa, MasterCard, American Express
Season: Early May through October. Open for hunting October through mid-November.
Activities: Guests will enjoy walking outside their cabins to cast a line into the Williams Fork River for brook, brown, and rainbow trout. Fishing gear available, weekly fly-fishing clinic. Guides available on request. Half-day and all-day riding, hiking (ask about the Lake Evelyn picnic hike), pack trips, seasonal hunting, mountain bikes available. Guests can participate in seasonal cattle work. Golf and ballooning, 30 miles. Ranch gymkhana, calf roping, and barrel racing in professional-size rodeo ring. Rafting on the Colorado River is available each week.
Children's Programs: Two gal wranglers teach kids 3 to 12 daily about horses, roping, and riding, both in the arena and on the trail. Other activities include crafts, hiking, fishing, picnicking, and gold-panning. Ask about the kids' cabin.
Dining: Hearty ranch cooking served family-style with a gourmet flair. Fresh trout, barbecues, and cookouts. Some wild game. Lunches include soups, salad bar, and sandwich buffet. House specialties: steaks, ribs, chicken, and freshly baked pies and cookies. BYOB.
Entertainment: Sing-alongs, square dancing, and modern country line dancing, tractor hayrides, and weekly rodeos in town with demonstration barrel racing and steer roping. Weekly wildlife, local history, and Indian talks.
Summary: Small, very friendly guest ranch for families, couples, and the right singles. Wonderful cabin amenities. Nearby: towns of Breckenridge, Vail, and Keystone for shopping, Rocky Mountain National Park, old mining towns of Georgetown and Fairplay.

Aspen Lodge Ranch Resort
Estes Park, Colorado

In 1992, Jill and Tom Hall became the proud new owners of Aspen Lodge Ranch Resort. Under their caring and sensitive direction, Aspen Lodge shines bright. Situated at the base of the Twin Sisters Mountains at 9,000 feet, the lodge and guest cabins look out to Longs Peak. Fresh air, spectacular views, and quiet surroundings provide an environment that make for a tremendously positive work/vacation opportunity for everyone. The focal point of the Aspen Lodge is the tremendous main lodge. Built of lodgepole pine, this magnificent 33,000-square-foot structure is one of the largest log buildings in Colorado. With access to more than 2,000 acres of wooded mountainside and alpine meadows, the Aspen Lodge Ranch Resort offers both summer and winter activities in rustic elegance.

Address: 6120 Highway 7K, Longs Peak Route, Estes Park, Colorado 80517
Telephone: (303) 586-8133, (800) 332-MTNS nationwide; fax: (303) 586-8133
Airport: Denver
Location: 10 minutes south of Estes Park, 65 miles northwest of Denver off I-25
Memberships: Colorado Dude and Guest Ranch Association
Award: Mobil 3 Star, AAA 3 Diamond
Medical: Estes Park Hospital, 7 miles
Conference: 150; excellent conference facilities
Guest Capacity: 150
Accommodations: The lodge features several hospitality suites and 36 guest rooms. Separate from the main lodge are twenty multiroom, quiet cabins with porches.
Rates: • $-$$. American Plan. Horseback riding and some equipment rentals (mountain bikes) extra. Children's, conference, and group rates available. Check with ranch for special winter rates. No minimum stay.
Credit Cards: Visa, MasterCard, American Express, Diners Club, Discover
Season: Year-round
Activities: Summer programs include an excellent horse plan, with rides for all levels. Various horseback packages available. Trail riding in adjoining Rocky Mountain National Park and also fast, open meadow riding available over 2,000 magnificent acres of a working cattle ranch surrounded by 33,000 acres of Roosevelt National Forest. Ask about the overnight horseback campout. Week-long instructional program for kids and adults. Fishing, hiking, climbing, and heated outdoor pool with whirlpool. Two lighted tennis courts, two racquetball courts, Health Club with weights and exercise room, Finnish sauna. River rafting and van tours can be arranged. Mountain bikes, volleyball, horseshoes. Eighteen-hole par 70 golf course nearby. Estes Park with 300 shops and galleries is ten minutes away. Winter brings cross-country skiing, snowmobiling, sleigh rides, ice skating, winter horseback riding.
Children's Programs: Extensive children's program that is fun as well as educational: Indian lore, pioneer lifestyles, and nature exploration. Baby-sitting available.
Dining: Beautiful Longs Peak is framed through the dining room windows. The dining lodge offers "casual continental" to Colorado cuisine prepared by creative chefs with imagination. Great western bar and outdoor patio café.
Entertainment: Hayrides, square dancing, barbecues, movies, weekend entertainers, two-stepping
Summary: Magnificent ranch resort with access to 30,000 acres of an old-time cattle ranch in Roosevelt National Forest. Exhilarating horseback riding opportunities in lake meadow country surrounded by the highest peaks in the Rockies.

See color photos, page 197

Avalanche Ranch
Redstone, Colorado

What does an ex-ski instructor/realtor and businessman who loves the mountains, the outdoors, people, and antiques do for an encore? Sharon and Jim Mollica created a year-round romantic getaway called Avalanche Ranch. Located about one hour south of world-famous Aspen, Colorado, this wonderful bed-and-breakfast ranch combines the charming qualities of a New England country inn and western cabins with the rugged splendor of Colorado's mountain peaks and rivers. Originally built in 1913, the red and white ranch house and log cabins look out to 12,953-foot Mt. Sopris and over the Crystal River, which provides great fishing. From antiques to apple orchards to Tony the donkey and Avi the dog (who gets fan mail), the Mollicas' country paradise is a unique and special getaway and one of Colorado's real mountain highs!

Address: 12863 Highway 133, Drawer K, Redstone, Colorado 81623
Telephone: (303) 963-2846
Airport: Aspen, 45 minutes; Denver, 3½ hours
Location: 30 minutes southeast of Glenwood Springs on Highway 133, 40 miles southwest of Aspen
Medical: Herrington & Knaus Medical Clinic in Carbondale, 10 miles; Valley View Hospital in Glenwood Springs, 30 miles
Conference: 24
Guest Capacity: 57
Accommodations: Eleven log cabins and four bed-and-breakfast rooms. The cozy cabins have lofts, wonderful kitchens and bathrooms, picnic tables, barbecues, some wood stoves, and great views. The inn offers four rooms, two with private baths and two that share a bath with claw-foot tub/shower. Sinks in rooms and robes provided. Common sitting area, library, and meeting/party barn. Lots of views!
Rates: • $. Call for details. Breakfast included with bed and breakfast, also available to cabins.
Credit Cards: Visa, MasterCard, Discover
Season: Year-round
Activities: There are no formal activities. Avalanche provides a launching pad for all kinds of outdoor adventures: fishing in the Crystal River, unlimited hiking and bicycling, horseback riding in Marble (20 minutes away by car), rafting with local outfitters on the Roaring Fork and Colorado rivers, volleyball, horseshoes, and badminton. Winter: Cross-country and downhill skiing at five ski areas within a one-hour drive, snowshoeing.
Children's Programs: This is a kid's wonderland with lots of animals (llama, donkey, goats, chickens, pigs, ducks, and rabbits). Treehouse and kids' play cabin. Parents are responsible for their children.
Dining: A healthy, continental-plus breakfast is served. It includes homemade granola, breads, muffins, fresh fruit, yogurt, cereals, juice, teas, and fresh-ground coffee. Breakfast included with inn and available to cabins. Pancakes on Sundays. Other meals are offered seasonally or catered.
Entertainment: Informal campfires. You are on your own.
Summary: A charming, year-round bed-and-breakfast ranch with cabins in the heart of the towering Colorado Rockies, located on a designated scenic byway. Ask about Sharon's Antiques Barn, the nearby famous working marble quarry, the Redstone Castle Tour, and nearby attractions. Less than one hour from Aspen. Lots of weddings and family reunions.

Bar Lazy J
Parshall, Colorado

The Bar Lazy J guest ranch began entertaining guests in 1912, when it was known as the Buckhorn Lodge. It is situated on the Colorado River at an elevation of 7,500 feet, about a half-mile from the little town of Parshall. In 1987, Larry and Barb Harmon bought the ranch. Like many, they had been guests at various dude ranches and fell in love with this wonderful way of life. A unique feature of the ranch is the beautiful Gold Medal trout river offering anglers the opportunity to fish right outside their cabin doors. Horseback riding is the main activity at the ranch. Small groups of riders have a choice of walking, trotting, or loping rides. Larry and Barb have put together a strong children's program with two children's counselors and two wranglers. At the Bar Lazy J you can ride, fish, read, or just get downright lazy and listen to the Colorado River sing its song right outside your cabin.

Address: P.O. Box NK, Parshall, Colorado 80468
Telephone: (303) 725-3437
Airport: Denver
Location: 15 miles west of Granby off Highway 40, 100 miles northwest of Denver
Memberships: Dude Ranchers' Association, Colorado Dude and Guest Ranch Association
Medical: Kremmling Hospital, 13 miles
Guest Capacity: 38
Accommodations: Guests stay in twelve cozy log cabins, accommodating two to eight people each. Each is named after wildflowers or fishing flies. Most have wooden floors (some squeaky), with paneling and enclosed covered porches overlooking the river, and all have rockers. Bathroom and thermostatically controlled heat in each. Nightly turn-down service and coffee makers in each cabin.
Rates: • \$-\$\$. American Plan. Children's and off-season rates available. Weekly minimum stay in June, July, and August. Three-day minimum stay in September.
Credit Cards: None. Personal checks and traveler's checks accepted.
Season: June through September
Activities: Each guest receives a rawhide bolo name tag on arrival which helps guests get to know each other, along with a personal welcome note from Barb. Gold Medal fishing with weekly fishing clinic. Stocked fishing pond for kids and those who don't wish to fish the river. Horseback riding for all levels of experience. Breakfast rides, half-day rides, and all-day rides through open cattle grazing fields dotted with sage. A favorite is the Cliff Ride. Usually small groups of 8 or fewer go out on each ride. Slow, medium, and fast rides in small groups. Hiking, outdoor heated swimming pool, large Jacuzzi, shuffleboard, horseshoes, volleyball. River rafting nearby. Jeep trips.
Children's Programs: "Ranch Fun" is for kids 3 years and older. It can be a full day of supervised ranch activity including horseback riding. The program is flexible and optional. Children's playroom where all craft activities take place. Young children may go on trail rides if the wranglers feel they are able to. Children eat with their parents. Baby-sitting available for very young children (extra).
Dining: Each meal is a joy, served family-style in a beautiful log dining room. Weekly steak fries, barbecue ribs, and Mexican buffet. Enjoy homemade soup, breads, pies, and cakes. BYOB.
Entertainment: Campfires, hayrides, volleyball, staff shows, and square dancing in the rec room barn.
Summary: One of the oldest guest ranches in Colorado located along the Colorado River. Great children's program, which allows parents to be on vacation, too. Great for families, couples, and singles who enjoy the outdoors and not a highly structured program.

Cherokee Park Ranch
Livermore, Colorado

What brings guests back to Cherokee Park Ranch is one simple thing—the superb staff. In 1991, this old historic ranch (one of the oldest in Colorado) took on a whole new direction and spirit. The lifeblood of dude ranching is people. I have said in my travels that numbers may run the world, but people make it. That is just the case here. The combinations of history, enthusiasm, love for life and nature, and a young staff with loads of energy make a week or two at Cherokee Park extra-special. Hosts and owners William (everyone calls him "B") and his wife, Eli, both met while working on a ranch. Both from the Carolinas, they finished college, headed west, fell in love, and the rest is history. It is their abundant joy that makes this ranch a winner. When asked for a quote that they might share with others, B and Eli offered this: "Love yourself, believe in yourself, be yourself." Cherokee Park Ranch is a wonderful place to do all three.

Address: P.O. Box 97K, Livermore, Colorado 80536
Telephone: (303) 493-6522; (800) 628-0949
Airport: Denver Stapleton International
Location: 100 miles northwest of Denver, 40 miles northwest of Fort Collins
Memberships: Dude Ranchers' Association, Colorado Dude and Guest Ranch Association
Medical: Fort Collins, 40 miles
Guest Capacity: 35
Accommodations: The main lodge and many of the cabins reflect the early Western history here—lots of authentic charm and a real cozy feel. All cabins and rooms have been restored with families in mind. The main lodge has four suites upstairs ranging in size from two to three bedrooms. All five cabins are situated along the river or creek with porches, wonderful relaxing swings, hummingbird feeders, and lots of bright flowers. All rooms are carpeted with full baths. Some have fireplaces. Daily maid service and homemade ranch treats.
Rates: • $$-$$$. American Plan. Children's rates. Off-season and group rates. One-week minimum stay, Saturday to Saturday arrival except in low-season.
Credit Cards: None. Personal checks accepted.
Season: May through September
Activities: Cherokee Park offers a tremendous diversity of activities for every age. With a staff of twenty, the ranch program allows lots of flexibility. What makes the riding special here is the mountain and prairie combination. You can ride abreast; because of the wide-open country, it is not all trail riding. Safety is number one, and those who are capable may lope. Five wranglers and a kids' riding counselor offer morning, afternoon, and all-day rides each day. Ask about the river ride to Turkey Roost. Fly-casting instruction for beginners and guided trips for experienced anglers. Ask B about float tube fishing and the Poudre fishing ride. River-rafting, Eli's nature hikes, informal trap shooting and old-time black powder shoots (guns provided). Swimming in heated pool, hot tub. Weekly trips to Rocky Mountain National Park and to Laramie, Wyoming.
Children's Programs: Extensive. Three full-time counselors for ages 3-12. Ask about the educational nature programs. No charge if you BYO nanny for kids under 3.
Dining: Top-notch home-cooked meals with lots of variety. BYOB.
Entertainment: Each night there is something planned. Mountain-man show and musical talent. Rodeo with riding games, square dancing, hayrides with hot chocolate and s'mores.
Summary: Family emphasis with diversity of activities for all ages. Very personal, caring attention. Young and energetic spirit prevails. Excellent, particularly for young families and single parents.

Colorado Trails Ranch
Durango, Colorado

Since 1960, Dick and Ginny Elder have been welcoming guests to their home, Colorado Trails Ranch. Their ranch and western village is complete with trading post, where they serve old-fashioned ice cream treats, an opera house, and a parlor furnished with antiques. With great fun and relaxation for families, couples, and singles, Colorado Trails offers western charm and hospitality high in the beautiful San Juan Mountains, just outside Durango. At 7,500 feet, don't worry about smog. The air is clean and sparkling with the scent of fresh pine. While the ranch offers many activities, it takes great pride in its comprehensive riding program. They offer both English and western riding instruction with certified riding instructors. Dick and Ginny have gone out of their way to give their ranch a real western flair. Guests love it and keep coming back. Among them are artists, financiers, surgeons, pilots, lots of families, and several astronauts. Artists and photographers are overwhelmed by the fall colors. At his weekly welcome dinner, Dick tells his guests, "You're guests in our home, and that's the way you'll be treated." Folks, this is one of the all-around champions.

Address: 12161 K County Road 240, Durango, Colorado 81301
Telephone: (800) 323-DUDE (3833), (303) 247-5055; fax: (303) 385-7372
Airport: La Plata County Airport, 18 miles from ranch
Location: 12 miles northeast of Durango on County Road 240; 200 miles north of Albuquerque, New Mexico
Memberships: Dude Ranchers' Association, Colorado Dude and Guest Ranch Association, American Quarter Horse Association, American Humane Association, American Riding Instructors Association, Durango Chamber of Commerce, U.S. Equestrian Team Supporter
Awards: *Family Circle* 1990 and 1991 Family Resort of the Year; 1988 American Humane Association's outstanding service in the field of humane education (Rosemary Ames Award)
Medical: Mercy Medical Center
Conference: 60; three different set-up rooms, 4,800 square feet; from early September
Guest Capacity: 75 (33 rooms)
Accommodations: Guests can stay in four types of comfortably furnished cabins surrounded by pine trees. All rooms have private bathrooms, carpeting, electric baseboard heat, and porches. Guest laundry service is available.
Rates: • $$-$$$. American Plan, family rates
Credit Cards: Visa, MasterCard, American Express, Discover, Diners Club
Season: Late May to October
Activities: One of the best riding programs in the country—both western and English instruction. Heated swimming pool, whirlpool spa, two tennis courts, fishing in stocked river pond or nearby lakes. Archery, rifle and trap shooting (guns provided), hiking, and water skiing on Lake Vallecito. Golf, rodeo, and float trips are available at extra cost.
Children's Programs: Extensive programs—three children's programs divided into age groups, each with full-time counselors. Game room with pool table and table tennis. Kids' groups usually eat together.
Dining: The dining room overlooks the scenic Shearer Creek Valley and Eagle Ridge. Hearty ranch food and plenty of it. No bar. Drinking permitted in cabins only.
Entertainment: A program every evening: staff show, hayrides, cookouts, dances, and melodrama in Durango. Adults enjoy the unique turn-of-the-century parlor.
Summary: Superb western and English horseback riding, one of the best programs in the country. Outstanding children's programs. Caring, personable staff. Wonderful entertainment. Adults-only weeks. Nearby: The famous narrow-gauge train ride to Silverton (this is loads of fun and really takes you back to the old days), guided tours to Mesa Verde National Park with Indian cliff dwellings, and pro rodeo in Durango.

See color photos, page 198

Coulter Lake Guest Ranch
Rifle, Colorado

Coulter Lake Guest Ranch is one of the few guest ranches in the West overlooking its own charming lake. The ranch is nestled in a small mountain valley on the western slope of the Rockies, deep in the White River National Forest at 8,100 feet. In operation since 1938, the ranch has tried to retain the Old West flavor. Norm Benzinger, his wife, Sue, Kim Sutton, and her late husband, Al, purchased the ranch in 1981 to escape southern California. Coulter Lake Guest Ranch is surrounded by some of Colorado's most spectacular mountain country stretching for miles in all directions, virtually unchanged since Indian times. Forests of quaking aspen and spruce overlook meadows of wildflowers. Deer, elk, and other wildlife are abundant. Norm and Sue are year-round residents and have purposefully kept the ranch small, intimate, and rustic. Family members of all ages, as well as singles, will immediately feel comfortable. Be prepared to make lasting friendships!

Address: P.O. Box 906 K, Rifle, Colorado 81650
Telephone: (800) 858-3046, (303) 625-1473; call ranch for fax information
Airport: Grand Junction, Colorado
Train: Amtrak to Glenwood Springs
Location: 21 miles northeast of Rifle beyond State Highway 325
Memberships: Dude Ranchers' Association, Colorado Dude and Guest Ranch Association, Rifle Area Chamber of Commerce
Medical: Clagett Memorial Hospital, Rifle
Conference: 25 (spring and fall only)
Guest Capacity: 25
Accommodations: Eight cabins stand on the mountainside among the quaking aspen; Lakeside and Forest Haven are by the lake. They vary in size and can sleep from two to nine people. Each has a private bath, some with fireplaces (the original log cabins, Lakeside, Hilltop, Woodland), and carpeting, and most have porches. Ranch generates its own power (curling irons and hair dryers not recommended).
Rates: • \$-\$\$. American Plan. Children's rates available. Off-season and group rates.
Credit Cards: None. Checks, cash, or money orders preferred.
Season: Late May to October, mid-December to early April
Activities: Good horses provide activities, from short to all-day rides. Mondays and Tuesdays have morning and afternoon rides to Little Box Canyon, Long Park, and Pot Holes (a big open meadow "bowl"). Wednesdays and Fridays feature all-day rides to Irish Point and Little Hill. Hamburger twilight rides to Coulter Mesa on Thursdays. Weekly four-wheel-drive trips, fishing in stocked lake or in alpine streams and lakes (some fishing poles at ranch). The famous Coulter Lake boat races take place on Saturdays. Hiking and horseshoes, occasional cattle drives. Eighteen-hole golf, tennis, rafting, and hot springs in nearby Rifle and Glenwood Springs. Photographers should bring a lot of film! Lots to do, and guests enjoy doing it together. Winter: Meals and lodging for snowmobilers and cross-country skiers. Guided snowmobile rentals and tours are available but extra.
Children's Programs: Baby-sitters are available with advance notice. No set program, but supervised kiddie rides are provided.
Dining: Hearty, family-style meals. Cookouts, including a supper ride to 10,000-foot Coulter Mesa. Everyone enjoys the Saturday buffet, Wednesday steak fry, and Friday trout dinner. Special diets can be accommodated. BYOB.
Entertainment: Sing-alongs, square dancing, and melodrama.
Summary: Delightful, small family ranch. Remote setting situated right on its own lake—no noise, no telephones. As Sue says, "We are low-key and off the cutting edge of technology." If you enjoy good people, riding, and nature, give the Benzingers a call. Adults-only weeks early summer and fall. Video available.

See color photos, page 199

C Lazy U Ranch
Granby, Colorado

The C Lazy U Ranch story began back in 1919. In 1988, the Murray family, who had been guests each year since 1959, bought their favorite home-away-from-home. They have ensured that the C Lazy U experience continues to be one of the best in the business today. C Lazy U mixes rustic luxury with old-fashioned informality. Facilities and food are western, comfortable, and of superb quality. The ranch continues to receive the prestigious Mobil 5-Star and AAA 5-Diamond ratings. This 2,000-acre ranch has it all, from designer soap to therapeutic massage that will soothe your tired muscles and help you to unwind. Very family oriented, the ranch has different programs for children and adults. Families eat breakfast together, then the kids go off to work—to work at having the most fun they have ever experienced.

Address: Box 379 K, Granby, Colorado 80446
Telephone: (303) 887-3344; fax: (303) 887-3917
Airport: Denver
Location: 6 miles northwest of Granby off Highway 125, 95 miles west of Denver
Memberships: Colorado Dude and Guest Ranch Association, Cross-Country Ski Association
Awards: Mobil 5 Star, AAA 5 Diamond
Medical: Granby Medical Center
Conference: 70; spring, winter, and fall
Guest Capacity: 120
Accommodations: Rustic elegance reigns supreme here. The accommodations are comfortable and casual. Many cabins have fireplaces and vary from single rooms to family suites. Some have Jacuzzi bathtubs with stocked complimentary refrigerators. Full amenities include hair dryers, bathrobes, nightly turn-down service, fruit basket that is replenished daily, and fire that is reset daily.
Rates: • \$\$-\$\$\$\$. Full American Plan includes everything. Off-season and group rates available.
Credit Cards: None. Personal checks or cash accepted.
Season: June through September and mid-December through March. September is adults only.
Activities: Summer brings a full riding program with 145 horses. There are fast, medium, and slow rides depending on rider's ability and instructional rides for every level. Morning, afternoon, and weekly picnic rides. Some English riding. Horses are assigned for the week and matched to rider's ability. Usually six to eight to a ride. Adults and children ride separately, with the exception of the weekly family rides. Two laykold tennis courts with tennis pro who gives complimentary tennis instruction, spring-fed, heated pool, indoor sauna and whirlpool, championship racquetball court, trap and skeet range, fishing in stocked pond or in Willow Creek (guided fishing can be arranged on the Colorado River), white water raft trips (30 minutes away, extra), and golf nearby. Winter: See Cross-Country Ranch section write-up.
Children's Programs: Kids and adults do their own thing. Parents and kids love it! Extensive children's and teens' program for ages 3 to 17. Kids' playroom and dining room. Children eat together at lunch and dinner. Families with children under age 3 must bring their own nanny/babysitter. Ask about designated baby weeks.
Dining: Guests enjoy happy hour before dinner in the cozy lodge bar, often accompanied by live grand piano background music. Prime rib, steaks, fresh vegetables, and homemade breads. Poolside cookouts twice weekly. Special meals on request. Full wine service with dinner.
Entertainment: Square dancing, cookouts, campfires, and sing-alongs. Cowboy singer, staff shows, Western band, and weekly "Shodeo"—part show, part rodeo.
Summary: One of the top year-round guest ranches in the world. Destination ranch resort. Premiere children's programs. Superb for families and couples.September is adults-only month. Spectacular Rocky Mountain National Park nearby. French, German, and Spanish spoken.

See color photos, page 200

Deer Valley Ranch
Nathrop, Colorado

Deer Valley Ranch is surrounded by 14,000-foot peaks, Mt. Princeton and Mt. Antero, with the Chalk Cliffs forming the backdrop. This Christian guest ranch has been in the same family since 1954. Harold DeWalt and John Woolmington, who now run the ranch, are committed to creating a very special atmosphere for all ages. The ranch places a strong emphasis on the family and does not allow any alcoholic beverages. Their ranch program is extensive, with special activities planned from dawn to late evening.

Address: Box K, Nathrop, Colorado 81236
Telephone: (719) 395-2353; fax: (719) 395-2394
Airport: Colorado Springs or Denver; private planes to Buena Vista, 10 miles
Location: 12 miles southwest of Buena Vista, 100 miles directly west of Colorado Springs on Highway 162
Memberships: Colorado Dude and Guest Ranch Association
Medical: Buena Vista Medical Clinic, 10 miles; Salida Hospital, 25 miles
Conference: 125 can meet in the two-story, 1,500-square-foot Centennial Hall or in two other meeting areas (off-season only).
Guest Capacity: 125
Accommodations: Ten-bedroom guest lodge with Western-decorated living area, attached to main dining rooms. Fifteen housekeeping cottages of two, three, or four bedrooms and one or two baths with fireplaces and spacious decks. The cottages are scattered in the trees around the main lodge. Cottage names like St. Elmo, Whitehorn, Tincup, and Pitkin reflect the Western mining heritage of the valley. Meeting and recreation rooms.
Rates: • $-$$. Full American Plan in the ranch lodge and a Modified European Plan in the cottages. Meals may be prepared in the cottages, though guests are asked to eat at least one meal each day in the lodge. Children's rates for ages 6-12 and 3-5. Horses are not included but may be rented by the hour or week.
Credit Cards: None. Personal checks accepted.
Season: Year-round, including all holidays
Activities: Full daily program including a complete horseback experience. Instructional riding, trail riding in the San Isabel National Forest, and high country riding above timberline. Tennis court. Free golf privileges at the Collegiate Peaks Golf Course in Buena Vista. Trout fishing in Chalk Creek, the stocked ranch lake, high country lakes, or the Arkansas River. Free fly-fishing instruction and trips to the Fryingpan, Roaring Fork, and South Platte rivers. Two hot spring pools (90°-95°), outdoor hot tub, and indoor whirlpool and sauna. Extensive hiking program. Orienteering program. Whitewater rafting on the nearby Arkansas is extra. Four-wheel-drive vehicles are available at the ranch for half-day and full-day rental.
Children's Programs: Family vacation ranch with most activities planned for families to be together. Children have their own program for two to six hours each day, at parent's discretion. Full-time children's director. Special play areas for children, including Western town. Babysitting extra. Game room.
Dining: Three meals daily in ranch dining room overlooking Mt. Antero. Box lunches, wrangler's breakfast, cookout lunch, and steak fry ride. Special diets accommodated.
Entertainment: Nightly programs, square dancing on the lodge deck, slide shows and history talks, campfires with western music, western staff show, big screen TV and many western videotapes. Sunday morning worship service and evening hymn sing.
Summary: Christian family guest ranch for families, couples, single parents, and singles, with full program of ranch activities. You determine your own activities and even adjust your expenses by determining how many meals you want in the dining room and what riding you do. A complete family destination vacation. Be sure to get a copy of the ranch cookbook.

Diamond J Guest Ranch
Meredith, Colorado

The Diamond J is a year-round, friendly, family-owned ranch for families, singles, and honeymoon couples who enjoy fresh air, tall pines, mountain peaks, and trout streams. The ranch is at 8,300 feet in the Frying Pan River Valley, surrounded by the White River National Forest. It has been owned and operated by the Sims family since 1981. Prior to that, it was a hunting and fishing lodge dating back to the early 1920s. The Diamond J offers full summer and winter programs with plenty of activities for all. Cross-country skiing enthusiasts will enjoy some of the best skiing in Colorado. The ranch is an overnight stop on the Tenth Mountain Division Trail between Aspen and Vail. Be sure to ask about the jeep ride to the Continental Divide. At 12,259 feet, the air is wonderfully fresh and the view . . .as far as the eye can see.

Address: 26604 Frying Pan Road, Drawer K, Meredith, Colorado 81642
Telephone: (303) 927-3222
Airport: Aspen via Denver
Location: 45 miles northeast of Aspen, 45 miles east of Glenwood Springs off Highway 82
Memberships: Colorado Dude and Guest Ranch Association, Colorado State Snowmobile Association
Medical: Aspen and Glenwood Springs, 45 minutes
Conference: 50
Guest Capacity: 72
Accommodations: The ranch has a cozy two-story, nine-room lodge and twelve log cabins. Each cabin is decorated in a rustic western style with fireplaces, stoves, and gas heat, and each has its own character and squeaky carpeted floors. Winter guests stay in the lodge. Laundry facilities available.
Rates: • $-$$. American and European plans. Children's rates available. No minimum stay.
Credit Cards: Visa, MasterCard, American Express
Season: All year, except Easter, Thanksgiving, and Christmas
Activities: Summer program includes horseback riding with instruction, and everyone gets instruction. Half-day and all-day group trail rides and pack trips. Summer activities abound at the Diamond J. The extensive horse program is handled by Dale and Gail Coombs, who have more than 25 years of experience with horses. Youngsters will also develop their riding skills under this couple's watchful eyes. Parents should know that by Friday their children will be participating in the ranch's fun and exciting guest rodeo. Trail rides with 10 to 15 guests are scheduled daily and last from two to six hours. Ask Martha or Bill about their spectacular Mt. Yakael ride or their easygoing Montgomery Flats ride. Fishing in the Fryingpan River (a gold medal stream), which runs through the ranch. White water rafting, four-wheel-drive trips, volleyball, hiking, horseshoes, and tennis on a clay court. Seasonal deer and elk hunting. Whirlpool year-round. Winter brings cross-country skiing. Snowshoeing, downhill skiing, and snowmobile trails nearby. Bring your own cross-country gear.
Children's Programs: The ranch encourages children to enjoy their ranch vacation with mom and dad. Supervised horse program. Baby-sitting available on request.
Dining: Western home cooking. Barbecued ribs a specialty. As Martha says, "Don't come here to lose weight." Special meals can be prepared. BYOB.
Entertainment: Most guests are so delightfully worn out by the end of the day that they retire to their cabins. Weekly ranch rodeo and staff shows.
Summary: Martha and Bill, along with their staff, set the stage for one heck of a great week. Warning: Your children may not want to go home with you. Year-round, friendly family ranch for families, singles, and honeymoon couples. Nearby: Victorian town of Aspen, hot springs pool in Glenwood. town of Marble with nearby quarry.

Don K Ranch
Pueblo, Colorado

The Don K Ranch is in southern Colorado, about thirty miles from Pueblo. From the main road, one takes a 2-mile drive through a canyon with sheer cliffs, which opens to the beautiful ranch valley. The ranch is owned by the Smith family, which hails from Columbia, South Carolina. In the late 1960s, the Smiths began looking for the perfect guest ranch. In 1987, they found it in the Don K. Over the years, the ranch has hosted notables including the ambassador to Uruguay. The Smiths exude southern hospitality in their western wonderland. The ranch is surrounded by the San Isabel National Forest. You can ride through meadows, over mountain trails, or through the forest. An abundance of pines surround the buildings. The two-story main lodge is reminiscent of days gone by, with its walkways, lawns, colorful flower boxes, and garden.

Address: 2677 South Siloam Road, Dept. K, Pueblo, Colorado 81005
Telephone: (719) 784-6600, (800) 879-0307; call for fax number
Airport: Pueblo, Colorado Springs
Location: 30 miles west of Pueblo off Highway 96, 60 miles south of Colorado Springs, 120 miles south of Denver. Call for directions.
Memberships: Dude Ranchers' Association, Colorado Dude and Guest Ranch Association
Medical: Parkview Hospital, 30 miles
Conference: 25
Guest Capacity: 60
Accommodations: The Don K Ranch, the home of Charles Bronson's movie *Mr. Majestyk*, has six upstairs lodge rooms, with names like Mr. Majestyk, War Wagon, and True Grit, and six cabins, with names like Jessie James, Billy the Kid, and Geronimo. All rooms are fully carpeted and have gas and electric heat and wood paneling. Cabins have private baths, while the lodge has large semiprivate baths. The cabins accommodate from two to six and feature colorful western and Indian decor. All units with porches offer mountain, forest, and central ranch views. Daily maid service. Laundry available.
Rates: • $$-$$$. American Plan. White water rafting extra. Children's, group, and off-season rates available. Sunday to Sunday arrival. Two-night minimum off-season.
Credit Cards: Visa, MasterCard, American Express; personal checks or cash preferred
Season: Mid-May through October
Activities: Guests are assigned a horse for their entire stay and are divided by ability—beginner, intermediate, and advanced. Five rides go out morning and afternoon, two for children and three for adults. Parents may ride with kids. Kids ride together. Ask about the Edge of the World, ghost town, and Red Shadow. Usually six to eight in a ride. Weekly brunch and all-day rides. Horses get the day off on Sunday. Heated pool, professional tennis court, volleyball, and hot tub. Hiking, white water rafting in Royal Gorge.
Children's Programs: Excellent program available for children ages 3 to 5 and 6 to 16. Children 3 to 5 ride under supervision around the ranch. Children's overnight camp-out, playground with swings. Kids rodeo, treasure hunts, arts and crafts, and playroom.
Dining: Delicious ranch meals served family-style. Daily fresh breads and pastries. Poolside barbecue cookouts. Optional children's dining table. Drinks and wine available at Bear Head Saloon in lodge. Weekly steak cookouts. Brunch on the trail.
Entertainment: Square dancing, country-western band, campfires, sing-alongs, western movies, games, rodeo awards night, and videos of the guests "in action." Ask about Indian night.
Summary: Wonderful, secluded family ranch where you will feel like a member of the family. Excellent children's program, thus parents are on vacation too. This is a family-oriented ranch. Couples and singles welcome. Adults-only weeks. Nearby: Colorado Springs and Royal Gorge.

See color photos, page 201

Drowsy Water Ranch
Granby, Colorado

The Drowsy Water Ranch is exactly what you imagine a classic mountain dude ranch would be. This 600-acre ranch is in the beautiful Rocky Mountains bordered by thousands of acres of backcountry and the Arapahoe National Forest. This ranch is situated in a valley at 8,200 feet and surrounded by shimmering aspen and scented pine. Drowsy Water is genuine and offers its guests great Colorado hospitality. The recently remodeled log cabins are situated along Drowsy Water Creek, which meanders through the ranch. The Foshas are hosts and owners of this mountain paradise. Ken and Randy Sue offer an outstanding horse program for experts and beginners and a full program for children of all ages. You won't forget their home-cooked meals, whether enjoyed at cookouts, on the trail, or at the main lodge. You'll eat plenty of homemade breads, tasty salads, baked chicken, and sizzling steaks, and you'll sleep like a baby. There is old-fashioned goodness to this ranch. It brings to mind another century when people were less hurried and really cared about each other.

Address: P.O. Box 147K, Granby, Colorado 80446
Telephone: (303) 725-3456
Airport: Denver
Train: Amtrak to Granby, 6 miles
Location: 90 miles west of Denver, 6 miles west of Granby off U.S. 40
Memberships: Dude Ranchers' Association, Colorado Dude and Guest Ranch Association
Medical: Granby Clinic, 6 miles
Conference: 40
Guest Capacity: 60
Accommodations: Guests enjoy comfortable and clean log cabins that are sheltered in stands of aspen and pine overlooking Drowsy Water Creek and the ranch ponds. Cabins have covered porches. The largest sleeps nine and looks out over the ranch's pond. The newly remodeled cabins accommodate from two to nine persons. There are also eight rooms in the main lodge. All have private baths.
Rates: • $$-$$$. Full American Plan; minimum one-week stay in high season, Sunday to Sunday. Family, children's, and off-season rates. Pack trips and river rafting extra.
Credit Cards: None. Cash, personal checks, or traveler's checks accepted.
Season: June to mid-September
Activities: One hundred fine horses provide all the riding you could possibly want. Ken and Randy Sue raise many of their own paint horses. Fast, slow, and all-day rides to beautiful vistas to 10,500 feet, pack trips, and cookout rides. Riding here will get you to some spectacular high country and views of the Continental Divide. Riding instruction available. River rafting on the Colorado River. Hayrides, fishing (equipment for beginners provided), heated pool, and whirlpool. Golf and tennis nearby. Seasonal hunting for elk and deer. Two championship golf courses down the road.
Children's Programs: This is one of the top children's ranch programs in the country. Supervised children's program for ages 6 to 13 with daily counseled games and crafts. Special horse program builds confident riders. Children under 5 have a special program that includes horseback riding and games, crafts, and picnic hikes. Weekly kids' gymkhana.
Dining: Lots of home-cooked, hearty meals, salad bar. BYOB in cabins only. Families usually eat together.
Entertainment: Something different each night. Monday, square dancing; Tuesday, hayride for kids with marshmallow toasting and adults-only dinner; Wednesday, country swing band; Thursday, carnival night; Friday, adults-only hayride; Saturday, staff show. Weekly rodeos in town.
Summary: Drowsy Water is one of the top family-owned and operated ranches in the country for parents with young children. It is also great for couples and singles. Lifelong friendships have been made here. Nearby: Rocky Mountain National Park.

Elk Mountain Ranch
Buena Vista, Colorado

Elk Mountain Ranch is a cozy hideaway, high in the Colorado Rockies at 9,535 feet. It is dedicated to excellence and provides wonderful hospitality and off-the-beaten-path charm. The ranch, ten miles into the beautiful San Isabel National Forest, is surrounded by lush aspens, evergreen forests, and distant snowcapped peaks. It has been in operation since 1981. Hosts Tom and Sue Murphy take great pride in pampering their guests, and they do! Elk Mountain is a family-oriented ranch with wonderful horseback rides and friendliness. Nature lovers and photographers will especially appreciate the abundance of deer, elk, and wildflowers. Everyone will take home fond memories and savor the peacefulness and relaxation. One family remarked, "It was quite simply the best time we've ever had!"

Address: P.O. Box 910K, Buena Vista, Colorado 81211
Telephone: (719) 539-4430
Airport: Denver
Location: 100 miles southwest of Denver, 70 miles west of Colorado Springs, 20 miles southeast of Buena Vista; ranch will send you a detailed map.
Memberships: Dude Ranchers' Association, Colorado Dude and Guest Ranch Association
Awards: *Hideaway Report*
Medical: Buena Vista Medical Clinic, Salida Hospital
Conference: 25 (early June or late September for less than one week)
Guest Capacity: 35
Accommodations: The main lodge houses the dining room with fireplace, cowboy and mining artifacts, sitting room, library, sun deck, and the upstairs Elk guest suite. There are six one- and two-bedroom log cottages with private baths and queen- and king-size beds, as well as the Pioneer Lodge with four private rooms and baths, all tastefully furnished. Fresh fruit is always in the rooms. Sue loves flowers and always has a colorful array hanging from cabin porches and on the main deck. The ranch generates its own electricity. Lights are out at 11:00 p.m.
Rates: • $$. American Plan with one-week minimum stay, Sunday to Sunday. Children's and off-season rates available.
Credit Cards: Visa, MasterCard, American Express. Personal and traveler's checks accepted.
Season: June through September
Activities: Horseback riding is wonderful at Elk Mountain with miles of trails and spectacular views of the distant Collegiate Peaks. Tom gives an excellent horse orientation program every Monday morning. Overnight wilderness pack trips to Cow Gulch 12 miles away. Be sure to ask Sue about the weekly brunch trail ride overlooking Brown's Canyon. White water rafting on the Arkansas River near the ranch. Weekly auto trips to Aspen for the views and shopping. Rifle marksmanship and trap shooting (guns provided), trout fishing in two stocked ponds (some fishing gear is available at the ranch's trading post), archery, horseshoes, and volleyball.
Children's Programs: Full children's program for ages 4 to 7. Ranch encourages parents to interact with kids. Children eat with grown-ups.
Dining: Great, hearty ranch food. Freshly baked breads and desserts, evening hors d'oeuvres, BYOB. Weekly barbecues and Saturday candlelight dinners. One guest described it best: "The food is super!" No smoking in dining room.
Entertainment: Old western and kids' movies, library, chess, backgammon, tractor hayrides, square dances, campfires, hammered dulcimer concert.
Summary: Wonderful, remote, small, family-oriented ranch. Delightful, energetic hosts and excellent staff, who love what they do and it shows. Riding is the main activity. Great for families, couples, and singles who enjoy outdoors and a remote wilderness setting. Great ranch store called the Trading Post.

See color photo, page 202

Everett Ranch
Salida, Colorado

The Everett Ranch was established in the 1890s by the great-grandparents of the present owners. This 15,000-acre working cattle ranch with 1,000 head of cross-bred hereford and angus cattle has stayed in the family and is now being operated by the third and fourth generations of Everetts. Northeast of Salida, the ranch covers many thousands of acres ranging from desert to alpine meadows, from rocky canyons to open spaces. The Ute Indians used to summer in the high country and come down to the valley in the winter. Over the years, many arrowheads have been found here. In September, the leaves are changing color and the bull elk are bugling. For serious cowboys and cowgirls only—it's the Old West here. You should be in good health and ready for the rough life at cow camp. If you are ready to get away from your fax machine and step back in time, the Everett family will show you how. Guests have come from as far as Germany, France, and Switzerland. If you expect electric blankets and need your hair dryer, ride on.

Address: 10615 County Road 150K, Salida, Colorado 81201
Telephone: (719) 539-4097
Airport: Denver, 150 miles; Colorado Springs, 100 miles
Location: Cow Camp 20 miles northeast of Salida, Winter Home 5 miles northwest of Salida, 150 miles south of Denver
Memberships: Colorado Outfitters Association, National Cattleman's Association, Colorado Cattleman's Association
Medical: Salida Hospital, 20 miles
Guest Capacity: 10
Accommodations: Three cow camp metal cabins. Each sleeps at least four (one double bed and one bunk bed). No electricity, running water, or telephone. Outhouse and solar-heated shower nearby. Bring your own bedroll and towels.
Rates: • $. American Plan. Children's rates available under 12.
Credit Cards: None. Personal and traveler's checks accepted.
Season: June to October
Activities: The Everetts provide excellent cow horses, which they try to match to the rider's ability. Lots of cattle work and some basic roping lessons. Depending on the day, guests may be in the saddle for six to eight hours, and that's one heck of a lot of riding for a tenderfoot! While the Everetts will take folks who have never ridden, it would be in your best interest to have put in at least 20 hours in the saddle (or whatever you can manage) before you arrive. Float trips can be arranged. Excellent fall hunting for elk and deer.
Children's Programs: Children are welcome but should be old enough to enjoy a full day in the saddle. Recommended for children over 9.
Dining: Wholesome meals are cooked on a wood stove in main cow camp cabin. Breakfast and dinner are the big meals of the day. Dining table seats 15, and everyone eats together.
Entertainment: Just the stars and Mother Nature. Horseshoe pitching and the famous Everett cow camp "cheat-your-neighbor" card game. May take in a local rodeo or roping once in a while.
Summary: Perhaps this guest's letter best sums it up: "I want to thank you so much for the wonderful time you showed me at your ranch. I enjoyed experiencing the lifestyle of getting up in the morning and getting on a horse instead of in a car and fighting rush hour traffic! I enjoyed the landscape and eating the delicious meals." Real cattle ranch. Abundant wildlife, including elk, mule deer, mountain sheep, coyotes, and antelope. Sixty miles away from the Royal Gorge Bridge, one of the highest suspension bridges in the world. No hookups but will take RVs.

4UR Ranch
Creede, Colorado

The present owners bought the 4UR in the early 1970s. Today the ranch is cheerfully managed by Rock Swenson and his wife, Kristen. The same timeless qualities of nature, history, and hospitality continue to make the 4UR Ranch a delightful experience. The ranch is high in the San Juan Mountains of southwestern Colorado. The old CF and I Fluorspar Mine from the early 1900s keeps a watchful eye over the ranch. For discriminating fly-fishing guests, there is private fishing on the Rio Grande and on Goose Creek. There are also the two Lost Lakes at 11,000 feet. July and August are the ranch's busiest months. September is a favorite for fishermen.

Address: P.O. Box 340K, Creede, Colorado 81130
Telephone: (719) 658-2202; fax: (719) 658-2308
Airport: Alamosa airport via Denver; 6,800-foot paved airstrip in Creede, nearby, with hangar facilities for guests
Location: 222 miles southwest of Denver, 60 miles west of Alamosa, 8 miles southeast of Creede off Highway 149
Medical: St. Joseph's Hospital in Del Norte, 40 miles
Conference: 50, June and September
Guest Capacity: 50
Accommodations: Guest facilities consist of three 1950s vintage cedar shake mini-lodges. Rooms share a common breezeway porch, but each has its own entrance. Numerous rockers are on each porch. All have private baths, thermostatic heating, and daily maid service. Each night beds are turned down. Two family cottages are available at certain times. The main lodge, with its dining and living room, splendid valley views, bar, and game room, is the center stage for evening socializing. Laundry service is available.
Rates: • $$-$$$. American Plan. Includes all activities on ranch except jeep trips, trap shooting, raft trips, guided hikes, and fly-fishing instruction. Children's rates available. Children under 4 free. Group and conference rates available. Seven-day minimum stay in July and August, Sunday to Sunday.
Credit Cards: Visa, MasterCard, American Express
Season: Early June through September
Activities: Fly-fishing on river and in alpine lakes with instruction available on request. Each evening fishermen roll the dice and select their own half-mile stretch of water for the following morning fishing. Bring your own gear. Some flies and equipment available. Breakfast, morning, afternoon, and all-day horseback rides through very scenic country; most rides are walking. Heated swimming pool, log bathhouse with sauna, hot sulfur baths, whirlpool. Exercise and massage room with licensed massage therapist available. Tennis court, hiking, rafting, and jeep trips available. Trap shooting (ranch prefers you bring your own guns).
Children's Programs: Counselor for kids over 6. Junior wrangler program teaches kids about horses. Baby-sitting provided with advance notice. Bring your own nanny if you wish full-time care.
Dining: Fisherman's early continental breakfast followed by regular full-course breakfast. Weekly breakfast ride along the Rio Grande with biscuits and gravy, scrambled eggs and ham, baked apples, and cowboy coffee. Once a week, the ranch features a high noon fish fry along Goose Creek. Gourmet backcountry picnics. Full-service bar and wine service available.
Entertainment: Unscheduled children's gymkhana, jeep-pulled hayrides, video movie classics (Westerns and Disney). Evening fly-tying.
Summary: Wonderful guest ranch on scenic Goose Creek, famous for its excellent fly-fishing. Eight and one-half miles of private waters. Family oriented during July and August. Mostly adults during September. Hot sulfur pool. Mel Krieger fly-fishing school in June. Old "Doc" buggy and six-seat surrey rides.

Forbes Trinchera Ranch
Fort Garland, Colorado

Malcolm Forbes was a man with a passion for business, people, and life. Forbes Trinchera Ranch was one of his hideaways where he would come to savor the tranquil wide open spaces, to think, reflect, and entertain. Today, the ranch is owned by *Forbes Magazine*. It is located in the famous Sangre de Cristo Mountains. It encompasses over 180,000 acres of spectacular mountain countryside. It has been developed into a facility for executive conferences. The main lodge and conference area is situated in the Trinchera Valley, which is dominated by 13,517-foot Trinchera Peak. The lodge itself is a virtual museum of art, seascapes, model ships, and bronzes that Malcolm collected over the years. With a warm family-like spirit, the Forbes Trinchera Ranch offers corporate and business groups, beauty, privacy, and luxury. It is a place to think, create, recharge, and have fun. Malcolm Forbes wouldn't have wanted it any other way.

Address: P.O. Box 149 K, Fort Garland, Colorado 81133
Telephone: (719) 379-3264; fax: (719) 379-3266
Airport: Alamosa Municipal Airport, 35 miles
Location: 2 miles east of Fort Garland, Colorado, on U.S. 160; 200 miles southwest of Denver
Medical: San Luis Valley Regional Medical Center
Conference: 46
Guest Capacity: 46
Accommodations: The lodge and accommodations have a Southwest flavor—adobe brown and white trim. The main lodge sleeps 30 with 16 luxurious bedrooms, most with two queen-size beds, several with king-size beds. Each has original art and cedar siding. The adobe house across the courtyard has four bedrooms, two with two queen-size beds, two with king-size beds. The motif is country. The original log house next to the adobe house has two bedrooms with queen-size bed. All rooms have telephones, alarm clocks, and comforters.
Rates: $$$$. American Plan. Six rooms, three-night minimum.
Credit Cards: None. Personal checks and cash accepted.
Season: January through August
Activities: Activities are tailored to individual groups. Over the years men and women alike have come to fish and horseback ride. Fishing in Trinchera, Ute, and Indian creeks for rainbow and brook trout. All small streams. All gear is provided. Horseback riding is limited to 8 riders at a time, at almost any hour of the day. All riding is done at a walk. Sporting clays (five stations—guns and ammunition provided). Eighteen-hole golf course nearby. Winter: Ice fishing in ponds, game spotting, guided snowmobile trips (four machines), sporting clays, cross-country skiing (rentals in Alamosa).
Children's Programs: None. Children not advised unless entire ranch is booked for family reunion.
Dining: Malcolm Forbes always appreciated good food. The tradition continues. The chef will accommodate your culinary wishes. Complimentary wine served with dinner.
Entertainment: You decide. The ranch's goal is to please you.
Summary: A world-class executive and group conference ranch/retreat. Family, reunions too!

Fryingpan River Ranch
Meredith, Colorado

Guest ranches began when visitors from other parts of the country came to stay with families in the west. That tradition is alive and well at the Fryingpan River Ranch. In early 1990, after a year-long search, Jim Rea found a ranch with great riding, great fishing, great views, and a great partner, Paula, who helps him share this very special place. This small historic ranch, located at 8,800 feet on the west side of Hagerman Pass and next to Nast Lake, accommodates guests who ride, fish, hike, mountain bike, and bask in the warmth of owners and staff. The ranch is the perfect spot for a vacation where some members of the family are avid fly-fishermen and others are more interested in the traditional guest ranch activities. Paula, an extremely talented wildlife artist, leads sketching hikes in fields of wildflowers that bloom in July and August. Personalized service and old-fashioned hospitality are served in abundance at the Fryingpan River Ranch.

Address: 32042 Fryingpan Road, Drawer K, Meredith, Colorado 81642
Telephone: (303) 927-3570; fax: (303) 927-9943
Airport: Aspen or Denver
Location: 31 miles east of Basalt on Fryingpan River Road, Colorado; 1¼ hours northeast of Aspen
Memberships: Dude Ranchers' Association, Colorado Dude and Guest Ranch Association
Awards: Orvis-Endorsed Lodge
Medical: Aspen or Glenwood Springs, 50 miles
Conference: 36
Guest Capacity: 36
Accommodations: Guests stay in six cabins and two two-bedroom lodge rooms. Each cabin has its own special charm. Some offer views of Nast Lake, while others overlook the Fryingpan River. Two are secluded in the pines away from the main activity of the lodge. Many of the rooms and cabins were redecorated recently with pine and antique furnishings, accented with art collected by Jim and Paula. Each has its own private bath and Paula's note cards in each room. The hot tub overlooks Nast Lake. No smoking in any of the buildings.
Rates: • $$$-$$$$. American Plan. Rates vary depending on the season. Ask about the fishing packages. Three-, four-, and seven-day stays.
Credit Cards: Visa, MasterCard. Personal checks and traveler's checks accepted.
Season: June to mid-October (summer); mid-October to mid-November (hunting); Thanksgiving to April (winter)
Activities: Summer brings a full horse program including instruction, half- and full-day rides, and a breakfast ride once a week. Overnight pack trips are available. Excellent fishing on the Gold Medal waters of the Fryingpan and Roaring Fork rivers. Nast Lake sits less than a hundred yards from the lodge and is full of brook and rainbow trout. Guided hiking and sketching hikes. Mountain biking, trap and rifle shooting, along with archery, river rafting, and four-wheel-drive trips are available. The hot tub is always open. Hardy swimmers enjoy Nast Lake. Winter activities: See cross-country write-up.
Children's Programs: No formal children's programs. Children are the responsibility of their parents. Paula has two children, so your children will be in good company.
Dining: The quality of the ranch food often attracts people from Aspen. The ranch features traditional foods cooked in healthy and creative ways. Wild game is often served along with beef, lamb, pork, chicken, and trout. BYOB.
Entertainment: Well-stocked library, VCR with a selection of videos, and a cozy log lodge.
Summary: You'll find lots of warmth and caring hospitality at this small family ranch located on Nast Lake. Great food and personal service. Good mountain horseback riding. Excellent fly-fishing on Gold Medal rivers. Be sure to talk with Paula about her art; she is a wonderful and very talented artist. Nearby: the famous mountain ski town of Aspen.

See color photos, pages 204-205

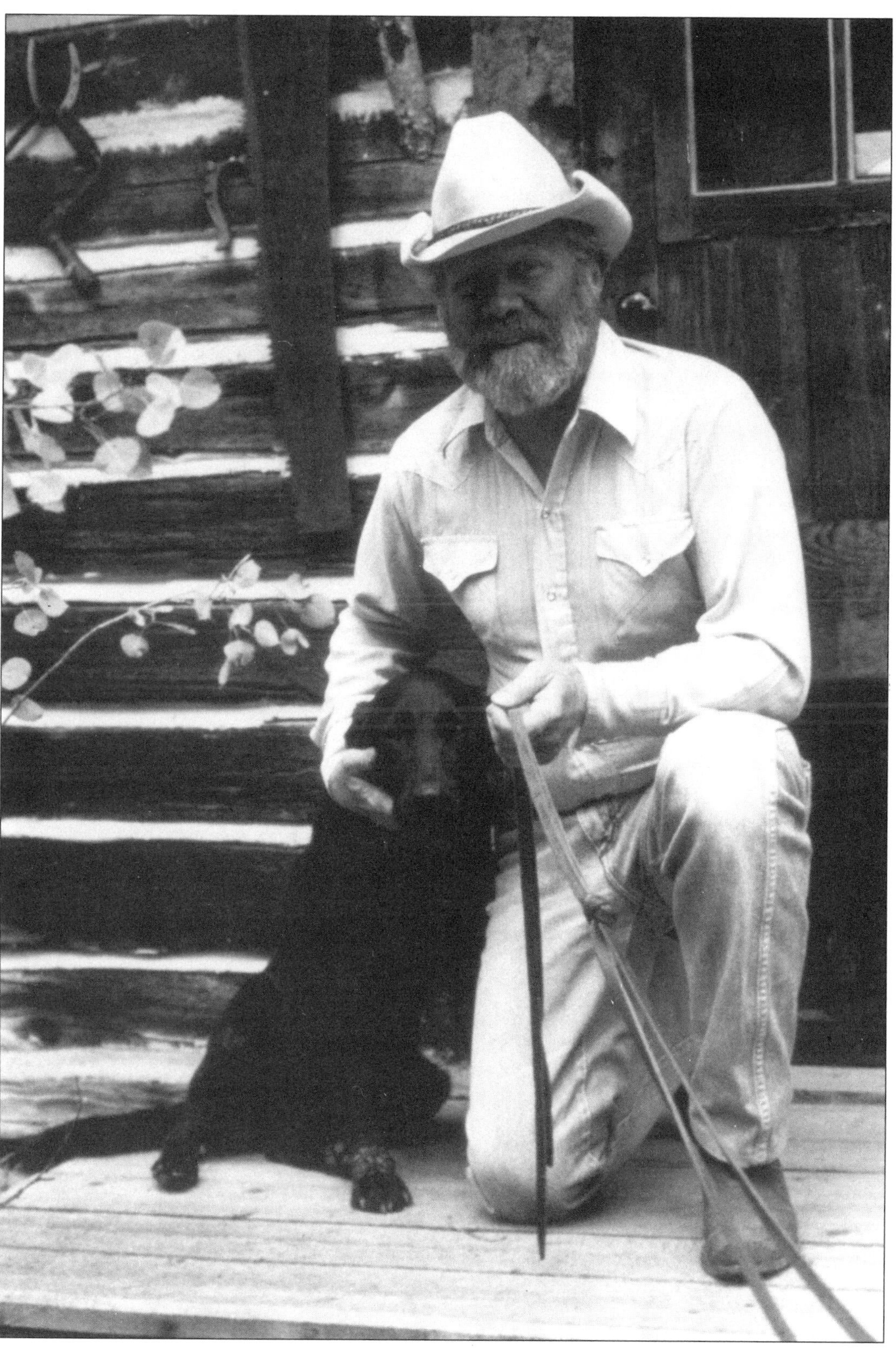

The Home Ranch
Clark, Colorado

As one drives up the gravel road to the ranch and sees the hand-hewn log buildings set among shimmering aspens, two words come to mind—paradise and, maybe better yet, heaven. The Home Ranch was the longtime dream of co-owner and builder Ken Jones, and his wife, Cile. Ken grew up on horses and got most of his guest ranch experience at the old Valley Ranch. While working there he met a guest who shared his enthusiasm. Ken and his partners, Steve and Ann Stranahan, have created a ranch so special that it boasts the highly coveted Relais and Chateaux membership, along with the Mobil 4-Star award. There is very little this ranch doesn't have for its guests. Best of all, it serves plenty of Old West rustic elegance and hospitality. The *Los Angeles Times* captured the essence when it said, "Here guests commune with a world as fresh as a Rocky Mountain raindrop."

Address: Box 822K, Clark, Colorado 80428
Telephone: (800) 223-7094, (303) 879-1780; fax: (303) 879-1795
Airport: Steamboat Springs via Denver
Location: 18 miles north of Steamboat Springs off Highway 129
Memberships: Dude Ranchers' Association, Colorado Dude and Guest Ranch Association, Relais and Chateaux
Awards: Mobil 4 Star
Medical: Steamboat Springs Hospital
Conference: 30
Guest Capacity: 45
Accommodations: Each beautiful log cabin is wonderfully furnished and set in a grove of aspen, ensuring privacy. Each has its own hot tub on a covered deck, great for total relaxation at the end of a day's ride or for warming up after cross-country skiing. There are also rooms on both levels in the handsome main lodge. A wonderful 2,500-square-foot, two-floor, hand-hewn log cabin for large families is available as well. All rooms with nightly turn-down service, wildflowers, and your own robe. Full laundry service available.
Rates: • $$$-$$$$. American Plan. Children's rates available.
Credit Cards: Visa, MasterCard, American Express. Personal checks accepted.
Season: Summer, June through mid-October; winter, mid-December through March
Activities: You are assigned your own horse for the duration of your stay. It's up to you how much you want to ride in the adjoining 1,000,000-acre Routt National Forest. Those who are interested will be taught how to saddle and bridle their horses. Rides go out in small groups each day accompanied by a wrangler. The ranch raises many of its own quarter horses. Ask Ken about his quarter horse breeding program. Heated swimming pool, fishing and fly casting in stocked pond or in the Elk River, all-inclusive fly-fishing program with instruction available for all guests. Extensive hiking program with two full-time nature guides. The hike to Gilpin lake is a favorite. Tennis and golf can be arranged nearby. Winter: See Cross-Country Skiing Ranches.
Children's Programs: Kiddie wrangler. Complete children's program for ages 3 through teens. Kids are completely looked after, breakfast to sunset. Riding starts at age 6. While the ranch is very flexible, there is a strict policy that absolutely no children under age 3 are allowed.
Dining: Excellent, mouth-watering gourmet meals. Younger children may eat dinner early. BYOB.
Entertainment: The Home Ranch features its own western band, which has recorded an album in Nashville. Ranch and Steamboat Springs rodeos, barrel racing. Top local entertainers.
Summary: A world-class guest ranch in a world-class setting! Ranch-raised quarter horses and breeding program. English riding, BYOH. Scottish Highland cattle. Full winter program.

See color photo, page 203

Lake Mancos Ranch
Mancos, Colorado

In the heart of southwestern Colorado's cowboy country is Lake Mancos Ranch. Since the early 1950s, the Sehnert family has hosted guests from around the country. One guest comes twice each year! Kathy, son Todd, and his wife, Robin, believe "American families still want to take a vacation in an atmosphere that isn't reeking of commercialism, with pinball machines and video games." The ranch leaves guests lots of leeway to enjoy all the activities, or to simply sit on the porch and watch the world go by. It is above the Mancos Valley at 8,000 feet, on a plateau between the West Mancos River and Chicken Creek, looking out to the La Plata Mountains. One family wrote, "Please know how grateful we are for the most relaxing and refreshing vacation ever." On their brochure they say, "Easygoin' vacation at its very best." And that's just the way it is.

Address: 42688 CR-N, Dept. K, Mancos, Colorado 81328
Telephone: (303) 533-7900, (800) 325-WHOA (9462)
Airport: Durango via Denver, Phoenix, or Albuquerque
Location: 5 miles north of Mancos, 35 miles west of Durango
Memberships: Dude Ranchers' Association, Colorado Dude and Guest Ranch Association
Medical: Cortez Hospital, 25 miles
Conference: 40
Guest Capacity: 55
Accommodations: There are seventeen bright red guest units with names like Spruce Mill, Golconda, and Lost Canyon, cabins of various sizes, and four spacious units with private bath in the ranch house for couples and singles. All heated family cabins have comfortable living rooms, bedrooms, bathrooms, private shady porches, king-size beds, refrigerators, and carpeting. Guest laundry available. Daily maid service.
Rates: • $$-$$$. American Plan. Nonriding, children's, and off-season rates available.
Credit Cards: Visa, MasterCard, Discover. Personal checks accepted.
Season: Early June to October. September is adults only.
Activities: Riding is the main activity at the ranch. A wide variety of scenic trails provide riders with a great opportunity to see some of Colorado's prettiest country. Many of the one- to six-hour trail rides explore shimmering aspen, spruce, and lush mountain meadows. Children and adults usually ride separately. Adults may ride with children if they like. Several times a week there are family rides. Because of the terrain, it is mostly walk and trot. Guests are assigned their own horses for their stay. Hiking and fishing (rods available for children) in Lake Mancos and nearby ranch stream. Heated pool and hot tub. Four-wheel-drive and wildflower trips. Wednesday is the open day. Many like to raft in Durango, golf in Cortez, or ride the spectacular Durango/Silverton steam train, which was started in 1882. Ask about the Anasazi Indian ruins.
Children's Programs: Children's program with counselors for ages 4 and up. Younger children not advised. Baby-sitting by special arrangement only. Movie nights and overnight cookout. Petting zoo and recreation room.
Dining: Home-style cooking and baking. Weekly barbecue creekside at Rendezvous Canyon. Cookies, coffee, and lemonade always plentiful. BYOB. Children may eat at children's table or with their parents.
Entertainment: You may just hear how the West was really won, or about wildflowers, or Anasazi Indian culture. Hayrides, cookouts, skits, and awards night.
Summary: Lake Mancos is for families who really enjoy being on vacation together. The Sehnert family is one of the oldest guest ranching families in Colorado. Very relaxed. Riding is the main activity. Many singles and couples enjoy the camaraderie of the family ranch. Adults only in September. Nearby: Old Durango and Silverton Railroad, Mesa Verde National Park, Telluride, Four Corners Monument, McPhea Dam and Dolores River.

See color photos, page 206

Lane Guest Ranch
Estes Park, Colorado

Lane Guest Ranch is a medium-size ranch that takes a maximum of seventy guests during the summer months. Previously inhabited by Arapaho Indians and later by mountain man Kit Carson, the area is known for its history, its abundance of wildlife, and its spectacular mountain scenery. Since 1954, Lloyd Lane and a staff of forty have received families, couples, and singles from around the country. The ranch sends potential guests plenty of information about the facilities. The motto here is, "We aim to please," and their brief poem that captures the spirit of the ranch goes like this: "Your time with us to relax, be at ease, time out from collars, ties, belts, and hose. There's no place here for city clothes, leave them home and give them a rest. Slacks are fine, but jeans are best. A jacket, a sweater will fill the bill to ward off the early morning chill. To hike, to ride, to leave cares behind, but remember to bring comfy shoes of any kind. So pack to play, enjoy your stay—there's something doing every day." As one guest put it, "I felt as if I had come home to a warm and cheerful large family." Welcome to the Lane Guest Ranch.

Address: P.O. Box 1766K, Estes Park, Colorado 80517
Telephone: (303) 747-2493
Airport: Denver International
Location: 67 miles northwest of Denver, 12 miles south of Estes Park off Highway 7
Memberships: American Hotel and Motel Association
Medical: Estes Park Hospital, 11 miles
Guest Capacity: 70
Accommodations: Log-sided units accommodate from two to six. Twenty-five units are comfortably furnished with queen-size beds, private baths, patios, hammocks, TV/VCR, stocked refrigerators, and radios. Eighteen units have their own hot tubs. Daily maid service. One-day laundry service provided (extra).
Rates: • $$-$$$. American Plan. Children's, senior, weekly, and honeymoon packages available. No minimum stay required (most guests stay at least a week).
Credit Cards: Visa, MasterCard
Season: June to early September
Activities: Daily ranch activity sign-up sheet, daily horseback riding (except Sunday) in Rocky Mountain and Roosevelt National Forests; 1½-hour to 2-hour morning and afternoon rides. Most riding is done at the walk, with occasional fast rides. Two overnight pack trips each week and wine and cheese rides for adults. Guided hikes, wildlife photography trips, fishing trips, riding instruction, four-wheel-drive, heated outdoor pool, hot tub, river rafting about two hours away. Two tennis courts nearby at Saint Malo. Eighteen-hole golf can be arranged. Massage available (masseuse on staff).
Children's Programs: Counselors, full child care available for infants and older children during the day. Kiddie wrangler. Baby-sitting available in the evening (extra). Playground with swings and sandbox.
Dining: Mealtimes are flexible. Menu offerings include fresh-squeezed orange juice, salad buffet, charcoal-broiled New York steaks, seafood dinners, broiled and poached salmon, prime rib, selection of California wines and mixed drinks (licensed bar), capuccino and espresso, poolside café, Sunday bar, complimentary house wine and beer.
Entertainment: Four nights of professional music at bar, shuffleboard, volleyball, horseshoes, well-stocked library, chess, table tennis, TV and over 500 video movies, Estes Park rodeos.
Summary: Lloyd Lane celebrated his 40th year in operation in 1992. The ranch is in one of the prettiest areas in Colorado, with high mountain peaks and natural splendor. If all you want to do is horseback ride, this is not the ranch for you. Come here to enjoy a wide variety of activities, food, and entertainment. High staff-to-guest ratio. Strong children's program for infants on up. Lots of families and couples. Video available on request. Pets allowed. Nearby: Estes Park for shopping—loaner cars available.

See color photo, page 207

Lazy H Guest Ranch
Allenspark, Colorado

Located on a mountain ridge, near the base of Mt. Meeker, Longs Peak, and Rocky Mountain National Park, the Lazy H Guest Ranch focuses its activities on horseback riding and children's programs. In 1992, Karen and Phil Olbert bought Lazy H Ranch. Along with their two daughters, Tami and Jenny, the Olberts have created an atmosphere for families and children to enjoy themselves without a highly regimented schedule. As Karen says, "We are very low-key in all aspects but are very hands-on." Riding is the main activity, but their educational mountain man talks in Owl Canyon and weekly Native American program give guests a wonderful feel for the Old West and nature. The Olbert family is excited about their ranch and their friendly spirit radiates throughout, right down to the Baron, Tina Turner, and M&M.

Address: P.O. Box 248K, 15747 Highway 7, Allenspark, Colorado 80510
Telephone: (800) 578-3598, (303) 747-2532; call for fax number
Airport: Denver, 65 miles
Location: 65 miles northwest of Denver, 16 miles south of Estes Park on Highway 7
Memberships: Colorado Dude and Guest Ranch Association
Medical: Estes Park Medical Center, 16 miles
Conference: 50
Guest Capacity: 50
Accommodations: The Navajo red and white trimmed, 13,000-square-foot log-sided and stone lodge was built in the 1930s. It is three stories and looks out across the valley. There are eleven guest rooms, each with its own individual charm. Rock Basin is the lovely honeymoon suite. There are three cabins; two are duplexes (Sundance and Cheyenne) that sleep up to 22 people. All cabins and rooms have private baths and twin, double, king-size, queen-size, and bunk beds.
Rates: • $$. American Plan. Children's and off-season rates. Three-day minimum stay in June. One-week minimum stay in July and August, Sunday to Sunday. Rafting and bicycle rental extra.
Credit Cards: Visa, MasterCard, Discover
Season: Year-round, May through September with horses
Activities: The main activities are horseback riding and the children's program. Horses have Sundays off. The length of the rides progresses over the course of the week. Guests are assigned the same horse for their entire stay, usually eight guests per wrangler. Most is walk-trot trail riding; some loping for advanced riders. Ask about the Meadow Mountain, Rock Creek breakfast, and Olive Ridge lunch rides. Overnight pack trip with advance reservations. Below the ranch in a little valley is Rock Creek where guests fish for browns and rainbows—all catch and release. Lots of unguided hiking in Roosevelt National Forest. Heated swimming pool in front of the lodge. Rafting on the Poudre or Colorado River with local outfitters.
Children's Programs: Experienced counselors help create memories your kids will have for a lifetime. Morning and afternoon program for kids 4 and up. Crafts, picnics, nature hikes, swimming, and the star-studded petting corral. Overnight camp-out in tepee a favorite with young kids. Beaver animal study.
Dining: Dining room looks out on Iron Clads and Meadow Mountain. Ranch-style, all-you-can-eat buffet and cookouts. Fully licensed bar. Wine available with dinner.
Entertainment: Usually something planned each evening. Marvelous Native American Indian magic show, singing cowboy, mountain man, campfire sing-alongs, country line dancing. Rec room with Ping-Pong, pool table, and video games.
Summary: Family-oriented, low-key ranch with plenty of riding, lots of children's activities (ask about Tina Turner), and nightly western entertainment. Wonderful Native American Indian show and mountain man talks. Ask about the mountain weddings and conference facilities. Nearby: Rocky Mountain National Park, Estes Park shopping.

See color photos, page 209

Latigo Ranch
Kremmling, Colorado

At 9,000 feet, the air is crisp, the view tremendous, and the hospitality sincere. Nature lovers will enjoy the breathtaking scenery and the abundance of wildflowers and wildlife on thousands of acres. Latigo Ranch runs a four-season program, from hayrides in the summer to snowshoeing in the winter. Here you can ride, hike, swim, fish, or interact with Salvadore or Pepe, the ranch llamas. Whether you and your family are at the ranch for the Fourth of July or Christmas, you can be sure of one thing—many special memories. If you want to have some interesting conversations, just ask your hosts about their educational backgrounds. It is not uncommon for guests to engage in high-level discussions. Mostly, though, everyone takes in nature's beauty and serenity.

Address: P.O. Box 237, Drawer K, Kremmling, Colorado 80459
Telephone: (303) 724-9008, (800) 227-9655; fax: (303) 724-9009 (call before sending)
Airport: Denver
Location: 130 miles northwest of Denver, 55 miles southeast of Steamboat Springs, 16 miles northwest of Kremmling
Memberships: Colorado Dude and Guest Ranch Association, Colorado Cross-Country Skiers Association, Dude Ranchers' Association
Awards: AAA 3 Diamond
Medical: Kremmling Memorial Hospital
Conference: 35
Guest Capacity: 35
Accommodations: Guests stay in contemporary log duplexes nestled in the pine forest and one fourplex that overlooks 75 miles of mountain ranges to the Continental Divide. Each is carpeted, with sitting room and fireplace or wood-burning stove. All have refrigerators and home-made caramel corn.
Rates: • \$\$-\$\$\$. American Plan. Children's rates available. Rates vary depending on the season. Three-day to one-week minimum stay.
Credit Cards: Visa, MasterCard, American Express
Season: Late May to mid-November (summer); late November to April (winter)
Activities: Summer offerings include heated swimming pool, fishing in streams and ranch pond, fly-fishing instruction, and day fishing trips. Horseback riding instruction for all levels on trails and in the arena. Breakfast and sunset rides; 1½-hour to 2½-hour rides go out twice a day and may vary from three to eight riders. Walk, trot, and lope. You may saddle your own horse here. Hot tub available for sore muscles. Pack trips, lots of hiking, and rafting nearby. In winter, there's cross-country skiing with instruction and snowshoeing. The ranch maintains 50 kilometers of trails with set track and skating lanes.
Children's Programs: Fully supervised program for ages 3 to 13 most of the day. Arts and crafts center. Kids under 6 do not ride on the trail. Babysitting available.
Dining: Excellent food both summer and winter ranging from ranch fare to gourmet. Weekly breakfast, lunch, and dinner cookouts. BYOB.
Entertainment: The three-story Social Club is a log-sided entertainment building, where guests enjoy happy hour (BYOB), square dancing, piano, pool room, and library.
Summary: Latigo Ranch is really known for three things: its hospitality (high staff-to-guest ratio), scenery, and horse program. The ranch is run by two families with very interesting backgrounds. High setting with excellent panoramic views. Photo workshops. Jim's geology and wildlife lectures. Be sure to see Jim Yost's movie on Ecuador, *Nomads of the Rain Forest*, a beautiful show seen on "Nova." Fall cattle roundup in late September.

See color photos, page 208

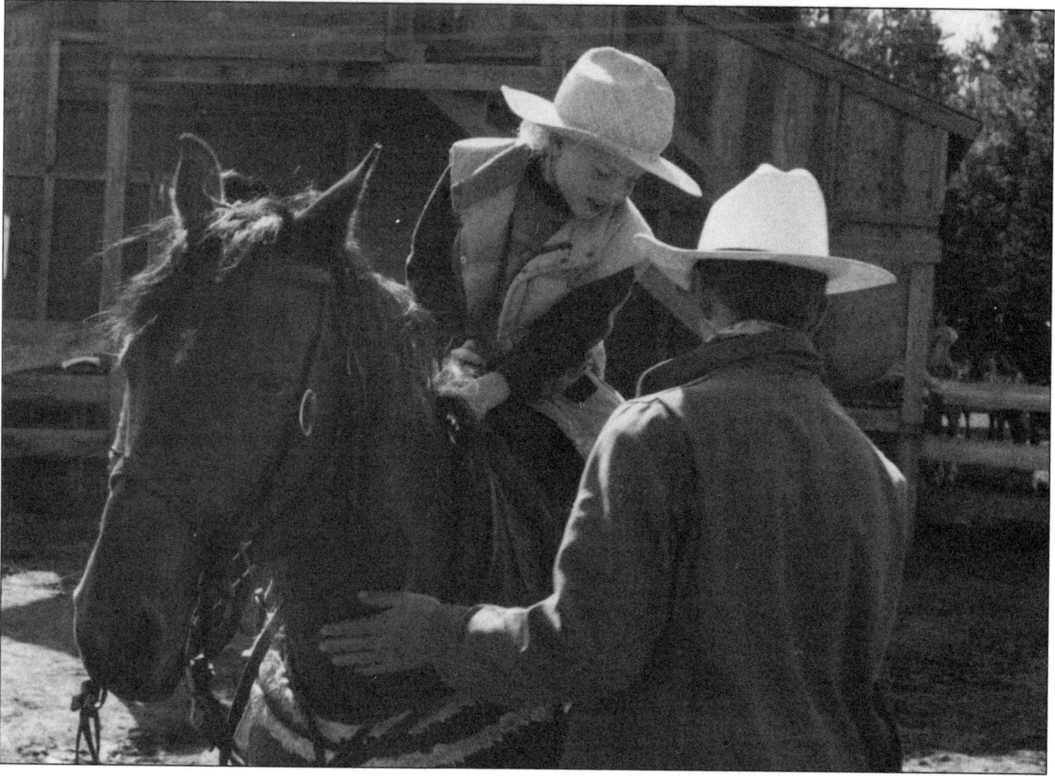

Lost Valley Ranch
Sedalia, Colorado

In the world of guest ranching, Lost Valley Ranch is right at the top. The qualities that make the Foster family's ranch so unique are their superb staff, excellent accommodations, and fabulous children's/teen program. Everyone at the ranch exudes a caring and enthusiastic spirit. Lost Valley has been in the ranching business for more than one hundred years and under the stewardship of two generations of Fosters for the past thirty years. This year-round cattle and horse ranch is set among tall pines on 40,000 acres of the Pike National Forest. At Lost Valley rugged adventure is combined with fun. Here guests become friends. If attendance and returning guests are any indication, the Fosters are doing everything right. Walt Disney stayed here years ago and said to the Fosters, "If I had this place, I would do all that I could not to change its character." The Fosters took his advice. The ranch is one of the best in the business.

Address: Route 2, Box K, Sedalia, Colorado 80135
Telephone: (303) 647-2311; fax: (303) 647-2315
Airport: Denver or Colorado Springs
Train: Amtrak to Denver
Location: 2 hours southwest of Denver, 1½-hours northwest of Colorado Springs, 12 miles southwest of Deckers
Memberships: Dude Ranchers' Association, Colorado Dude and Guest Ranch Association
Awards: AAA 4 Diamond; Mobil 3 Star
Medical: Langstaff-Brown Medical Clinic, 1 hour
Conference: 70, fall and spring only; largest room 1,800 square feet
Guest Capacity: 95
Accommodations: The twenty-four cabin suites (one to three bedrooms) are some of the finest in the business. All have living rooms, fireplaces, refrigerators, covered porches with swings, full private tub/shower baths, and amenities such as daily maid service, oversized towels, and a delightful cowboy hat amenities basket. To ensure peace and quiet, the cabins are nicely spaced among the pines. No TVs or telephones. Laundry facilities are available.
Rates: • $$-$$$. American Plan. Children's and spring/fall rates available. During summer there is a 7-day minimum stay policy, Sunday arrival.
Credit Cards: None
Season: February through November
Activities: At Lost Valley, guests learn to be better riders and gain a greater knowledge of Western riding skills. With 150 horses and 200 head of cows and calves, guests are encouraged to participate in ranch and cattle work. Fish in Goose Creek, which runs through the ranch, or drive 20 minutes and wet your fly in the world-famous Cheasman Canyon on the South Platte River. Orvis fishing guides are available. Heated outdoor swimming pool, two whirlpool spas, two plexi-paved tennis courts, trap shooting, and hiking.
Children's Programs: This is one of Lost Valley's strongest attractions. Children are looked after by fully trained staff members. This program provides tremendous fun for children, yet gives parents peace of mind knowing their children are safe and happy. The teens operate within a framework of freedom, friendship, and fun provided by the collegiate staff.
Dining: The Fosters and their staff eat with the guests. This is a wonderful tradition and one that is a real treat. Enjoy roast beef carved to your preference, fresh salads, homemade breads and desserts, wrangler breakfast, evening cookouts and steak fries. Nonsmoking dining room.
Entertainment: Entertainment is second to none. Lost Valley's staff is exceedingly talented. Enjoy musical entertainment, melodramas with shootouts, square dancing, hayrides, campfires, and sing-alongs.
Summary: Without question, this is one of the top guest ranches in North America. Excellent staff and superb children's and teens' programs. Year-round riding spring and fall, cattle roundups, special horsemanship weeks with top professional reining and cutting horse trainers, ranch store. A true destination vacation.

See color photos, page 210

JVL
LOST VALLEY RANCH
JVL
MEMBER - COLO.
DUDE & GUEST
RANCH ASSN.
AAA
APPROVED
POSTED

North Fork Guest Ranch
Shawnee, Colorado

North Fork Guest Ranch is located on the South Platte River. This ranch is for families who like to spend their vacation together. Dean and Karen May are the hosts and owners of this delightful riverside ranch. Like many others, they moved out West in the early 1980's, met, fell in love with each other and with Colorado, and stayed. Today, North Fork offers single parents and families a chance to ride, fish, hike, river raft, swim, play, and have wholesome fun together. President Eisenhower made this part of the country famous when he came to fish and relax in this valley. North Fork is a 520-acre turn-of-the-century property. The original homestead date back to the 1890s. One of the unique features of North Fork is the beautiful estate built out of native rock which looks out over the river and the ranch. Dean has a background in forestry and Karen in nursing, and together they share with their guests an understanding of the land and a compassion for all those who travel through their ranch gates. What makes North Fork unique is that the Mays encourage children and their parents to spend quality time together. North Fork Ranch is wonderful for young and older families who love the outdoors and being together.

Address: P.O. Box B-K, Shawnee, Colorado 80475
Telephone: (303) 838-9873, (800) 843-7895
Airport: Denver
Location: 50 miles southwest of Denver, 6 miles west of Bailey
Memberships: Dude Ranchers' Association, Colorado Dude and Guest Ranch Association
Medical: Conifer Mountain Medical Center, 20 miles. Karen May is a registered nurse.
Conference: 20, spring and fall
Guest Capacity: 43
Accommodations: The main lodge offers eight rooms, each with private bath. The Homestead cabin offers accommodations for three families of four people; each of the units has two bedrooms and a private bath. The Klondike cabin is a spacious duplex log cabin for families of four or six. Stonehenge, the three-story mansion, offers several sleeping arrangements for families. All accommodations are decorated in a unique style with antiques and western art. Daily maid service.
Rates: • $$-$$$. American Plan. Children's, off-season, and group rates available. Minimum one-week stay, Saturday to Saturday. Shorter stays in off-season.
Credit Cards: None
Season: May through September
Activities: Weekly program. Experienced wranglers guide groups of 6 to 8 on half-day and all-day rides, champagne brunch rides, and overnight pack trips. Rafting on the Arkansas River with certified outfitters. Target and trap shooting, fishing in the stocked pond or on the North Fork of the South Platte River. Weekly Orvis fishing class. Guiding and fishing equipment available. Swimming in heated pool next to the river, or relaxing in the spa at Stonehenge.
Children's Programs: Dean and Karen feel that the ranch is a place for parents and children to be together. Counselors and baby-sitters are available for kids under 8 when parents are riding or rafting.
Dining: Everyone eats together. Enjoy fresh breads, roast beef with bernaise sauce, full turkey dinners, barbecues, steak, and hamburger lunches. Friday farewell dinner features fresh trout or upland duck, quail, or pheasant. Special diets catered to. BYOB.
Entertainment: Square dancing with live caller. Campfire sing-alongs, evening fishing, and hayrides.
Summary: Located in a beautiful valley along the river. Great small family ranch for families who like to vacation with their children. North Fork was included on a "Good Morning America" segment and in *Good Housekeeping*.

See color photos, page 211

McNamara Ranch
Florissant, Colorado

McNamara Ranch takes only three guests, offers unlimited riding opportunities, and attracts mostly women. In fact, over 90 percent of the guests are women. As Sheila says, "I am a single parent. For several years my daughter helped me here. Now she is off on her own. I feel a kinship with women and have developed my program for women (and some couples) of all ages to come, relax, and ride this magnificent country with me." And when it comes to riding, the sky is the limit. Sheila is quite a horsewoman. She spent 25 years in Maryland showing hunters and jumpers and fox hunting. In fact, she still prefers an English saddle. As she says, "I haven't been off a horse in 30 years!" If lots of undivided attention, a riding program completely tailored to your riding abilities, and delicious barbecued lamb chops (lamb is her specialty) sounds like what you are looking for, read no further! Pick up the telephone and give Sheila a call.

Address: 4620 County Road 100, Drawer K, P.O. Box 702K, Florissant, Colorado 80816
Telephone: (719) 748-3466
Airport: Colorado Springs, 55 miles
Location: 55 miles west of Colorado Springs, 13 miles south of Florissant
Medical: St. Francis Hospital, Colorado Springs
Guest Capacity: 3
Accommodations: There are two bedrooms in the main house, one with a double bed and loft, the other with a double bed. Both share one bath in the laundry room with Dixie, the pet rabbit.
Rates: $. American Plan. Side trips extra. No minimum stay (most guests stay about four days).
Credit Cards: None. Personal checks or cash accepted.
Season: May through October
Activities: This is a working sheep ranch. In the morning and evening, there are always things to be done. Sheila gets up about 5:30 a.m. and hits the sack about 9:00 p.m. You are welcome to help tend the 9 head of horses and 100 head of sheep. After the morning chores are done, Sheila is yours. There are no set riding schedules. If you wish to ride to 14,000 feet and put nine nice hours in the saddle, you may do so. If you wish to ride bareback around the ranch, just ask Sheila. No nose to tail riding here. Just about the only thing you can't do here on horseback is ride on your own. With Sheila's knowledge of horses, the country, and friendly, caring spirit, I don't know why anyone would ever consider it.
Children's Program: There are a number of single parents who bring their children. Kids should be old enough to ride. More important, they should enjoy riding.
Dining: Sheila admits that riding is really her forte. She's a meat and potatoes chef. Enjoy hearty ranch cooking. Lamb is her specialty: scrumptious steaks, chops, and leg of lamb. Don't come here to lose weight. Sheila will ask you what your preferences are, including beverages and wine. BYOL.
Entertainment: By day's end and after a big dinner, usually everyone is pretty tuckered out. Early to bed and early to rise is a good rule of thumb.
Summary: This is a small, working sheep ranch run by a woman mostly for women and some couples. Sheila would like you to feel like you are visiting a friend in Colorado. Unlimited riding opportunities for all riding abilities.

Old Glendevey Ranch
Glendevey, Colorado

Garth and Olivia Peterson have traveled all over the world. Garth is a senior captain for one of the major airlines and flies only international routes. At 40,000 feet, one has a chance to reflect and really think about the important things in life. For Garth, that is the great outdoors and the backcountry of Colorado. He was raised in the country and has always appreciated wildlife and the unspoiled wilderness. To fulfill his passion and love for the outdoors, he began his wilderness pack trip business in 1975. In 1985, Garth and Olivia bought Old Glendevey Ranch so they could share their love for the great outdoors with families and single people from around the world. Old Glendevey Ranch is special in that it combines ranch stays with wilderness pack trips. For those who really want to get away from it all and experience nature at its best, the wilderness pack trip is a must. Old Glendevey Ranch is for those who would like a true wilderness experience and a ranch stay as well.

Address: Old Glendevey Ranch Ltd., Glendevey Colorado Route P.O., Drawer K, Jelm, Wyoming 82063
Telephone: (303) 435-5701
Airport: Laramie, Wyoming, 55 miles. Pick-up available (extra).
Location: Approximately 100 miles northwest of Ft. Collins, Colorado, off Laramie River Road; 55 miles southwest of Laramie, Wyoming, off Larimer 190
Memberships: Dude Ranchers' Association, Colorado Dude and Guest Ranch Association, Colorado Outfitters Association
Medical: Ivinson Memorial Hospital, Laramie, 55 miles
Conference: 18 overnight
Guest Capacity: 18
Accommodations: The two-story lodge offers a large dining room, lounging area with stone fireplace, and seven bedrooms upstairs, all newly carpeted and remodeled and very comfortable. Large men's bathroom facilities and separate large women's facilities. A game room plus library. Also large guest porch to take in the scenery.
Rates: $$. American Plan. Children's, group, and nonrider rates. Minimum three-night stay. Arrivals any day.
Credit Cards: None. Personal checks and cash accepted.
Season: June through mid-September, October to mid-November (hunting)
Activities: Horseback riding, fishing, hiking, and relaxing are the main activities. The Petersons offer a flexible program. Many stay a few days at the ranch, then go off on a pack trip. Some come specifically for pack trips. Others prefer to stay at the ranch all week. Half-day, morning, and afternoon rides go to North Middle Mountain and around the ranch. All-day wilderness rides (8 hours) with lunch go out daily except Sunday to Pine Creek, Base Camp, and the West Branch. Fishing is challenging. Three miles of private shoreline of McIntyre Creek run through the ranch. The creek has native trout. Serious fishermen should ask about the all-day and overnight fishing trips to high wilderness lakes. Hikers can enjoy all kinds of hiking trails and old logging roads.
Children's Programs: None. Children are welcome but must be supervised by parents. Usually kids under 10 do not ride. Nannies encouraged.
Dining: Family-style meals served in the dining room; traditional outdoor western-style barbecues. Homemade soups, breads, and desserts. BYOB.
Entertainment: Very informal. Evening hayrides, wildlife viewing, and just plain relaxing by the fire with a good book from the library. Game room, horseshoes, volleyball, and occasional cowboy poetry.
Summary: The Petersons' ranch focuses on horseback riding and horse-related activities, specializing in wilderness pack trips. The Petersons share the natural beauty that abounds in a relaxed western style. Complete hunting and outfitting services offered in the fall.

See color photos, page 212

Peaceful Valley Lodge and Ranch Resort
Lyons, Colorado

Peaceful Valley Lodge and Ranch Resort is a year-round resort providing hospitality and personal attention in a Rocky Mountain setting. Since 1953, the Boehm family has delighted guests at their western/Austrian-style ranch. Near Rocky Mountain National Park and St. Vrain Canyon, Peaceful Valley offers easygoing western lifestyle and Old World charm. During summer, enjoy extensive riding on quarter and Arabian horses. Lessons for all skill levels and scenic mountain trails ensure riding enjoyment. Hiking, llama treks, breakfast on the mountain, riverside picnics, and backcountry tours of ghost towns and gold mines display Colorado's beauty. The Paul F. Boehm Memorial Chapel's 1,000-pound bell imported from Holland calls to worshipers on Sunday and Wednesday (summer only). The blend of American ranch life and European charm is carried on by Mabel, daughter Debbie, and Debbie's husband, Randy Eubanks. As they say at Peaceful Valley, "He who enters is a stranger but once."

Address: Star Route, Box 2811K, Lyons, Colorado 80540
Telephone: (303) 747-2881, (800) 95-LODGE (955-6343) for reservations only; fax: (303) 747-2167
Airport: Denver
Location: 60 miles northwest of Denver
Memberships: Dude Ranchers' Association, Colorado Dude and Guest Ranch Association
Awards: AAA 3 Diamond, Mobil 3 Star
Medical: Longmont Community Hospital, 28 miles
Conference: 80-100. Brochure available.
Guest Capacity: 130
Accommodations: Eleven cabins and thirty-one lodge rooms. Moderate units are cozy and informal. Superior units are roomy with full tub/shower baths, telephones, and sitting areas with view. The best rooms are beautifully appointed with Jacuzzi-style bathtubs, private balconies, telephones, desks, and refrigerators. The best cabins have living rooms, fireplaces, and hot tubs. Coin-operated laundry.
Rates: • $$-$$$. American Plan. Children's, pack trip, and conference rates available. Children under age 3 free (baby-sitting available for fee). Minimum: seven nights mid-July through August.
Credit Cards: Visa, MasterCard, American Express, Diners Club, Discover
Season: Mid-March to January
Activities: Extensive riding with indoor arena, overnight pack trips, chuck wagon breakfast rides, and lunch rides to Continental Divide. Daily mountain trail rides vary, from one to seven hours, with eight to ten guests on a ride. No Sunday riding. Hiking, poolside barbecues, indoor swimming pool, Jacuzzi, sauna, tennis, mountain biking, and llama treks. Winter: See Cross Country Ranchs.
Children's Program: Extensive program for kids 3 through teens. Nursery and supervised children's program in summer. Strong teen program. Children's petting farm (summer).
Dining: Year-round hearty, healthy Continental and American cuisine. Beer, wine, and liquor available.
Entertainment: In summer, square dancing, gymkhana, sing-alongs, hayrides, naturalist talks, talent shows, melodrama.
Summary: Wonderful ranch resort emphasizes personal service (2-to-1 guest to staff ratio). Ideal for families, couples, and singles. Riding, hiking, and communing with the great outdoors. Lots for nonriders as well. Beautiful alpine chapel and gift shop. Visit ghost towns, old mining camps, and Rocky Mountain National Park (elk, deer, and bighorn sheep sometimes seen). Summer video available.

See color photos, pages 214-215

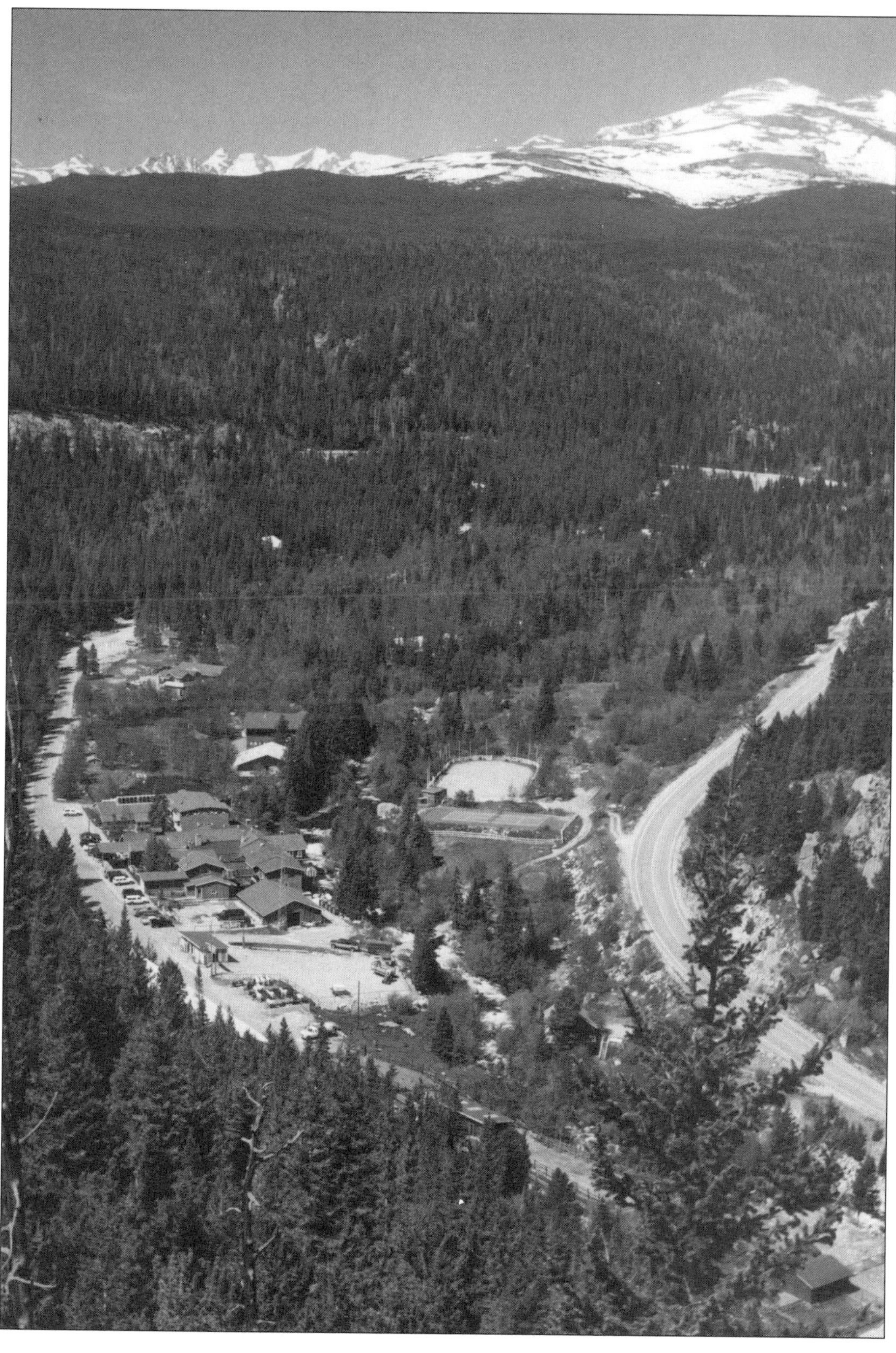

The Pines Ranch
Westcliffe, Colorado

Driving to the Pines Ranch one comes over Hardscrabble Pass down to Wet Mountain Valley with the majestic Sangre de Cristo mountains looming to the west. The ranch celebrated its 100th birthday in 1993. It was built by Regy Cusack, an Englishman. Cusack ran the ranch for 50 years. In 1984, the Rusks purchased the property. Dean, his wife, Casey, and their five children, undertook a three-year renovation and rebuilding of the ranch. The clean air, high altitude (8,700 feet), and breathtaking views bring guests back again and again. "Our guests just can't believe how magnificent these mountains are," says Casey. "We really have a paradise, with tremendous views of Pikes Peak to the northeast and New Mexico to the south." Westcliffe and the Wet Mountain Valley comprise one of Colorado's oldest yet least-known resort areas. When visiting the Pines, you will take advantage of one of the prettiest areas in the Rockies. Guests arrive as strangers but depart as members of the Rusk family.

Address: P.O. Box 311 K, Westcliffe, Colorado 81252
Telephone: (800) 446-WHOA, (719) 783-9261; fax: (719) 783-2977
Airport: Pueblo or Colorado Springs
Location: 8 miles northwest of Westcliffe off Highway 69 North, 70 miles west of Pueblo, 95 miles southwest of Colorado Springs
Memberships: Colorado Dude and Guest Ranch Association
Medical: Clinic, 8 miles; Thomas More Hospital, 50 miles
Conference: 40
Guest Capacity: 40
Accommodations: The renovated 1890s lodge has four second-floor rooms and two large common areas on the main floor as well as two shared bathrooms. The lodge is furnished with Victorian antiques and is ideal for singles, couples, and small groups. The other four cabins, all built in the 1980s, are modern with motel-like rooms, private baths, and living rooms with TVs and VCRs. Laundry facilities available.
Rates: • $-$$. American Plan. Children's rates available. Baby-sitting included during high season.
Credit Cards: Visa, MasterCard, American Express
Season: May through October for ranch activities, December through March for cross-country and downhill skiing and sleigh rides.
Activities: Fishing in the ranch's streams, ponds, and in the mountain lakes. Half-day and all-day rides. Ten to fifteen people per ride, with pack trips into the high country on Tuesday nights (extra charge). Horses available for all levels of riders. Riding at the Pines is especially scenic as it is all alpine riding, going through streams, meadows, and lush high-country areas. Raft trips can be arranged. Hiking trails available. Seasonal hunting, eight-person whirlpool, and two saunas year-round. Downhill skiing, 18 km of groomed cross-country trails, and sleigh rides highlight the winter activities. Each Presidents' Day Weekend, the Pines presents its Winterfest, with Nordic ski competitions, skijoring races, sleigh rides, hamburger cookout, and lots of fun. A special Victorian Christmas celebration takes place in the historic lodge.
Children's Programs: Children 3 to 8 have scheduled activities. Two playhouses and video game room. Baby-sitting available.
Dining: PRHC (Pines Ranch Home Cookin')—home-baked, home-cooked, served buffet-style. BYOB.
Entertainment: Square dancing, staff shows, sing-alongs, campfires, breakfast wagon rides, cookouts, Saturday guest rodeos at the ranch and in town during July.
Summary: Young families, couples, and singles come to the Pines, as do the young at heart. Wonderful high-country scenery and riding. Ranch at 8,700 feet. Pine Cone General Store. Ranch originally an English settlement. Nearby: Royal Gorge "Little Grand Canyon."

See color photos, page 213

Powderhorn Guest Ranch
Powderhorn, Colorado

Powderhorn Guest Ranch has a picture-perfect setting in a narrow mountain valley. Powderhorn is a love story between two people who had a dream way back in high school. It took a while, but in 1984, Jim and Bonnie bought the ranch and began a tradition along the banks of the Cebolla (pronounced sa-VOY-a) Creek in southern Colorado. The Cooks fell in love with Powderhorn because of its riverside location (it used to be a fishing retreat) and its seclusion. They take an active role in managing the ranch with their son, Jeff, and his wife, Jill (who oversee the horse program). Second to riding, fishing is the most popular activity. Bonnie is famous for her wildflower hike and Jim for his jeep trips. Powderhorn attracts lots of families during July and August. Couples and singles tend to come during June and September. Perhaps one family summed it up best: "You are very special people to be able to bring such happiness to others. When we turn that curve and see the big red barn, we just know we're 'home' again."

Address: County Highway 27, Drawer K, Powderhorn, Colorado 81243
Telephone: (303) 641-0220, (800) 786-1220
Airport: Gunnison via Denver, complimentary pick-up at Gunnison
Location: 38 miles southwest of Gunnison
Memberships: Dude Ranchers' Association, Colorado Dude and Guest Ranch Association
Medical: Gunnison Valley Hospital
Conference: 35
Guest Capacity: 30
Accommodations: Thirteen individual, green-roofed log cabins with names like Snoopy, Peanuts, Prancer, Dancer, and Bashful. All have refrigerators and coffee makers, as well as front porches with lawn chairs. All are carpeted and have private baths. Daily maid service is provided, with laundry facilities available.
Rates: • $-$$. American Plan. Children's and off-season rates. Five-day minimum stay, one week preferred. Sunday arrivals.
Credit Cards: American Express. Personal checks and cash accepted.
Season: Early June to mid-September
Activities: Horseback riding is the main activity with emphasis on safety and pleasure. Excellent instruction in the arena, weekly gymkhana, supper ride, all-day ride to East Fork, with fresh fish caught for lunch. Groups are usually about six people, but rides will go out even if only one person is signed up. Special attention is given to children and novice riders. Fishing in the creek as well as two stocked ponds. Equipment is provided, and licenses are available. Swimming in large heated pool. Twelve-person hot tub, hiking, wildflower walk, four-wheel-drive trips. River raft trip is included.
Children's Programs: Kids must be 6 years old for the trail rides, but Lightning, the Appaloosa pony, happily carries the little ones around in the arena. Here it is easy for parents to vacation with their children. Ask about occasional baby-sitting.
Dining: Three delicious home-cooked meals a day are served family-style or buffet, all you can eat. Several cookouts during the week on the picnic island. Everyone eats together, including the staff. Vegetarian and special diets are happily accommodated.
Entertainment: Classic Western movies (with popcorn), square dancing with a caller who teaches, campfire sing-alongs, weekly guest gymkhana (games on horseback), lodge with pool table, jukebox, and table tennis. Saturday night is Jim's special "VCR Movie of the Week."
Summary: Small and friendly, for down-home friendly guests in a beautiful river valley setting. Family-owned and operated guest ranch. Remote and peaceful, without a strictly regimented program. Families, couples, singles, and single parents become one big family very quickly.

See color photo, page 216

Rainbow Trout Ranch
Antonito, Colorado

Rainbow Trout Ranch was a sleeping giant. No longer! In 1993, this marvelous paradise was reopened to the world. Rainbow Trout was built back in the 1920s. The 18,000-square-foot log lodge and cabins were used as an exclusive sportsman's retreat by successful businessmen who liked to fish—thus, its name. Today its great tradition is carried on in a number of ways. First and foremost, it is a haven for families who come to rejoice in natural beauty and in being together. The RTR serves up plenty of warm and friendly hospitality. When staff members say they're glad you came, they mean it. Guests can ride the historic Cumbres and Toltec Scenic Railroad, visit Santa Fe or Taos, fish the Conejos River, or just savor all the family fun. At the RTR, you can have it all—the best of the Colorado Rockies and northern New Mexico.

Address: 1484 FDR 250, Drawer K, Antonito, Colorado 81120 (May 1-October 1); P.O. Box 249 K, Winter Park, Colorado 80482 (October 2-April 30)
Telephone: (800) 633-3397
Airport: Alamosa, Colorado, is the closest (available pick-up extra); guests also fly into Denver, Colorado Springs, and Albuquerque
Location: Two miles off Highway 17 between Antonito, Colorado (22 miles), and Chama, New Mexico (39 miles)
Memberships: Dude Ranchers' Association, Colorado Dude and Guest Ranch Association
Medical: Regional hospital, Alamosa, 1 hour
Conference: 60, late May and September
Guest Capacity: 60
Accommodations: Seventeen old-time cabins with names like Deer, Birch, Cottonwood, and Cougar are situated above the main lodge and interspersed among the aspen and pines. They range in size from two bedrooms and one bath to three bedrooms and two baths. Larger cabins have living rooms and fireplaces. All have covered porches. Daily maid service. Guest laundry room.
Rates: • $$. American Plan. Children's and group rates. Sunday to Sunday stays June through August. Rafting, pack trips, and train rides extra.
Credit Cards: None. Personal checks, traveler's checks, and cash accepted.
Season: Late May through September
Activities: Horseback riding and fishing are the most popular ranch activities. You will have your own horse for the week. Six to ten riders per ride, divided according to the wishes and abilities of the guests. Sometimes individual families may ride together. Weekly pack trip for teenagers and adults. The ranch's Conejos River is known for its fishing. Some instruction and gear available, limited guiding. Heated swimming pool, volleyball, basketball, and hiking. Ask about white water rafting near Taos, New Mexico.
Children's Programs: Supervised children's program for ages 3-5, 6-11, and teens. Kids 3-5 take pony rides with a counselor; ages 6-11 have their own horse for the week and take trail rides. Crafts, hiking, swimming, and kids' cookouts also offered. Parents welcome to join in children's activities. Programs for children not mandatory.
Dining: Hearty ranch food family-style. All-you-can-eat turkey dinner and twilight steak ride are favorites. This is home-cooking in the traditional sense. BYOB.
Entertainment: Something is planned each evening: weekly square dance, hayride, movie night, and sing-along. Games and cards in the lodge.
Summary: At Rainbow Trout you will find the best of Colorado and New Mexico. Great for families who want to be together but enjoy different activites for different interests and ages. Magnificent lodge with views to the valley. Lots of horseback riding; fishing in the Conejos River. Located 2½ hours north of Santa Fe, 1½ hours northwest of Taos.

See color photos, page 217

Rawah Ranch
Glendevey, Colorado

Rawah (ray-wah) is Ute for "abundance." At 8,400 feet, the ranch sits at the edge of the 76,000-acre Rawah Wilderness with the Laramie River steps from its door. Rawah is relaxed and, unlike most ranches, is quite a distance from the closest town. It caters to folks who want to escape the hectic pace of urban life and enjoy nature and wonderful hospitality. Rawah is owned and operated by the Kunz family, who were guests themselves at dude ranches for over 15 years. You can ride, fish, hike, photograph, pitch a few horseshoes, just loaf, or rock yourself to sleep in one of the rocking chairs on the front porch of the main lodge—it's your vacation. Whatever you decide to do, you are in good hands at Rawah. It's one of the best.

Address: Glendevey, Colorado Route, Dept. K, Jelm, Wyoming 82063 (summer); 1612 Adriel Cr., Dept. K, Ft. Collins, Colorado 80524 (winter). (The ranch is in Colorado, but the nearest post office is in Wyoming.)
Telephone: (800) 820-3152; (303) 435-5715 (summer), (303) 484-8288 (winter)
Airport: Denver, with commuter air service to Laramie, Wyoming
Location: 60 miles southwest of Laramie, Wyoming; 75 miles northwest of Fort Collins, Colorado
Memberships: Dude Ranchers' Association, Colorado Dude and Guest Ranch Association
Medical: Laramie Ivinson Memorial Hospital; staff EMT
Conference: 32
Guest Capacity: 32 (with a caring staff of 18)
Accommodations: The log lodge is the hub of activity, with stone fireplaces in the living and dining rooms and a wonderful rocking chair porch overlooking Middle Mountain. There are five rooms with baths in the lodge and six single or duplex log cabins scattered around the ranch. Cabins have fireplace, electricity, full bath. All rooms have choice of twin or king-size beds. Lodge rooms are carpeted, and cabins have the original, beautiful wood floors.
Rates: • $$. American Plan. Lower rates for kids 6 to 9 and during off-season.
Credit Cards: None. Personal checks, traveler's checks, and cash accepted.
Season: Early June through September. Adults only in September.
Activities: Rawah goes out of its way to accommodate guests' riding preferences and takes great pride in its horses for all levels of riding experience. Its many wranglers help you enjoy mountain trail, breakfast, and loping rides, plus arena riding and instruction. Wild trout fishing on the Laramie River, which runs through the ranch, the Poudre River nearby, more than 25 alpine lakes, and the ranch's stocked pond. Some fishing equipment available. Each week includes a full afternoon fly-fishing clinic with professional instruction. Great hiking (June Wheeler's "Trail Guide" provided). Lawn sports, skeet shooting, rafting, and other notable excursions. Seasonal hunting for elk, deer, and moose.
Children's Programs: No formal children's programs. Children 6 and older are welcome and ride with their families or each other. Fishing pond, playground equipment, separate recreation building.
Dining: Wonderful ranch food, including many specialties. Everything is home-baked. Guests actually complain that Rawah's food is too good. Morning beverages delivered to guest rooms. Special diets with advance notice. BYOB.
Entertainment: Cowboy singers, square dancing, geology presentation, "roll-o-roper," numerous parlor games in lodge.
Summary: This ranch is one of the best! A terrific combination of riding, fishing, hiking, and western hospitality. One guest wrote, "Once again Rawah gave our family a '10' vacation. Log cabins, wood fires, superb horses, lovely people, wonderful home-cooked food, and crisp Rocky Mountain air. Fantastic." Video available. Norwegian spoken.

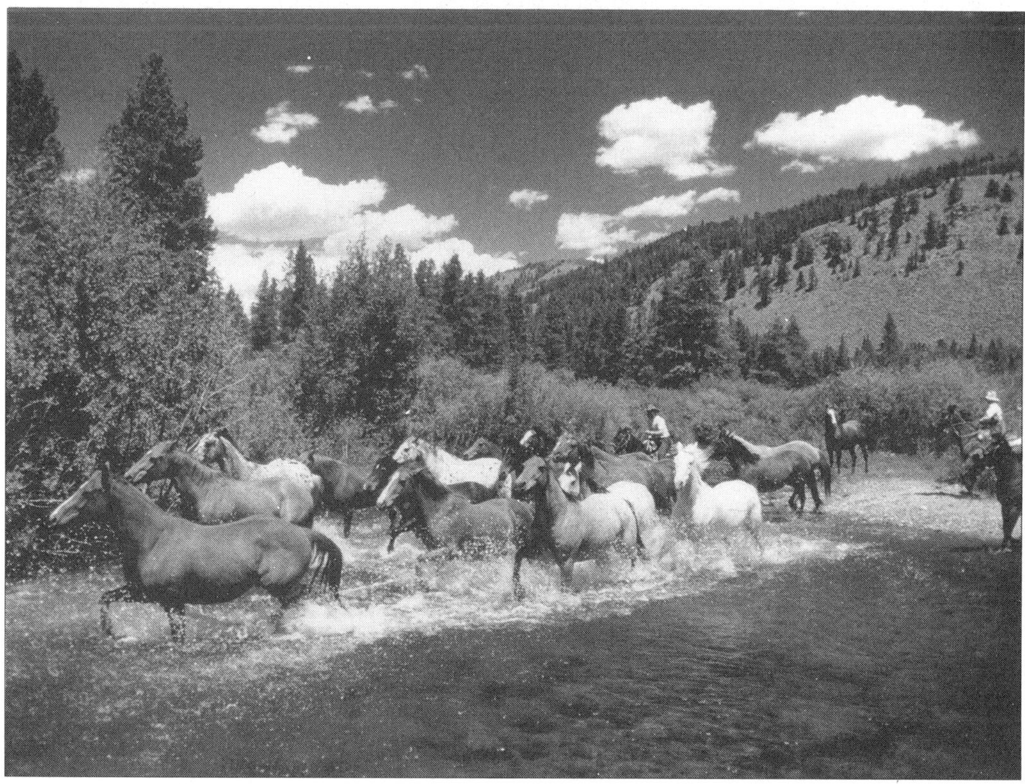

The Ranch on Sweetwater
Gypsum, Colorado

At 7,600 feet, Sweetwater looks out from the valley floor to striking geological rock formations, giving the area its name—the Flat Top Wilderness Area. Sweetwater is managed by Layne and Jeanne Wing, a young couple with a great love and understanding for this part of Colorado. Layne used to be a cowboy on a neighboring cattle ranch. Sweetwater offers families, couples, and singles an environment to explore, ride, swim, hike, and interact with other people who appreciate caring hospitality and a laid-back way of life.

Address: 2650 Sweetwater Lake Road, Drawer K, Gypsum, Colorado 81637
Telephone: (800) 321-7639, (303) 524-7676
Airport: Grand Junction or Aspen (summer); Eagle (winter)
Train: Amtrak to Glenwood Springs, 33 miles west
Location: 55 miles northwest of Vail, 33 miles east of Glenwood Springs, 155 miles west of Denver
Memberships: Dude Ranchers' Association, Colorado Dude and Guest Ranch Association
Medical: Valley View Hospital, Glenwood Springs, 33 miles
Conference: Groups of up to 28
Guest Capacity: 28
Accommodations: There are two types of cabins at the ranch—three log-sided cabins that can hold a maximum of six people and two duplex cabins that can hold a maximum of ten people and are ideal for two families who want to vacation together. All cabin units have private baths, panelling, queen or double beds, and a sitting area (some with fireplaces). Some are carpeted; some have wooden floors. As Jeanne says, "We might not be fancy, but we are very comfortable."
Rates: • $-$$. American Plan. Off-season, children's, group, and daily rates available. Six-day week, Sunday to Saturday. Three-day minimum stay.
Credit Cards: None. Personal checks and traveler's checks accepted.
Season: Late May to late September (summer); Mid-December through March (winter)
Activities: Ranch programs are flexible and arranged according to the wishes of the guests. Horse program includes instruction in the arena and half-day and all-day rides to surrounding 10,000-foot elevations. Lunch rides to the wilderness camp. Trotting and loping rides for those who are capable or wish to learn. Guests may saddle their own horses. Overnight and longer pack trips can be arranged. Fly-fishing on two miles of the ranch's own Sweetwater Creek (catch and release only), or you may fish in the ranch pond (two trout per day limit). Heated pool and hot tub. Rustic tennis court on ranch for beginners. White-water rafting can be arranged. In the winter the ranch provides meals and lodging for cross-country skiers and snowmobilers.
Children's Programs: Optional programs, including pony rides, nature hikes, and western arts and crafts, for children between the ages of 3 and 12. Baby-sitting available.
Dining: Family-style meals served in the beautifully restored historic lodge or on the deck. At breakfast and dinner cookouts held on the mountain, you can watch the sun rise or set. BYOB. Once a week, the ranch has separate seatings—a cookout with hotdogs and s'mores for the kids, a candlelight dinner with complimentary wine for adults. The cookie jar is always full of fresh cookies!
Entertainment: Evening games and slide show, horseshoe tournaments, square dancing with live caller, campfires, sing-alongs, stargazing.
Summary: Great for young couples, singles, and families who enjoy relaxing and exploring. Riding and fishing are the main activities. Sweetwater Lake is next door. Hikers like to visit the Ute Indian Cave and Hanging Lake. Day trips to Glenwood Springs, Aspen, Vail.

7W Guest Ranch
Gypsum, Colorado

History, hospitality, and the ever-changing splendor of the Rockies await you at the 7W Guest Ranch, which has been in operation since the early 1920s, making it one of the oldest guest ranches in Colorado. This 210-acre ranch, perched on a high mountain bench, lies between Vail and Glenwood Springs on the border of the White River National Forest. The 7W has a variety of activities for families; however, 60 percent of the guests are couples and singles. Horseback riding is the main feature here. Surrounding the 7W is a lot of history and terrific sightseeing in the nearby towns of Vail, Glenwood Springs, and Aspen. Whether you want to sleep under the stars, cast for trout, explore, or just relax, you can do it all here. A warning, though—tranquillity at the ranch is broken only by fun, laughter, and enjoyment.

Address: 3412 County Road 151K, Gypsum, Colorado 81637
Telephone: (303) 524-9328, (800) 524-1286; fax available on request
Airport: Eagle, Grand Junction, and Denver, Colorado
Train: Amtrak to Glenwood Springs, 37 miles east
Location: 30 miles northwest of Eagle off I-70, 60 miles northwest of Vail, 165 miles west of Denver. Pickup service available from Grand Junction, but extra.
Memberships: Dude Ranchers' Association, Colorado Dude and Guest Ranch Association
Medical: Valley View Hospital, Glenwood Springs, 37 miles
Conference: Groups of up to 15
Guest Capacity: 18
Accommodations: Guests enjoy six log cabins decorated à la Ralph Lauren, each with a splendid view of the private, stocked 5-acre ranch lake. Each has its own bathroom and a wood-burning stove, braided throw rugs, and pitched 10-foot ceilings. Welcome homemade cookies on arrival. Awake to the wonderful aroma of cowboy coffee, which is delivered to your front porch each morning. Wait for the friendly knock on your cabin door.
Rates: • $$-$$$. American Plan. Off-season, children's, and group rates available.
Credit Cards: None. Personal checks accepted.
Season: Early June to late September
Activities: Summer features horseback riding with excellent instruction available. Guest to wrangler ratio is five to one. Small group rides. Morning, afternoon, and all-day rides. Be sure to ask about the Deep Creek wine and cheese ride, the evening ride, or the famous Bushwacking ride (for advanced riders only). No riding on Sundays. Overnight and longer pack trips available. Fishing in stocked lake or in nearby streams and alpine lakes. Serious fishermen should bring their own equipment. Seasonal hunting for deer and elk. Hiking, white-water float trips on the Colorado River 17 miles away. Challenging mountain croquet course, volleyball, badminton, and horseshoes.
Children's Programs: No structured program. Children's play area. Baby-sitting available. Not recommended for children under age 7. Pony rides available.
Dining: Family-style home cooking. Ranch specialties: beef ribs, Mexican fiesta, fresh locally grown apple pie. Weekly steak fry with guests arriving by horseback. Breakfast ride to Riland Lake with Forest Service nature specialist. BYOB.
Entertainment: Weekly square dancing, country-western singing, cookouts, campfires under the stars. Weekly guest rodeo.
Summary: Best for singles and couples and families with older children. Riding and fishing are the main activities. Bring a smile, and they'll do the rest! Nearby: hot springs at Glenwood, historic tours to Carbondale, Aspen, and Vail.

See color photos, page 218

San Juan Guest Ranch
Ridgway, Colorado

San Juan Guest Ranch is surrounded by more 14,000-foot peaks than any other spot in the United States. The ranch is in southwestern Colorado in the incomparable Uncompahgre Valley, which has been called "the Switzerland of America." It is also just four miles north of quaint, Victorian Ouray, which has been carefully preserved to keep this century-old mining town's special qualities. While the ranch is small, catering to 30 guests, it is big in personal service and hospitality, overseen by owners and hosts Pat MacTiernan, her son, Scott, and his wife, Cristy. In the western tradition, San Juan Ranch excels in horseback riding with superbly trained horses. Fall is a wonderful time to visit, as the aspens display a magnificent array of gold before the winter snows. To capture this beauty, Scott has created a 35mm photo adventure/workshop for adults only. The special spirit of teaching and sharing passed down to Scott from his father makes San Juan one of the best.

Address: 2882 Highway 23, Dept. K, Ridgway, Colorado 81432
Telephone: (800) 331-3015, (303) 626-5360
Airport: Montrose or Telluride via Denver
Location: 5 miles north of Ouray, 6 hours southwest of Denver by car
Memberships: Dude Ranchers' Association, Colorado Dude and Guest Ranch Association
Medical: Ouray Clinic, Montrose Hospital, 30 miles; in-house EMT
Conference: 30, off-season only
Guest Capacity: 30
Accommodations: Guests stay in the comfortable two-story Lodge. It is fully carpeted and comfortable, with nine individual apartments on both levels decorated with lots of country charm, with common decks and views of the ranch and valley. Private baths and daily maid service. Queen-size, doubles, and bunk beds. Refrigerators and native flowers in all rooms.
Rates: • $$-$$$. American Plan. Children's, off-season, and group rates available. Six-day minimum stay, Sunday to Saturday. Three-day minimum stay in winter.
Credit Cards: Visa, MasterCard. Personal checks accepted.
Season: June through September, open Christmas. Off-season for groups.
Activities: Summer brings a full riding program with lessons available in the arena. Weekly half-day and full-day rides and overnight high country pack trip. Jeep trips to ghost towns and abandoned gold mines in the heart of the San Juan Mountains. Fishing in the Uncompahgre River or private stocked ponds. Trap shooting and rifle range (guns available). Hiking, eight-person hot tub, volleyball, horseshoes, and horse-drawn hay-wagon rides. Tennis and huge natural hot springs in Ouray. Balloon rides available (extra). Winter offers antique one-horse sleigh rides, snowshoeing, tobogganing, and guided cross-country skiing. Downhill skiing at world-famous Telluride ski area, 45 minutes away.
Children's Programs: A child's paradise, with supervised activities including feeding animals and petting zoo. Baby-sitting included.
Dining: Hearty meals served family-style. Traditional turkey dinner starts each week. Lots of vegetables and salads. Fresh trout served weekly. Weekly cookouts and barbecues. BYOB.
Entertainment: Bonfire with cowboy singing and professional Western dance instruction. Shopping in Ouray and Telluride. Scott's team roping demonstrations are really exciting. Ask the MacTiernans about the narrow gauge train to Silverton with free pickup at Silverton.
Summary: Family owned and operated with an intimacy that is contagious. Great for families, those without families, and single parents. Very strong children's program for all ages. Photography workshop, ballooning. Nearby: Victorian mining town of Ouray, ghost towns, Telluride.

Sky Corral Ranch
Bellvue, Colorado

Sky Corral Ranch is a friendly, family-owned and operated guest ranch remotely situated on 450 acres of secluded mountain meadow nestled in and around the 780,000-acre Roosevelt National Forest. The 3-mile drive into Sky Corral takes you past abandoned cabins built by other homesteaders in the early 1880s. The flexible schedule here allows families to have a meaningful, unforgettable time together. The famous Cache La Poudre River, which is only minutes away and travels through the Poudre Canyon, is filled with scenery and history. Sky Corral is a ranch for those who appreciate a strong family atmosphere and goodness that comes from many years of working the land. It is a ranch with low-key charm and modern-day amenities.

Address: 8233 Old Flowers Road, Dept. K, Bellvue, Colorado 80512
Telephone: (303) 484-1362; call for fax number
Airport: Denver, airport express bus to Fort Collins
Location: 2 hours northwest of Denver, 24 miles west of Fort Collins off Rist Canyon Road
Memberships: Dude Ranchers' Association, Colorado Dude and Guest Ranch Association
Medical: Poudre Valley Hospital, Fort Collins; Sharon Vannice is a registered pharmacist.
Conference: 50
Guest Capacity: 38
Accommodations: The main lodge has great views overlooking the pond, the valley, and on to Mt. Ethel, a sitting room, large deck, and six upper rooms with private baths, twin and double beds, carpeting, electric heat, daily maid service, and nightly bed turn-down. Lots of flowers inside and out. Large recreational hall for gatherings, pool, Ping-Pong, and children's activities. Older cabins are rustic and range in size from one to three bedrooms, some with wood stoves or fireplaces.
Rates: • $$. American Plan. Children's rates available. Spring and fall discounts. Hunting rates. Three-day minimum stay with arrivals on Sunday or Wednesday.
Credit Cards: MasterCard, Visa (with service charge). Personal checks accepted.
Season: Open year-round and all holidays
Activities: A full, varied, and flexible horseback riding program. Families may ride together or separately. Homestead trail to overnight campsite, fishing in ranch ponds or Cache La Poudre River, archery, hiking, horseshoes, tennis, volleyball, hayrides, white-water rafting on the Poudre, rodeo, hot tub, sauna, heated swimming pool, van trips, and more.
Children's Programs: Qualified children's counselors during the summer season. Baby-sitting available. Kiddie tepee campout. Children's play area. Petting farm (ask Dave about this) and supervised feeding. Kids 6 and over ride on trails.
Dining: Bring your appetite. Family-style home-cooked meals are a specialty at Sky Corral. Tried and proven mountain recipes will keep you coming back. Several meals on the deck. Steak dinner on the campout. Home-made ice cream and desserts. BYOB, in rooms and cabins only.
Entertainment: Campfires, sing-alongs, shoot-outs, skits, popcorn, and an evening at the movies, square dancing, ice cream social, night sounds in the mountains, and nights under the stars.
Summary: This is a family ranch for families only. Here you will share Old West hospitality with modern-day comforts. Here a handshake is a handshake and the coffee pot is always on.

Skyline Guest Ranch
Telluride, Colorado

When Dave and Sherry Farny bought Skyline Guest Ranch in 1968, their first concern was to preserve the natural beauty so that generations to come could enjoy this magnificent and breathtaking mountain paradise. They succeeded by deeding the property to the great wilderness protector, the Nature Conservancy. Thus, the ambience and tranquillity at Skyline will be savored for years to come. In the southwestern corner of the state, Skyline is nestled in the high meadows and aspen-rich peaks of the San Juan Mountains. The crisp air and the crystal-clear mountain water, not to mention the snowcapped 14,000-foot peaks, make this ranch one of the most beautiful. Dave and Sherry, their son, Mike, and his wife, Sheila, and young son Luke have preserved their "mountain joy" tradition, a spirit on which guest ranching was founded—honest and friendly hospitality. Privacy and comfort are yours in abundance here. This is one of the best guest ranches in the West.

Address: Box 67K, Telluride, Colorado 81435
Telephone: (303) 728-3757; fax: (303) 728-6728
Airport: Telluride
Location: 15 minutes from Telluride
Memberships: Dude Ranchers' Association, Colorado Dude and Guest Ranch Association
Medical: Telluride Clinic, 8 miles
Conference: 35
Guest Capacity: 35
Accommodations: Guests stay in ten comfortable lodge rooms or six housekeeping cabins. All the rooms have magnificent views, private baths, and excellent beds with down comforters and sheepskin mattress pads. Awaken in the morning to sweet aromas from Skyline's famous kitchen. Laundry is done at your request. No smoking in buildings.
Rates: • $$-$$$. American Plan. One-week minimum stay, Sunday to Sunday.
Credit Cards: Visa, MasterCard, American Express. Personal checks preferred, traveler's checks accepted.
Season: June to mid-October (summer); mid-December to April (winter); open Christmas
Activities: Summer brings a full horse program with "natural horsemanship" instruction for all levels. Guests may become as involved as they wish—grooming, saddling, and wrangling. Usually 6 to 8 per ride. Beginner, intermediate, and advanced rides. Be sure to ask about the Calico Trail, Lizard Head, and Wilson Mesa rides. Also ask the Farnys about their magnificent hideaway—High Camp. Pack trips available. Fishing is superb in the ranch's three mountain lakes and nearby streams. Lake swimming for the brave, guided mountain biking, hiking, mountain climbing, photography, white water adventures, four-wheel-drive trips over Ophir Pass and the abandoned gold and silver mining camps, Tomboy and Alta. Hot tub and sauna. Massage available. See Cross-Country Skiing Ranches for winter activities.
Children's Programs: No children's program, but kids can participate with parents. Kids under 6 do not ride on trails. Really best for older children.
Dining: Skyline's cuisine is fresh and scrumptious. Vegetarian and special dietary requests are no problem. Dave's breakfast cookout and picnic rides are favorites. Complimentary beer and wine served with happy hour and dinner.
Entertainment: Dave plays a mean accordion. Sing-alongs, square dancing, slide shows. Terrific library and cozy main lodge.
Summary: The Fabulous Farny Family and their spectacular mountain setting. This family will hook you for life. Best for older children, singles, couples, and families who appreciate nature's best. Four-day pack trip for experienced riders in both June and September. Adult week in July. Dry goods store with boots, hats, chaps, T-shirts, and sweatshirts. Telluride, filled with museums, galleries, music, and shopping, just 15 minutes away.

See color photos, pages 220-221

Sylvan Dale Ranch
Loveland, Colorado

There are not many ranches in the country that combine all the qualities and activities of Sylvan Dale Ranch: cattle ranching, fishing, delightful country decor, and new cabins. Sylvan Dale is a working cattle ranch with charm and loads of friendly hospitality on the banks of the Thompson River, discovered by Maurice Jessup in the 1930s. Daughter Susan now oversees all ranch activities. Under her enthusiastic direction, Sylvan Dale offers a delightful blend of working cattle ranch and resort recreation for families in the summer months and for business groups the rest of the year. Susan's partner, David (who teaches biology during the school year), hosts an informal weekly naturalist program. The ranch is terrific for grandparents, too. Those who wish to experience calving and/or fly-fishing should ask Susan about the opportunities in March, April, and May. At Sylvan Dale you will experience good fun, good food, good folks, and lots of western hospitality.

Address: 2939 N. County Road 31D, Dept. K, Loveland, Colorado 80538
Telephone: (303) 667-3915 (You may call collect)
Airport: Stapleton International, Denver. Shuttle service available through Continental into Loveland where the ranch van will meet you.
Location: 55 miles northwest of Denver, 18 miles east of Estes Park off Highway 34
Memberships: Colorado Dude and Guest Ranch Association
Medical: McKee Medical Center, Loveland, 8 miles
Conference: September through mid-June
Guest Capacity: 60
Accommodations: Comfortable country! Individual and family units in nine cabins and the two-story Wagon Wheel Barn. No television or telephones in rooms. Cabins are carpeted and accented with antique furnishings. With its large gathering room, wood-burning fireplace, raised stage, and kitchen for midnight snacks, the Wagon Wheel is ideal for family reunions
Rates: • $. American Plan, six-night package Sunday to Saturday. Off-season "Bunk" and breakfast rates. No-tip policy for dude ranch guests.
Credit Cards: None. Personal checks welcome.
Season: Year-round. Full-program dude ranch June through Labor Day.
Activities: There is a wide variety of activities. When you arrive expect a wagon tour of the ranch—just to get your bearings. Ranch chores are posted each morning after breakfast, such as bringing in a load of hay, feeding the cattle, gathering eggs, moving irrigation pipe, or fixing fences. You can assist with moving cattle from one pasture to another and try your hand at team penning. The horse care clinic teaches guests to groom and saddle their own horses. Tennis, swimming, river rafting, shopping trips, tours to Rocky Mountain National Park, hikes, and nature walks. The program is flexible. You set your own schedule.
Children's Programs: Ranch chores, horsemanship, nature hikes, and fishing for children 6 and older. Baby-sitting available for younger children.
Dining: Wholesome family-style meals. Home-baked favorites by Mrs. Jessup—cherry pie, cinnamon rolls, and a weekly Thanksgiving feast. Box lunches packed for all-day excursions. BYOB, in cabins only.
Entertainment: Evenings are family affairs. Foot tappin' and square dancin'. S'mores round the campfire, hayride to Green Ridge for the buffalo roast, or up to the Field of Dreams for family softball, watermelon seed-spitting contests and live country music at the Friday night ranch party. Mountain man show.
Summary: Sylvan Dale Ranch is a gentle place for people of all ages right on the Thompson River. A comfortable blend of authentic working ranch activities and resort recreation for families who want to vacation together. Excellent fly-fishing. Terrific for off-season seminars and conferences.

Tumbling River Ranch
Grant, Colorado

Tumbling River is second to none! It is the year-round home of Jim and Mary Dale Gordon, two very friendly Texans who serve southern hospitality high in the Colorado Rockies. At 9,200 feet, the ranch is in Indian country on the banks of Geneva Creek and in the middle of Pike National Forest. This secluded spot is well known for the Ute Indians and trappers who once roamed these parts. The property is divided into an upper ranch (where most of the activities take place), built as a mountain retreat by a former mayor of Denver, and a lower ranch house, the Pueblo, built by Native Americans with carved beams and adobe walls, for the daughter of Adolph Coors. You will find a warm, informal atmosphere here and plenty of natural ambience and wildlife. Elk, deer, sheep, and mountain goats may be seen. One of the best features at Tumbling River is the children's program. One guest said, "A family can spend its vacation together and still get away from one another." Tumbling River, in one word, is terrific.

Address: P.O. Box 30K, Grant, Colorado 80448
Telephone: (800) 654-8770, (303) 838-5981
Airport: Denver Stapleton International
Location: 4 miles north of Grant, 62 miles southwest of Denver
Memberships: Dude Ranchers' Association, Colorado Dude and Guest Ranch Association
Medical: Denver hospitals
Conference: 40, off-season only
Guest Capacity: 55
Accommodations: Accommodations are in two clusters: the upper ranch and the lower ranch, about a quarter mile apart. Eight cabins (one is bilevel) have names like Indian Hogan, the Frenchman's Cabin, Big Horn, and Tomahawk. Most have fireplaces; twin, queen-size, or bunk beds for kids; and arching ceilings. Some are real log; some log-sided; all the porches have swings and hanging geranium planters, and many bird feeders are scattered about. There are also fourteen rooms in the two upper and lower ranch lodges, each with its own fireplace.
Rates: • $$$. American Plan. Children's, off-season, and group rates available. One-week minimum stay, Sunday to Sunday.
Credit Cards: None
Season: Mid-May through September
Activities: The Gordons offer a wide variety of activities: excellent riding with a string of 80 horses, half-day and all-day rides, pack trips, and riding instruction. Four-wheel-drive trips and hiking to breathtaking 11,000-foot vistas. Fly-fishing with instruction in stocked ponds, streams, and mountain lakes, and black powder plus trap shooting (guns and ammunition provided). The heated swimming pool has a full-length cabana with tables and an eight-person hot tub with nearby old-time steam sauna. Weekly river rafting.
Children's Programs: Kiddie wrangler and programs for children 3 years old and up. Separate programs for children 3 to 5, 6 to 11, and teens. Baby-sitting available for kids under 3. Children 5 and under ride with supervision.
Dining: Complimentary coffee served in your cabin each morning. Every day, except Wednesday, there is a cookout. Favorites include apple pancakes with apple cider syrup and luncheon cookouts with homemade soup. Weekly "Gordon's hamburgers" poolside. Two adult candlelight dinners. Entrées include shrimp Dijon, chicken Florentine, and weekly Thanksgiving dinner. Pecan pies and lemon mousse. BYOB.
Entertainment: Every night there is something different: hayrides, mountain campfires with hot chocolate, square dancing, ranch rodeos, and talent shows. Old-fashioned farewell hootenanny.
Summary: Diverse program with lots of activities. Excellent family ranch with something for every member of the family. Hosts and staff are tops! Wait until you see the old barn and marvelous old ranch trading post. Nearby: a historic narrow gauge train and the towns of Georgetown and Fairplay.

See color photos, page 219

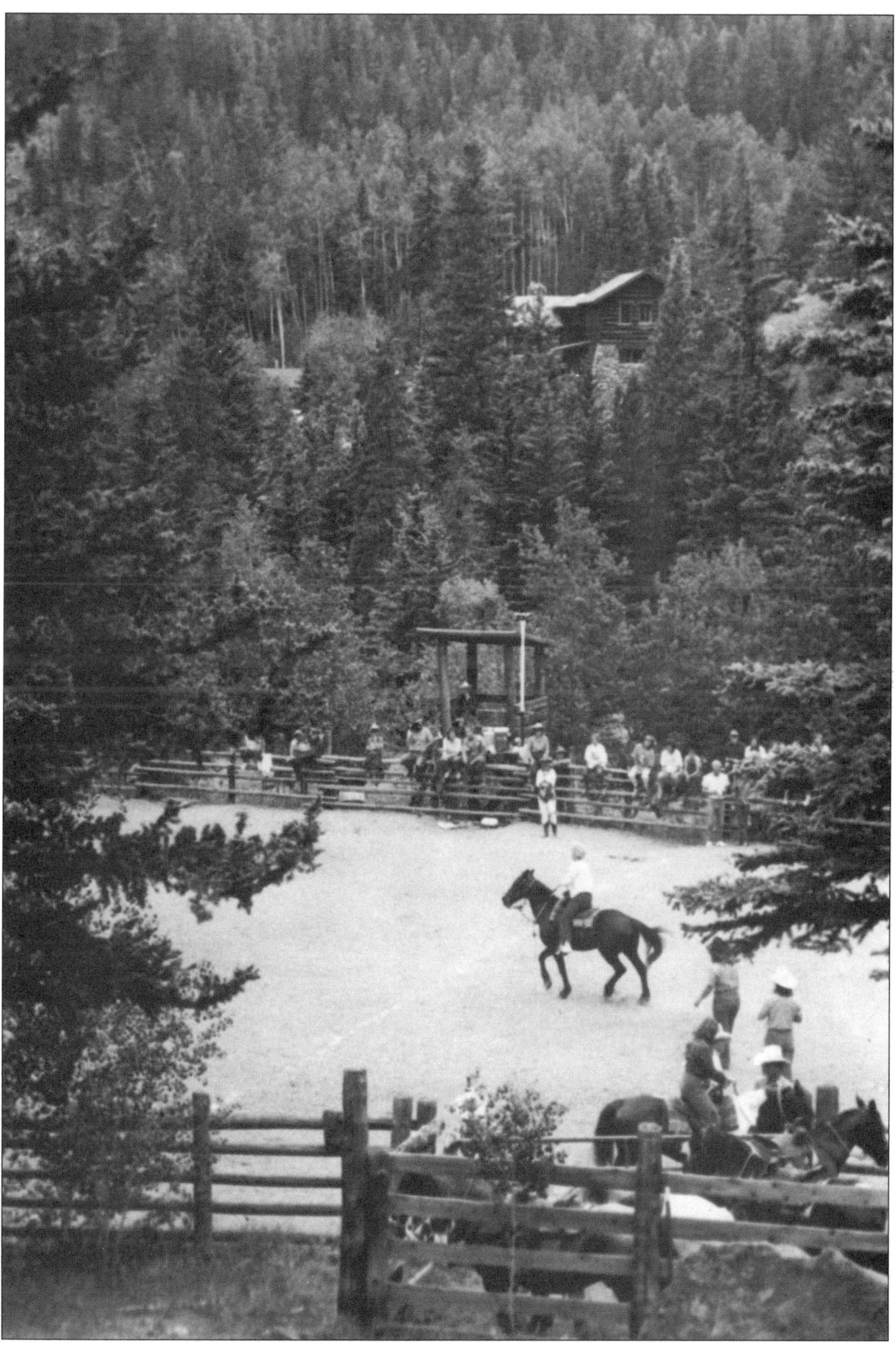

Vista Verde Guest and Ski Touring Ranch
Steamboat Springs, Colorado

In his business career, John Munn made a specialty of buying companies and making them better. When John and his wife, Suzanne, escaped the Midwest in 1991 to fulfill their dream, they took the same approach with Vista Verde. As John says, "The ranch was already a wonderful property. What we have done has simply made it better." And so they have. With a new lodge, upgraded cabins, a culinary institute chef, and lots of energy, Vista Verde is indeed better than ever and one of the best year-round guest ranches in North America. Set in a secluded valley with hay meadows and mountain vistas, Vista Verde is not just a riding ranch. It offers tremendous diversity for those who want to do other things like river rafting, fly-fishing, rock climbing and hot-air ballooning. The Munns have kept their ranch small and charming—a hideaway to forget your worries and savor a piece of paradise.

Address: Box 465K, Steamboat Springs, Colorado 80477
Telephone: (303) 879-3858 or (800) 526-RIDE (7433); fax: (303) 879-1413
Airport: The ranch is remote, yet very accessible, with the Steamboat Airport just 25 miles away. Ranch Suburbans meet you there.
Train: Amtrak to Granby, Colorado
Location: 25 miles north of Steamboat Springs, off Seed House Road.
Memberships: Dude Ranchers' Association, Colorado Dude and Guest Ranch Association
Medical: Steamboat Springs Hospital
Conference: 25, September through May
Guest Capacity: 35
Accommodations: Named after surrounding mountains, log cabins are nestled in aspens and pines. Handsomely furnished, they include wood stoves, full baths, and comfortable porches that overlook the meadows and forest. Three rooms with splendid views are available in the new lodge. Wildflowers are provided in each cabin, along with a great assortment of books.
Rates: • $$$-$$$$. American Plan. Children's, low-season, and winter rates available. Hot air balloon rides, guided fly-fishing, and overnight packtrips (extra). One-week minimum.
Credit Cards: None. Personal or traveler's checks accepted.
Season: Summer, June to mid-September. Winter, Christmas to mid-March.
Activities: Riding program includes in-depth arena instruction for all levels of experience. Numerous trail rides (such as Hole-in-the-Wall Canyon, The Cliffs, Indian Hills) through the adjoining national forest go out daily. Rock-climbing with instruction for all provides an exhilarating experience. Rafting on the Colorado, professional rodeo (in town), ranch rodeo, extensive guided hiking and nature program in the Zirkel Wilderness, mountain biking, on- and off-ranch fishing, hot air ballooning. Cattle drives in June and September. Spa building with indoor and outdoor hot tubs, exercise equipment, and beautiful mountain views.
Children's Program: Complete supervised program structured to provide some activities with the parents (riding, rock-climbing, rodeo, most meals) and gold-panning, fire engine rides, Indian lore, animal feeding, and treasure hunts. Fort Smiles for outdoor activities and the Hole-in-the-Wall for indoor games.
Dining: Culinary institute-trained chefs present gourmet meals prepared with a touch of country. Home-grown vegetables, homemade, just-baked everything, hand-cranked ice cream. Special dietary needs accommodated. Wine and beer available.
Entertainment: Reception Sunday evenings hosted by the Munns. Something is planned each night: folk music, cowboy poetry, barn dancing, staff show, pro rodeo.
Summary: One of the top year-round ranches in North America near the famous ski town of Steamboat Springs. With many on- and off-ranch activities, this is not just a riding ranch. Lots of wilderness, lots of great food, and lots of good company.

See color photos, page 222

Tall Timber
Durango, Colorado

Perched high in the splendor of the San Juan Mountains at 7,500 feet, Tall Timber is a hidden retreat. This Mobil 5 Star hideaway is so secluded that guests arrive by the Silverton, one of the last narrow gauge trains in the United States, or by helicopter. Dennis and Judy Beggrow discovered this remote spot in 1970. Since then, they have, with a lot of time and work, developed this world-class property. Tall Timber is surrounded with history and beauty. The early Ute Indians used the meadows as hunting grounds, and later miners came in search of gold. In recent years the countryside has been used in countless movies, including *Around the World in 80 Days* and *Butch Cassidy and the Sundance Kid*, just to name a couple. No roads, no telephones, no stress, no deadlines. Tall Timber equals seclusion, beauty, and, maybe most of all, a marriage of luxury and nature.

Address: S.S.R. Box 90 K, Durango, Colorado 81301
Telephone: (303) 259-4813 (radio telephone; be patient as there may be lots of static)
Airport: Durango/La Plata; private planes to Animas Air Park with 5,000-foot paved runway
Location: 26 miles north of Durango
Awards: Mobil 5 Star
Medical: Mercy Medical Center, Durango; emergency helicopter available
Conference: 24
Guest Capacity: 24
Accommodations: All ten wood-paneled condominium-style units are private and surrounded by quaking aspen. Each year the Beggrows and staff plant more than 25,000 petunias, pansies, and snapdragons. There are eight one-bedroom and two two-bedroom suites. Each has its own living room, wet bar, floor-to-ceiling stone fireplace, and balcony. Turn-down service is provided each evening. Furnishings emphasize casual elegance and comfort. The main lodge is a massive three-story structure with a wine cellar, wet bar, lounge, dining room.
Rates: $$$$-$$$$$. American Plan. Four- and seven-day packages, special low season and children's rates available. Four-day minimum stay.
Credit Cards: None. Personal checks accepted.
Season: Mid-May through October (summer); mid-December through mid-January (winter)
Activities: In the summer, there is a heated pool (ask one of the staff to tell you how the pool arrived), three outdoor whirlpools (one overlooks the Animas River), sauna, putting green, driving range, nine-hole, par 29 golf course, tennis court, trout fishing, Nautilus fitness room, jogging trail, plenty of hiking, helicopter picnics, hikes, and tours. All horse activities begin at a sister property about a mile away. Guided horseback riding to high mountain lakes, Silver Falls (a wonderful seasonal waterfall); morning, picnic, or afternoon rides; riding instruction available. The Christmas and New Year's activities are among the special winter events. All suites are decorated with Christmas trees. It's a happy and festive time. While winter is a short season, there is cross-country skiing, ice skating (equipment available), and a daily helicopter shuttle to Purgatory for downhill skiing. Some snowmobiling.
Children's Programs: Well-behaved children welcome. No program. Tall Timber is great for families who can enjoy the outdoors together.
Dining: Food is not taken lightly. Each table in the dining room has its own picture window. Meals are served from a pre-selected menu and feature eggs Benedict, grilled salmon, beef Wellington, steak and trout, lots of fresh breads, and pastries. Many vegetables and herbs are fresh from the garden. Dinners are by candlelight with crystal and gold-rimmed china. Picnic lunches will be prepared on request. Stocked bar and wine cellar.
Entertainment: You are on your own.
Summary: Exclusive wilderness hideaway. Arrive by the exciting and historic Durango-Silverton narrow gauge train or by helicopter.

Whistling Acres Guest Ranch
Paonia, Colorado

Whistling Acres Guest Ranch is situated in Colorado's Minnesota Creek Valley. To the south of the ranch is 11,600-foot Mt. Lamborn. Here cedar trees and sage dot the hills and willows and cottonwoods follow the creek that winds its way through this expansive valley. This is a working cattle ranch that runs about 200 head of cattle on 6,200 acres and grows its own hay. In 1984, Whistling Acres was opened to families who wish to be with their children or small groups (family reunions) who book the entire ranch to ride, relax, and explore. In addition to horseback riding, hayrides, and cookouts, guests like to explore the Black Canyon of the Gunnison National Monument and enjoy jet boating, rafting, or fishing on the Gunnison River. Your hosts, Jerry and Roberta Bradley, have children themselves. Unlike many ranches, there is no set age requirement for children to ride. It is completely up to Jerry's discretion. If you are looking for a highly regimented resort or rustic old-time ranch, this is not for you. If you would like to relax, ride horses, enjoy a low-key warm, comfortable family environment, give the Bradleys a call.

Address: 4397 "050" Drive, P.O. Box 88K, Paonia, Colorado 81428
Telephone: (303) 527-4560; fax: (303) 527-6397
Airport: Montrose, 60 miles; Grand Junction, 70 miles; Denver, 240 miles
Location: 240 miles west of Denver, 70 miles southeast of Grand Junction, 2 hours west of Aspen
Memberships: Colorado Dude and Guest Ranch Association
Medical: North Fork Medical Clinic, 3 miles
Conference: 21
Guest Capacity: 21
Accommodations: The spacious six-bedroom, four-bath ranch house and pavilion area are the center for all activities, lodging, and dining. Each of the modern bedrooms has carpeting, paneling, and double and twin beds. There is a fireplace in each of the three living room areas, a sun room, hot tub, pool table, jukebox, and player piano. The front patio is a gathering area in the afternoon and evening.
Rates: • $$. American Plan. Children's and off-season rates. No minimum stay. Three- or six-night stays preferred.
Credit Cards: Visa, MasterCard
Season: May to October (summer); December to April (winter)
Activities: Meadow and mountain rides usually go out twice a day lasting 1½ hours to 2½ hours. All-day rides by prior arrangement. Most riding is done at a walk. Ask about the Valley, Turner Ditch, Burn, Oak Ridge, and Jumbo Mountain rides. This is a working cattle/hay ranch. There are some opportunities for guest participation. Fishermen should ask about the gold medal waters on the Gunnison River, 15 miles away. There are two jeeps available for rent. Winter offers snowmobiling on Grand Mesa or on the ranch (15 snowmobiles), cross-country skiing, sledding, and inner-tubing.
Children's Programs: No formal program. Families are encouraged to interact together. Children of all ages are able to ride depending on their ability. Call for details.
Dining: Hearty, home-cooked meals are served family-style in the ranch house or at the pavilion. BYOB. Weekly hayride cookout.
Entertainment: Weekly homemade hand-cranked ice cream social. Evening sing-alongs and campfires. Pool table, Ping-Pong, big screen satellite television, player piano, jukebox. Sit out on the veranda and visit or read your favorite book.
Summary: Small working cattle/hay and guest ranch. Warm and friendly with bed-and-breakfast atmosphere. Very family oriented. Ideal for families, couples, and small groups. Riding is the main activity. Nearby Gunnison River Pleasure Park, Black Canyon and backcountry jeep tours, scenic trips over McClure Pass on Highway 133, a Scenic Byway. Ask about Grand Mesa, which has more than 200 lakes. Aspen, 2 hours by car.

Waunita Hot Springs Ranch
Gunnison, Colorado

Since the early 1960s, the Pringles have hosted families, couples, and singles who are looking for an enriching western experience. Near the Continental Divide at 8,946 feet, the ranch is adjacent to mountain meadows and the Gunnison National Forest. A noted health spa in the early 1900s, the Waunita is where guests will enjoy colorful history and beautiful scenery along miles of riding trails or on four-wheel-drive trips. The swimming pool, fed by crystal-clear Waunita Hot Springs, is naturally soothing. The ranch has maintained the flavor of the Old West but is modern in all respects. Three generations of the Pringle family are actively involved with the ranch and its activities, seeking to provide a western experience as well as a haven for their guests in a wholesome, family atmosphere. Nondenominational service on Sunday mornings.

Address: 8007 County Road 887, Dept. K, Gunnison, Colorado 81230
Telephone: (303) 641-1266
Airport: Gunnison
Location: 27 miles northeast of Gunnison, 150 miles west of Colorado Springs off Highway 50
Memberships: Dude Ranchers' Association, Colorado Dude and Guest Ranch Association
Awards: Mobil 2 Star
Medical: Gunnison, 27 miles
Conference: 25, informal
Guest Capacity: 50
Accommodations: Two lodges are fashioned somewhat like old Western town buildings. Rooms are paneled and carpeted, with private baths and thermal heating. There are double, queen, and some bunk beds for kids. Laundry facilities available. Recreation center in top floor of new log barn.
Rates: • $-$$. American Plan. Children's rates available. Minimum stay policy. Special winter group rates.
Credit Cards: None. Personal checks and cash accepted.
Season: June through September; December through March for groups only
Activities: Planned activities include daily horseback rides on a variety of trails, from flowered meadows to snowcapped mountain ridges. Guided rides are scheduled in small groups, and rides vary from beginner walking rides to more advanced rides with loping. Arena games are scheduled one morning each week. The all-day ride to the 12,000-foot summit of Stella Mountain and lunch on its highest ridge is an unforgettable event. Three cookout rides and an overnight at the forest camp on Canyon Creek are weekly highlights. Scenic four-wheel-drive trips to North Star Mine, Fairview Peak, and Alpine Tunnel. Gunnison River float and white water trips, hayrides, and marshmallow roasts. Hiking and a weekly softball game in the front yard. Four stocked ponds and lakes, with stream fishing available on Tomichi Creek and the Gunnison River. Winter offers cross-country skiing and snowmobiling.
Children's Programs: Children are welcome and included in most activities. Five-year-old children can begin riding by themselves; 3- and 4-year-olds are led in the arena. Special children's rides. Part-time child care is available. Small animal petting farm. The ranch is a natural playground.
Dining: Wholesome meals served buffet- and family-style. Fruit, coffee, tea, punch, and cookies always available. The Pringles have a no-alcohol policy.
Entertainment: Cookouts at three different forest camps. Recreation room. Something special each night. The musically talented Pringle family features a night of western music.
Summary: Waunita Hot Springs Ranch is a Christian, family-owned and operated ranch featuring riding and activities for all ages. Located at the site of a natural hot springs that provides thermal heat for buildings and water for the pool. Historic, yet modern. Ranch emphasis is on families enjoying the ranch and activities together. One guest summed it up, "Thanks for the best week of the year."

Wilderness Trails Ranch
Durango, Colorado

A soaring eagle, the song of coyotes, a deer bounding across the meadow, horses grazing in the front pasture, and millions of twinkling stars in the clear mountain skies—this is Wilderness Trails Ranch. Since 1970, Gene and Jan Roberts have owned and operated this lovely ranch in the Colorado Rockies. Today, with the help of their children, Lance and Erika, and an enthusiastic college staff, the Roberts offer one of the finest ranch vacation experiences in the country. Gene and Jan are both very athletic and blend their enthusiasm for life with their athletic zest in a host of different ways. Wilderness Trails is snuggled in the Pine River Valley not far from beautiful Vallecito Lake. The main lodge looks out over a beautiful meadow and on to the distant mountains. Wilderness Trails offers a wonderful family-oriented, personalized, wilderness experience.

Address: 776 County Road 300 K, Durango, Colorado 81301
Telephone: (303) 247-0722, (800) 527-2624; fax: (303) 247-1006
Airport: La Plata Airport in Durango via Denver, Albuquerque, or Phoenix
Location: 35 miles northeast of Durango in southwest Colorado, 190 miles northwest of Albuquerque
Memberships: Dude Ranchers' Association, Colorado Dude and Guest Ranch Association
Medical: Mercy Medical Center, Durango, 35 miles; local rescue service
Guest Capacity: 50
Accommodations: Comfortable, well-appointed two-, three-, and five-bedroom log cabins with porches, nestled among pines, spruce, and aspen. Lovely country furnishings, queen, king, or single beds, modern private baths with shower/tub combinations, amenity packet, individually controlled heat. Three-bedroom, three-bath deluxe cabins feature wood-burning stoves in living rooms, separate room with coffee bar, refrigerator, robes, nightly turn-down service. Laundry facilities available.
Rates: • $$$. American Plan. Family and children's rates. Discounts June and September. Seven-day, seven-night minimum stay, Sunday arrival.
Credit Cards: Visa, MasterCard
Season: June through September
Activities: Most come here to ride. Morning, afternoon, all-day, and weekly family rides into the San Juan Mountains. Ask about the Lake Lookout and Vista Grande rides. No more than eight to a ride, and rides are divided according to ability—"Sidekicks," "Trailhands," and "Trailblazers." Daily riding instruction. Boot rental available. Seventy-two-foot heated pool. Weekly jeep trip to Middle Mountain, tour to Mesa Verde cliff dwellings. River rafting, water skiing, mountain biking, and hiking. Historic Durango/Silverton Steam Train.
Children's Programs: Exceptional programs for children 3 to 17. Kids and teens have their own wranglers. Waterskiing at Lake Vallecito. Riding instruction, trail rides, hayrides, and a variety of other activities keep the kids happy and entertained all day. Parents may do as much or as little as they wish with their children.
Dining: Young children may eat with counselors if parents desire. A weekly gourmet candlelight dinner is a very special evening for adults. A vegetarian menu, along with hearty, healthy ranch cuisine. BYOB.
Entertainment: Experience a variety of fun each evening—a hilarious staff show, intriguing magic show, two-stepping, country swing, square dancing, horse-drawn hayrides.
Summary: Beautiful setting! Family-owned and operated since 1970. Great hosts and staff attracting 95 percent families. Wide variety of activities and weekly adventure trips. Excellent kids programs. One guest wrote, "Neither words nor pictures can capture the depth of our enjoyment. By unanimous vote, Wilderness Trails Ranch has been selected as our favorite ranch. We'll be back."

See color photos, page 223

Wit's End Guest and Resort Ranch
Bayfield, Colorado

Wit's End Guest and Resort Ranch is the creation of Jim and Lynn Custer, a couple with impeccable taste! Wit's End is located in the beautiful Vallecito Lake Valley just off County Road 500. Set amid thousands of aspens and pines, it offers guests a host of activities, all in a setting of luxury, charm, and quality. Wait until you see the beautifully restored, century-old, main lodge. The craftsmanship and decor is exquisite. The ranch is surrounded by 12,000- to 14,000-foot mountains and looks out over its own Chain O'Lakes and meadows. At Wit's End you can do as much, or as little, as you wish. Unlike many guest ranches, Wit's End offers rustic elegance with all the freedoms that you might find at a resort. The theme is luxury at the edge of the wilderness. It's a wonderful haven for families, singles, couples, children of all ages, and groups.

Address: 254 C.R. 500 K, Bayfield, Colorado 81122
Telephone: (303) 884-4113; fax: (303) 884-4114
Airport: Durango, La Plata Airport
Location: 24 miles northeast of Durango directly off County Road 500 and U.S. Highway 160
Awards: Country Inn's 12 Best Award, 1991; Country Living's Top 25, 1992; Official Hotel Guide's Superior First Class, 1993
Medical: Mercy Medical Center, 24 miles; local rescue service
Conference: 80 (overnight), 150 for the day
Guest Capacity: 80
Accommodations: All of the one-, two-, three-, and four-bedroom log cabins are luxuriously decorated for the most discriminating taste: knotty pine interiors, native stone fireplaces, queen-size brass beds, custom bed coverings, plush carpets, balloon draperies, French doors, television, telephones, china dishes, attractive kitchens with separate dining areas, and swings and willow furniture on the porches. Be sure to ask about the 7,500-square-foot Trout House on the water.
Rates: • $$-$$$$. American Plan and limited European Plan June, July, and August. Off-season and group rates available.
Credit Cards: Visa, MasterCard, Discover. Traveler's and personal checks accepted.
Season: Year-round (limited services mid-January to late April, call for details)
Activities: A host of outdoor activities are available. Depending on the package you select, you can ride, fly-fish, hike, swim in the heated pool or in Lake Vallecito, play tennis, take a mountain motor tour, mountain bike, or soak in one of the hot tubs. Horseback riding from Wits End or its sister ranch, Meadowlark. Wilderness pack trips, Durango/Silverton train, Jeep tours, whitewater rafting, Indian ruin trips, golf, and rodeos are offered for an additional charge. Winter offers untracked cross-country skiing, sleigh rides, snowmobile tours to the top of Middle Mountain, pond skating, and occasional dog sledding.
Children's Programs: Children's counselors and special programs during summer season.
Dining: Jim and Lynn travel a great deal and appreciate fine cuisine. Scrumptious meals are served in the century-old exquisite lodge. Breakfast and dinner rides, western barbecue. Fine wine and candlelight dinner served nightly. Choice of menu and full bar.
Entertainment: Beautiful century-old main lodge and Colorado Tavern with cut-glass mirrors from the Crystal Palace of the London World Exposition of 1853. Huge stone fireplace, upstairs library, and game room with a custom antique billiard table. Weekly seasonal live entertainment.
Summary: Luxury ranch resort at the edge of the wilderness in Vallecito Lake Valley. Superb cuisine and wonderful accommodations. Excellent for family reunions, corporate retreats, weddings, and honeymoons. Beautifully restored century-old main lodge. At Wit's End, you can do your own thing. Activities coordinated by ranch staff if you wish. Wilderness pack trips. Nearby: Durango/Silverton narrow gauge railway and Mesa Verde Indian dwellings. Fully stocked general store.

See color photos, pages 224-229

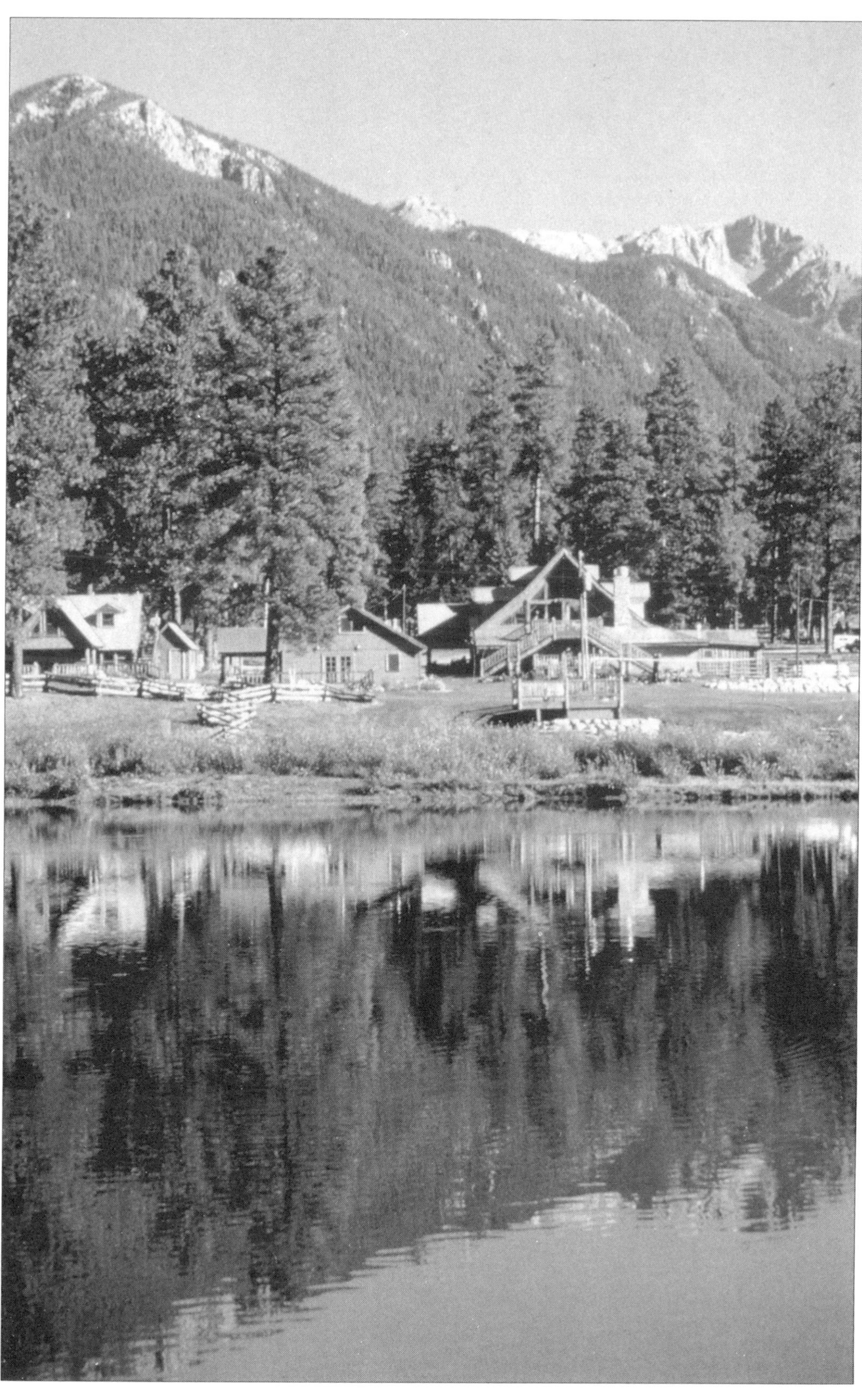

Wind River Ranch
Estes Park, Colorado

At 9,200 feet, the ranch overlooks the rugged peaks of Rocky Mountain National Park. It has been in operation for more than fifty years and in the Irvin family since 1973. Today, the ranch is run by Rob and his wife, Jere, along with their two children, Richard and Alyisa. The "WRR" has wonderfully preserved the Old West with its rustic setting, antiques, and Indian artifacts. Wind River is for the busy executive and his or her family who wants to get away from it all. Be as busy as you want, or just sit back with a good book and relax. One guest wrote, "Wind River was our pick because of its beautiful location, smaller size, and wide range of activities."

Address: P.O. Box 3410 K, Estes Park, Colorado 80517
Telephone: (303) 586-4212, (800) 523-4212
Airport: Denver
Location: 7 miles south of Estes Park off Highway 7, 75 miles northwest of Denver
Memberships: Dude Ranchers' Association, Colorado Dude and Guest Ranch Association
Awards: Mobil 3 Star
Medical: Estes Park Hospital, 7 miles
Conference: 52, early June and early September
Guest Capacity: 54
Accommodations: All of the eleven country-decorated cabins and five lodge rooms have modern comforts, including private baths with oversize towels, individually controlled heat, and carpeting. Some have fireplaces or wood-burning stoves. All have a nice western feel. Each has a porch or a patio. There are always hanging baskets with colorful flowers around the main lodge and pool. Daily maid service.
Rates: • $$-$$$. American Plan. Children's and family reunion rates available. Minimum 3-day stay policy, with arrivals and departures on Sunday. Nonriding rates available.
Credit Cards: Visa, MasterCard, Discover
Season: Early June to mid-September
Activities: Most come to ride. Two-hour, half-day, and all-day rides, as well as breakfast rides. Ask about the magnificent Chasm Lake ride. Instruction is available, as are weekly horsemanship clinics. Hiking on more than 600 miles of trails in the surrounding area. Guided hikes once a week. Swimming in the outdoor heated pool or hot tub. Fishing on and off the property (bring your own equipment). Ranch has its own stocked pond. Tennis, 18-hole golf course, and river rafting nearby.
Children's Program: Organized program for children ages 4 to 12, all day or mornings and afternoons; children under 6 ride in an arena only. Full fenced-in children's playground.
Dining: Families eat together. BYOB happy hour each evening with your hosts at the main house. Delicious buffets, fine steak dinners, filet mignon, and shrimp scampi. Breathtaking upper meadow cookout. Wind River's famous coffee cake, pastries, cheesecakes, and cherry pies. Patio picnics. Fine wine and beer available.
Entertainment: For those who wish to relax, the ranch has an extensive library in the lovely, rustic, circa 1920 ranch house. There is something planned each evening: reading or playing cards in front of the cozy fireplace, family movies, country-western singing with marshmallow roasts, evening naturalist talks with slides, bingo, hayrides with Belgian draft horse team.
Summary: Rob and Jere provide a place where busy professionals can relax and get away from it all. Magnificent mountain views. Most visitors come here to ride, hike, and completely relax. Stimulating ideas and conversation abound here. Nearby: Rocky Mountain National Park and 12,200-foot-high Trail Ridge Road, mining town of Central City on the spectacular "peak to peak" highway, now designated as a National Scenic By-Way, town of Estes Park with many attractions.

Outdoor Resorts River Ranch
River Ranch, Florida

Outdoor Resorts River Ranch is a modern resort community that caters to both RVers and non-RVers who are seeking western activities as well as recreation more typical of central Florida. River Ranch encompasses more than 1,700 acres of beautifully varied landscape. The roster of activities is long and diverse. The setting is conducive to the recreation that families and retired people traveling in recreational vehicles enjoy. River Ranch, near Lake Wales, was purchased by Outdoor Resorts of America. After an ambitious renovation that included upgrading all facilities, the ranch again opened its doors. The record attendance at this facility can be attributed to comfortable accommodations and a variety of recreational opportunities. The theme of the resort is definitely western, even though a few water birds are interspersed with barns, stables, a golf course, and a full marina. River Ranch is an RVers' haven that combines western flavor with a Floridian life-style. It also appeals to seniors, families, corporate and international groups, and bus tours because of the variety of accommodations and activities.

Address: P.O. Box 30030, Dept. K, ORA River Ranch, Florida 33867
Telephone: Nationwide (800) 654-8575; in Florida (800) 282-7935; local (813) 692-1321
Airport: Orlando or Tampa International; private 5,000-foot paved, lighted airstrip at ranch
Location: 24 miles east of Lake Wales on Highway 60, 65 miles south of Orlando
Medical: Lake Wales Hospital, 24 miles; EMT on staff at ranch
Conference: 500; 5,000-square-foot meeting facility
Guest Capacity: 186 units plus over 400 RV sites
Accommodations: Rooms, suites, efficiencies, cottages, and RV sites with full hookups. Call for availability and full description.
Rates: • $, RV rates; $-$$$, hotel accommodations, meals not included in overnight rates. Group rates available. Some activities not included (riding and golf).
Credit Cards: Visa, MasterCard, American Express, Discover
Season: Year-round including Thanksgiving, Christmas, and Easter
Activities: There is a recreation director on the property who makes suggestions for guest activities. There is something here for everyone to do. Special events, holiday programs; escorted horseback rides that go out daily, usually about 45 minutes to one hour. Sign-up sheet at front desk. All riding at a walk. Four pools, three Jacuzzis, five lighted tennis courts, 9-hole par 36 golf course, miniature golf, horseshoes, archery, ranch marina where guests can launch their own boats or rent skiffs, fishing, trap and skeet shooting, archery, aerobics, a nicely furnished Mustang Center health spa with saunas, steam rooms, tanning booths, weight room, hair salon, and post office. Exotic game hunting at nearby FX Bar Ranch for deer, wild boar, and quail.
Children's Programs: No program per se. Kids are the responsibility of parents. Petting corral with rabbits, sheep, goats, chickens, turkeys, calves; children's playground; hayrides, pony riding. Arts and crafts. Full recreation room with video games. Rental bikes available. Kids can safely run free; 24-hour security on property.
Dining: Ranch Branding Iron Restaurant, Ranch Harbor Bar and Grill, fully stocked country store with deli. Liquor available.
Entertainment: River Ranch Saloon, weekend country-western live entertainment, square dancing, bingo, arts and crafts, card tournaments.
Summary: Appeals to a variety of people—families, seniors, groups, and bus tours. Laid-back country atmosphere. Resort for RVers and non-RVers. Pets allowed in RV area only. Ranch airstrip. Western wear and gift shop; professional ranch rodeos; square dancing; live country-western bands; weekly River Ranch newspaper outlining all activities. Nearby: Cypress Gardens, 35 miles; Walt Disney World Vacation Kingdom, 65 miles; Kennedy Space Center, 100 miles; Bok Tower Gardens with chiming bells.

Allison Ranch
Boise, Idaho

In the 1880s, the Allison Ranch was the pioneer homestead of Joe Myers, a miner. Today, Allison Ranch is a private guest facility surrounded by the Frank Church River of No Return Wilderness Area—the largest designated wilderness area in the United States except for Alaska. The ranch prides itself on taking only small families or parties of eight people. The Thomases make the ranch available also during the summer months to missionaries home on furlough. The only way into this secluded natural wonder is by small plane, jet boat, or a string of horses and mules. There are still some places in the world where roads have not penetrated, and this is one of them. The pilots who fly you in are experienced backcountry commercial pilots. This is a land where the pine-scented air is clear and the only footprints are your own or those of moose, elk, or deer and an occasional bear and even cougar. Allison Ranch, on the Salmon River, is a place where all the trappings of a mechanized world have been kept at bay. Don't expect to find television, automobiles, or telephones—there are none. The only communication with the outside world is by radio. Otherwise, you and seven other lucky guests and Marvin Thomas, the son and ranch manager, are on your own.

Address: 7259 Cascade Drive, Dept. K, Boise, Idaho 83704
Telephone: (208) 376-5270; fax: (208) 345-3431
Airport: Charter aircraft from Boise or McCall directly to the ranch
Location: 1 hour north of Boise by air, 30 miles south of Elk City on the Salmon River. The Thomases will explain everything to you.
Memberships: Idaho Outfitters and Guides
Medical: No medical facilities nearby; emergency plane or helicopter can be arranged.
Guest Capacity: 8
Accommodations: There are two two-story hand-hewn log guest cabins—one with three bedrooms overlooking the Salmon River which sleeps up to seven and a two-bedroom ridge unit. Propane lights and wood-burning stoves. Ranch has own hydroelectric plant. Summers are usually pretty warm.
Rates: • $. American Plan. Children under 6, no charge. Special missionary packages. Jet boat ride or plane ride in and out extra.
Credit Cards: None. Personal checks accepted.
Season: May to September; October through November for steelhead fishing
Activities: Horseback riding along the river is completely tailored to your own desires. All riding is done at a walk upstream or downstream. You won't mind, though, because the scenery is spectacular. In July, August, and September, fly-fishermen will enjoy catching six-inch to eight-inch rainbow trout on Bargamin Creek. In October and November, the big steelhead arrive. Enjoy swimming in Idaho's famous Salmon River, which runs right by the ranch, hike to the spectacular Myers Creek 100-foot waterfall, and enjoy plenty of fishing on a sandy beach along the Salmon River.
Children's Programs: No special programs. Children are welcome. All kids are the responsibility of parents. Not recommended for children age 2 and younger.
Dining: Hearty Idaho food, occasional venison and bear, all served family-style. Many meals during the summer are served outside on the deck overlooking the Salmon River. BYOB.
Activities: Peace and tranquillity, the melodic Salmon River, and abundant birds and wildlife.
Summary: Secluded ranch accessible only by plane, pack string, or jet boat, in a beautiful wilderness setting located on the Salmon River. Best for families and small family reunions wanting a secluded experience on one of Idaho's most scenic rivers. You might even get to share a story or two with folks floating the river. Great for very small business retreats. One couple even booked the ranch completely for themselves for two weeks. Special arrangements made for missionaries on furlough. Private airstrip.

Bar H Bar Ranch
Soda Springs, Idaho

The Bar H Bar Ranch is steeped in pioneer history. It is one of the oldest ranches in southeastern Idaho and was homesteaded by the Mormon church. Their unique irrigation system is still used today by owners McGee and Janet Harris. The deep ruts of the Oregon Trail are visible as they follow the Bear River, which runs through the ranch. The ranch consists of 9,000 acres. It is located in the Bear River Range of the Wasatch Mountains and borders the Caribou Cache National Forest. You will see Idaho in all its beauty—a splendid variety of stately pine, shimmering aspen, cold streams, wildlife, breathtaking panorama of wildflowers in June and July, and beautiful hay meadows. This is a real working cattle ranch that runs 2,000 head of beef cattle, pasturing most of them on private land. The Harris family keeps busy each day riding fence lines, doctoring cattle, and making sure the cattle are well fed. There is always plenty to do.

Address: 1501 Eight Mile Creek Road, Drawer K, Soda Springs, Idaho 83276
Telephone: (208) 547-3082, (800) 743-9505
Airport: Salt Lake International, 184 miles; Idaho Falls International, 120 miles; Pocatello Municipal, 60 miles; Jackson Airport, 100 miles
Location: 60 miles west of Pocatello off Highway 30 to Soda Springs
Medical: Caribou Memorial Hospital, 8 miles
Guest Capacity: 8
Accommodations: Four rooms in an old-fashioned, rustic bunkhouse. Each room has a private entrance. Recently renovated and furnished with native lodgepole furniture with a sprinkling of antiques that reflect the early years of this pioneer ranch. From a full-length porch, you will enjoy relaxing in comfortable rocking chairs and find pleasure in the sights and sounds of nature.
Rates: • $$. American Plan. Family rates available.
Credit Cards: None. Cashier's, traveler's, and personal checks accepted.
Season: May through November
Activities: Activities will vary according to the season. You may expect calving, branding, fence repair, and moving cattle to spring and summer ranges. There will also be salting and doctoring cattle, irrigating and preparing cattle for market, and moving to winter range. Other activities are nature hikes (on which you can expect to see a variety of wildlife), fishing on and off the ranch, and just relaxing. Hunting packages available September to late November.
Children's Programs: Children are welcome under the supervision of parents. Best for children over 10.
Dining: You will eat with the Harris family. Most meals will be cooked and served family-style in the old ranch cook house. You will enjoy three hearty meals a day in the tradition of the West which may include homemade bread, pies, and other goodies, Dutch oven cookouts, a steak fry, and depending on the weather, breakfast cooked out in the pines. The cook house is open to guests 24 hours a day, just in case someone gets the midnight munchies.
Entertainment: Everyone is usually pretty tired at the end of the day.
Summary: The Harrises have been in the cattle ranching business for four generations. In 1993, they opened the ranch gates to the world to share their special love of the West and their way of life. If you are looking for a real hands-on working ranch vacation with plenty of good food and wholesome time, give the Harrises a call.

See color photos, page 230

Hidden Creek Ranch
Harrison, Idaho

Idaho is a nature-lover's paradise, nicknamed "The Gem State." Hidden Creek Ranch is one of Idaho's new treasures. It has been created with great care by a couple who bring love, respect, and understanding for nature to their guests. John Muir and Iris Behr searched the Rockies for a ranch offering a base camp for a variety of outdoor activities. As Iris says, "When we arrived at Hidden Creek, we felt the magic right away." In 1993, Hidden Creek opened its gates to the world. With tremendous enthusiasm and a private mountain valley, John and Iris bring to dude ranching a unique respect for nature and the environment. They offer an adventure reminiscent of the time when man listened to nature and did not try to control it. With European attention to detail, new accommodations, and beautiful Idaho landscape, Hidden Creek Ranch is a gem!

Address: 7600 East Blue Lake Road, Drawer K, Harrison, Idaho 83833
Telephone: (208) 689-3209, (800) 446-DUDE (3833); fax: (208) 689-9115
Airport: Spokane, Washington
Location: 5 miles east of Harrison, 78 miles southeast of Spokane, 40 miles southeast of Coeur d'Alene, Idaho
Memberships: Dude Ranchers' Association, Idaho Guest and Dude Ranchers' Association, Idaho Outfitters and Guides Association, Audubon Society, Sierra Club, National Wildlife Federation, American Quarter Horse Association, Arabian Horse Registry of America
Medical: Kootenai Medical Center, Coeur d'Alene, 40 miles
Conference: 36; must book entire ranch, excellent for corporate retreats
Guest Capacity: 40
Accommodations: The lodge houses facilities for dining, living room, library, deck, and four guest rooms on the second floor, each with private bath. Six log cabins overlook the valley and mountains. All cabins have two or four units, each with private baths and queen-size beds. Children can sleep in bunkbeds. The ranch's "Chocolate Fairy" turns down your bed each night.
Rates: • $-$$$. American Plan. Children's, off-season, and group rates available. Three-day minimum stay, six-day or longer stay preferred.
Credit Cards: Visa and MasterCard. Personal checks and traveler's checks accepted.
Season: May to November. Limited selective hunting mid-October through December.
Activities: Daily horseback rides, a sunset ride, a champagne brunch ride, team-drawn hayride, and a barrel-racing and meadow games rodeo. A string of mountain bikes, fishing in Blue Lake, trap-shooting (extra), and archery. Campfire activities, barbecue and steak cookouts, an all-day hike to a gold mine, and optional "Dirty Dudes Day" where you participate in ranch work. Your stay concludes with an awards night, a candlelight dinner, and entertainment at the lodge. At Hidden Creek Ranch, "There isn't enough time to do it all!"
Children's Programs: Full programs for children from 3 to teens. Special activities for kids. Campfire with story-telling, marshmallow roasting, lots of hot chocolate, and an overnight in Indian tepees. Children 6 years and up normally can join the trail rides. Baby-sitting for children under 3 is available (extra).
Dining: Iris and John believe that good food is one of the greater pleasures in life. Hearty gourmet meals are homemade with fresh-baked goods and sinfully delicious desserts. Children eat with parents or may eat earlier.
Entertainment: Hosted cocktail hour with wine each evening. BYOB, in cabins only. Staff skits and talent night, awards night, hot tubs, campfire activities, evening stars, and Mother Nature.
Summary: Hidden Creek Ranch is one of Idaho's treasures. Emphasis is on horseback riding, nature, and excellent cuisine. It celebrates life and adventure. Pets allowed. Handicapped facilities. Video available.

See color photos, pages 234-235

Diamond D Ranch
Clayton, Idaho

The Diamond D is located in one of Idaho's hidden valleys. Many guests come by car and savor the long and winding gravel road up and over Loon Creek Summit that eventually switches back down into the rugged Salmon River mountain valley. This slow but scenic drive is breathtaking and gives everyone a chance to slow down and unwind to the pace that they will enjoy for their week or two, or more, at the ranch. The Diamond D is remote. On all sides it is surrounded by millions of acres of wilderness and plenty of wildlife. Arriving at the ranch, one feels the same exhilarating feeling the early gold miners must have felt when they exclaimed, "Eureka! We found it!" The Demorest family has been running this wonderful ranch since the 1950s. No telephones, no schedules. Nothing but pure Idaho wilderness and a lot of friendly hospitality. If this strikes your fancy, write or call for their brochure, which is filled with color photographs.

Address: P.O. Box 1 K, Clayton, Idaho 83227 (summer); P.O. Box 1555K, Boise, Idaho 83701 (winter)
Telephone: Summer: Radio telephone (208) 879-2364 for emergencies only. The voice answering will probably say "Bob's Aircraft." Note: You may not be able to get through to the ranch. Best to call (208) 336-9772 summer and winter.
Airport: Boise, 45 minutes by charter plane, 5 hours by car. Air charter service available from Boise, Twin Falls, Idaho Falls, and Challis to the 2,800-foot dirt airstrip just 4 miles from the ranch. Private pilots: DO NOT attempt to fly in without contacting the Demorests for specifics.
Location: 75 miles north of Sun Valley off Highway 75. Ranch will send you a map.
Medical: Emergency helicopter service available
Conference: 35; must book entire ranch
Guest Capacity: 35
Accommodations: Three comfortable two-bedroom cabins a short walk from the main lodge and near Loon Creek. One large four-bedroom cabin that sleeps 10. Several one-bedroom suites including the honeymoon/anniversary suite. Several upstairs lodge rooms. All rooms and cabins have electricity and modern bathroom facilities. Ranch powered by a hydroelectric generator. Guest laundry.
Rates: • $$. American Plan. Children's rates available.
Credit Cards: None. Personal checks and cash.
Season: Mid-June through early September
Activities: No schedules, but lots of activities are available each day. Evening and morning sign-up sheets for horseback riding and gold panning (very popular and all supplies are provided). Ask about Rob's Hot Springs and Pinyon Peak (tremendous lookout point at 10,000 feet) rides. The Diamond D offers two- to seven-day pack trips to hot springs, mountain lakes, and historic ranches. Hiking, swimming in modern pool with adjacent hot tub. Ranch has own lake with rowboats and fishing. Volleyball, badminton, and horseshoes on the green lawn in front of the lodge.
Children's Programs: Full supervision can be provided. Most kids under 6 do not ride.
Dining: Wholesome ranch cooking. Special diets will be catered to with advance notice. Birthdays and anniversaries are always special. BYOB.
Entertainment: Campfire sing-alongs. Cards, games, video movies, and fireside conversation in the lodge.
Summary: Lovely remote ranch with all the comforts of home. Area full of western lore, gold mines, and Indian stories. If you drive, you will want to see the old mining town of Custer and the Yankee Fork Gold Dredge. Be sure to ask Linda about her wonderful "Sparkling T-shirts" and crafts program. Private pilots should call Tom or Linda for details.

See color photos, pages 232-233

Idaho Rocky Mountain Ranch
Stanley, Idaho

The Sawtooth and White Cloud mountain ranges of central Idaho are among the most spectacular regions of North America. Here lies the Idaho Rocky Mountain Ranch, constructed in the 1930s by Winston Paul. In 1951, Edmund and Ruth Bogert acquired the ranch. Since that time the ranch has been operated under the guidance of their daughter, Rozalys B. Smith. At present, Bill and Jeana Leavell manage the ranch. The ranch is almost exactly as it was, right down to the monogrammed china. All furniture is handcrafted, and period photographs and animal trophies grace the log walls. From the lodge front porch you look out to the jagged, snowcapped peaks of the Sawtooth Mountains. At the Idaho Rocky Mountain Ranch, you will be surrounded with beauty.

Address: HC 64, Box 9934K, Stanley, Idaho 83278
Telephone: (208) 774-3544
Airport: Boise, 130 miles; Sun Valley (Hailey), 65 miles; private grass airstrip in Stanley, 10 miles
Location: 50 miles north of Sun Valley/Ketchum
Memberships: Cross-Country Ski Areas Association, National Trust for Historic Preservation, Idaho Outfitters and Guides Association Special Places
Medical: Medical clinic in Stanley, 9 miles; Moritz Hospital in Sun Valley
Conference: 43
Guest Capacity: 43
Accommodations: Beautifully preserved, 8,000-square-foot hand-hewn log main lodge houses a large sitting room, dining room, and four rooms with double or twin beds and private baths. The lodge porch provides spectacular vistas of the valley below and mountains beyond. The porch oak and wicker rockers are well used throughout the summer. Nine duplex cabins offer handcrafted furniture, stone fireplaces, private baths, and choice of twin or queen beds. Winter accommodations on the lower ranch include comfortable one- and three-bedroom cabins with wood stoves, private baths, kitchens, and great views.
Rates: \$-\$\$. Modified American Plan or Bed and Breakfast Plan. All activities are á la carte. No minimum stay.
Credit Cards: Visa, MasterCard, Discover
Season: Early June through September (summer); November to April (winter). Open Thanksgiving and Christmas.
Activities: Summer activities on the ranch include a horseback riding program, hot springs swimming pool (within a short walk or drive), fishing, short walking trails, horseshoes, volleyball, and wildlife viewing. Myriad activities await you on the surrounding public forest lands. Water activities include rafting on the Salmon and Payette rivers and fishing in the Salmon River and numerous pristine mountain lakes. Many hiking or mountain biking trails begin on the ranch or within a short drive. Rock climbing, photography, nature study, wildlife viewing, ghost town tours, and browsing around world-famous Sun Valley are other popular activities. Winter programs include cross-country skiing on groomed trails, backcountry hut-to-hut skiing, alpine skiing, and wildlife viewing nearby.
Children's Programs: None
Dining: Continental and hot breakfast is offered to all ranch guests. Dinner consists of four to five entrées served nightly. This is Idaho country cuisine at its best, featuring fresh Idaho trout, tender steaks, and succulent lamb, pastas, and a chef's special. Vegetarian options available. Western barbecue once a week. Open to the public by reservation.
Entertainment: Library, contemporary and live western music, wonderful local musicians, singalongs, stargazing. Entertainment in Stanley on Friday and Saturday nights.
Summary: One of the most beautiful lodges in the country. Incredible log and iron architecture. Run much like a large country inn. Most activities are á la carte. Excellent cuisine. Spectacular views, individualized service, cultural events in Sun Valley area, hot springs-heated pool. Bring your own horse.

See color photos, page 231

Indian Creek Ranch
Northfork, Idaho

This ranch is small and cozy, surrounded by Forest Service land and bordering an Idaho Primitive Area. It's a 2-mile drive into the ranch from the main road. Here there is no schedule and nothing that you have to do. Indian Creek is secluded and powered with propane and used to be actor Burgess Meredith's hideaway in the 1940s. If you need a hair dryer, this is not the place for you. After you have been at the ranch for a while, when the city is behind you, when you are beginning to feel the pine needles under your feet, when you've really relaxed, owners Jack Briggs and his daughter Theresa will pick up the pace with activities. With only ten guests at a time, the Briggses can tailor things just for you. Since the mid-1960s, they have created an atmosphere so natural that you can't help but relax and enjoy the things that enhance the spirit, soothe the soul, and rekindle inner strength. They are easygoing western folks who realize the importance of R&R and are ready to share their hospitality with you. When they say, "Relax up here," they mean it!

Address: HC 64, Box 105 K, Northfork, Idaho 83466
Telephone: (208) 394-2126
Airport: Missoula, small private airplanes to Salmon Airport
Location: 35 miles north of Salmon off Highway 93, 130 miles south of Missoula. Inquire at Northfork Store in Northfork, Idaho, for directions.
Memberships: Idaho Packers and Guides Association
Medical: Salmon Clinic, 35 miles; emergency helicopter service
Guest Capacity: 10
Accommodations: The ranch has a main lodge and four cabins. Each cabin is rustic but comfortable and complete with private bath and shower, and as Jack says, "We never run out of hot water!" No TVs or telephones here.
Rates: American Plan. Bed-and-breakfast rates available. No minimum stay.
Credit Cards: None. Personal checks accepted.
Season: April to November
Activities: Lots of mountain country for half-day and all-day rides. Jack plays it by ear. As he says, "It depends on the guests," and it really does. Some guests can take a half-day ride, and some can take an all-day ride. All riding in this country is at a walk. It's too rough for anything else. Fishing on and off the property, hiking, four-wheel-drive trips, seasonal hunting. Many guests enjoy venturing out and visiting by car other beautiful areas close to the ranch. Ask Jack about the gold-mining town. One day float boat trips can be arranged on the Salmon River.
Children's Programs: None
Dining: This is a real Idaho steak and potato outfit: prime rib, steaks, chicken, home-baked breads, biscuits, and muffins. BYOB.
Entertainment: After all these years Jack has some great stories to tell, or many just enjoy star-gazing and nature's solitude.
Summary: Indian Creek Ranch is for anyone who enjoys the outdoors in a very low-key, rustic environment. Very small ranch 2 miles from the Salmon River. Great story-telling. Jack is a character and also an expert on Lewis and Clark history. No electricity, powered by propane. Bed-and-breakfast or week stays. Trips to the ghost town of Ulysses. Float trips on the Salmon River, Idaho's "River of No Return." Pets allowed.

Shepp Ranch
Boise, Idaho

The only way to Shepp Ranch is by jet boat or charter plane service out of Boise. The ranch is in mountainous central Idaho, isolated deep in backcountry 15 miles from the closest road. It is a haven of comfort, healthy meals, good fellowship, and Western traditions. In the roadless wilderness of the Nez Perce Forest, the ranch lies on the north bank of the main Salmon River, at its confluence with Crooked Creek. This spot was homesteaded at the turn of the century by miners Charlie Shepp and Peter Klinkhammer, who built the rustic whip-sawed ranch house still in use today. In 1950, Pete sold the property to Paul Filer, who, with his wife, Marybelle, built a sawmill and new buildings using electricity from the hydropower plant. Fresh spring water comes from a large tank they floated downstream and installed high on a hillside. A sense of history prevails here in the buildings, the orchard, rare hand tools, a fence made of elk horns, antique guns, and horse-drawn farm implements. Paul Resnick, the present owner, purchased the ranch in 1979. It is run by Lynn and Michael Demerse.

Address: P.O. Box 5446K, Boise, Idaho 83705
Telephone: (208) 343-7729 (radio telephone at the ranch)
Airport: Boise
Train: Amtrak to Boise. Contact Jinny regarding transportation to ranch.
Location: 45 miles east of Riggins, Idaho; 200 miles northwest of Boise
Memberships: Idaho Outfitters and Guides Association
Awards: *Hideaway Report*
Medical: McCall Hospital, 100 miles; emergency helicopter service
Guest Capacity: 16
Accommodations: Six rustic individual log cabins with showers, wood-burning stoves, and porches. Each sleeps four comfortably. Of these six, there are two deluxe cabins (the Filer and Shepp cabins), with separate bedrooms. A marvelous hot tub overlooks the Salmon River—right on the river's edge. A sauna is also available. The ranch has its own generator. Lights out at 11 p.m., although almost everyone is sound asleep by then anyway. The paneled main lodge has a nice fireplace. The walls are decorated with a bearskin rug and hunting trophies. There are also books and a small piano. In the spring and early summer, before it warms up, there is an abundance of wildflowers, wildlife, and many hanging geranium baskets.
Rates: • $$-$$$. American Plan. Charter flight to ranch additional. Children age 13 and under half-price. One-day, weekend, and five-day packages available.
Credit Cards: None. Personal checks accepted.
Season: March through November
Activities: The Salmon River (Lewis and Clark called it the "River of No Return") is right out the front door. It offers the opportunity for many water sports. Guests enjoy sunbathing on sandy beaches, jet boating, white water rafting, hiking, and exploring. Trail riding on the ranch's sure-footed mules and horses. All riding done at a walk due to the terrain. Trout fishing in the summer and steelhead fishing in the spring and fall. Seasonal big game hunting.
Children's Programs: None. Recommended for ages 6 and older. Children are the responsibility of their parents.
Dining: Family-style meals. Many ranch-grown vegetables, barbecued steaks and pork chops, freshly baked breads, hand-cranked ice cream. Special diets with advance notice. BYOB.
Entertainment: Volleyball, horseshoes, archery, and skeet shooting. Very casual.
Summary: Wilderness lodge on Salmon River accessible only by small charter plane or jet boat. No TV or telephones. Warm hospitality. Everybody feels like family. The Salmon River Canyon is one of the deepest river canyons on the North American continent. Families or corporations with a minimum of 12 guests may rent the entire ranch.

Wapiti Meadow Ranch
Cascade, Idaho

Wapiti Meadow Ranch is a historic outpost in the remote and majestic Salmon River Mountains of central Idaho. One of just a handful of private properties in this magnificent Wilderness Area, it was originally homesteaded during the great Thunder Mountain gold rush. The lodge was built in 1926 by the Cox family, and it became the first Idaho guest ranch, famous as the Cox Dude Ranch until the mid-1970s. Diana Haynes bought the ranch in 1986. At 5,000 feet and surrounded by 8,000-foot ridges and peaks, Wapiti Meadow is cradled by heavily forested mountains, crystal clear streams, and lush valley meadows that are home to herds of elk, mule deer, and a fine string of horses and pack mules. What makes Wapiti Meadow special is its rugged seclusion coupled with its gracious elegance in accommodations and dining.

Address: H.C. 72 K, Cascade, Idaho 83611
Telephone: (208) 382-4336 year-round (radio telephone), (208) 382-3217 (November-May)
Airport: Boise. Contact ranch for air charter details.
Location: 130 miles north of Boise, 60 miles east of McCall, 140 miles northwest of Sun Valley
Awards: Orvis endorsed
Memberships: Dude Ranchers' Association, Idaho Outfitters and Guides Association, Idaho Conservation League, Cross-Country Ski Areas Association, Idaho Guest and Dude Ranch Association
Medical: McCall Hospital, 60 miles; Life Flight helicopter from Boise
Guest Capacity: 15
Accommodations: The main lodge is a hand-hewn log structure. In it is Diana's collection of antiques from her days in Virginia and a handsome stone fireplace. There are three newer two-bedroom cabins and one one-bedroom cabin. All feature large porches with twin, double, or queen beds, living room, bath, and kitchen. Singles usually stay in the lodge rooms.
Rates: • $$-$$$. American Plan. Pack trip and group rates. Three-day minimum stay, seven-day stays encouraged.
Credit Cards: None. Personal checks accepted.
Season: Year-round
Activities: Horseback riding a few hours or all day, superb fly-fishing on the blue ribbon waters of the Middle Fork of the Salmon, hike to "No Name" lake where the absence of any trail testifies to the few people who enjoy its deep green waters and bountiful supply of native trout, or four-wheel-drive to the historic Thunder Mountain area to explore and pan for gold. Also two- to five-day pack trips, backpacking with mules for equipment, over a dozen high mountain lakes. River rafting on the North Fork of the Payette and the Middle Fork of the Salmon. Cross-country skiing (see Cross-Country Skiing Ranches).
Children's Programs: None. Kids under 10 not advised.
Dining: Cocktails, hors d'oeuvres on the porch. Fine, hearty gourmet cuisine. A California Culinary Academy-trained chef is on hand year-round. Gourmet meals with fresh vegetables and exotic desserts. Complimentary wine and beer. Special diets accommodated. BYOL.
Entertainment: Relaxing on the main lodge porch, good conversation, watching the horses and game graze in the meadow, hot tub stargazing, informal roping contests, foal and yearling training sessions, horseshoes, volleyball, campfires.
Summary: Remote (60 miles from the nearest town)! Small family-owned and operated ranch. Personal service and intimate atmosphere. Delightful hosts who combine the best of city and country living. Wilderness skills, historic gold mines, Thunder Mountain Road, Middle Fork of the Salmon River. Small business retreats May, early June, and after Labor Day.

See color photos, page 237

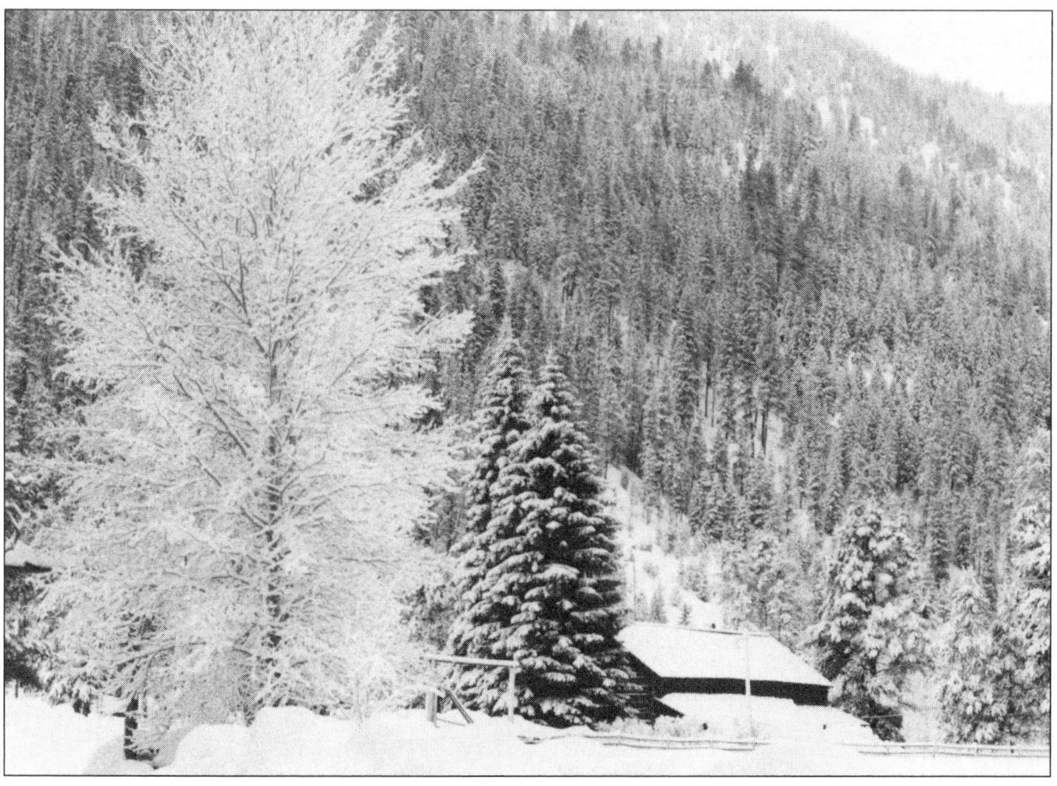

Twin Peaks Ranch
Salmon, Idaho

Little was left out when E. Dupont developed one of Idaho's first authentic dude ranches from a hay ranch dating back to 1923. After being closed for decades, this secluded private ranch, 18 miles south of Salmon, was opened to guests in the late 1980s by Allen and Lenabelle Davis. Its impressive setting, nestled in a mile-high valley in the shadow of surrounding peaks jutting up thousands of feet, has been described by guests as "unreal" and "hard to duplicate." The 2,200-acre ranch is wedged between the Salmon "River of No Return" and the largest wilderness and national forest area in the lower 48 states. Rarely can a dude ranch offer three days of scenic floating, drift fishing, and the white-water rapids of a world-class rafting river. Trails along the river wind up into the pine forest where elk, deer, and big horn sheep can occasionally be seen. Twin Peaks Ranch has it all—wilderness, white-water rafting, horseback riding, and fly-fishing. A writer for *House and Garden* magazine wrote it was "the guest ranch of my imagination."

Address: P.O. Box 774, Dept. K, Salmon, Idaho 83467

Telephone: (208) 894-2290, (800) 659-4899; fax: (208) 894-2429

Airport: Missoula, Montana, or Idaho Falls, Idaho. Complimentary transportation Sunday to and from Idaho Falls.

Location: 18 miles south of Salmon off Highway 93, 3 hours south of Missoula

Memberships: Dude Ranchers' Association, Idaho Outfitters and Guides Association, Idaho Guest and Dude Rancher's Association

Medical: Steele Memorial Hospital, Salmon, 18 miles; emergency helicopter service

Conference: 40, off-season only

Guest Capacity: 40

Accommodations: The original six rustic cabins have their own three-quarter baths for two or four persons. The deluxe cabin units have one or two bedrooms with Jacuzzi tubs. One room of the two-bedroom unit has a bath, murphy bed, and game table and becomes a sitting room. Six persons can be accommodated in these adjoining units. The lodge has a spacious lounge with stone fireplace, trophies, and numerous artifacts. An adjoining large heated pool and hot tub are surrounded by a sun deck and spectacular views.

Rates: • $$$-$$$$. American Plan. Children's, group, and off-season rates. One-week minimum stay, Sunday to Sunday.

Credit Cards: None. Personal and traveler's checks accepted.

Season: April through November

Activities: This traditional dude ranch offers the choice of taking raft trips on the Salmon River every other day. This provides a chance to enjoy every type of scenic riding terrain and also the Salmon Gorge, which combines many panoramas with the excitement of white-water rafting. Trail rides range from half-day to all-day. Instruction is available for improving riding skills and getting the knack of herding cattle and barrel racing in the new arena.

Children's Programs: No set program. Kids should be old enough to ride. Kids may eat together.

Dining: The view from the dining room is magnificent. Delicious western cuisine is offered buffet-style with scrumptious desserts. Weekly breakfast cookout and dinner steak fry barbecue served chuck wagon-style. BYOB, in cabins. Beer and wine are available in the lodge.

Entertainment: Weekly dancing to country-western music. Guest rodeo competition Saturday night. Nightly campfires, marshmallow roasting, and sing-alongs.

Summary: Here you have the best of three worlds—riding, river rafting, and relaxing. Ideal for a family adventure! The Davis family takes great pride in providing every opportunity for you to have an exciting vacation that will beckon you back. Be sure to ask about the 1936 touring bus that the Davises completely restored.

See color photo, page 236

Double JJ Ranch
Rothbury, Michigan

Double JJ Ranch is 25 miles outside Muskegon in west Michigan right on Big Wildcat and Carpenter lakes. This is one of the few adults-only ranches in the country and has entertained thousands of midwestern guests. It has a wonderful atmosphere, where people over the age of 18 can relax and be themselves. The ranch was started in the 1930s. Since then, it has grown to be a full-service ranch resort, which includes the Thoroughbred, an 18-hole championship golf course designed by noted architect Arthur Hill. Today, it is owned and operated by Bob and Joan Lipsitz. Since the early 1970s, both have been involved in the outdoor recreation field. The Double JJ accommodates up to 250 adults who participate in everything from horseback riding to organized sports. Said to be America's friendliest resort for "big kids," the ranch has 1,200 wooded acres set in a natural pine forest. There are hundreds of acres of trails and thousands of acres of the Manistee National Forest. Here the beauty of native Michigan is evident. Move fast or slow, whichever you like. The Double JJ is like being on a cruise ship without the boat.

Address: Box 94 K, Rothbury, Michigan 49452
Telephone: (616) 894-4444; fax: (616) 893-5355
Airport: Muskegon, 25 miles; Grand Rapids International, 45 miles; private airstrip on ranch
Location: 25 miles north of Muskegon off U.S. 31, 189 miles east of Chicago, 200 miles west of Detroit
Memberships: Michigan Appaloosa Horse Association
Medical: Muskegon General Hospital
Conference: 400; 10,000 square feet of conference space
Guest Capacity: 250
Accommodations: Guests sleep in cabins and lodge rooms with double and single beds, private baths, and showers. All 100 rooms have carpeting and daily housekeeping. Some deluxe ranch accommodations available with the development of the golf course. Condominium rentals are also available.
Rates: • \$-\$\$. American Plan. Two-, three-, and seven-night packages. Call regarding golf packages. Daily and weekend rates available. Conference and group rates. Holiday packages.
Credit Cards: Visa, MasterCard, Discover
Season: Year-round. Full programs May-November; limited programs rest of the year.
Activities: Daily riding with weekly breakfast and steak rides. Individual lessons and horse training available. Rides go out according to experience. Advanced riders can lope. All those who claim to be advanced riders are tested first for ability. Rides are typically one hour and 45 minutes and go out four times per day in small groups. Private lake fishing for bass and pike. Canoeing, outdoor heated swimming pool, 12-person hot tub spa, two tennis courts, hiking, rifle and archery range, baseball diamond, minigolf. Here there are many organized sports. All sports equipment, except fishing poles (fishing licenses are not required), is provided. Golfers, be sure to inquire about the new 18-hole championship Thoroughbred Golf Club.
Children's Programs: No children allowed.
Dining: Three meals per day are included. Plenty of down-home cooking! All you can eat. Weekly breakfast and steak rides. Full-service bar.
Entertainment: Nightly entertainment, including dances with live bands and deejays, musicians, comedians, staff, and game shows. Ranch rodeo each week with contest. Tractor hay wagon rides, game and video room, horseshoes. All-night volleyball. Theme weeks with costume parties.
Summary: Adults-exclusive resort ranch, full group adult activities with director and staff. This ranch will keep you entertained from morning until night. Single individuals always feel a part of this big Double JJ family. Health and fitness workshops. Motor coach tours welcome. Corporate Management Training, theme weeks, gift shop. Video available on request. Nearby: Lake Michigan, 6 miles; Silver Lake Sand Dunes, 15 miles; antique shops.

El Rancho Stevens
Gaylord, Michigan

El Rancho Stevens is in northern Michigan, on Dixon Lake, known for its cool, refreshing waters and sandy beaches. This ranch was started by "Doc" and Candy Stevens in 1948. Doc had been an automotive engineer and bought the property with the intent of building a Michigan dude ranch. Today, this ranch/lake resort is run by Doc's son, Steve. It encompasses about one thousand acres with good lakeside access, well-kept lawns, and open pastures. The Stevenses cater to couples and families with children 6 years old and up. Those who enjoy water activities and horseback riding will enjoy El Rancho Stevens.

Address: P.O. Box 495 K, Gaylord, Michigan 49735
Telephone: (517) 732-5090
Airport: Traverse City, 60 miles; private planes to Gaylord Airport, 5 miles
Location: 225 miles north of Detroit off I-75, 50 miles south of the famous Mackinaw Bridge, 5 miles southeast of Gaylord off McCoy Road
Memberships: West Michigan Tourist Association, Michigan Travel & Tourism, Otsego County Chamber of Commerce
Medical: Otsego Memorial Hospital, 6 miles
Conference: 100 (Ox Yoke Beach Building)
Guest Capacity: 100
Accommodations: There are two two-story lodges and two one-story lodges with 30 motel-style rooms. Each is comfortable, carpeted, with private bath and double beds. There is one two-bedroom suite with full bath and living room. No televisions or telephones in rooms.
Rates: • $. Modified American Plan. Children's, holiday, and off-season rates available. Two-night minimum stay.
Credit Cards: Visa, MasterCard
Season: June through September
Activities: Riding and hiking trails wander through the ranch and onto state lands with forested areas. All rides are on a per hour basis and divided into beginner, intermediate, and advanced. All guests are guaranteed one ride each day. Rides usually go out on an hourly basis. Two breakfast rides each week. Large indoor riding arena. Heated swimming pool. Full lake activities including paddle boats and small sailboats, waterskiing, fishing, and canoeing. You may bring your own boat if you wish. Softball, archery, and volleyball. Gaylord is fast becoming the golf capital of northern Michigan, with ten 18-hole golf courses nearby (packages available). Tractor hayrides and cookouts.
Children's Programs: Counselors and daily junior wrangler programs for kids 6 and up mornings and afternoons. Riding, waterskiing, crafts, and other activities. Kids may eat with counselors at dinner or with parents for lunch and dinner. Evening entertainment after dinner for children. Kids have a great time with games, riding, arts and crafts. They really love the independence, and so do their parents. Baby-sitters available (extra).
Dining: Meals from the dining room are ordered from a menu and served on an individual basis. Cookouts and beach barbecues of chicken and ribs are the ranch favorites. Breakfast rides. Licensed cocktail lounge in dining room and the Silver Dollar Saloon at the beach.
Entertainment: There is usually something every night: hayrides, country dancing, sing-alongs with marshmallow roasts. Corral capers, in which guests compete against each other in games like egg and spoon races. Recreation room with video games, table tennis, and pool tables.
Summary: Affordable, friendly ranch resort on two-mile-long Dixon Lake. Great for families and single parents. Junior wrangler program for children 6 and up. Some baby-sitting available for kids under 6. This ranch attracts families from lower Michigan, Ohio, Indiana, and Illinois. Indoor riding arena. Bring your own horse. Nearby: Mackinaw Island and Bridge, Hartwick Pines State Park, canoeing down Ausable River.

Turkey Creek Ranch
Theodosia, Missouri

Overlooking Bull Shoals Lake in the heart of Ozark Mountain Country is the Edwards' Turkey Creek Ranch. Run by the founders, Dick and Elda Edwards, and their oldest son and daughter-in-law, Robert and Loretta, this 400-acre working ranch and lake resort is a far cry from the dilapidated old farm purchased by the Edwards family in 1953. Turkey Creek Ranch offers affordable family fun with activities that appeal to anyone from one to one hundred. Here you can indulge in serious fishing or just serious fun! The Edwardses welcome you to Turkey Creek—"a place with hills, hollows, trees and lake, where you can do as little or as much as you like."

Address: H.C. 3, Box 3180 K, Theodosia, Missouri 65761
Telephone: (417) 273-4362
Airport: Springfield, Missouri, 85 miles
Location: 47 miles east of Branson, Missouri; 47 miles northwest of Mountain Home, Arkansas
Memberships: AAA, Missouri Bull Shoals Lake Association, Ozark Mountain Region, Branson Chamber of Commerce
Awards: Mobil 2 Star, AAA 3 Diamond
Medical: Baxter County Hospital, Mountain Home, 47 miles
Guest Capacity: 140
Accommodations: There are twenty-four cabins and casitas. All cabins have kitchens complete with microwave and full-size appliances, air-conditioning, color television, carpeted bedrooms, daily paper, screened porch, picnic table, and barbecue grill. The cabin size varies from four- to ten-person capacity. Daily maid service is available. Some cabins are handicapped accessible.
Rates: • $. Riding, restaurant meals, and motor rentals extra.
Credit Cards: None. Personal checks accepted.
Season: Mid-March to mid-November
Activities: Guided trail rides daily except Saturday offer enough variety for both beginner and advanced riders. The hiking trails follow the bridle paths and go through the forest and along the lake. Lake activities include boating, fishing, skiing, and diving (Scuba gear available locally). The lake offers a wide variety of game and pan fish (bass, crappie, walleye, trout, sunfish, etc.) to tempt any fisherman. Resort activities include an indoor heated pool and whirlpool spa, outdoor pool with kiddie pool, tennis, shuffleboard, horseshoes, volleyball, and a golf putting area (golf course nearby). Ranch activities vary according to time of year and guest experience. Turkey Creek has its own riding horses and herd of Angus/Simmental cross-bred beef cattle.
Children's Programs: No formal program. Children are encouraged to participate in activities with their parents. Children too young for trail rides (under age 8) may be led on rides around the resort grounds. There is also a large playground area. Baby-sitting available with advance notice.
Dining: The Chuckwagon offers a full menu for lunch and dinner; seafood, steaks, salads and fresh-baked goods are featured. A special occasion meal can be arranged with advance reservation, and special diets can be accommodated.
Entertainment: It's all up to you. Do a little or a lot. The 3,000-square-foot recreation building has two fireplaces, a piano and organ for singalongs, indoor heated pool and spa, pool tables, video games, shuffleboard, table tennis, air hockey, and much more. Plus Turkey Creek has some of the best Ozark Mountain scenery to be found.
Summary: Family-owned and family-oriented vacation ranch resort on Bull Shoals Lake in the heart of beautiful Ozark Mountain country offering a wide variety of ranch and lake activities for all ages and abilities. Near the famous country music town of Branson, Missouri, with its wide variety of music shows; Silver Dollar City, Shepherd of the Hills, and White Water theme parks; Springfield, Missouri, with Bass Pro Shops Outdoor World Headquarters, and Dickerson Park Zoo.

Beartooth Ranch and JLX
Nye, Montana

As you drive up Stillwater Canyon on your way to Beartooth Ranch, the Woodbine Falls signal your arrival. These magnificent falls plummet more than 1,000 feet before striking the river below. As you drive in the ranch gate, you will probably be greeted by Jim and Ellen Langston, who are your hosts at this wonderful, historic ranch. Jim, who is a native-born Montanan, is a past president of the Dude Ranchers' Association. Both Jim and Ellen exude the friendly spirit of the Old West and have friends from around the world who have been through their ranch gates to savor and cherish their very special Montana hospitality and ranching goodness. Beartooth Ranch is one of the charter members of the Dude Ranchers' Association and began serving guests in 1904. At 5,058 feet, this 160-acre homesteaded ranch is four miles within the Custer National Forest boundary and adjacent to nearly one million acres of the Absaroka Beartooth Wilderness Area. Jim and Ellen have been in the dude ranch business since 1956. Here you will live the history of Montana and savor the spirit of the Old West. With great fishing, scenic horseback riding, and down-home friendly hospitality, Beartooth Ranch is one of the best.

Address: HC 54, Box 350 K, Nye, Montana 59061
Telephone: (406) 328-6194 or (406) 328-6205; call for fax number
Airport: Billings Logan International Airport
Location: 23 miles west of Fishtail, 45 miles south of Columbus, 90 miles southwest of Billings
Memberships: Dude Ranchers' Association, Montana Outfitters and Guides Association
Medical: Absarokee Medical Clinic, 30 miles; Stillwater Community Hospital, 45 miles; HELP helicopter from Billings, 90 miles
Conference: Available
Guest Capacity: 30
Accommodations: Twelve log and native rock, heated cabins varying from one to four bedrooms, most with living rooms, some with fireplaces, and all with baths; one two-story lodge with eleven rooms, each with its own bath. Laundry facilities available. Daily maid service.
Rates: $. American Plan. Family and group rates available, one-week minimum stay, Sunday to Sunday.
Credit Cards: American Express, MasterCard, Visa
Season: June through Labor Day
Activities: Horseback riding is the main daily activity. Ask Jim and Ellen about their rides to Sioux Charley, Horseman Flat, and Nye Basin. Instruction available. Advanced riders may help wrangle horses. Excellent fly-fishing in the Stillwater River for rainbow, German brown, and brook trout. Fishing licenses available. Pack trips, hiking, swimming in the ranch pond. Horseshoe pitching tournaments, volleyball, softball, badminton, table tennis, billiards, bird-watching, and rock-climbing.
Children's Programs: Children's supervisors and wranglers arrange treasure hunts on horseback, melodramas, pageants, variety shows, lawn games, crafts, swimming, nature hikes, and trail rides. Children usually interact with families.
Dining: Breakfast is served short-order style. A buffet luncheon is ready at noon. Dinner, served family-style, begins at 6:30 p.m. and features western ranch cooking. At 5:30 p.m., guests gather at the Happy Hour Circle by the chuck wagon. BYOB. Luncheon rides and steak or hamburger barbecues at the riverside picnic area are held several times a week.
Entertainment: Campfires with western singing, evenings in the lodge with western dancing, melodramas, pageants, variety shows.
Summary: Jim and Ellen Langston's Beartooth Ranch offers excellent old Montana hospitality, great fishing, scenic horseback riding, warmth and kindness. Ask Ellen about the interesting geology here. Nearby: Memorial Day rodeos, Festival of Nations in Red Lodge, and Western Days in Billings in mid-June.

Blue Spruce Lodge and Guest Ranch
Trout Creek, Montana

Russ Milleson was injured in an industrial accident in 1974 at the age of 23. Suddenly confined to a wheelchair for life and unable to find places that were wheelchair accessible for hunting, fishing, and other outdoor activities, with the help of his family, he designed and built the Blue Spruce Lodge. Completed in June 1986, the Blue Spruce is in the foothills of the Bitterroot Mountains of northwest Montana and is run today by Russ and his wife, Karen. Open year-round, the lodge offers a wide variety of recreational activities for all. River raft trips begin in May. Russ also operates a 24-foot pontoon boat on the Noxon Reservoir, with sightseeing and fishing trips on Lake Pend Oreille. Fall brings the hunting season, with a large variety of big game and birds. There is a special program for wheelchair hunters. Cross-country skiing is good December through March, and there are many miles of trails that provide entertainment and challenge. The warm lodge interior features family-style dining, a wet bar, and a pool table. The cozy wood stove creates a homey environment in a scenic Montana setting. Blue Spruce Lodge is a place for families, couples, and singles who may or may not be wheelchair-bound and who appreciate the outdoors and a family environment.

Address: 451 Marten Creek Road, Dept. K, Trout Creek, Montana 59874
Telephone: (406) 827-4762, (800) 831-4797; call for fax number
Airport: Missoula, Montana, or Spokane, Washington
Location: 25 miles west of Thompson Falls off Highway 200, 140 miles northwest of Missoula, 140 miles northeast of Spokane
Medical: Plains, Montana, 75 miles; Sandpoint Hospital in Idaho, 65 miles; helicopter ambulance from Missoula or Spokane
Conference: Up to 16
Guest Capacity: 16
Accommodations: The two-story main lodge has been designed for wheelchair access and maneuverability. The main floor is serviced by wide entrances and generous porches. There are few obstacles or hindrances. Sleeping accommodations are provided on the second floor, and there is an elevator for convenience. Several of the nine bedrooms have private balconies. There are five rooms with queen beds, three rooms with bunk beds, and a sleeping loft with a double bed. Laundry service is available. No minimum stay.
Rates: • $. American Plan. Children's and group rates available.
Credit Cards: Visa, MasterCard, American Express
Season: Year-round
Activities: Week-long programs and activities are tailored to the groups or individuals at the ranch. Trail rides, white water raft trips, and float fishing trips are available for everyone. Even big game and bird hunting are possible for guests in wheelchairs. Winter program includes cross-country skiing, sit skiing for the disabled, sledding, snowmobiling, ice fishing.
Children's Programs: Children go on most outings with parents; baby-sitting available.
Dining: Home-cooked meals served family-style; special diets on request. BYOB.
Entertainment: Fiddle and guitar music around campfire some evenings.
Summary: A unique, small, family ranch designed and built to give individuals confined to wheelchairs and their families full enjoyment of ranch life and a rustic wilderness experience. The lodge is totally wheelchair accessible, as are most activities. Russ's philosophy is to make as many wilderness activities as possible available for those with physical and developmental disabilities. As Russ says, "Life is short, and nature is perhaps our greatest healer." Blue Spruce Lodge is a very special place for very special people.

Boulder River Ranch
McLeod, Montana

In a rugged mountain valley, surrounded by the Absaroka Mountains at 5,050 feet, Boulder River Ranch is a neat old ranch on the banks of the beautiful Boulder River. This family owned and operated ranch is on one of the most productive trout streams in North America. Since 1918, the Aller family has played host to families from around the world who return year after year. Now run by third and fourth generations, the Allers take only 30 guests at a time and specialize in superb fishing and horseback riding. Experienced and novice anglers will enjoy tremendous fishing in the cold, crystal clear waters of the Boulder River. Hearty swimmers love the river's natural pools. Riders savor the beautiful high country and meadow trail rides to abandoned mines, homesteads, and the Indian caves. June is for bird-watchers, with more than seventy species of birds in the area. Deer, elk, and hundreds of wildflowers also abound. No matter which month you choose, fishermen and riders alike will enjoy every moment with the Allers.

Address: Box 210 K, McLeod, Montana 59052
Telephone: (406) 932-6406
Airport: Billings or Bozeman
Location: 110 miles southwest of Billings, 87 miles southeast of Bozeman, 28 miles south of Big Timber
Memberships: Dude Ranchers' Association
Medical: Certified EMT at ranch
Conference: Up to 25
Guest Capacity: 30
Accommodations: Most of the fifteen individual cabins are arranged in a semicircle around the front lawn; each is comfortable, with fresh wildflowers, private baths, and daily maid service. Each looks to the Absaroka Mountains across the river. Happy hour at the end of the day brings guests onto the front lawn for tale swapping. It is a nice family arrangement. Laundry services available. Cabin girls will do your laundry if you wish (extra).
Rates: • $. American Plan. Children's and family rates available. Children under age 3, free.
Credit Cards: None. Personal checks and cash accepted.
Season: June to mid-September
Activities: Fishing and horseback riding are the main activities here. The ranch raises and trains its own quarter horses. Half-day and all-day guided rides to Green Mountain, West Boulder Plateau, and Pruitt Park. Walk, trot, lope depending on your level of experience. No riding on Sundays. Catch-and-release fly-fishing. Boulder River is a haven for families who like to fish. Most fish on their own, but the Allers are always delighted to show a novice the ropes. Guides are available (extra). Limited fishing gear available. Hiking and swimming in the river. Seasonal deer and elk hunting.
Children's Programs: Very limited children's program. Kiddie wrangler; stocked pond for swimming and fishing. Baby-sitting on request.
Dining: Scrumptious family-style meals. Ranch-raised beef, cookouts. Ranch chef will cook your freshly caught pond trout. Once-a-week breakfast rides with famous ranch "fry" bread. BYOB.
Entertainment: Most guests like to retreat to the porches of their cabins and reminisce about their experiences of the day. There is no formal entertainment at the ranch.
Summary: Delightful, very relaxed, very informal family owned and operated ranch on 2½ miles of the Boulder River; 90 percent return guests. Most come to fish and ride. Single and couples week. June and September art workshops. Fly-fishing clinics available on request. Nearby: Yellowstone National Park, Big Timber Professional Rodeo in June and world championship pack horse race in August.

C-B Cattle and Guest Ranch
Cameron, Montana

This family-owned cattle ranch is in the famous Madison River Valley. Fly-fishermen know this river for its trophy brown and rainbow trout. The C-B Cattle and Guest Ranch was established in 1971 by Mrs. Cynthia Boomhower of Palm Beach, Florida, who as a young girl fell in love with the West and dude ranching. Today her daughter, Sandy, and son-in-law, Chris, are the hosts. The ranch encompasses 21,000 acres and raises 200 head of Charolais crosses and a small herd of longhorn cattle. At 5,000 feet, the ranch lodge and cabins are situated where Indian Creek comes out of the Madison Range, which rises to 11,000 feet behind the property. You will have a great feeling of Western nostalgia as you pass under the C-B Ranch gate and experience the grandeur of Montana's Big Sky Country.

Address: P.O. Box 604 K, Cameron, Montana 59720
Telephone: (406) 682-4954 (summer); (619) 723-1932 (winter)
Airport: West Yellowstone or Bozeman
Location: 20 miles southeast of Ennis off U.S. 287, 60 miles southwest of Bozeman
Memberships: Dude Ranchers' Association
Medical: Ennis Hospital
Guest Capacity: 12-14
Accommodations: Three large double log cabins, each with two double beds and a fold-out couch, with private entrances. All cabins have private baths and open fireplaces or Franklin stoves, with fire starter in a little bucket. Furnished with real Navajo rugs, clip-on reading lights, candles, and fresh flowers. Additional electric heat and air-conditioning (which is seldom needed) in all cabins.
Rates: $-$$. American Plan. One-week minimum stay July and August, Sunday to Sunday arrival. Three-day minimum stay early June.
Credit Cards: None. Personal checks or cash accepted.
Season: Mid-June to early September
Activities: There are no planned activities at the C-B Ranch. Traditionally, the men have fished morning, noon, and night, and the ladies have enjoyed horseback riding, walking, and reading. Today more women are fly-fishing, and so they should. The fishing in this part of the country is superb. If you wish to float the famous Madison River, Sandy will put you in touch with one of the local guides (extra). You may also fish the waters of the Henry's Fork. Horseback riders are assigned their own horses for the length of their stay. Guided rides go out daily. Because the ranch is small, riding is flexible but always guided. Ask about the Indian Creek Waterfall ride. Weekly lunch ride with barbecue, weather permitting. Most of all, families usually do things together.
Children's Programs: Kiddie wrangler is available. This is not a child-oriented place. Better for older children.
Dining: All meals are prepared fresh. There is always plenty of food. This is a meat, potatoes, fresh salad kind of place. Sandy is proud of the fare here. Fresh berries, melons, vegetables, cakes, pies, Sunday turkey dinner. BYOB.
Entertainment: The howls of coyotes at night. You may see deer, antelope, coyotes, elk, moose, and bears.
Summary: C-B is quiet and relaxing. Here you will truly feel a part of Montana's Big Sky Country. Eighty percent are repeat guests. No planned activities. Most come to fly-fish the famous Madison River or the Henry's Fork, ride, or relax. Very occasional cattle work that guests can help with. Nearby: Yellowstone National Park, Virginia City, Lewis and Clark Caverns, Intercollegiate Rodeo Finals in Bozeman, local rodeos in Ennis.

See color photos, page 238

Circle Bar Guest Ranch
Utica, Montana

The Circle Bar Ranch is a dude/working cattle ranch in central Montana where the scenery ranges from dry prairie to towering mountains. Host and owner Sarah Hollatz bought the ranch in the early 1980s. It had been a dude ranch since 1930 and a cattle ranch since 1890. While her first love is guest ranching, she is very talented and, among other things, has written and performed children's records and is currently working on a Broadway musical. The ranch takes 35 guests at a time and is bordered on two sides by the Lewis and Clark National Forest. The ranch encourages full participation in ranch activities or just plain relaxing and savoring the goodness of ranch life. As Sarah says, "If you have a song in your heart, and love the wide-open spaces of the West, come and see us!"

Address: P.O. Box K, Utica, Montana 59452
Telephone: (406) 423-5454; fax: (406) 423-5686
Airport: Great Falls
Location: 90 miles south of Great Falls, 13 miles southwest of Utica near Route 87
Memberships: Dude Ranchers' Association, Montana Outfitters and Guides Association
Medical: EMT on premises; Lewistown Central Montana Hospital, 50 miles
Conference: 40
Guest Capacity: 35
Accommodations: There are nine one- to four-bedroom log cabins; all have propane or electric heat and private baths. Most cabins have their own fireplace or wood stove. The exquisite lodge has a huge fieldstone fireplace and three suites for guests. All cabins have porches or decks and names such as Buffalo, Eagle, and Corral. The artwork in each cabin exemplifies its name. You will probably find a bouquet of fresh wildflowers in your room. Laundry facilities are available.
Rates: $$. American Plan. Conference, winter, hunting, and pack trip rates available on request. One-week minimum stay. Arrivals any day.
Credit Cards: None. Personal checks or cash accepted.
Season: Year-round, including Thanksgiving and Easter
Activities: In summer, riders will enjoy the ranch's fine string of horses. All-day and half-day rides in groups no larger than 8 to 10 persons. Moonlight rides through open meadows and pines once a week. Ask about Blackfood Indian Cave, Elk Game, or Hole-in-the-Ground rides. Riding instruction is available. Pack trips with advance notice. Light harness carriage driving with instruction. Fishing on the Judith River, which runs through the ranch. Hiking, volleyball, indoor top of the barn basketball, horseshoes, heated swimming pool, and hot tub. Fall hunting. In winter, provided there is snow, wilderness cross-country skiing, sleigh rides, ice skating, and snowmobiling are available. (BYOS.)
Children's Programs: Parents are responsible for children. Young children ride with supervision.
Dining: All meals served in the lodge, buffet and family-style. The ranch is proud of the fresh breads and homegrown herbs and vegetables used in preparing the daily meals. Ranch specialties: Caribbean chicken, homegrown steak, fresh rhubarb pies. Sunday barbecue. BYOB. Cocktails on the deck.
Entertainment: Team-drawn hayrides, occasional square dances, campfire sing-alongs. Evening swimming.
Summary: A wonderful, working ranch that raises cattle, horses, buffalo, chickens, and a few milk cows. Sarah is a multi-talented woman who loves people, creative energy, and the outdoors. Flexibility to cater to specific interests. Families, couples, and singles all feel comfortable. Fossil hunting, horse-drawn carriage driving with instruction. Artist workshops. Ask Sarah about the historic four-day Charlie Russell horseback ride. Branding in May and roundups in June and October. Nearby: Sapphire and gold mining, trips to Charles M. Russell Museum, castle ghost town. Some rusty French spoken.

Covered Wagon Ranch
Gallatin Gateway, Montana

In 1982, Vic Benson, the patriarch of this old-time ranch, realized that he was getting on in years. A young fellow by the name of Will King worked at the ranch and expressed his desire to carry on what Vic's family had started. Today, Vic and Will, along with Will's brother, Bruce, share their home and way of life with guests from all over the United States and Europe. It's a great story of love and devotion to one another and to the spirit of dude ranching. Since 1925, the Covered Wagon Ranch has operated as a western mountain ranch, experienced by four generations of guests. The ranch is located just off the road in the Gallatin Canyon three miles from the northwest corner of Yellowstone National Park between the Madison and Gallatin ranges. Horseback riding is the principal activity, although stream trout fishing is equally important to many, along with hiking and relaxing. Vic and Will operate their ranch as if they were entertaining personal house guests. As Will says, "Our purpose is to provide a pleasant visit as a family in a comfortable and enjoyable manner." Covered Wagon Ranch offers old-time charm and real, sincere hospitality, just the way it used to be.

Address: 34035 K Gallatin Road, Gallatin Gateway, Montana 59730
Telephone: (406) 995-4237
Airport: Bozeman, 60 miles; West Yellowstone, 34 miles. A ranch car will meet guests on arrival at either airport.
Location: 54 miles south of Bozeman and 34 miles north of West Yellowstone on Highway 191
Memberships: Dude Ranchers' Association
Medical: Bozeman Deaconess Hospital, 54 miles
Conference: 24
Guest Capacity: 24
Accommodations: Eight one- and two-bedroom, nifty old-time log cabins, all with private baths and covered porches, sleep from two to six persons. Accommodations are attractively and comfortably furnished, including good beds. A large recreation lodge, with fireplace, provides a place for easy living and for gathering and relaxing.
Rates: • $$. Full American Plan. Children's, off-season, and nonriding rates available.
Credit Cards: American Express. Personal checks preferred.
Season: May to October (summer), February to April (winter)
Activities: Activities are self-structured. Guests enjoy horseback riding, fishing, hiking. Mountain bikes available. Nearby nonranch activities include white water rafting, golf, and tennis. In winter, the ranch is open to skiing guests. The upper Gallatin has the most reliable snow in the northern Rockies, both tracked cross-country and ski touring. Downhill skiing is available nearby. Snow coach trips into Yellowstone National Park by prior arrangement.
Children's Programs: No structured children's program. Children are treated as part of the daily ranch program.
Dining: Hearty ranch cuisine. Family-style meals served in the central dining room. BYOB.
Entertainment: Evenings include campfire visits to discuss the day's happenings and plans for the coming day's activities. A guitar often encourages song during the evening. The recreation hall inspires action with table tennis, pool, foosball.
Summary: This is a wonderful little ranch with the old-time dude ranch spirit, rich in western hospitality, warmth, and kindness. Located along the Yellowstone Highway only three miles from the northwest corner of Yellowstone National Park and near the confluence of the Taylor Fork and Gallatin rivers.

Diamond J Ranch
Ennis, Montana

In 1959, Peter and Jinny Combs were on their way to Alaska, looking to move from the ever-increasing development of southern California. They stopped at the Diamond J Ranch, and the rest is history. The Diamond J was built in 1930 by Julia Bennett and run as a guest ranch. It was her masterpiece, located in the Madison River Valley, famous for cattle ranching and fly-fishing. The ranch is surrounded by the Lee Metcalf Wilderness Area and is nestled in a separate canyon at 5,800 feet with Jack Creek running alongside. Jinny and her son, Tim, run a great operation. Families return to the Diamond J Ranch year after year.

Address: P.O. Box 577 K, Ennis, Montana 59729
Telephone: (406) 682-4867; fax: (406) 682-4106
Airport: Bozeman, commercial; Ennis, 4,800-foot paved airstrip 12 miles away for light aircraft
Location: 14 miles east of Ennis off Highway 287, 60 miles south of Bozeman
Memberships: Dude Ranchers' Association
Awards: Orvis-Endorsed Lodge, Fishing and Wing Shooting Lodge
Medical: Ennis Hospital, 12 miles
Conference: 36 (June, September, October, November)
Guest Capacity: 36
Accommodations: The ten log cabins are constructed with lodgepole pine logs. Each has its own rock fireplace, tongue-and-groove hardwood floors, matching furniture, and beds. Each cabin features a few of Julia Bennett's personal big game trophies, a full bath with separate shower stall, and cast iron tub. The bedroom-living rooms feature twin beds, writing desks, and front porches, each with different railing designs. No television or telephones in cabins.
Rates: • $$-$$$$$. American Plan. Children's and seasonal rates available. Skeet and trap shooting, sporting clays, pack trips, guided fly-fishing and wing shooting/water fowl packages available. July and August, one-week minimum stay, Sunday to Sunday.
Credit Cards: MasterCard, Visa
Season: June through November
Activities: Activities can be tailored to individual or family needs, as schedules are flexible. The ranch emphasizes a relaxed, unstructured atmosphere. The Diamond J has great children's horses. Breakfast, half-day, all-day rides. Annual June horse drive for expert riders only. Ask about the Yellowstone National Park ride. Mountain pack trips are possible. Hiking. Excellent fly-fishing: the ranch is near some of the best blue ribbon streams in Montana, like the Madison, Gallatin, Jefferson, Beaverhead, and Missouri, 70 miles away. Private two-acre lake with rainbow trout. Full-time guides are available. Indoor tennis, mountain bike trails, heated swimming pool, hot tub. Float trips arranged. Massage available. Wing shooting (guns provided) and ten-station sporting clay course.
Children's Programs: Kiddie wrangler and riding instruction. Usually children ride together. Baby-sitter available.
Dining: Meals served family-style in three rooms. At lunch and dinner, children and adults usually eat separately (not mandatory). House specialties: fruit pancakes, tostadas, ham loaf with honey mustard, and steak barbecue. Special diets catered to with advance notice. Cookouts. Prefer no smoking in dining room. A BYOB happy hour.
Entertainment: Square dancing, campfire, sing-alongs, games, and an excellent library (ranch subscribes to best-seller list).
Summary: Lovely unstructured family owned and operated guest/fly-fishing and wing shooting ranch. Very flexible programs; do as much or as little as you wish. Horses for children, ten-station sporting clay course, float trips, indoor tennis, June horse drives. Fluent Spanish spoken. Orvis-endorsed. Nearby: Yellowstone National Park, Museum of the Rockies in Bozeman, historic Virginia City.

See color photos, page 239

Elk Canyon Ranch
White Sulphur Springs, Montana

John and Kay Eckhardt and the Texas-based Schoellkopf family all shared a dream, a love, and a vision. Together, in 1985, they created a guest ranch masterpiece along the Smith River in central Montana. The Eckhardts have been in the guest ranching business since the early 1960s. From their beautifully laid out brochure to nightly bed turndown service, John and Kay, along with their son, Bob, and his wife, Mandy, have not forgotten a thing. In addition to their luxurious amenities, they recruit some of the nicest collegiate staff in the business. Elk Canyon Ranch is a "top gun."

Address: 1151 Smith River Road, Drawer K, White Sulphur Springs, Montana 59645
Telephone: (406) 547-3373; fax: (406) 547-3719
Airport: Bozeman. Private planes may land at the 6,000-foot paved airstrip at White Sulphur Springs, Montana
Location: 30 miles northwest of White Sulphur Springs off Highway 360, 110 miles north of Bozeman
Medical: White Sulphur Springs Hospital; emergency helicopter service available
Conference: 24; off-season only
Guest Capacity: 42
Accommodations: Eight sensational one- to four-bedroom deluxe log cabins among manicured lawns and beside a small man-made creek. The cabins have 15- to 20-foot peaked ceilings and fieldstone fireplaces, pine interiors, large country windows, and sitting areas or living rooms. Each bedroom is carpeted and has its own private bath. All the cabins have front porches. Each cabin also features washer/dryer, private telephones with direct outside lines, baseboard heating, air-conditioning, and old-fashioned overhead fans and brass bathroom fixtures. A few deluxe cabins even have full kitchens, but they are not used by the guests. One cabin even has a wheelchair-access shower. To top it off, your handmade log bed will be turned down each night.
Rates: • $$$-$$$$. Full American Plan. Children's rates available. One-week minimum stay, Sunday to Sunday.
Credit Cards: None
Season: Early June to mid-October. Conference groups in the off-season.
Activities: Each guest is assigned a horse for the entire length of stay. Beginners receive full instruction. Experienced riders cover more territory. Rides usually go out in groups of five to seven. Hourly, half-day, and all-day rides, cookouts and breakfast rides to Spring Creek and Songsters Divide. Twenty-five-foot by fifty-foot outdoor heated swimming pool with lifeguard on duty during the day. Two professional tennis courts; a breathtaking trap and skeet shooting range. Excellent catch-and-release fly-fishing only. Limited fishing equipment available. There is a stocked meadow pond for those who wish fresh trout at breakfast. Golf carts are available for those who truly need them.
Children's Programs: Terrific, but nonmandatory, program from 9:00 a.m. to 2:00 p.m. and again from 6:00 p.m. to 9:00 p.m. each day for children ages 4 to 13. Baby-sitting for younger children on a limited basis.
Dining: Full breakfast, lunch buffets, and wonderful salads poolside (weather permitting). Weekly noon and evening cookouts. Children eat with other children and counselors. Dinner entrées include wonderfully prepared beef, fish, lamb, veal, and poultry served with fresh vegetables and California wine.
Entertainment: After dinner, parents reunite with their children. Some go for short walks, others sit on their porches or just drift off to sleep.
Summary: A luxury guest ranch. Excellence in every way. Fully appointed individual cabins with complete amenities. Sundry items available. Nearby: Museum of the Rockies, Charles M. Russell Museum, and Glacier, Teton, and Yellowstone national parks.

See color photos, page 240

Elkhorn Ranch
Gallatin Gateway, Montana

The Elkhorn Ranch is one of the old-time, no-nonsense dude ranches. A ranch steeped in history, it was started in the early 1920s by Ernest and Grace Miller. Located one mile from the northwest corner of Yellowstone Park, Elkhorn is at 7,000 feet in a beautiful valley surrounded by the Gallatin National Forest and the Lee Metcalf Wilderness. It is a gateway to incredible natural beauty, mountain scenery, and loads of wildlife. From the ranch headquarters rides go out in all directions. Since the early days, the ranch has been famous for its superb riding program, its dedication to preserving our Western heritage, and to uniting families. Today, as in years gone by, the Elkhorn combines old-fashioned Montana-style hospitality, rustic warmth, and natural beauty. At the Elkhorn Ranch, they still serve up the West that used to be.

Address: 33133 Gallatin Road, Drawer K, Gallatin Gateway, Montana 59730
Telephone: (406) 995-4291; call for fax number
Airport: Bozeman and West Yellowstone
Location: 60 miles south of Bozeman off Highway 191, 30 miles north of the west entrance to Yellowstone Park
Memberships: Dude Ranchers' Association
Medical: Bozeman Deaconess Hospital, 60 miles
Conference: 45; June and September only
Guest Capacity: 45
Accommodations: Sixteen original log cabins radiate old-time western charm and the early spirit of dude ranching. Most were built in the 1930s. Each is set apart from the others and varies in size, sleeping one to eight persons. Most have colorful Hudson Bay foot blankets and comforters; some even have squeaky wooden floors. Most have electric heat in the bathrooms and wood stoves in the sitting areas. All have porches, most covered, and guests spend a good deal of time on them relaxing, reading, reflecting, and visiting. Limited laundry facilities.
Rates: $$-$$$. American Plan. Children's rates available. One-week minimum stay, Sunday to Sunday, in July and August. Shorter stays available in June and September.
Credit Cards: None. Personal checks or traveler's checks.
Season: Mid-June to October
Activities: This is a western riding ranch. Beginners will feel just as much at home as do experienced riders. A great emphasis is placed on safety. Each morning at breakfast, guests are individually signed up for the day's riding. Riding starts each morning at 10:00. Groups usually go out with 6 to 8 people and two wranglers. All-day rides three times a week. Fishing rides twice a week. No riding on Sundays. Because there is such a diversity of riding, guests will seldom go on the same ride twice. Fly-fishing enthusiasts will enjoy the Madison, Gallatin, and Yellowstone rivers, all blue ribbon trout streams. Swimming in the ranch spring-fed pond, for the brave, and limited hiking, but keep an eye out because this is bear country.
Children's Program: Peanut Butter Mother is with children ages 6 to 12 all day for dining, riding, and activities. Teenager "Jets," as they are called, ride and eat together. Baby-sitting available with advance notice.
Dining: Home-cooked meals served buffet family-style in the big dining room located in central lodge. Children dine at their own table. Weekly breakfast, lunch, and dinner on the trail. BYOB (no liquor in dining room). Guests usually have cocktails on their porches with other guests.
Entertainment: Weekly bonfires with singing and marshmallows, square dancing, and speakers on topics of local interest (grizzly bears, wildflowers, etc.).
Summary: One of the classic, old-time dude ranches with lots of real authentic old Western charm! Emphasis on horseback riding. Excellent fly-fishing on nearby blue ribbon waters. Many guests take advantage of being able to stay two to three weeks.

Flathead Lake Lodge
Big Fork, Montana

Flathead Lake Lodge is on the shores of the largest freshwater lake in the West, surrounded by 2,000 private acres of riding trails that border national forest. Written up in *Better Homes & Gardens*, *Sunset*, and *Bon Apetit* magazines (to name a few) and a Mobil 4 Star property, this full-service dude ranch features the best of two worlds. For those who like the water, there are all kinds of lake activities. If you would rather be on horseback than on a pair of water skis or in a sailboat, there are plenty of horses and many scenic trails. In the lake and timber country of northwestern Montana, the lodge is 35 miles from one of nature's greatest wonders—Glacier National Park—and 1 mile from the tiny "Western" village of Big Fork. Built in 1945 by Les Averill, a former airline pilot, and his wife, Ginny, the ranch has been operated by Doug and Maureen Averill since the early 1970s. What makes Flathead Lake Lodge great is that the Averills love people, know the cattle ranching, rodeo, and dude ranch business, and have friendly personalities that make you feel at home. *Travel & Leisure* rated the ranch as the "best do-everything vacation in Montana."

Address: Box 248 K, Big Fork, Montana 59911
Telephone: (406) 837-4391; fax: (406) 837-6977
Airport: Kalispell
Train: Whitefish, 25 miles
Location: 1 mile south of Big Fork, 17 miles south of Kalispell
Memberships: Dude Ranchers' Association
Awards: Mobil 4 Star
Medical: Big Fork Medical Center, 1 mile
Conference: 130, with five meeting rooms, one that can seat 180 convention-style. Conference video and packet available.
Guest Capacity: 130
Accommodations: There are three lodges and twenty two- and three-bedroom cottages/cabins set amid the well-kept lawns. The log cabins can sleep four to six people. Built in the 1940s, each cabin is carpeted, has original handmade log furniture and a living room, bathroom, and two or three bedrooms. The lodge rooms overlook the lake. The main lodge is a beauty, with a huge rock fireplace. Everything at the ranch radiates warmth and charm.
Rates: • $$-$$$. American Plan. Children's, corporate, off-season, group, and convention rates available. One-week minimum stay summer season.
Credit Cards: Visa, MasterCard, American Express. Personal checks preferred.
Season: May through October
Activities: Horseback riding, instruction, and ranch rodeo. Breakfast rides. Heated pool right next to Flathead Lake. Four tennis courts. Extensive lake activities and beach. Sailing (classic 50-foot sloops), canoeing, lake cruising, water-skiing, wind surfing. Tremendous lake and river fishing for native trout. Wilderness hiking. White water rafting and float fishing available.
Children's Programs: Daily kids' program for ages 3-6 and 7-12. Nature program with arts and crafts. Complete recreation room and games. Kids' overnight camp. Kids under 6 ride in stable area.
Dining: Family-style meals with plenty of home-baked bread, pies, and preserves made from fresh mountain huckleberries. Steak fry. Salmon seafood barbecues, whole roast pigs weekly. Social hour each evening before dinner in the Saddle Sore Saloon.
Entertainment: Campfires with sing-alongs, Western barn dance, guest rodeo once a week with various horse games twice weekly, team roping with local cowboys, canoe and sailboat races. Evening cruises and volleyball games.
Summary: The ranch is unique in that it combines a complete horse program and all aspects of riding, instruction, and rodeo with full lake activities. Beautiful world-class dude ranch on 28-mile-long Flathead Lake. Nearby: Glacier National Park, Big Fork Summer Theatre (has featured such musicals as *Oklahoma!* and *Sugar*) 1 mile away. Language interpreters available. Be sure to have a huckleberry milkshake at the Dairy Queen.

See color photos, page 241

G Bar M Ranch
Clyde Park, Montana

Sage-covered, rolling foothills of the Bridger Mountains are a part of Brackett Creek Valley, home to the G Bar M guest ranch. The Leffingwell family has operated this no-nonsense 3,200-acre cattle ranch since 1900 and has welcomed guests since the early 1930s. This part of the country was made famous by one of North America's early explorers and mountain men, Jim Bridger. The Leffingwells make no bones about it: "We have no golf, no pool, no tennis, and no structured entertainment." At the G Bar M, you can join in the daily activities that are part of this 100-head cattle/guest ranch or you can enjoy everything at your own pace. Part of the ranch has been designated as a game reserve; no hunting is allowed. George Leffingwell points out to his guests, "We here at the G Bar M think it is important to live in harmony with the land." Eagles, elk, deer, and even hummingbirds frequent the ranch. While most guests come from the United States, many have come from as far away as Europe, Australia, and other parts of the world.

Address: Box AE, Dept. K, Clyde Park, Montana 59018
Telephone: (406) 686-4423
Airport: Bozeman
Location: 26 miles northeast of Bozeman off State Highway 86
Memberships: Dude Ranchers' Association
Medical: Deaconess Hospital in Bozeman, 26 miles
Guest Capacity: 15
Accommodations: The G Bar M accommodates guests in two rustic cabins (one is actually a log house), both with full bathrooms and hot and cold running water, and four rooms (three downstairs and one upstairs called the "Family Loft") in the ranch house, with private baths, double and twin beds, and carpeting.
Rates: $. Full American Plan. Rates include everything, including pickup at airport. Children's rates available. Sunday to Sunday minimum stay.
Credit Cards: None. Personal checks accepted.
Season: May through September
Activities: Your horse is matched to your riding ability. Guests may participate in various kinds of cattle work, mostly herding, changing pastures, or ranch chores like checking fences or placing salt licks for the cattle. Because this is an operating cattle ranch, you are expected to fit into the varied daily program unless you wish to entertain yourself by reading, hiking, or fishing for part of or the entire day. Ranch fishing for rainbow trout in Brackett Creek. Limited fishing gear available.
Children's Programs: Children enjoy helping to milk cows and feed the 50 chickens. Children are the responsibility of parents.
Dining: Families, ranch hands, and wranglers all eat together, except at breakfast. Eggs and milk, as well as beef and pork, are all ranch fresh. There are two dairy cows milked daily. Mary Leffingwell has been cooking for 60 years and is well known for many specialties. Be sure to get copies of Mrs. Leffingwell's *Sage Brush and Snow Drifts* cookbook and *Diamonds in the Snow*, an account of her life growing up in Montana.
Entertainment: No organized entertainment. Occasionally, colt training, on-the-ground roping, and horseshoeing, but the best is listening to George and Mary tell their "kitchen table tales" (ranch stories). Once-a-week steak fry.
Summary: Small family cattle ranch, with wonderful old-time Montana hospitality. "The coffee pot is always on here." Here you are welcomed into the family. Great for families as well as singles and couples. George insists on visiting with all new guests on the telephone before they make a reservation. Nearby: Yellowstone National Park, 90 miles; Museum of the Rockies; Lewis and Clark Caverns. Ask about the family cookbook.

Grassy Mountain Ranch
Townsend, Montana

In 1992, the reins of this wonderful ranch were passed on to Brad and Trish Dana who, along with their young children, have brought a young spirit to an old tradition. Just like before, Grassy Mountain Ranch is a small, family-oriented ranch combining both a guest and cattle ranch operation. Here, on its 6,000 acres, guests will enjoy wide-open country (exactly what Montana is famous for), lots of friendly hospitality, watching the sun rise over the distant Crazy Mountains, and at night listening to the coyote lullaby as you drift off to sleep. The ranch encompasses both forest and open cattle range. The main ranch headquarters is right at the foot of the Grassy Mountains, thus its name. The ranch setting is a natural haven for families with children who can run free in front of their cabins or around the main lodge. Here, everyone becomes part of the Dana ranch family and new, lifetime friendships are made. You may participate as much or as little as you wish, help with occasional cattle work, watch the wranglers ride young colts, walk through fields of wildflowers, take a moonlight horseback ride, or do nothing. Families, singles, and young couples will regenerate, recharge, and get a new outlook on life after spending a week at Grassy Mountain Ranch.

Address: P.O. Box C, Dept. K, Townsend, Montana 59644
Telephone: (406) 547-3402
Airport: Helena
Location: 50 miles southeast of Helena
Memberships: Dude Ranchers' Association
Medical: Townsend Hospital, 24 miles; White Sulphur Springs, 19 miles; EMT on ranch
Guest Capacity: 24
Accommodations: Four cozy triplex log cabins with names like Little Wolf, Running Face, Sitting Bull, and Chief Joseph are scattered near the aspen and pine trees. All have rock fireplaces, comfortable twin and queen-size beds, carpeting, porches, and private baths. The main lodge is the hub of activity.
Rates: • $$. Children's and off-season rates.One-week minimum stay in July and August, Sunday to Sunday. Two-night minimum stay, June and September.
Credit Cards: None. Personal checks or cash accepted.
Season: June to after Labor Day
Activities: Riding is the main activity here. Each day guests sign up for a variety of activities. Rides are divided according to ability. There are morning and afternoon rides and an all-day picnic ride into the Grassy Mountains. Usually each week guests can help with some cattle work (the ranch has about 400 head). This is very low-key and may involve doctoring cattle or moving them. Each week there is a breakfast/late lunch ride combination and arena games and steer activities on Saturdays. No riding on Sundays. For history buffs, one of the local hands takes guests on a wonderful homestead tour. Be sure to ask Trish about this. Swimming in heated pool, fishing in nearby lakes and streams, hiking, and volleyball.
Children's Programs: No specific program. All children welcome. Riding for ages 3 to 5 limited to arena or leadline. Ages 6 and older may participate in the regular riding program. Instruction in roping. Kids' overnight camping trip, playhouse, sandbox, and swing. Lots of animals to enjoy—geese, goats, donkeys, pigs, rabbits, and dogs.
Dining: Hearty ranch food served buffet-style. Variety of fresh food including ranch-raised beef and home-made breads and desserts. Everyone eats together. Weekly cookouts. BYOB.
Entertainment: Campfire sing-alongs with guitar and harmonica players, Ping-Pong, pool, horseshoe pitching. Rodeos nearby throughout the summer.
Summary: Small family ranch. Relaxed, friendly atmosphere with emphasis on horseback riding. Nearby: Yellowstone National Park and the town of Helena.

See color photos, page 242

Hargrave Cattle and Guest Ranch
Marion, Montana

When the original homesteader retired in the 1960s, he handed the reins of this historic cattle ranch to the Hargraves. The ranch is nestled in a valley shouldered by tall pines and bordered by national forests. The Thompson River flows through its broad green meadows. It's the kind of beauty that gives peace, interrupted occasionally by the cry of a coyote on the crystal evening air or muffled honks of Canada geese in the morning mist. The log buildings date from the 1930s and 1940s, hewn by true craftsmen. You walk amid history in the huge log house barn. Hargrave Ranch is a working cattle operation on 87,000 acres. Leo, Ellen, and local cowboys welcome guests year-round. Guests can thrill at new life as calves are born, join in brandings, drive cattle to the summer range, and ride roundup in fall. You can ride to check fences or simply check out the two miles of private trout stream. For those seeking more adventure, there are pack trips in the proposed Cube Iron Wilderness among alpine lakes, flowers, and wildlife. Your trips are led by your host, Ellen, who always has an eye out for photographic opportunities. The ranch limit of 14 guests means personalized attention. Here there is lots of love and warmth, nature and understanding!

Address: 300 Thompson River Valley, Dept. K, Marion, Montana 59925
Telephone: (406) 858-2284; call for fax number
Airport: Kalispell, 48 miles
Location: 40 miles west of Kalispell, off Highway 2 West
Memberships: Dude Ranchers' Association, Montana Guides and Outfitters Association, National Cattlemen's Association
Medical: Kalispell Regional Hospital, 40 miles; emergency helicopter service available
Guest Capacity: 14
Accommodations: "The Stable" has a bedroom, loft, fireplace, kitchen, and bath and houses 2 to 6 guests. Rooms for 2 to 6 people in the main ranch house, "Headquarters." Not far away is "Grandfather's Cabin," a small cabin with twin beds. Bathroom and shower are about 100 feet away. Ask Ellen about the newly built log cabin, called the "Chicken House," with red carpet, stained glass, and quarters for 5 buckaroos. Ellen likes color and usually has planted red petunias and geraniums.
Rates: $$-$$$. American Plan. Children and off-season rates. Wilderness pack trips additional. One-week minimum stay in the summer, Saturday to Saturday.
Credit Cards: Visa, MasterCard. Personal checks preferred.
Season: Year-round, including all holidays
Activities: This is a working ranch where you can be up with the cowboys or sleep in. Spring—newborn calves everywhere. Women's week. Summer—hiking, riding, timber barbecues, overnight campouts, four-wheel-drive jeep trips to mountaintop fire lookout, cattle drives, fishing in private stream or nearby lakes. Fly-fishing river float trip can be arranged. Ellen's weekly overnight campout. Friday trip to Glacier National Park is a must! "Artists of the Mountains" studio tours arranged. Fall—cattle roundups, guided big game hunting. Winter—cross-country skiing, cedar sauna. Many just come to relax.
Children's Programs: None; children welcome. Children under 7 do not ride. Nanny rates.
Dining: Your hosts enjoy fine food: ranch-raised beef, local lamb and pork, fresh vegetables, and homemade desserts. Western fare and plenty of it. Happy hours with creative hors d'oeuvres. BYOB.
Entertainment: Remember that this is a working ranch. Very low-key, no evening schedule, mostly visting with other guests about the day's adventures. Practice roping and horseshoes.
Summary: This is a cattle ranch that welcomes guests. Here you will learn what it takes to raise cattle in Montana. Great folks sharing a way of life they love and cherish! Come to learn, enjoy, and relax! Ask about the Great Montana Cattle Drive and Women's Week. Nearby: Glacier National Park, National Bison Range, and western shopping.

See color photos, page 243

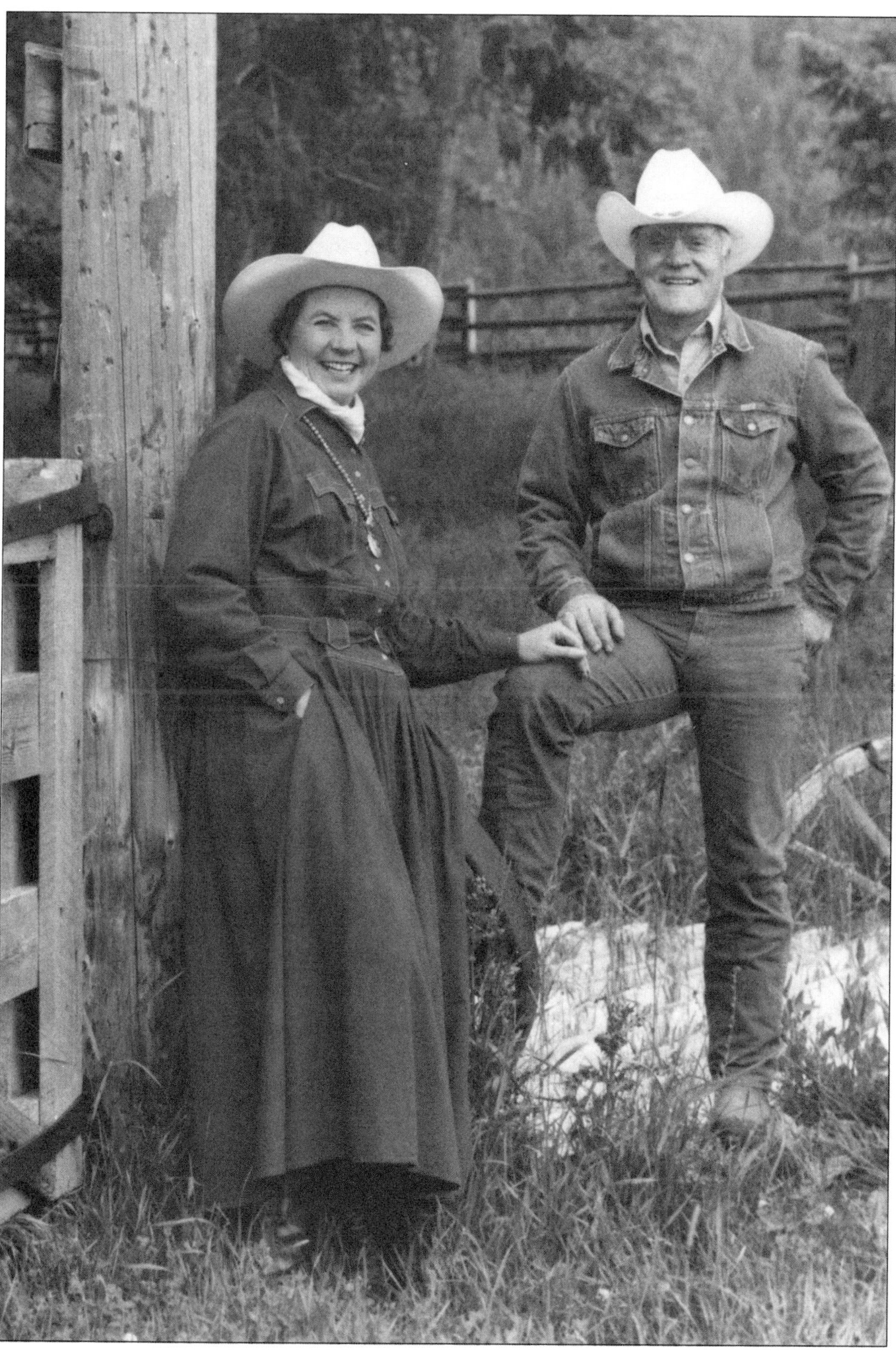

J J J Wilderness Ranch
Augusta, Montana

The "Triple J" Ranch is run by the Barker family—Max and Ann and Ernie and Kim. They cater to a very limited number of guests each season. Here in the pure mountain air, the emphasis is on enjoying the great outdoors, unwinding, relaxing, and having fun. The ranch lies in a valley at 5,500 feet in the Rocky Mountain Front Range of the Lewis and Clark National Forest, above the beautiful Sun River Canyon and Gibson Lake (7 miles long). The Barkers specialize in family vacations and emphasize horseback riding, hiking, and trout fishing. For the more adventurous and pioneers at heart, Ernie takes pack trips to remote mountain lakes and through pine forests of the famous Bob Marshall Wilderness. These trips offer riding excursions deep into remote and unspoiled wilderness areas. The Barkers have hosted people from around the country over the years. They have a saying, "Let us show you some new horizons." Indeed, they will! Guests leave refreshed and renewed, realizing just how special the Barkers are and how very special life can be.

Address: Box 310 K, Augusta, Montana 59410
Telephone: (406) 562-3653 or (406) 562-3651 (winter)
Airport: Great Falls
Location: 80 miles west of Great Falls, 25 miles northwest of Augusta at the end of Sun River Canyon Road
Memberships: Dude Ranchers' Association, Professional Wilderness Outfitters Association
Medical: Teton County Hospital in Choteau, 45 miles; Great Falls, 80 miles; emergency helicopter available
Guest Capacity: 20
Accommodations: The ranch has six cozy cabins with modern baths, private bedrooms or loft, and spacious living areas with carpeted floors randomly situated among the aspen and pine trees. The lodge has a loafing area complete with dining area, fireplace, library, and piano downstairs, and a three-bedroom guest quarters upstairs.
Rates: $-$$. American Plan. Week-long stays encouraged (Sunday to Sunday). Children's and pack trip rates available.
Credit Cards: None. Personal checks and traveler's checks accepted.
Season: June through mid-October
Activities: The emphasis is on horseback riding consisting of horsemanship instruction followed by half-day and all-day rides on new trails each day. Also, there are hiking opportunities, guided nontechnical mountain climbing, and nature hikes to learn to identify wildflowers, trees, and birds. Trout fishing in the ranch trout ponds or nearby Gibson Lake and Sun River. Cookouts on Mortimer Vista, 4 miles north of the ranch. Hayrides and optional overnight pack trips. Also available are 5- to 8-day-long pack trips that take in the incredible beauty and mystique of the Bob Marshall Wilderness. Wildlife includes mountain goats and bighorn sheep.
Children's Programs: Horseback instruction with experienced ranch wranglers. Trail rides, gymkhanas, and other games. Baby-sitting available at no extra charge.
Dining: Healthful meals served family-style in the main lodge with fresh home-baked breads and vegetables from the garden accompanying each meal. Coffee is delivered to your cabin each morning.
Entertainment: Evening outdoor campfires, occasional sing-alongs, and tall-tale-telling. Seasonal rodeos in Augusta. Choteau and Great Falls.
Summary: The "Triple J" is a small and personal ranch that allows the Barkers to offer a variety of activity options. You make the choices. You will discover new dimensions to life after spending a week or more with the Barkers. The ranch was included in a feature article on Bob Marshall (of Bob Marshall Wilderness fame), in the 1985 issue of *National Geographic*. Nearby: Glacier National Park, Plains Indian Museum, and Charles Russell Museum.

Laughing Water Ranch
Fortine, Montana

If you are looking for a small, family owned and operated guest ranch where you will actually live with the family in their modern ranch-style home, then keep reading. Since 1988, Laughing Water Ranch has provided a private and personal ranch experience. Guests here become part of the Mikita family and will enjoy not only great home-cooked meals but friendly Montana-style hospitality. Laughing Water is a 200-acre ranch surrounded by evergreen trees. In fact, at one time this used to be a Christmas tree ranch. As you drive in you will pass the old barn and a lovely meadow, and up on a rise you will see the large extended main ranch house that is their lodge and headquarters. Surrounded by the Kootenai National Forest, the Mikitas' ranch offers singles, couples, and families a low-key Western experience. You might also be interested in knowing that Ted Jr. is a commercial pilot and flies regularly to Europe and Asia. Both he and Ted Sr. are licensed ham radio operators and communicate all over the world. The ranch's call letters are N7JKF (N7AYG).

Address: P.O. Box 157 K, Deep Creek Road, Fortine, Montana 59918
Telephone: (406) 882-4680, (800) 847-5095; fax: (406) 882-4880. Computer buffs may call up Ted's Compuserve electronic mail, no. 70634,45.
Airport: Kalispell
Location: 50 miles north of Kalispell off Highway 93 near the Canadian border
Memberships: Dude Ranchers' Association
Medical: North Valley Hospital in Whitefish, 40 miles; emergency helicopter available
Guest Capacity: 24
Accommodations: Four two-room "suites" in the family's modern, one-story, log-sided, ranch-style house. Each room varies, with comfortable furnishings, full baths, carpeting, and baseboard heating. Family-style dining room and open-beamed living room with parquet floors. Fully equipped recreation room with fireplace. Deck and Jacuzzi off living room. There is also a three-bedroom "original homestead" cabin with loft about 300 feet down the hill which can sleep up to six people and is great for families.
Rates: • $-$$. American Plan. Children's, family, and off-season rates available. Three-day minimum stay.
Season: May through October; winter bed and breakfast
Activities: Two guided 2- to 4-hour horseback rides each day. Riding instruction is tailored to individual guests. Riding through scenic mountainous terrain. Loping in arena only. Open to the public for daily horseback rides. Fishing in two stocked trout ponds. Fishing gear, fly-casting, and off-ranch fishing can be arranged with prior notice. Weekly white water rafting day trips to Glacier National Park and into Canada to see the historic Canadian Mounted Police post. Winter—snowmobiling and cross-country skiing.
Children's Programs: Morning activity program with Native American/Western theme the Mikitas call "Kamp Kootenai," which includes corral rides, beaded crafts, nature walks, and Native American food.
Dining: Some of Shirley's guests call her the "best chef north of Yellowstone." Wholesome, hearty ranch cooking. Her menus include prime rib, trout fish fry, huckleberry muffins, and delicious pies. BYOB.
Entertainment: Cowboy singing and storytelling. Ping-Pong, pool table, game tables, and a large video library with a tremendous selection of Westerns, musicals, and classics.
Summary: Small, easygoing, very friendly, low-key family-operated guest ranch. Be sure to ask about Kamp Kootenai for children 2-12. Adults-only week. Access to Glacier National Park, British Columbia. Be sure to ask the Mikitas about their beautiful Christmas wreaths, which they make each Christmas and send to customers all over the country.

Klicks' K Bar L Ranch
Augusta, Montana

The K Bar L Ranch is warm, cozy, friendly, and "beyond all roads!" To get to the ranch, you take a half-hour jet boat ride across Gibson Lake or ride by saddle horse on a scenic mountain trail. If you arrive by jet boat, you may be picked up lakeside in a mule-drawn surrey with a fringe on top for a short ride to the ranch. The ranch was founded in 1927 by the senior Klicks, and today's owners and hosts, Dick and Nancy, along with their son, Todd, and his wife, Jean, welcome you. The ranch is in a magnificent setting, almost right on Gibson Lake and near the Bob Marshall Wilderness. The ranch buildings are wonderfully old and weathered. Inside and out they exude comfort and the spirit of the old American West. You know that each one has a story to tell you. Colorful Indian rugs are on many of the floors. The ranch is like the hub of a huge wheel, with miles of mountain trails leading in every direction. The wilderness area is all scenic fish and game country. One of the highlights at the K Bar L is the natural hot springs pool (86° year-round)—great for total relaxation with the stars and fireflies twinkling overhead at night. A good piece of advice: make your reservations early; others have also discovered the Klicks' high-country hideaway.

Address: Box 287 K, Augusta, Montana 59410
Telephone: (406) 467-2771 (summer); (406) 562-3589 (winter)
Airport: Great Falls; ranch will pick you up (extra)
Location: 75 miles west of Great Falls, 35 miles west of Augusta. If you are driving, be sure to call Nancy or Dick for directions.
Memberships: Dude Ranchers' Association
Medical: Great Falls
Conference: 35
Guest Capacity: 35
Accommodations: The main lodge houses the kitchen, dining room, and library in a comfortable fireside setting. There are thirteen cabins, five single, five double, and three triple, each with single and double beds and rustic furnishings including Hudson Bay blankets and Navajo rugs. Clean, separate cabins provide hot showers and modern toilet facilities. Water is piped to each cabin door, and a pitcher and wash basin is provided just like in the "good old days" (cabins do not have running water). Laundry facilities available.
Rates: $-$$. American Plan. Six-day minimum stay. Three-day minimum stay in June.
Credit Cards: None. Personal and traveler's checks accepted.
Season: June to mid-October
Activities: Superb catch-and-release fly-fishing right at the ranch. Your daily catch of wild rainbow trout will vary from 12 to 20 inches. You can keep three fish (under 12 inches) per person per day. Pack trips for the more adventurous are usually planned as loop excursions, leaving the ranch one way and returning another, over trails leading to the Chinese Wall and Continental Divide. Each guest is assigned his or her own saddle horse. Dick is a master guide and in the fall offers superb hunting. Swimming in natural warm-water pool or in the crystal clear Sun River.
Children's Program: Children under age 6 not recommended.
Dining: As Nancy Klick says, "Never had a complaint." Good, wholesome food served family-style. Occasional pig roast and barbecues. She will explain her beverage plan. Weekly barbecues.
Entertainment: Sing-alongs, volleyball, baseball.
Summary: One of the best and oldest dude ranches in the West. Remote ranch accessible only by saddle horse or jet boat. Great for adventuresome families, couples, and "Western folks" as Nancy says, who like the outdoors and like meeting people from all over. Many come here to fly-fish and enjoy the quiet of the wilderness. Beautiful day rides to Slate Goat, Bear Lake, and Pretty Prairie. Be sure to ask about the June horse and mule roundup moving ranch stock to summer pastures. Naturally warm swimming pool. Nearby: Yellowstone and Glacier national parks.

See color photos, pages 244-245

Lazy K Bar Ranch
Big Timber, Montana

In southern Montana where the Crazy Mountains pierce blue sky at 11,178 feet, families have returned year after year to one of the oldest and most celebrated guest ranches—the Lazy K Bar. With endless meadows and hundred-mile views, this historic ranch is tucked at the end of an unmarked, mountain dirt road at 6,000 feet. For guests, the appeal is serious riding on registered quarter horses and a chance to experience authentic ranch life. Established by the Van Cleve family in 1880, the ranch became a founding member of the Dude Ranchers' Association back in 1926. The ranch is run today by Barbara Van Cleve and Barbie, Tack, and Carol. Her late husband, Spike, was a legendary horseman. Chairman of the board of directors of the Cowboy Hall of Fame, Spike was also a gifted writer and story-teller. Regarding horses, he used to say, "If God had meant man to walk, He would have given him four feet." For spectacular Big Sky scenery, unlimited riding on 42,000 private acres, and plenty of genuine ranch hospitality, the Lazy K Bar and the Van Cleve family are one of a kind.

Address: P.O. Box 550 K, Big Timber, Montana 59011
Telephone: (406) 537-4404
Airport: Bozeman or Billings; Big Timber Airport will accommodate small private jets
Location: 25 miles northwest of Big Timber off U.S. 191 North, 85 miles northeast of Bozeman, 100 miles west of Billings
Memberships: Dude Ranchers' Association
Medical: Big Timber Clinic, 25 miles
Guest Capacity: 40
Accommodations: Nineteen hand-hewn one-to four-bedroom log cabins have rustic but cozy furniture. Some have living rooms. All have fireplaces or wood stoves and names like Palmer, Miles, Ross-Lewn, and Stockade and views of the mountains. Two are without baths. Wonderful old log main lodge with 1880 Brunswick billiards table. Personal laundry service available; coin operated machines as well.
Rates: • $-$$. American Plan. Rates vary with size and type of cabin and number of occupants. Special rates for children under 6. References required. One-week minimum stay. Arrival any day except Sunday.
Credit Cards: None. Personal checks always accepted.
Season: June 23 through Labor Day
Activities: Unlimited riding through high alpine country or open rangeland. Overnight rides on request. Guests may help with cattle and ranch work when there is work to be done. Mountain streams and lake fishing (kitchen will cook your catch), hiking, swimming pool (unheated but refreshing). No organized activities except Saturday night square dance and weekly campfire dinner.
Children's Programs: Wrangler for children ages 6 to 14. Ranch requires parents to bring a governess for children under 6.
Dining: Milk, cheese, butter, and meat are all fresh from the ranch. Children eat first at dinner with their wrangler. Guests may drink and entertain in their own cabins. Sunday campfire breakfast walk option.
Entertainment: 1880s grand piano, billiards table, extensive and unusual library, occasional slide shows and talent shows, local rodeos. Nearby Cowboy Poet gathering each August.
Summary: Historic working ranch not open to the general public—references required. This is one of the granddaddies of dude ranching. If you need a program director and an amenity basket, ride on! Ranch store. Trips to Yellowstone Park, ghost towns, Indian reservation, Hutterite colony, Custer Battlefield, Lewis and Clark Caverns. Be sure to ask one of the Van Cleves about *A Day Late and A Dollar Short* and *Forty Years' Gatherin's*, books written by their late father, Spike Van Cleve. Spanish spoken.

Lost Fork Ranch
Cameron, Montana

It has been said that until you have visited Montana's beautiful Madison River Valley, you just haven't experienced all of life's pleasures. Merritt and Barbara Pride's Lost Fork Ranch sits on a scenic bluff overlooking the Madison River Valley. With Big Sky views, Lost Fork is a riding and fly-fishing ranch that attracts families, couples, and groups. Merritt grew up in the horse racing business and holds a master's degree in animal science from Montana State University. The Prides found this beautiful piece of property and built their ranch in 1989. Their daughter, Kerry, is a regular rodeo participant and works with many of the kids (and adults) who wish to learn about barrel racing, pole bending, and roping. If you like to fish and ride and want to see lots of Big Sky Country, give the Prides a call.

Address: Highway 287, Drawer K, Cameron, Montana 59720
Telephone: (406) 682-7690; fax: (406) 682-7515
Airport: Bozeman, 100 miles; West Yellowstone, 32 miles
Location: 40 miles south of Ennis, Montana, off Highway 287
Memberships: Dude Ranchers' Association, Montana Outfitters and Guides Association, Rocky Mountain Elk Foundation, Foundation for North American Wild Sheep
Medical: Ennis, 40 miles
Conference: 24
Guest Capacity: 34
Accommodations: Four duplex cabins, two lodge rooms. The cabins are situated along Pine Butte Creek in the shadows of the Madison Mountains. On the ranch property the view is spectacular in all directions, encompassing five different mountain ranges. All buildings are of native log and stone with porches and electric heat. They are fully carpeted and comfortably decorated in western style. The main lodge has a spacious living room (with a 12-foot stone fireplace) which looks out over the lawn and pasture to the distant mountain ranges. The back deck is a favorite gathering point.
Rates: • $$. American Plan. Children's, corporate, and group rates are available. Sunday to Sunday and Wednesday to Wednesday arrivals. Three-night minimum. Rates include three days of guided walk/wade fishing. Drift boat fishing extra.
Credit Cards: None. Personal checks or cash accepted.
Season: May through October
Activities: The main activities are riding and fly-fishing. Rides go out daily, half-day and two all-day rides each week and 6 a.m. breakfast ride. Meadow and alpine country riding. Ask about Squaw Creek, Kirby Place, and Raspberry Ridge rides. Guests may have a different horse each day. Supervised saddling of horses is optional. Limited cattle work for intermediate and advanced riders. The fishing program is in conjunction with Craig Matthews Blue Ribbon Fly Shop. Most like to fish the Madison. Yellowstone, Gallatin, and Yellowstone Park fishing available. Extensive fly shop in lodge. Full guide service.
Children's Programs: No structured programs. A family-oriented ranch where kids and parents interact. Horsemanship program offered for children 8 and older. Depending on ability, children may ride while parents are fishing.
Dining: Family-style and buffet meals feature ranch cooking. Complimentary wine and beer served with some evening meals. BYOB.
Entertainment: Informal weekly kids' rodeos, lectures/slide shows on fly-fishing and horsemanship topics. Team roping and team penning several evenings a week in the arena. Volleyball and hayrides.
Summary: New ranch built in 1989 with commanding views overlooking the upper Madison River Valley. Two kinds of people come to Lost Fork Ranch—those who love to ride and others who fish morning, noon, and night. Ask about the horsemanship and packing school. Mostly families in July and August, singles and couples in June and September.

Lone Mountain Ranch
Big Sky, Montana

Lone Mountain Ranch is one of the premier, year-round, family-run guest ranches in the country with a unique and very strong naturalist program. What makes this ranch so special is that it offers nature enthusiasts from around the world the opportunity to enjoy first-rate guest ranching in the summer, a world-class cross-country skiing program in the winter, and year-round fly-fishing. The ranch is in Montana's famous Gallatin Canyon, just down the road from Chet Huntley's Big Sky Ski Resort and Yellowstone National Park. The Schaap family acquired the ranch after a long search for a property with all the attributes of Lone Mountain. Lone Mountain's naturalist program is an increasingly popular ranch activity. Throughout each week, naturalists lead hikes that give opportunities to learn about the spectacular natural history of the Yellowstone area. Activities are varied, including spotting soaring eagles, wildflower identification, geology, learning about old Indian trails, early morning trips to hear bugling elk, or Yellowstone trips. Whether you are riding, hiking, skiing, fishing, or just daydreaming, the Lone Mountain crew will show you Montana's best.

Address: P.O. Box 160069 K, Big Sky, Montana 59716
Telephone: (406) 995-4644; fax: (406) 995-4670
Airport: Bozeman
Location: 40 miles south of Bozeman
Memberships: Cross-Country Ski Area Association, Greater Yellowstone Coalition
Awards: *Hideaway Report*
Medical: Bozeman Deaconess Hospital, 40 miles
Conference: 50
Guest Capacity: 70
Accommodations: Twenty-three well-maintained, fully insulated one- and two-bedroom log cabins sleep up to nine. Each features comfortable beds, electric heat, modern bathrooms with tub/shower, and a rock fireplace or a wood stove. The cabins are close to the clear mountain stream that winds through the property, and all have front porches for relaxing.
Rates: • $$$. American Plan. Children under age 2 stay free. Special rates for white water rafting, guided fishing. Normally, minimum one-week stay, Sunday to Sunday.
Credit Cards: Visa, MasterCard, Discover
Season: Late May to mid-October (summer); early December to early April (winter)
Activities: Horses are a way of life at the ranch. Summer guests enjoy daily rides (except Sundays) to the surrounding wilderness with experienced wranglers. Riding instruction, with usually less than 8 on a ride, and pack trips offered. Exceptional fishing on the Madison, Gallatin, and Yellowstone rivers and the lakes and streams of Yellowstone National Park. All fly-fishing guides are experienced on the local waters and will bring you a variety of fishing opportunities. Half-day and full-day walk/wade trips, drift boat fishing, float tubing, and back-country horse trips to alpine lakes. Fly-fishing equipment may be rented or purchased at the ranch. Tennis and swimming pool nearby. In winter, the ranch offers a variety of cross-country skiing (see Cross-Country Skiing Ranches). Outdoor whirlpool.
Children's Programs: Full program for ages over 6. Nannies encouraged.
Dining: Ranch cooking with a gourmet flair served in the dining lodge—nutritious, wholesome, and widely acclaimed. Cookouts, stream-side dinners. Special diets catered to. Restaurant open to the public. Full bar. No smoking.
Entertainment: Naturalist. Barbecue sing-alongs. Evening fly-tying demonstrations, dancing to country-western music.
Summary: Excellent, world-class, year-round guest ranch. Fly-fishing with guides and instruction, top cross-country skiing program. Retail shop. Video of winter program available. Orvis-endorsed lodge. Be sure to ask about the extensive naturalist program.

See color photos, page 246

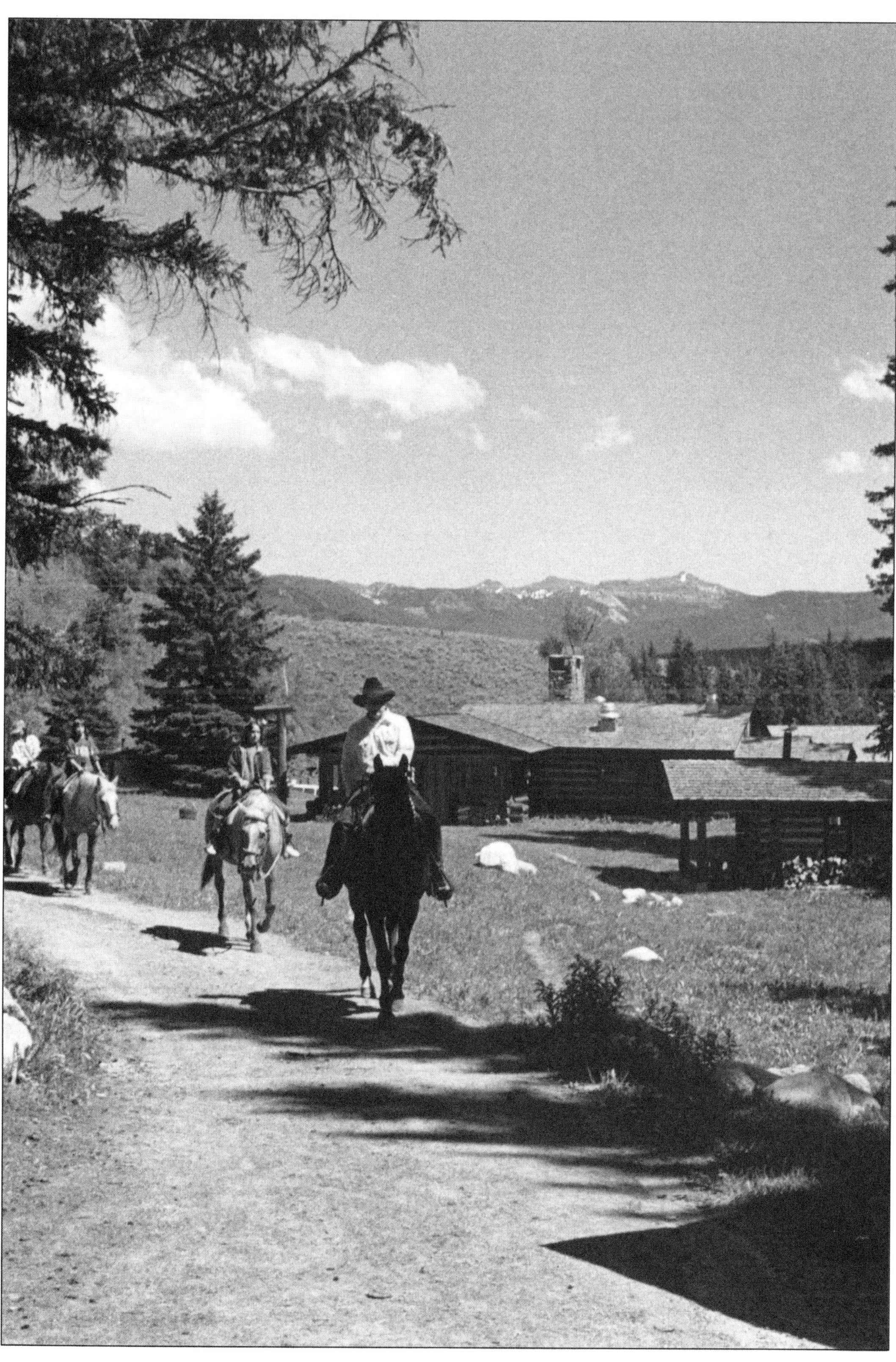

Mountain Sky Guest Ranch
Bozeman, Montana

The Mountain Sky goes way back to the early days of dude ranching. Originally it was the famed Ox Yoke Ranch, run by an old Montana family. Today, under the ownership of Alan and Mary Brutger, the ranch has guests hailing from around the globe. Alan, who has owned and operated hotels in the past, has succeeded in blending the competence and service that one customarily expects in a fine hotel with the casualness and sincerity of a Western ranch. Mountain Sky Ranch has undergone extensive renovation and has emerged as a premier ranch. It is in the magnificent Paradise Valley, home of the famous Yellowstone River. Just as in the early days, there is great emphasis placed on the family. The wranglers and staff go out of their way to ensure that both young and the young at heart are happy and having one of the greatest experiences of their lives. Mountain Sky offers outstanding scenery, clean, fresh air, tranquillity, lovely accommodations, and fine dining. At this ranch, the "Sky's" the limit.

Address: Box 1128 K, Bozeman, Montana 59715
Telephone: (800) 548-3392, (406) 587-1244; fax: (406) 587-3977
Airport: Bozeman
Location: 60 miles southeast of Bozeman, 30 miles south of Livingston
Memberships: Dude Ranchers' Association
Awards: AAA 4 Diamond
Medical: Livingston Clinic, 30 miles; Bozeman Deaconess Hospital, 60 miles
Conference: 75 (off-season only)
Guest Capacity: 75
Accommodations: There are twenty-seven guest cabins, some new, with carpeting, modern baths (with bathrobes), large picture windows, and sitting rooms that can sleep up to seven. The older, more rustic cabins have been preserved, keeping the Old West charm with stone fireplaces or wood-burning stoves, pine furniture, and small front decks. All of the cabins have inviting front porches with hanging flower baskets. A bowl of fresh fruit is brought to each cabin daily. Yellowstone City, the newly rebuilt main lodge, radiates warmth and comfort with three stone fireplaces, a hand-hewn trussed ceiling, and braided rugs. It has a lounge, intimate bar, dining room, and for those who are musically inclined, a Yamaha grand piano.
Rates: • $$$-$$$$. American Plan. Children's and group rates. One-week minimum stay, Sunday to Sunday.
Credit Cards: Visa, MasterCard. Personal checks accepted.
Season: Late May to mid-October
Activities: Extensive riding program. Rides go out daily, except Sunday. Swimming in heated pool. Whirlpool and sauna. Guided nature hikes. Tennis on two championship courts. Fishing on the Yellowstone River with guides available. Fishing on the ranch in a stocked trout pond. Big Creek is minutes from your cabin door.
Children's Programs: Children of all ages are well looked after here. Kiddie wrangler, kids' cookouts and meals, hiking, swimming, and fishing. Children can eat separately. Outstanding all-around program.
Dining: The food is wonderful and fresh. Gourmet, five-course dinners Tuesday and Saturday nights, featuring favorites like poached salmon or rack of lamb with fine wine. Hearty breakfasts; lunch is buffet-style. Poolside barbecues. Children's meals with counselor are available. Special diets catered to.
Entertainment: Evening country-western dancing and folk singing in front of the fire. Light, relaxing music with the twice-weekly gourmet dinners. Saturday ranch "shodeos." Volleyball, billiards. Monday night get-acquainted session with western dancing. Plenty of spots to curl up in and snooze or read a favorite book.
Summary: World-class ranch with superb children's program. Excellent fly-fishing and horseback riding. River rafting on the Yellowstone River. Horse and fly-fishing clinic. Nearby: Yellowstone National Park, 30 miles.

See color photos, page 247

Nez Perce Ranch
Darby, Montana

Nez Perce Ranch, located in the Bitterroot Mountains in a private setting, is owned and operated by Bob and Judy Kline. Bob was formerly a corporate pilot, and Judy was raised on a farm in Iowa. The lodge and homes are next to the Selway-Bitterroot Wilderness Area, the largest federally classified wilderness in the continental United States, with millions of acres. In addition, the property is on the historic Nez Perce Trail, with the Nez Perce Fork of the Bitterroot River running through it. Here, Bob and Judy blend unspoiled nature, comfortable accommodations, and healthy outdoor activities. You are completely on your own. There are no planned activities. Plenty of fishing, hunting, eating, and relaxing can be found here, along with access to nearby hot springs. If you want to get away from the tensions of modern life and spend time pretty much on your own in this beautiful part of Montana, consider the Nez Perce, a special, do-your-own-thing retreat for the discriminating traveler.

Address: West Fork Route, Dept. K, Darby, Montana 59829 (summer); 19802 North 32nd Street, 8K, Phoenix, Arizona 85024 (winter)
Telephone: (406) 349-2100 (summer), (602) 569-6776 (winter); call for fax number
Airport: Johnson/Bell Field in Missoula; 4,000-foot paved runway in Hamilton for smaller aircraft
Location: 40 miles south of Hamilton off Highway 93, 84 miles south of Missoula. Ranch will send detailed directions.
Medical: Hamilton Hospital, 40 miles north; paramedics, 10 miles
Guest Capacity: 18
Accommodations: Three log homes with lofts can sleep up to six. Each has a large family room with fireplace, open beam ceiling, and efficiency kitchen. These homes are completely and comfortably furnished. All have covered decks and charcoal barbecues.
Rates: • $-$$. The three completely furnished log homes are rented by the week to individuals or families.
Credit Cards: None. Personal checks accepted.
Season: June through September
Activities: Absolutely no planned activities. You are on your own. Fly-fishing in large and small streams, rivers, reservoirs, and high mountain lakes. Miles of horseback riding can be arranged through a local outfitter. Hiking, swimming in several area mineral hot springs, bird-watching, wildlife (deer, mountain sheep, elk, mountain goats, bear, and moose depending on the season and location). A photographers' paradise.
Children's Programs: Parents must look after their children. Sitters are available with advance notice.
Dining: Guests dine in the privacy of their own cabin (most eat breakfast and lunch in their cabin). Dinners are available at area restaurants within a 10- to 40-mile radius. Judy or Bob will give you a list of restaurants.
Entertainment: When guests arrive, Judy and Bob host an informal evening meal. Relax on your porch, take an evening drive up the valley. Most go fishing in the evenings.
Summary: Many couples and families come here to fly-fish, relax, and do their own thing. No set program. Three individual log homes rented.

Nine Quarter Circle Ranch
Gallatin Gateway, Montana

Since 1946, from early June to mid-September, the Nine Quarter Circle Ranch has been doing what it does best—dude ranching. High in the Montana Rockies and nestled among lodgepole pines, the Nine Quarter Circle has a 4,000-foot airstrip on the property and raises and trains Appaloosa horses. The ranch is seven miles from the northwest corner of Yellowstone National Park. There is a five-mile drive up a winding, scenic, dirt road until the ranch is visible in its secluded valley. Taylor Fork, a fly-fishing river, runs through the ranch, and most of the log structures overlook the green, grassy meadows to the striking mountain peaks in the distance. This lovely ranch is run by Kim and Kelly Kelsey and their two young sons, Konnor and Kameron. They are the son and daughter-in-law of the founders, Howard and Martha Kelsey. As the Kelseys say, "Two things can never change or end, the goodness of nature and man's love for a friend." You will find both here.

Address: 5000 Taylor Fork Road, Box K, Gallatin Gateway, Montana 59730
Telephone: (406) 995-4276
Airport: Bozeman or the ranch airstrip. Contact ranch for airstrip fact sheet.
Location: 60 miles south of Bozeman
Memberships: Dude Ranchers' Association
Medical: Bozeman Deaconess Hospital, 60 miles
Conference: 75; off-season only
Guest Capacity: 75
Accommodations: Twenty one- to four-bedroom log cabins with wood stoves and porches. Most of the cabins are named after guests, for example, Hubbards' Cupboard and Wihtol's Wickiup. Cabin furnishings are simple but comfortable; all cabins have private or family baths. The main lodge has one of the largest rock fireplaces you will ever see. The Kelseys have a clever "Medallion" award board for guests who have returned year after year. It's hanging in the dining room. Some guests have medals representing over 30 years. Guest laundry facilities.
Rates: • $$. American Plan. Children's and off-season rates available. Minimum one-week stay policy, usually Sunday to Sunday.
Credit Cards: None. Personal or traveler's checks accepted.
Season: Mid-June through mid-September
Activities: Plenty of horses. The ranch raises and trains over 120 Appaloosas. Four or five rides, ranging from kiddie rides to advanced rides daily, that go to vistas like Inspiration Point, Sunken Forest, and Alp Basin. Two all-day rides and an over-night pack trip go out weekly, including the Kelsey Killers "for those who want a real thrill." Great fly-fishing in the Gallatin, east of Taylor Fork, which runs through the ranch with the ranch fishing guides. Individualized instruction and local fishing trips available with ranch guides. Stocked trout pond for casting and kids catch-and-release fishing. Kids under 12 can catch their breakfast. Limited loaner fly-fishing rods and retail fishing shop on ranch. A spring-fed "swimming pool" for hardy swimmers.
Children's Programs: Full program for kids under age 10. Talk to the Kelseys about their program for children under 6. Kiddie wrangler for children ages 6 to 9. Walking-led rides for kids 5 and under around ranch pasture. Playground and playroom. Weekly kids' picnic. Child supervision is provided during the morning and afternoon rides, as well as lunch and dinner.
Dining: Children and teens eat early while parents enjoy happy hour. BYOB. Meals are home-cooked and family-style. Weekly barbecues and cookouts.
Entertainment: Live music, square dancing, weekly western movies, volleyball, softball, and games on horseback (a big hit with the kids).
Summary: Wonderful family-run ranch for families, many of whom have returned year after year. Ideal for young families with kids 2 to 15 and for grandparents, too. Appaloosas bred and trained on the ranch. Private airstrip. Ranch store. Nearby: Yellowstone National Park, the western college town of Bozeman, and Museum of the Rockies in Bozeman.

See color photos, page 248

Pine Butte Guest Ranch
Choteau, Montana

This is one of only two Nature Conservancy retreats offering lodging. Pine Butte is the former Circle 8 Guest Ranch that was privately owned before the Conservancy took it over in 1978. The ranch is surrounded by wilderness—18,000 acres managed by the Conservancy and an additional one million plus acres in the Bob Marshall Wilderness, one of the largest wilderness expanses in the continental United States. The Pine Butte Swamp, adjacent to the ranch, is one of the largest wetland complexes along the eastern slope of the Rockies. Also, it happens to be one of the last grizzly bear strongholds in the lower 48 states. The ranch hosts a variety of nature adventures. Each spring and fall, there are week-long, custom nature tours and workshops led by regional experts. This is a ranch for those who love to hike and commune with nature. Pine Butte offers one of the best naturalist programs of any guest ranch in North America.

Address: HC 58, Box 34C, Dept. K, Choteau, Montana 59422
Telephone: (406) 466-2158
Airport: Great Falls, 90 miles
Location: 90 miles northwest of Great Falls, 27 miles west of Choteau off Highway 89
Memberships: Dude Ranchers' Association, Nature Conservancy, Audubon Society
Medical: Choteau Clinic, 27 miles
Conference: 25
Guest Capacity: 25
Accommodations: Ten rustic cabins and two lodge rooms. The cabins are set among the aspens, cottonwoods, and firs that line the South Fork of the Teton River. Built of native stone and wood, each cabin is complete with fireplace, private full bath, and hand-made hardwood furniture. The central lodge, with its huge fireplace and homey front porch, provides a perfect spot for guests to gather and get to know each other.
Rates: • $$-$$$ American Plan. Children's and off-season rates available. Group rates in spring and fall. One-week minimum stay, Sunday to Sunday. Two-night minimum stay in spring and fall.
Credit Cards: None
Season: May through September
Activities: A traditional Western guest ranch atmosphere is combined at Pine Butte with an in-depth natural history program available to guests interested in furthering their knowledge of the outdoors. During the summer, a full-time naturalist conducts daily treks that focus on local plants, animals, geology, and paleontology. Enjoy fishing and a heated outdoor swimming pool. Rides go out twice a day with a wrangler and last two to four hours. All-day rides, breakfast rides, and steak fry rides go out weekly.
Children's Programs: None. Children under 8 not recommended. Ask about the schoolhouse nature program in the summer for children.
Dining: Family-style meals served in the lodge dining room, featuring healthy food (homemade soups, breads, and pastries) presented with simple grace. Fresh, homegrown vegetables are featured. BYOB.
Entertainment: Weekly square dance; slide shows and lectures four to five evenings. Tour of Egg Mountain dinosaur nesting site with evening lecture/slide show given by a paleontologist from the Museum of the Rockies. Beaver watching.
Summary: Marvelous ranch for those who love to hike and commune with nature. Excellent natural history tours with naturalists and workshops include birding, mammal tracking, nature photography, paleontology (dinosaur dig), wildflower identification. Ask about the Montana grizzly bear spring and fall workshop. Nearby: Glacier National Park.

Schively Ranch
Billings, Montana

Ever dream of being a cowboy? At Joe and Iris Bassett's Schively Ranch, you will experience firsthand a real cattle operation. No more than 18 guests at a time saddle up and help drive cattle. Each year, the spring cattle drive starts the middle of April and continues through mid-May. It begins at the ranch's winter feedlot in Lovell, Wyoming, and ends at their summer pastures in south central Montana on the Crow Indian Reservation, 52 miles north. During this drive, you will cross the Shoshone River, the Big Horn Recreational Area (famous for its wild horse range), and eventually arrive at the foot of the Pryor Mountains. You will enjoy chuck wagon meals and bed down in real tepees under the stars. From mid-May until mid-October, nights are spent at the ranches, one-half of the week at the Upper Ranch, and one-half at the lower Dry Head Ranch, named after the Indian buffalo jump. In October, cattle are driven by horseback from Montana to Lovell. During the drives, Iris and Joe, along with their cowhands, set up cow camps along the trail. Depending on the time of year, you will experience branding, doctoring, roping, gathering, sorting, weaning, and rotating pastures. You pick the time. The Bassetts will give you one of the greatest western experiences of your life.

Address: 1062 Road 15, Dept. K, Lovell, Wyoming 82431
Telephone: (307) 548-6688 (winter); (406) 259-8866 (summer)
Airport: Billings International Airport, off Montana Highway 416
Location: 50 miles south of Billings; all guests, whether flying or driving, are picked up at the airport
Memberships: Dude Ranchers' Association, National Cattlemen's Association
Medical: Deaconess Hospital in Billings, 50 miles; Med Evac helicopter available
Guest Capacity: 16
Accommodations: Large divided log bunkhouse at lower Dry Head Ranch; cabins at Upper Ranch. Small cabins with electric heat. Each cabin is close enough that you can hear the creek and directly behind the main house, which has shower and bathroom facilities. Not to worry, you will not be spending much time in the bunkhouse or cabins. Ask Iris about the cowboy bedrolls she rents.
Rates: • $-$$. American Plan. Ranch and cattle drive rates. Children's rates for kids under 12.
Credit Cards: None. Personal checks, money orders, and cash accepted.
Season: Mid-April through mid-November
Activities: This is a real ranch, caring for many cattle, and they offer you the opportunity to participate in as much of it as you wish—five to six hours of riding each day when possible (it may rain or snow).
Children's Programs: No organized children's program, just a vast experience of life on a ranch. Children are welcome but are the responsibility of the parents. Kids should like horses and be good riders. Iris will advise you accordingly about your kids.
Dining: Home-cooked, ranch-type meals served family-style with ranch's own antibiotic-free beef, served summers in the ranch house dining room and spring and fall on the trail. Specialties include real ranch breakfasts, steak, and homemade bread and rolls.
Entertainment: A Big Sky heaven full of stars, a peaceful, well-earned sleep. A weekly video of your week will be shown on Fridays.
Summary: Real working cattle ranch for those who love horses, love the outdoors, and want to experience a little bit of what it's like to be a cowboy. Cattle drives, great horses, wide open spaces (looks like it did 100 years ago), vast cattle experiences. (Author's note: Be in good physical shape and get as much riding in as you can before you arrive.)

63 Ranch
Livingston, Montana

One of the first dude ranches in the country to be chosen as a National Historic Site, the 63 Ranch is one of the oldest ranches in the business. It is still run by the same family that started it in 1930. At an altitude of 5,600 feet, one listens to the soothing sounds of Mission Creek as it tumbles down its rocky course through the ranch on its way to the Yellowstone River. The 63 offers guests an eye-opening view of what the early West was all about. Depending on the time of year, one can join the cattle roundup and branding. The 63 features summer pack trips into the Absaroka-Beartooth Wilderness. There is also plenty of riding, fishing, hiking, and Indian lore. Sandra, Bud, their son, Jeff, and Sandra's mother, Jinnie (who founded the ranch with her husband, the late Paul Christensen), know the meaning and spirit of Western hospitality and serve up plenty of it to guests from all over the United States and many foreign countries.

Address: Box 979 K, Livingston, Montana 59047
Telephone: (406) 222-0570
Airport: Bozeman, 50 miles; or a small airstrip for private planes, 6 miles
Location: 12 miles southeast of Livingston
Memberships: Dude Ranchers' Association, Gallatin Outfitters Association
Awards: National Register of Historic Places
Medical: Livingston Hospital, 20 minutes
Conference: Off-season only, October to June
Guest Capacity: 30
Accommodations: Eight comfortable one- to four-bedroom cabins with wonderful log furniture, all different and unique. All have baths and showers; some are heated with gas, others with electricity or by wood stoves. Double and twin beds. All arriving guests receive in their cabin a ranch-colored cotton bandana on their pillow, fresh seasonal wildflowers, and the 63 Ranch newspaper. Coin-operated laundry facilities. Pay telephone and soda machine.
Rates: • \$-\$\$. American Plan. Rates vary depending on the season. Children's rates. One-week minimum stay, Sunday to Sunday arrival.
Credit Cards: None. Personal checks, traveler's checks, cash accepted.
Season: Summer runs mid-June to mid-September. Winter by special arrangement.
Activities: The 63 is known for its horses and excellent riding. Sidesaddle and Western lessons available. Arena for beginners learning to lope. Picnic and barbecue rides. Blue ribbon fly-fishing (ask Sandra for her "Montana's First Best Place for Fishing" pamphlet). Ranch pond also stocked with cutthroat trout for children. Wagon rides, swimming in a pond for the courageous, hiking, Sandra's history lesson, homestead ride, and evening nature walk. Photography workshops in spring and fall.
Children's Programs: No formal program. Each week is planned around the particular guests who are at the ranch, and children are always included. Recreation room, baby-sitter available. The ranch will teach 4-year-olds to ride if they want to learn and go out on trail rides with families.
Dining: Hearty ranch cooking with plenty of fresh fruits and vegetables. Dining room in the lovely, old, cozy log lodge with porch cookouts. House specialties are prime rib and full turkey dinners. BYOB.
Entertainment: Square dancing to records each week, rodeos in town, or just peaceful reading and relaxing.
Summary: Wonderful old-time historic dude ranch with emphasis on riding. Great for the person who wants to enjoy good horses, scenery and relax! Be sure to see their beautiful new brochure. Seasonal cattle work. First Montana dude ranch to be listed in the National Register of Historic Places. Fourth of July rodeo, museums, and nine-hole golf course in Livingston. Video available on request.

See color photo, page 249

Seven Lazy P Ranch
Choteau, Montana

Chuck and Sharon Blixrud have been in the guest ranch and pack trip business since the 1950s. What makes their operation special is that they combine their love for the great outdoors with a tremendous respect for nature and knowledge of the Bob Marshall Wilderness. Right against this million-acre area that Montanans call "The Bob" is the Seven Lazy P Ranch, right on the north fork of the Teton River. Chuck grew up not far from where the Seven Lazy P is headquartered. This part of Montana has some of the most spectacularly rugged geological formations in the country. The Seven Lazy P couples an excellent pack trip program with friendly ranch hospitality. Singles, couples, and families all get along here.

Address: P.O. Box 178 K, Choteau, Montana 59422
Telephone: (406) 466-2044
Airport: Great Falls, Montana; a paved and lighted runway for small planes in Choteau
Location: 30 miles west of Choteau off Highway 89, 80 miles northwest of Great Falls, 100 miles south of Glacier Park
Memberships: Dude Ranchers' Association, Professional Wilderness Outfitters Association, Montana Wilderness Association
Medical: Choteau, 30 miles
Conference: 20
Guest Capacity: 20
Accommodations: The ranch has a large main lodge with a huge stone fireplace, lobby, dining room. The covered porch looking out toward the mountains is where most of the evening visiting is done. There are six rustic cabins, one of which is an A-frame with loft. Five have private shower/baths, and two have fireplaces. Most have queen and twin beds. Four cabins are nestled in the spruce; two are across the small footbridge over the creek. Laundry facilities available.
Rates: • $-$$. American Plan. Children's, off-season, and pack trip rates. Three-day minimum stay.
Credit Cards: None. Personal checks, traveler's checks, and cash accepted.
Season: May through November
Activities: Horses and mules provide a terrific combination for superb riding and pack trips into the high country. This and their sincere hospitality, is what makes the Blixrud's program so special. With a fine wrangling staff, Chuck combines his knowledge and love for the back-country with excellent riding horses and pack mules. Here you will experience Montana's beautiful Big Sky wilderness country. If you are interested in an unforgettable experience, talk with Sharon or Chuck about their trips. If you simply wish to spend your entire time at the home ranch reading, relaxing, riding, snoozing, or watching hummingbirds, you can do that too. Guests return year after year and range in age from 30 to 75. Other activities include fishing in the Sun River and in alpine lakes and September and October hunting for elk and deer.
Children's Programs: No special programs. Children under 8 do not go on pack trips.
Dining: Hearty, scrumptious, ranch cooking. Special diets catered to.
Entertainment: Library and wildlife movies. Most guests like to visit with each other, go for an evening walk, or drift off to sleep.
Summary: At the Seven Lazy P, you will slow down, relax, and enjoy the sounds of nature. Low-key family owned and operated ranch specializing in scenic mountain pack trips, with more than 40 years of experience. New guests and singles always feel like part of the family. If you expect to be constantly entertained, this is not the ranch for you. Many couples, singles and older families. Nearby: Glacier National Park, C. M. Russell Museum, Egg Mountain Dinosaur Archaeological Site.

See color photos, page 250

Sweet Grass Ranch
Big Timber, Montana

"We are an operating cattle ranch, not a resort, with unlimited riding as our main emphasis. Guests are welcome to take part in all pleasures of ranch life," say Sweet Grass hosts and owners, Bill and Shelly Carroccia, who radiate warmth and sincere western hospitality. The Sweet Grass Ranch is secluded in the Crazy Mountains 40 miles outside the small town of Big Timber. Cattle and dude ranching have been in the family for five generations. The Carroccias limit the number of guests so that everyone will actually feel like family. As you might expect, families from all over have come to enjoy the 20,000 acres of beautiful foothills and alpine country. Share in the ranch activities if you like, or do your own thing. Life is unstructured. The Sweet Grass Ranch is a place where the whole family can enjoy the great outdoors, the real Old West, and the fabulous Carroccia hospitality.

Address: Melville Route, Box 161 K, Big Timber, Montana 59011
Telephone: (406) 537-4477; call for fax number
Airport: Billings or Bozeman. Pick-up service available (extra).
Location: 120 miles northwest of Billings, 40 miles northwest of Big Timber. Driving directions will be sent to you.
Memberships: Dude Ranchers' Association, National Register of Historic Places, National Cattlemen's Association, Stewards of the Range
Medical: Clinic, hospital, in Big Timber, 40 miles; advanced first-aid on ranch
Guest Capacity: 20
Accommodations: Guests are housed in nine rustic log cabins (built between 1928 and 1935) or in four rooms on the second floor of the main house, some with living rooms and fireplaces. Lots of rustic comfort here. Private baths in six cabins, bath/shower house for two cabins. Coin-operated laundry facilities available. Early photographs of the ranch in the main house, along with a marvelous burl second-floor railing and banister.
Rates: • \$-\$\$. American Plan. Children's rates available. One-week minimum stay. Many guests stay ten days to two weeks. You may arrive on any day; most arrive on Sunday.
Credit Cards: None. Traveler's checks and personal checks accepted.
Season: Mid-June through Labor Day
Activities: Each morning one of the Carroccias' sons discusses ranch activities and options for the day. Every day is different. Those who wish to participate in ranch work may do so, like checking livestock, riding the fence, salting cattle, trail clearing, and doctoring cattle. In addition, half-day and all-day rides go out every day except Sundays. These may be working or scenic, walking, trotting, and loping rides. Bareback and dinner rides along with pack trips and cattle work are things you may enjoy, too. Riding instruction is available on request. Fishing in alpine lakes and on the Sweet Grass River, which runs through the ranch. Swimming in the creek for the hearty and brave, bird-watching. Photographers should bring lots of film.
Children's Programs: No special programs. Children are welcome and are included in all ranch activities. Baby-sitting can be arranged.
Dining: The meals and bread are home cooked and served family-style in the circa 1925 main lodge. Ranch-raised Montana beef, fresh milk, cream, and homemade ice cream. Weekly dinner ride. Picnic lunches are served on all-day rides and trips. BYOB.
Entertainment: As Shelly says, "Whatever guests would like to do." Some swap stories or go for an evening stroll. Both sons (Rocco and Tony) play guitar. Piano and pool table in lodge. Occasional square-dancing, western swing, or campfires.
Summary: Bill and Shelly are two of the nicest people you'll ever meet. Their rustic ranch serves up plenty of western spirit and genuine hospitality. Sweet Grass is a riding ranch. No set schedule; do as much or as little as you please. Cattle work. Most guests don't wish to leave the ranch.

Triple Creek Ranch
Darby, Montana

Triple Creek Ranch is an exclusive, mountain hideaway almost at the foot of beautiful Trapper Peak just outside the tiny town of Darby. This modern "diamond in the rough" (adults-only property) was built in 1986 to create a wilderness retreat for those who yearned for nature's wildness but wanted to experience it with luxurious amenities. Triple Creek is managed by Wayne and Judy Kilpatrick, and, together with their wonderful staff, they have created a haven of rest, relaxation, and mountain splendor.

Address: West Fork Stage Route K, Darby, Montana 59829
Telephone: (406) 821-4664; fax: (406) 821-4666
Airport: Missoula Airport; private planes to Hamilton Airport with 4,200-foot airstrip; helicopter pad at ranch. Airport pickup also available.
Location: 12 miles south of Darby, 74 miles south of Missoula
Awards: *Hideaway Report:* Hideaway of the Year 1988, 1992; *Hideaway Report:* One of Six U.S. Hideaways of the Decade; *Hideaway Report:* Distinguished Staff and Service Award 1990
Medical: Marcus Daly Memorial Hospital, Hamilton; emergency helicopter service available.
Conference: 23; 23 singles or 16 couples
Guest Capacity: 23 singles, 16 couples
Accommodations: Plush, cozy, spruce log cabins, deluxe cabins, poolside suites, and several luxury cabins (with everything). Each is tastefully furnished with wall-to-wall carpets, dressers, breakfast tables, and small kitchenettes. Refrigerators are fully stocked with an array of beverages, and there is a full complimentary supply of liquor. For those who wish, there is satellite TV. VCR units are available. In the larger cabin suites, there are massive handcrafted log king-size beds. For the romantic, there are double showers and a private hot tub on the deck that looks out into the forest. Daily housekeeping and laundry service.
Rates: • \$\$\$\$-\$\$\$\$\$. American Plan, per night per couple. Single rates available. Not included are guided river rafting, guided fishing, or guided winter snowmobiling service. No minimum stay required.
Credit Cards: Visa, MasterCard, American Express
Season: May through October (summer); December through February (winter), not open Christmas Day. If rented in full, Triple Creek is available year-round.
Activities: For summer, there is an informal program that caters to each couple or individual. Horseback riding, hiking, fly-fishing, white-water river rafting (call for detailed information), helicopter tours, swimming in the lovely outdoor heated pool. Bird and wildlife viewing and photography. Serious golfers can drive to the Hamilton 18-hole golf course. In winter, Triple Creek comes alive with the spirit of Christmas: hot buttered rum, sleigh rides with bells, and horseback riding in freshly fallen snow. Snowmobiling is one of Triple Creek's specialties. Wilderness cross-country skiing (limited instruction available), downhill skiing, 28 miles away. The ranch will tell you what you will need.
Children's Programs: Children under 16 are allowed only when ranch is reserved in total by a family or group.
Dining: All meals are varied and designed to tempt even the most finicky diners. Complimentary wine served. Special diets not a problem. Triple Creek will help you celebrate your birthday or anniversary.
Entertainment: Lovely upstairs bar in the main lodge with occasional live music. Many go for a stroll under the stars or enjoy a glass of fine cognac in the hot tub.
Summary: Luxurious, adults-only mountaintop guest ranch. Superb and friendly staff with personalized service second to none. Quiet, restful, intimate, romantic atmosphere (great for honeymoons), with gourmet cuisine. Triple Creek may be booked for family reunions and corporate retreats. Rental cars encouraged.

See color photos, page 251

West Fork Meadows Ranch
Darby, Montana

As a young boy growing up in Germany, Guido Oberdorfer dreamed of America's West—cowboys, cattle, mountain air, and ranch food. He promised himself that he would work very hard for his family's international manufacturing company, and one day he would have a ranch. It took him years to realize that dream, but in 1989 Guido and his soft-spoken Swiss bride, Hanny (pronounced Honey), one of the newest guest ranches in the business and are proudly welcoming guests from around the world. Set in a picturesque valley with a meadow in front and mountains behind, West Fork Meadows Ranch combines American Old West tradition with European style and comfort. The Oberdorfers cater especially to families, individuals, and the ever-growing European market. The successful combination of the rough outdoors and the cultured interior and fine culinary experience makes this place unique.

Address: Coal Creek Road, Drawer K, Darby, Montana 59828
Telephone: (406) 349-2468, (800) 800-1437; fax: (406) 349-2031
Airport: Commercial jets to Missoula; 4,000-foot paved runway in Hamilton for small aircraft. Helicopter and airport pickup available.
Location: 93 miles south of Missoula (two-hour drive), 50 miles south of Hamilton, 31 miles southwest of Darby
Medical: Hamilton Hospital, 50 miles
Conference: 34
Guest Capacity: 34
Accommodations: Three brand-new three-bedroom log cabins, with two separate showers and baths, comfortable living room/sitting area, and fireplace. Wonderful covered balconies overlooking the meadow. Four remodeled one-bedroom cabins behind the main lodge, each with private bath, wood stove, and covered balcony. A three-bedroom log house is also available. The newly built 6,000-square-foot log main lodge combines a main level dining/living room with decks with an upstairs "watering hole" and apartment. Ask Guido to show you his wine cellar.
Rates: • $$-$$$. American and European Plans. Corporate rates available.
Credit Cards: Visa, MasterCard, American Express, Diners Club
Season: May through September
Activities: Western horseback riding with instruction. Trail rides, all-day picnic rides, and pack trips. Guests are assigned their own horse to use while at the ranch. Guided river rafting, hiking, wildlife viewing (deer, elk, moose), and photography. Fishing in stocked pond, in the West Fork of the Bitterroot River (which runs through the property), in nearby streams and mountain lakes. Boating, swimming, and jet-skiing in Painted Rock Lake. Mountain biking, jeep excursions (jeeps provided). Ask about the Nez Perce Trail pack trip. Mountain biking.
Children's Programs: No specific program. Well-behaved children are welcome to share activities with their families.
Dining: Superb food prepared by great chefs. Wine, beer, and liquor available. Breakfasts and lunches casual. All food is fresh and locally grown; organic produce in season. Breads, pies, cakes, pastries, and Italian ice cream are all made fresh daily. Guido and Hanny are very proud of their deluxe kitchen.
Entertainment: Horseshoes, bottle-shooting contests, hot tub, and billiards. Mostly just relaxing and making friends from around the world.
Summary: Beautiful ranch hosted by Europeans, catering especially to individuals, families, Europeans, and international guests. Fine food and accommodations. German, French, Italian, and English spoken.

See color photos, page 252

White Tail Ranch
Ovando, Montana

"You touched my heart and your wilderness captivated my soul," wrote one guest, and so it goes at the White Tail Ranch in Ovando, Montana. This small Montana ranch is owned and operated by Jack and Karen Hooker, along with their son, Bill, and his wife, Dena. Together, they offer a combination ranch operation specializing in high-country pack trips for those who want to get away from everything and intimate ranch stays. Over the years Jack and Karen have built quite a reputation for their wilderness pack trips and big game hunting. Once Jack reported that he and a group of guests silently crept up on a herd of sixty elk feeding in a high mountain meadow. Later that day he came up over a high pass, around a bend, and there were grizzlies feeding on huckleberries. Before the day was over, they had seen nine grizzlies, five black bears, a coyote, several mountain goats, eagles, deer, and elk. While that is not always the case, both Jack and Bill know this country very well, and they know how to find animals if they are there. For years, Jack and Karen have worked as a team sharing their love of the high country. Now Bill takes out his own pack trips and Dena holds down the fort, sharing the ranch activities with those who would rather ride locally than high into the mountains. If you like backcountry horsepack trips and a low-key ranch visit, give the Hookers and White Tail Ranch a call. And one last thing, if you want to hear some really great stories, be sure to ask Jack about his Iditarod dog-sled races. He has been a contestant twice!

Address: 82 White Tail Ranch Road, Dept. K, Ovando, Montana 59854
Telephone: (406) 793-5666
Airport: Missoula
Location: 65 miles east of Missoula, 15 miles east of Ovando
Memberships: Montana Outfitters and Guides, Professional Wilderness Outfitters Association
Medical: St. Patrick's Hospital, Missoula, 65 miles
Guest Capacity: 20 (ranch), 10 (pack trips)
Accommodations: Ranch guests stay in nine cabins, four set along the creek. Three have plumbing, and the others use a central bath house. All are heated and comfortable. All bedding is provided. Pack trip guests spend their first night at the ranch, then most nights will be spent sleeping under the stars in the land of crystal clear lakes, winding streams, rugged peaks, and gorgeous flowering alpine meadows. You must bring your own sleeping gear.
Rates: • $$-$$$. Group and children's rates available.
Credit Cards: None. Personal checks and cash accepted.
Season: Late June through August; hunting season, mid-September to November
Activities: Wilderness pack trips and hunting trips on horseback. Most trips begin some distance from the ranch. This is one of the few ranches that have permits to send trips to the four national forests that comprise the Bob Marshall Wilderness Complex. Jack gives wonderful mini-horse seminars at the ranch and during the pack trips. Enjoy the pristine wilderness and wildlife, photography, and fishing. All ranch activities are primarily horse-related.
Children's Programs: None, but children are welcome. Children under 6 are not recommended on pack trips.
Dining: Karen and Dena cook excellent down-home high-country meals, including mountain chow mein, barbecued chicken, corn on the cob, roast beef, tacos, stew, and steak. Special diets catered to with advance notice. BYOB.
Entertainment: Jack's high adventure wilderness stories. Primitive fire demonstration and fireside horsemanship.
Summary: The ranch specializes in exciting wilderness pack trips into the Bob Marshall Wilderness Complex. Guests should like the outdoors and be reasonably athletic. Lots of friendly hospitality. Great for single women, couples, and families. Nearby: C. M. Russell Museum, buffalo preserve.

Cottonwood Ranch
Wells, Nevada

At 6,200 feet, the Cottonwood Ranch is in Nevada's high desert country on Cottonwood Creek in the O'Neil Basin of Elko County, one of the largest cattle-producing counties in the United States. This working ranch runs 500 head of cows, calves, and bulls and 80 head of horses over 2,000 acres. The fourth-generation Smith family leases more than 30,000 acres from the forest service and Bureau of Land Management. Horace Smith, his wife, Renie, and their adult children, Kim, Agee, and his wife, Vicki, go out of their way to ensure that each guest is well looked after. Cottonwood offers city folks a chance to really get away from it all and experience life the way it used to be. The Smiths have been in the cattle ranching business and in this part of Nevada since the 1920s. Today, their guests travel a good distance to experience their hospitality at this way-off-the-road paradise. Depending on the time of the year, guests may (are encouraged to) participate in a variety of ranch/cattle activities. The high mountain cow camp is right in the middle of Nevada's summer home to hundreds of elk and mule deer. Here the air is so clean and it's so quiet that you may just think you have gone to heaven. Wilderness pack trips lasting almost a week take guests into the isolated and beautiful Jarbidge Wilderness, where one can see dramatic views of mountain peaks, quaking aspen, willows, and meadows filled with sunflowers and lupine. The only sounds you'll hear in this country are those of nature.

Address: O'Neil Basin, Drawer K, Wells, Nevada 89835
Telephone: (702) 752-3604 (this is a radio telephone and you may have difficulty getting through); (916) 832-4861 (winter)
Airport: Elko, Nevada, or Twin Falls, Idaho; private airstrip, 7 miles west of Jackpot, 120 miles northeast of Elko, 120 miles south of Twin Falls, 75 miles northwest of Wells
Memberships: Nevada Outfitters and Guides Association, Nevada Cattleman's Association
Medical: Magic Valley Regional Medical Center, Twin Falls, Idaho
Guest Capacity: 10
Accommodations: A comfortable seven-bedroom, open-beam lodge with a deck offering panoramic views has three rooms with double beds, four rooms with twin beds and bunk beds. Bathrooms are both private and shared. Once on the trail, the ranch provides all your gear, except sleeping bags and personal belongings. High mountain cow camp—everything is provided except a sleeping bag and personal gear. Check with the Smiths for exactly what you need.
Rates: • $-$$. American Plan. Pack trip, cow camp, children's, and group rates available. Two-day minimum stay at ranch.
Credit Cards: Visa, MasterCard
Season: May to September
Activities: For many years the Smiths have been known for their high country pack trips. Recently they have been welcoming guests to participate in their weekly cattle ranch activities. The Smiths and their expert guides will show you some of Nevada's magnificent backcountry. Seasonal cattle roundup and horse drive, trap shooting at ranch. Seasonal big game and bird hunting.
Children's Programs: Children welcome, but check with ranch. Kids should be out of diapers.
Dining: Hearty, home-cooked, real ranch meals, BYOB. Cooking under the stars pack trips. Wine served.
Entertainment: Hay wagon and buggy rides, cookouts, occasional sing-alongs, cowboy poetry. Nature and wildlife are most of the entertainment here.
Summary: One of Nevada's old-time ranching families. Authentic working cattle ranch serving up wonderful western hospitality. The long drive in is worth every minute! Tremendous high desert beauty, with the Jarbidge Mountains forming the backdrop. Cattle work, horse drives, wilderness pack trips, and high mountain cow camp. Ask about Jarbidge Wilderness, Cougar, Jumbo, God's Pocket, and Mary's River peaks.

Red's Ranch
Lamoille, Nevada

At the foot of the Ruby Mountains, also known as Nevada's "Little Yosemite," there is a very private place—a retreat for both work and play. Red's Ranch consists of 125 acres of meadowland located four miles from Lamoille Canyon, the entrance to the Ruby Mountains. Lamoille was named by *Outside Magazine* as one of the "Ten Best Places" to live in the next decade. The house, patterned after the great hunting lodges of the Rockies, provides tremendous views of the mountains and is surrounded by wonderful hunting and fishing opportunities. Red's Ranch is, without question, one of the most beautiful, charming, and rustically elegant, private ranch estates I have ever seen. And to top it off, the setting is even more magnificent. Built in 1988 by the Ellis family, longtime Nevada hoteliers, and operated by their daughter, Mimi, it is the height of luxury, built with vision and impeccable taste. It is also a sanctuary where rustic elegance reigns supreme and nature captivates and soothes the soul. The Double R is open to the public on a very limited basis. In fact, its ranch gate only opens for individuals, families, and corporate or professional groups who are willing to book the entire ranch. If you are not in one of those categories, no need to read any further. If you are, however, here is a place where you can truly rest and recharge, where the spectacular setting can inspire and promote creativity. Red's Ranch, simply put, is magnificent.

Address: P.O. Box 281406 K, Lamoille, Nevada 89828
Telephone: (702) 753-6281
Airport: Elko, Nevada, 20 miles
Location: 20 miles southeast of Elko, Nevada, 1 mile off the Lamoille Highway
Memberships: Trust for Public Lands, High Country News, Western Folklife Center
Medical: Elko Regional Medical Clinic, Elko General Hospital, 20 miles
Conference: 25-35
Guest Capacity: 20-35
Accommodations: The 10,000-square-foot main house, with its commanding, awe-inspiring views and lofty log accents, is rich in western heritage. The ten upper and lower bedrooms with eight accompanying baths reflect Mimi's superb taste and attention to detail. The guest house has three bedrooms, two baths, and a full kitchen. The conference barn, with its boardroom, office, kitchen/dining room, and five bedrooms, has been carefully thought out
Rates: $$$$$. American Plan.
Credit Cards: None. Cash or personal checks accepted
Season: Late June to late October (summer); Mid-January to mid-April (winter)
Activities: Your biggest activity here should be taking in the view and recharging. During the summer many swim in the heated pool, walk, soak in the Jacuzzi looking out to Old Man of the Mountain, play horseshoes, croquet, and badminton, or rest in the hammock. Horseback riding, helicopter sight-seeing tours, fishing, and pack trips can be arranged. In winter the main activity is helicopter skiing and soaking in the Jacuzzi.
Children's Programs: None. Children over 12 are welcome as part of a family gathering.
Dining: The chef will prepare just about anything. Meals have a western flair. Call for specifics. Fine California wines.
Entertainment: No planned evening entertainment. It is completely up to you: visit in front of the fireplace, or read a good book from the extensive library. For the adventuresome, the ranch is 20 miles from Elko. Ask Mimi about her family hotel in Elko, The Commercial, one of the oldest gaming casinos in Nevada.
Summary: Private ranch-estate for individuals, small family reunions, and excellent for small corporate and professional retreats. One-of-a-kind, rustic luxury. Captivating view. References required.

See color photos, page 253

The Ponderosa Ranch
Incline Village, Nevada

The Ponderosa Ranch is a day ranch known to millions as home to *Bonanza*, one of the world's most famous television series. Although you cannot stay overnight, you can tour the Cartwright Ranch House and ramble through the streets of this re-created western town, which features a saloon, general store, church (you can even get married), antique barber shop, photo studio, and much more. View carriages, horse-drawn farm equipment, vintage cars, steamrollers, tractors, and thousands of other pieces of western memorabilia. There is also lots to do. Take a hay wagon breakfast ride, pet the animals in the petting farm, go through the mystery mine, try the shooting gallery, savor a Hoss burger, and then belly up to the bar in the authentic western saloon. You can browse through the souvenir shop or go for a hike on trails that take in the spectacular beauty of Lake Tahoe. The Ponderosa Ranch is owned by Bill and Joyce Anderson, who founded the ranch in 1967. Since the opening, they have worked tirelessly to make it as memorable an attraction as possible for the 250,000 visitors annually. The Ponderosa Ranch is still a family-run operation, with the emphasis on giving guests good, old-fashioned western hospitality and an unforgettable memory.

Address: 100 Ponderosa Ranch Road, Incline Village, Nevada 89451
Telephone: (702) 831-0691; fax: (702) 831-0113
Airport: Reno Canon International, 35 miles
Location: On the north shore of Lake Tahoe in Incline Village, 35 miles southwest of Reno, 20 miles from South Lake Tahoe
Medical: Incline Village, 5 minutes
Conference: 2,000
Guest Capacity: 3,000
Accommodations: None. Six thousand beds available within 5-mile radius.
Rates: • $. Check with ranch for general admission and group rates. Hay wagon breakfast extra.
Credit Cards: Visa, MasterCard, Discovery, American Express
Season: General admission May through October; hay wagon breakfast late May through Labor Day
Activities: There are all kinds of activities at Lake Tahoe and in the surrounding Sierras. Contact the Incline Village/Crystal Bay Convention and Visitors Bureau, 969 Tahoe Boulevard, Incline Village, NV 89451, or call (800) 468-2463 (out of state) or (702) 831-4440 (in Nevada), for further information.
Dining: Daily, all-you-can-eat cowboy breakfast on the hay wagon ride; barbecue lunches including Hoss burger, hot dogs, corn dogs, and deep-pit beef barbecue sandwiches. Special dinner arrangements can be made for large groups.
Entertainment: Shopping, souvenirs, and specialty stores. Petting zoo and arcade.
Summary: Famous day ranch where television series *Bonanza* was filmed. (*Bonanza II* is also being filmed here.) Excellent for large groups and tours. Overlooking beautiful Lake Tahoe. Close to Reno, Nevada. Free pony rides, gunfights Labor Day weekend.

The Spur Cross Ranch
Golconda, Nevada

Long before Nevada became known for its neon lights and one-armed bandits, this far-reaching state had developed quite a reputation in the cattle industry. Still today, many of the country's largest cattle operations are found in the Silver State. While the Spur Cross Ranch is by no means one of Nevada's largest cattle spreads, this 585-acre ranch shares 100 miles of BLM rangeland and offers guests an authentic hands-on cattle ranch experience. Rich in history, this ranch was homesteaded in 1864. Today, the ranch is run by Richard Hubbard, who likes to be called "Hubb." He is an experienced, easygoing man who loves the cowboy life and the peace and beauty of this wide-open country. Here you will go back in time: no telephone, no television, no stress. Just the call of the wild and the call of calves for their mothers and other animals including miniature donkeys, milk cows, goats and baby goats, sheep and lambs, geese, chickens, pigs, cats, and dogs.

Address: P.O. Box 38K, Golconda, Nevada 89414
Telephone: None. Emergency radio telephone on ranch.
Airport: Reno, 190 miles; Winnemucca, 36 miles; Elko, 125 miles
Location: 36 miles east of Winnemucca off Interstate 80, look for Mile Marker 194
Medical: Winnemucca, 36 miles
Guest Capacity: 12
Accommodations: Five-room "station" house with two separate indoor bathrooms with showers/tubs or two private cabins with shared bathroom. These accommodations are old-time western rustic.
Rates: • $. American Plan. Includes three meals and all activities. Free transportation from Winnemucca to the ranch. Three-day minimum say.
Credit Cards: None. Personal checks accepted.
Season: March through November
Activities: There is no structured schedule. You can become as involved as you wish. At breakfast each morning, Hubb will discuss the day's activities. This is a working ranch, and you ought to enjoy some ranch work. Daily activities keep the ranch in good working order. Guests should bring their own gloves, jeans, and boots. Included during the week may be cattle work such as branding and herding (on or off a horse). Freshwater, large-mouth bass fishing is available on the ranch's pond (there are always a few poles at the ranch). Overnight trips to the ranch's cow camp, where you will see many species of birds, are offered. Four-wheel-drive trips to old mining sites can be scheduled. Seasonal hunting is available by special arrangement.
Children's Programs: None. Children are the responsibility of parents. Not recommended for children under 10.
Dining: Traditional ranch-style, sit-down meals including ranch-raised beef, lamb, pork, vegetables, and eggs. Some wild game. Fresh-baked desserts. BYOB.
Entertainment: After-dinner table games, stargazing, and listening to the call of the coyotes. Some guests with lots of energy visit the casinos in Winnemucca. Most of the time Hubb and his crew are swapping stories about their ranching experiences.
Summary: A working cattle ranch where you will experience a week or more in a cowboy's life. No set schedules; do as you like. Here you will share a way of life and leave fulfilled and enlightened. Beautiful, wide-open, Nevada landscape. Nearby: city of Winnemucca (38 miles).

Soldier Meadows Ranch
Gerlach, Nevada

Soldier Meadows Ranch is part of the 70,000-acre Spanish Springs Ranch. It is an authentic working cattle ranch encompassing almost 14,000 acres. Located at the top of the Black Rock Desert, it is one of the early ranches in Nevada history. The ruts of the historic Applegate/Lassen Emigrant Trail blazed in 1849 by some 30,000 emigrants cross the ranch. Soldier Meadows got its name over 100 years ago when it was Camp McGarry (1865-68), a calvary outpost used as winter quarters for soldiers. Guests live and work alongside the ranch staff. Depending on the time of year, you may tag along driving Hereford-cross cattle to pasture or brand a corral full of calves, or just ride through the vast, open country just checking on things. Unique here is the opportunity to view small herds of wild horses running free. The remoteness, privacy, and authenticity is best suited for families, singles, and intermediate and advanced riders who are looking for one of the most unique western cowboy experiences anywhere in the world.

Address: Bookings are made through Spanish Springs Ranch, P.O. Box 70, Ravendale, California 96123 (reservations)
Telephone: (800) 272-8282 (California), (800) 282-0279 (out-of-state), (916) 234-2050 (ranch phone); fax: (916) 234-2041
Airport: Reno; private gravel airstrip at ranch
Location: 165 miles north of Reno through Gerlach, approximately 62 miles by mostly unpaved road northeast from Spanish Springs Ranch, about 3½ hours
Medical: Reno, 1 hour by air, 3 to 4 hours by road
Guest Capacity: 20 overnight in ten double-occupancy rooms. Well-developed tent camping facilities available for 50-100.
Accommodations: Comfortable, modern, ten-bedroom bunkhouse with cookhouse, dining room, and meeting room. Also available are deluxe accommodations for one or two couples in the "Stone House," one of the refurbished original buildings. Tent area uses a portable shower and toilet facility. Concrete dance floor and band shell with microphone system. Fully stocked gift shop.
Rates: • $$. American Plan. Children's rates and special package/group rates available.
Credit Cards: Visa, MasterCard, American Express, Discover
Season: Year-round, weather permitting, including Thanksgiving, Christmas, and Easter
Activities: Regular working ranch activities plus day trips or overnight camping at Summer and Stanley camps. Abundant wildlife. Seasonal hunting and fishing. Natural hot springs pool close by. For those who really want to see and experience the Old West, the Buckaroo Camp, held every year, is an unbelievable five days! Call for dates. All of the regular ranch activities plus horsemanship clinics, wild horse taming, big loop roping, team penning, horse-drawn wagons, western art, cowboy poetry, authentic western crafts, and more!
Children's Programs: Not advised for children under 10.
Dining: Delicious home-cooked meals are served ranch-style in the cookhouse in the morning and evening. Sack lunches are available at noon. BYOB.
Entertainment: No organized entertainment. Lots of visiting and relaxing.
Summary: Soldier Meadows is remote, isolated, wild, and authentic. There is nothing quite like it. This is a once-in-a-lifetime experience. Be sure to ask about the wild horses and the Buckaroo Camp.

See color photos, page 256

Bear Mountain Guest Ranch
Silver City, New Mexico

Bear Mountain Guest Ranch is not the typical dude ranch. Horseback riding is not provided. This is a small ranch for southwestern nature lovers. It is on the north edge of Silver City, once a mining town. Here, a century ago, the streets teemed with miners, freighters, prospectors, and outlaws (boyhood home of Billy the Kid). Parts of Silver City still retain its Victorian elegance, reflecting the prosperous mining years. Bear Mountain is southwestern in architecture and landscape. This 160-acre property sits in the mountains high above the desert. This was once the territory of prehistoric Indians who hunted and fished in the surrounding Gila Wilderness, the nation's first designated wilderness area. These pine-clad mountains are testament to a highly developed civilization with their Gila Cliff Dwellings, a community that was suddenly abandoned centuries ago. Bear Mountain Ranch is hosted and owned by Myra McCormick. Myra loves nature, respects its peace and tranquillity, and cares about people. Her nature program is highly regarded by her guests. One of Myra's most treasured guests was the late actor Steve McQueen. Said Myra, "We just sat in the kitchen and traded stories."

Address: P.O. Box 1163 K, Silver City, New Mexico 88062
Telephone: (505) 538-2538
Airport: Silver City, Grant County Airport
Location: 2.8 miles north of Silver City, 325 miles southwest of Santa Fe, 160 miles northwest of El Paso, Texas
Memberships: Nature Conservancy, National Audubon Society, International Wildlife Wilderness Society
Medical: Gila Regional Medical Center
Conference: 30
Guest Capacity: 40
Accommodations: Built in the traditional southwestern style to provide shady, cool rooms in the summer as well as snug, warm winter quarters, the guest houses are off-white plaster with dark brown trim. They reflect the decor of the 1920s and 1930s but provide modern comforts, electric blankets, modern baths, antique furniture, and twin or double beds and a king-size bed. There are guest rooms and suites in the two-story ranch house, two one-bedroom cottages, and a full five-bedroom house.
Rates: • $-$$. American Plan. Contact ranch for children's and group rates. No minimum stay required.
Credit Cards: None
Season: Year-round, including Thanksgiving, Christmas, and Easter
Activities: "The big one is enjoying nature," says Myra. Gila Cliff Dwellings National Monument is enjoyed by everyone. Fishing in nearby lakes and Gila River, bird-watching, wild plant identification, archaeological exploration, and bicycling (can be rented nearby).
Children's Programs: None. Baby-sitting available.
Dining: The high-windowed dining room is designed to give the best view of an aviary. Nutritious, home-cooked food with home-baked breads. Favorite is enchilada pie. Desserts include peanut butter pie and carrot cake. BYOB.
Entertainment: "After a full day in the field, most people are happily pooped," says Myra.
Summary: Friendly and very low-key "ranch" at 6,250 feet run as a bed and breakfast. If you need a TV, this is not the place for you. Great for active adults and for children who like the same things their parents do. Bring your own horse. Lodge and learn program, workshops (pottery, archaeology, birding). Nearby: Glenwood Catwalk over White Water Creek, Gila Cliff Dwellings, City of Rocks State Park.

Bishop's Lodge
Santa Fe, New Mexico

Bishop's Lodge is nestled in the foothills of the Sangre de Cristo mountains. This world-class oasis of southwestern hospitality has been under the active stewardship of the Thorpe family for years. In 1917, Denver mining man James R. Thorpe discovered Old Santa Fe. He bought the property and began creating a world-class resort that preserved southwestern ambience, simplicity, and comfort. Today, Bishop's Lodge is one of the great jewels of the Southwest. This Mobil 4 Star property can host up to 160 guests and offers a wide range of activities. It is situated on 1,000 privately owned acres that back up to the Santa Fe National Forest. At 7,000 feet, the high desert scenery includes red sun-baked soil, juniper and native shrubs dotting the hills, fresh desert air, and plenty of sunshine. Service and kindness reign supreme. The informal, relaxed atmosphere at Bishop's Lodge combined with its proximity to Santa Fe, the cultural center of the Southwest, make it ideal for families and corporations.

Address: Box 2367 K, Santa Fe, New Mexico 87504
Telephone: (800) 732-2240 (reservations only), (505) 983-6377; fax: (505) 989-8739
Airport: Albuquerque
Location: 3 miles north of Santa Fe off Bishop's Lodge Road
Awards: Mobil 4 Star, AAA 3 Diamond
Medical: St. Vincent Hospital in Santa Fe, 5 miles
Conference: 200; five conference rooms, executive conference facilities, the largest of which is 1,924 square feet. Full conference brochure.
Guest Capacity: 160
Accommodations: The adobe-style buildings blend comfortably with the ranch property. Rooms are decorated Santa Fe style with southwestern motifs, soft accents, locally sculpted furniture, air-conditioning, telephones, and television. Deluxe rooms and suites all have traditional corner fireplaces, open beamed ceilings, and plenty of private patio space. Each room has a selection of southwestern magazines.
Rates: • $$-$$$$. European Plan and Modified American Plan June through August; $-$$$. European Plan the rest of the season. Rates vary depending on time of year. Horseback riding, tennis, and skeet and trap shooting are extra.
Credit Cards: Visa and MasterCard
Season: April through January
Activities: Tennis courts with teaching professional and full pro shop; pool complex includes large heated swimming pool with lifeguard, whirlpool, sauna and exercise room. Stable of fine riding horses with morning and afternoon rides lasting about 1½ hours. Breakfast and evening rides. All-day rides on request. Usually slow, scenic rides, eight to ten riders per group. Trap and skeet shooting (guns provided), plenty of hiking trails, and guest tennis tournaments. Golf privileges nearby.
Children's Programs: A summer children's program keeps kids ages 4 to 12 happily occupied and parents free to sightsee and browse in Santa Fe 8:00 a.m. to 4:00 p.m. and 6:00 p.m. to 9:00 p.m. Limited program for teens. Baby-sitting available on request.
Dining: Breakfast buffets and luncheon menues. Dinner features fresh fish and regional specialties (southwestern cuisine); jackets and dresses are suggested attire. Daily room service available. Fully licensed bar.
Entertainment: Live guitar, harp, mariachi music in summer months.
Summary: A charming southwestern resort ranch just outside Santa Fe. Mobil 4 Star, AAA 3 Diamond Resort Ranch. Conference facilities. Golf nearby. Archbishop Lamy's lovely Chapel on hill above lodge. Nearby: Santa Fe, the cultural mecca of the Southwest, including Santa Fe Opera and six museums; Indian pueblos; old mining ghost towns; ancient pueblo ruins; and traditional Spanish mountain villages (Truchas, Chimayo).

The Lodge at Chama
Chama, New Mexico

More than ever I have been asked by corporations, boards of directors, incentive meeting planners, and families to identify ranches that offer nothing less than excellence. Welcome to the Lodge at Chama. It is here that men and women come to enjoy privacy amid 32,000 acres of unspoiled mountain and forest scenery. The Lodge at Chama provides first-rate amenities and excellent service—in a few words, rustic luxury. Over the years, the Lodge has hosted many leaders in business and industry. Because it takes only twenty-four people at any one time, guests quickly feel at home. Whether it's a high-level board meeting or plain old rest and relaxation, the Lodge at Chama has what it takes for groups or families who appreciate beauty, kindness, and a host of recreational opportunities. The Lodge at Chama's fine staff go out of their way to tailor everything to the preferences of each group.

Address: Box 127 K, Chama, New Mexico 87520
Telephone: (505) 756-2133; fax: available on request
Airport: Albuquerque International; private jets to Pagosa Springs. Call regarding ranch airstrip.
Location: 100 miles north of Santa Fe, 90 miles west of Taos, 45 miles southeast of Pagosa Springs
Awards: *Hideaway Report:* 1986 Fishing/Hunting Lodge of the Year; *Hideaway Report:* 1990 Best Sporting Retreat
Medical: Local clinic; hospital in Española; emergency helicopter service available
Conference: 24 in boardroom, 50 for day meetings. Fax, speaker telephones, copy room, overhead projection, flip chart. Ask for conference brochure.
Guest Capacity: 24
Accommodations: Vaulted ceilings, full animal mounts, and views of the Chama Valley overlooking the well-kept lawns are the first thing you see as you enter the 13,500-foot main lodge. Just off the Great Room are ten rooms, each with private bath and upscale amenities (bathrobes, hair dryers, and oversized towels), and two suites with fireplaces, television, and vanity baths. All rooms have telephones.
Rates: • $$$$. Full American Plan. Special rates for full lodge rental. Winter rates available. No minimum stay required.
Credit Cards: None. Personal/corporate checks accepted.
Season: Year-round
Activities: The Lodge will send you a detailed brochure outlining all the activities. During the summer months guests enjoy fishing, hiking, drives through the ranch property to view spectacular vistas and wild game, horseback riding, wildlife photography, and sporting clays. Be sure to ask about the historic steam-powered train ride from Chama to Antonito, Colorado. Limited hunting of elk, deer, buffalo, bear, and grouse is offered September to December. Photographers will go through many rolls of film shooting the magnificent fall colors. Winter activities November to March include cross-country skiing (gear, guides, and instruction available), snowmobiling, sleigh rides to view wildlife, snowshoeing, and snow tours.
Children's Programs: Minimum age of 12 or by special arrangement
Dining: Hearty ranch fare. Special requests and diets accommodated. Ask about Chama's delicious northern New Mexico dishes. Complimentary bar, wine separate.
Entertainment: Enjoy the spectacular sunsets, take an evening stroll, watch wide screen TV, relax in front of the fire or in the huge indoor whirlpool and sauna, or read yourself to sleep. Hayrides, picnics, and country-western band available on special request.
Summary: Excellent for small group/corporate/family retreats. Personalized service, delicious cuisine, and tremendous wilderness recreational activities. Superb fishing and hunting. Tremendous wildlife viewing. One of the world's largest private elk herds. Large buffalo herd also.

See color photos, pages 254-255

Los Pinos Ranch
Tererro, New Mexico

Los Pinos is "where the road ends and the trail begins." In 1910, a Santa Fe family purchased the property as a family hideaway. One of the daughters fell in love with an Easterner and returned to build this wonderful mountain ranch. Perched 500 feet above the Pecos River, the ranch has been in operation since the late 1920s. In 1964, Bill McSweeney, an architect from New Jersey, bought the property. He and his wife, Alice (who loves cooking, arts and crafts, and singing), and their daughter, Alice, run their special Los Pinos Ranch. Small, informal, and limited to 16 guests, Los Pinos is in the heart of the Sangre de Cristo Range. It is near the headwaters of the Pecos River at an elevation of 8,500 feet, surrounded by distant peaks rising to 13,000 feet and higher. The average summer temperature is 76 degrees at noon and 40 degrees at night. The quaint and historic cities of Santa Fe and Taos with colonial artists, Indian pueblos, and ruins are all within a few hours of Los Pinos by car over fine roads. Los Pinos is said to be located in "the most interesting fifty-mile square in America."

Address: Route 3, Box 8 K, Tererro, New Mexico 87573 (summer); P.O. Box 24 K, Glorieta, New Mexico 87535 (winter)
Telephone: (505) 757-6213 (summer); (505) 757-6679 (winter)
Airport: Albuquerque
Location: 45 miles northeast of Santa Fe off I-25. Maps sent on request.
Medical: Medical clinic in Pecos, 23 miles
Guest Capacity: 12-16
Accommodations: The four original log cabins (three one-bedroom, one two-bedroom) are rustic but comfortable. All are heated with wood stoves and have plenty of blankets, private bathroom and shower. The main lodge is old and rustic. The outside screened and glassed-in porch looks out to the magnificent scenery. Inside there are a piano, artifacts, and paintings given to Alice and Bill by their artist friends. Laundry available.
Rates: $. Includes three meals. Riding is extra. Alice runs this program and you deal directly with her. Two-night minimum stay.
Credit Cards: None. Personal checks or cash accepted.
Season: Late May to mid-August (Labor Day)
Activities: Horseback riding is one of the main activities at Los Pinos. Horses are sure-footed and gentle. All-day and half-day guided rides through dense pine, quaking aspen forests, and meadows. Alice runs the horse program. The many sparkling streams with their deep pools and swift riffles and tiny hidden lakes make the upper Pecos region a tempting spot for the trout fisherman. Bring your own fishing gear and purchase a license on your way to the ranch at Terrero General Store. Plenty of hiking and bird-watching.
Children's Programs: No children under 6 years of age. Family reunions are an exception. Children are the responsibility of parents.
Dining: "Best Chef West of the Pecos River." Be sure to get Alice's cookbook, *Los Pinos Ranch Brand of Cooking*. Hot breads at breakfast. Lamb, chicken; Italian, Irish, German dishes. BYOB.
Entertainment: A wonderful library of local history and nature references. Evening stars and Mother Nature.
Summary: Lots of peace and quiet here. Rustic, cozy, and very friendly. If you like the outdoors and no planned activities (you are completely on your own time), Los Pinos and the McSweeneys are terrific. Wonderful scenery, food, and fellowship. Nearby: Old Santa Fe Trail, Pecos National Monument, Indian pueblos, and Spanish villages. RV campsites within two miles.

Pinegrove Resort Ranch
Kerhonkson, New York

Pinegrove is nestled in the peaceful, gentle, rolling hills of upstate New York's Catskill Mountains with miles of mountain trails for riding. Pinegrove is a year-round family vacation wonderland that serves up western hospitality. Dick and Debbie started Pinegrove Dude Ranch in 1971. Today, it is one of the most family-oriented resort ranches in the Northeast. In 1992, the ranch won the *Family Circle* "Ranch of the Year" award, and ABC Eyewitness News sent Scott Clark up for Memorial Day weekend to sample Pinegrove's "City Slickers II." CNN rated them "Best Family Vacations." Pinegrove Resort Ranch was mentioned in *Child Magazine* (June/July 1993 issue) as a dude ranch hosting many activities for kids. The ranch specializes in children's activities, and the full-time children's programs enables parents to enjoy themselves as well.

Address: Box 209 K, Kerhonkson, New York 12446
Telephone: (914) 626-7345, (800) 346-4626; fax: (914) 626-7365
Airport: JFK, New York; Newark, Newburgh
Train: Poughkeepsie, 25 miles
Location: 100 miles northwest of New York City, 1 mile west of Kerhonkson off Route 209
Memberships: American Hotel and Motel Association, Association for Horsemanship Safety Education, Camp Horsemanship Association certified wranglers
Medical: Ellenville Hospital, 6 miles
Conference: Up to 300; 5,000 square feet of meeting space
Guest Capacity: 350
Accommodations: Guests sleep in comfortable, modern rooms with wall-to-wall carpeting, TV, telephone, air-conditioning, and private baths. All 125 rooms are in three connected two-story lodge buildings.
Rates: • $-$$ American plan. Children ages 4-16 half price. Kids under 4 free. Single parent, group, and senior discounts. Ask about Get Acquainted special.
Credit Cards: Visa, MasterCard, American Express
Season: Year-round
Activities: Nightly riding video and lecture for all newcomers. In summer, free beginner and advanced group riding instruction available. Ride over acres of picturesque rolling hills. Most trails are quite wide. You can go deep into the forest for miles of secluded trails crossing streams and affording distant views. Most rides have 15-20 people. Rides go out on the hour, all day. Cattle driving (call for information), bass fishing in stocked lakes, boating, hiking—all on the property. Indoor facilities, tennis, heated swimming pool, miniature golf, bocci ball, archery, basketball, rifle range, volleyball, paddle and handball, table tennis, and shuffleboard. Outdoor Olympic-size swimming pool. Free 18-hole golf nearby. In winter, downhill skiing on two slopes, ice skating. Free equipment at ranch. Ranch has its own snowmaking equipment.
Children's Program: Children's day camp with arts and crafts. Teen program. Baby-sitting available, including "night patrol." Baby animal farm, cow milking, and calf feeding.
Dining: Three meals daily from menu are served in the main dining room, which has a view of the Shawangunk Mountains. Sunday barbecue in season. Parents eat with their kids. Complimentary snack bar 10:00 a.m. to midnight.
Entertainment: Hayride, night club with show, and cocktail lounge with live music plus square dancing. Western saloon with swinging doors and popcorn machine. Hitching Post Pool Bar. Game nights. Steer roping and leather carving demonstrations.
Summary: A comfortable family-oriented, family-owned and operated, full ranch resort, specializing in families and children. Guided nature walks, cattle calling, feeding and petting baby animals. Fifty new family rooms and a total multimillion-dollar renovation of all other facilities in 1992.

See color photos, page 257

See ranch description on page 425

See ranch description on page 8

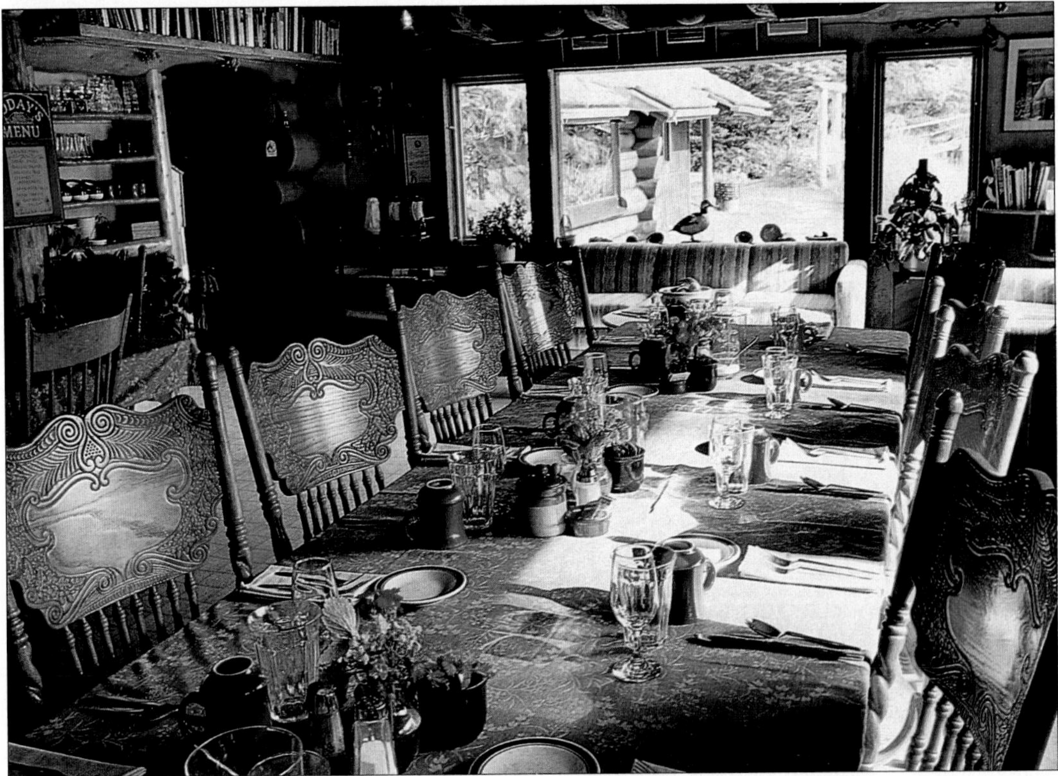

See ranch description on page 9

Circle Z Ranch, Arizona

See ranch description on page 10

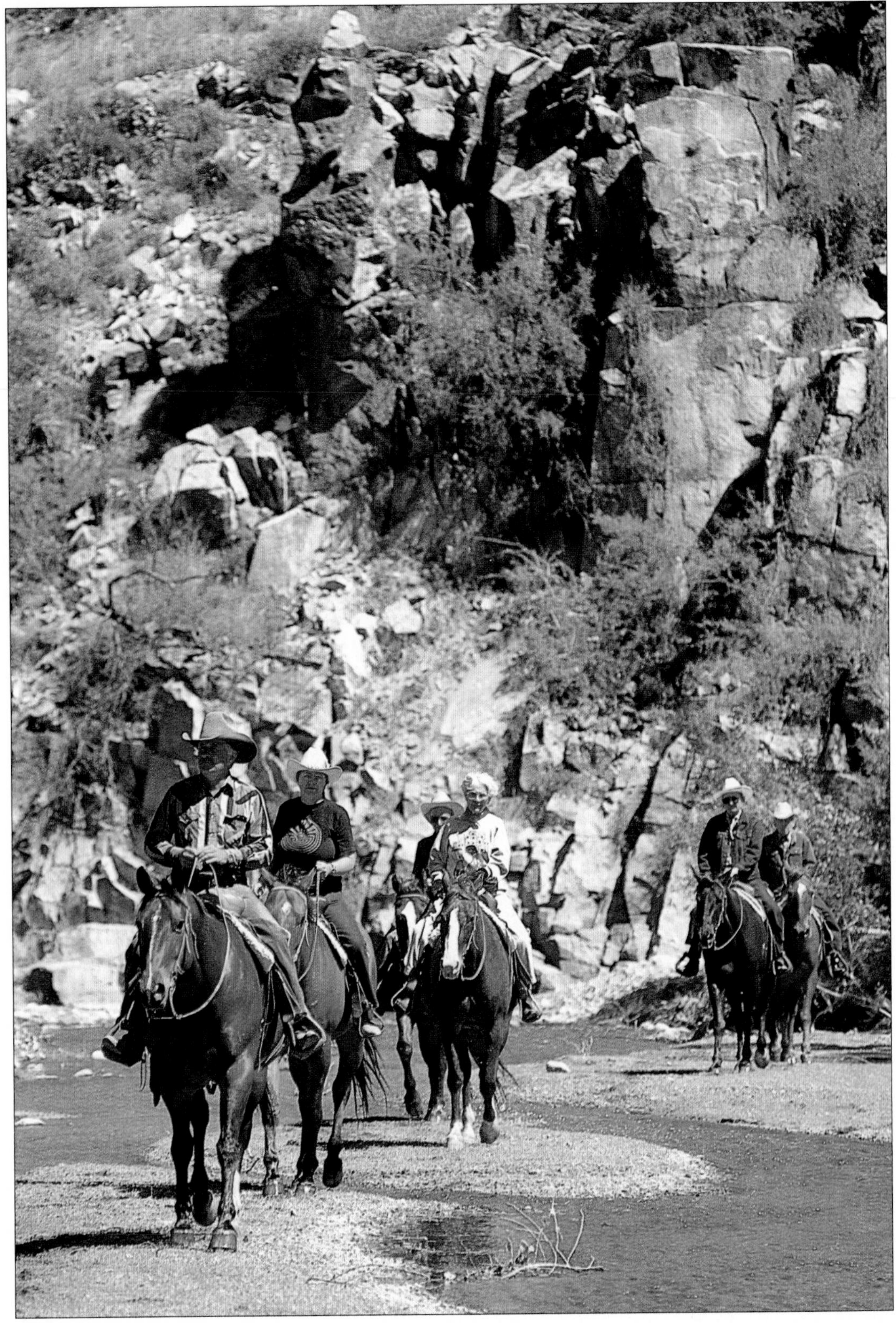

See ranch description on page 12

Flying E Ranch, Arizona

See ranch description on page 13

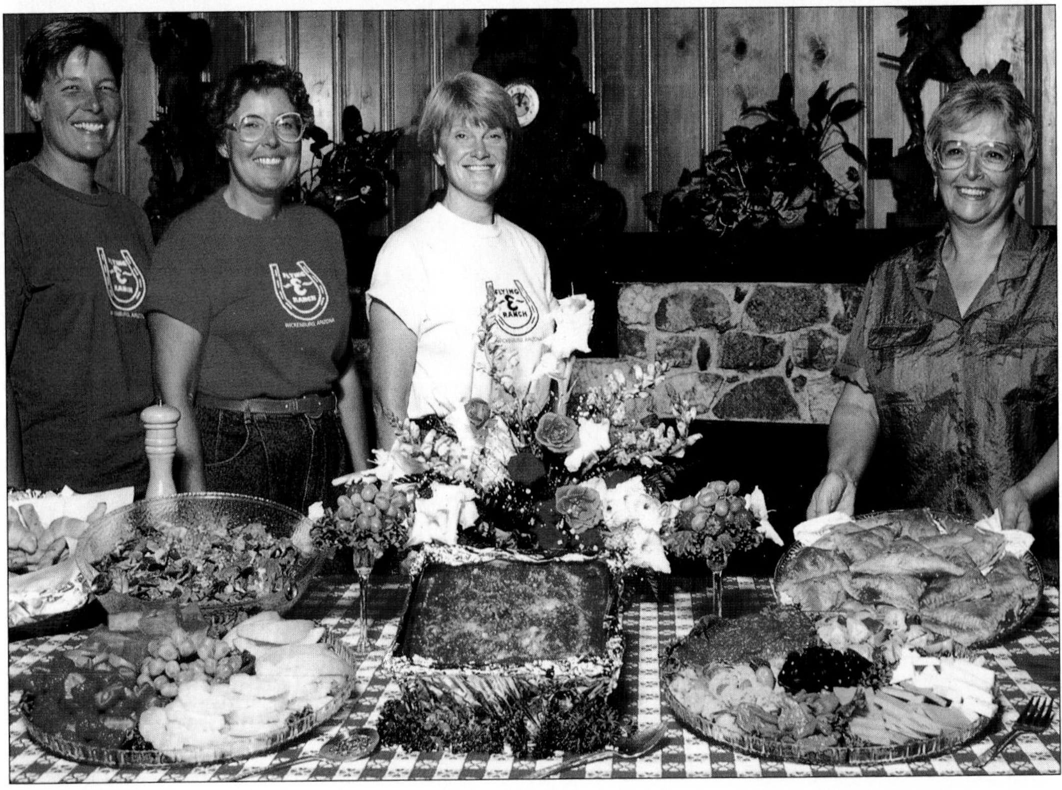

Lazy K Bar Guest Ranch, Arizona

See ranch description on page 17

Grapevine Canyon Ranch, Arizona

See ranch description on page 15

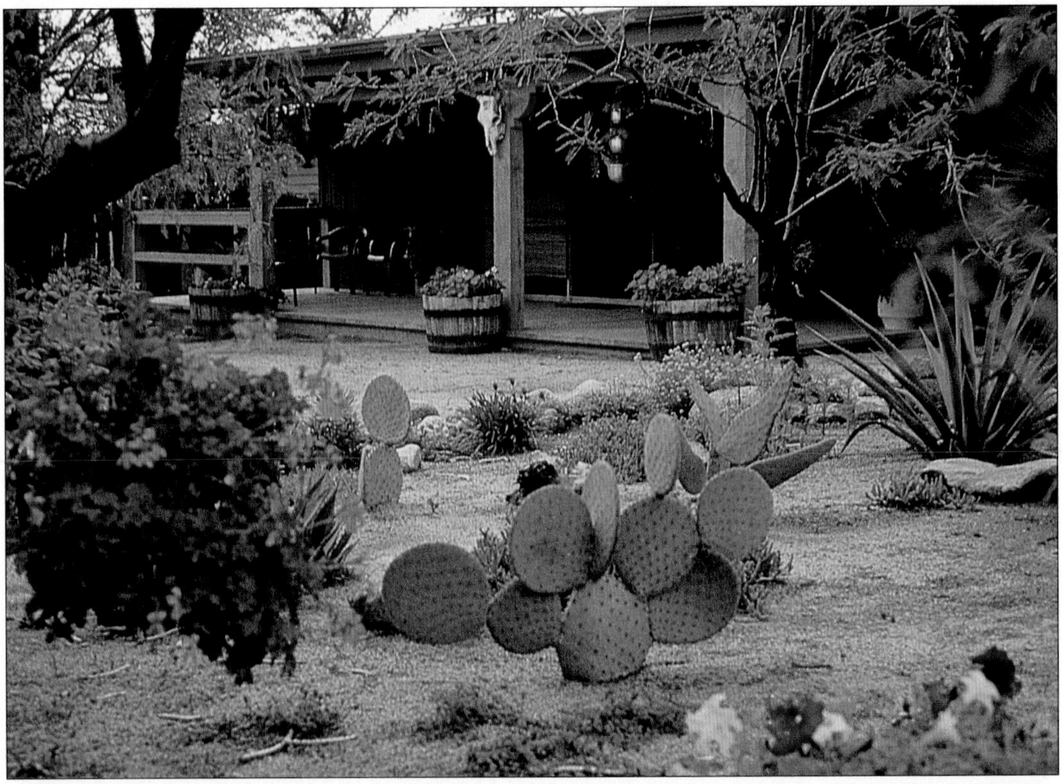

Grapevine Canyon Ranch, Arizona

See ranch description on page 15

Tanque Verde Ranch, Arizona

See ranch description on page 24

White Stallion Ranch, Arizona

See ranch description on page 28

Scott Valley Resort and Guest Ranch, Arkansas

See ranch description on page 30

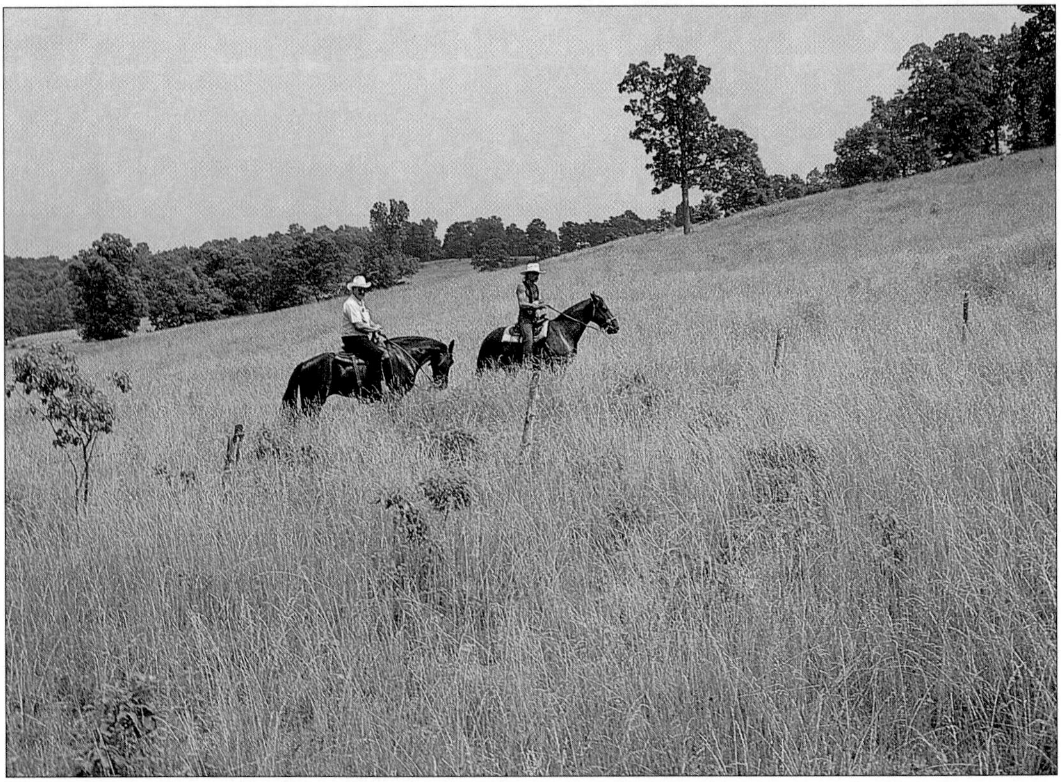

Circle Bar B Guest Ranch, California

See ranch description on page 34

Alisal Guest Ranch, California

See ranch description on page 32

Alisal Guest Ranch, California

See ranch description on page 32

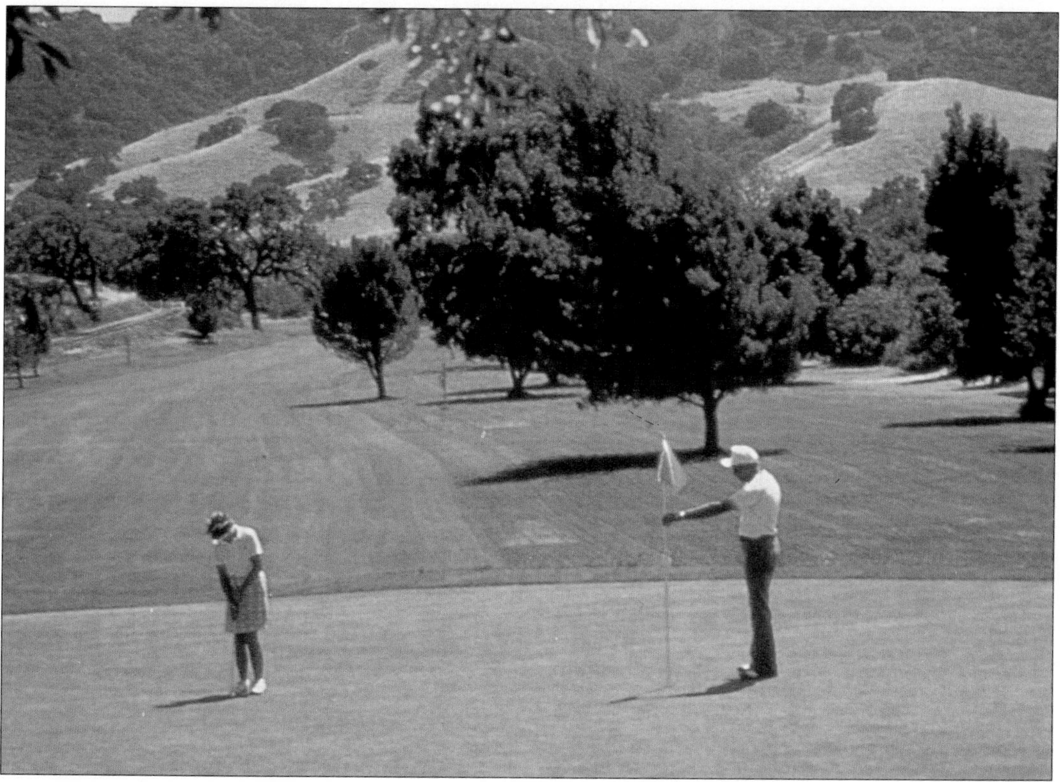

Coffee Creek Ranch, California

See ranch description on page 36

See ranch description on page 38

Hunewill Circle H Ranch, California

See ranch description on page 40

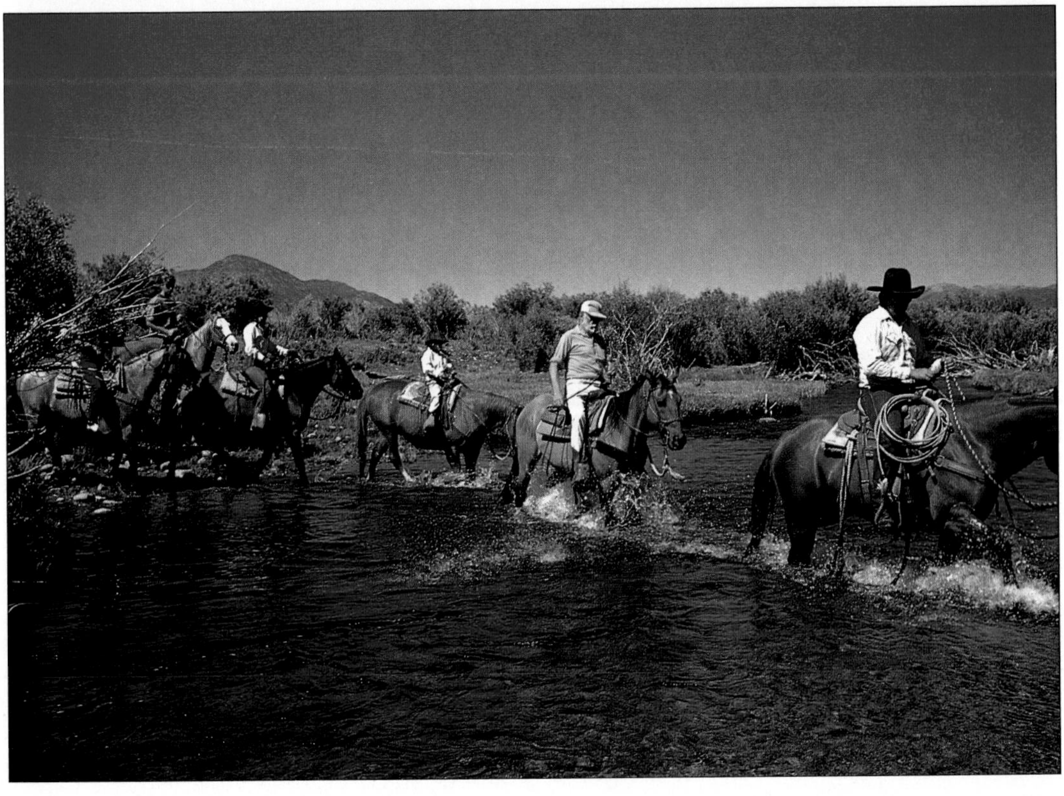

Rankin Ranch, California

See ranch description on page 42

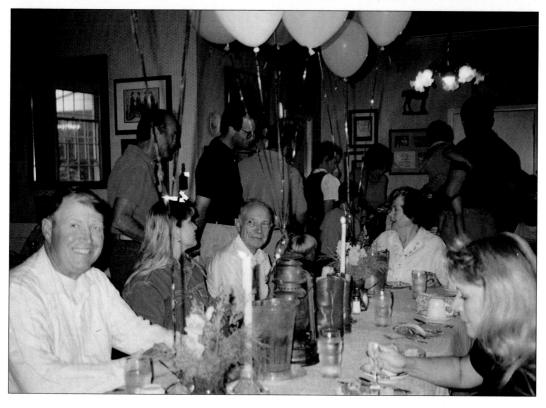

Spanish Springs Ranch, California

See ranch description on page 44

Aspen Lodge Ranch Resort, Colorado

See ranch description on page 48

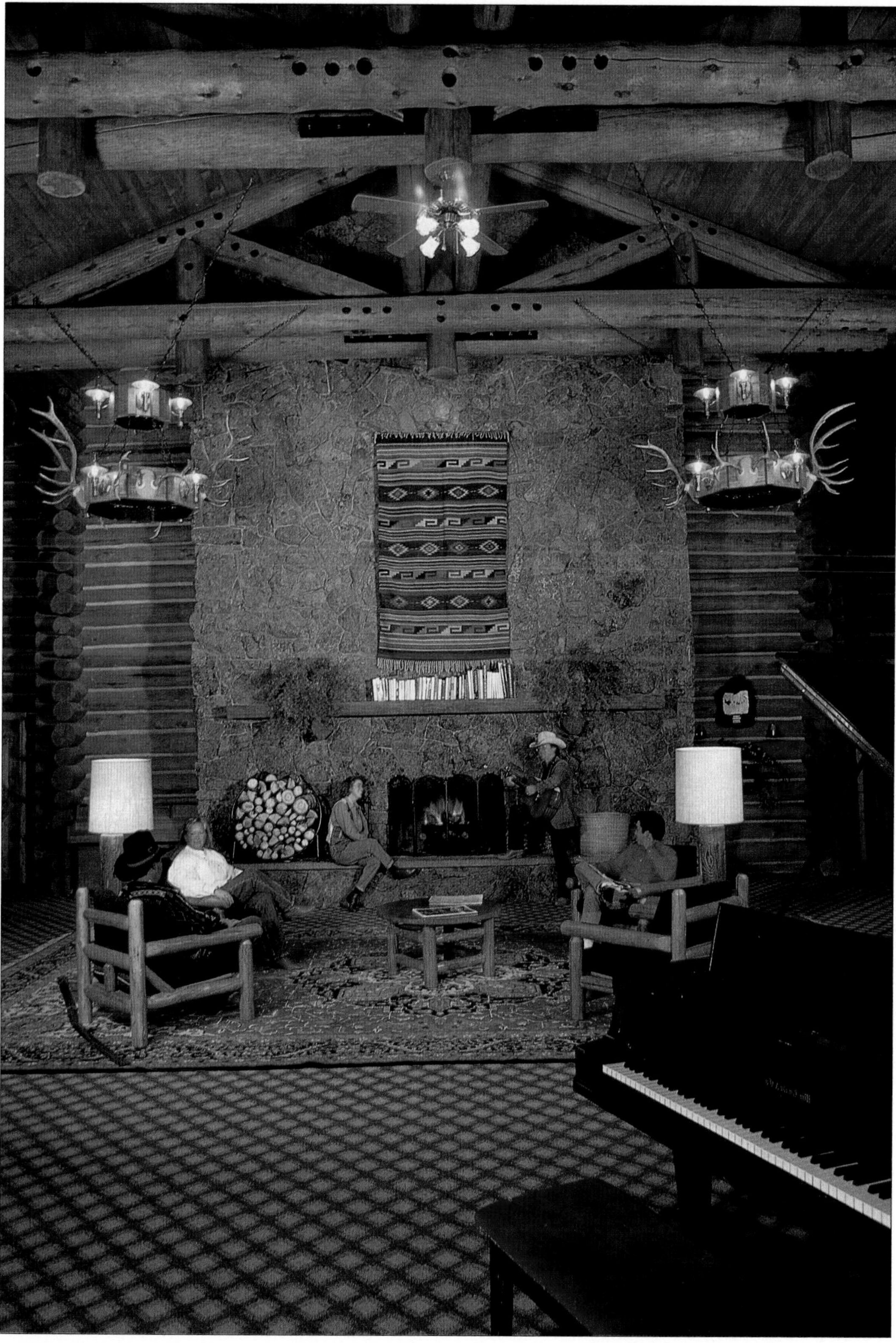

Colorado Trails Ranch, Colorado

See ranch description on page 54

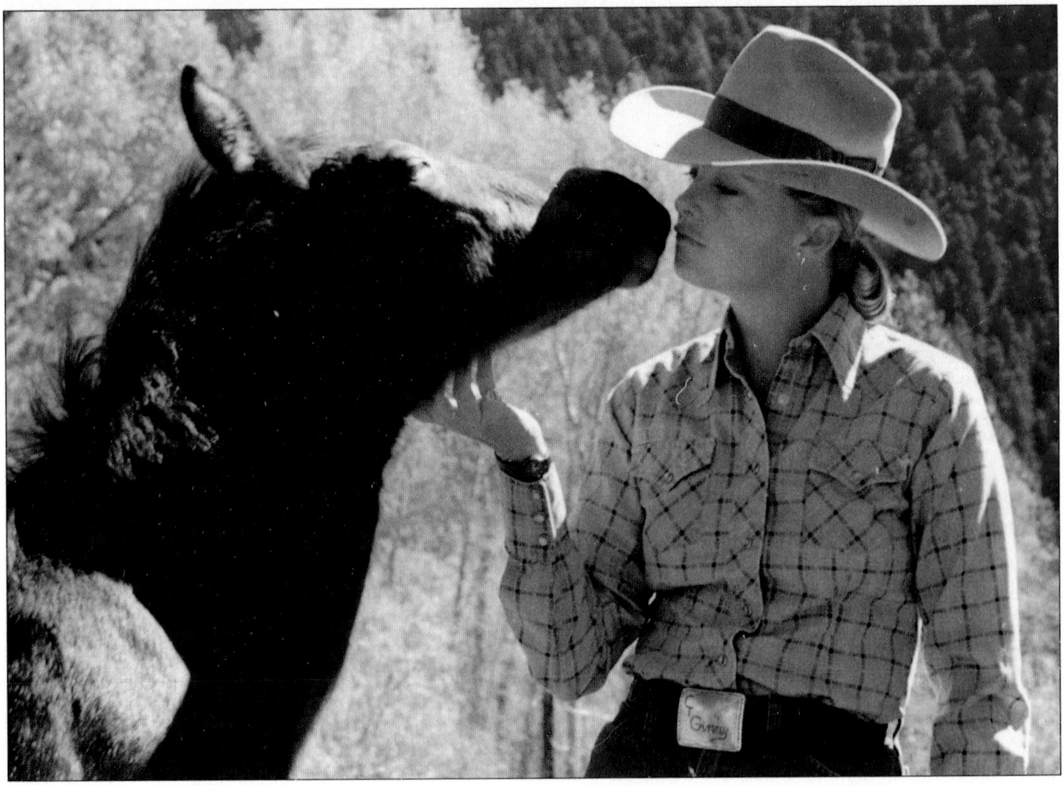

See ranch description on page 55

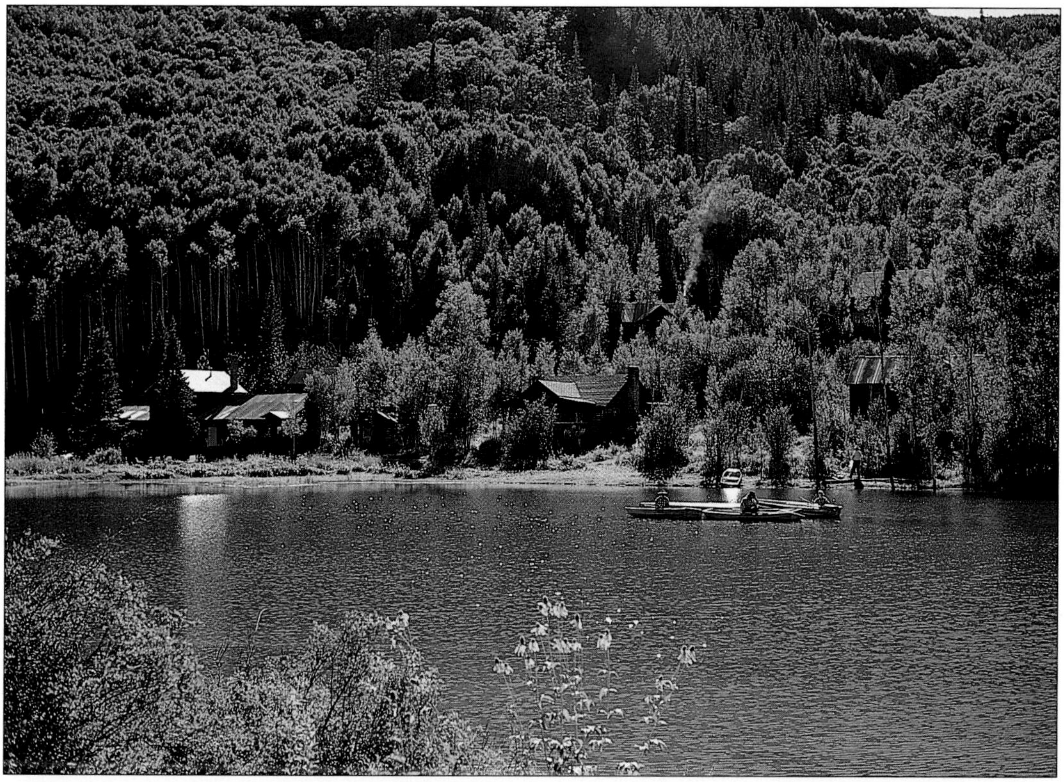

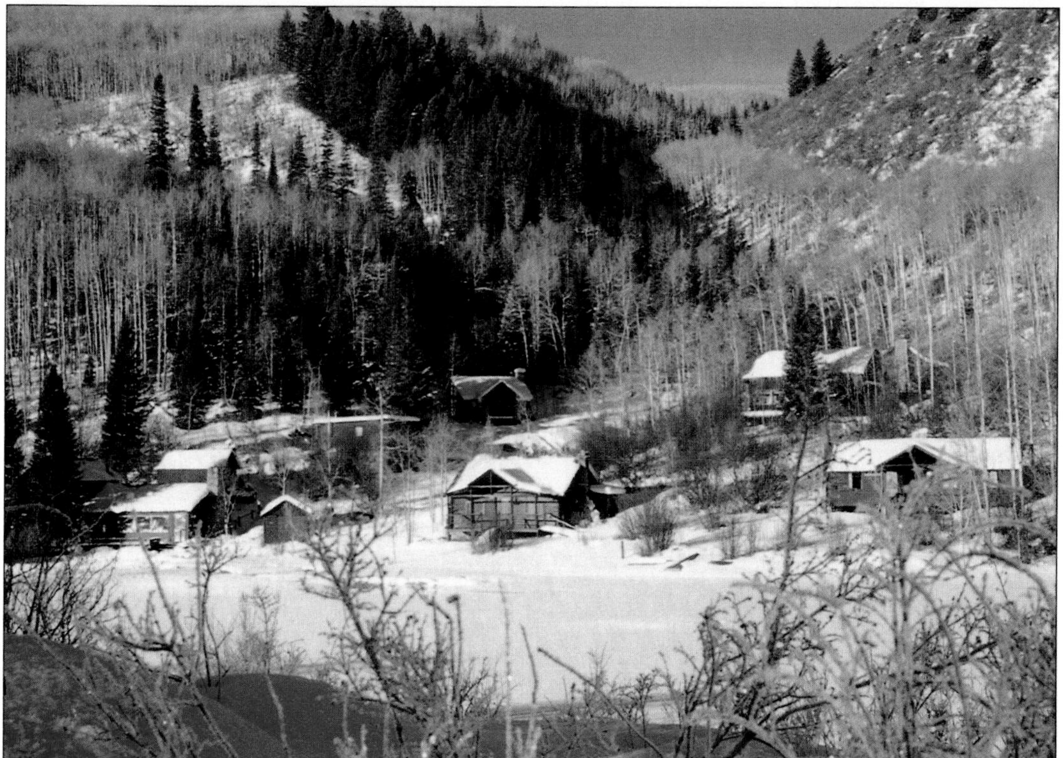

See ranch description on page 56

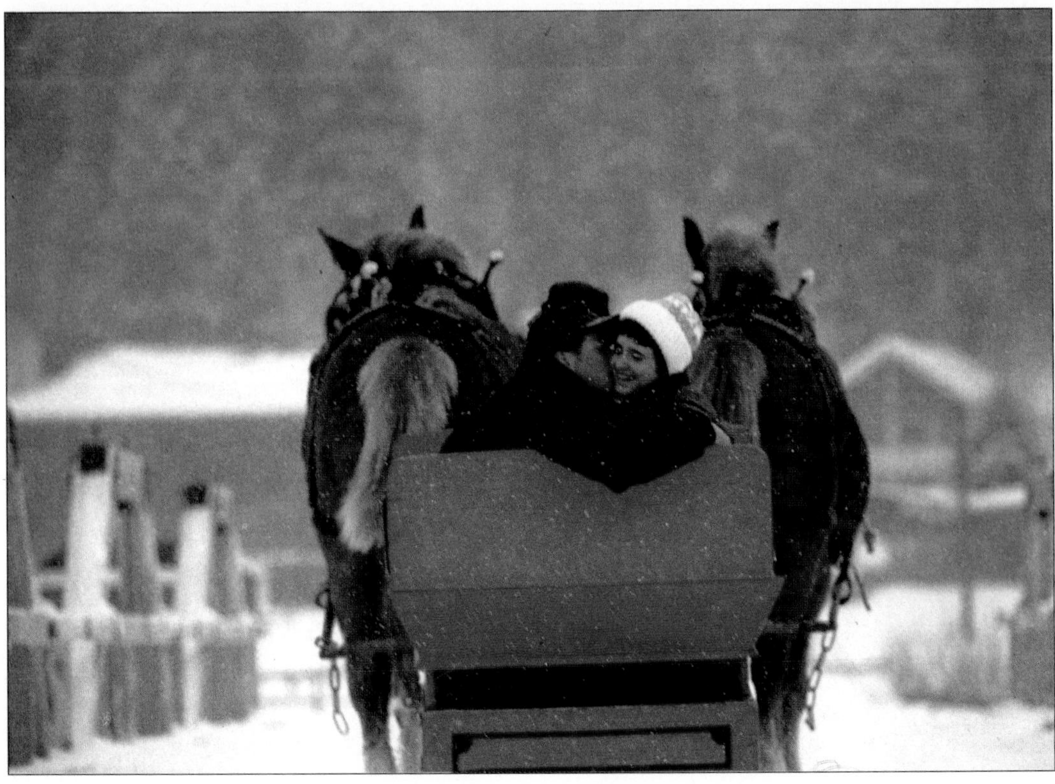

Don K Ranch, Colorado

See ranch description on page 60

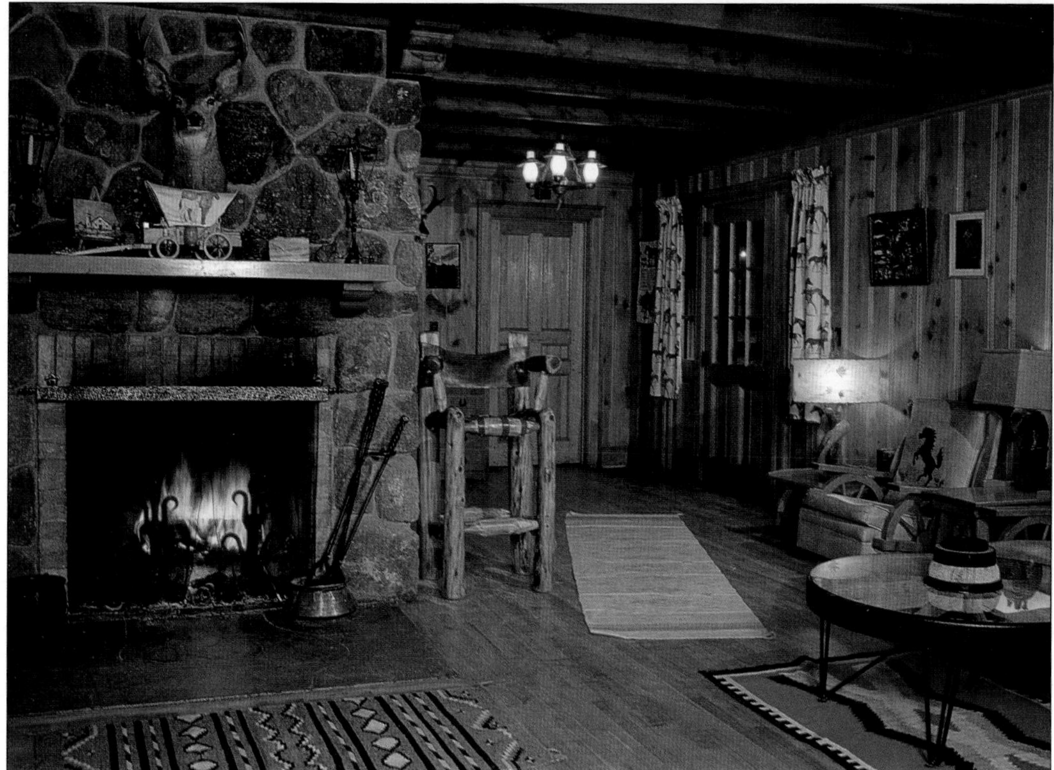

Elk Mountain Ranch, Colorado

See ranch description on page 64

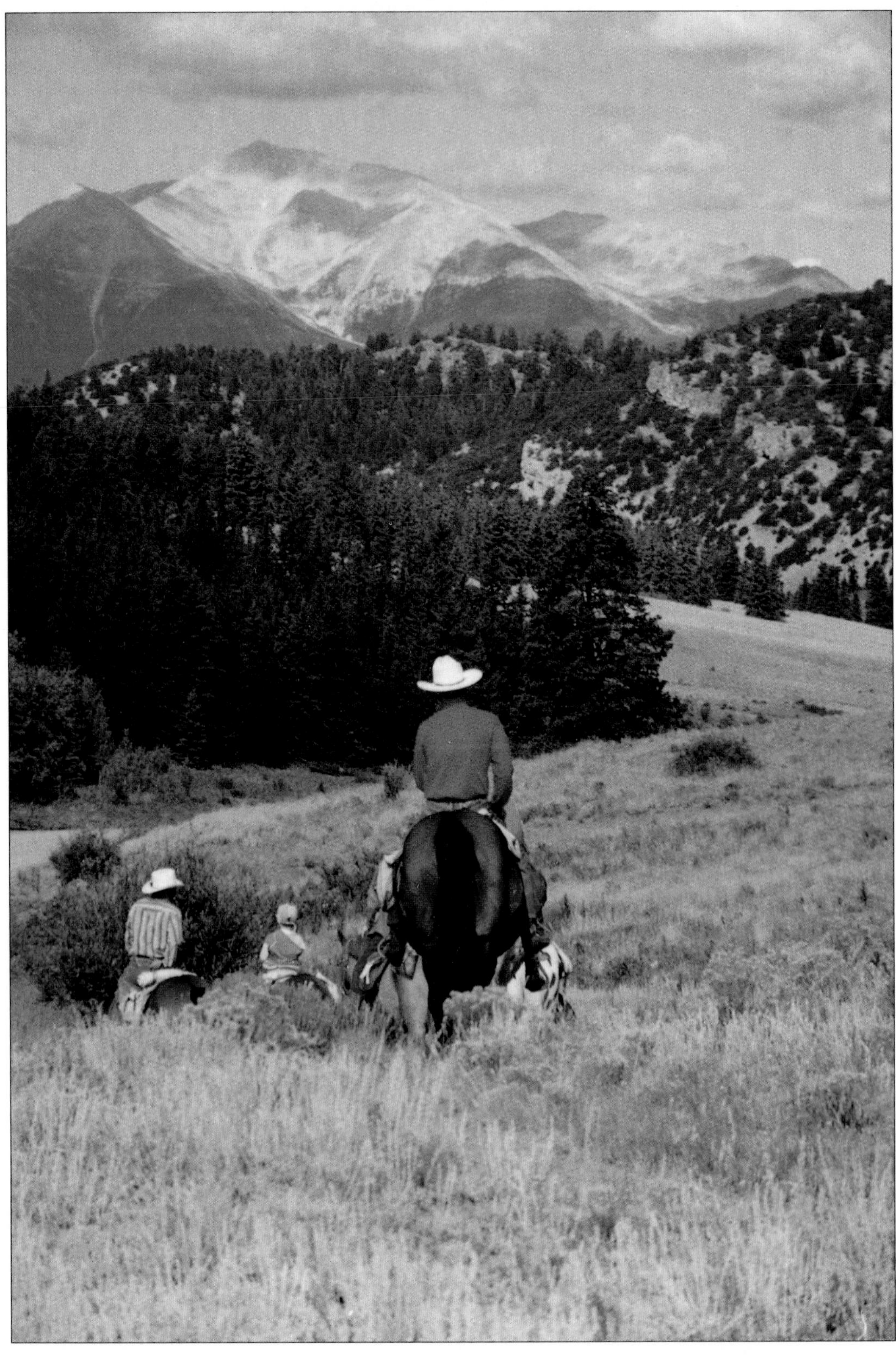

The Home Ranch, Colorado

See ranch description on page 70

Fryingpan River Ranch, Colorado

See ranch description on page 68

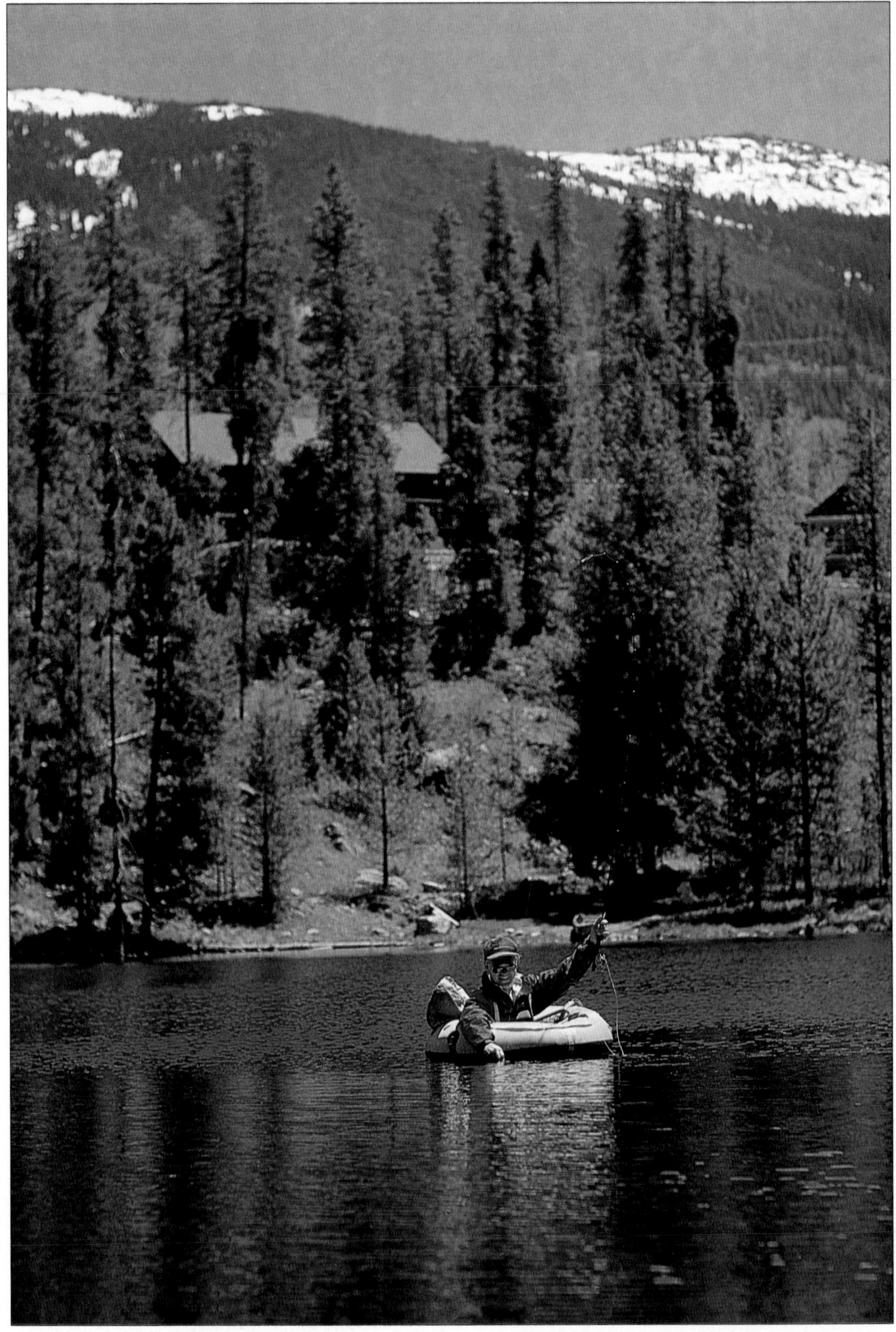

See ranch description on page 68

Lake Mancos Ranch, Colorado

See ranch description on page 71

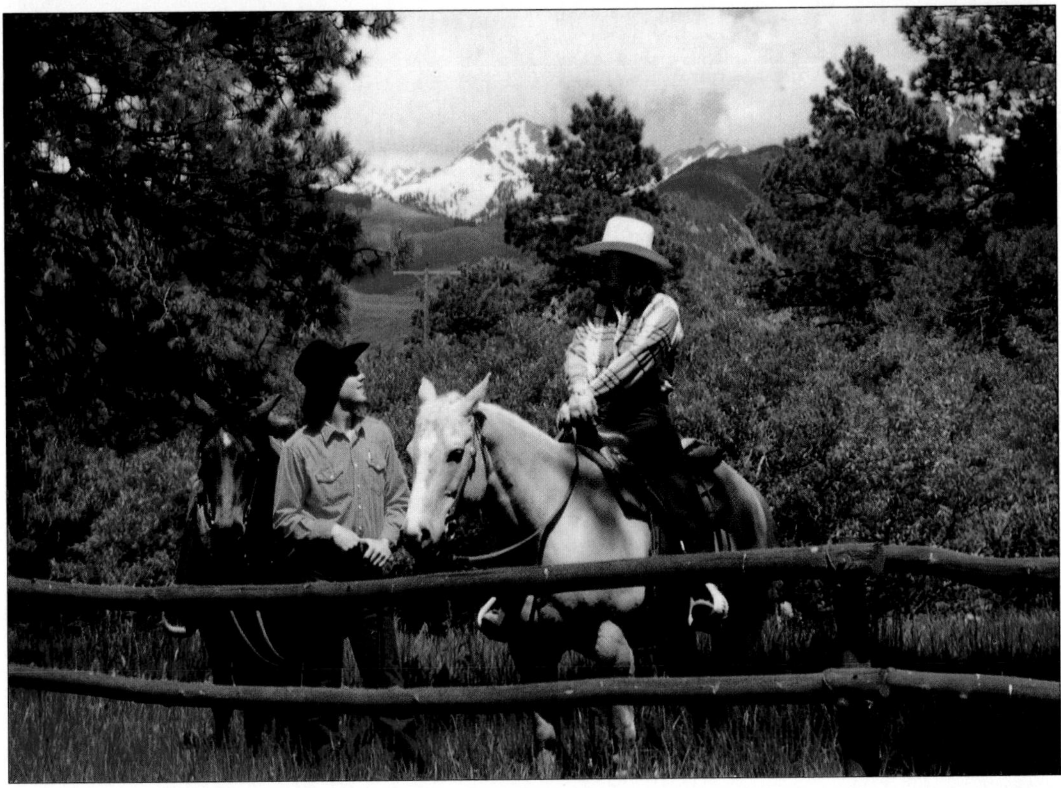

Lane Guest Ranch, Colorado

See ranch description on page 72

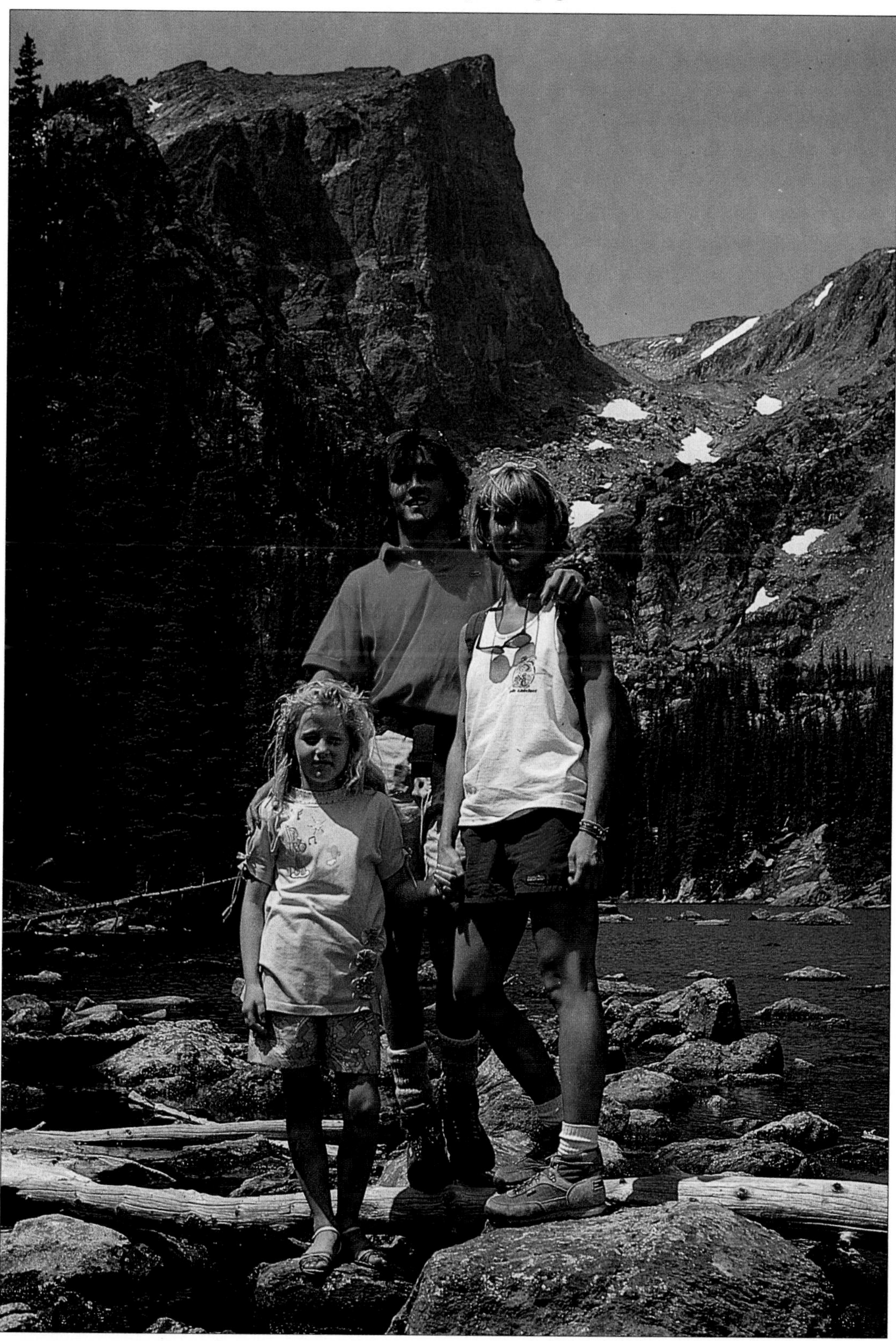

Latigo Ranch, Colorado

See ranch description on page 74

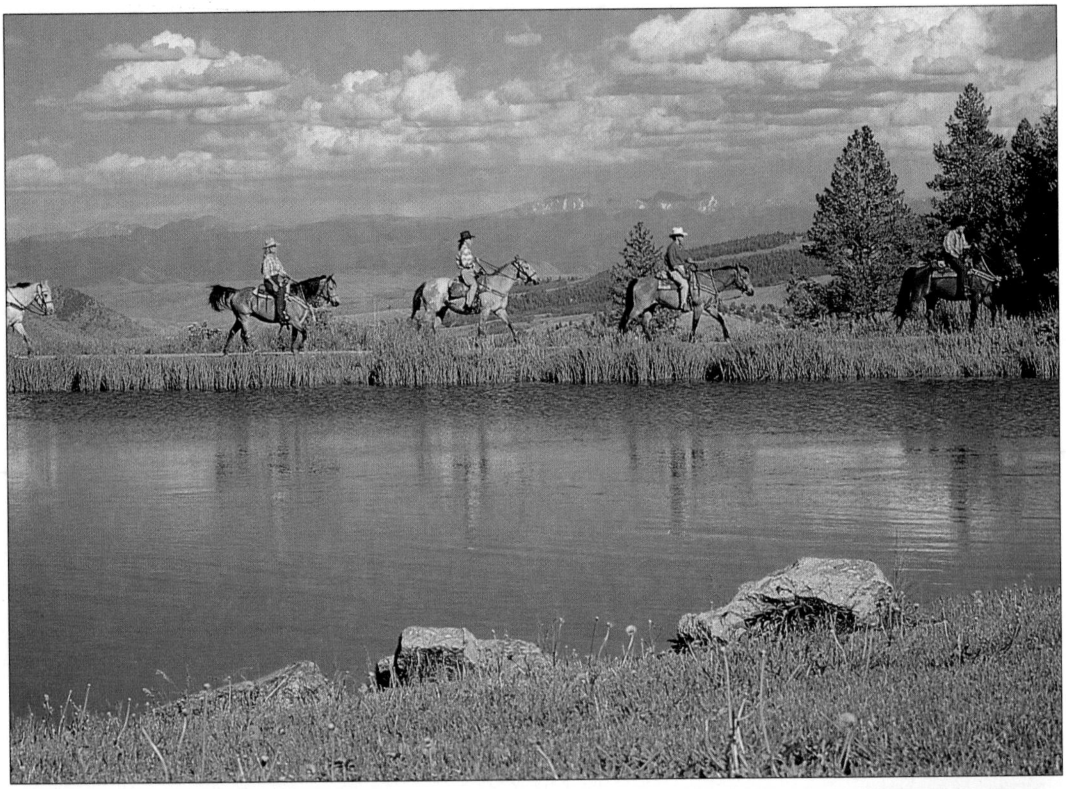

Lazy H Guest Ranch, Colorado

See ranch description on page 73

Lost Valley Ranch, Colorado

See ranch description on page 76

North Fork Guest Ranch, Colorado

See ranch description on page 78

Old Glendevey Ranch, Colorado

See ranch description on page 81

The Pines Ranch, Colorado

See ranch description on page 84

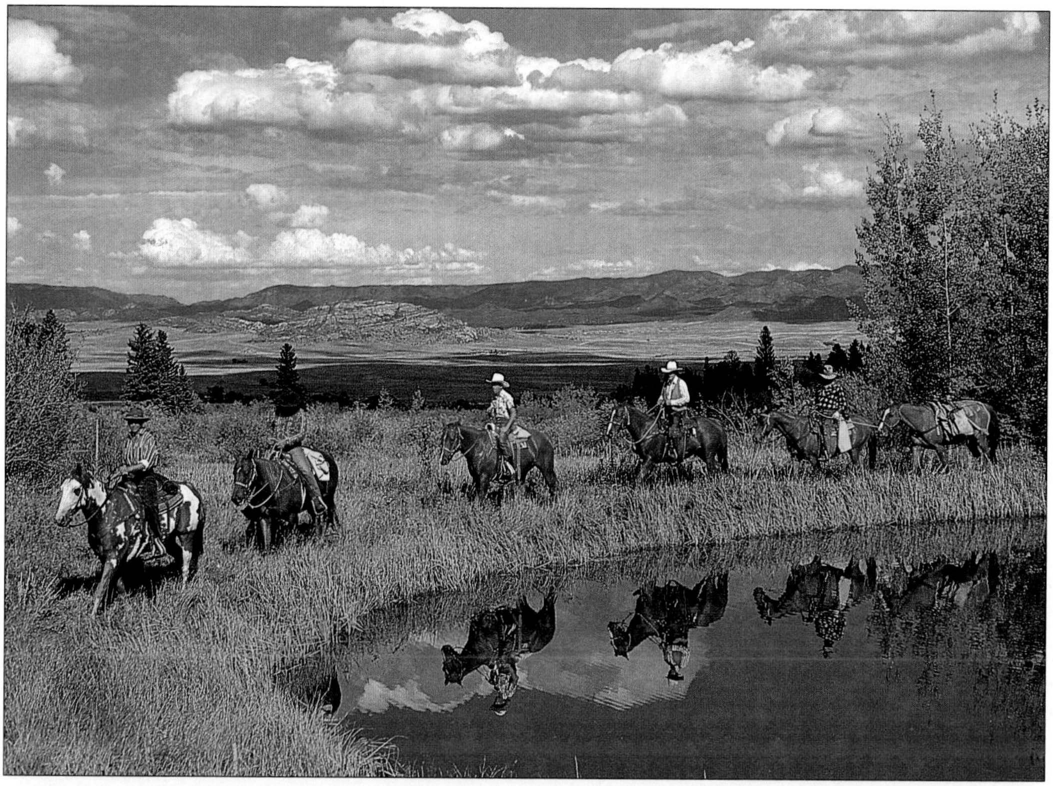

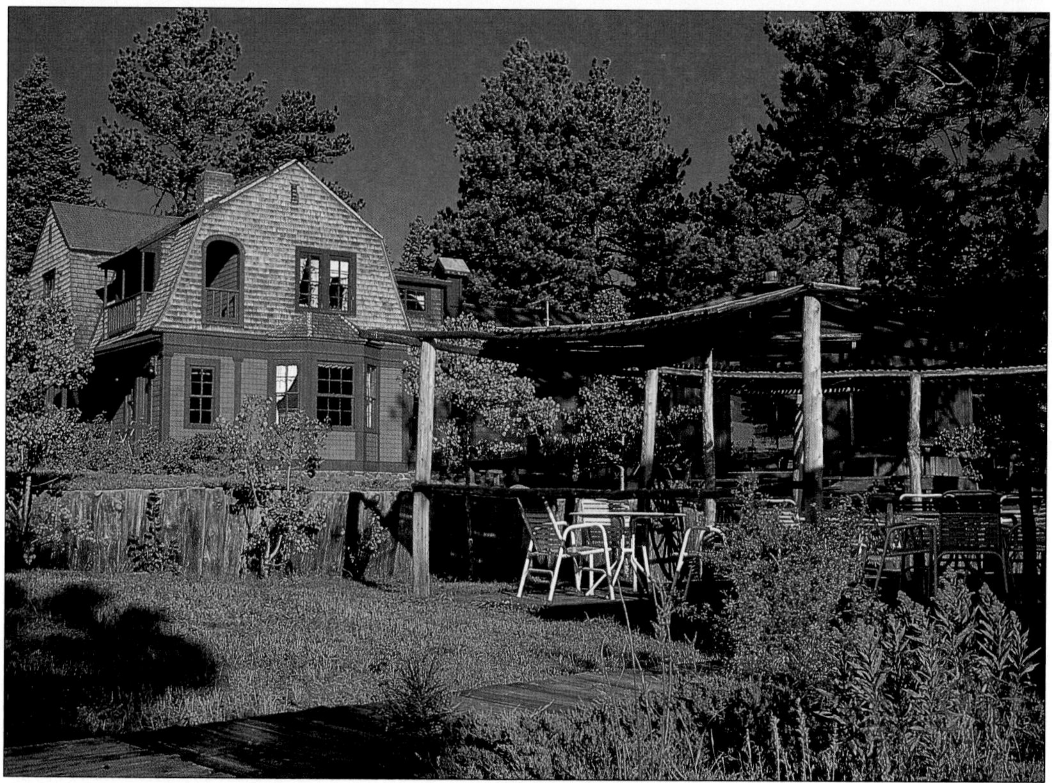

Peaceful Valley Lodge and Ranch Resort, Colorado

See ranch description on page 82

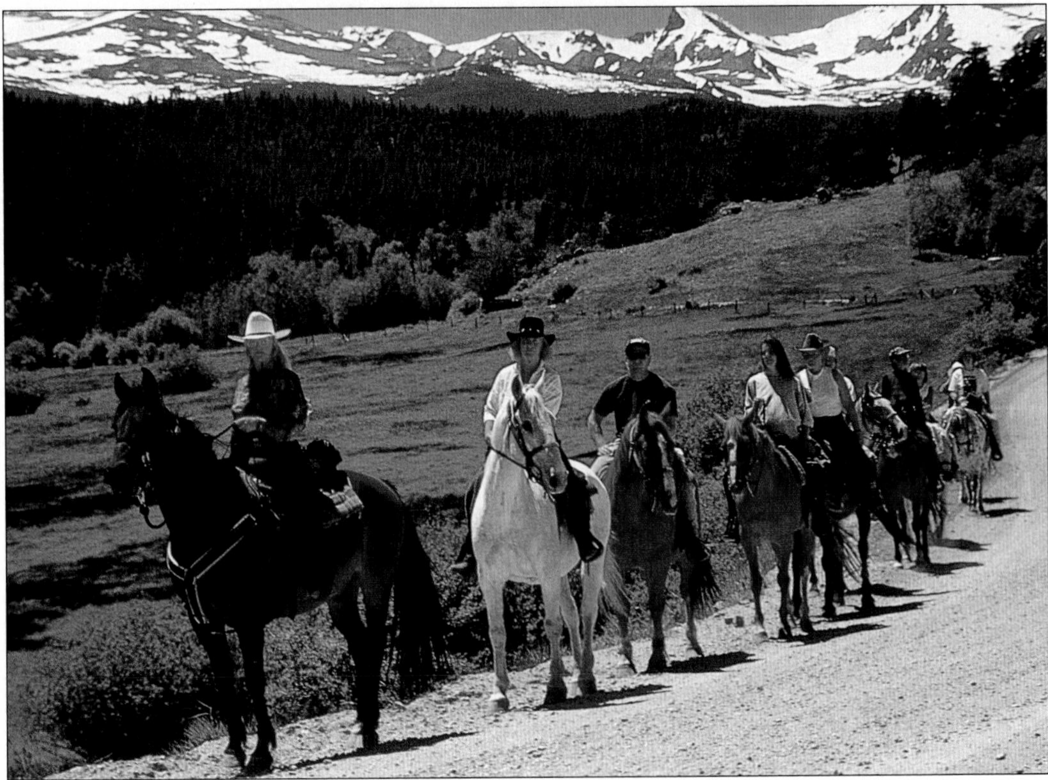

See ranch description on page 82

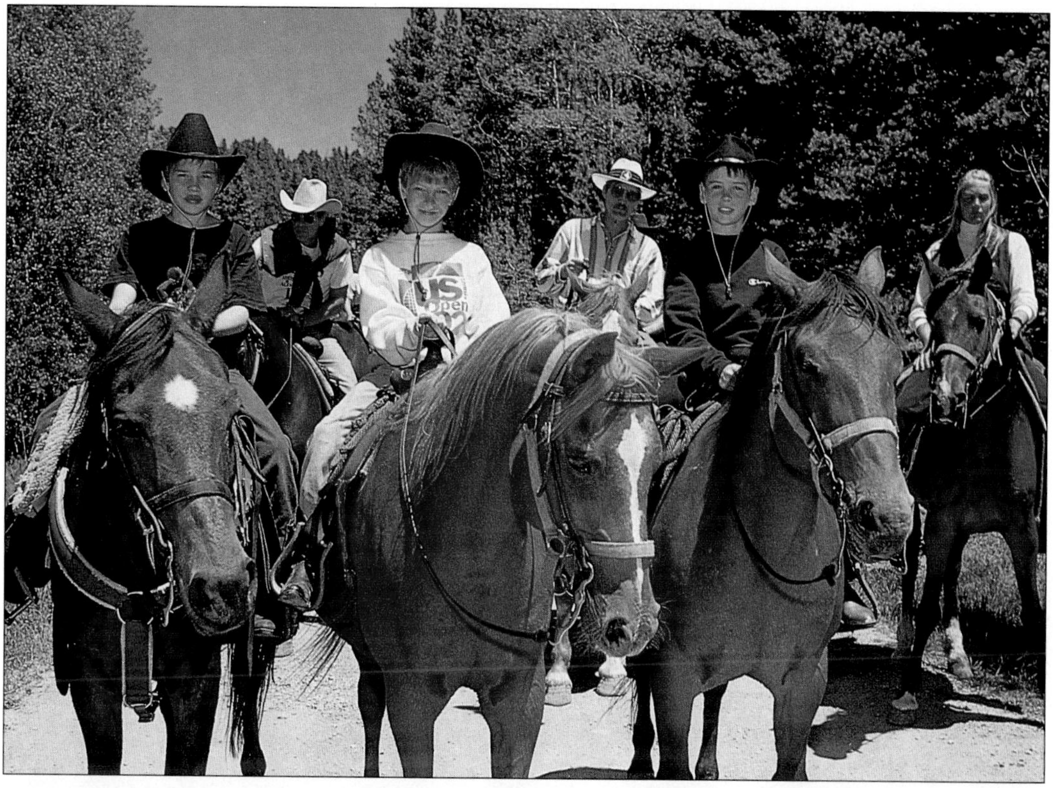

Powderhorn Guest Ranch, Colorado

See ranch description on page 86

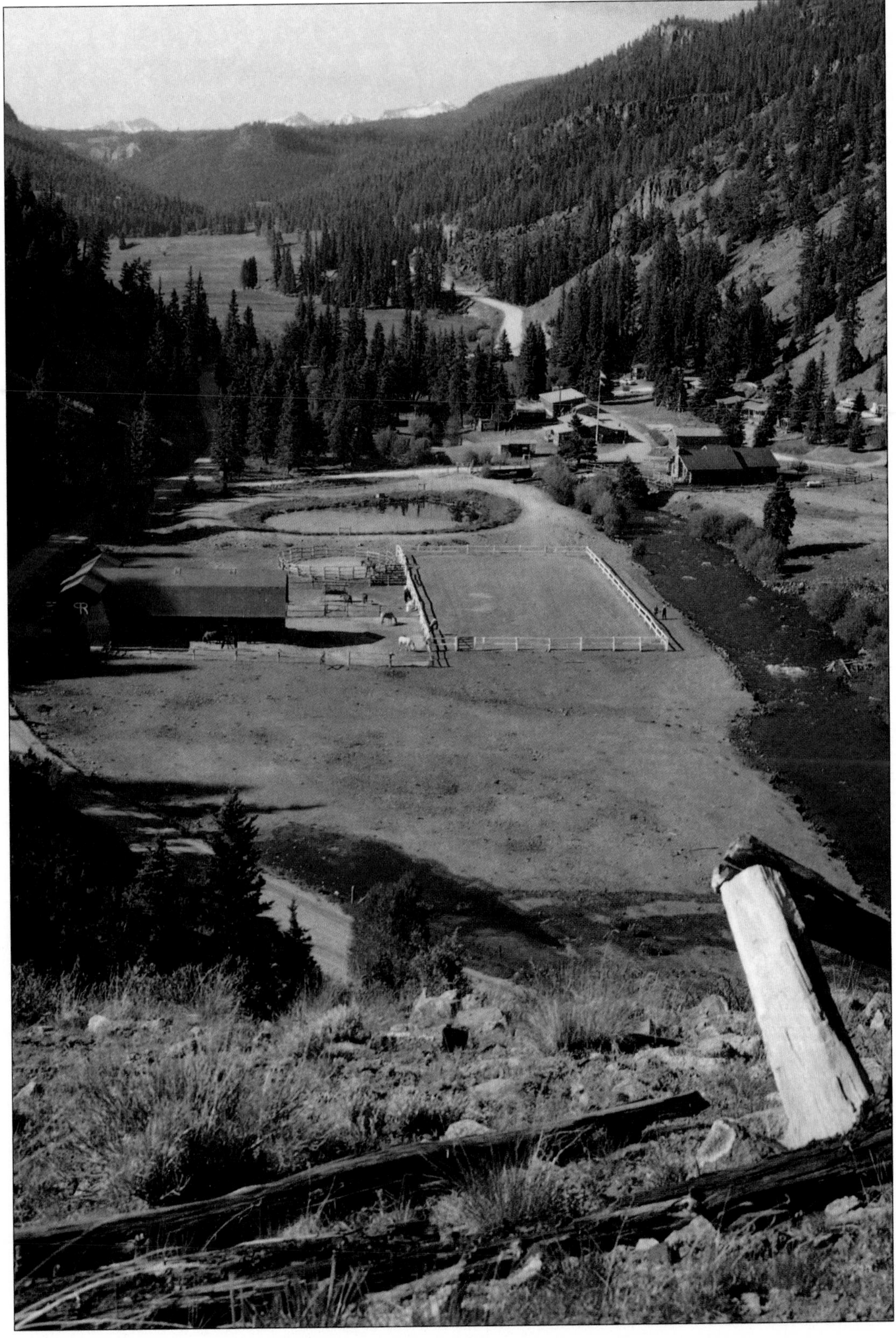

See ranch description on page 87

7W Guest Ranch, Colorado

See ranch description on page 91

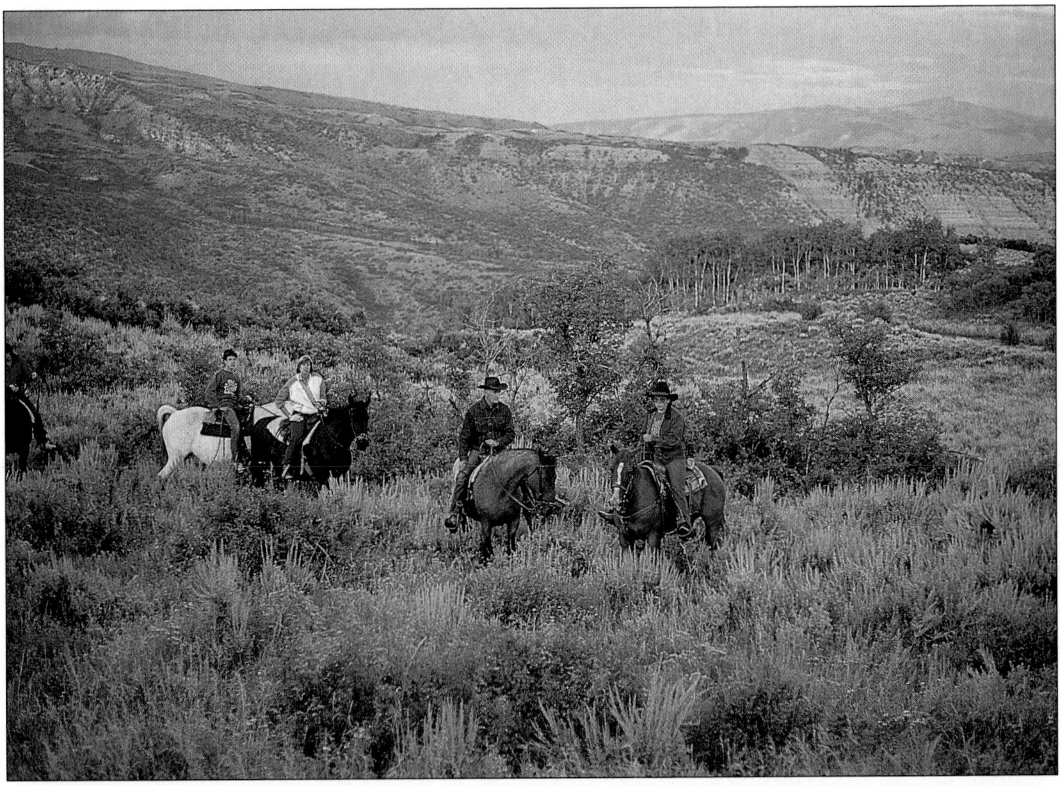

See ranch description on page 98

Skyline Guest Ranch, Colorado

See ranch description on page 95

See ranch description on page 95

Vista Verde Guest and Ski Touring Ranch, Colorado

See ranch description on page 100

Wilderness Trails Ranch, Colorado

See ranch description on page 106

Wit's End Guest and Resort Ranch, Colorado

See ranch description on page 108

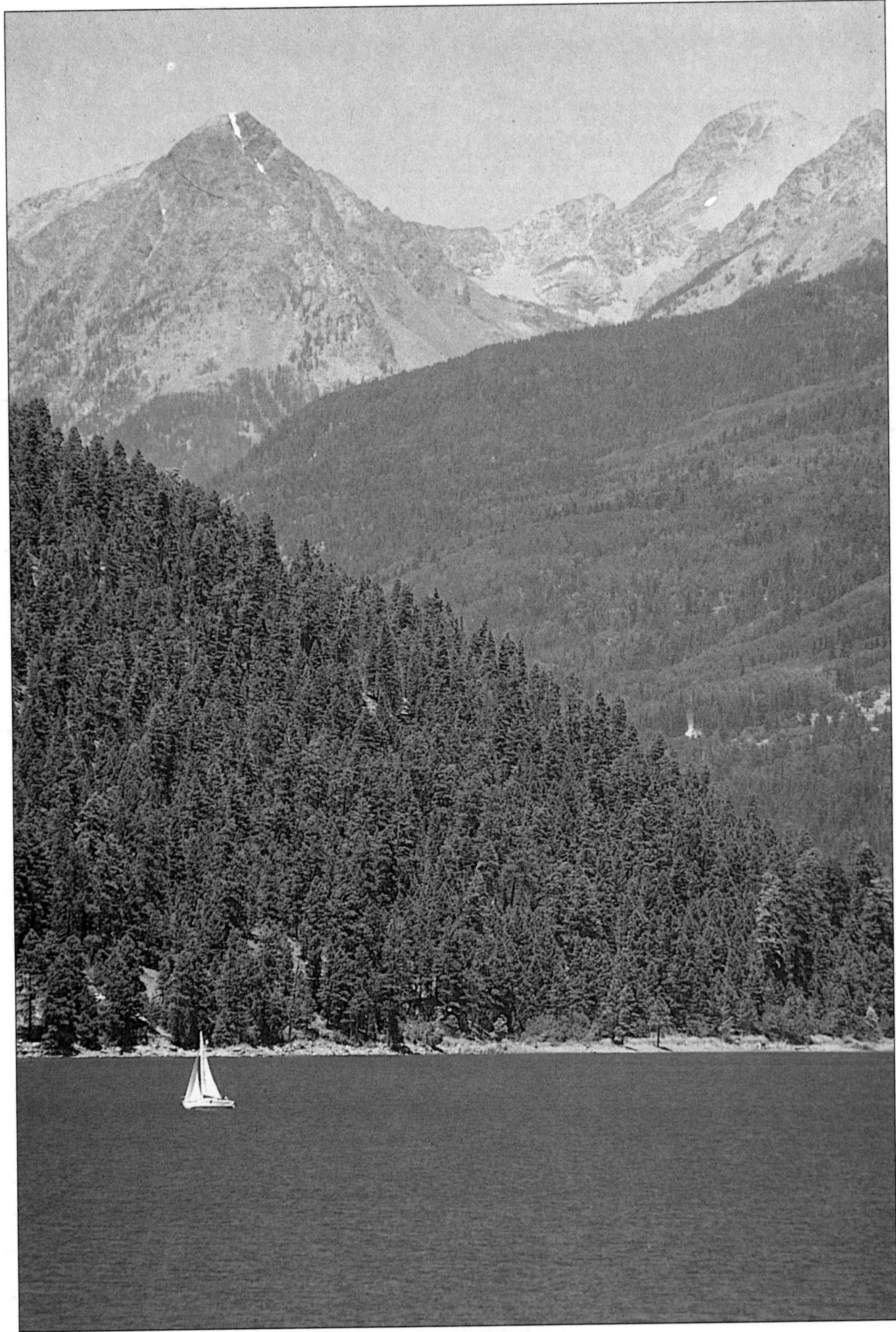

See ranch description on page 108

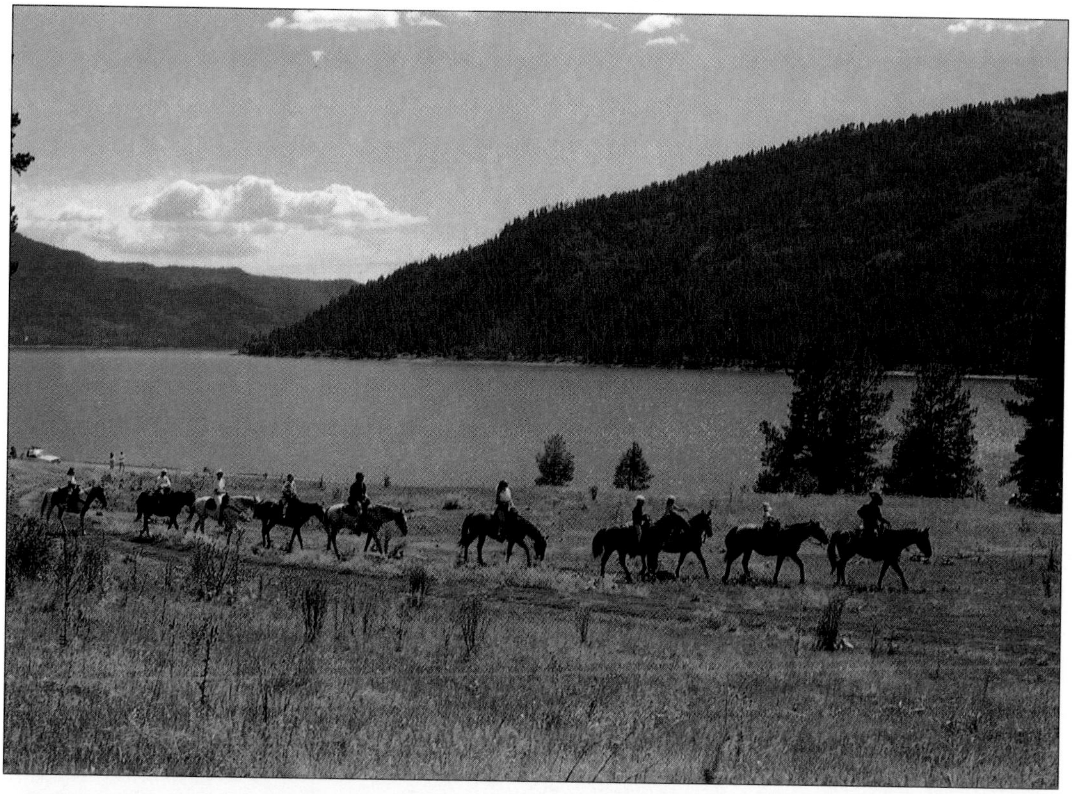

Wit's End Guest and Resort Ranch, Colorado

See ranch description on page 108

Wit's End Guest and Resort Ranch, Colorado

See ranch description on page 108

Wit's End Guest and Resort Ranch, Colorado

See ranch description on page 108

Wit's End Guest and Resort Ranch, Colorado

See ranch description on page 108

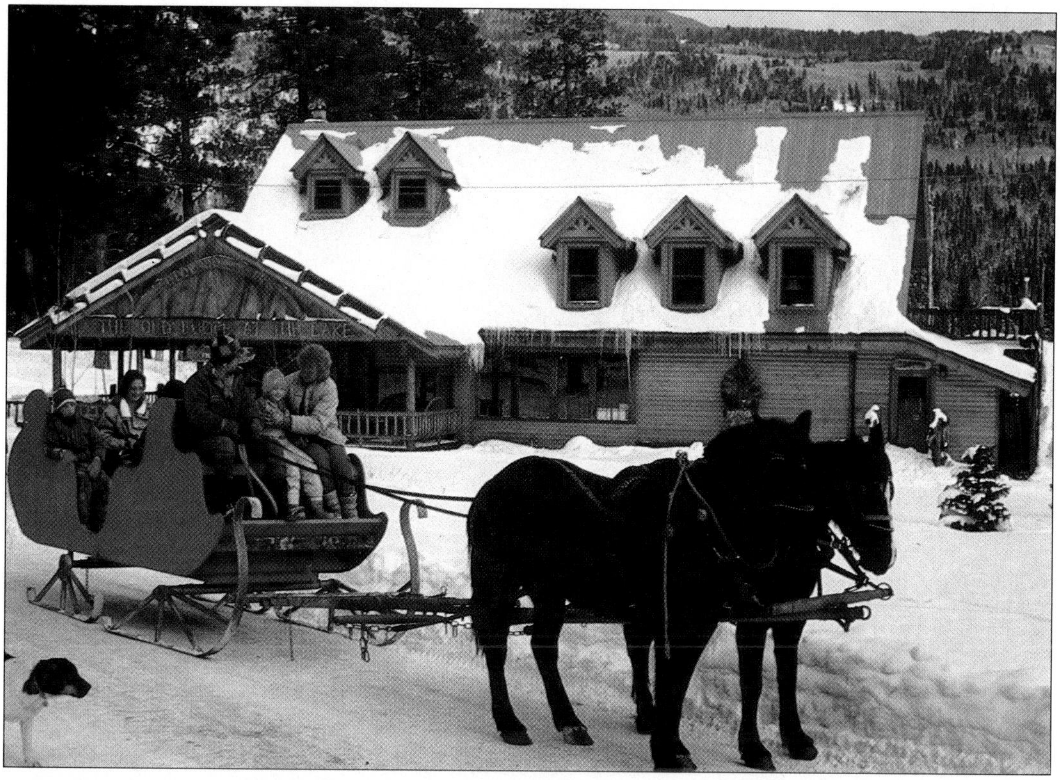

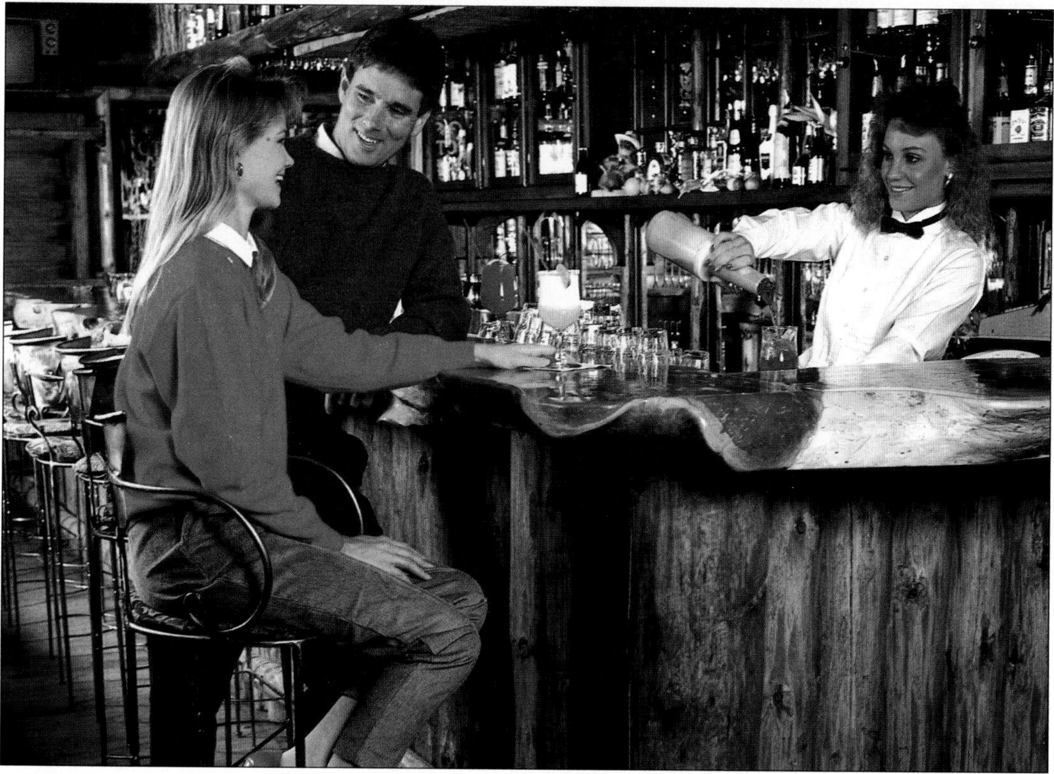

Bar H Bar Ranch, Idaho

See ranch description on page 113

See ranch description on page 117

Diamond D Ranch, Idaho

See ranch description on page 116

Diamond D Ranch, Idaho

See ranch description on page 116

Hidden Creek Ranch, Idaho

See ranch description on page 114

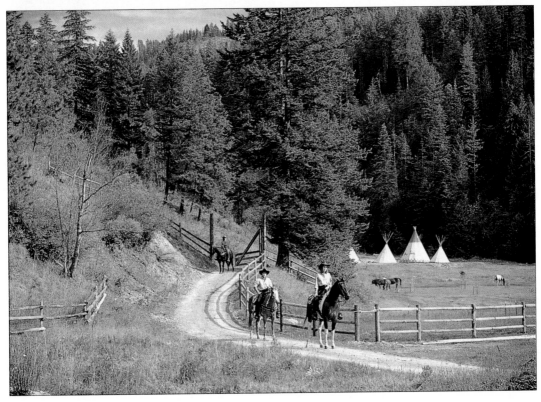

See ranch description on page 114

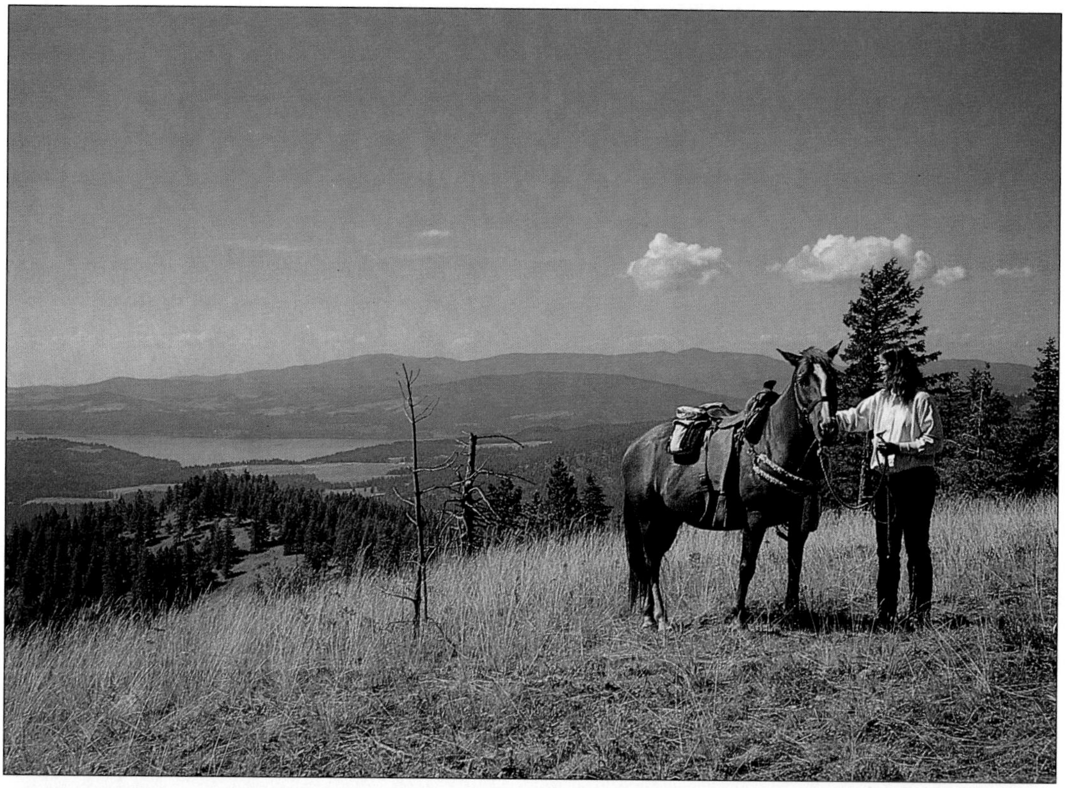

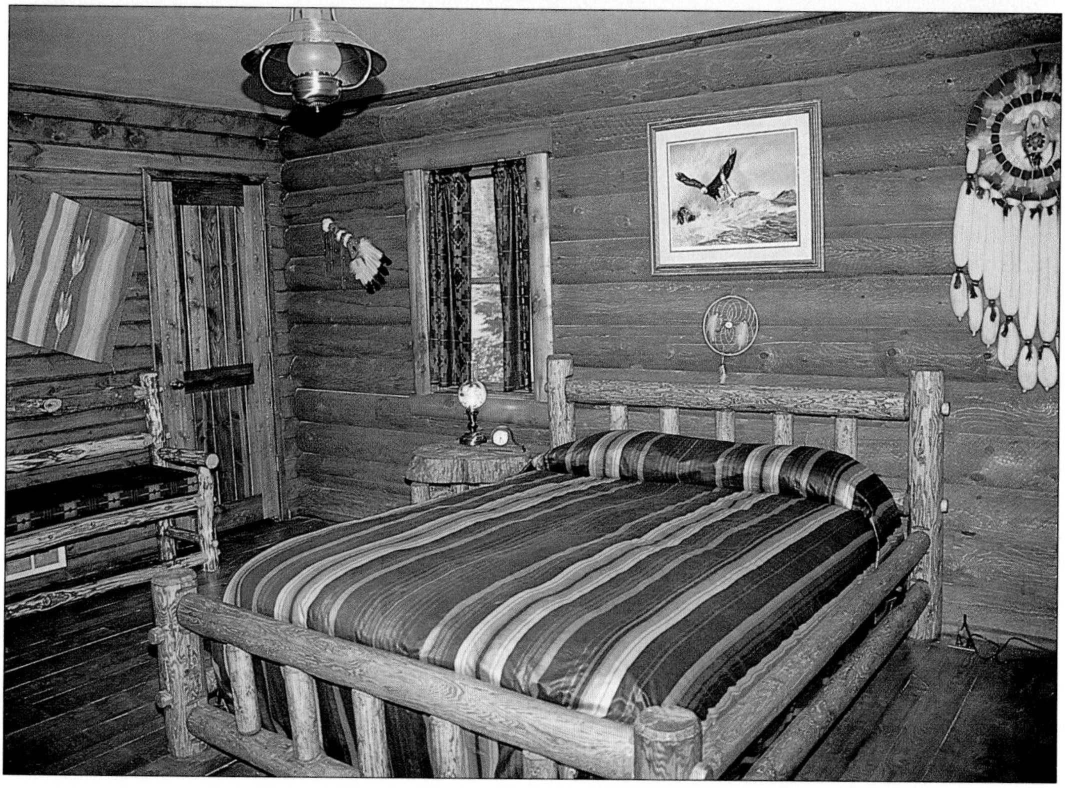

Twin Peaks Ranch, Idaho

See ranch description on page 122

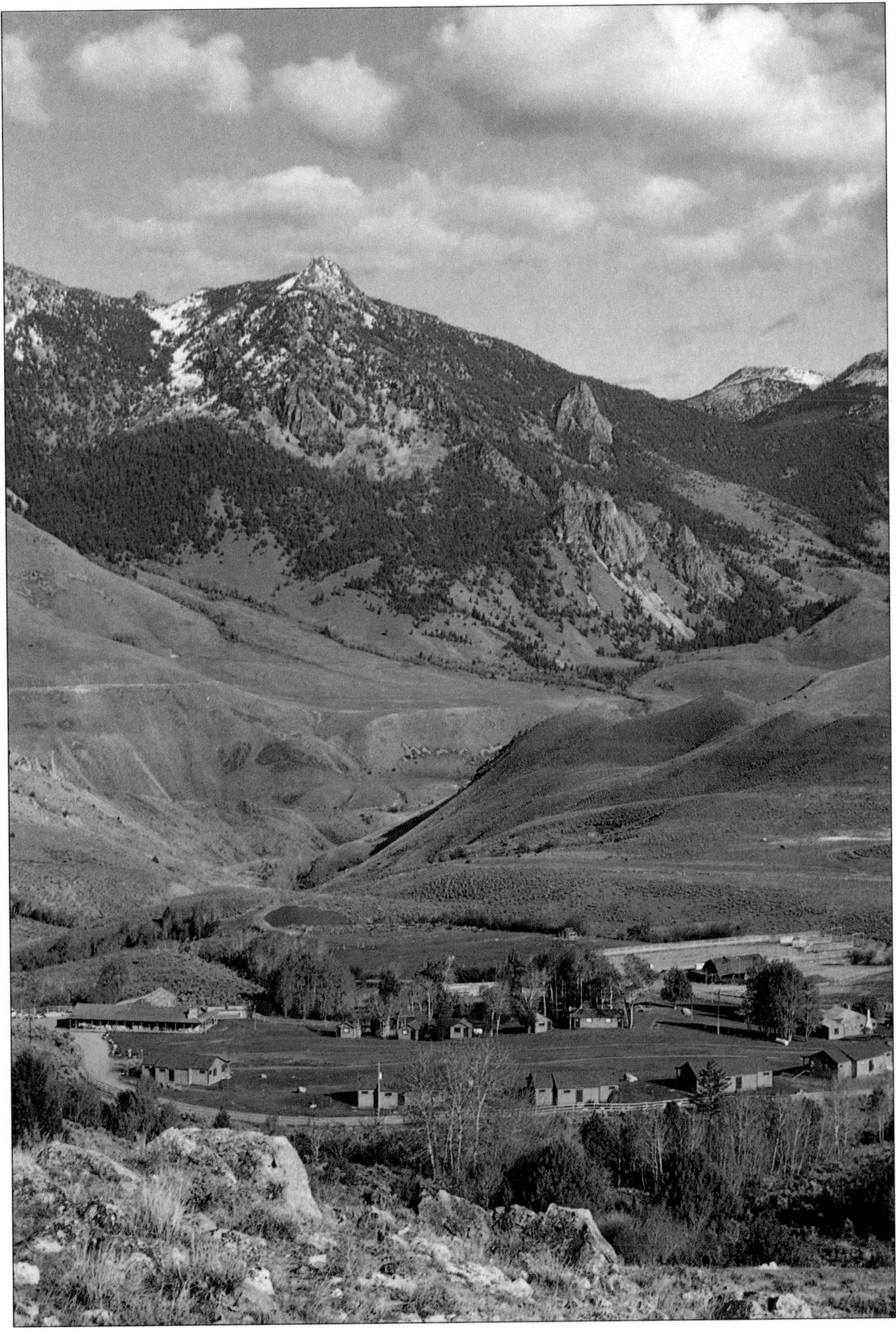

Wapiti Meadow Ranch, Idaho

See ranch description on page 120

C-B Cattle and Guest Ranch, Montana

See ranch description on page 131

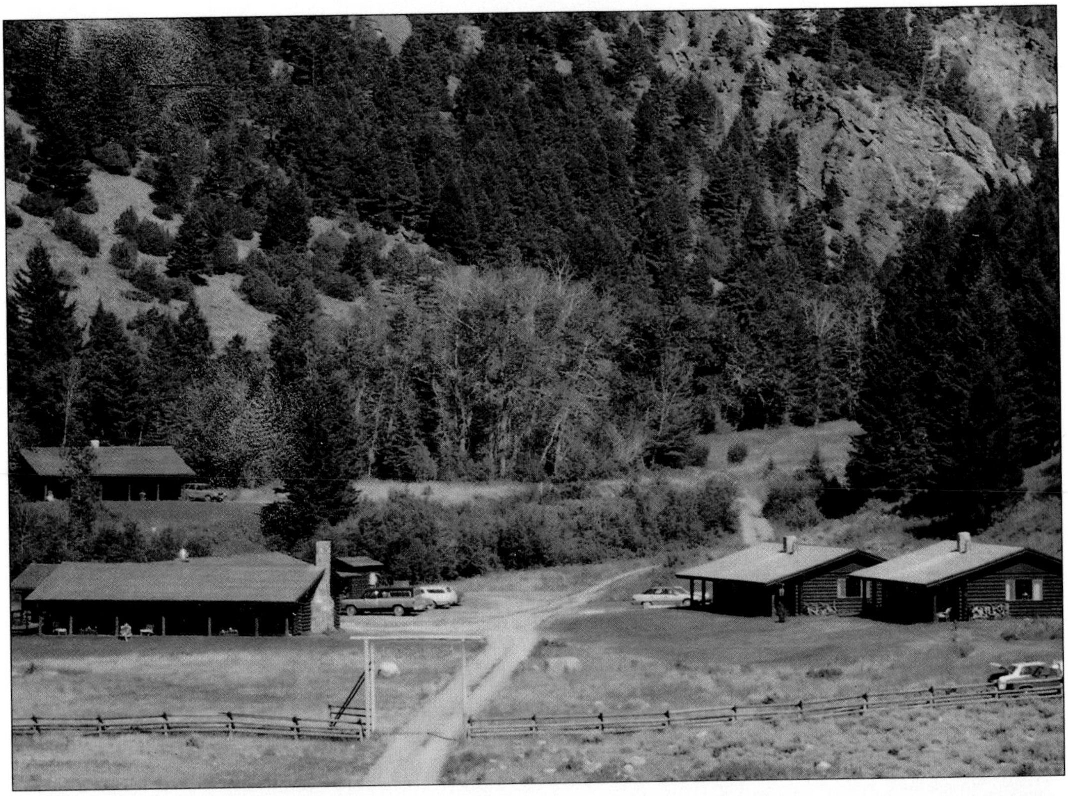

Diamond J Ranch, Montana

See ranch description on page 134

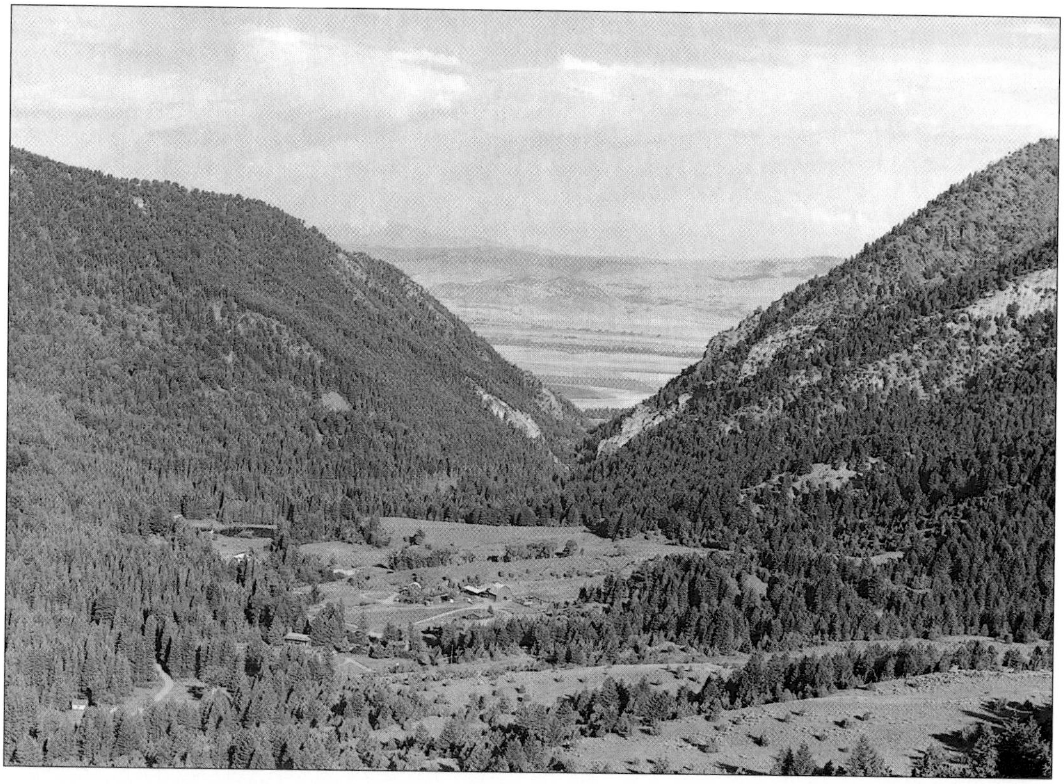

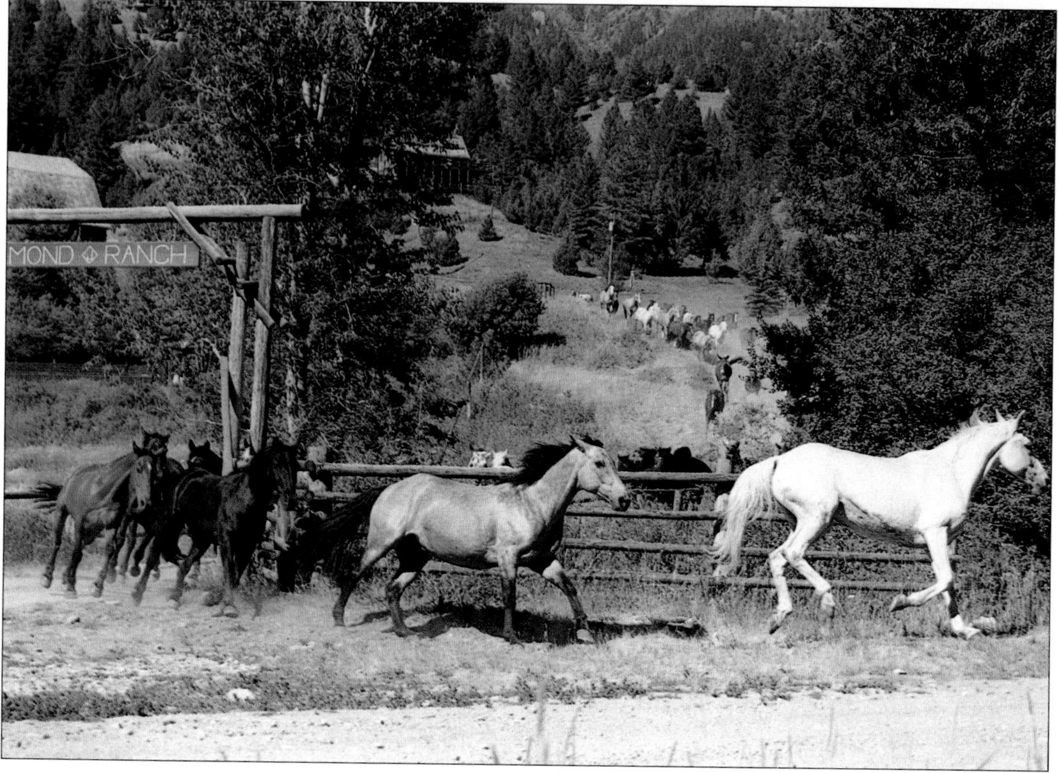

Elk Canyon Ranch, Montana

See ranch description on page 136

See ranch description on page 138

Grassy Mountain Ranch, Montana

See ranch description on page 141

Hargrave Cattle and Guest Ranch, Montana

See ranch description on page 142

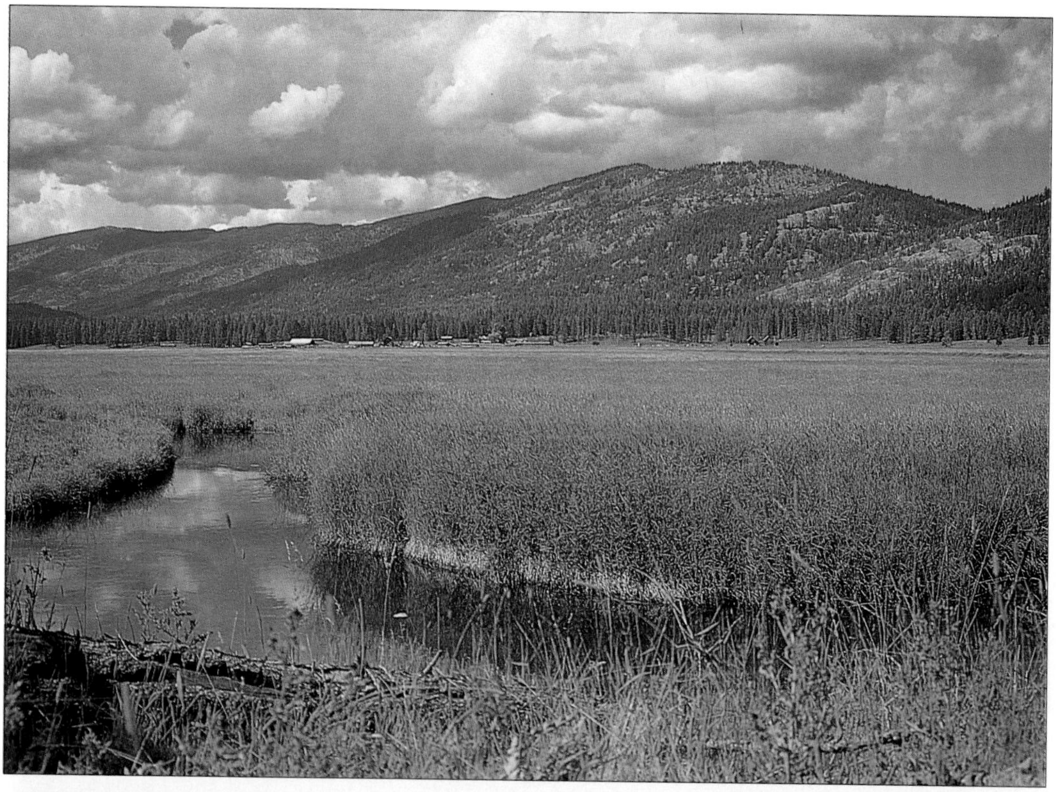

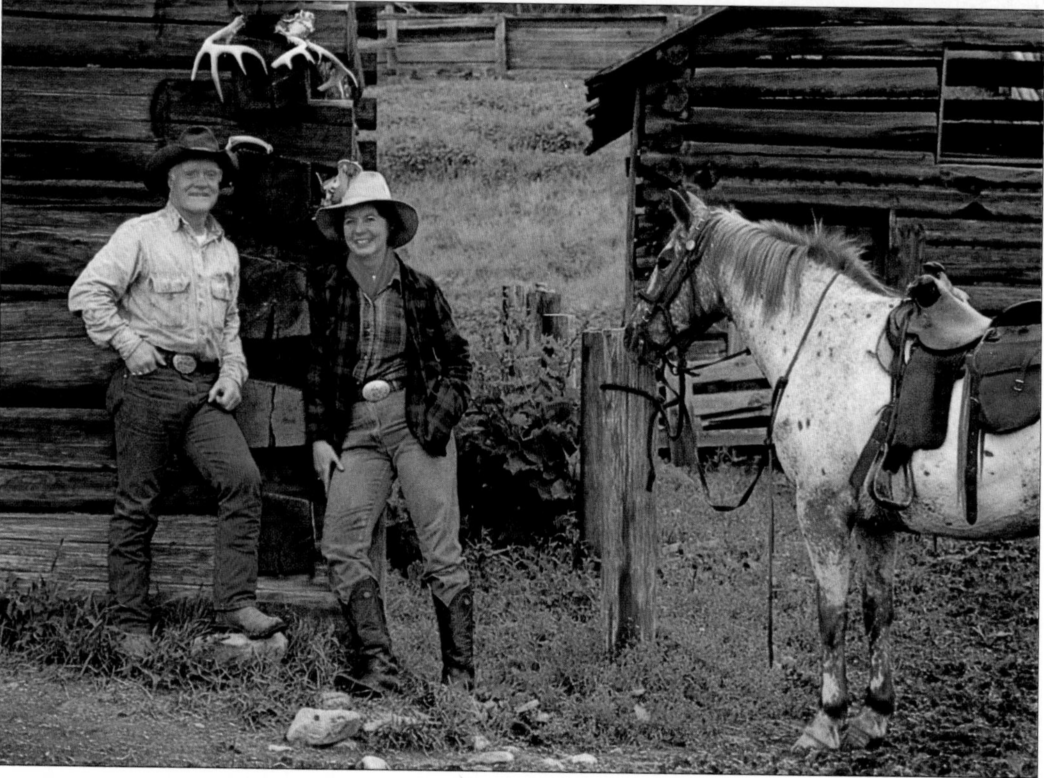

Klicks' K Bar L Ranch, Montana

See ranch description on page 146

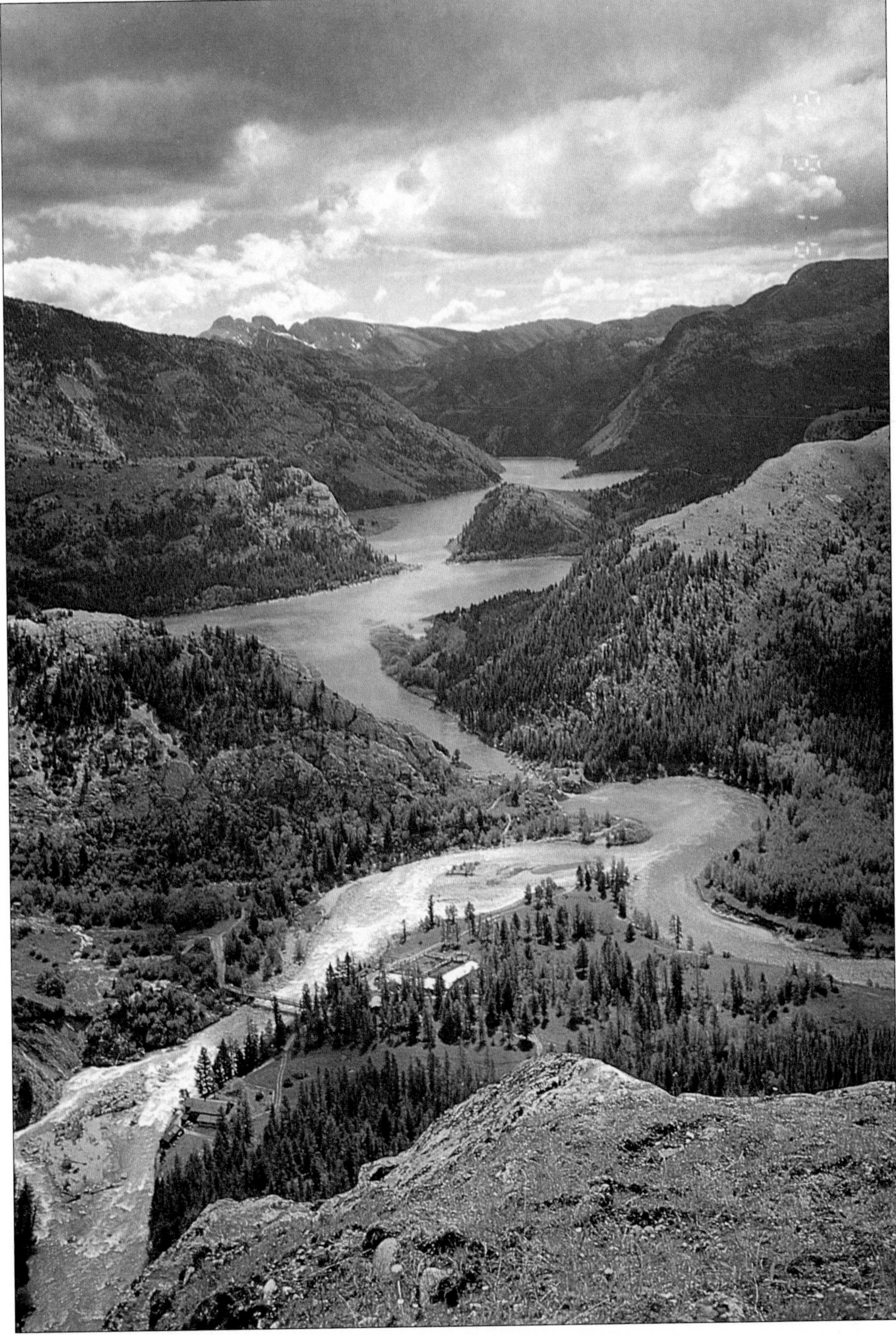

See ranch description on page 146

Lone Mountain Ranch, Montana

See ranch description on page 150

Mountain Sky Guest Ranch, Montana

See ranch description on page 152

Nine Quarter Circle Ranch, Montana

See ranch description on page 155

63 Ranch, Montana

See ranch description on page 158

Seven Lazy P Ranch, Montana

See ranch description on page 160

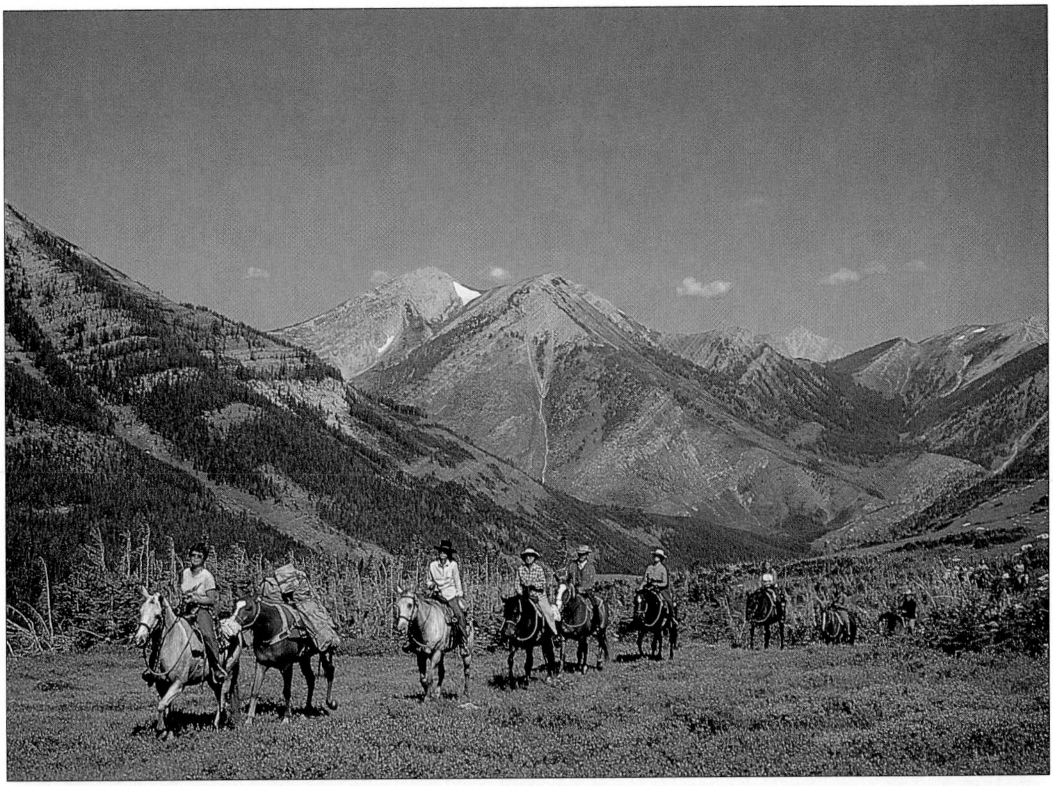

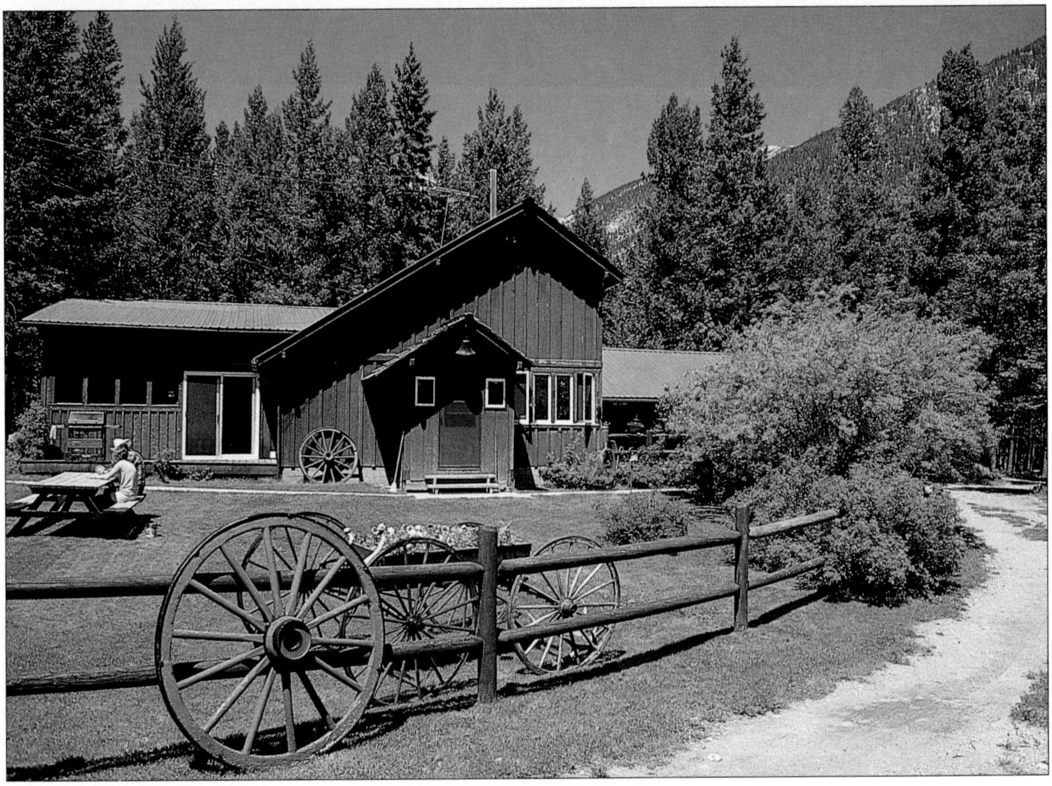

See ranch description on page 162

West Fork Meadows Ranch, Montana

See ranch description on page 163

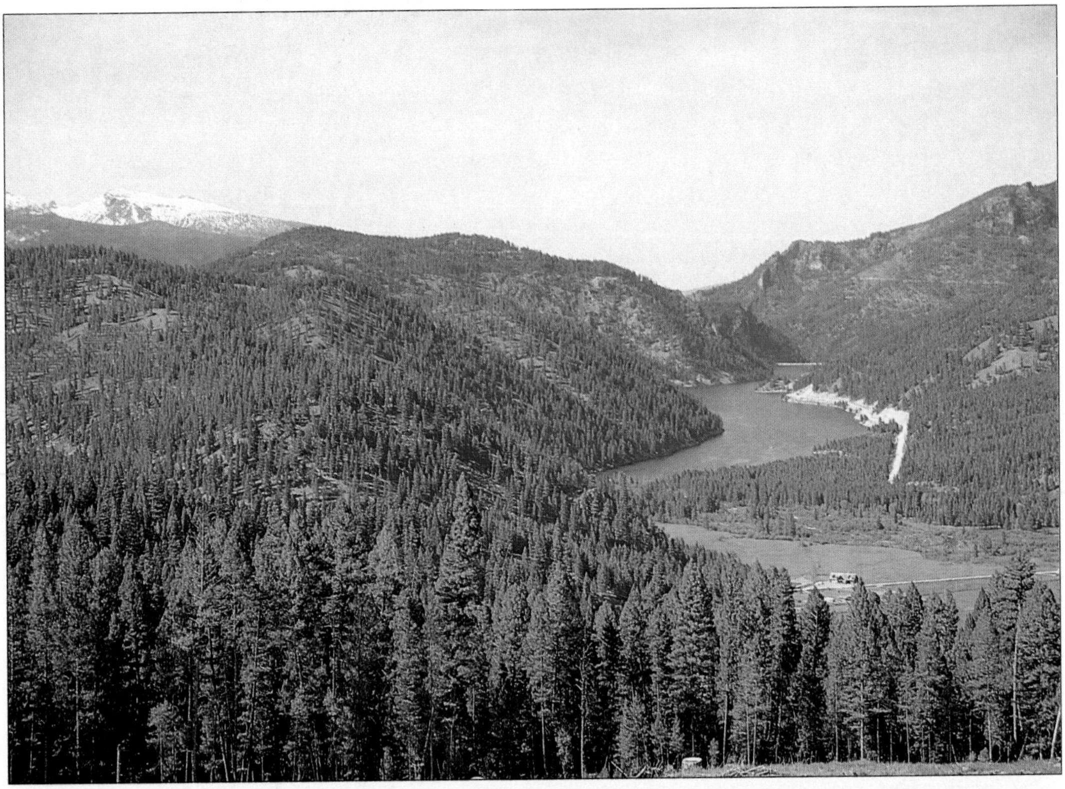

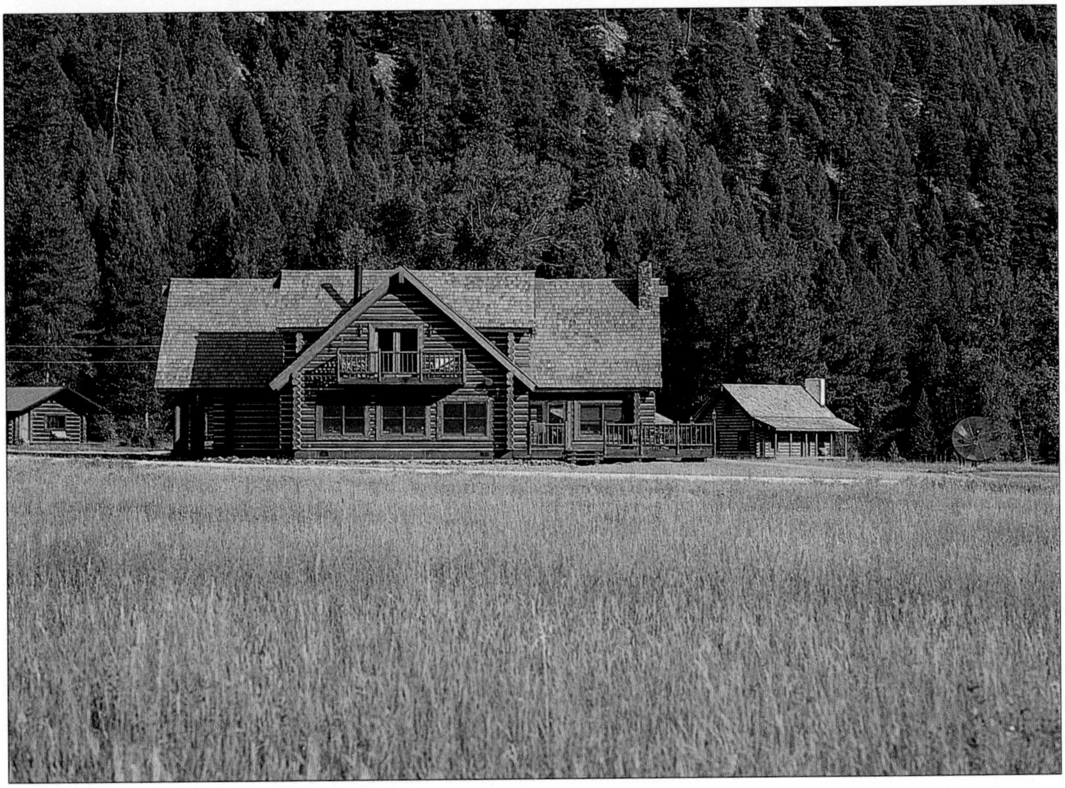

Red's Ranch, Nevada

See ranch description on page 166

The Lodge at Chama, New Mexico

See ranch description on page 174

See ranch description on page 174

Soldier Meadows Ranch, Nevada

See ranch description on page 170

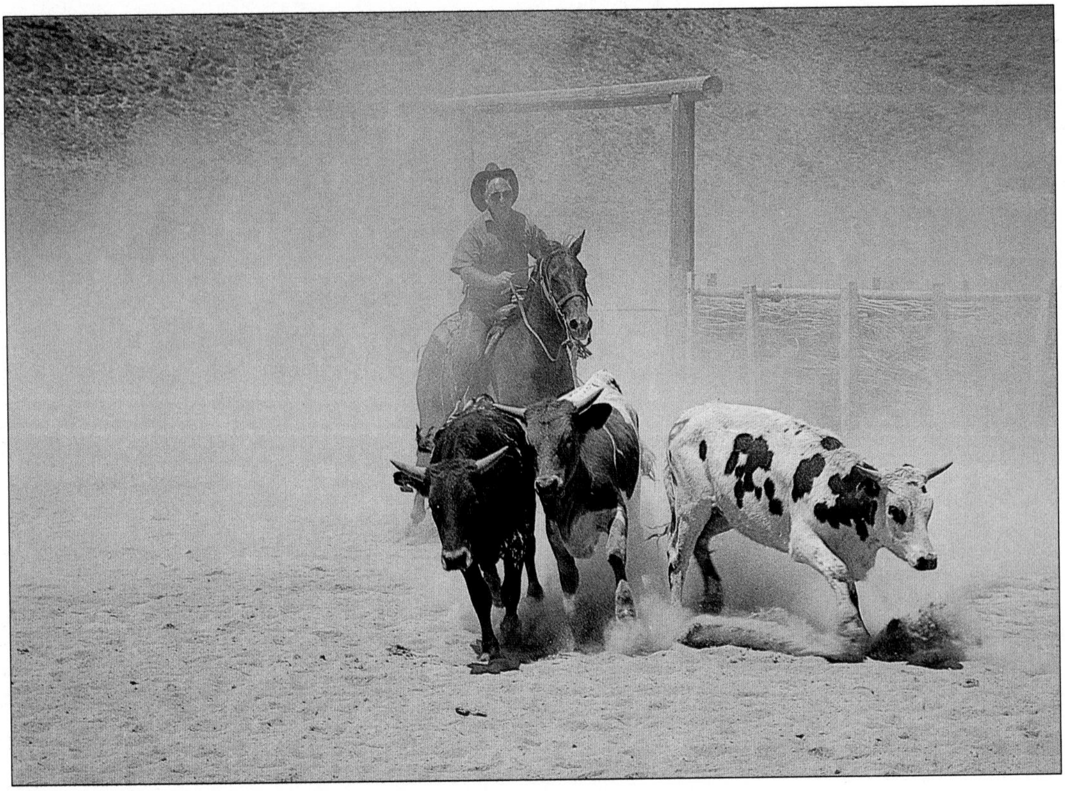

See ranch description on page 176

Rocking Horse Ranch, New York

See ranch description on page 308

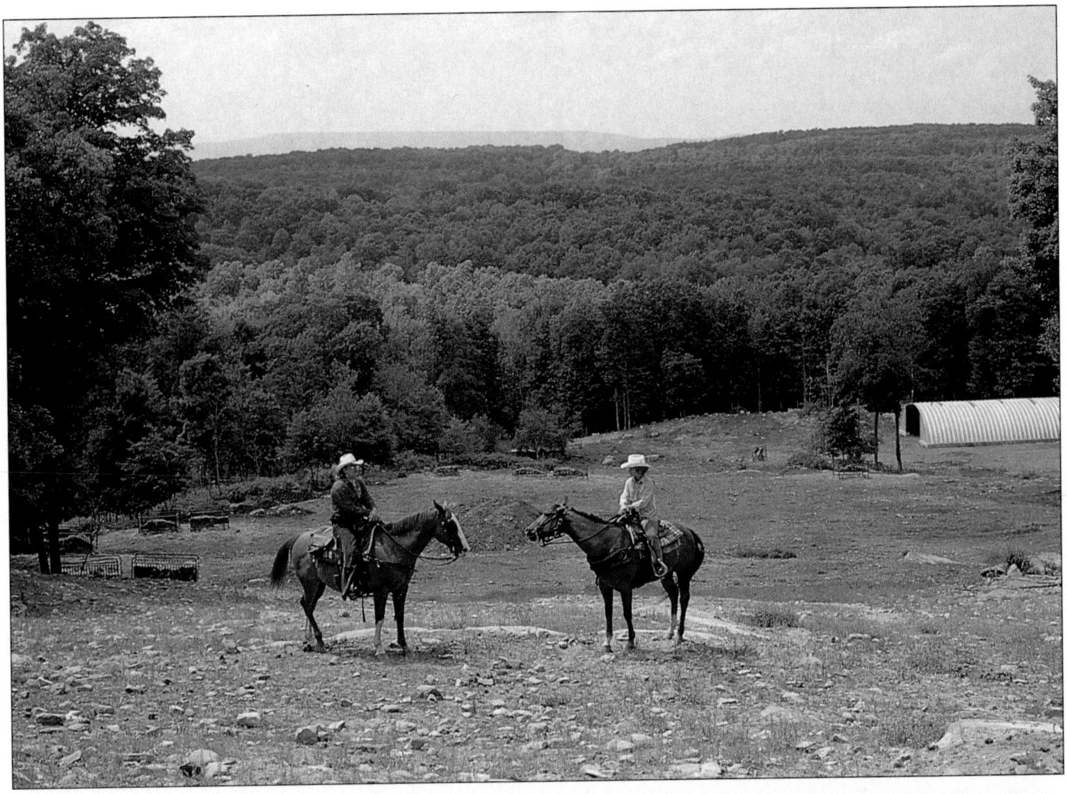

See ranch description on page 310

Ponderosa Cattle Company and Guest Ranch, Oregon

See ranch description on page 319

Ponderosa Cattle Company and Guest Ranch, Oregon

See ranch description on page 319

Rock Springs Guest Ranch, Oregon

See ranch description on page 320

See ranch description on page 320

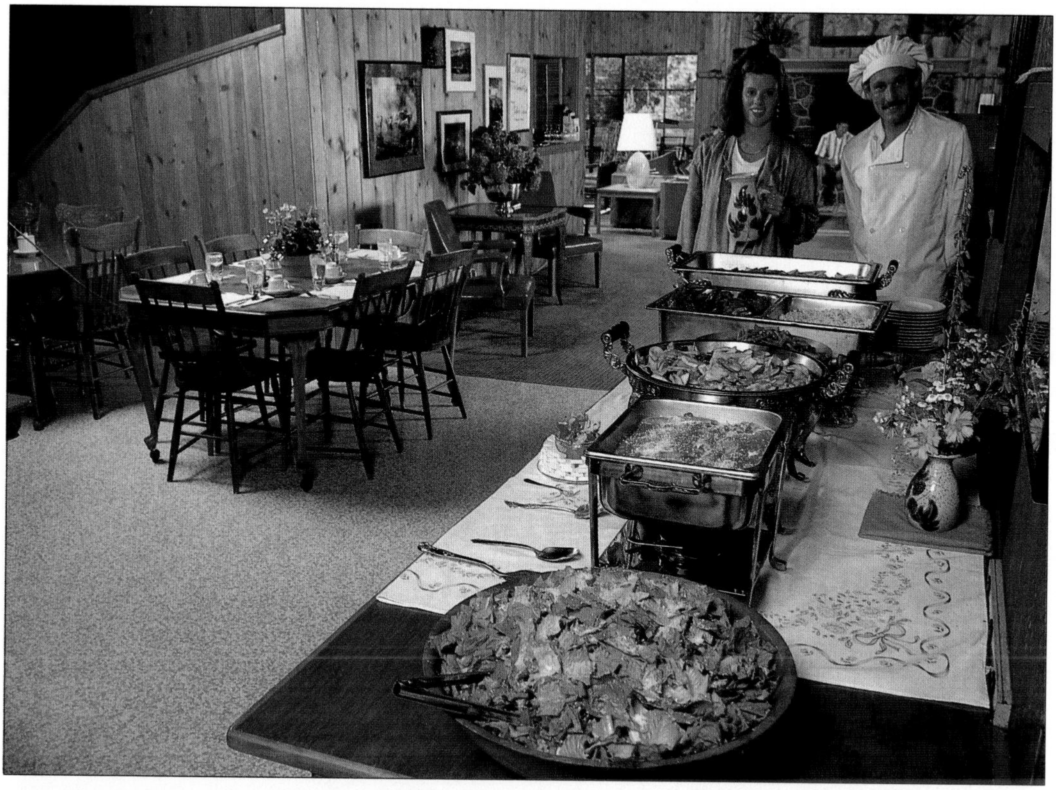

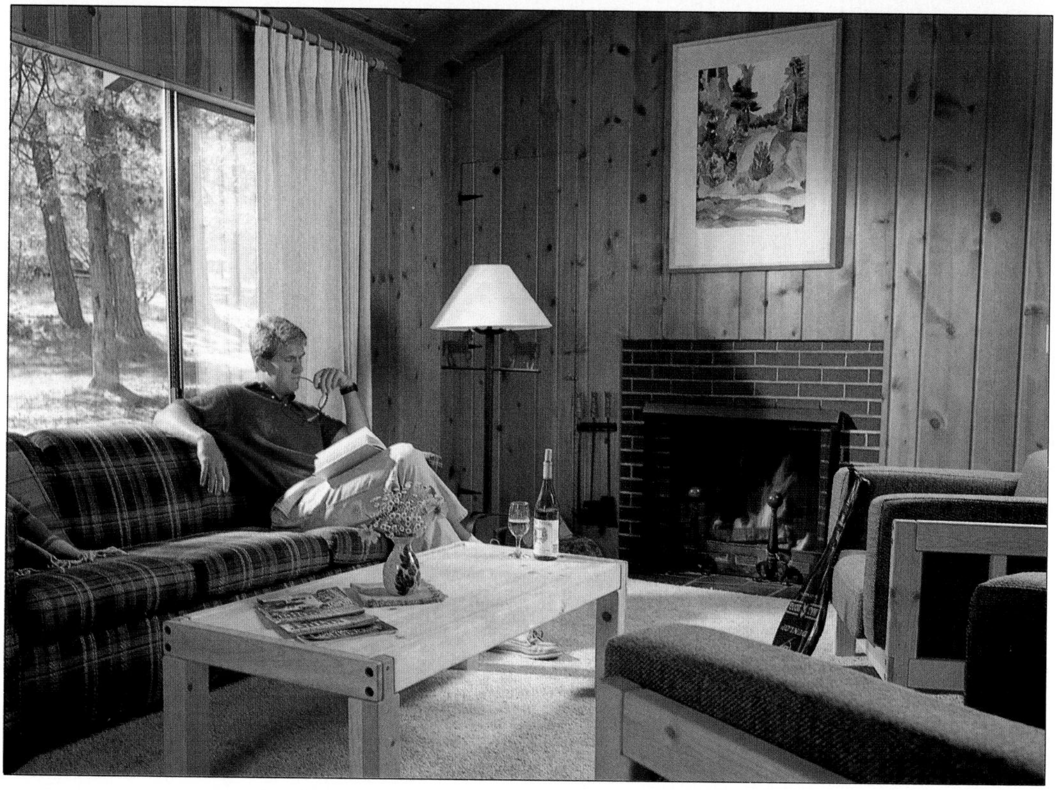

Baker's Bar M Ranch, Oregon

See ranch description on page 316

See ranch description on page 323

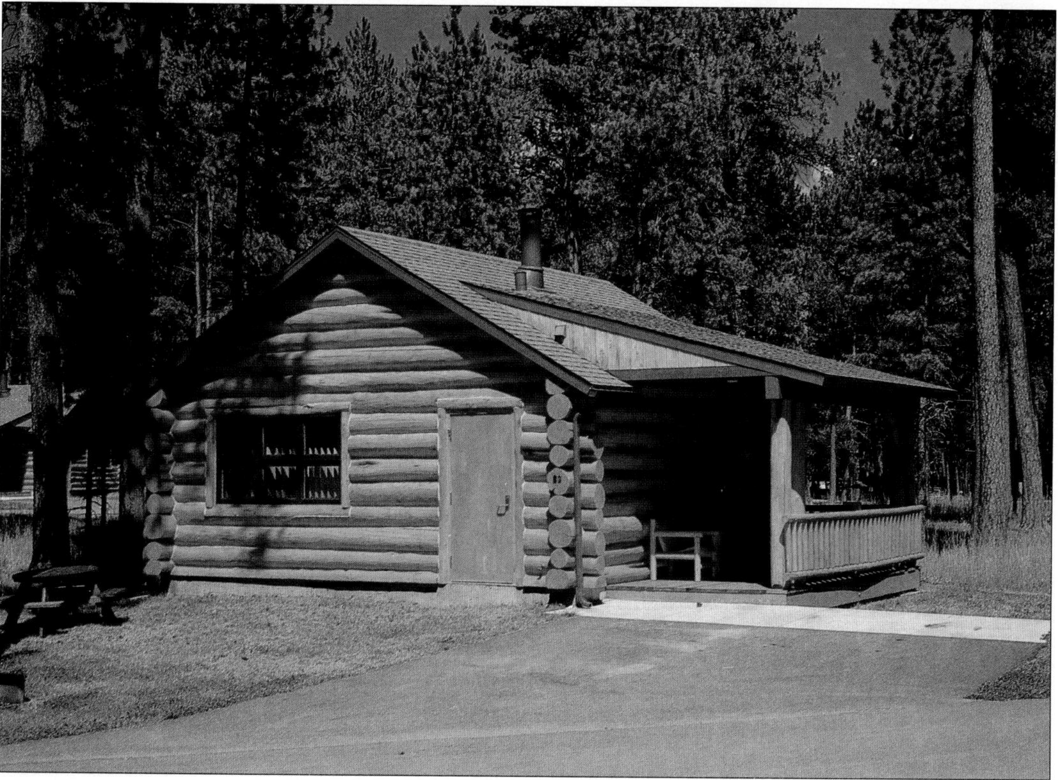

Nemo Guest Ranch, South Dakota

See ranch description on page 324

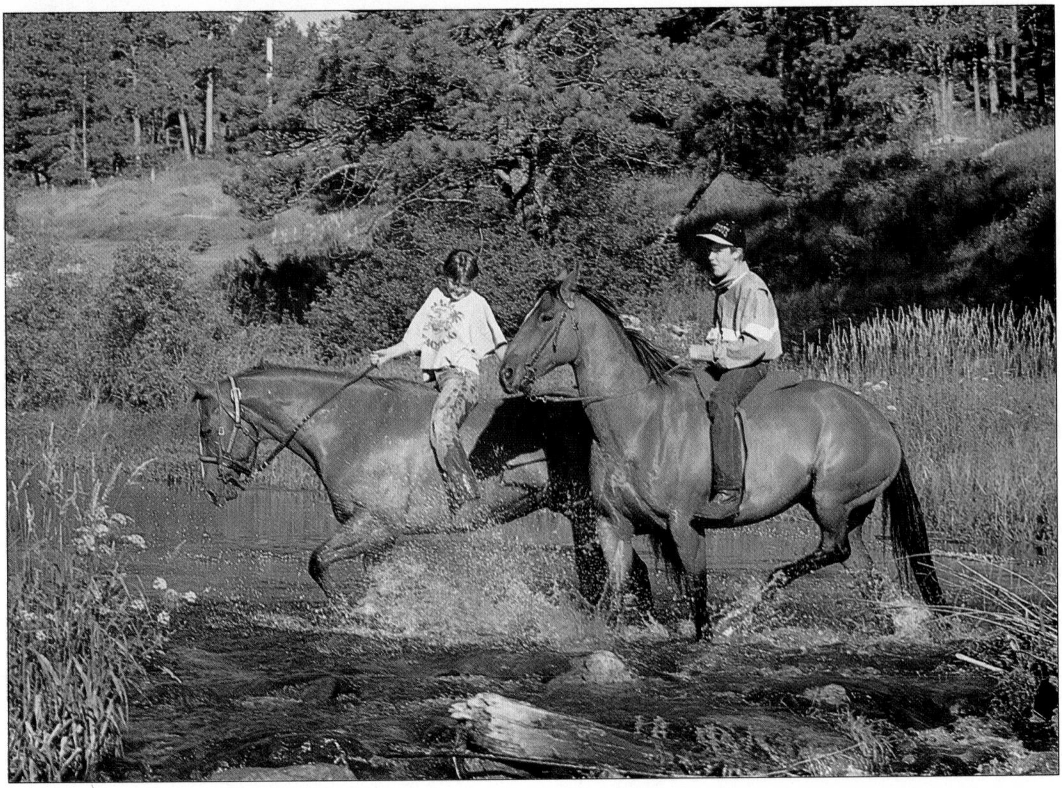

Flying L Guest Ranch, Texas

See ranch description on page 330

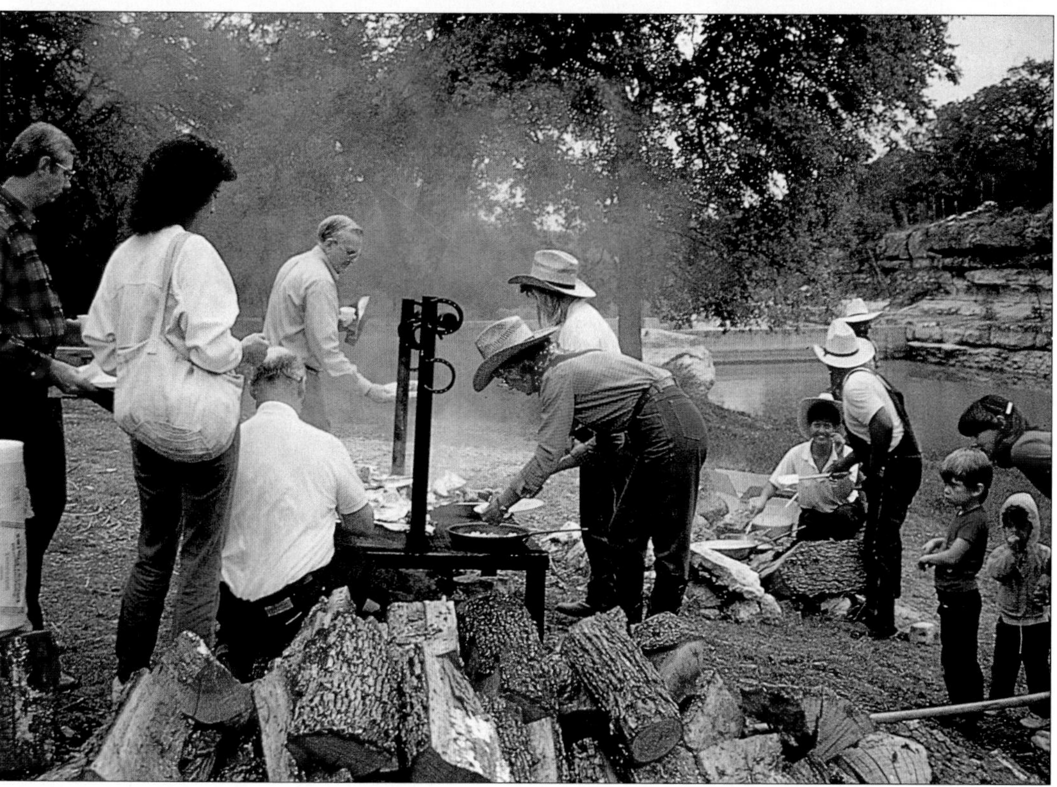

Silver Spur Dude Ranch, Texas

See ranch description on page 335

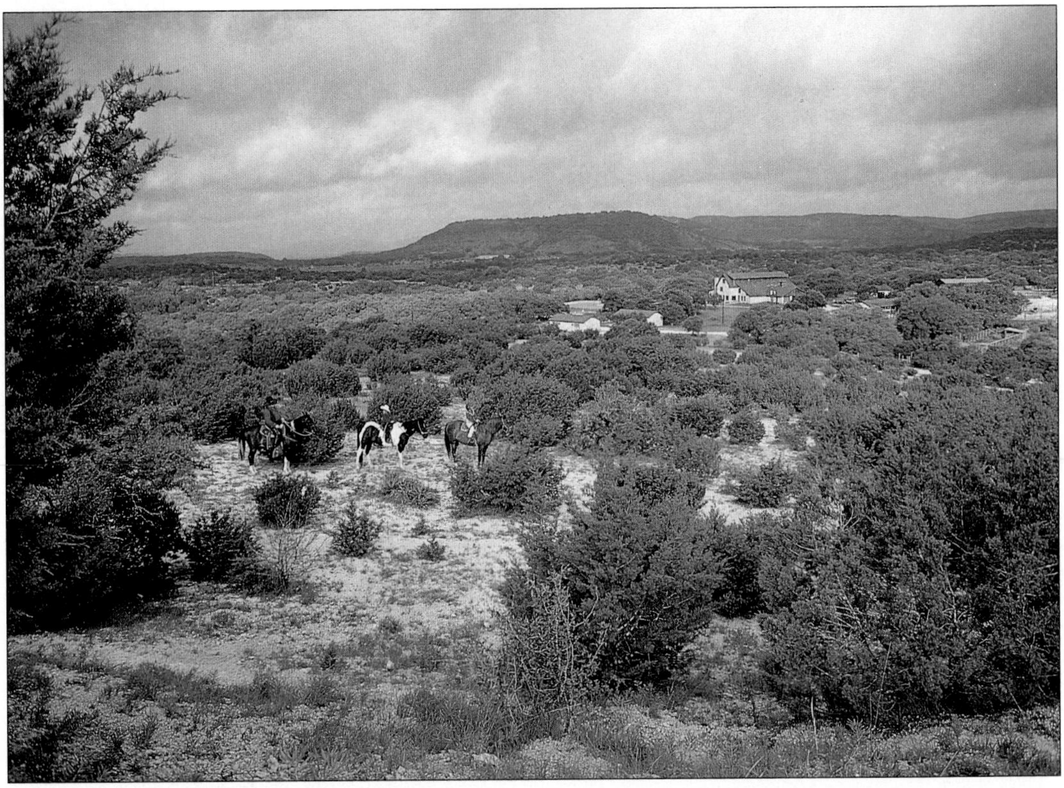

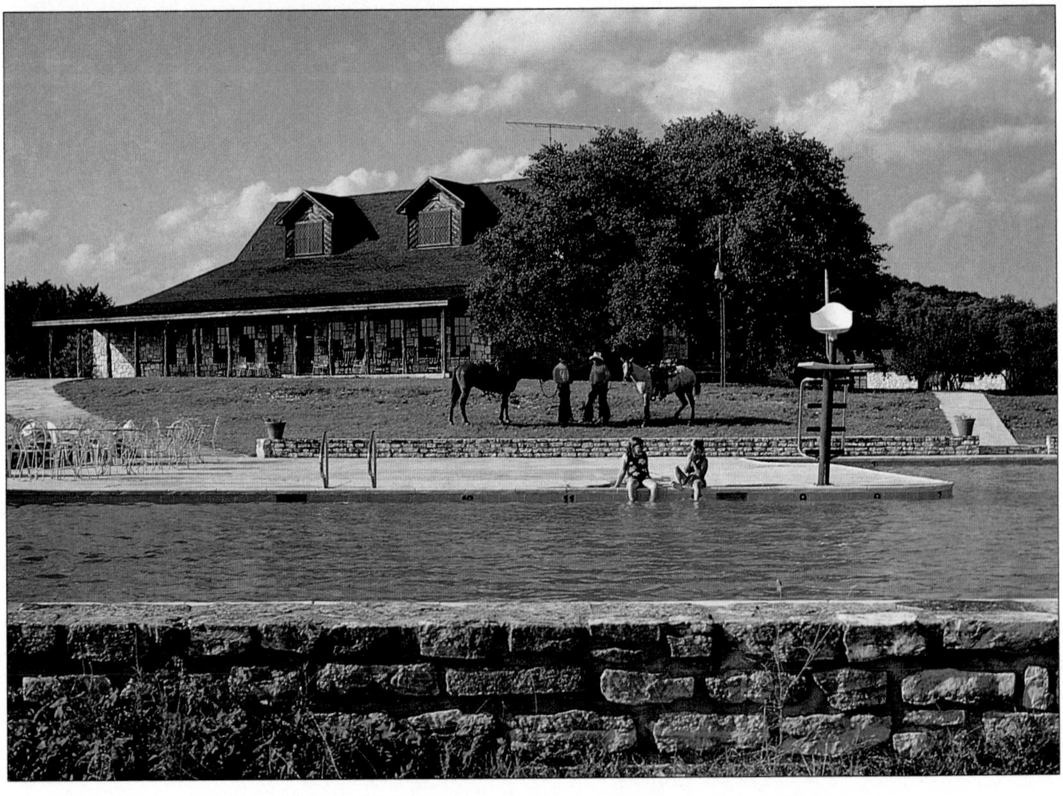

Reid Ranch, Utah

See ranch description on page 342

Hidden Valley Guest Ranch, Washington

See ranch description on page 347

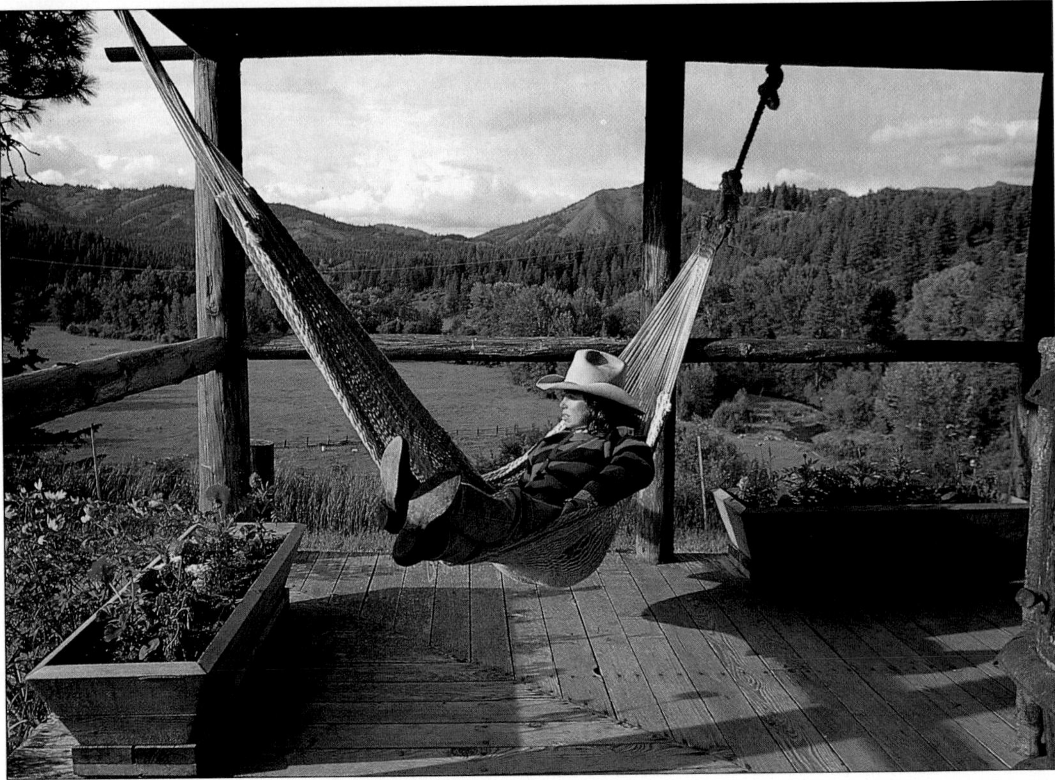

See ranch description on page 351

Brooks Lake Lodge, Wyoming

See ranch description on page 353

Brooks Lake Lodge, Wyoming

See ranch description on page 353

Brush Creek Ranch, Wyoming

See ranch description on page 356

See ranch description on page 356

Bitterroot Ranch, Wyoming

See ranch description on page 352

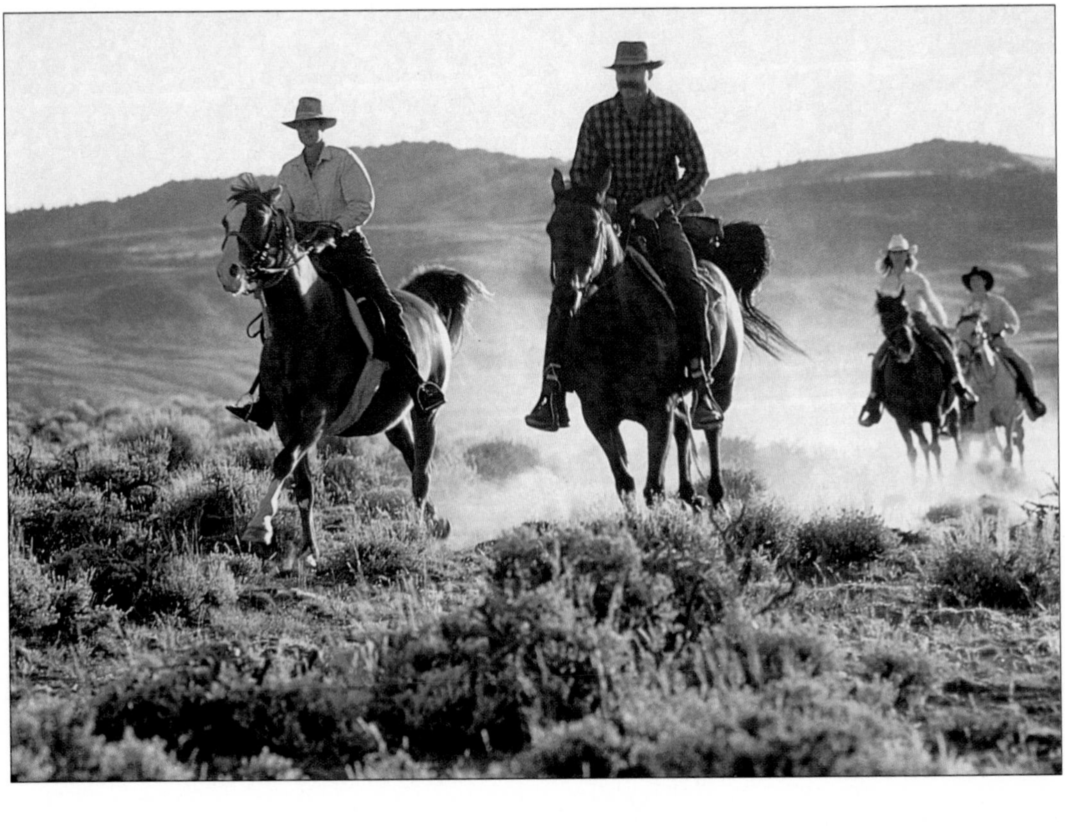

See ranch description on page 360

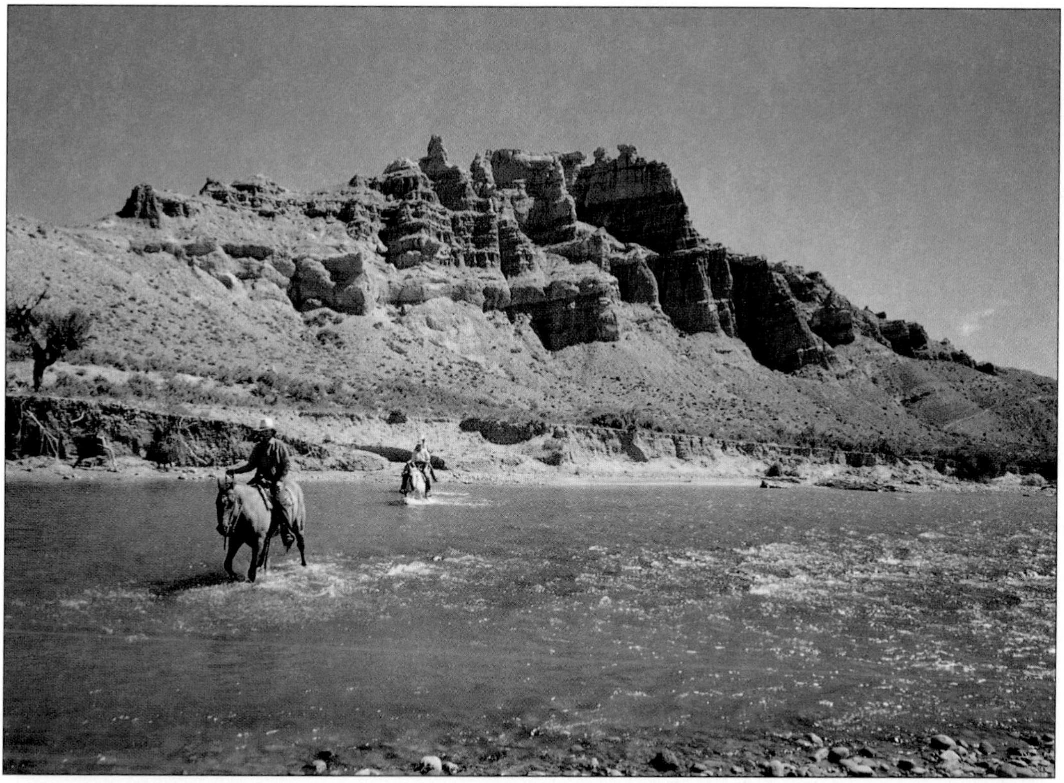

Crescent H Ranch, Wyoming

See ranch description on page 444

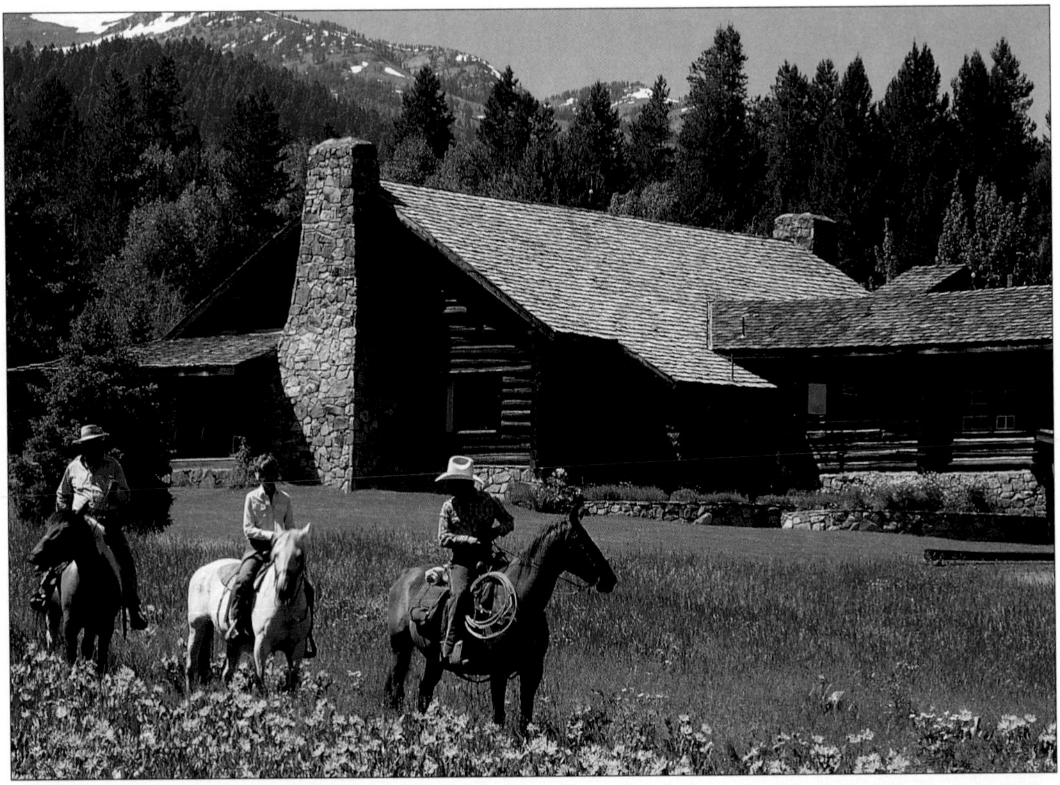

Crescent H Ranch, Wyoming

See ranch description on page 444

Crossed Sabres Ranch, Wyoming

See ranch description on page 362

Darwin Ranch, Wyoming

See ranch description on page 363

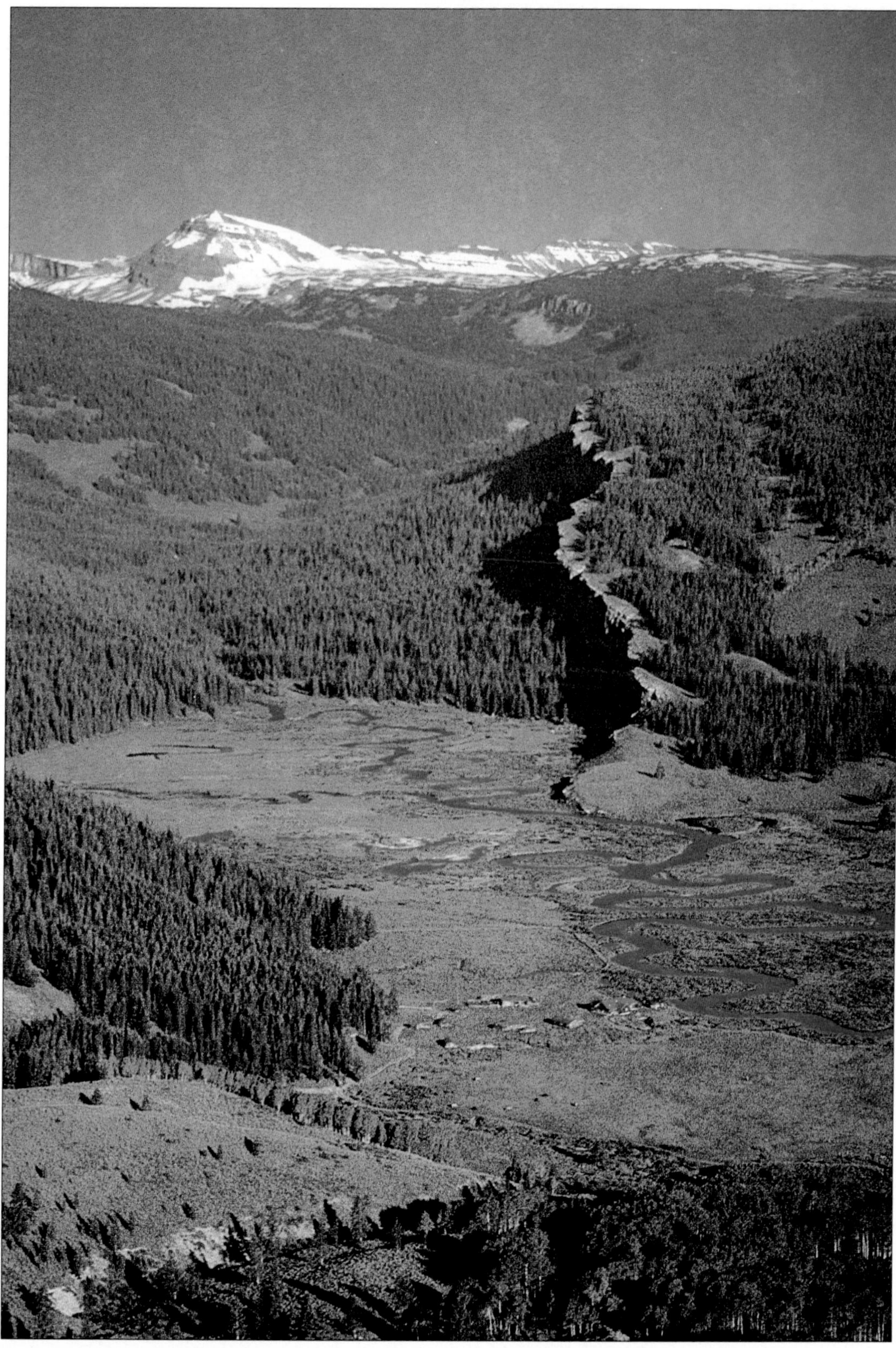

Gros Ventre River Ranch, Wyoming

See ranch description on page 368

Gros Ventre River Ranch, Wyoming

See ranch description on page 368

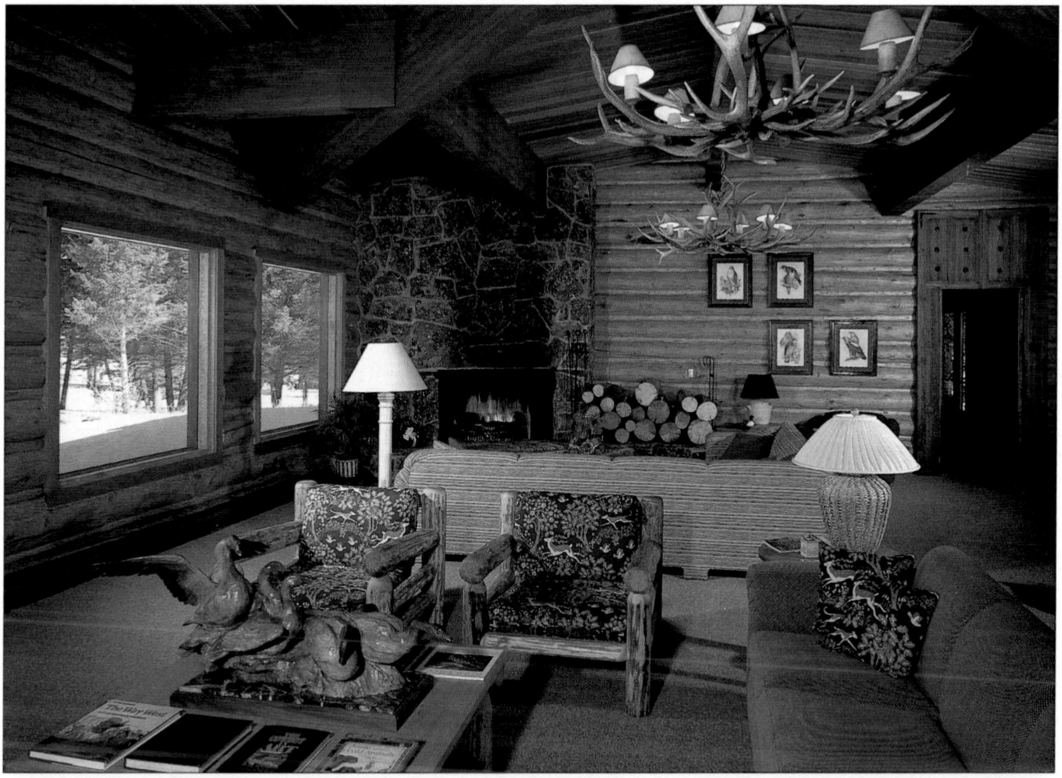

High Island Ranch and Cattle Company, Wyoming

See ranch description on page 372

See ranch description on page 380

Lost Creek Ranch, Wyoming

See ranch description on page 376

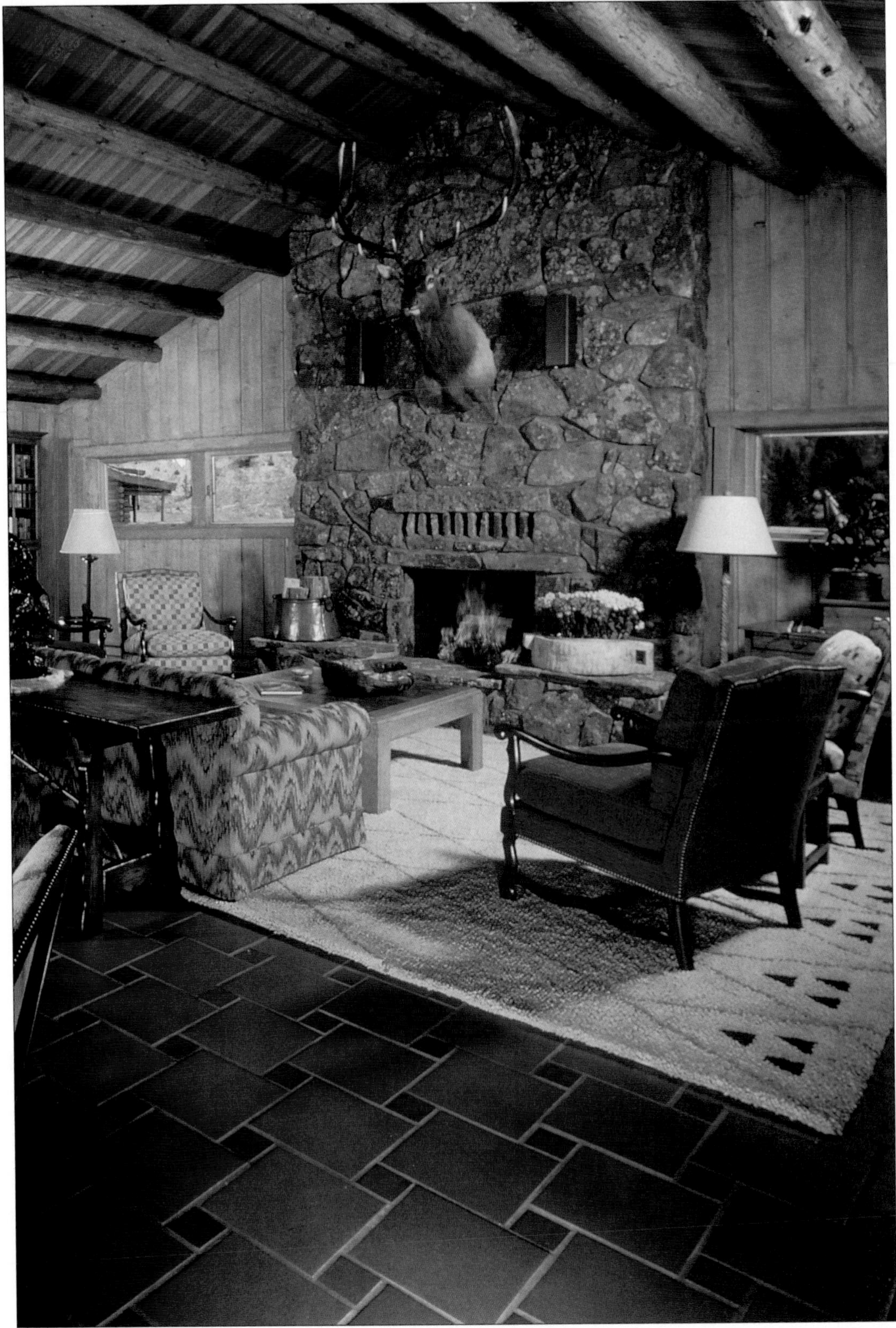

See ranch description on page 376

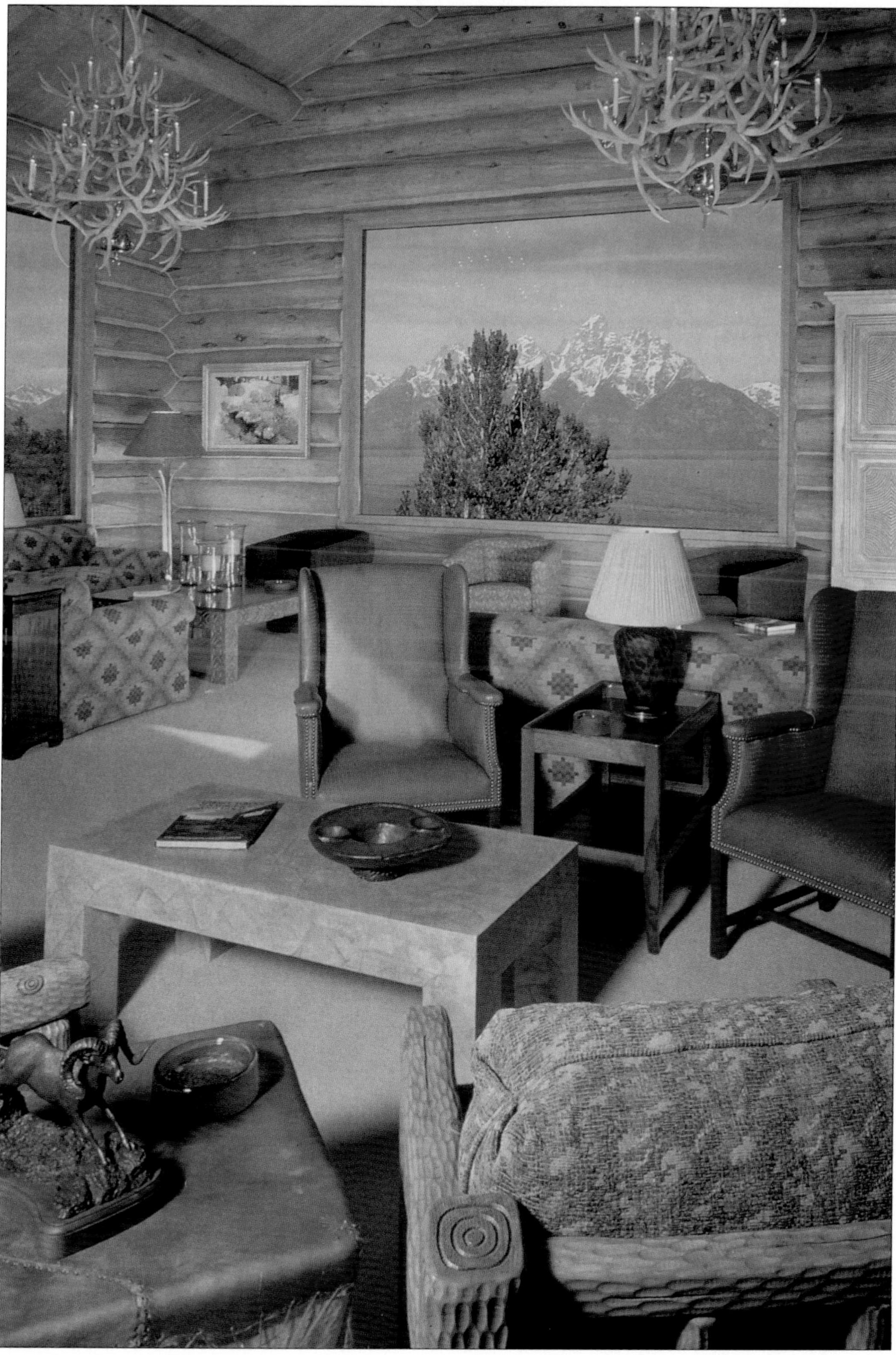

Lazy L & B Ranch, Wyoming

See ranch description on page 374

See ranch description on page 378

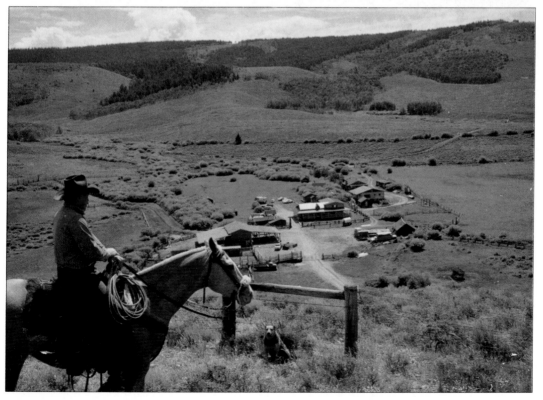

Paradise Guest Ranch, Wyoming

See ranch description on page 382

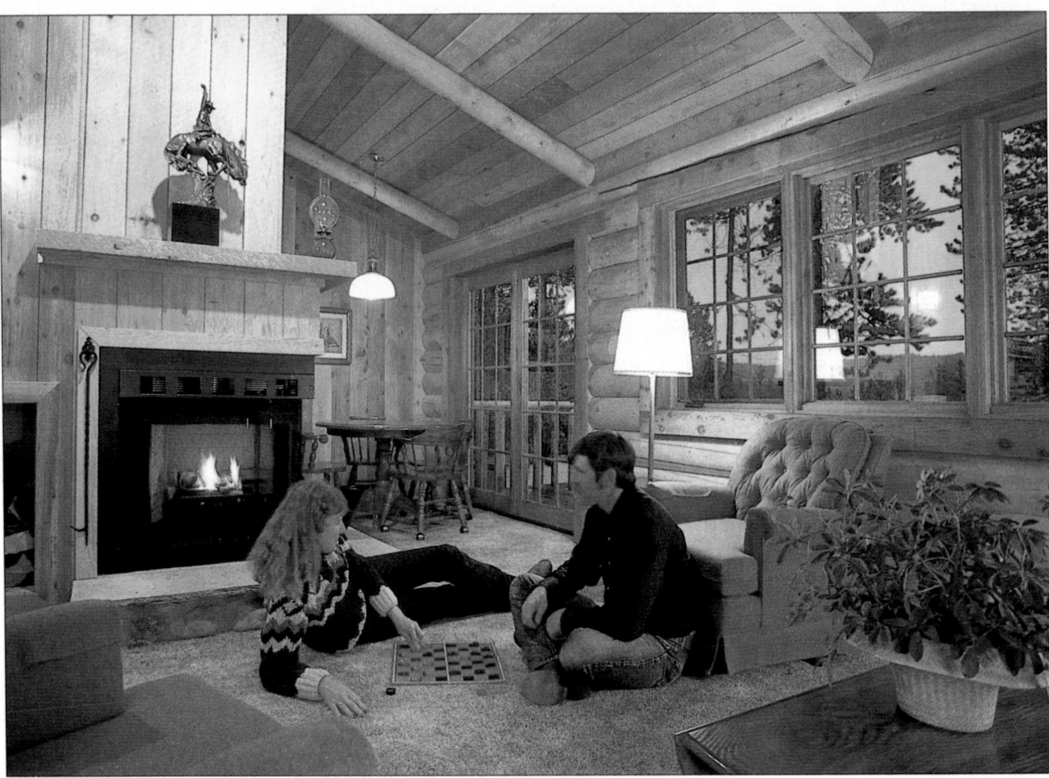

See ranch description on page 382

Red Rock Ranch, Wyoming

See ranch description on page 386

Rimrock Ranch, Wyoming

See ranch description on page 385

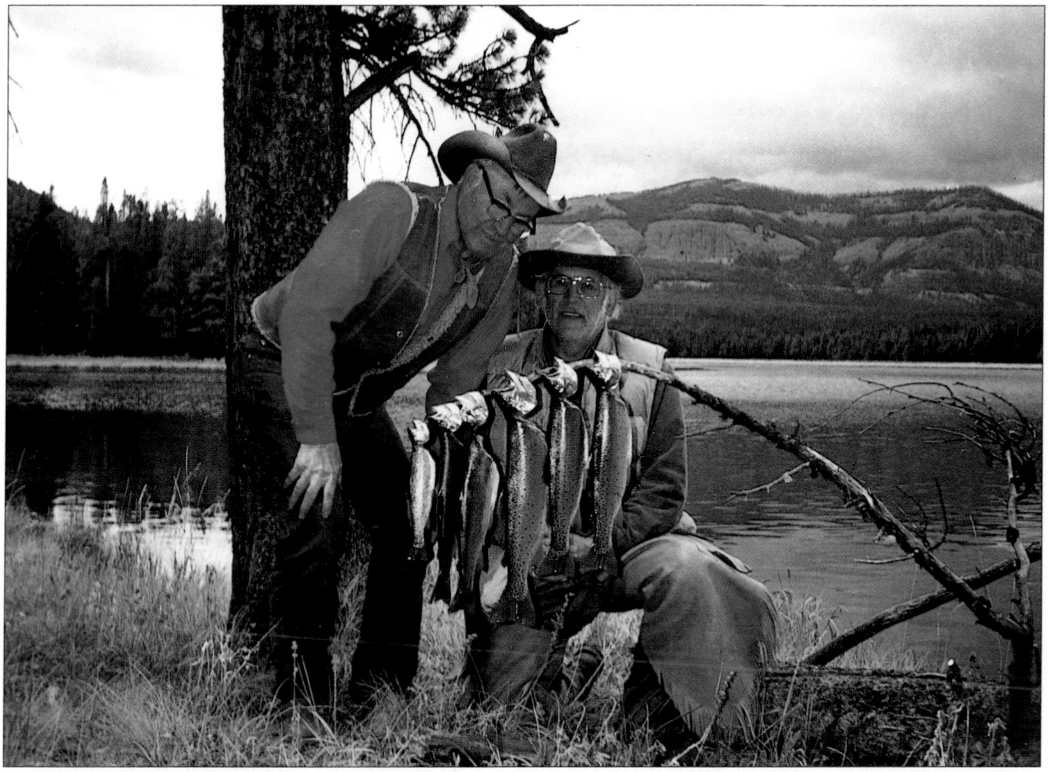

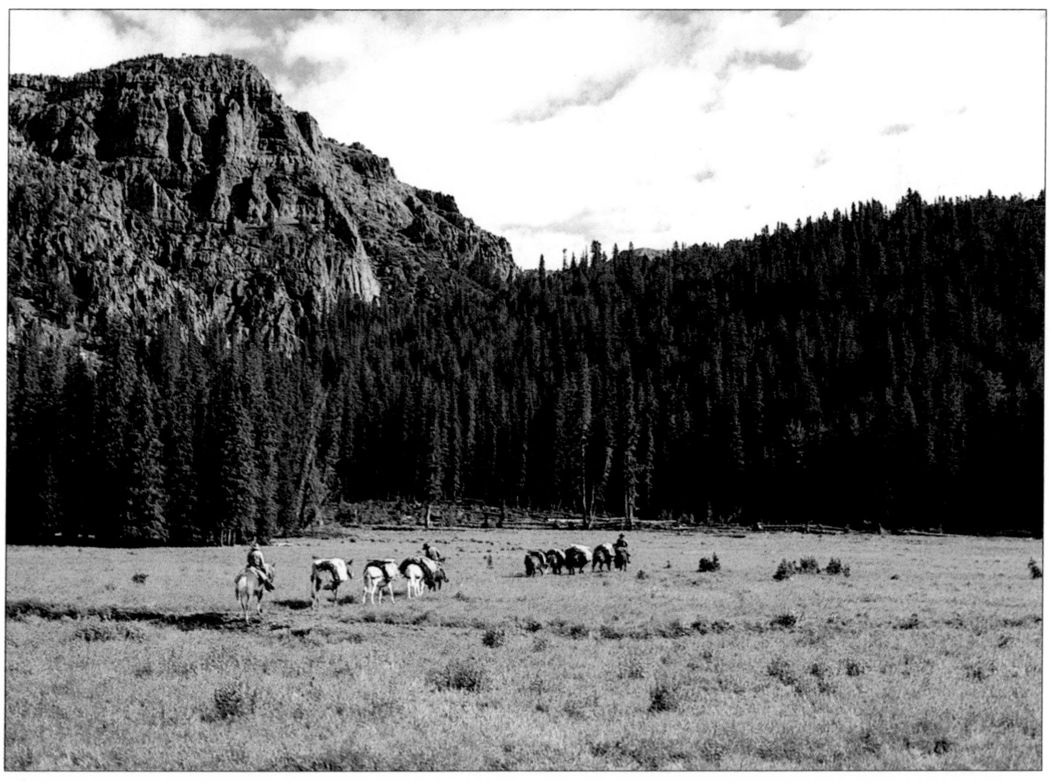

Savery Creek Thoroughbred Ranch, Wyoming

See ranch description on page 389

See ranch description on page 391

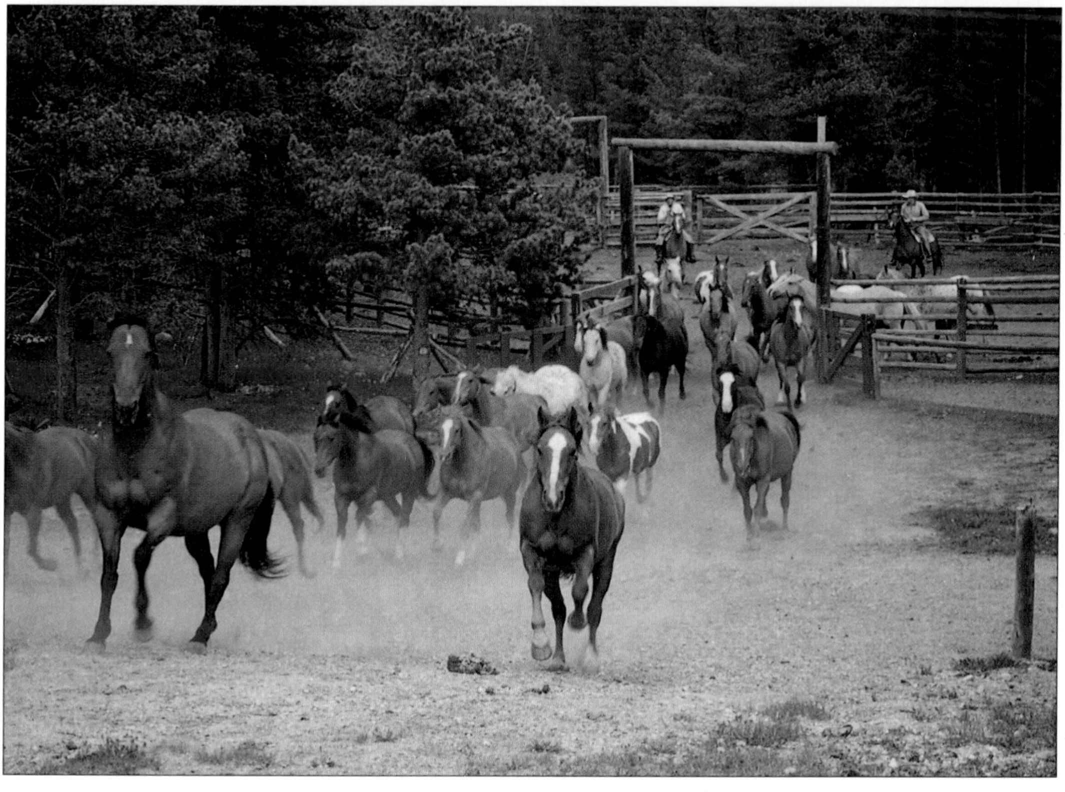

T-Cross Ranch, Wyoming

See ranch description on page 394

Trail Creek Ranch, Wyoming

See ranch description on page 396

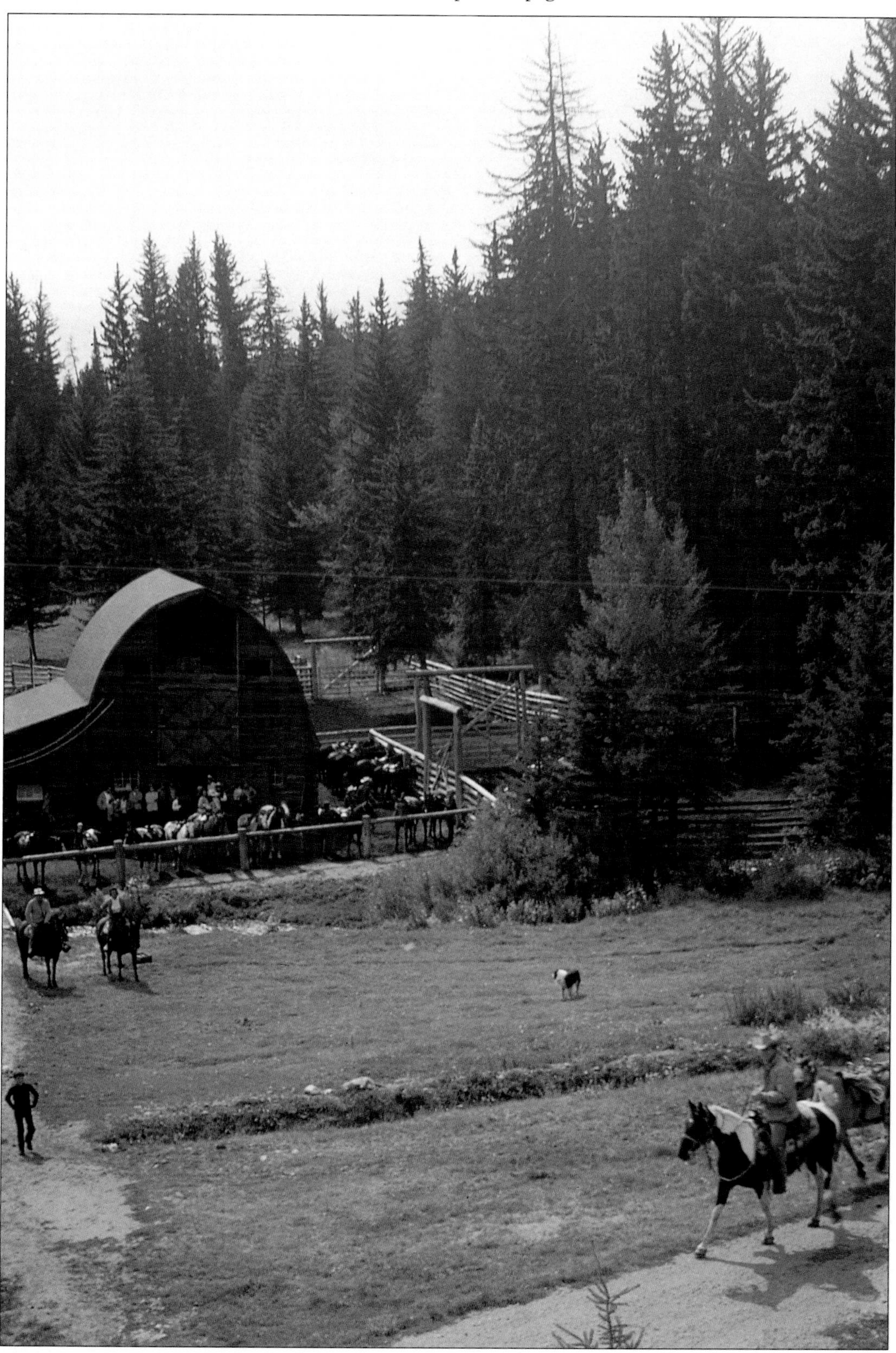

V-Bar Guest Ranch, Wyoming

See ranch description on page 398

V-Bar Guest Ranch, Wyoming

See ranch description on page 398

Rafter Six Ranch Resort, Alberta, Canada

See ranch description on page 405

TL Bar Ranch, Alberta, Canada

See ranch description on page 404

Flying U Ranch, British Columbia, Canada

See ranch description on page 413

See ranch description on page 416

Top of the World Guest Ranch, British Columbia, Canada

See ranch description on page 417

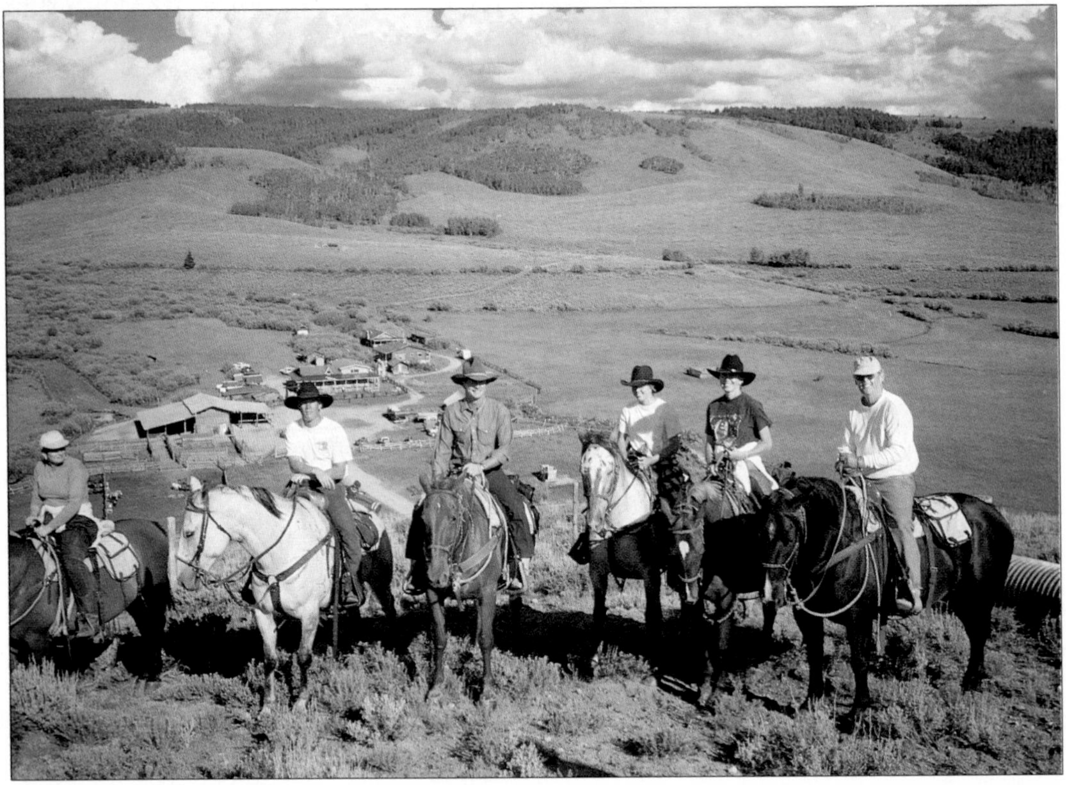

Roaring Brook Ranch and Tennis Resort
Lake George, New York

Roaring Brook Ranch and Tennis Resort is one of the country's largest destination ranch resorts. Roaring Brook is fortunate in having an ideal location in the township of Lake George in New York's Adirondack Mountains. It has been a ranch for families and vacationers since the turn of the century. This area of the country has historic significance. In fact, when President Thomas Jefferson first saw Lake George, he called it "the queen of the American lakes," suggested by its purity and picturesque setting. The ranch has been under the continuous stewardship of one family since 1946 and is run today by George Greene. This picturesque 500-acre estate specializes in family, group, and corporate activities with accommodations for 300. The high percentage of repeat guests appreciate the all-inclusive vacation package. Although the ranch spirit prevails, tennis and poolside relaxation appeal to many. Roaring Brook has recently added a large conference facility that can seat up to 1,000. The ranch draws most of its guests from metropolitan New York and New England.

Address: P.O. Box K, Lake George, New York 12845
Telephone: (518) 668-5767, (800) 88-BROOK (800-882-7665) only for New York and New England; fax: (518) 668-4019
Airport: Albany, 60 miles
Location: 2 miles south of Lake George, 60 miles north of Albany, 200 miles north of New York City
Memberships: New York State Hotel/Motel Association
Awards: Mobil 3 Star, AAA 3 Diamond
Medical: Glen Falls Hospital, 7 miles
Conference: 300; a total of 17,000 square feet of conference space. Full audiovisual equipment available. On-staff conference coordinator.
Guest Capacity: 300
Accommodations: There are 140 motel-style rooms in nine buildings spread out around the property. All rooms have private baths, wall-to-wall carpeting, heat and air-conditioning, color television, and telephones. Most have deck areas. There are several two-room suites available.
Rates: • $-$$. Modified American Plan. Children's, riding, and conference rates available. Two-day minimum stay.
Credit Cards: Visa, MasterCard
Season: Mid-May to mid-October; conference year-round
Activities: The ranch always recruits Montana wranglers who oversee the riding program. Four scheduled rides go out daily. All rides last about 1½ hours. Groups of 25-30 go out at a time, split into experienced and inexperienced riders. New riders are encouraged, and group instruction is available. There are five tennis courts, two lighted. The ranch tennis pro (who splits his tennis year between Boca Raton, Florida, and the ranch) offers a variety of tennis instruction. Private instruction available. Three swimming pools (both outdoor and indoor), badminton, archery, hiking, volleyball, table tennis, horseshoes, weight room.
Children's Programs: Children's playground and counselor for children ages 4-7 morning and afternoons, summer season only. Every effort is made to work with families, and baby-sitting arrangements can be made.
Dining: Full-service, licensed, dining room, coffee shop; choose from varied menu. Full bar.
Entertainment: Two cocktail lounges with musical entertainment. Table tennis, billiards, movies.
Summary: Full-service destination ranch and tennis resort that appeals to families and couples. Singles will enjoy the ranch as well. All-inclusive packages offered. Nearby: shoreline cruise on Lake George, Fort William Henry, National Museum of Racing, hot air balloon festival, and dinner theater.

Ridin-Hy Ranch Resort
Warrensburg, New York

This is a year-round family resort ranch in the timberlands of Adirondack State Park and along the shores of beautiful spring-fed Sherman Lake. The ranch is owned and operated by Andy and Susan Beadnell and their three sons. Since 1940, when the ranch was started by Susan's father, the property and guest accommodations have grown. Today, the ranch hosts 175 guests who enjoy the privacy of the resort's 800 acres. Most guests come from New York, Connecticut, New Jersey, and Massachusetts. As one happy guest said, "There are not many resorts where you can catch good-sized bass in the morning, trail ride in the afternoon, have a swim before dinner, enjoy an after-dinner drink, and square dance to your heart's content." The lake activities, including fishing, are complemented by a friendly staff and a year-round riding program. Ask the Beadnells about their beautiful fall colors; many love to ride at this time of year.

Address: Box 369K, Sherman Lake, Warrensburg, New York 12885
Telephone: (518) 494-2742; fax: (518) 494-7181
Airport: Albany
Location: 65 miles north of Albany, 15 miles north of Lake George off Route 87
Memberships: New York State Tourism Association
Medical: Glens Falls Hospital, 20 miles
Guest Capacity: 175
Accommodations: Rooms range from budget singles to deluxe private cottages. All are clean and comfortable, heated, with private baths, and not far from the main lodge, beach, and pool. The main lodge has a large stone fireplace that provides a warm and cozy atmosphere. It is situated on the lake with views to the Adirondacks.
Rates: • $. American Plan. Summer riding and nonriding rates. Children's rates according to age. Winter rates and various ranch packages offered. Off-season rates.
Credit Cards: Visa, MasterCard, American Express, Discover. Personal checks accepted.
Season: Year-round, including Thanksgiving and Easter
Activities: Horseback riding for the whole family, with pony rides for the young. Fast, slow, and intermediate mountain trail rides. Rides go out for a minimum of two hours daily. A favorite ranch activity is the weekly guest "rodeo." Riding during the fall colors is breathtaking. Lessons available from experienced wranglers. Fishing for trout, pike, and small- and large-mouth bass. Plenty of water sports on Sherman Lake, including paddleboats and rowboats. Swimming in lake or heated pool, archery, two tennis courts, and whirlpool. Golf nearby. Full winter program including cross-country skiing, sleigh rides, snowshoeing, ice skating, downhill skiing with instruction, snowmobiling, indoor pool, and horseback riding.
Children's Programs: Children's activities director. Organized activities year-round. Baby-sitting available. Under age 7 ride in arena.
Dining: The large country-style dining room looks out over Sherman Lake. Enjoy poolside steak barbecues and weekly smorgasbord dinners featuring ham and turkey roasts. Full weekly menu. Families eat together at assigned tables. Three meals daily from a choice of menus.
Entertainment: Nightly entertainment with social program year-round. The main lodge has a dance floor, cocktail lounge, TV, card tables, and complete game room. Jackpot rodeo at ranch with professional contestants, mid-week mini-rodeo for guests.
Summary: Run by the Beadnell family for families. One-stop, one-price family vacation. Nearby: Lake George, Fort William Henry, Adirondack Museum, Stone Bridge Caves, Gore Mountain gondola.

Rocking Horse Ranch
Highland, New York

Just 90 minutes north of New York City, the Rocking Horse Ranch is one of the largest year-round dude ranches for the entire family. Rocking Horse was started by Bucky and Toolie Turk, two brothers from Manhattan, who bought a small hotel and over the years created their resort ranch, complete with everything from a full riding program, tennis, and swimming in the summer to skiing and sleigh rides in the winter. Since 1958, the Turk family has operated this 500-acre ranch. Most guests come from New York, Pennsylvania, New Jersey, and Connecticut. With no hidden costs, the ranch recognizes that not everyone wants to ride, so there are plenty of options. For those who love western activity, there are square dances, hayrides, horseshoes, bonfires, marshmallow roasts, and lots of riding supervised by professional wranglers. Kids and parents will find a lot to do together and apart, at an affordable price.

Address: Route 44-55, Dept. K, Highland, New York 12528
Telephone: (914) 691-2927, (800) 647-2624; fax: (914) 691-6434
Airport: Stewart Airport in Newburgh, John F. Kennedy, Newark, and La Guardia airports in New York area
Train: Poughkeepsie
Bus: To New Paltz
Location: 75 miles north of New York City
Memberships: New York State Hotel Association
Awards: Mobil 3 Star; *Family Circle:* 1990, 1991 and 1992 readers voted "My Favorite Ranch Resort."
Medical: Vassar and St. Francis hospitals (Poughkeepsie), 6 miles
Conference: 250 in 2,800-square-foot auditorium
Guest Capacity: 400
Accommodations: Twenty motel-style rooms and 100 rooms in main lodge with two wings that sleep up to 6 people each room. All rooms have television, telephone, air-conditioning, carpeting, double and king-size beds, private baths with showers, and daily maid service.
Rates: • $-$$. American Plan and Modified American Plan depending on season. Group rates available. Free children's specials (up to age 16).
Credit Cards: Visa, MasterCard, American Express, Discover
Season: Year-round
Activities: Full-time activity director; over 100 horses give everyone the opportunity for plenty of rides. Riding instruction available. As safety always comes first, guests are tested on their riding skills. Guided trail rides are divided into levels of experience. Several rides, lasting one hour, go out daily. Outdoor and indoor heated pools, two professional tennis courts, waterskiing, canoeing, volleyball, basketball, rifle range, archery, softball, paddleboats, fitness program with aerobics every morning. Winter program includes cross-country skiing, downhill skiing, sleigh rides, ice skating, horseback riding, tobogganing. Equipment and instruction provided for all sports. Three swimming pools (one for children only).
Children's Programs: Full program with counselors. Milk and cookies every afternoon. Babysitting available. Day camp for children ages 5 and older. Nursery for others.
Dining: Rotating menus, all you can eat, great salad bar, fresh fruit and dessert assortment. Licensed bar and nightclub.
Entertainment: Dances every night, band and disco, magic-comedy stage shows, square dancing, great talent shows, movies on big screen television, backgammon, cards, karaoke, social directors.
Summary: Year-round destination resort ranch. Large ranch with wonderful spirit and service. The Turk family and their staff do a first-rate job. Single parents weekend. Ceramics workshop run by Miriam, a retired teacher who travels to the ranch most weekends from Manhattan. 1990 *Family Circle* winner. Outdoor group barbecues for up to 1,000. Nearby: oldest street in America, Kingston, Roosevelt's Hyde Park Mansion and Library, West Point Military Academy.

See color photos, page 258

The Timberlock
Sabael, New York

As a young boy, Dick Catlin used to spend his summers with his family at Timberlock. Dick went on to graduate from Middlebury College with a degree in biochemistry. Not long after, he became a navy fighter pilot. But it was at Timberlock, way back in his youth, that a seed was planted. So when this beautiful Adirondack retreat on Indian Lake came up for sale, Dick and his young bride, Barbara, didn't think twice. They bought it and have been carrying on the great Timberlock tradition since the mid-1960s and together with son Bruce and daughter-in-law Holly (both naturalists), do a great job. As the Catlins say, "Timberlock is unique among today's small resorts. We are informal, rustic, woodsy, one menu American Plan, unprogrammed, relaxed. We are not a luxury place, and we are not for everyone." They may not be for everyone, but over 70 percent of those who discover Timberlock return. In fact, some return year after year, bringing third and fourth generations. If you are looking for a vacation retreat where the pace is slow, the folks are friendly, and life is the way it used to be, give the Catlins a call. Don't wait too long, though. Timberlock books up months in advance. (Note: The Catlins will not confirm your reservation until they are sure you have read their brochure.)

Address: Indian Lake, Dept. K, Sabael, New York 12864 (summer); RR 1, Box 630 K, Woodstock, Vermont 05091 (winter)
Telephone: (518) 648-5494 (summer), (802) 457-1621 (winter)
Airport: Glens Falls, New York, 50 miles; small planes to Lake Pleasant (Piseco)
Bus: Adirondack Trailways leaves via the Port Authority or connects in Albany
Location: 250 miles north of New York City, 10 miles south of Indian Lake on Route 30. Brochure gives good directions with map.
Medical: Health center with doctor, 10 miles.
Guest Capacity: 65
Accommodations: Cabins with and without baths. The only electricity is in the main kitchen. If you cannot live without your hair dryer, Timberlock is not for you. Gas lamps provide light, and propane provides hot water. Wood stoves heat cabins when necessary. The Catlin's 24-page brochure is excellent and has a map that locates all the cabins.
Rates: • $. American Plan. All-inclusive, except horseback riding and motor boat rentals. Daily, weekly, off-season, group, and senior rates available. Two-day minimum.
Credit Cards: None. Personal checks accepted.
Season: Late June to October
Activities: As Dick says, "Everything on the place is on a take it or leave it basis. There are no preplanned programs other than meals. Do what you want when you want." Sleep, read, cool off in the lake, canoe, sail, ride (English or western) on one of seven horses (except Saturday), water ski, play tennis on clay courts, or enjoy archery or golf on 9-hole courses 10 miles away. Many enjoy the nature walks and birding. Several naturalist guided hiking and canoeing trips offered each week. Be sure to ask Dick about his fully staffed woodshop where you can make your own paddle.
Children's Programs: Bring your own high school sitter if you want your children to be completely looked after. Ask about the adventure camp for ages 11 to 15.
Dining: Family-style. Eat under the covered porch overlooking the lake. Sunday noon special, full turkey dinner. BYOB, in cabins only.
Entertainment: The Catlins attract a wide variety of guests with varied intellectual backgrounds. Evening discussions and music make for rich artistic and educational environment.
Summary: The wonderful Catlin family. Timberlock is a rustic lakeside paradise. The 24-page brochure tells you everything you could possibly want to know. Ask about special foliage weekends, Elderhostel, ladies-only hiking trips, fall inn-to-inn, and naturalist-guided canoe trips.

Cataloochee Ranch
Maggie Valley, North Carolina

In 1939, Tom Alexander, a young forester, began the tradition and spirit of Cataloochee Ranch. A mile high in the Great Smoky Mountains of western North Carolina, Cataloochee (Cherokee for "wave upon wave") is a 1,000-acre spread bordered by half a million acres of the Great Smoky Mountains National Park. For half a century, the Alexander family has been sharing their Southern warmth and hospitality. This southern ranch looks out over the rolling hills of Maggie Valley, providing guests with a ringside seat for the four seasons as they unfold. Cataloochee offers an unhurried pace with the Smoky and Blue Ridge mountains as a wonderful backdrop. Today your hosts are Alice and Tom Aumen and their sister, Judy Coker. For those who would rather not ride, the ranch is in the middle of western North Carolina's year-round recreational playground. In less than a day's drive, you can see everything from clogging to Appalachian folk art.

Address: Route 1, Box 500 K, Maggie Valley, North Carolina 28751
Telephone: (704) 926-9249, (800) 868-1401; fax: (704) 926-0737
Airport: Asheville
Location: 35 miles west of Asheville, 150 miles northwest of Charlotte off Interstate 40 and U.S. 19, 185 miles north of Atlanta
Memberships: American Forestry Association, Southeast Tourism Society, North Carolina Travel Council, Smoky Mountain Hosts
Awards: Mobil 3 Star
Medical: Waynesville Hospital, 10 miles
Conference: 50
Guest Capacity: 65
Accommodations: Open fireplaces, handmade quilts, and antiques set the tone for each of the eight cabins, some with kitchenettes. There is no air-conditioning, as the mile-high elevation brings lots of cool mountain air. Guests enjoy electric heaters, midmorning fires, and warm summer days of about 75 degrees. Silverbell Lodge has six units, two of which have full kitchens. The main lodge is the heart of the ranch, with an impressive stone fireplace and chandeliers made from ox yokes. There are a number of rooms on the second floor. Fresh wildflowers are provided in the rooms in the summer.
Rates: • \$-\$\$. Modified American Plan. Horseback riding is extra. Children's and low- and high-season rates available. Group rates by request. Two-night minimum.
Credit Cards: Visa, MasterCard, American Express. Personal checks accepted.
Season: Summer, May through October; winter, late December to March
Activities: Slow, easygoing mountain horseback riding, but experienced riders can trot and lope; half-day and all-day rides, usually with eight to ten guests to a ride. Ask about the Hemphill Bald ride. Riding instruction available. Each spring the ranch offers two week-long backcountry pack trips. Fishing in ranch pond. Croquet, hiking, heated swim-spa, tennis, wagon rides. Float trips and six golf courses nearby. In winter, weather permitting, very casual cross-country skiing; downhill ski area one mile away is the main attraction.
Children's Programs: Not recommended for infants or children under 6.
Dining: Weekly outdoor barbecue, fresh garden vegetables (lettuce, broccoli, cabbage, squash, and spinach), fresh homemade jams and jellies, Richard's ribs, mountain trout, fall harvest game feast, including venison and rabbit. Beer and wine available.
Entertainment: Nearby regional mountain music, clogging, folk/ballad singer. Horse-drawn wagon rides at ranch. Informal evening entertainment.
Summary: Family-oriented ranch with great southern charm. Many professional families and family reunions. Off-season business seminars. Spectacular southeastern scenery, cool climate, hospitality, twice yearly week-long pack trips. Nearby: Cherokee Indian Village, Biltmore House, Mountain Heritage Center, clogging, Blue Ridge Parkway.

See color photos, page 259

Pisgah View Ranch
Candler, North Carolina

Pisgah View Ranch has been in the Davis family since the 1700s. Initially, the ranch was a farm and later became a boarding house for local loggers and the well-known traveling dentist, Dr. Lee Davis. The present ranch really began to take shape in 1940, when Chester Cogburn, a distinguished attorney, found he no longer wished to battle away in court. Instead, he decided to play host to people from around the world. Together with his wife, Ruby Davis Cogburn, he bought out other family members and began today's Pisgah View Ranch. Named appropriately, the ranch is overshadowed by 5,749-foot Pisgah Mountain. Chester definitely had his own style. He began to build cabins each year, designing and building each differently. There is everything from a log cabin to a New England-style white clapboard lodge. When the book on southern hospitality was written, it may well have been drafted at Pisgah View Ranch. Today, Ruby, the ranch's matriarch, her daughter, Phyllis, son, Max, and son-in-law, Sam, welcome their guests, as always, with an outpouring of southern warmth. Folks return year after year and feel like they are coming back home to grandma's house.

Address: Route 1, Box K, Candler, North Carolina 28715
Telephone: (704) 667-9100
Airport: Asheville, 45 minutes
Location: 15 miles southwest of Asheville, 100 miles west of Charlotte off NC 151
Memberships: National Forest Recreation Association
Medical: Memorial Mission Hospital, 15 miles
Conference: 110
Guest Capacity: 110
Accommodations: There are twenty-three cottages that range in style from log cabin and A-frame to several duplexes, triplexes, fourplexes, and one eightplex. Most rooms have two double beds and hardwood floors; all have private baths, heat, and air-conditioning. Some have front porches with wooden rockers to pass the time southern-style. Laundry facilities available.
Rates: • $-$$. American Plan. Half-rate for children under age 7. Horseback riding not included.
Credit Cards: None
Season: May to November
Activities: Two thousand acres of hiking and riding trails. Riding caters mostly to beginners and intermediate riders. Rides geared to least experienced riders. Four one-hour rides each day, with fewer than 10 riders going out on a ride. Many guests enjoy sight-seeing throughout the area and driving the Blue Ridge Parkway. Outdoor, heated, L-shaped pool, tennis court, softball games, shuffleboard, horseshoes.
Children's Programs: Children are the responsibility of their parents. Children under age 8 must ride with adults. Baby-sitting can be arranged. Children under 4 do not ride.
Dining: Next to its fine southern hospitality, Pisgah is renowned for its southern cooking. Fresh vegetables come from the garden, including rhubarb, corn, and asparagus. Breakfast includes sawmill gravy and biscuits; light lunches. For dinner, enjoy old favorites like southern fried chicken, country ham, cornbread dressing, homemade rolls, and sweet potato soufflé. For dessert—Grandma's apple cake and famous oatmeal and buttermilk pies. The food is so popular, the restaurant is open to the public. Picnic lunches included. Dieters beware. Ask about the fresh applesauce and fall cider.
Entertainment: Different entertainment every night in the barn loft with weekly square dancing, clogging, country and bluegrass music with local fiddlers, professional magician, men's and women's barbershop choruses, and bingo.
Summary: It's a family affair with lots of great southern meals and hospitality. Some people have been coming for 35 and 40 years. Two ranch gift shops—the Pioneer Museum and the Gift Stall. Nearby: Vanderbilts' Biltmore House (much like Hearst's Castle in California), Blue Ridge Parkway, Sliding Rock, Cherokee Indian Reservation, Mount Mitchell, folk art center, RV campground, Great Smoky Mountains National Park, lots of outlet shopping.

Snowbird Mountain Lodge
Robbinsville, North Carolina

Snowbird caters to two groups—those wanting to relax and look at the mountains and those wanting to hike. Bing Crosby visited here back in the 1940s shortly after it was built and savored the peace and ambience. Designed in harmony with the great hardwood forest that surrounds this 100-acre paradise, Snowbird Mountain Lodge is one of America's great hideaways. A haven for naturalists, bird-watchers, botanists, hikers, fishermen, and those who just want peace and quiet. At an elevation of 2,880 feet, this mountain retreat offers privacy, relaxation, and rustic but elegant comfort. One will find cathedral ceilings, chestnut logs, two huge native stone fireplaces, paneling in butternut and cherry woods, and handmade custom furniture in most rooms. Forty-two guests enjoy the marvelous southern hospitality and intimate informality here. Hosts Eleanor and Jim Burbank go out of their way to share their love of the South and their special mountain hospitality. Jim's background in wildlife management and forestry is shared with guests during his weekly hikes. For an interesting discussion, ask Jim about his red deer and wolf projects. For magnificent scenery, a relaxing way of life, and, most of all, time out from traffic noise, telephones, and the heat of the cities, escape to this marvelous mountain hideaway. You'll enjoy fantastic views and incredible, serene peace and quiet.

Address: 275 Santeetlah Road, Dept. K, Robbinsville, North Carolina 28771
Telephone: (704) 479-3433
Airport: Charlotte, 250 miles east; Knoxville, 75 miles north; Asheville, 100 miles east
Location: 75 miles south of Knoxville, Tennessee
Memberships: National Parks and Conservation Association, Sierra Club, Natural History Association
Awards: Mobil 2 Star, AAA 3 Star
Medical: Andrews Hospital, 25 miles
Guest Capacity: 42
Accommodations: Fifteen guest rooms in the main lodge are paneled in a variety of native woods with custom-made furniture to match bare floors, steam heat, comfortable beds with reading lamps, and mountain air to induce sound sleep. There are also six rooms in two newer separate cottages close to the main lodge. The Wolfe Cottage looks out to Snowbird Mountain. All rooms have private baths. No smoking in buildings.
Rates: $. Full American Plan.
Credit Cards: Visa, MasterCard, Discover. Personal and traveler's checks and cash preferred.
Season: Late April to mid-November
Activities: Hiking and wildflower walks are extremely popular. Families, couples, and singles return year after year just for these. Mountain stream swimming, lake and stream fishing (boats can be rented nearby), shuffleboard, table tennis, horseshoes, billiards, miniature indoor bowling, old-fashioned skittles, cards, library, white water rafting on the Nantahala River, guided wildflower hikes, and horseback riding nearby.
Dining: Wholesome hearty American favorites. French toast, blueberry pancakes, Cornish game hens, rib eye steak, prime rib, BYOB. Lunch and dinner open to public by reservation only.
Entertainment: Sing-alongs, guided nature walks in late April and early May. Jim also occasionally shows slides on their travels and the natural features of the area.
Summary: Snowbird Mountain Lodge is for those who appreciate the beauty of the Southern mountains in a quiet, relaxing atmosphere. Most guests stay an average of two to three days. Secluded hideaway with views to Snowbird Mountains, spring wildflowers, and bird spotting hikes with prominent experts. Hiking week led by director in June. Wildflower and Dulcimer workshops. Nearby: Joyce Kilmer Memorial Forest, logging road in Nantahala Forest, Fontana Dam, Great Smoky Mountains National Park, Cherokee Indian Reservation.

Logging Camp Ranch
Bowman, North Dakota

Logging Camp Ranch was established in 1884 as a horse trading company. Early on, the ranch property, because of its proximity to the Little Missouri River, became the center from which commerce, settlement, and socializing evolved. Timber products were floated down to the ranch—thus the name Logging Camp. Since 1904, the Hanson family has ranched these parts, running cattle over more than 10,000 acres. John Hanson's ancestors, who settled this part of the country, were stockmen and farmers who came from as far away as the Falkland Islands, wanting to experience firsthand North America's Wild West. In 1983, Logging Camp Ranch extended its stewardship and began welcoming paying guests. The ranch offers guests a magnificent glimpse of the multidimensional North Dakota landscape. It also offers an informal eco-naturalist ranch stay for guests who wish to see this part of the country. If you want to experience real cattle ranch life in an unstructured way with personal attention, give John or Jennifer Hanson a call.

Address: HC1 Box 27 K, Bowman, North Dakota 58623
Telephone: (701) 279-5501; (701) 279-5702, bed and breakfast only
Airport: Bismarck, 180 miles
Location: Amidon, 18 miles off Highway 85, 30 miles south of Medora off I-94, 180 miles west of Bismarck
Memberships: Old West Trails Association, National Cattleman's Association
Medical: St. Lukes Hospital in Bowman, 45 miles
Conference: 50; day groups only
Guest Capacity: 30
Accommodations: Guest accommodations are about 2½ miles from the main ranch. Two cabins have electricity and wood-burning stoves but no running water or bathrooms. Two communal lodge/cabins. One sleeps six, and the other sleeps twenty bunk bed-style. Both have full bathroom and full kitchen. All accommodations constructed of native pine. Bed and breakfast stays with John's father available.
Rates: • $. Various ranch and horseback riding packages available. Bed-and-breakfast rates also available. Bow hunters, call about fall hunting rates.
Credit Cards: None. Cash, personal checks, and traveler's checks accepted.
Season: Year-round, including Thanksgiving, Christmas, and Easter
Activities: Most guests come to commune with nature and relax. Many hike, study the geology and biology, and watch an abundance of wildlife, particularly song and game birds and deer. You will be able to see ranch life firsthand and participate in ranch activities depending on the time of the year. Horseback riding is unstructured. You may ride as much or as little as you wish. Usually only six riders at a time. Ask John about his horse problem-solving clinic. Ask about the three- to five-day packages. Fall bow hunting from September to December, trap shooting. The ranch caters to individuals and small groups.
Children's Programs: No special program. Best for kids who love the outdoors and lots of animals. Kids are the responsibility of their parents.
Dining: Cook your own meals in the communal lodge kitchen. With prior arrangements, the Hansons will provide meals.
Entertainment: Environmental/historical and ecological seminars by local authorities, if arranged in advance with the Hansons.
Summary: Logging Camp Ranch is located in a unique part of North Dakota. Your hosts are John and Jennifer Hanson, along with their three young children. Located in the heart of cowboy/ranch country, this 10,000-acre working cattle ranch runs a little over 500 head of cattle. Come here to enjoy the scenery and get a firsthand experience of what ranch life is all about. Cook for yourself, or the Hansons will prepare your meals. Diverse landscapes and ecosystems rich in history. The Hansons have a strong fall bow hunting program. Nearby: Roosevelt National Park, historic HT Ranch, Tepee Buttes, and dinosaur at Marmarth.

Allen Ranch
Bixby, Oklahoma

The Allen Ranch is an 800-acre day and evening ranch open to the public on weekends during June, July, and August. During these months the Allens run a Christian ranch camp during the week. The rest of the season it is open to adults full-time. The Allen Ranch, fifteen miles south of Tulsa, is the creation of Ted and Fern Allen. Together with four grown children, the Allens have built a ranch that is a launching pad for a variety of western experiences. The Allens offer groups, families, and corporations everything from hayrides, public and private rodeos, and breakfast and moonlight horseback rides to Halloween "Trail of Fear" hayrides as well as the Kids' Cowboy Ranch Camp in the summer. The Allens have become famous for their old-fashioned chuck wagon suppers and cowboy music shows. You will experience cowboy meals followed by musical entertainment by the Allen Ranch Wranglers—lots of singing and yodeling of some of your favorite cowboy tunes. The Allen Ranch has lots of western entertainment and fun for all ages. As you drive in, keep an eye out for the longhorn cattle and buffalo, or visit the children's barnyard once inside.

Address: 19600 South Memorial Drive, Drawer K, Bixby, Oklahoma 74008
Telephone: (918) 366-3010; fax: (918) 366-3027
Airport: Tulsa International
Location: 15 miles south of Tulsa on Highway 64 (Memorial Drive)
Medical: St. Francis Hospital in Tulsa, 11 miles
Conference: Indoor seating for 600, outdoor seating for 5,000
Guest Capacity: 60 (30 women/30 men in bunkhouses)
Accommodations: There is a modern one-story bunkhouse facility that accommodates 30 men and 30 women. Full shower and bathroom facilities. Bring your own bedroll and towels—cowboy style. RV hookups and some camping permitted.
Rates: $. Overnight including three meals and two hours of riding. Small and large group rates available. Check with ranch.
Credit Cards: Visa, MasterCard
Season: Year-round (closed Thanksgiving and Christmas and New Year's day). Open New Year's eve for nonalcoholic western party.
Activities: The main attractions are the Saturday "Chuck Wagon Supper and Cowboy Music Show." Hourly horseback riding, breakfast and evening rides can be arranged. Horse-drawn hayride available. Carriage and horse-drawn vehicle. Rentals for weddings, parades, and birthday party packages. Ask about the gospel roundup every other Friday. Memorial Day and Labor Day 3-day cattle drives.
Children's Programs: Birthday party packages for all ages. Boy and Girl Scout outings and campouts. Summer Ranch Camp June, July, and August for ages 8 and up. Kids can spend the week riding horses, swimming, and doing all types of ranch activities.
Dining: Tremendous. Weekend western barbecue feed. As Ted says, "We can feed an army." Steaks, hamburger fries, and hot dog roasts. Be sure to ask the Allens about their famous biscuits. Special meals on request. Absolutely no liquor is served or allowed at the Allen Ranch. This is a Christian-run ranch.
Entertainment: The Allens can arrange just about any kind of western or Indian entertainment. Private and public rodeos, cowboy, gospel, and country bands with dancing. Ask about the ranch games.
Summary: Christian ranch open to the public on weekends for western experience June, July, and August. Open full-time to the public September through May. Ideal for people (families, groups and companies) looking for a day, a week, or just a weekend outing with a western theme. Great for parties, small and large. The Allens will customize a western package to suit you.

Western Hills Guest Ranch
Wagoner, Oklahoma

Western Hills Guest Ranch is a 150-room state resort located in Sequoyah State Park in scenic eastern Oklahoma. Not far from Oklahoma's first frontier post, Fort Gibson, and right on 19,000-acre Fort Gibson Lake, this resort property is in the heart of Oklahoma's vacationland. This modern horseshoe-shaped facility specializes in family vacation fun with an emphasis on the Western heritage so unique to Oklahoma. Western Hills is well known in this part of the country for its comfortable accommodations, good hearty food, complimentary recreation, and Western programming, all at affordable family rates. A bonus is the state park, which offers interpretive naturalist programs, a nature center with resident naturalist, and a one-day "cowboy camp" program right at Western Hills. The property was acquired from a private company in 1955 and has been operated by the state ever since. Western Hills operates with the philosophy of a theme destination, friendly service and fair rates. A strong emphasis is placed on history, conservation, safety, and education with activities oriented to children, families, and convention groups.

Address: Box 509 K, Wagoner, Oklahoma 74477
Telephone: (918) 722-2545 (ranch), (800) 654-8240 (nationwide reservation/information service)
Airport: Tulsa International; 2,800-foot lighted airstrip in the park
Location: 8 miles east of Wagoner, 52 miles east of Tulsa
Memberships: Oklahoma Hotel/Motel Association
Medical: Wagoner Municipal Hospital, 8 miles
Conference: 750
Guest Capacity: 450
Accommodations: Two-story lodge with rooms, cabanas, and suites situated around the huge keyhole-shaped outdoor swimming pool. Poolside and lakefront views are available. All are heat-controlled/air-conditioned rooms, with carpeting, color television and telephones, full bathrooms with amenities, and daily maid service. Cottages complement the main lodge accommodations and feature carpeting and air-conditioning, and some have kitchenettes.
Rates: • $-$$. American and European plans. Group, corporate, and off-season rates available. Children under 18 stay free in same room with parents.
Credit Cards: Visa, MasterCard, American Express, Discover
Season: Year-round, all holidays
Activities: Cowboy day camp featuring full horse program. Full horse care is taught. Riding is also available on an hourly basis with instruction. Stagecoach and covered wagon rides, 18-hole, par-70 golf course, two lighted tennis courts, miniature golf, marina and nature boat tours, hiking and bicycle trails.
Children's Programs: Full summer recreation office. Depending on time of year, there are swimming lessons, nature hikes, nature programs, arts and crafts, story telling, little wranglers' night out (program for children 6-12 that gives parents time off during parts of the day and evening). Baby-sitting available with advance notice.
Dining: Full-service Calico Crossing restaurant. Specialties include pecan pancakes, smoked barbecue meats, brisket of beef and chicken, fried catfish, and grilled steaks. Poolside lunches and cookouts. Ask about the Oklahoma Meal and breakfast hayrides. Liquor and wine available.
Entertainment: Black Jack's saloon with jukebox. Annual Blue Grass Festival in January.
Summary: Full-service resort on Fort Gibson Lake with Western activities and cowboy day camp—best for families and small groups. Nearby: Fort Gibson, Tsa-La-Gi (an accurate reconstruction of a 1600s Cherokee Indian village), Five Civilized Tribes Indian Museum in Muskogee, scenic canoe trips on the Illinois River.

Baker's Bar M Ranch
Adams, Oregon

Since the 1930s, the Baker family has owned and operated the Bar M Ranch. This 2500-acre ranch is in the Blue Mountains of northeastern Oregon on the Umatilla River. Three generations of Bakers live and work this traditional guest ranch with emphasis on good family fun. The main lodge, built in 1864 as a stagecoach stop, is a vital part of the ranch. The notched, weathered logs were hewn while the Civil War raged. An old ledger shows that Teddy Roosevelt stayed here, and you will still find marks of the old stage road. There are five special things that bring guests back year after year—the Baker family, the riding, the excellent food, the geothermal warm springs pool, and the peaceful river setting. The soothing water stays an almost constant 90 degrees. After a long day in the saddle, the pool is heaven. The Bar M is a family operation. When you walk in the front door you may be a stranger, but when you have been there just a day, you feel like a part of the family. Baker's Bar M is one of the best!

Address: Route 1, Box 263 K, Adams, Oregon 97810-9704
Telephone: (503) 566-3381
Airport: Pendleton, Oregon, and Pasco, Washington
Train: Amtrak to Pendleton (many enjoy the scenic ride); ranch will pick you up
Location: 31 miles east of Pendleton
Memberships: Dude Ranchers' Association
Medical: Pendleton, 31 miles
Conference: Up to 45 people off-season only
Guest Capacity: 32
Accommodations: Guests stay in the old homestead with four two-room apartments; the circa 1864 ranch house with eight rooms in period furnishings (bathrooms down the hall); the two-bedroom Brookside cabins; or three-bedroom Lakeside cabins with porches looking to the pine-studded hills. There are queen-size beds in most rooms.
Rates: • $-$$. American Plan. Family and children's rates available. Six-night minimum stay mid-June through August. Arrivals noon Sundays.
Credit Cards: None. Cash or personal checks accepted.
Season: May through September; March, April, May, and September for conferences
Activities: There are no schedules except for mealtimes. The emphasis is on family activities, horseback riding, warm springs pool, and river swimming. Guests are assigned a horse for the week and are invited to saddle and groom it. Usually no more than 10 go out on rides. Two rides daily plus weekly all-day rides and occasional overnight trips to Little Bear Camp. Bareback riding, weekly horseback games, fishing in the Umatilla River on ranch (some gear available), hiking trails, natural 40-by-60-foot warm springs pool.
Children's Programs: There is no separate children's program, as the emphasis is on family activities. However, the ranch does allow them much freedom to play and explore. Children under 6 ride only with parents.
Dining: The food is wonderful! Marvelous meals with Gene's famous raspberries, homemade bread, and ranch-raised beef and pork. Occasional Mexican fare. Always freshly baked cookies. No preservatives. BYOB.
Entertainment: Square dancing, basketball, and volleyball in the log recreation barn. Sing-alongs on the porch and evening swimming.
Summary: One of the great family-owned and operated guest ranches for families, couples, and singles. It just doesn't get any better. Started in 1938 by the late Howard and Bonnie Baker, the ranch tradition is now carried on by their children, grandchildren, and great-grandchildren. Lots of friendly Oregon hospitality and rich in history. Nearby: Pendleton Roundup in mid-September. Spanish spoken.

See color photos, page 264

Flying M Ranch
Yamhill, Oregon

It's not called the Flying M for nothing. In Oregon's beautiful northwest corner in the heart of wine country, the Mitchell family ranch has its own 2,200-foot turf airstrip. Many private pilots and guests savor this grass landing strip, making travel to the ranch so convenient. The center of the ranch is the hand-hewn log lodge built in 1985. The lodge rests at the edge of a meadow where the North Yamhill River and Hanna Creek join under alder and maple trees cloaked with moss. A bar in the lodge was handmade from a six-ton Douglas fir log. Some of the lounge tables surrounding the dance floor are made from cross cuts of myrtle, cedar, walnut, and maple. Hanging from the ceiling of the Sawtooth Room is Mitchell surrey, which came from the early homestead. While most guests come from surrounding counties, the Flying M has had visitors from as far away as South Africa and Australia.

Address: 23029 N.W. Flying M Road, Dept. K, Yamhill, Oregon 97148
Telephone: (503) 662-3222; fax: (503) 662-3202
Airport: Portland International; 2,200-foot turf/gravel airstrip at ranch
Location: 45 miles southwest of Portland off Highway 47
Memberships: Oregon Guides and Packers, Unique Northwest Country Inns, Portland Oregon Visitors Association
Medical: McMinnville Hospital, 15 miles; Life Flight helicopter available
Conference: 150
Guest Capacity: 150
Accommodations: Eight cabins with kitchens, twenty-four rooms in the "bunkhouse" motel, and four rooms in the line shack. These rooms vary considerably; some have queen-size beds and are painted brown and orange; all have full baths and electric heat. The cabins have wood-burning stoves. The tiny honeymoon cabin is wonderful with fireplace, queen-size bed, two-person indoor bath/whirlpool, television, carpeting, and a wonderful private deck overlooking the North Yamhill River. Ask about the overnight to weekly camping facilities. Many guests bring their own horses and camp. If this is of interest to you, ask about Big, Little, and Old Horse camps.
Rates: • $-$$$. Meals and horseback riding extra. Family and group rates. Daily picnic rates, too. Two-night minimum stay in cabins April-September.
Credit Cards: Visa, MasterCard, American Express, Discover, Diners Club
Season: Year-round, including Thanksgiving and Easter. Closed for Christmas, December 24 and 25.
Activities: Horses rent by the hour. There are overnight trail rides to Trask Mountain cabin usually once a month. Great spring steelhead fishing in the North Yamhill River, lighted blacktop tennis court, and pond for swimming. Seasonal hunting of elk and deer. In winter, the ranch doesn't get much snow, and there is no specific program. Most people come to enjoy the fine dining, visit wineries, listen to country music, and ride horses.
Children's Programs: The Flying M has a children's horse camp each year. Otherwise no special program.
Dining: Ranch cooking ordered from a menu, homemade desserts, weekly steak fries and cookouts, lots of seafood. Wonderful selection of local wines; mixed drinks available. Dining room seats 180, open to the public. Monthly brunch. Winter dinners at Elk Camp (rain or shine) along the river.
Entertainment: Tractor-drawn hayrides. Nightly music.
Summary: A wonderful setting in the beautiful northwest corner of Oregon. The property has been in the Mitchell family since the early 1930s. Charming cabins and magnificent log lodge. Great for singles, couples, families, and groups. Bring your own horse. Wonderful horse camping facilities. Dining open to public, private airstrip, and steelhead fishing. Nearby: local wineries, the Gallery Players of Oregon theater company, horse shows in the DeLashmutt Equestrian Center.

Minam River Lodge
Joseph, Oregon

Minam River Lodge is deep in northeastern Oregon's Eagle Cap Wilderness. This magnificent country contains over fifty lakes and many streams, including the Minam River, which runs along the ranch property. The lodge was started in the early 1960s. Since then it has changed hands several times. Today Cal and Betsy Henry run their isolated, rustic hideaway accessible only by small plane or horseback. You may not meet them, though, as they run two other pack stations and are on the go all summer and fall. Don't worry, though, as they always have friendly staff on hand. The ranch has its own 3,000-foot dirt and grass airstrip. The horseback ride into the ranch is eight miles. Either way you arrive, as you catch a glimpse of the property, you will feel as though you are out in the middle of God's country with mountains, evergreen trees, and the wonderful Minam River. There are wonderful elements of backcountry peace and rustic simplicity. Except for the wind sock and a few planes, you might think you have come upon some old-time cattle rustlers' hideaway.

Address: P.O. Box 26, Dept. K, Joseph, Oregon 97846
Telephone: (503) 432-9171 for reservations (they will answer "High Country Outfitters"); there is only an emergency radio telephone at the ranch. From September to December, don't expect your calls to be returned immediately, but they will be returned.
Airport: 3,000-foot dirt/grass airstrip; charter flights to ranch available; contact ranch for specifics
Location: 260 miles east of Portland, 45 miles southeast of Pendleton off I-5. Call for details.
Memberships: Oregon Outfitters and Guides
Medical: Grand Round Hospital, 18-minute flight
Conference: 16; very low-key and rustic
Guest Capacity: 16
Accommodations: Rustic but comfortable cabins by the Minam River. Each has a wood stove and hot shower and single and double beds. These cabins were built with timbers from the lodge and are lighted by generator and Coleman lanterns. You can hear and see the river from the cabin. Daily maid service. Laundry service available.
Rates: • $$. American Plan. Children under age 3 free. Children 4 to 6 20% off. Includes transportation in and out by horse. Charter flights to and from the ranch are extra. Group rates available. Two-day minimum.
Credit Cards: Visa, MasterCard
Season: Mid-May to November
Activities: Cal and Betsy specialize in pack trips, fishing, and hunting trips, but those who would like to just enjoy the peace at the ranch can do so as well. Horses are furnished to guests of all ages, or you can bring your own. Daily rides from lodge leave hourly, all day long. Fishing in Minam River or mountain lakes (bring your own gear). Combination horseback and float trips on the Snake River in Hell's Canyon are separate from the ranch but can be arranged. Seasonal hunting for elk, deer, bear, cougar, and bighorn sheep. Ask Cal about his drop camps, deluxe hunts, and lodge hunts.
Children's Programs: None. Kids are welcome and encouraged but are the responsibility of parents.
Dining: Home cooking, served family-style. BYOB.
Entertainment: You are on your own. Guitar music occasionally.
Summary: Secluded lodge accessible by small plane or 2-hour horseback ride. Remote, peaceful, private river setting. Very low-key. Magnificent views. You can bring your own horse. Nearby: Chief Joseph Memorial, artists' foundry, Wallowa Lake, Hell's Canyon (deepest gorge in North America).

Ponderosa Cattle Company and Guest Ranch
Seneca, Oregon

The Ponderosa Cattle Company and Guest Ranch is in one of the most beautiful wide-open valleys in the West. That is exactly what attracted the Fleming and Oren families to this area. Lush green meadows, forests, creeks, sagebrush, snow-capped mountains, along with 3,000 head of cattle and 120,000 acres make this a cowboy's paradise. In 1988, these two families (the Fleming family has been in the cattle business for two generations) purchased this incredible property and built a brand-new guest ranch facility overlooking the Silvies Valley. Izzy Oren, who oversees the entire operation, grew up in Europe and has had a fascinating business career. His wife, Nancy, grew up in California and taught skiing and high school. Together with local cowboys they offer guests (must be 18 or older) the chance to ride the range and experience a variety of cattle and outdoor adventures. As Izzy says in his deep European accent, "We offer an incredible adult experience that is completely geared to our guests' riding abilities." Come to Ponderosa with an open mind, and with some time in the saddle you'll leave a cowboy. Well, almost!

Address: P.O. Box 190 K, Seneca, Oregon 97873
Telephone: (800) 331-1012, (503) 542-2403; fax: (503) 542-2713
Airport: Redmond, Oregon; private 4,000-foot airstrip (3,250 feet are paved)
Location: 35 miles northeast of Burns, 35 miles southwest of John Day, 160 miles east of Redmond, 230 miles southeast of Portland
Medical: Blue Mountain Hospital, 35 miles; Air Life Helicopter
Conference: 48
Guest Capacity: 48
Accommodations: The eight three-plex log cabins are arranged in the pines behind and to the west of the lodge with valley views. Each has common covered porches, individual entrances, two double beds, wood floors, a country motif, individual baths/showers. No televisions or telephones in rooms. The 5,000-square-foot main log lodge with the beautiful hand-carved front door has a dining room, bar, and gift shop. The covered veranda overlooks the picturesque Silvies Valley.
Rates: • $$$. American Plan. Corporate and group rates. Special holiday packages. Special family weeks.
Credit Cards: Visa, MasterCard, American Express
Season: Year-round
Activities: Riding and cattle work in the summer. Riding geared to ability level. All levels of riders welcome. Previous riding experience not required. You may (depending on your ability) participate in ranch activities. Cattle work includes herding, changing pastures (60 different pastures), checking fences, roundups, and practice roping. Fishing in creeks and on the Silvies River, hiking, golf nearby. Seasonal deer, elk, antelope, goose, and duck hunting. Winter: Cross-country skiing and snowmobiling.
Children's Programs: None. Must be 18 years or older, except during special family weeks.
Dining: Hearty family-style ranch cooking. "Cookie" is famous in this part of the country. Chuck wagon lunches on the trail. Hiking with sack lunches provided.
Entertainment: Jukebox music, pool table, and large-screen television in lodge. Occasional line dancing and mountain man story-telling.
Summary: Historic 120,000-acre cattle ranch. Guest ranch built in 1993. Located in magnificent valley in eastern Oregon. Unlimited riding and cattle experiences depending on your abilities. No children under 18 except during special family weeks. Private elk herd in 7,500-acre enclosure.

See color photos, pages 260-261

Rock Springs Guest Ranch
Bend, Oregon

Just outside Bend, Oregon, in the foothills of the Cascade Mountains, Rock Springs Guest Ranch was founded by the late Donna Gill. A schoolteacher, Donna developed an early love for young people, their parents, and the great outdoors. Her spirit and the tradition she inspired are carried on by her nephew, John Gill, and his wife, Eva, along with their fine staff. "Our goal is to provide the highest quality vacation experience for each of our guests, with an emphasis on the family," says Gill. Rock Springs attracts guests from all over the world. With the snowcapped peaks of the Three Sisters Mountains behind, Rock Springs provides trappings of the West as well as modern conveniences. The result—Rock Springs Ranch is one of the best guest ranches in the West. The ranch is abundant with natural beauty, radiant with hospitality, cozy with warmth, and as for activities—you name it, they've got it. Rock Springs is also popular for business meetings and retreats during the nonsummer months.

Address: 64201 Tyler Road, Drawer K, Bend, Oregon 97701
Telephone: (503) 382-1957, (800) 225-DUDE (3833); fax: (503) 382-7774
Airport: Redmond/Bend Airport, 19 miles
Location: 9 miles northwest of Bend, 180 miles southeast of Portland
Memberships: Dude Ranchers' Association, Meeting Planners International
Medical: St. Charles Hospital, Bend, 9 miles
Conference: 50; ask for the detailed conference information packet
Guest Capacity: 50
Accommodations: Individual cabins and duplex-triplex units with large suites and bedroom cottages nestled in the ponderosa pines. Rooms are finished in knotty pine, and many are newly remodeled. All cabins have decks, and most have fireplaces and refrigerators.
Rates: • $$-$$$. Full American Plan in summer. One-week minimum stay. Modified American Plan Thanksgiving, Christmas, and Memorial Day weekend. Corporate meeting packages available.
Credit Cards: Visa, MasterCard, Diners Club, American Express, Discover
Season: Late June through Labor Day; Thanksgiving, Christmas, and Memorial Day. All other times are dedicated to corporate conferences, retreats, and seminars.
Activities: Horseback riding is the ranch's summer specialty. Heated, hourglass-shaped swimming pool, 2 lighted professional tennis courts, stream and lake fishing, hiking, nature walks. Everyone enjoys relaxing in the huge free-form whirlpool with spectacular 15-foot waterfall over volcanic boulders. Golf and white water rafting nearby. Downhill and Nordic skiing at Mount Bachelor. Trapshooting, billiards, table tennis, and volleyball. Fly-fishing clinic.
Children's Programs: During the summer, children ages 3 to 5 and 6 to 12 have youth counselors to help them enjoy a variety of activities and adventures. Lunch and dinner are available in their own dining room or out on the trail. Counselors on duty from 9:00 a.m. to 1:00 p.m. and again from 5:30 p.m. to 9:00 p.m. Children under 6 do not take trail rides. Special infant and nanny rates available. Ask about kids' overnight campout.
Dining: All meals are served buffet-style, offering a wide variety of cuisine. Entrées of prime rib and fresh Northwest seafood. Special dietary preferences are always accommodated. Hors d'oeuvres precede dinner. Fresh fruit, homemade cookies, and beverages always available in the dining room. Domestic and imported wines and beer available. BYOB in cabins only.
Entertainment: Tractor-drawn hayrides, nightly volleyball, western dancing, pool table, table tennis, and a variety of game tables and games.
Summary: One of the premiere guest ranches for families. Superb corporate meeting ranch offering exclusive use of all facilities for each group. Nearby: Mount Bachelor ski area, High Desert Museum (wildlife and cultural museum).

See color photos, pages 262-263

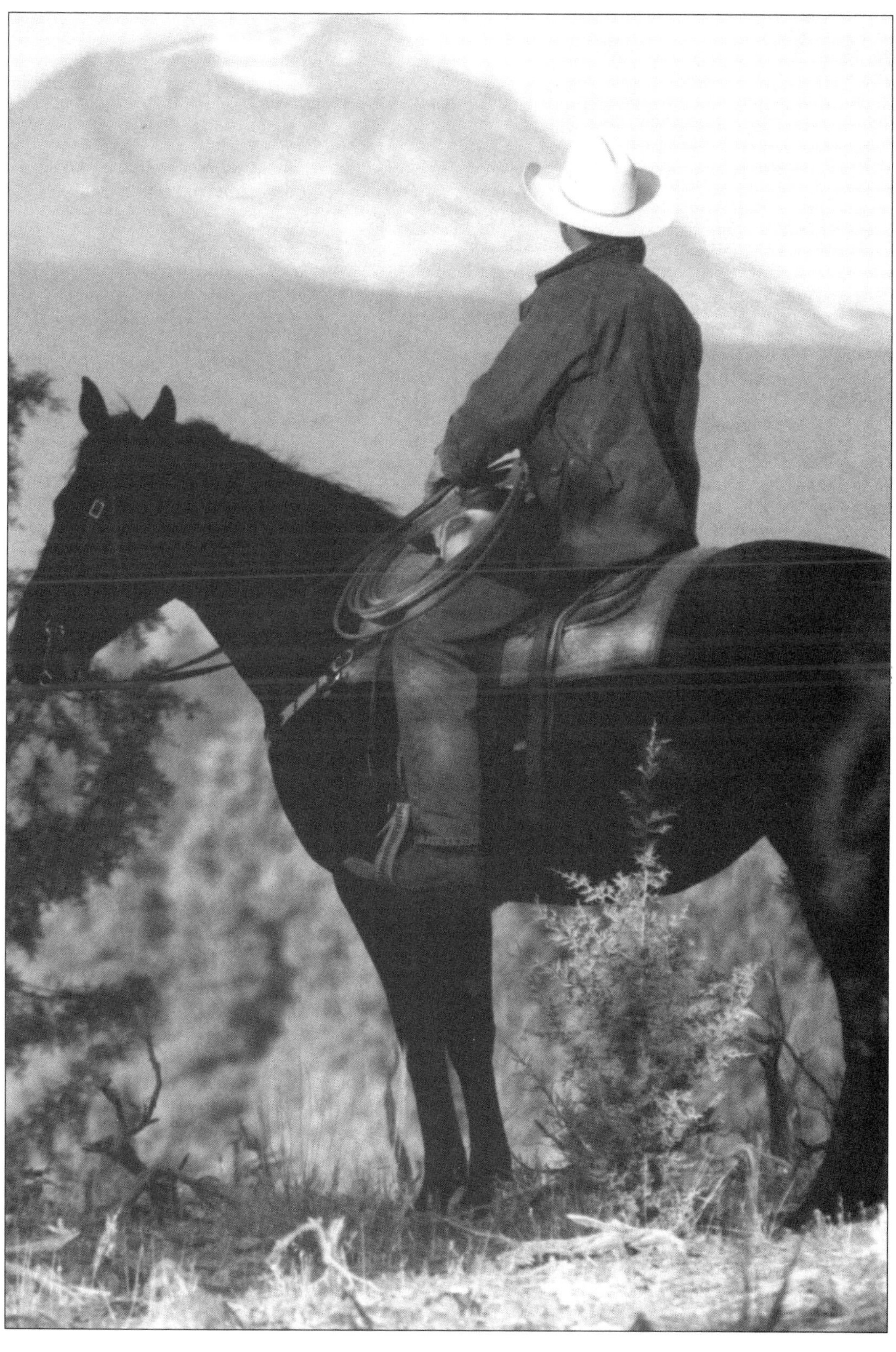

Flying W Ranch
Tionesta, Pennsylvania

Near the remote northern town of Tionesta is the Weller family's 500-acre Flying W Ranch, home of the Allegheny Mountain Annual Championship Rodeo. Each year, this professional rodeo attracts over 15,000 visitors and professional cowboys from around the country. In 1965, the Flying W ran Hereford cattle. Today, this working ranch, surrounded by a half-million acres of the Allegheny National Forest, offers secluded peace, hay fields, rolling hills, and timbered forests to individuals as well as groups. Unique to the Flying W is its "à la carte" riding program, which includes horse camping and a bring-your-own-horse program. Each summer, children enjoy the western riding camp for beginner to intermediate riders. At the Flying W, one can ride for an hour, stay for a weekend, spend a week, or enjoy the ranch's own professional rodeo in July.

Address: Star Route 2, Box 150 K, Tionesta, Pennsylvania 16353 (summer)
Telephone: (814) 463-7663; fax: (814) 463-5003
Airport: Pittsburgh
Location: 150 miles north of Pittsburgh, 40 miles south of Warren, 14 miles northeast of Tionesta
Memberships: International Professional Rodeo Association
Medical: Titusville Hospital, 30 miles
Conference: 90
Guest Capacity: 100
Accommodations: Sleeping arrangements vary greatly. The campground has RV hookups, a bathhouse with showers, and a coin-operated laundry. There are three heated bunkhouses with a bathhouse nearby. Each sleeps 16. There are also three duplex cabins and one three-bedroom, one-bath lodge with full kitchen and fireplace.
Rates: • \$-\$\$. Five-day ranch vacation package available. Other package rates available for adults and children. Most activities are à la carte.
Credit Cards: Visa, MasterCard
Season: April through mid-December. Late December through March by reservation only.
Activities: More than a half-dozen riding opportunities, from hourly rides with instruction to overnight trips through the Allegheny National Forest. All trail riding done at a walk. You may bring your own horse (stall rental extra). Ask about the 5-day, 4-night ranch vacation package. Outdoor unheated pool, canoeing at Tionesta Creek and Allegheny River, hiking on the North Country Hiking Trail, fishing and seasonal hunting for bear, white-tailed deer, turkey, and small game.
Children's Programs: Youth (age 9-16) camp program summer months only. Contact ranch for specifics.
Dining: Restaurant open to the public. Eat in the Trails End dining room. Pennsylvania ranch cooking, including chicken and biscuit dinners, steaks, prime rib, stuffed pork chops, cod, and haddock. Snack bar and ice cream parlor. Drinks (wine, beer, liquor) available in restaurant.
Entertainment: Live country-western music most weekends, tractor hayrides, game room with pool table, electric games.
Summary: Family-run ranch. Great for families, scouts, and church groups. Five-day, four-night ranch vacation package. Bring-your-own-horse program, RV hookups. On-site professional Allegheny Mountain Championship Rodeo in July, Pennsylvania High School Rodeo Memorial Day weekend, American Indian powwow, western tack and gift shop. Nearby: Sawmill Museum, Music Museum in Franklin, Blair Company Clothing Outlet.

Blue Bell Lodge & Resort
Custer, South Dakota

South Dakota was put on the map by Kevin Costner's film, *Dances with Wolves*. It is a state rich in early American history and diverse in its stunning landscape. Blue Bell Lodge is in the heart of the 73,000-acre Custer State Park. It is owned and operated by Phil and Sue Lampert. Blue Bell was built back in the 1920s and offers travelers a home base for a diverse combination of recreational activities. The lodge, along with its old and new cabins, offers families and couples a place to be on their own in the midst of panhandling wild burros, the world's largest herd of buffalo, and scenic drives. At Blue Bell you are, for the most part, on your own and free to roam as you wish. One of the unique things about this lodge is the horse camping and horse boarding programs. For those traveling through South Dakota by car or RV, Blue Bell offers rustic and modern comfort in the heart of magnificent Custer State Park.

Address: HCR 83, Box 63K, Custer, South Dakota 57730
Telephone: (605) 255-4531, (800) 658-3530; fax: (605) 255-4706
Airport: Rapid City Regional Airport, 50 miles
Location: South on Highway 87 toward Wind Cave National Park and Hot Springs, 44 miles southwest of Rapid City off Highway 36
Memberships: National Tour Association, AAA, Mobil Travel Guide
Medical: Custer General Hospital, 11 miles
Conference: 90; very large gatherings as well
Guest Capacity: 72-148
Accommodations: Blue Bell has 29 cabins, 11 of which were built in the 1920s. All of the older cabins have one main room with kitchenette, a modern bathroom, and electric heat. There are 16 new log cabins that are very spacious—one large room with two beds and sitting areas, modern bathroom, refrigerator, microwave, coffee makers, and fireplaces. All cabins have outdoor fire grates and picnic tables.
Rates: $. Food and activities à la carte.
Credit Cards: Visa, MasterCard, American Express, Discover
Season: May through September (some cabins are kept open during the winter months, but most activities are closed)
Activities: Guided trail rides throughout the day, offering one-hour, two-hour, half-day, and all-day rides. Breakfast and dinner rides and overnight pack trips can be scheduled with advance notice. Trout fishing in French Creek or one of the nearby lakes. Swimming beaches also at nearby lakes. There are paddleboats and rowboat rentals available nearby, or you can rent a mountain bike. Excellent hiking throughout the park. The Park Service offers interpretive programs.
Children's Programs: No special programs.
Dining: The rustic Buffalo Dining Room and Buffalo Wallow Lounge are popular gathering places. Home-cooked meals, served family-style. Buffalo, fresh trout, chicken, and beef steaks are specialties. Ask about the hay wagon rides in the wildlife area. Full bar.
Entertainment: Old-fashioned hayride and chuck wagon cookout, with sing-along entertainment scheduled most evenings.
Summary: Located in the heart of Custer State Park. Rustic and modern cabins. Phil and Sue Lampert were both born and raised in South Dakota and know the history very well. Very informal program—you are on your own with lots to do. Depending on the time of year, there are lots of buffalo and elk. Horse boarding and camping available.

See color photos, page 265

Nemo Guest Ranch
Nemo, South Dakota

In the late 1970s, Dale Deverman and his family traveled from Springfield, Illinois, to Colorado for vacations. On the way they came upon the old 4-T Ranch. Each summer on their way west, they would stop over. As Dale says, "There was just something about the ranch that I loved." So in 1985, he bought it! Nemo Guest Ranch still maintains its rustic "old town" charm. In the late 1800s, along with the old general store, Nemo was a company town for Homestake Gold Mine's timber camp. Of note is that the father of William Randolph Hearst, of publishing fame, was one of the original stockholders in the Homestake Mine. Today, as before, Nemo offers people traveling through South Dakota on their way to Mt. Rushmore or Deadwood (the new old frontier gambling town) a place to put their feet up and rest for a while. Nemo is just off County Road 2335. There are small ranches and laid-back homes that surround the ranch property. In the summer, the days are warm and the nights cool—you'll always need covers. In Sioux, Nemo means "open valley in wooded area." Nemo is relaxed, peaceful, and a great place to spend a couple of days or more.

Address: Box 77K, Nemo, South Dakota 57759
Telephone: (605) 578-2708
Location: 16 miles northwest of Rapid City, 21 miles southeast of Deadwood
Memberships: Rapid City Chamber of Commerce
Medical: Rapid City Regional Hospital, 20 miles
Conference: 70
Guest Capacity: 86; ask about the campground
Accommodations: There are a total of fourteen cabins and homes, all of which have kept their authentic charm. Troxeli, Circle 6, Big House, and 4T House all have three to five bedrooms. The boardinghouse has four individual bedrooms. Many of the units have kitchen facilities. An RV campground with hookups is available.
Rates: • $. Lodging, meals, horseback riding, all extra. One-night minimum stay.
Credit Cards: Visa, MasterCard, American Express
Season: May to October
Activities: A relaxed and casual atmosphere prevails at Nemo. The only formal activity is horseback riding, and that is done on an hourly basis by reservation at the general store or at the barn (one-, two- and three-hour rides). Ask about the Whiskey Gulch and Nemo Mountain rides. Riding is geared for the beginner and done at a walk. Fishing in Boxelder Creek (the general store has some fishing gear), which runs through the ranch. Many combine a few of the ranch activities with local sightseeing, including Mount Rushmore and Deadwood.
Children's Program: No structured program. Kids are the responsibility of their parents. Kids are free to roam the ranch and end up doing just that. Small video arcade in general store.
Dining: The restaurant is open to the public from 8:00 a.m. to 10:00 p.m., serving general American/western cuisine.
Entertainment: You are on your own in the evening, except on Friday and Saturday nights, when you can relax in the Ponderosa Bar. Country-western music.
Summary: Here the pace is slow and the atmosphere relaxed and friendly. Nemo Ranch has a charming turn-of-the-century Old West, small town feel. You are on your own to do whatever you wish. Nearby: Mount Rushmore (one hour), Deadwood (45 minutes). Arrangements can be made for family reunions and weddings.

See color photos, page 266

Western Dakota Ranch Vacations
Wall, South Dakota

When the farm and ranch economy became depressed in the mid-1980s, Lavon and Dorothy Shearer put their heads together. Since they enjoyed people and always seemed to have someone visiting, they decided to open their 15,000-acre ranch and their way of life to fellow Americans and guests from around the world. Lavon, a Texan, and Dorothy, from the Badlands, have been in the ranching business since the early 1950s. The Shearers and their son, Grant, and his wife, Jodee, run a bed and breakfast and offer a wide range of western activities for a handful of guests. The ranch is located along the Cheyenne River, with alfalfa fields on the bottomlands and cedar tree canyons extending up to grass-covered, rolling prairies. The area is rugged enough for good deer hunting and yet protected for the 800 Angus, registered Texas longhorns, and cross-bred cattle. Lavon and Dorothy serve a low-key real ranch vacation—nothing fancy, just lots of down-home goodness. As outfitters for movies and commercials, Kevin Costner rode with them on the ranch in search of locations for the movie *Dances with Wolves*. Grant was a driver in this movie. Another son did a television commercial for Winchester ammunition.

Address: HCR 1, Dept. K, Wall, South Dakota 57790
Telephone: (605) 279-2198
Airport: Rapid City Airport; 3,500-foot lighted paved airstrip in Wall, 9 miles
Location: 1 hour east of Rapid City, 10 minutes north of Wall
Memberships: American Quarter Horse Association; Black Hills, Badlands and Lakes Association; Old West Trails Association
Medical: Rapid City Regional Hospital, 60 miles; Wall clinic, 9 miles
Conference: 75 for chuck wagon cookouts
Guest Capacity: 20 comfortably
Accommodations: "People sleep here, there, and everywhere," says Dorothy. The Shearers' split-level home provides comfortable lodging. Some rooms have private baths and patio entrances in a sunken garden or one large deck looking across the plains. The ranch also has a rustic cabin with a wood stove, outdoor plumbing, and lantern-light; several Indian tepees used in *Dances with Wolves*; and a sheepherders' wagon in a cedar canyon away from everything.
Rates: • $. Bed and breakfast. Family and weekly rates available. Horseback riding, wagon rides, and hunting extra. No minimum stay.
Credit Cards: None. Personal and traveler's checks accepted.
Season: Year-round
Activities: Guests who stay three days or more can do as little or as much as they desire. Lavon and Dorothy and their family go out of their way to make you a part of their ranch. They prefer that all riders are good to experienced. Many horses to choose from, guests may help with occasional cattle work. All riding 20 minutes away. You may ride on your own here, fish for catfish in the Cheyenne River running through the property or ponds stocked with bass, hike, or hunt fossils. This ranch is well known for trophy deer, antelope, turkey, prairie dog, and coyote hunting.
Children's Programs: No specific program. Children are welcome.
Dining: Dorothy cooks great meals, including her famous sourdough pancakes. Chuck wagon suppers are prepared by a cowboy over an open fire along the river for small or large groups. You will really feel like you are on the range in the 1800s. BYOB.
Entertainment: People talk in this part of the country. The Shearers have time to listen and share. Large recreation room with trampoline; wagon rides and chuck wagon dinners.
Summary: Overnight bed and breakfast or weekly ranch vacation. Wagon train trips (10 person minimum), guided bow and trophy deer hunts, famous 1880 desperado trek with shoot-out, and western artist ride, ranch antiques, Indian and homemade crafts at the Ranch Trading Post. Video available.

Triple R Ranch
Keystone, South Dakota

The Triple R Ranch is a low-key guest ranch only eight miles from world-famous Mount Rushmore. The ranch is in the heart of the 27,000-acre Norbeck Wildlife Preserve, surrounded by Black Hills National Forest and only two miles from the 10,000-acre Black Elk Wilderness, the only wilderness area in the Black Hills. The Triple R's mile-high elevation assures cool evenings to enjoy pine-scented air, a star-speckled sky, peace, and quiet. The ranch offers an eye-opening look into the Old West of South Dakota, and host Jack Bradt has lots of wonderful stories and history to share. Names like Wild Bill Hickok, Calamity Jane, General Custer, and General Crook, along with Indian Chiefs Crazy Horse and Sitting Bull, are synonymous with the Wild West. The Black Hills were opened for settlement during the gold rush period, thus creating the last frontier in the lower 48 states. In 1967, Jack and his wife, Cherrylee, moved to South Dakota from nearby Nebraska. Since 1977, they have been receiving guests. Their love for the unique beauty of the Black Hills is evident, as they extend their warmth and hospitality to you at Triple R. One professor and his wife wrote from Wisconsin, "We've traveled all over the world, and you are the best hosts we've ever had."

Address: Highway 16A, Box 124 K, Keystone, South Dakota 57751-0124
Telephone: (605) 666-4605. If Jack and Cherrylee are not in, Slim always answers the phone; (800) 843-1300, ext. 3600 (evenings only)
Airport: Rapid City
Location: 28 miles southwest of Rapid City off Highway 16A
Memberships: Dude Ranchers' Association
Medical: Rapid City Regional Hospital, 28 miles
Guest Capacity: 15
Accommodations: Small, carpeted, air-conditioned, wood-sided, flattop simple cabins, with refrigerators for snacks. Each cabin is modestly decorated. Some have air-conditioning. Guests traveling by RV may park in the RV camp area.
Rates: • $$. American Plan. Six-day stay is usual, with four-day minimum.
Credit Cards: Visa, MasterCard, American Express, Diners Club. Personal checks and cash accepted.
Season: Mid-May through mid-September
Activities: Daily, planned activities. Most guests come here to ride. Rides to old mines and ghost towns. Half-day, all-day, and breakfast rides. This is rugged country, so most riding is done at a walk. Fishing for trout in Lakota Lake and Iron Creek, adjacent to the ranch. Solar-heated swimming pool, horse-drawn wagon rides. Hiking trails abound.
Children's Programs: No children's program. Ranch activities are suited to children 7 years and older.
Dining: Delicious home-cooked meals, family-style. Ranch specialties are barbecued ribs and South Dakota steaks. Meals are served in a "sit down, pass around, down-home" manner. All meals are hearty and wholesome. Beer available, BYOL.
Entertainment: Recreation and dining hall in Rendezvous Lodge. Cowboy chuck wagon supper and musical show near Rapid City, Mount Rushmore lighting ceremony. Cowboy poetry.
Summary: Riding is the main activity here. Jack Bradt offers tremendous hospitality in a low-key atmosphere. Nearby world-famous Mount Rushmore. RV camping and hookups available. Both the Norbeck Wildlife Preserve and the Black Elk Wilderness Area are abundant with wildlife and vegetation. Be sure to ask about the Iron Mountain road and the Mount Rushmore trail ride. Guests go each week to the Mount Rushmore lighting ceremony. Buffalo herds in Custer State Park; trips to the historic town of Deadwood now with legalized gambling.

Cibolo Creek Ranch
Shafter, Texas

Luxurious, authentic, historical, beautiful. It is hard to describe Cibolo Creek Ranch, but this is a beginning. With the same vision and passion that brought Milton Faver, ranching pioneer, to West Texas and the Chinati Mountains back in 1857, Faver's three crumbling old forts have been restored to world-class luxury and historical accuracy right to the last square nail and peach tree. Milton Faver is often referred to as the "mystery man of the Big Bend," and the present owner has also elected to avoid the spotlight. But the result of his and his team's work is apparent in the three National Historic Site designations and five Texas State Historical Markers that the ranch has been awarded. This magnificent property was rediscovered in 1988, and the seemingly impossible restoration task was begun soon afterward. Fueled with energy and vision second to none, a team of archaeologists, architects, builders, and ranch hands set out to prove what Walt Disney said years ago, "All our dreams can come true if we have the courage to pursue them." The dream came true! In 1993, the ranch gates were opened to the world. If you have ever read the book, *In Search of Excellence*, this is what it is all about.

Address: P.O. Box 44K, Shafter, Texas 79850
Telephone: (915) 229-3507; fax: (915) 229-3653
Airport: Midland, Texas, 200 miles; El Paso, Texas, 200 miles; Alpine, Texas, 60 miles. Private 5,000-foot airstrip on ranch. Beechcraft King Air Charter from nearby airports direct to the ranch.
Location: Off Texas Highway 67, 200 miles southwest of Midland, 32 miles south of Marfa, 5 miles north of Shafter
Medical: Big Bend Medical Center, 60 miles
Conference: 20
Guest Capacity: 23 total at Cibolo Creek Ranch, La Cienega, and La Morita
Accommodations: Three separate guest areas. All rooms are furnished with authentic Mexican and Spanish antiques. Ceilings with traditional vigas and latillas. Each bedroom has all the amenities of a deluxe hotel—down pillows, fluffy towels, most with fireplaces.
Rates: • $$$. American Plan.
Credit Cards: Visa, MasterCard, American Express
Season: Year-round
Activities: Touring the forts, walking, horseback riding, and wildlife viewing are the main activities. Nothing is structured. More challenging rides through remote and rugged areas of the Chinati Mountains. Team-drawn chuck wagon for those who may not wish to ride. Mountain wildlife is plentiful. Buffalo, elk, longhorns, and Hi Jolly, the camel, can be watched from deluxe vehicles. Many Indian caves in the area. Off-ranch activities include visits to McDonald Observatory, Fort Davis National Monument, Fort Leaton, Big Bend National Park, Big Bend Ranch State Natural Area, rafting through the Rio Grand Rapids, the ghost town of Shafter, and shopping across the border in Mexico, 25 miles away.
Children's Programs: None. Children are the responsibility of parents.
Dining: Superb! Served at the forts, at the Hacienda, and on the trail. Flexibility in menus arranged for groups. Excellent wine cellar and cuisine features southwestern and Mexican specialties.
Entertainment: An evening stroll in the cool evening air. Stimulating conversation. Occasional mariachis, historical and contemporary library.
Summary: This 25,000-acre ranch/fort/hacienda is world-class in every way. For those who appreciate beauty, privacy, history, and excellence. Superb for couples and individuals. Small corporate retreats, high-level meetings, and family reunions. Average ranch elevation of 5,000 feet and low humidity result in a comfortable year-round climate.

Dixie Dude Ranch
Bandera, Texas

Five generations of the same family have operated this nostalgic working ranch since 1901. The ranch was co-founded by Rose Crowell and her father, William Wallace Whitley, and today is run by her grandson, Clay Conoly, and his wife, Diane. A dude ranch since 1937, the Dixie Dude captures the authentic Old West. Over 700 acres make up the setting for scenic horseback rides through the Texas Hill Country. Hearty Texas cuisine is served daily in the family-style dining room, occasionally on the range, or poolside. Dixie Dude is a great place for rest and relaxation or taking part in daily planned activities. No one remains a stranger long. Folks gather in the Round-Up Room, play games, dance, or just get acquainted by the fireplace. Guests return year after year for the family atmosphere, delicious food, and scenic rides. One guest has returned every year since the ranch was opened.

Address: P.O. Box 548K, Bandera, Texas 78003
Telephone: (800) 375-Y'ALL (9255), (210) 796-4481; fax: (210) 796-3067
Airport: San Antonio International
Location: 9 miles southwest of Bandera
Memberships: Texas Hotel & Motel Association, Texas Longhorn Breeders Association
Medical: Bandera Medical Clinic, Sid Peterson Hospital, Kerrville, 34 miles
Conference: 50
Guest Capacity: 70
Accommodations: Guests stay in comfortable motel-like rooms in the main lodge and in individual rustic and modern duplex log and stone cabins. Many are of early Texas architecture. All complete with air-conditioning, vented heat, and television but no telephone. Mostly double beds, all with private baths and tiled floors.
Rates: • $. American Plan. Children's, weekly, low-season, and group rates available.
Credit Cards: Visa, MasterCard, American Express
Season: Year-round except Christmas day
Activities: Each guest is entitled to two supervised morning and afternoon rides each day. There are trails on over 1,500 acres. Usually you will see the ranch longhorns and sometimes native wildlife such as whitetail deer. This is rocky hill country, so most riding is done at a walk. Outdoor pool, hayrides, bonfires, cookouts, river tubing in Medina River in Bandera, hiking, volleyball, table tennis, horseshoe pitching, tetherball. Winter program is the same, weather permitting. Bandera Gun Club for skeet shooting. Shotguns can be rented.
Children's Programs: Riding instruction and baby-sitting available but extra. Children under 6 ride with adult or parent. Shallow children's pool. Large ranch playground. Weekly piñata party and calf roping.
Dining: Family-style and buffet. Texas ranch-style meals served, briskets and pork rib barbecues, and Dixie Dude Ranch's famous fried chicken dinners. Weekly breakfast rides. Hamburgers and hot dogs at poolside. BYOB.
Entertainment: Old ranch tractor hayrides through hill country. Cowboy poetry and guitar-playing cowboys around the bonfire. Bandera rodeos and country-western dance lessons. Will Rogers-type trick roping show. Be sure to ask Clay about the ranch's snake handling exhibition.
Summary: Old-time western stock ranch turned guest ranch with lots of Old West charm. Best for families who wish to introduce their children to the Old West and a simpler way of life. Couples and singles will enjoy Dixie Dude as well. Century-old barn and the surrounding Texas Hill Country. Be sure to buy a copy of Dixie Dude Ranch's cookbook. Fluent Spanish spoken. Nearby: Frontier Times Museum, Cowboy Artists of America Museum, and Bandera Downs thoroughbred racing, Sea World of Texas and Fiesta Texas in San Antonio.

Flying L Guest Ranch
Bandera, Texas

The Flying L Guest Ranch offers warm southern hospitality as well as the modern comforts of a resort. This 542-acre ranch in Bandera (referred to as the Cowboy Capital of the World), is known for limestone cliffs and live oak and mesquite trees. Winters are mild and brief, which attracts many visitors from the north. The Flying L continues a wonderful tradition of treating each guest as a star. Parents with strollers and older couples who enjoy walking like the paved roads and sprawling manicured lawns. The countryside is flat, so one can get around easily. One guest wrote, "We enjoyed the facility, the food, and especially the kindness of your staff." When they say, "Ya'll come back," people do!

Address: HCR 1 Box 32K, Bandera, Texas 78003
Telephone: (210) 796-3001; (800) 292-5134; fax: (210) 796-8455
Airport: San Antonio International
Location: 45 miles northwest of San Antonio, 1 mile south of Bandera
Memberships: Texas Tourism Council, Meeting Planners International
Awards: AAA 3 Diamond
Medical: University of Texas Medical Center, 35 minutes
Conference: 110; 2,500-square-foot conference center; audiovisual equipment available
Guest Capacity: 150
Accommodations: Among the private homes scattered around the property, there are 38 guest houses that accommodate 76 people, double occupancy. All are comfortable and spacious suites with color TV, small refrigerators, microwaves, and air-conditioners. All have living, dining, and bedroom areas. There are golf and ranch view suites. Villa suites are the most basic. Ranch view and villa units come in pairs—small and large—and are great for families.
Rates: • $-$$. Modified American Plan (breakfast and dinner included); an à la carte lunch is offered. Rates also include golf, horseback rides and lessons, children's activities, as well as nightly entertainment, and use of all other amenities. Rates for children and groups available. Children under 3 stay free. Senior, military, and AAA discounts.
Credit Cards: Visa, MasterCard, American Express
Season: Year-round
Activities: Here you sign up for which ride you wish. A 35-horse stable provides morning, guided rides. While adults enjoy a leisurely trail ride, children ages 6 to 9 are given riding lessons in the round pen. Pony rides are offered to children between the ages of 3 and 5. Adult riding lessons and private family rides are available in the evenings (extra charge for private rides). Everyone is guaranteed one ride per day. Enjoy the Texas-size pool and hot tub. Fish in the San Julian Creek, as well as Medina Lake. Year-round 18-hole, 72-par golf course with carts and golf clubhouse (cart rental extra). Two lighted tennis courts and basketball court. Horseshoes, shuffleboard, volleyball, table tennis, softball, and water volleyball.
Children's Programs: Full children's program during summer and holidays. Supervised activities such as pony rides, story telling, fishing, arts and crafts, nature program in new greenhouse. Baby-sitter list available.
Dining: Breakfast is served creekside three mornings a week. Weekly creekside barbecues with beef brisket and chicken, cole slaw, potato salad, corn-on-the-cob, beans, and homemade fruit cobbler. Weekly Mexican fare, steak night, and home-cookin' night! Fully licensed Branding Iron Saloon.
Entertainment: Old West town, rodeo, Wild West shows, sing-alongs, dances. Ask about holdups.
Summary: Texas-style resort ranch with 18-hole golf course and driving range, horseback riding and roping lessons, and western-style entertainment. Perfect for corporate meetings/retreats and family reunions. Entire ranch can be reserved for your group.

See color photos, page 267

Garrett Creek Ranch
Paradise, Texas

Garrett Creek Ranch is, without a doubt, one of the top executive conference ranches. Veteran meeting planner Leslie Schultz came up with the idea after years of conference work. Her goal was to create an environment where executives and business groups could meet away from city life—one that would lend itself to creative thinking and would foster positive intellectual interaction with the very best in professional service and amenities. Today the ranch is managed by Burl and LaNelle Kirkland, and along with their staff, they host groups from around the country, with most coming from the Dallas/Ft. Worth area. Just off the foyer is a wall that is filled with letters of praise from company heads and meeting planners. This is a ranch exclusively for business and professional groups. The information that the ranch sends to prospective groups is extremely thorough and well thought out. Included is a detailed planning guide, description of facilities, price and billing information, and a well-illustrated color brochure. Perhaps the ranch motto says it best: "Paradise is closer than you think."

Address: Route 2, Box 235K, Paradise, Texas 76073
Telephone: (817) 433-2055 (ranch); (214) 680-8679 (sales)
Airport: Dallas/Ft. Worth International, 45 miles
Location: 45 miles northwest of Dallas/Ft. Worth
Memberships: International Association of Conference Centers, Meeting Planners International, Texas Society of Association Executives
Medical: First-aid-trained staff; Decatur Hospital, 14 miles; emergency helicopter available, helipad
Conference: 100
Guest Capacity: 86
Conference Accommodations: The ranch tries to book one large group or several small groups at a time. It has been designed to provide a wide range of meeting formats. There are seven conference rooms seating 10 to 100 comfortably. Standard audiovisual equipment and comfortable padded, swivel-reclining meeting chairs.
Accommodations: Six clustered log cabins with four to six rooms per cabin, with covered porches and rocking chairs. Each is decorated individually with high ceilings, hardwood floors, business telephones, and color TV. Adjacent is the "Old West town" called Paradise Junction, with sixteen rooms and a parlor. There are a total of forty-three guest rooms and two studios on the ranch.
Rates: • $$$. Full American Plan, complete meeting package. One-night minimum stay.
Credit Cards: Visa, MasterCard, American Express. Master billing preferred.
Season: Year-round. Closed Christmas through New Year's.
Activities: Swimming, jogging, par course, high/low ropes course, limited horseback riding, volleyball, basketball, bicycles, and two paddle tennis courts, driving range and putting green.
Children's Programs: None. Adults only.
Dining: Delicious food and a variety of menus. Breakfast and lunch buffets and sit-down dinners. Ask about the special menus, which include South of the Border Mexican Fiesta, Paradise Luau, Cattle Baron's Steak, and Bunkhouse Spread. Full bar.
Entertainment: Ranch will arrange any entertainment you desire. Theme nights, campfires, and cowboy singers.
Summary: One of the top conference ranches in the United States. Designed by a meeting planner for business and professional groups. Be sure to get a copy of the *Garrett Ranch Cookbook* and a packet of their ranch wildflower seeds.

Lazy Hills Guest Ranch
Ingram, Texas

In 1959, Bob and Carol Steinruck were in Venezuela. Bob, who is from Pennsylvania, was working for Gulf Oil. Most of their colleagues at Gulf were Texans. Through the grapevine, they heard that Lazy Hills Guest Ranch was for sale. In 1959, they mustered enough money to buy it. Today, Lazy Hills is run by the Steinruck family. This 750-acre ranch is in the Texas Hill Country, surrounded by oaks and sycamores. The ranch, very family oriented, is a children's haven, with lots of riding, always under the supervision of a wrangler. Lazy Hills is not far from the LBJ Ranch and National Park. Summer temperatures reach into the mid-90s with low humidity and light breezes. The countryside is tranquil, the pace slow. Listen to nature's peace, or watch deer or an occasional armadillo. Lazy Hills is a great family holiday!

Address: Box K, Ingram, Texas 78025
Telephone: (210) 367-5600, (800) 880-0632; fax: (210) 367-5667
Airport: San Antonio International
Location: 70 miles northwest of San Antonio off Interstate 10, 105 miles southwest of Austin
Memberships: Texas Hill Country Tourism Association, Texas Hotel-Motel Association
Medical: Sid Peterson Memorial Hospital, Kerrville, 10 miles
Conference: 100
Guest Capacity: 100
Accommodations: Lazy Hills' accommodations consist of 26 air-conditioned guest rooms, each with blue jean bedspreads, twin or queen beds, some with bunk beds and wood-burning fireplaces, all with showers. Most sleep four easily, some six. Room also available in ranch house. Most have covered porches.
Rates: • $. American Plan. Corporate and group rates available. Three-day minimum stay in summer.
Credit Cards: Visa, MasterCard, Discover
Season: Year-round, including Thanksgiving, Christmas, and Easter
Activities: Informal. Only scheduled activities are meals and horseback riding. Over 30 miles of wooded hiking and horseback riding trails, with four guided trail rides daily. Experienced riders may find the riding a bit tame, but the scenery and wildlife more than compensate. No more than 16 to a ride; everyone usually rides together. First-rate wranglers carefully supervise children. Olympic-size swimming pool, children's wading pool, hot tub, two lighted tennis courts, archery, fishing for bass and catfish, volleyball, basketball, shuffleboard, table tennis, hayrides, seasonal hunting.
Children's Programs: Activities for children are scheduled in the morning during the summer. Plenty to keep children busy: playground with tree house, sandbar, merry-go-round. Babysitting extra.
Dining: Family-style or buffet, hearty Texas meals, chicken-fried steak with mashed potatoes and cream gravy, biscuits, beef brisket, sausage and chicken barbecue, weekly Mexican dinners, Lazy Hills grilled catfish, cookouts, pecan pie, buttermilk pie, chocolate-pumpkin cake. Get the picture? No dieting here! Picnic lunches always available. BYOB.
Entertainment: Entertainment is planned each night in the summer. Bonfires with s'mores, Crider's Rodeo on Guadalupe River, hay wagon rides pulled by Belgian draft horses or tractor.
Summary: A wonderful family-owned and operated ranch in the Hill Country of Texas. The guests who come and return are people with high family values. The majority are from Texas and the surrounding states. A good number come from Europe. Also, ideal for small groups and family reunions. RV hookups available. Group barbecues. Off-season bed and breakfast. Spanish spoken. Nearby: Cowboy Artists Museum of America, Kerrville, Fredericksburg (Little Europe U.S.A.), LBJ Ranch and National Park, Fiesta Texas, Sea World, San Antonio River Walk.

Mayan Dude Ranch
Bandera, Texas

The Mayan Dude Ranch is along the Medina River in the heart of Texas Hill Country near the town of Bandera. This ranch delivers warm hospitality; it has been doing so since the early 1950s. Judy and Don Hicks and their children (all 12 of them) quickly make you feel like family. Guests come mostly from Texas, though some come from England and Germany. Summers are on the warm side. Winters are short and mild. From little buckaroos to older cowpokes—there is something for everyone.

Address: P.O. Box 577 K, Bandera, Texas 78003-0577
Telephone: (210) 796-3312, 796-3036; fax: (210) 796-8205
Airport: San Antonio
Location: 47 miles northwest of San Antonio off Highway 16, 260 miles south of Dallas
Memberships: Texas Travel Industry Association, Texas Hotel-Motel Association
Awards: Texas Governor's Award for Hospitality 1985
Medical: Bandera Clinic, Kerrville Hospital, 24 miles
Conference: 150 classroom-style in 2,500-square-foot conference facility with 600 square feet of deck; audiovisual equipment available
Guest Capacity: 167
Accommodations: Twenty-nine Texas rock air-conditioned cottages, carpeted and decorated with many handmade furnishings. Six cottages with fireplaces nestle under old cedar trees. There are two two-story lodges with carpeted motel rooms and handmade western furniture. All rooms have private baths and color televisions but no telephone. Daily maid service. Laundry facilities available.
Rates: • \$-\$\$. American Plan. Children's and weekly rates available. Corporate, group, and government rates. Two-day minimum stay.
Credit Cards: Visa, MasterCard, Diners Club, Discover, American Express
Season: Year-round
Activities: Structured activities program (optional) during the summer. All kinds of contests for guests. One-hour morning and afternoon trail rides, 25 guests per ride with 2 wranglers. All riding done at a walk. Guests usually get two rides a day. The cool, clear Medina River offers swimming, tubing, and fishing (cane fishing poles available). Unheated swimming pool, two tennis courts, and a nearby fitness center with Nautilus weight machines; 18-hole golf nearby. The Hicks will send you their activity chart filled with lots of information.
Children's Programs: Summer season only. Children's arts and crafts, games, and outings, varied and well-planned program. Kids are watched two hours in the morning and two hours in the afternoon. Kids' roping lessons. Twice a week children eat separately. Children under 6 ride in corral.
Dining: Open to the public by reservation only. The Mayan Cocktail Lounge features happy time from 6:00 to 7:00 p.m. Steak fries, barbecues, and cookouts along the river. Theme nights including Indian night, Mexican fiesta, weekly musical nights. Lunches may be served poolside. The cowboy breakfast is truly a big affair.
Entertainment: Planned entertainment each night, western dancing at ranch "ghost town," truck and horse-drawn hayrides to cowboy breakfasts. Entertainment in the bar several evenings a week. Your children are supervised in the summer months.
Summary: The heart and soul of the Mayan Ranch is the family spirit and tradition. There is no ranch that I know of that has so many family members involved each day sharing their ranch with so many guests. Ranch attracts many Texas families and guests from Europe. Lots of food and plenty of activities—morning, noon, and night. Be sure to ask for a copy of the Mayan Ranch newspaper. Nearby: Frontier Times Museum in Bandera; Cowboy Artists' Museum in Kerrville, 24 miles; former President Johnson's ranch, 60 miles; Sea World, 45 minutes; Fiesta Texas, 30 minutes.

Silver Spur Dude Ranch
Bandera, Texas

Tom Winchell grew up in Kansas, lived as a boy on a farm in Arkansas, and spent most of his adult career as a building contractor in Houston. During vacations he would come to the Bandera area to ride as a guest at other dude ranches. In 1979, he bought a wonderful piece of property overlooking Texas Hill Country and built Silver Spur Guest Ranch on a plateau between two hills. The ranch features a huge native stone lodge with guest rooms and an equally large swimming pool that looks out to Saddleback Mountain. The relaxed atmosphere here enables guests to do as they wish. And one last thing, Tom is big on closing gates. On your drive in you'll see what happened to the last guest who forgot to shut the gate.

Address: P.O. Box 1657K, Bandera, Texas 78003
Telephone: (210) 796-3639; fax: (210) 796-7170
Airport: San Antonio
Location: 40 miles northwest of San Antonio, 10 miles south of Bandera off Highway 10-77
Memberships: Dude Ranchers' Association
Medical: Sid Peterson Hospital, Kerrville, 32 miles
Conference: 20
Guest Capacity: 20
Accommodations: There are three duplex stone cabins with names like Wyatt Earp and The Dalton Gang. Each has one king and one double bed, a television, but no telephones. Each has a covered porch.There are also nine single guest rooms in the 14,000-square-foot, three-story main ranch house. The ranch house rooms have double and king-size beds, private baths, color television, air-conditioning, heating, carpeting, and wood paneling.
Rates: • $. American Plan. Children's, group, and off-season rates available. Two-day minimum stay.
Credit Cards: Visa, MasterCard, Discover
Season: Year-round
Activities: Riding, swimming, and relaxing are the main activities. Rides go out daily, morning and afternoon. One-and-one-half-hour to three-hour rides into the park. Mostly quarter horses, a few fox trotters. The average ride has 15 guests. Most of the guests who come are beginners or have never ridden. Advanced riders should call and talk to Tom about the morning rides that offer a wrangling opportunity. Guests may unsaddle horses. Almost every guest spends a good deal of time in or around the junior Olympic-size pool overlooking the Hill Country. Lots of trails for hikers. Nearby tubing and fishing in the Medina River. Horseshoes, volleyball, trampoline, and swings. You may see white-tailed deer, armadillos, and jackrabbits.
Children's Programs: No special program. Families interact together. Shetland pony for very young children. Six years and older may go on trail rides. All the kids enjoy the swimming pool and the pool table in the lodge.
Dining: On-the-trail ranch meals served family-style in the huge dining room with vaulted ceiling which seats 125. Cowboy breakfasts with eggs and biscuits and gravy on the trail. Afternoon and evening meals feature cookouts and Texas barbecues with brisket of beef, German link sausage, and chicken. Warning: This is not the ranch for dieters. Ice available at the bar in the lodge. BYOB.
Entertainment: Hay wagons pulled by a "cowboy Cadillac" (Tom says, "That's cowboy for pickup truck"), campfire cookouts. Occasionally someone will pick and sing. Maybe a trick roper. Most guests go into Bandera in the evening for entertainment. Ask about Bandera's Arkie Blue's Silver Dollar Saloon, Cabaret & Dance Hall in Bandera.
Summary: Beautiful setting overlooking Texas Hill Country. A big Texas view. Riding, swimming, and relaxing by the pool are the main things here. Families usually stay a couple of days. Singles and European guests stay longer. Mostly beginner rides, some advanced rides. Call Tom and talk to him about his program.

See color photos, page 268

Prude Ranch
Fort Davis, Texas

The Prude Ranch was established as a cattle ranch in the late 1800s. Over the years, the Prude family became involved in the "people business." Since the late 1920s, guests and cattle ranching have been the main concerns of six generations of the Prude family. The Prudes specialize in tour groups, retreats, family reunions, and business workshops; they also welcome individuals and families all year long. This ranch is recognized throughout West Texas as a fun place for the entire family. Guests enjoy open range riding and many other activities. There are 50 horses and 100 head of cattle on over 3,000 acres. Many guests visit the ranch in their RVs, and the Prudes have 42 hookups. From single parents to business groups of 250, the Prudes make guests feel at home Texas-style with their warm, gracious, and sincere hospitality. As the Prudes say, "We are one mile high in elevation and a darn good place to spend any vacation."

Address: Box 1431K, Fort Davis, Texas 79734
Telephone: (915) 426-3202, (800) 458-6232; fax: (915) 426-3502
Airport: El Paso, Midland, or Alpine; private plane to Marfa Municipal Airport, 25 miles
Location: 6 miles west of Fort Davis off Highway 17 North, 210 miles east of El Paso, 150 miles west of Midland
Memberships: Discover Texas Association, AAA
Medical: Big Bend Memorial Hospital, 25 miles; EMT, 5 minutes
Conference: 250; 4,000 square feet
Guest Capacity: 250
Accommodations: Guests stay in batten and board ranch-style cottages with 35 spacious bedrooms. Single, double, and king-size beds, carpeting and Mexican tile, private bathrooms, and private porches. There are an additional 15 family cabins. There are several bunkhouses for singles, youths, and tour groups, with 10 to 20 bunk beds per room. Multiple baths and single stall showers.
Rates: • \$-\$\$. Rates depend on group and individual packages. Ask ranch for specifics. Riding may be extra depending on package selected. No minimum stay.
Credit Cards: Visa, MasterCard, American Express
Season: Year-round, including Thanksgiving, Christmas, and Easter
Activities: Activities are planned according to the size and interest of the group. Sign-up sheet in main lodge for guests to fill out daily. Four rides a day, all-day luncheon rides with advance notice. Families ride together. Two lighted tennis courts, large indoor/outdoor heated pool. Float trips on Rio Grande and 18-hole golf nearby can be arranged. Guests will see working ranch activities. Ask about corporate City Slicker programs and the chance to "play" cowboy.
Children's Programs: Summer ranch camp for kids 7 to 16 mid-July to early August. Babysitting available.
Dining: Cafeteria-style suitable for large groups. Chuck wagon dinners with pepper steak, squash, green beans, and chili beans. Mexican dishes, chicken, turkey, catfish, and white cod. BYOB.
Entertainment: Hayrides, sing-alongs, country-western dancing with fiddler and caller. Stargazing at world-famous McDonald Observatory. Mysterious Marfa lights. Steer roping and rodeos.
Summary: The Prude Ranch specializes in large groups, corporate, family, and foreign/domestic tour bus groups. Tremendous hospitality! Elderhostel super-site, art school. RV hookups. Nearby: Carlsbad Caverns and Big Bend National Park; side trips to Mexico, Chihuahua Desert Research Project. Video available on request.

Texas Lil's Diamond A Ranch
Justin, Texas

They call her Texas Lil, and she calls her ranch the Diamond A. If you are a business group, family, or individual looking to savor some mighty friendly Texas hospitality, with a western flair, for a day or an evening, better keep reading. Texas Lil is all Texan and has that marvelous "Ya'll come back now" personality that goes with being a good Texan. Originally, Lil got her start in the corporate catering business. Before too long she recognized that her clients wanted a relaxed ranch atmosphere to hold company and business gatherings. With no shortage of ideas and energy, it wasn't long before she found her Diamond A Ranch just outside Justin, a small town between Denton and Fort Worth. Today, her ranch offers a host of day and evening activities for groups and individuals alike. If you are in Texas or traveling that way and want to enjoy the West, Texas-style, give the ranch a call. If by chance you are held up by the Diamond A gang when you arrive, tell these ole boys they can holster their pistols. Texas Lil sent you!

Address: P.O. Box 656K, Justin, Texas 76247
Telephone: (800) LIL-VILL (545-8455), (817) 430-0192; fax: (817) 430-0984
Location: 24 miles northwest of Dallas/Ft. Worth Airport, 30 miles north of Ft. Worth off Highway 35 West
Memberships: Dallas and Fort Worth Chambers of Commerce
Medical: Denton Medical Center, 12 miles
Conference: 1,000
Guest Capacity: 2,500
Accommodations: For small groups only, Lil offers a two-day, one-night City Slickers Cattle Drive.
Rates: • $-$$. Rates vary greatly with individual and group packages. Call ranch for details.
Credit Cards: None. Cash, traveler's checks, or corporate checks for groups.
Season: Year-round (closed Mondays May through October and Sundays November through April)
Activities: Individuals and families: most arrive before noon and will engage in a luncheon and afternoon activity program including hourly horseback riding, swimming (seasonal), fishing (Lil provides the water and the fish, you bring the rest), softball, and volleyball. A late afternoon hayride tops off the day. Group (tours, travel clubs, bus tours, and corporate groups): participation in a variety of activities depending on the group package chosen. Ask about the following packages: City Slickers Cattle Drive, Day at a Dude Ranch, Texas Experience Cookout, and the Cowboy Breakfast. Twenty-five tee cowboy golf driving range (everything provided).
Children's Programs: No specific program. Special activities can be arranged for children's groups. Old-fashioned playground with giant tree slide, trampolines, swings, horseshoe pitching, cable trolley, bucking barrel, tire swings.
Dining: Ranch specializes in Texas-style barbecues and steaks. Everything is home-baked. A private club (the Longhorn Saloon) is open to guests and serves mixed beverages, beer, and wine.
Entertainment: Country music with guitar-picking, singing cowboys. Country swing dancing, shootouts, wild outlaws, arena games with competitions and prizes, rodeos, and Wild West shows.
Summary: The Diamond A Ranch is a day ranch offering customized western packages/activities for groups and individuals. Plenty of Texas hospitality and exciting western fun located in the Dallas-Ft. Worth Metroplex. Nearby: Six Flags Over Texas, Southfork Ranch, historic West End District of Dallas, and the old stockyards of Ft. Worth.

Y.O. Ranch
Mountain Home, Texas

Y.O. Ranch is in the heart of the Texas Hill Country near San Antonio. It is one of Texas' largest working ranches and the largest exotic wildlife ranch in North America. Today, fourth-generation Gus Schreiner oversees all guest activities. The Y.O. is famous for its herd of 1,500 Texas longhorns and over 10,000 animals, representing 55 species, that inhabit 40,000 acres of ranchland. Visitors come to see native white-tailed deer and turkeys, as well as giraffe, ostrich, wildebeest, scimitar-horned oryx, addax, European fallow deer, Japanese sika, axis, aoudad, Iranian red sheep and Indian black buck antelope, zebra, and African Watusi cattle. The Y.O. is very conservation oriented and runs a wonderful educational program and summer camp for children. At its 2,200-foot elevation, the Y.O. is dry and temperate most of the year. Evenings are usually cool.

Address: Drawer K, Mountain Home, Texas 78058
Telephone: (210) 640-3222; fax: (210) 640-3227
Airport: San Antonio International and Kerrville; small 2,200-foot airstrip at the ranch
Location: 1½ hours northwest of San Antonio off I-10, 30 minutes northwest of Kerrville
Memberships: International Wildlife Ranchers' Association, Texas Longhorn Breeders Association
Medical: Sid Peterson Hospital, Kerrville
Conference: Up to 2,500 for an afternoon or evening visit with meal
Guest Capacity: 30-35 overnight
Accommodations: Four renovated log cabins, each over a century old with names like Wells Fargo, Boone, Crockett, and Sam Houston. Each is individually decorated with Old West relics and furnishings and sports Texas Historical Markers. Each has a fireplace, gas and electric heat/air-conditioning, and a front sitting porch. There are also four rooms in the former Schreiner home. There are no telephones or televisions in any of the rooms.
Rates: • $-$$. American Plan. Children's rates; children under 4 free. Wildlife tours, horseback riding, photo safaris, and hunting rates available. No minimum stay.
Credit Cards: Visa, Mastercard, American Express
Season: Year-round. Closed Christmas Eve and Christmas Day.
Activities: Most come here to relax, enjoy Texas hospitality, and view all the animals. No scheduled programs unless requested. Limited horseback riding opportunities on a reservation basis only. You should book this before you arrive. Rides go out for a minimum of one hour. Most guests go on the daily guided ranch tours or relax and swim in the beautiful Y.O. pool with adjoining hot tub. The ranch offers photographic safaris and an adventure nature trail. Texas longhorn cattle drive each spring. Limited year-round hunting is available.
Children's Programs: Ranch adventure camp June, July, and August. Ask ranch about environmental programs for children 9 to 14 during the school year.
Dining: Bertie, the ranch chef, has been featured five times on "Great Chefs of the Southwest." Breakfast, lunch, and dinner served at the Chuckwagon Dining Room. Serve yourself buffet-style —all you can eat. Be sure to try the world-famous Y.O. Ranch-style Beans. Liquor available.
Entertainment: Game viewing from pool deck. Piano, pool table, and shuffleboard. Wait until you see the main lodge. Ask about the Y.O. Social Club and other special events.
Summary: Famous 100-year-old, 40,000-acre working cattle/wildlife ranch with 10,000 game animals from around the world and large herd of Texas longhorns. Most come to view wildlife and relax. The Y.O. is rich in history and serves up tremendous Texas hospitality. Photo safaris and cattle drive each spring. Summer camp for children. Limited big game hunting. Special note: The Y.O. has a family landowner program. Ask ranch for details. Nearby: The Alamo, LBJ State Park, Cowboy Artists of America Museum.

Pack Creek Ranch
Moab, Utah

Pack Creek Ranch is wonderful! Fifteen miles southeast of Moab and within easy driving distance of Arches and Canyonlands national parks, this rustic hideaway is in the foothills of the 12,721-foot La Sal Mountains. Hosts Ken and Jane Sleight met some years ago on a whitewater raft trip. In 1987, they bought their 300-acre ranch to complement a lifetime devoted to river running and horse packing. Pack Creek Ranch is in the heart of beautiful riding, hiking, rafting, and mountain bike country. Here you call your own shots. Most come here to commune with nature, enjoy the peaceful setting, savor good, friendly company, and relax for a day, a week, or more. If beautiful sunsets are your thing, wait until you see the sunsets over the distant Moab Rim.

Address: Box 1270 K, Moab, Utah 84532
Telephone: (801) 259-5505; fax: (801) 259-8879
Airport: Grand Junction, Colorado, 100 miles; commercial flights to Moab Airport, 30 miles
Location: 15 miles southeast of Moab, 5 hours south of Salt Lake City, look for La Sal Mountain Loop Road off Highway 191
Memberships: Utah Guide and Outfitters Association
Medical: Allen Memorial Hospital in Moab, 16 miles
Conference: 50
Guest Capacity: 50
Accommodations: Nine red-roofed cabins are of log or log-sided construction. Each has a living room, full kitchen, hide-a-bed, electric blankets or quilts, and carpeting; most have fireplaces. Cabins vary in size, sleeping from 2 to 12 people. Ask ranch for details. Laundry can be sent out.
Rates: • \$-\$\$. Includes breakfast, dinner, and sack lunch. Riding extra. No minimum stay.
Credit Cards: Visa, MasterCard, American Express, Discover
Season: Cabins available year-round. Restaurant open to public and guests April through October. Call for group and holiday activities.
Activities: The ranch is a base camp for many different kinds of activities on and off the property. Some guests arrive and do absolutely nothing. Others hike or ride in the canyons or the La Sal Mountains or swim in the pool or soak in the hot tub/sauna. Horseback riding is available, but extra. Guided rides go out by reservation from April through October. Ken offers 1- to 3-night pack trips to a mountain hideaway (South Mountain Cabin) or to Amasa's Back and into Grand Gulch. Exciting river rafting trips arranged through local outfitters. Ask about their backpacking and horse packing trips. Also available are scenic flights, jeep trips, mountain bike (BYO and rentals available in town) tours, and fishing. Cross-country skiing in the winter.
Children's Programs: Children welcome but no special program.
Dining: Hearty breakfast. Lunch sack—make your own buffet at breakfast. Candlelight dinners include fresh seafood, Swedish cream topped with raspberries. Crab, pasta, and fresh fruit salads, barbecued chicken, steaks, and vegetarian specialties. Wine available.
Entertainment: Few organized activities. You may hear country-western or piano music or a poetry reading at dinner. Lots of books.
Summary: Come to Pack Creek to relax. No telephones and no televisions. If you need to be entertained around the clock, ride on. Jane and Ken offer a low-key environment away from all social pressures. Host Ken Sleight is very knowledgeable about Utah's backcountry. Ranch is open to the public for dining and horseback riding. Massage available. Much like a guest ranch run like a country inn. Nearby: Canyonlands National Park, the wild Colorado River, and the biggest attraction—Arches National Park. Pack Creek takes rides into the park in the summer.

Reid Ranch
Salt Lake City, Utah

The Reid Ranch sits at 7,800 feet, on the slopes of the Uinta Mountains, once home to the Uinta Ouray Indians. Since it was originally homesteaded in the late 1800s, the property has had four owners, all of whom savored the abundance of wildlife and nature's tranquillity. Today, this modern ranch is owned by Mervin and Ethna Reid, both Ph.D.'s, and managed by their son, Gardner. Only two hours east of Salt Lake City, the ranch owns 400 acres and is surrounded by state and federal forest land. The Reids, both from Utah, have a very successful Reading Center that attracts people nationwide. They bought the ranch to host visitors from around the world and to establish a learning environment where individuals, teachers, students, and professionals could have fun studying in nature's setting. It is ideal for business conventions, executive meetings, and relaxing vacations. The ranch offers lodge facilities for seminars, family reunions, and group retreats.

Address: 3310 South 2700 East K, Salt Lake City, Utah 84109
Telephone: (800) 468-3274, (801) 848-5776 (summer); (801) 486-5083 (winter); fax: (801) 485-0561
Airport: Salt Lake City International
Location: 50 miles east of Heber City off I-40, 100 miles east of Salt Lake City
Memberships: International Reading Association
Awards: United States Department of Education, Nationally Validated Reading and Computer programs
Medical: Heber City Hospital, 50 miles
Conference: 110; two 2,000-square-foot meeting rooms/dining rooms
Guest Capacity: 110
Accommodations: Two modern lodges and two newly built homes. One lodge, The Bunkhouse, has two rooms that sleep 26 each in bunk beds and a 2,000-square-foot dining/meeting room. The main three-story lodge has seven large bedrooms that sleep up to 7 adults each. The 24-foot cathedral ceilings, spacious entry, library with adult and children's books, large dining area, and decks provide a wonderful atmosphere.
Rates: • $. American Plan. Children's rates available; children 6 and younger free. Family, corporate, and group rates available. No minimum stay.
Credit Cards: American Express
Season: June through September
Activities: Adults and children can participate in activities like horseback riding (half-hour and hour rides). Riding sign-up sheets for one-hour to all-day rides on the ranch's limited number of horses. Rides are mostly walking, guided rides. Fishing, hiking, fossil hunting, swimming in kidney-shaped heated pool and whirlpool spa, one lighted sports court for tennis, volleyball, and basketball. Photography, archery, and four-wheel-drive trips.
Children's Programs: Excellent setting for family reunions. Kids are the complete responsibility of their parents or nanny. Reading camp program each summer with teachers and counselors.
Dining: Buffet breakfast and lunch; dinner under chandeliers on formally set tables. Barbecues, special meals on request, weekly cookouts. Groups should contact ranch in advance. BYOB.
Entertainment: Campfires, tractor hayrides, occasional forest ranger talks.
Summary: Excellent group/conference ranch facility, great for church, business groups, family reunions. Individual families call regarding two cabins available for rent in late June and early July. Seminars for teachers in teaching methods and leadership workshops for administrators, reading/computer camp for students, English and reading classes taught as a second language for adults. Nearby largest piñon and juniper forest in the world. Only east-west mountain range in the United States, Dinosaur National Monument. Spanish spoken fluently.

See color photos, page 269

Rockin' R Ranch
Antimony, Utah

The Rockin' R is in Grass Valley on the outskirts of the little village of Antimony, just north of Bryce Canyon. Burns Black is the patriarch of the ranch. Early in his ranching career, Burns realized that the best way to stay afloat in the cattle business was to diversify. In 1970, the ranch opened its doors to the public. A 21,000-square-foot, three-story, barnlike lodge was built in 1985. Since then, more rooms and facilities have been added. The Rockin' R is operated by Burns, his wife, Mona, two sons, and close family friends. The Blacks run nearly 1,000 head of cattle on the privately owned 1,000 acres and on 40,000 acres of leased grazing land. The ranch hosts guests at the lodge, lake, and river, and offers trail rides up on the Aquarius Plateau where you can "see forever." The Kids & Colts Summer Camp experience, a program to make good kids better, is something the Blacks have been doing since 1970. Executive retreats, family reunions, youth groups, and business conferences are all welcome at the ranch.

Address: 9160 S. 1850 West, #20, Sandy, Utah 84070 (office); Antimony, Utah (ranch)
Telephone: (800)RNR-4FUN (767-4386), (801) 565-8588; fax: (801) 565-8526
Airport: Bryce Canyon airstrip, 35 miles south; Salt Lake City, Las Vegas, or Cedar City
Location: 200 miles south of Salt Lake City, 60 miles south of Richfield, just east of Highway 89, 37 miles north of Bryce Canyon
Medical: Richfield Hospital, 60 miles
Conference: 120
Guest Capacity: 250
Accommodations: The lodge is surrounded by lawns and ball fields. It features a full three-story fireplace with a huge, rock-floor fire pit. There are 22 private rooms, all carpeted, plus two large dormitories that sleep 55 each. Guests use large, tiled restrooms with both private and group showers. Laundry facilities are available nearby.
Rates: • $-$$. American Plan. Children under 4 free. Youth rates. Special youth group and family reunion rates available.
Credit Cards: Visa, MasterCard, American Express, Discover
Season: Year-round
Activities: The Rockin' R Ranch offers a host of outdoor and lake activities, including cattle drives and roundups. Guests may participate in cattle drives at the 10,000-foot cow camp or take half-day or all-day rides on one of forty saddle horses. Pack trips and riding instructions are available. Near the lodge, there is a bungie sling, basketball, softball, football, lawn hockey, tennis court, zip lines, bull-barrel ride, and more. Just three miles from the main lodge is six-mile-long Otter Creek Lake, a popular fishing lake. Sailboarding, canoeing, sailing, and water skiing are some of the lake activities.
Children's Programs: Games and activities for all ages. Kids are the responsibility of parents. Baby-sitting is available. Kids & Colts Summer Camp in June, July, and August for ages 9 through 17 who really want a unique, one-of-a-kind ranch experience.
Dining: Buffet, cafeteria-style food in the lodge dining room and solarium. Dutch oven chicken, barbecued steak with mushrooms, Rockin' R pizza, fresh fruits and vegetables, etc. Nonalcoholic beverages served. BYOB.
Entertainment: Hayride, dancing, cowboy poetry and singing, and fun times around the campfire or fireplace.
Summary: Excellent for foreign and domestic tour groups, vacationing families, small to medium-sized conference groups. (Lodge may be booked exclusively for larger groups.) Cattle drives available. Video available on request. Nearby: Zion, Capitol Reef, Bryce, and other national parks and monuments.

Tavaputs Plateau Ranch
Green River, Utah

Tavaputs ("Rising Sun" in Ute) Plateau Ranch takes in some 15,000 acres along the rim and plateaus bordering Desolation Canyon. At 9,100 feet, the main guest lodge is surrounded by rolling meadows, steep mountains, and red rock canyons. The view is endless—the Uinta Mountains to the north, Colorado and Arizona to the east and south. Four generations of the Wilcox family have owned and operated Tavaputs Ranch. Today, it is run by Jenette and Don. This part of the country is full of early American folklore. Butch Cassidy and his wild bunch rode the same trails you will ride. Don is an expert on local history. Nearby are the remains of the Fremont Indian culture. Relaxing is easy here. Soft country music after a hearty dinner, combined with brisk night air, makes sleep effortless. If you arrive by car, the ranch will meet you in East Carbon City as the gates to the ranch are kept locked, and it's one heck of a drive in.

Address: Box 418 K, Green River, Utah 84525
Telephone: (801) 454-8955 (summer radio telephone); (801) 564-3463 (winter)
Airport: Salt Lake City, Utah; Grand Junction, Colorado
Location: 200 miles southeast of Salt Lake City, 65 miles east of Price, off Highway 6/50
Memberships: Utah Cattleman's Association
Medical: Castleview Hospital, 65 miles; Life Flight helicopter available
Conference: 15
Guest Capacity: 15
Accommodations: A variety of accommodations for singles, couples, and families in the main building, as well as in several cabins that sleep up to 6. Each has private bath, carpeting, homemade comforters. The ranch makes its own electricity, and the ranch generator runs continuously.
Rates: • $$$. American Plan. White water trips extra.
Credit Cards: None
Season: June through September
Activities: Riding, relaxing, hiking, and rafting are the main attractions here. Combination ranch and rafting packages available. If you enjoy walking, you can take strolls through fields and aspen woods as well as ambitious hikes along the rim country or in the canyons. Four-wheel-drive trips to breathtaking vistas and canyons. Plenty of horseback riding on saddle mules and quarter horses—slow, easy rides taking in the scenery. Ask about the Desolation Canyon and Range Valley rides. Rafting trips in conjunction with rafting outfitter—Western River Expeditions. Jenette will have them send you information. Outdoor whirlpool.
Children's Programs: None. Older children are welcome. Children under 5 do not ride.
Dining: Great ranch food. Meals are carefully planned and well balanced. Stone-ground whole wheat breads and rolls, fresh scones, apple strudel. Roast beef, steaks, fresh fruits and vegetables. Special diets catered to with advance notice.
Entertainment: Depends on group. Occasional guitar music, sing-alongs, or player piano.
Summary: If you want to truly get away from it all and be literally on top of the world, give Jenette and Don a call. Very, very remote ranch offering ranch and rafting package vacations. The drive to Tavaputs is magnificent but very slow going, approximately an hour and a half by four-wheel-drive vehicle from East Carbon City. You should let Don or Jenette pick you up. Spectacular views, lots of wildlife, and brilliant sunrises and sunsets. Wildlife photographers' paradise, nightly bear watch, Fremont Indian pictographs, Butch Cassidy country, western river expeditions.

Firefly Ranch
Bristol, Vermont

In 1980, Marie Louise Link (she likes to be called "Issy"), not knowing the first thing about horses but having lots of people experience at her restaurant in upstate New York, began the Firefly Ranch. A native of Germany, she came to the United States in 1962. After 13 years in a successful but pressured restaurant business, she sought a way of relaxing. And so, Firefly was born. Taking only eight guests at a time, Firefly serves warm and friendly New England hospitality in the Green Mountains with their rolling farmlands, beaver ponds, and woodland glades. The atmosphere is casual. Said one guest, "We felt not like guests but like members of the family." A stay at Firefly is much like finding a friend in a beautiful part of the country. Riding here is by choice, not by chance.

Address: P.O. Box 152 K, Bristol, Vermont 05443
Telephone: (802) 453-2223
Airport: Burlington International, 26 miles; pickup available at a small charge
Location: 16 miles northeast of Middlebury off Route 7 or Route 116
Medical: Porter Hospital in Middlebury, 20 minutes
Guest Capacity: 6
Accommodations: Inn-type lodging with views from each of the three rooms. The main house overlooks Mount Abraham, Vermont's second-highest mountain, and sleeps six. Double and single beds, shared baths, homemade quilts, electric blankets. Spa room with hot tub that seats five.
Rates: • $$. American Plan. Two-day minimum for riding. Bed and breakfast during the winter months. Tuesday through Sunday riding packages. Arrive after 4:00 p.m.
Credit Cards: None. Personal checks accepted.
Season: May to October (summer); December through March (winter)
Activities: In summer, there is unlimited English and western riding. You may ride 5 to 6 hours per day. For those who are out all day, Issy will prepare a lovely picnic including homemade soup. Rides cater to intermediate and experienced riders. All rides accompanied by experienced guides. Lots of hiking and fishing off the property, spring-fed pond for swimming, hot tub, tennis nearby. In winter, Firefly turns into an informal ski lodge, offering coziness, cross-country skiing, snowshoeing, and downhill skiing at Mad River Glen and Sugar Bush, 12 miles away.
Children's Programs: No children please. Teenagers must definitely be experienced riders.
Dining: Wonderful fresh gourmet German-American food served on bone china, with crystal glasses, sterling silver, and cloth napkins. As Issy says, "I may not ride well, but I do cook well!" Complimentary cocktails and wine served. Vegetarian and macrobiotic and modified kosher diets catered to.
Entertainment: Most guests are too tired after an all-day ride to do anything except relax, eat, and climb into bed for deep sleep.
Summary: Firefly specializes in the three R's—riding, rest, and relaxation. Most come here for riding, the privacy, and the quiet atmosphere. Ranch country inn/B&B. You may bring your own horse if you wish. English riding lessons. Massage available by appointment only. Families of four or more with children may book the entire ranch as a home-away-from-home, and many do. Local arts and crafts shops, the University of Vermont Morgan Horse Farm in Middlebury. Ask Issy about leaf peeping. Tremendous shopping in the marketplace of downtown Burlington. Dutch, French, and German spoken.

Flying L Ranch & Country Inn
Glenwood, Washington

Flying L Ranch is located in one of the prettiest mountain valleys in the Pacific Northwest. With commanding views of nearby Mt. Adams (second highest peak in the Northwest at 12,276 feet), this lush green paradise offers individuals, families, and groups country inn charm. The Flying L is a 160-acre retreat. In the mid-1940s, Les Lloyd, a forestry engineer, and his wife, Ilse, bought the Flying L Ranch to be their family home. The Flying L opened its doors in 1960. Today, the Lloyds' sons, Darvel and Darryl, both accomplished mountain climbers and outdoor educators, run the ranch. Most guests come from the Pacific Northwest and stay just a couple of days. Many art and business groups and organizations have found the Flying L ideal for retreats. The emphasis here is on hiking, cycling, nature watching, relaxing, and mountain gazing. As one guest said so well, "The Flying L is a place of peace and beauty, and what a mountain!"

Address: 25 Flying L Lane, Dept. K, Glenwood, Washington 98619
Telephone: (509) 364-3488
Airport: Portland, Oregon, 90 miles
Location: 35 miles north of Hood River off SR 141, Oregon; 100 miles northeast of Portland; 265 miles southeast of Seattle
Memberships: Professional Association of Innkeepers International, Washington Bed & Breakfast Guild
Medical: Mid-Columbia Medical Center, 32 miles
Conference: 30
Guest Capacity: 30
Accommodations: The main lodge sleeps 12 to 15 in six country-appointed rooms; a two-story guest house sleeps 12 in five rooms; and two-room cabins sleep 6 to 8. Most rooms have private bathrooms. Rooms are named after famous western personalities like Will Rogers, Charlie Russell, and Yakima Canutt. Full breakfasts are served to all overnight guests. Guests cook lunch and dinner for themselves or choose from wonderful restaurants nearby. Cooking facilities are provided. Complete meals can be arranged for groups.
Rates: • $. European Plan. Children's and weekly rates available. Ask about the summer midweek hiking package. Two-night minimum on certain weekends and holidays.
Credit Cards: Visa, MasterCard, Diners Club, American Express. Personal checks and cash accepted.
Season: Year-round
Activities: In summer hiking, cycling, and back-road exploring are the main activities. Bicycles are provided. Bring your own horse. Horse boarding facility is nearby. Steelhead trout fishing in the Klickitat River or berry picking in season. There are miles of ranch hiking trails and loop trails on national wildlife refuge. There are also many beautiful trails in the Mount Adams Wilderness and float trips on the wild White Salmon and Klickitat rivers. Local guides and outfitters can be arranged for white-water rafting, fishing, and llama pack trips. Ask Darvel about their three-day Mt. Adams hiking program. In winter, enjoy cross-country skiing on marked and groomed ranch and forest service trails. Year-round hot tub.
Children's Programs: No special programs. Children are welcome.
Dining: Cook for yourself in several shared kitchens. The ranch serves a hearty breakfast, including Mount Adams Huckleberry Hot Cakes. Restaurants in nearby Glenwood and Trout Lake. Full meal service can be arranged for groups of 15 or more.
Entertainment: Guests regularly gather in the warm living room to read by the fireplace. The Lloyds have a great collection of books on travel, history, wildlife, and mountaineering.
Summary: Beautiful setting and magnificent mountain views. Ranch bed and breakfast. Bring your own horse. Short stays OK; great place to host workshops and family reunions. Nearby: Glenwood rodeo in late June.

Hidden Valley Guest Ranch
Cle Elum, Washington

Hidden Valley Guest Ranch is a shining star. With charm, character, and lots of personality and hospitality, this ranch is terrific. It offers a year-round getaway in a relaxing atmosphere. The ranch is nestled in the Swauk Valley of eastern Washington in the foothills of the Wenatchee Mountains, at 2,500 feet. On 750 acres of canyon and rolling range, the ranch has been continuously operated as a guest ranch since 1947, when Hollywood cowboy and entertainer Tom Whited carved Hidden Valley from an old homestead dating to 1887. Many original buildings, including the homestead cabin, form the nucleus of the lodging facilities. Today Hidden Valley is owned and operated by the Coe family, Bruce and his wife, Kim, and Matt and his wife, Julie. The main features here are riding, relaxing, visiting, and enjoying the old-time serenity.

Address: HC 61, Box 2060K, Cle Elum, Washington 98922
Telephone: (509) 857-2344
Airport: Cle Elum Municipal Airport, 8 miles; commuter flights via Seattle to Yakima; DeVere Field (private), 6 miles
Location: 8 miles northeast of Cle Elum off Highway 970, 85 miles east of Seattle
Memberships: Cascade Mountain Lodging Association
Awards: Northwest Best Places 2 Stars
Medical: Kittitas Valley Community Hospital, 20 miles
Conference: 33
Guest Capacity: 40
Accommodations: One- to two-bedroom cabins and two fourplex cabins, each with its own personality and names like Cedar, Aspen, Apple Tree, Spruce, or Elk Horn. The cabins are wonderful! All are fully furnished with private bath and entry, gas heat, some fireplaces, and private porches.
Rates: • $-$$. American Plan. Horseback riding, hayrides, and bar tab extra. Off-season rates. Two-night minimum stay during summer and major holidays.
Credit Cards: Visa, MasterCard
Season: Year-round, including all holidays
Activities: Heated pool, ten-person hot tub, hiking, wagon rides, chuck wagon barbecues, and breakfast rides, fishing in Swauk Creek and trout farm nearby, wildflower/bird-watching. Good mountain biking, but BYO. New sports court. In winter, cross-country skiing, sleigh rides, sledding, and snowshoeing. Bring your own gear. The riding program is under the direction of Matt Coe and his wife, Julie. Matt is a champion horse trainer and has traveled internationally showing horses on the A-Circuit. Riding here is geared for all levels on excellent quarter horses. Daily 1½ hour and half-day rides. Ask about Lookout Mountain and Swauk Canyon rides. Because of Matt's experience, people do come for the day to ride on a reservation-only basis. From June through September team-drawn hayrides are offered.
Children's Programs: Family participation in all activities is encouraged. No organized children's program. Baby-sitting available during certain hours of the day. Children under 6 do not go on trail rides.
Dining: Guests eat in the cook house. Family-style dining served from a single-entrée buffet; all you can eat. Home-baked bread and pies, hearty western cuisine. Ranch specialties include Hidden Valley pork chops, barbecue, and Bruce's Mexican dishes. Vegetarian fare provided cheerfully on request. Beer and wine served.
Entertainment: Recreation lounge overlooks the pool and resembles a hunting lodge with fireplace, pool table, honky-tonk piano, and loads of atmosphere. Poker rides and play days, western fantasy weekends, gold panning and special events.
Summary: The Coes' Hidden Valley Guest Ranch is a diamond in the rough! Lots of Old West charm, warmth, and hospitality. Great setting and views. Excellent for two-day, three-day, and week-long ranch getaways and retreats. You may bring your own horse.

See color photos, page 270

Woodside Ranch
Mauston, Wisconsin

The 1,000-acre Woodside Ranch is open year-round and offers plenty of country-style activities for families. This is one of the few ranches in the country with a small buffalo herd. Woodside sits in the upper Dells on a high wooded hillside with panoramic views of the Lemonweir Valley. Woodside is a family-run guest ranch. It was started in 1914 by William Feldmann as a family farm. Soon the Feldmanns and their half-dozen children had friends wanting to be part of their fun. Grandpa Feldmann started charging guests $10 a week, and they still kept coming, so in 1926 he put an ad in the *Chicago Tribune* and the rest is history. Each year the ranch grew, until there were twenty-one cabins with fireplaces and a lodge. In 1952, the ranch was incorporated. It is managed today by the Feldmanns' youngest daughter, Lucille Nichols, and two grandsons, Rick and Ray Feldmann. You are part of the family at Woodside.

Address: Highway 82, Box K, Mauston, Wisconsin 53948
Telephone: (608) 847-4275, (800) 626-4275
Airport: Madison; small private airport in Mauston-New Lisbon, 11 miles
Train: Wisconsin Dells, 20 miles
Bus: Greyhound to Mauston, 4 miles
Location: 20 miles northwest of Wisconsin Dells, 70 miles north of Madison, 220 miles north of Chicago, 200 miles south of Minneapolis on Interstate 90/94.
Memberships: Wisconsin Innkeepers Association
Awards: Mobil 2 Star
Medical: Hess Memorial Hospital, 6 miles
Conference: 100
Guest Capacity: 150
Accommodations: Woodside offers rustic, informal accommodations. There are 21 one-, two-, and three-bedroom cabins with fireplaces, of which half are authentic log cabins. The main house has rooms with private baths that accommodate up to four people. All rooms have thermostatically controlled heat and air-conditioning. You must bring your own towels.
Rates: $-$$. American Plan. Three-day, six-day, and weekly rates available. Minimum three-day, two-night stay. Children's rates. Pet owners ask about pet rates.
Credit Cards: Visa, MasterCard
Season: Year-round except Thanksgiving
Activities: Summer recreation director on staff. Eight one-hour rides go out daily for novice to experienced riders. Daily breakfast rides and covered wagon and hayrides. Eighteen to twenty guests go out on trail rides. Experienced riders should ask about the advanced ride (must pass corral riding test). Three tennis courts, miniature golf, volleyball, large sauna. Fishing; several loaner poles, but you have to dig your own worms. Horseshoes, new outdoor heated pool, and paddleboats. Canoeing nearby. In winter, beginner alpine skiing with rope tow, night skiing, extensive cross-country skiing with 12 miles of tracked trails, horseback riding, sleigh rides, ice skating. Ski equipment rental.
Children's Programs: Pony rides in ring for children of all ages. Supervised play school during the day. Baby-sitting available but extra.
Dining: Barbecues, buffalo cookouts; family-style meals with everyone assigned to a table. Traditional country-style, like going to grandma's house, chicken dinners. Trading Post Cocktail Bar.
Entertainment: Square dancing and line dancing, polkas, 1950s music, sing-alongs, campfires with marshmallow roasts. Amateur night talent shows and guest rodeos.
Summary: Family owned and operated ranch for families, featuring log cabins with fireplaces, year-round horseback riding, horse-drawn wagon rides, sleigh rides. If you need to get dressed up for dinner or have television or telephones in your room, Woodside is not for you. Open seven days a week in the summer, weekends the rest of the year. Winter program. Small buffalo herd. Adults-only week at end of August.

Absaroka Ranch
Dubois, Wyoming

Absaroka Ranch is at the base of the spectacular Absaroka Mountains, yet just 25 minutes from the town of Dubois and just 45 minutes from the world-famous valley of Jackson Hole. The dirt road to the ranch offers exhilarating mountain views. The ranch hosts only sixteen guests at a time. Budd and Emi Betts and their terrific staff specialize in the personal touch. At 8,000 feet, the ranch is big on outdoor space, with thousands of acres and miles of trails, mountain streams, and valleys. Wildlife abounds; it is not uncommon to see elk, moose, deer, eagles, and even an occasional bear. The valley is surrounded by the Shoshone National Forest and wilderness, offering all the elements conducive to total rest and relaxation. If this kind of catches your fancy, better get on the telephone quickly—Budd and Emi book up quickly. Absaroka (named after the Crow Indians) is a very special place and attracts people who want a very personalized and secluded old-time guest ranch experience. Guests come from around the country, and most who travel through Budd and Emi's gates are families.

Address: Star Route, Dept. K, Dubois, Wyoming 82513
Telephone: (307) 455-2275
Airport: Jackson or Riverton via Denver or Salt Lake City
Location: 75 miles east of Jackson Airport, 16 miles northwest of Dubois off U.S. 26/287
Memberships: Dude Ranchers' Association
Awards: *Hideaway Report*: 1990 Family Guest Ranch of the Year
Medical: Emergency Clinic in Dubois, 16 miles
Guest Capacity: 16
Accommodations: Four cabins (Delta Whiskey, Six Point, Five Mile, and Detimore), are snug, heated, with two bedrooms and adjoining baths, comforters, full carpeting. One cabin has a fireplace. All cabins have covered porches with views of the Wind River Mountains and the manicured lawn in front where kids and families gather.
Rates: $$$. American Plan. Group, family, and children's rates available. Special rates for return guests.
Credit Cards: None
Season: Mid-June to mid-September
Activities: Activities center around guided horseback riding, guided hiking, and guided fly-fishing. Morning, afternoon, and weekly all-day, breakfast, and evening cookout rides. All levels of riding. Ask about Six Mile Overlook, Jackson Nob, and the beaver pond rides. For those who are not inclined to ride, hikes go out as requested to the Continental Divide and to Louise Lake with picnic lunches. Experienced fishermen should talk to Budd about his all-day fishing trips. The trout streams in this area are challenging. Limited fishing gear available. The ranch chef will gladly cook your fish for you. Float trips in Jackson Hole can be arranged. Ask about walking and horse pack trips (the ranch has a brochure on these). Photo enthusiasts should bring lots of film. Swimming in crystal clear but chilly streams and lakes. Many guests like to warm up in the redwood dry heat sauna at the end of the day.
Children's Programs: The Gold Pinch Palace recreation room has a pool table, a juke box, and a pop machine. Children's games, instructional horseback rides, and game rides. Baby-sitting can be arranged.
Dining: Delicious meals served family-style. Beef tenderloin and lasagna are two ranch specialties. Complimentary wine with dinner. BYOB.
Entertainment: Something is usually planned every evening. Gymkhanas, square dancing, card games, horseshoes, campfires, slide shows, weekly rodeos in Jackson, cowboy poetry.
Summary: Small, rustic, secluded, very personal and family-oriented, right at the base of the Absaroka Mountains. Walking and horse pack trips (ask for brochure), float trips. Saturday night in the western town of Dubois. Nearby: Yellowstone National Park, Teton National Park.

Allen's Diamond 4 Ranch
Lander, Wyoming

A rugged, high mountain ranch, a necklace of mountain lakes, and two salt-of-the-earth people: that's what makes this ranch sparkle. Jim and Mary Allen will welcome you to Diamond 4 Ranch, which is remote, pristine, and simple—and close to heaven. The Allens' paradise is best-suited for families, groups, and individuals who are adventuresome and love to fish, hike, and ride. The most important quality of all is to have a great spirit. You should go with an open mind so that you may fill it to the brim with beauty and images you will savor all your life. Jim and Mary are famous for their wilderness pack trips into Wyoming's Wind River Range. They have guided some of the country's top brass. They also share their ranch with those who choose not to go on pack trips. For many years Jim ran the horse program for the National Outdoor Leadership School. He is a leader and a man who loves to share his knowledge of the wilderness. He believes deeply that if we are capable of appreciation and self-reliance, we will be better people. The Diamond 4 Ranch is for those with great spirits who love the great outdoors.

Address: P.O. Box 243-K, Lander, Wyoming 82520
Telephone: (307) 332-2995
Airport: Riverton, Wyoming, 50 miles
Location: 35 miles west of Lander and 120 miles southeast of Yellowstone off Highway 287
Memberships: Wyoming Dude Rancher's Association; Wyoming Outfitters Association
Medical: Lander Valley Medical Center
Conference: 10
Guest Capacity: 10
Accommodations: Three log cabins with beds and bunks. Each cabin has propane lights (no electricity on ranch), sink, wood stove, rustic furniture, and covered porches with marvelous burl poles. Each is nestled among the lodgepole pines. The main lodge is the gathering place for visiting and home-style meals. Central shower house and lavatory has hot and cold water.
Rates: • $$-$$$. American Plan. Children's and pack trip rates. Three-night minimum stay.
Credit Cards: None. Personal and traveler's checks accepted.
Season: June through September
Activities: Unstructured. Wilderness fishing, unlimited horseback riding, sparkling high mountain lakes, pristine forests, wildflowers, and perennial snow fields, all within riding distance of your cabin. Wilderness pack trips for one or more by advance reservation. Hiking and relaxing. Big game hunting in the fall.
Children's Programs: Children are expected to participate with parents in the daily activities. Baby-sitters are available with advance notice. Talk with Jim or Mary about kids on pack trips.
Dining: Hearty family-style meals served in main lodge. Ranch cowboys and cowgirls sit together with guests. Meals always include meat, fresh salads and vegetables, home-baked breads, biscuits, and desserts—all you can eat. Special diets by advance request. Coffee and cookies always available. BYOB.
Entertainment: Visit at the main lodge, or sit on the porch of your cabin. Listen to the wilderness and the horse bells.
Summary: A small wilderness ranch with excellent pack trips and ranch stay. Remote comfort. Jim and Mary Allen offer the same sincere hospitality as Jim's grandfather did in the 1920s. Ask about the trips for kids age 9 to 15 in June.

Cody's Ranch Resort
Cody, Wyoming

Not far from the famous town of Cody, Wyoming, is Cody's Ranch Resort, a small, informal, friendly property that gives you the freedom to do as you wish. Many stop over here for several days when traveling to or from Yellowstone or Grand Teton national parks. Here the horseback riding is varied. Several rides leave from the back of the ranch. For many, though, horses and riders are trailered to locations up to 45 minutes away. Ask about the Eagle, Blackwater, Elk's Creek, and Green Creek rides. The seven-day-a-week riding program here is strict. All riding is done at a walk. That's fine for those who visit because many have never been on the back of a horse. And most come here to take in the beautiful scenery. If you wish a structured ranch program, better turn the page. If you wish a program that is less regimented in a very low-key atmosphere, where you can do pretty much as you wish, when you wish, you may want to give Barbara Cody a call. As she says, "It's your vacation," and she's happy to help you out in any way that she can.

Address: 2604 Yellowstone Highway, Dept. K, Cody, Wyoming 82414
Telephone: (307) 587-6271
Airport: Cody, Wyoming, or Billings, Montana
Location: 26 miles west of Cody just off U.S. Highway 14/16/20
Awards: AAA 3 Diamond
Medical: West Park Hospital in Cody, 26 miles
Conference: 30
Guest Capacity: 76
Accommodations: The lodge and guest facilities are nestled in a valley shaded by tall pines. Cottages are log-sided with motel-like western interiors, some with two bedrooms. All are spotless and very comfortable. All rooms have private baths; no television or telephone. All have covered porches.
Rates: • $$. American Plan. All-inclusive packages and family and off-season rates available. Minimum three-day stay.
Credit Cards: Visa, MasterCard, Discover
Season: Year-round, including Thanksgiving, Christmas, and Easter
Activities: Scheduled and unscheduled riding is the main activity at the ranch. Rides go out morning, noon, and evening. Riders and horses are trailered to points near Yellowstone National Park to provide a variety of riding terrain, but horses are allowed to walk only. There is one wrangler for every eight guests. Usually small groups of no more than ten go out on one ride. There is a small hot tub, volleyball, horseshoe pitching, hiking, and fishing off the property. Two-hour float trips can be arranged with a local professional rafting company. In the winter, the ranch becomes a base camp for snowmobiling and Yellowstone National Park. Ask Barbara for details.
Children's Programs: Children age 5 and older ride their own horses; baby-sitting available for children under age 5 while parents ride. Children are the responsibility of their parents.
Dining: Happy hour each evening at ranch lounge bar. Varied menus with daily steaks and fresh trout weekly. Cookouts by the ranch stream (3 times a week). Daily cookouts on the trail and afternoon ranch teas.
Entertainment: Evening rides; unscheduled musical entertainment, which could be a cowboy singer or a guest with a guitar.
Summary: A friendly ranch that attracts many families who travel with their AAA tour book close at hand. Riding is the main activity. Many come for three days; some stay for up to a week or longer. Strict riding program. Nearby: River rafting, Buffalo Bill Historical Center, Yellowstone and Grand Teton national parks.

See color photos, page 271

Bitterroot Ranch
Dubois, Wyoming

Bitterroot Ranch offers one of the premiere riding experiences in North America. It is bordered by the Shoshone National Forest to the north, the Wind River Indian Reservation to the east, and a 30,000-acre game habitat area to the south and west. The ranch is owned and operated by Bayard and Mel Fox. Bayard is a Yale graduate who has lived for many years in Europe, Africa, the Middle East, and the South Pacific. Mel was brought up on a farm in Tanzania and spent many years working with wildlife. Bayard and Mel place a strong emphasis on their riding program and provide at least two horses per guest, splitting rides into small groups according to ability. They provide both English and western tack, offer a jumping course for advanced riders, and give formal instruction twice per week. They raise and train their purebred Arabian horses exclusively for the use of their guests. The riding terrain is extremely varied. Sagebrush, plains, grassy meadows, and colorful rocky gorges give way to forested mountains and alpine clearings. With the Absaroka Range at the back door, riders are immediately immersed in wilderness settings. Because of their international backgrounds and strong equestrian program, Mel and Bayard get many European guests. When you get their brochure, you will also learn about their sister company, Equitour, which runs riding tours in twenty-eight countries around the world.

Address: Route 66, Box 807 K, Dubois, Wyoming 82513
Telephone: (800) 545-0019 (nationwide); (307) 455-2778; fax: (307) 455-2354
Airport: Riverton or Jackson
Location: 26 miles northeast of Dubois, 80 miles west of Riverton, 100 miles east of Jackson off Routes 287 and 26
Memberships: Dude Ranchers' Association
Medical: Medic in Dubois; Riverton Hospital, 80 miles
Guest Capacity: 29
Accommodations: Accommodations are provided in eleven cabins, many of which are old-time log cabins. Most have wood-burning stoves; all have electric heat, full bathrooms, and views of the mountains and river. The rustic main lodge offers a big stone fireplace, library and card room, and small bar. Laundry facilities.
Rates: • $$$. American Plan. Group and children's rates available. One-week minimum stay, Sunday to Sunday.
Credit Cards: None. Personal checks and traveler's checks accepted.
Season: Last weekend in May through third week in September
Activities: Besides a full riding program, with half-day and all-day rides, pack trips (extra), and optional videotaped riding instruction, there are week-long cross-country horseback rides: the Pony Express, Outlaw Trail, and Wild Horse Mountain rides. Telephone the ranch for more information. Bayard is a keen fly-fisherman. There is good catch-and-release fly fishing on the ranch in the East Fork of the Wind River, which is full of cutthroat trout. They also have two stocked trout ponds. Nature walks and hiking.
Children's Programs: Kiddie wrangler; no special programs. Young children ride at discretion of ranch.
Dining: As many of the guests are European, the standards of the cuisine are high. Complimentary wine with dinner.
Entertainment: Informal cocktail hour before dinner hosted by Bayard. Weekly square dancing in Dubois. Piano and extensive video library in main lodge, pool table.
Summary: This ranch offers an excellent equestrian program with both English and western tack. Expert instruction. Ranch-raised Arabians. Most who come are experienced riders. Unstructured and remote (it's a good drive into the ranch). Its sister company, Equitour, organizes exciting riding holidays in 28 countries for riders of almost all abilities. Lots of single people and families, many Europeans. Fluent German and French spoken.

See color photos, page 276

Brooks Lake Lodge
Dubois, Wyoming

Brooks Lake Lodge is in a world of its own. Recent guests have described the ambience in the following terms: enchantment, splendor, the greatest place in North America, a spiritual place, Heaven on earth. It is all of these! Now, for the rest of the story. Built in 1922, the lodge was an overnight stop for bus travelers on their way to Yellowstone National park. It later became a dude ranch, known as the Diamond G Ranch. Through a series of owners, the lodge deteriorated and eventually closed its doors. In 1988, the Carlsberg family discovered what Bryant B. Brooks had written about in 1889. "Among the pines glistened a lake . . . what a sight! Tracks of elk and bear. Where I sat on my horse stretched a broad, peaceful valley. I stood closer that day to nature's heart than ever before." Rehabilitation began, and its new doors opened in 1989. Dick Carlsberg's first words were, "Gee whiz, this is a very special place." I think you will agree!

Address: 458 Brooks Lake Road, Drawer K, Dubois, Wyoming 82513
Telephone: (307) 455-2121; fax: (307) 455-2121 (call first)
Airport: Jackson, 60 miles
Location: 60 miles northeast of Jackson off Highway 287/26, 23 miles west of Dubois off Highway 287/26
Memberships: Dude Ranchers' Association, Wyoming Dude Rancher's Association, Association of Historic Hotels of the Rocky Mountain West
Medical: Jackson, 60 miles
Conference: 26 (overnight); 250, day only
Guest Capacity: 26
Accommodations: Six comfortable lodge rooms with a distinctive motif and exquisite handcrafted lodgepole furnishings. There are also six cabins nestled in the spruce behind the lodge which offer wood-burning stoves, electric heat, and private baths with bathrobes. Several have wonderful old clawfoot bathtubs. The massive log lodge is furnished with wicker, antiques, and handcrafted works by Wyoming artists. No telephones or televisions. The Great Hall houses a collection of game mounts from throughout the world. The front lobby, with its large stone fireplace, serves as a gathering spot for afternoon tea and evening poetry readings or other entertainment. A separate spa cabin provides welcome relief after a hard day of riding, hiking, or in winter, cross-country skiing.
Rates: • $$$. American Plan. Children's, group, and winter rates available. Three-day minimum stay in summer.
Credit Cards: Visa, MasterCard, American Express
Season: Mid-June to mid-September (summer); late December to mid-April (winter)
Activities: In summer, an unstructured, informal program of daily horseback rides. The lush green meadows with an abundance of wildflowers lure the hiker, while Brooks Lake and nearby lakes and streams offer superb fishing. Canoes, fly-fishing rods, and tackle available. See Cross-Country Skiing Ranches for winter activities.
Children's Programs: None. Children must be 7 or older to ride horses. Kids are the responsibility of their parents. Nannies encouraged.
Dining: At 4:00 p.m. tea is served in the front lobby which includes English finger sandwiches, cookies, banana bread, or other baked pastries. Simply put—superb.
Entertainment: Before or after dinner, the Diamond G Saloon offers a full bar beginning at 6:00 p.m. with hors d'oeuvres, pool, darts, or perhaps a video. Forest Service naturalists provide evening talks weekly. Campfire singing and poetry reading as the mood strikes.
Summary: The spectacular scenery and warm hospitality leave guests with memories they treasure for years. Superb hiking, riding, and abundance of wild game provide daily viewing of deer, elk, moose, and bighorn sheep. This ranch is in a world of its own. Summer and winter presents an unforgettable experience. A great adventure back in time offering rustic luxury. Listed in the National Register of Historic Places. Be sure to ask about the old Yellowstone touring bus.

See color photos, pages 272-273

Breteche Creek Ranch Retreat
Cody, Wyoming

Breteche Creek is a unique, nonprofit educational ranch just east of Yellowstone National Park located on the edge of the Shoshone National Forest and the 18-million acre wilderness system that encompasses Yellowstone. The area is dramatically rugged, has a very remote feeling, and teems with wildlife, including an active grizzly bear population. Breteche Creek combines the recreation of a guest ranch with educational programs in areas ranging from ornithology and astronomy to writing and photography. Each day, various activities, workshops, and educational rides and hikes are offered. Guests may choose between the day's activities or go hiking, fishing, or exploring on their own. As Breteche Creek Ranch is a 7,000-acre working cattle and horse ranch, there are opportunities to "play cowboy," wrangling cattle or horses (for those who are able). As Chase Reynolds, director of guest programs says, "Breteche Creek is a remarkably beautiful, untrammeled area, and in keeping with its pristine nature, we direct our guests' attention to the natural world around us. In creating a camplike atmosphere, we sacrifice certain conveniences, such as electricity (we *do* have hot showers, propane lighting, flannel sheets, and gourmet meals)." The Breteche Creek Ranch experience is like going on a high country pack trip with the comforts of a mountain-based ranch camp retreat. There, the marvelous outward bound spirit prevails.

Address: P.O. Box 596 K, Cody, Wyoming 82414
Telephone: (307) 587-3844; fax: (307) 527-7032
Airport: Cody, Wyoming, or Billings, Montana. Pick-up service available from Cody.
Location: 18 miles west of Cody and 30 miles east of Yellowstone Park, off the Yellowstone Highway 14-16
Memberships: Cody Chamber of Commerce, Nature Conservancy, Greater Yellowstone Coalition
Medical: West Park Hospital, 18 miles
Conference: 16; no electricity or telephones, more appropriate for a "team performance enhancement retreat" than a traditional conference
Guest Capacity: 16-21
Accommodations: Seven "tent cabins" (wooden frame buildings with canvas roofs, some heated with wood stoves) are scattered along the creek, each one tucked among aspens for privacy. Each accommodates from one person to a family of four. A central lodge of native lodgepole and aspen houses the dining room. There are comfortable washrooms with hot and cold running water. All powered with propane.
Rates: • $$-$$$. American Plan. Children's and group rates available. Three-night minimum stay.
Credit Cards: None. Personal checks, traveler's checks, and cash accepted.
Season: June through September. Special sessions in wildlife viewing via cross-country skis with a naturalist offered in late November/December.
Activities: Traditional dude ranch activities—riding, hiking, fly-fishing, swimming, horse and cattle drives. Educational horseback rides and hikes have been offered in such subjects as ornithology, ecology, botany, astronomy, wildlife tracking, Plains Indian mythology, photography, and nature writing. Call for details.
Children's Programs: None. Children over 6 are welcome. Call ranch for details.
Dining: Healthful, fresh cuisine. Family-style meals. Classically trained chef. BYOB.
Entertainment: Lectures and lessons (fly-fishing, astronomy, photography), several evenings a week. Naturalist-guided day tours of Yellowstone National Park are offered each week.
Summary: As Chase Reynolds says, "This is not a place for those who need to blow-dry their hair every morning." This is a place for those who want to try something totally different from the traditional guest ranch, who love or would like to learn more about the outdoors, who want to be in a place that gets more traffic from elk and bears than it does from vehicles.

Brush Creek Ranch
Saratoga, Wyoming

Nestled in dramatic granite rock outcroppings in the southeast portion of Wyoming, Brush Creek Ranch for generations was home to western families like the Uihlein and, most recently, the Caldwell families. Mr. Uihlein built the main lodge in the early 1900s and consolidated several cow camps into the 6,000-acre Brush Creek Ranch, as it is today. When the Caldwells took over in the mid-1950s, they continued the western traditions. They continued the cattle operations, and only since 1991 have they allowed guests. At Brush Creek, traditions such as cattle drives, roping, branding, and roundups still endure.

Address: Star Route, Box 10 K, Saratoga, Wyoming 82331
Telephone: (800) Ranch-WY (726-2499), (307) 327-5241; fax: (307) 327-5384
Airport: Denver International Airport, 195 miles; Laramie Airport, 65 miles. Airport pick-up is extra.
Location: 65 miles west of Laramie off the Snowy Range Road, Wyoming Route 130; 16 miles northeast of Saratoga off Highway 130
Memberships: Dude Ranchers' Association, Wyoming Dude Rancher's Association
Medical: Clinic in Saratoga, 16 miles
Conference: 22
Guest Capacity: 22
Accommodations: 1900s-style, white-sided, green-trimmed spacious lodge or rustic cabins. The lodge is fronted by a small fountain and cascading flower garden and pine trees planted by the Uihlein family. The lodge features a native stone fireplace in the library and western murals in the dining and family rooms on the first floor. Sleeping accommodations are on the second and third floors. Each room is unique. All have private baths and entrances. Most have private, screened porches. These rooms have a turn-of-the-century feel. Cabin rooms are located near the main lodge but offer more privacy. These were used as the cowboy bunkhouses and the original Uihlein family cabin. All have private bathrooms, queen-sized beds.
Rates: • $$. Full American Plan. Children's, group, and off-season rates.
Credit Cards: None. Personal checks or cash accepted.
Season: Year-round
Activities: The ranch caters to the traditional ranch activities. This is a working cattle operation with over 500 head of cattle. Guests are always welcome to help with cattle work or, if they prefer, they may ride independent of the cattle. Daily morning and afternoon rides. All-day rides on request. No riding Sunday mornings. Ask about Francis Draw, Homestead Cabin, and Barrett Ridge rides. Fishing is available on three miles of Brush Creek or on the nearby North Platte or Encampment rivers. Hiking and mountain biking. Also available in the area are golf, tennis, float trips, and a natural hot springs. Winter cross-country skiing and snowmobiling.
Children's Programs: Half-day programs planned three times a week. Local baby-sitting available.
Dining: Served family-style with the ranch staff in the main lodge. Hearty western-style food. BYOB.
Entertainment: Informal barn dances in the hayloft of the old log barn. Campfire sing-alongs. Horse-drawn hay rides, breakfast rides, creekside barbecues, and pitching horseshoes.
Summary: Wonderful ranch for those who want authentic western charm at a working cattle ranch. This is wide-open cattle country. The real, down-home ranch goodness and Old West charm make Brush Creek Ranch a winner.

See color photos, pages 274-275

Castle Rock Ranch
Cody, Wyoming

Castle Rock Ranch offers a host of wilderness adventures in the magnificent South Fork Valley of the Shoshone River. It is bordered by the Shoshone River; by Castle Rock, which keeps a watchful eye over the property, pinnacles, and rocks of the desert; and by evergreen forests and distant snowcapped peaks. Today, Castle Rock is hosted by Derek and Gina McGovern, who purchased the ranch in 1993. Castle Rock offers guests an adventure experience. Guests who come to Castle Rock, both novice and expert, love outdoor adventures, along with western dude ranch activities. Here you can raft, kayak, mountain "technical" climb, mountain bike, as well as horseback ride and fish (both spin and fly-fishing). Some prefer to sit on their porches and watch the day go by, and that's just fine too.

Address: 412 County Road 6NS, Dept. K, Cody, Wyoming 82414
Telephone: (307) 587-2076 or (800) 356-9965
Airport: Cody
Location: 17 miles southwest of Cody
Memberships: Dude Ranchers' Association
Awards: Mobil 3-Star, AAA 3-Diamond
Medical: West Park Hospital in Cody, 17 miles
Conference: 32
Guest Capacity: 32
Accommodations: Ten log cabins sleep up to 6, feature handmade furniture, bright Pendleton blankets, and modern private baths with showers, and are decorated with Native American objects, pioneer era artifacts, and original paintings. All are insulated and heated, and most have either wood-burning stoves or fireplaces. The octagonal main lodge has a peaked roof and is decorated in a similar fashion. Floor-to-ceiling windows offer wonderful views of the mountains. Laundry service available.
Rates: • $-$$. American Plan, all-inclusive. Children's, family, and group rates. One-week minimum stay, Sunday to Sunday.
Credit Cards: None
Season: June through September. Open for special programs in winter.
Activities: In summer, there is an unusually wide range of activities supported by a large staff. Horsemanship instruction, including half-day and all-day rides, overnight pack trips. Outdoor experiences include kayaking, technical climbing, mountain biking, tubing, archery, rafting, Yellowstone guided trips, sailing, sailboarding, heated outdoor swimming pool, sauna, and stocked trout pond. Call for details concerning winter activities.
Children's Programs: Daily organized activities. "Kids' Club" for 3-year-olds and older. Swimming, arts and crafts, nature hikes, horseback riding, games, and skits. Children's tepees, game room, fishing pond. Baby-sitting available.
Dining: Guests enjoy the Saddle Saloon in the main lodge before dinner. BYOB. Western "gourmet" meals for all diets. No smoking in dining room. Everyone eats together.
Entertainment: Square dancing, musicians, cowboy balladry, game room in main lodge, rodeo nights in Cody, Buffalo Bill Historical Center.
Summary: Families, couples, and single people enjoy Castle Rock for the diversity of activities offered. It is a ranch with multiple outdoor adventure programs. Nearby: Yellowstone National Park and the Absaroka Range of the Rocky Mountains.

Cheyenne River Ranch
Douglas, Wyoming

Cheyenne River Ranch is in the wide-open prairie country of eastern Wyoming. Here sagebrush and prickly pear cactus dot the landscape. The wind blows the tumbleweeds, and you can see forever. For many, this is the Old West—the way it was and still is. Don, Betty, and Chuck Pellatz have welcomed guests to their 8,000-acre cattle and sheep ranch since the 1970s, usually only one family or couple at a time to ensure a real hands-on experience. Here the aroma of country cooking and the land are surpassed only by the warm, sincere western hospitality that the Pellatz family shares. There is nothing fancy at all about Cheyenne River Ranch, but then that is one of the reasons guests return. Don was raised in this part of the country. Betty, his bride and partner for over 40 years, came originally from Illinois. Together they raised five children and have devoted their lives to each other and the ranching tradition of the West. As Betty says, "It does get warm and the wind does blow, but we think this is God's country. When you ride the prairie you get the whole view of the landscape. The air is clean and the smell of the sage—it's wonderful." Here you will put things in perspective and share the rhythm of ranch life with a family who cares. When you stay with the Pellatz family, their home is your home!

Address: 1031 Steinle Road, Dept. K, Douglas, Wyoming 82633
Telephone: (307) 358-2380
Airport: Casper International Airport, 100 miles
Location: 50 miles northeast of Douglas, Wyoming, off Highway 59 and County Road 40
Memberships: WHOA-Bed and Breakfast and Ranch Recreation Establishments of Wyoming, Wyoming Stock Growers and Wool Growers Association, AAA approved
Medical: Converse County Memorial Hospital, 50 miles
Guest Capacity: 12 (usually only one family/couple at a time)
Accommodations: Both the ranch house and bunkhouse are beige with rust-colored trim. The bunkhouse has two bunk beds and a full bed with private bath. Three bedrooms are in the ranch house, two with full beds, one with twin beds; two have shared baths. All are immaculate, with quilts on the beds. There is a sheep wagon for those who want to experience the real West.
Rates: • $. American Plan. Children's, family, bed and breakfast, and cattle drive rates. No minimum stay. Most guests arrive Sunday and leave Saturday.
Credit Cards: None. Personal checks and cash accepted.
Season: April to October
Activities: The rooster lets you know the day has begun. This is a real working cattle and sheep ranch. April is calving and sheep-shearing time. May is branding and lambing. During May through October, there are six cattle drives, moving cattle from winter pasture to summer range. The program here completely depends on what you wish to do and what ranch work must be done. Chuck will teach you about horses. There is swimming in an aboveground pool.
Children's Programs: No organized program. Bottle-feeding lambs three times a day, gathering eggs, swimming.
Dining: Ranch cooking. Lasagna, barbecue steaks, pork chops, and casseroles. If you like lamb, let Betty know. The Pellatzes are nonsmokers and nondrinkers.
Entertainment: Lots of visiting. Lots of rock and fossil hunting. Tours of one of the largest open-pit coal mines. Stargazing. Learn to rope.
Summary: This is an 8,000-acre working cattle and sheep ranch in the wide-open prairie of eastern Wyoming. Usually one family/couple at a time. Warm, friendly, sincere ranch hospitality! Cattle and sheep work, cattle drives.

CM Ranch
Dubois, Wyoming

Life is simple on the CM Ranch, but then that's what makes ranch life so wonderful. The ranch's objective is to provide comfortable headquarters where guests can relax and enjoy informal, wholesome pleasures in the magnificent mountain country of the West. This classic ranch is one of the oldest dude ranches in the United States, with a fine reputation. The ranch and its Simpson Lake cabins in the Fitzpatrick Wilderness were recently honored with inclusion in the National Register of Historic Places. Pete and Lisa Petersen operate the CM with a wonderful staff of college students. The 7,000-foot altitude results in a predominantly dry and sunny summer climate. Rock hounds and geology buffs will be fascinated with the extraordinary red sandstone and geological displays.

Address: P.O. Box 217 K, Dubois, Wyoming 82513
Telephone: (307) 455-2331 or (307) 455-2266
Airport: Jackson or Riverton; private, surfaced airstrip 10 miles outside Dubois, 10 miles from ranch (large enough for small private jets)
Location: 6 miles southwest of Dubois
Medical: Clinic in Dubois, supervised by brand-new, fully equipped hospital in Jackson Hole
Conference: 25, small business groups
Guest Capacity: 50-55
Accommodations: Large, well-kept lawns surround 12 log cabins along Jakey's Fork, a branch of the Wind River. The green-roofed cabins have one-, two- and three-bedrooms, rustic wood furniture, wood-burning stoves, and small, comfortable porches with views of the meadows and the Badlands. Three beautifully decorated log houses with full amenities sleep up to six—East House, West House, and Hardie House. The CM employs a baby-sitter and laundress. Daily maid service for cabins and houses.
Rates: • $$. American Plan. Reduced rate for children under 12. One-week minimum stay, Sunday to Sunday arrival. Many guests stay two weeks.
Credit Cards: None. Personal checks, traveler's checks, or cash accepted.
Season: Mid-June to end of August
Activities: You can ride, fish, hike, swim in the outdoor heated pool, picnic, or relax with a book. Horses are matched to your ability. Usually six guests on each ride. Rides go out twice a day except Sundays. Weekly all-day picnic rides to Whiskey Mountain, which is, as Pete says, "home to the largest herd of bighorn sheep in North America." Excellent pack trips to Simpson Lake in the Fitzpatrick Wilderness. Five miles of stream run through the property, so anglers can fish privately for brook, rainbow, and brown trout. Fishing guides and tackle shop. Private fishing also available on the Wind River. Torrey, Ring, and Trail lakes are a short drive by auto. Tennis and golf nearby. Float trips on Snake River can be arranged. Parents must supervise their children at the pool.
Children's Programs: Kiddie wrangler, baby-sitting available (extra). No set program. A lot of family interaction.
Dining: Dining room decorated with Native American treasures. Menu includes traditional western meals that are carefully planned, well balanced, light, and healthy. Fresh mountain trout added to the menu frequently. Homemade breads and vegetarian dishes. BYOB. Welcome cocktail gatherings Monday evenings.
Entertainment: The recreation building has rooms for reading and games, two pianos, Ping-Pong, geology room, and small library, weekly square dancing in town, volleyball and softball with guests and crew, occasional musical evenings. Emphasis on spontaneity.
Summary: One of the most beautiful, really old-time historic ranches in North America. Tremendous warmth and personality. Second, third, and fourth generations come to the CM each summer. Great for families and large family reunions.

See color photos, page 277

The Cottonwoods
Moose, Wyoming

A little more than a two-day ride on horseback from Lost Creek Ranch, the Halpin family's showplace overlooking the Jackson Hole Valley, the Cottonwoods, is a stark contrast to Lost Creek. It is a rustic outpost located north of the Gros Ventre River, just south of Gunsight Pass and northeast of Coal Mine draw. The property was U. S. government patented to Edward Hill in 1909. In 1945, Bill Robinson established a small hunting camp for guests. Today, as Mike Halpin says, "This is a place for people to relive the Old West with a slow pace and an unstructured environment." During a stay at the ranch, you can ride, fish, explore the wilderness, or just relax by the campfire. Cottonwoods is a wonderful journey back in time.

Address: P.O. Box 95K, Moose, Wyoming 83012
Telephone: (307) 733-0945; fax (307) 733-1954
Airport: Jackson via Denver or Salt Lake City
Location: 40 miles northeast of Jackson. Accessible by four-wheel drive on the Gros Ventre River Road or by horse from Lost Creek Ranch.
Medical: First-aid assistance at ranch; St. John's Hospital, Jackson; emergency helicopter service available.
Guest Capacity: 16
Accommodations: Six sheltered rustic cabins and a main lodge shaded by tall cottonwood trees and adorned with western relics and furnishings. Navajo rugs on wooden floors, handmade quilts, flannel sheets, and wood stoves to keep you warm. Coleman lanterns and candles to show the way. Newly constructed bathhouse. Electricity generated at the ranch. No telephones or TV.
Rates: $$-$$$. American Plan, includes airport pickup. Mid-June to early September, four-night minimum stay.
Credit Cards: None. Personal checks or cash accepted.
Season: Mid-June to early September or until the snow falls.
Activities: Nonstructured and designed for each individual guest or group. Daily riding, your choice of half-day or all-day rides, pack trips. Experienced riders may ride alone once they have demonstrated competence. Trout fishing in Fish Creek (bring your own gear), hiking, and nature photography.
Children's Programs: Children 6 years of age and older are welcome but are the sole responsibility of parents. No planned activities.
Dining: Hearty, wholesome ranch-style food, including Dutch oven cooking and unexpected culinary surprises on authentic wood stoves. Evening barbecues and weekly picnics. Plenty of fresh fruits and vegetables. Special meals prepared with advanced notice. Families or groups who book entire ranch may help select their menu.
Entertainment: Cowboy coffee around a campfire, moonlight rides, occasional guitar strumming, and the yip-yipping of coyotes.
Summary: A wonderful adventure into Wyoming's Old West way back in the Gros Ventre Wilderness. Arrive by four-wheel drive or on overnight horseback trip from sister property, Lost Creek Ranch. Great for family reunions and groups of friends. Nearby: Jackson Hole, the Tetons, and the Snake River for rafting.

Crossed Sabres Ranch
Wapiti, Wyoming

Crossed Sabres Ranch was established in 1898 by Tex Holm as a stagecoach stop. As you walk around this historic ranch, you can imagine the old stagecoach with a team of six stout horses chomping at the bit as they wait for passengers. Crossed Sabres exudes life and rugged character the minute you lay eyes on the place. Besides the "years gone by" ambience, the ranch has a special feature: it is built alongside a wonderful stream that serenades all the cabins as it makes its way down the mountain. Fred could well have been a western movie star with his blue eyes and mustache. He and Alvie have seen a lot of guests over their 30 years in the guest ranch business. Today, as before, families come to be rejuvenated and share in each other's joy and excitement. Many love to sit in the rocking chairs on the porch of the main house, listening, watching, and remembering. Crossed Sabres has Old West charm and two of the nicest ranchers—Fred and Alvie Norris.

Address: P.O. Box K, Wapiti, Wyoming 82450
Telephone: (307) 587-3750
Airport: Cody, Wyoming, or Billings, Montana
Location: 43 miles west of Cody off U.S. Highway 14/16/20
Memberships: Dude Ranchers' Association, Wyoming Outfitters Association, Wyoming Dude Ranchers Association
Medical: Cody Hospital
Guest Capacity: 45
Accommodations: All seventeen cabins, half of which are along Libby Creek, have names like Red Cloud, Yellow Hand, Indian Echo, and Rides on Clouds. Each is rustic but comfortable and heated, with double and single beds and wooden floors. One hand-hewn pine rocking chair sits on each porch.
Rates: • $$. American Plan. Children's rates; children under age 2 free. Everything included. One-week minimum stay, Sunday to Sunday. Do not arrive before 3:00 p.m.
Credit Cards: None. Personal checks or traveler's checks accepted.
Season: Late May to October
Activities: Over the years, Fred and Alvie have developed a weekly program that gives guests a chance to relive history and to see what makes this part of Wyoming so famous. Sunday evening after the welcome barbecue beef and rib dinner, Fred discusses the week's calendar of events, which includes daily horseback riding (mostly slow and easy scenic riding), a day in Cody, an overnight pack trip into the Shoshone National Forest, and an all-day guided trip to Yellowstone National Park. This is really special because Fred is one of the few men alive who really knows the history of the park—his great-uncle was the second administrator. Also available are river rafting on the Shoshone River, fishing in nearby streams, and relaxing.
Children's Programs: No special program. Geared around family operation. Everyone rides and eats together. Younger children may ride with parents.
Dining: Wholesome family meals in the beautiful authentic old western main lodge built in 1906 with unique burl posts and beams. As Fred says, "Our food is just good. I eat it all the time. Nothing fancy, just hearty ranch cooking."
Entertainment: Cody rodeo, square dancing, movies, sing-alongs with wrangler, game room.
Summary: One of the most historic dude ranches in the country. Tremendous Old West charm. Fred Norris and his wife, Alvie, are old-time westerners and cattle ranchers with hearts of gold. Fred is a cowboy through and through. His famous Yellowstone Park tour is an absolute must. Weekly ranch program with on- and off-ranch activities.

See color photos, page 280

Darwin Ranch
Jackson, Wyoming

In a valley of its own, Darwin Ranch is one of the highest and most remote guest ranches in the Wyoming Rockies. It is a year-round hideaway surrounded by the magnificent Gros Ventre Wilderness. The property was first homesteaded by Fred Darwin in 1904. As the story goes, his Rough Rider friend, Teddy Roosevelt, gave Fred these 160 acres by presidential decree. In 1964, the old, rundown homestead was purchased and renovated. Today Darwin Ranch, at an altitude of 8,200 feet, welcomes 20 guests at a time during the summer and private gatherings of 6 to 12 people in the winter. Because the ranch is so small, there is great flexibility for guests and their desired activities. Though the ranch is secluded, guests can count on plumbing, electricity by a silent water turbine that runs 24 hours a day, a library, a piano, and a fine kitchen. Darwin Ranch offers an escape from hectic city life. It is today as it always has been—remote, low-key, serene, and beautiful.

Address: P.O. Box 511 K, Jackson, Wyoming 83001
Telephone: (307) 733-5588
Airport: Jackson. Call ranch for charter flights to ranch airstrip or helicopter flights from Jackson Airport.
Location: 30 miles east of Jackson, 50 miles northwest of Pinedale
Memberships: Dude Ranchers' Association, Wyoming Dude Ranchers Association, Wyoming Outfitters Association
Medical: St. John's Hospital in Jackson. Inquire about medical helicopter service.
Conference: 16
Guest Capacity: 20, summer; 12, winter (no less than 6)
Accommodations: Four rustic, comfortable log cabins. One with four bedrooms and two baths can sleep eight. One loft apartment with skylights and private bath in the main lodge is great for a couple. Each private cabin has its own bath (the old-fashioned kind), hot and cold running water, wood stoves, and sitting porches. No telephones. The main lodge with its vaulted ceilings has handmade furniture, large stone fireplace, sitting room, informal bar, dining room, and kitchen. From the lodge, there is a 360-degree view of wilderness.
Rates: $$-$$$. American Plan. One-week minimum stay policy during winter and high season in summer (late July to late August), Saturday to Saturday.
Credit Cards: None. Personal checks or cash accepted.
Season: Mid-June to late October; late December to early April
Activities: Individualized and nonstructured. In summer, enjoy this wilderness wonderland on foot or by horseback. Daily riding, fishing, pack trips. Experienced riders can ride without a guide once they have demonstrated competence. Riding program completely tailored to guests. It is totally flexible. Ask Loring about Sportsman's, Bacon, and Red Bluff Ridge rides. Also Brewster Lake! In winter, guided cross-country tours, snowshoeing. Five-person rustic log sauna by the ice-cold Gros Ventre River.
Children's Programs: Children are welcome, but they are the sole responsibility of parents. Many guests bring their own nannies. Better for children who can ride comfortably.
Dining: Continental and ethnic cuisine of considerable variety. Ask about Melody's specialties. Gourmet meals in the winter, even Chinese. BYOB.
Entertainment: The main lodge has a piano, lots of books and games, and a stereo tape deck with a variety of classical tapes and records. Most guests entertain themselves.
Summary: Rustic and isolated wilderness ranch in the heart of Jackson Hole's backcountry. Best for folks who are outdoor oriented and who enjoy an informal, beautiful setting, interacting with family or small groups of people. Very relaxing. Activities tailored to guests. Fluent French, Mandarin and Taiwanese, and some German spoken.

See color photo, page 281

David Ranch
Daniel, Wyoming

David Ranch was established in 1938 by Milton David, the present owner's father. Located on an 8,000-foot mountain plain. It is open country here with lots of room to breathe. Sublette County, where the ranch is located, is cattle country and is named after one of the early explorers and mountain men, Bill Sublette. Cattle ranches in this part of the country go way back and run thousands of head of cattle. The David Ranch leases its pastureland to some of these ranches and looks after about 3,000 head. Cattle work begins in late May and runs through September. Hosts Melvin and Toni David have been running the ranch since 1961. They have an excellent horse program and take great pride in teaching their guests about horsemanship. Adults are given tremendous appreciation for well-trained cow horses.

Address: Box 5, Dept. K, Daniel, Wyoming 83115
Telephone: (307) 859-8228; call for fax number
Airport: Jackson Hole, private planes to Pinedale
Location: 80 miles southeast of Jackson, 36 miles west of Pinedale off Highway 189
Memberships: Dude Ranchers' Association, Wyoming Outfitters Association, Green River Valley Cattleman Association, Wyoming Dude Ranchers' Association
Medical: Pinedale Medical Clinic, 36 miles east
Guest Capacity: 10
Accommodations: The ranch has four log cabins. One large two-room cabin was built in 1982 of native logs and timbers. Trappers cabin is about 20 by 20 feet, with shower. The old School House cabin was rebuilt in 1986 and also has a full shower. The last cabin is the old ranch house with three bedrooms and two bathrooms. The main ranch house serves as the kitchen, dining room, and living room and general gathering area. Handmade quilts on each bed.
Rates: • $$. American Plan. Minimum one-week stay.
Credit Cards: None. Personal checks accepted.
Season: Summer: June to mid-September; hunting in October; winter: mid-December to April
Activities: This is a working cattle outfit. As such, one has to have a good deal of flexibility because ranches like this are dealing with livestock and nature, and each day something unpredictable may occur. At the David Ranch there is a wide range of opportunities involving cattle and horses, provided you keep in mind the need for flexibility. Depending on the week and depending on the season, you may be herding, doctoring, and branding or cutting cattle, or you may just as easily be asked to fix a broken fence or learn how to rope. The main thing here that the Davids are particularly proud of is their well-trained and responsive horses. Here you will learn how a true cattle horse should perform, and perhaps most of all, you will learn that if you try to understand and respect a horse it will bring you tremendous pleasure and will take care of you as well. Other activities include fishing (you may catch your supper), horseshoe pitching, hiking, pack trips, wildflowers, and lots of photography.
Children's Programs: Children under 12 not recommended.
Dining: Served in the ranch house, hearty, filling, ranch-style food, weekly cookouts. Everything is cooked from scratch. Ranch specialties include full turkey dinners, steak barbecues, homemade pies. BYOB.
Entertainment: You are on your own. Occasional old western video movies and sing-alongs, horseshoe pitching.
Summary: Working cattle ranch. Great for experienced single adult riders and particularly for singles and couples who want to learn and work with horses and cattle (novice riders should talk with Melvin). Children not recommended. Superb horses. Hunting in the fall.

Eaton Ranch
Wolf, Wyoming

The Eaton Ranch is the granddaddy of dude ranches. Started in 1879 in North Dakota by three brothers, Howard, Willis, and Alden, the ranch relocated to its present site, 18 miles west of Sheridan, in 1904 to provide "more suitable and varied riding." Run now by the third and fourth generations, this 7,000-acre ranch has over 200 head of horses with daily rides for every type of rider. This is a no-frills spread—no telephones, no nightlife. There is no end to the varied riding terrain. You can hike or ride through open rangeland and wildflower-studded trails that traverse the intricate Big Horn Mountains just west of the ranch. One guest said, "What makes the Eatons' ranch such a success is that it has just enough structure to draw a family together but enough beautiful wide open spaces to give us our reins."

Address: P.O. Box K, Wolf, Wyoming 82844
Telephone: (307) 655-9285 or (307) 655-9552
Airport: Sheridan
Location: 18 miles west of Sheridan. Ask for a map if you have any questions.
Memberships: Dude Ranchers' Association
Medical: Sheridan Memorial Hospital, 18 miles
Conference: 15 to 20 (June, late August, and September)
Guest Capacity: 125
Accommodations: Guests stay in one-, two-, and three-bedroom cabins suitable for large and small families, couples, and singles. Most have twin beds, and all have private baths. Several have living rooms with fireplaces and real old-fashioned outdoor iceboxes, stocked and delivered the way they always have been with big blocks of ice onboard a '20s vintage Model A pickup. Most of the original cabins were built by and named after many of the early guests. Laundry facilities available.
Rates: $$-$$$. American Plan. Children age 2 and under free; other children's rates. Late June through early September, one-week minimum stay. You may arrive any day of the week.
Credit Cards: Visa, MasterCard. Personal checks preferred.
Season: June to October
Activities: The Eaton Ranch is one of just a handful of ranches left in the country that allow you to ride on your own (if you wish), only after the corral boss is confident that you are ready. Daily rides go out twice a day except Sunday. Pack trips, picnics, and riding instruction available. Fishing in Wolf Creek, hiking, bird-watching, and swimming in the heated outdoor pool. Golfers will enjoy the 9-hole course at a neighboring ranch or two courses in Sheridan.
Children's Programs: Children enjoy a variety of ranch activities. There is no children's counselor per se. Kids go to Howard Hall for crafts, games, and treasure hunts. Kids must be 6 years old to go on trail rides.
Dining: Huge dining room. Hearty western ranch cooking, barbecues, noon cookouts. At your first meal look for your personalized wooden napkin ring marking your place. BYOB in cabins.
Entertainment: Team roping, bingo, weekly country-western dancing at Howard Hall, the ranch's recreation building. Staff vs. guests softball games. Occasional rodeos in town. Books are available in the main ranch house.
Summary: First official dude ranch. The ranch exudes history and intrigue. Many multigeneration families return the same week each summer, year after year. There are still some families who spend more than a month at the ranch each summer. Wonderful ranch store and post office. Ride on your own. Nearby: Custer Battlefield, Fort Phil Kearney, polo tournaments in Big Horn, and the Bradford Brinton Museum in Big Horn, 20 miles away.

Flying A Guest Ranch
Pinedale, Wyoming

In 1965, Lowell Hansen went to Wyoming on a hunting trip. He returned with the Flying A Guest Ranch. Today, Hansen's daughter, Debbie, offers the discerning adult a distinctive western vacation. Located just 50 miles southeast of Jackson Hole at 8,200 feet, the Flying A is near the base of the Gros Ventre Mountains in a magnificent, wide-open meadow. The drive into the ranch is slow and beautiful. The ranch offers an unstructured casual western atmosphere. You can ride through the quiet seclusion of groves of aspens and pines; fish in the abundant ponds and mountain streams; and enjoy the wonder of moose, deer, and elk in their natural habitat and spectacular sunsets on the distant peaks. Built in 1929, the Flying A Guest Ranch has undergone complete renovation. It has been tastefully restored and offers exquisitely comfortable facilities. The Flying A reopened for guests in 1989 and hosts guests from across the United States and abroad.

Address: Route 1, Box 7 K, Pinedale, Wyoming 82941
Telephone: (307) 367-2385 (summer); (800) 678-6543 (reservations only). Don't be surprised if someone answers "Jack Rabbit Charters." Jack Rabbit Charters is owned by the Hansen family.
Airport: Jackson; airport for private planes in Pinedale; ranch has private 3,600-foot dirt airstrip. All pilots must telephone the ranch.
Location: 50 miles southeast of Jackson off Highway 191, 27 miles north of Pinedale
Memberships: Dude Ranchers' Association
Medical: St. John's Hospital in Jackson, medical center in Pinedale, helicopter service available
Guest Capacity: 12
Accommodations: Six completely renovated rustic cabins are named after the colorful characters who settled in the valley. Original hand-carved native pine furniture blends beautifully with new oak floors, tasteful art, and cozy flannel sheets and comforters. Cabins have living rooms, modern bathrooms with a shower or shower/tub combination, full-sized kitchens and bedrooms, and each has a fireplace or wood-burning stove in addition to electric heat. Kitchens contain everything from coffeemakers to wine glasses. Each cabin also has one or two private porches for relaxed viewing of the little stream and the grassy meadow where wildlife come to graze.
Rates: • $\$-\$\$\$. American Plan. Off-season rates. One-week minimum stay in July and August, Sunday to Sunday.
Credit Cards: None
Season: Mid-June through September
Activities: Very relaxed and unstructured. Guests are encouraged to set their own schedules. Debbie, her husband, Keith, and their staff make each guest's stay enjoyable. Trout fishing on ranch property or mountain streams, along with unlimited horseback riding or hiking to explore the high country. The riding program is completely tailored to ranch guests. Ask Debbie about her favorite rides to Jack Creek, Rock Creek, and Bartlett Canyon. Mountain bikes are also available. Hot tub.
Children's Programs: None. Adults only.
Dining: Three meals served with a casual, yet gourmet, flair. For that added touch, china is used for the daily settings. Weekly barbecues with silverhead trout appetizer. Each evening the ranch serves appetizers in their Gilded Moose Saloon, which overlooks the ranch pond and farther off, the Wind River and Gros Ventre mountain ranges. BYOB.
Entertainment: Visiting with other guests, lots of R&R, video library, horseshoes, volleyball, and croquet.
Summary: Small, adults-only guest ranch. Peaceful, remote setting. Do exactly as you like, no structured program. Warm and cozy accommodations with lovely interior decoration touches. Tremendous wildflowers in June and July and the beautiful colors of changing aspen trees and abundance of wildlife in the fall. Nearby: Yellowstone and the Tetons.

Gros Ventre River Ranch
Moose, Wyoming

At 7,000 feet, Gros Ventre River Ranch is a great place to savor the mighty Tetons, take quiet walks, fish, ride, explore, or just relax and enjoy this year-round paradise. This old ranch has been in the guest ranching business since the early 1950s but was bought by Karl and Tina Weber in 1987. They have given the place a real face lift but without diminishing the Old West charm. In fact, the Webers and their fine staff have enhanced what was and created a world-class guest ranch. Guests will enjoy a new lodge with views that capture the splendor of the Tetons, magnificent wilderness scenery, and the rushing Gros Ventre River. While preserving the past, the Webers have made it possible for people from around the world to settle in and enjoy rustic elegance and nature at its best.

Address: P.O. Box 151 K, Moose, Wyoming 83012
Telephone: (307) 733-4138; fax: (307) 733-4272
Airport: Jackson
Location: 18 miles northeast of Jackson. You will be sent a map with your confirmation.
Memberships: Dude Ranchers' Association, Wyoming Dude Ranchers' Association, American Quarter Horse Association
Medical: St. John's Hospital in Jackson, 18 miles
Conference: 35; May to June, mid-September to October
Guest Capacity: 35
Accommodations: There are nine log cabins, five of them renovated, three new, all winterized. The new cabins have ten-foot ceilings, fireplaces, sliding glass doors that open to decks with magnificent views of the Tetons, and kitchenettes. Your beds are turned down each evening. Laundry facilities available. The handsome lodge could well be on the cover of Architectural Digest and features original art, two decks overlooking the Gros Ventre River with views of the distant Tetons, a lovely dining room, living room, and bar area. On the lower level is a rec room/conference room that opens out to a landscaped area overlooking the river.
Rates: $$$-$$$$. American Plan. Children's and off-season rates. Weekly minimum stay mid-June to mid-September, Sunday to Sunday arrivals.
Credit Cards: None. Cash, personal checks, and traveler's checks accepted.
Season: May through October; December through March, open at Christmas
Activities: In summer, horseback riding with slow to fast, half-day, all-day, and lunch rides. Fly-fishing in the legendary Snake River, Crystal Creek, or Gros Ventre River, which runs through the ranch (some fishing gear available). The stocked beaver ponds provide a sure catch for fishermen and are enjoyed by all. Ranch swimming hole, canoeing in Slide Lake, hiking, mountain biking at ranch. (Bikes available.) Golf and tennis ten miles away. Winter activities include cross-country skiing (bring your own gear), snowmobiling, and downhill skiing in Jackson.
Children's Programs: No set programs. Children under 7 do not go on trail rides. Occasional baby-sitting available at an extra charge. If child-care is a must, bring your own nanny.
Dining: Rack of lamb, chops, baked trout, barbecued chicken and ribs, grilled-to-order New York steaks. Breakfast includes steak, eggs, and hash browns. Complimentary California wine with dinner. BYOB happy hour.
Entertainment: Cards or quiet music. Weekly rodeos in Jackson, campfires and marshmallow roasts, weekly cookouts with country-western singing by local entertainers.
Summary: World-class guest ranch with emphasis on horseback riding, fly-fishing, and relaxation. Excellent for families, couples, singles, and small corporate groups. Magnificent view of the Tetons and Gros Ventre River. Nearby: Grand Teton and Yellowstone national parks, National Elk Refuge, the town of Jackson, and Gros Ventre Slide (largest landslide in the United States).

See color photos, pages 282-283

GROS VENTRE RIVER RANCH

Heart 6 Ranch
Moran, Wyoming

The cover of the Garnicks' Heart 6 Ranch brochure really says it all. "If you are lookin' for a life where the air is sweeter, the folks friendlier, and the gallopin' years slow to a trot, we're playing your tune." Heart 6 Ranch looks out over the Buffalo River Valley and on to the Teton Range. It is just five miles east of the gateway to Grand Teton and Yellowstone national parks. The Buffalo Valley is a lush, wide open valley and offers guests at Heart 6 a variety of ranch activities. The Garnicks are an easygoing western family who serve downright friendly hospitality. They love kids, families, and life. Billie and Bill, along with their son, Cameron (who has six wonderful children), run the ranch. As Billie says, "We are mellow, easygoing folks who enjoy people who want to get away from it all." If you need a television or telephone in your cabin, this is not the ranch for you.

Address: P.O. Box 70 K, Moran, Wyoming 83013
Telephone: (307) 543-2477, (307) 739-9477
Airport: Jackson
Location: 35 miles northeast of Jackson off Highway 26
Memberships: Dude Ranchers' Association
Medical: Hospital in Jackson
Conference: 50
Guest Capacity: 50
Accommodations: Fifteen comfortable red-roofed log cabins with western decor. One-, two-, and three-bedrooms sleep up to 12. Almost all have wood stoves or fireplaces, and twin and double beds. Cozy main lodge with large fireplace and picture windows looking out over the valley. Laundry facilities.
Rates: • $$. American Plan. Family reunion and children's rates available. Snowmobile and hunting rates available on request. Six-day minimum stay, June to early September; arrivals on Monday, departures on Sunday.
Credit Cards: MasterCard, Visa, Discover, Diners Club
Season: June to mid-October, mid-December to mid-April. Open Easter.
Activities: In summer, riders sign up each evening for the ride they would like to take the next day. Morning, afternoon, all-day rides twice a week except Sunday. Ask the Garnicks about the Davis Mountain and Soda Fork rides. You may bring your own horse. Each summer the Garnicks have a Forest Service naturalist on staff who teaches guests (kids, too) all about the flora and fauna. Hiking, swimming in heated pool or in the Buffalo River—ask about the "polar bear club." Lots of great fishing in the Buffalo and Snake rivers and in Jackson Lake. Fly-fishing guide and float trips available. Pack trips by prior arrangement. In winter, the Garnicks offer fabulous guided one- to five-day snowmobile trips into Yellowstone.
Children's Programs: Cameron Garnick has six children, so your kids will always be in good company and well looked after—great for parents and single parents. Ask about their awards programs—wrangler, naturalist, and outdoorsman.
Dining: As Billie says, "It is not high gourmet because there are so many kids." Delicious, hearty ranch fare. Food served mainly banquet-style, some buffet. Prime rib, barbecued ribs, and trout almondine. Thursday night steak ride on Mt. Davis. Weekly breakfast ride and "polar bear swim." Happy hour each evening at 5:00 p.m. in the BYOB Beaver Slide Saloon.
Entertainment: Local guest speakers discuss area topics. Authentic Indian dancing, hayrides, talks by forest service personnel. Jackson Hole weekly rodeo and the best entertainment west of the Black Hills at the Garnicks' Jackson Hole Playhouse in Jackson.
Summary: Great family owned and operated ranch overlooking a lush river valley and to the distant Tetons. Terrific for families and single parents. The Garnicks' son has six children who will keep close tabs on your kids. Nothing fancy, just one heck of a guest ranch experience. Fly-fishing and photography lectures available. Pack trips and winter snowmobiling into Yellowstone. German, Spanish, and some French spoken.

H F Bar Ranch
Saddlestring, Wyoming

The H F Bar Ranch, one of the great old dude ranches in America, has preserved that old ranch feeling. Since the late 1920s, this 10,000-acre ranch has received distinguished guests from around the world. The ranch is owned and run today by Margi Bliss and her daughter, Lily. The H F Bar's horse corrals, barns, and ranch headquarters haven't changed much over the years, nor have the surrounding pastures with native grasses rising to meet the timbered hills leading into the Big Horn Mountains. Margi has tried to keep things as they always have been, and guests keep returning year after year. As Margi says, "I've made a tremendous effort to bring guests comfortable amenities and still maintain our old western traditions here." Don't be surprised if you find out from Margi that they are booked months in advance.

Address: P.O. Box K, Saddlestring, Wyoming 82840
Telephone: (307) 684-2487; fax: (307) 684-7144
Airport: Sheridan
Location: 12 miles northwest of Buffalo, 35 southwest of Sheridan
Medical: Family Medical Center, Buffalo
Conference: 95, audiovisual equipment available
Guest Capacity: 95
Accommodations: Guests stay in twenty-six older rustic cabins built from local timber. Each has its own charm, with names like Brookside, Meadowlark, and Round-Up. Each has a living room, fireplace, and one to seven bedrooms. Ten are heated with propane or electricity. Most have that days-gone-by feeling. The ranch stream sings outside many of the cabins. A horse-drawn wagon delivers old-fashioned blocks of ice to your cabin each morning as well as any items that are requested from town or the ranch general store, an old H F Bar tradition.
Rates: $$. American Plan. Children's rates. The ranch encourages families to bring their own nannies and offers a 50 percent discount for them. One-week minimum stay, no set arrival day.
Credit Cards: None. Personal checks or traveler's checks accepted.
Season: Mid-June to mid-September
Activities: It's a relaxed atmosphere, and guests can do as they please. With 150 horses and 10,000 acres, there is plenty of riding for beginners as well as experienced horsemen, who can ride on unsupervised only after their riding ability has been checked out completely by the cowboys. Half-day and all-day rides, pack trips, and riding instruction available. All rides customized to families or individuals. Excellent fishing in the North and South forks of Rock Creek, which runs through the ranch. Swimming in heated pool, hiking, and "sporting clays" shooting (flush, driven pheasant, and double courses). Guns available (extra).
Children's Programs: The ranch goes all out for families with young children. Two staff baby-sitters available with advance notice. Margi encourages you to bring your own nanny for very small kids. Hayrides, craft days, hamburger cookouts. Children's rides called the "Mosquito Fleet." Parents are encouraged to interact together. Baby-sitters available with advance notice.
Dining: Each family is assigned its own table. Children may eat earlier and have their own menu. Sunday is lavish country fare; otherwise it's hearty, standard American cuisine with extraordinary desserts. Special diets catered to. BYOB.
Entertainment: Weekly country dancing to live music, roping, and occasional bronc riding at ranch, rodeos in town.
Summary: A great ranch for the entire family and children of all ages. Lots of high-quality family time here. Many second- and third-generation families return year after year. First-time families receive a hearty welcome. Fascinating geology with Indian sites on ranch. Nearby: "Sporting clay" shooting, Big Horn Polo Club, King's Saddlery and Museum.

High Island Ranch and Cattle Company
Dome, Wyoming

High Island Ranch and Cattle Company is the dream of a keen businessman from Massachusetts. Since the mid-1960s, George Nelson has operated a successful steel fabrication plant. When time permits, he goes West to hunt. Not long ago he bought 43,000-acre High Island and began running Hereford and Angus cattle. Soon his Eastern friends were asking if they could help with the cattle work. This is exactly how the guest ranching business was born almost a century ago. High Island has become known for its authentic cattle drives and May branding week. The ranch now takes summer guests and offers week-long stays to individuals and families for daily riding and pack trips. You will experience a tremendous diversity of terrain, from 4,000-foot prairie to 11,000-foot mountains. This working cattle ranch is beautiful, remote, and rugged, in crisp mountain air, and surrounded by pungent sage. High Island is for those who want to experience the West the way it used to be but with a few modern conveniences.

Address: Box 71 K, Hamilton, Wyoming 82427
Telephone: (307) 867-2374; fax: (307) 867-2374
Airport: Cody
Location: 35 miles north of Thermopolis, 75 miles south of Cody
Memberships: Dude Ranchers' Association, Wyoming Dude Ranchers Association
Medical: Hot Springs Memorial Hospital, Thermopolis
Conference: 25 (very rustic)
Guest Capacity: 25
Accommodations: The upper ranch is powered by propane. It has six rustic four-wall canvas tents, one private cabin, and comfortable lodge rooms furnished with log beds, blanket rugs, and wood stoves. There are men's and women's outhouses and shower houses. Bring your own sleeping bag, towels, soap, and toiletries. The lodge, nestled in the timber, has a broad porch overlooking the campfire and a trout stream called Rock Creek. The lodge features comfortable seating and a dining area accented by prints and numerous animal mounts. The lower ranch has a smaller lodge, two bunkhouses, and four-wall canvas tents.
Rates: • $$$. American Plan. Children's rates available.
Credit Cards: None
Season: May to October; hunting season, October to November
Activities: Branding week; guests get to participate in all the cattle work including branding and doctoring calves. Spring and fall cattle drives 35 miles moving 220 head of cows and calves to new pastures. This is the real thing. For those who want to experience long days in the saddle, bedrolls, and hearty ranch food cooked over the campfire on the trail, this will be an adventure you will never forget. Pack trips and unlimited riding packages are also available between the brandings and cattle drives. Fishing for cutthroat trout. (Bring your own gear.)
Children's Programs: Children 16 and older go on cattle drives. Children 12 and older are welcome on roundup weeks. This is not a ranch for children who need a tremendous amount of attention. Children should be experienced riders.
Dining: While on the trail, an old-fashioned chuck wagon pulled by two stout draft horses follows with plenty of hearty food, including fresh fruit, vegetables, cold drinks, and cowboy coffee or tea. Almost everything is cooked on an open fire. Standard western fare at the upper and lower lodges. A nonsmoking, nonalcohol environment is promoted.
Entertainment: Listening to the call of the coyotes or cows calling for their young. Campfire sing-alongs. Finale barbecue and dance.
Summary: Old-fashioned cattle drives. Bring your own sleeping gear. If George is at the ranch, ask him to get out his banjo. Groups and corporations may rent ranch for entire weeks. (Author's note: If you go on the cattle drive, it is advisable to do a good bit of riding before you arrive. Novices should get some instruction.) Inexperienced riders not advised.

See color photos, page 284

Hunter Peak Ranch
Cody, Wyoming

Nestled in the pines at the base of Hunter Peak lies Hunter Peak Ranch at an elevation of 6,700 feet. Homesteaded in 1907, the ranch has evolved into a relaxing, family-oriented dude ranch. The hand-hewn lodge offers a warm and cozy atmosphere for guests, whether on vacation, attending a family reunion, celebrating a wedding or anniversary, or attending business meetings. The lodge is appointed with Indian rugs, a beautiful cinnamon bear rug, head mounts of elk, deer, and antelope, tack, and antique tools. Hunter Peak is situated near the spectacular Sunlight Basin, Beartooth Plateau, and Yellowstone Park. The Clarksfork River divides the property with 20 acres on one side, home to the buildings and pastures, and 100 acres on the other side for pastures and irrigated hay meadows. A hand-powered trolley provides transportation across the river. The ranch is within the Shoshone National Forest and adjacent to the North Absaroka Wilderness Areas. Pack trips into these areas and Yellowstone Park are a highlight. Louis Cary is the third generation to be running the ranch, with his wife, Shelley, who is from Wisconsin. Guests appreciate Louis's lifelong knowledge of the area—he knows a good deal about the local history and geography—and enjoy his tales and stories. A unique feature of Hunter Peak is the flexible cooking and meal program. Because each cabin has its own kitchen, guests can eat in the ranch dining room or cook their own meals. Most choose to combine the cooking privileges.

Address: Box 1731 K, Painter Route, Cody, Wyoming 82414
Telephone: (307) 587-3711 (summer); (307) 754-5878 (winter)
Airport: Cody, Wyoming; Billings, Montana
Location: 60 miles northwest of Cody, 120 miles southwest of Billings
Memberships: Dude Ranchers' Association
Medical: West Park County Hospital, 60 miles
Conference: 25
Guest Capacity: 35
Accommodations: The 30-year-old cabins, one log, the other framed and finished in wood paneling, are wood heated and close to the river. The log cabin sleeps two; the framed cabin sleeps four in 2 bedrooms. The main motel-like lodge, built in 1972, has 6 rooms with carpeting and steam heat. No TV or telephone. Laundry facilities available.
Rates: $-$$. American and European plans.
Credit Cards: None. Traveler's checks, cash, and money orders accepted. Personal checks accepted for deposit.
Season: June to mid-December
Activities: Activities are very flexible. Shelley and Louis try to cater to individual desires. Choose from hiking, scenic four-wheel-drive trips, hourly, half-, or all-day horseback rides, pack trips, and fishing for rainbow, cutthroat, brook, and golden trout. Big game hunting.
Children's Programs: No special program. Babysitting and child care available.
Dining: Enjoy home-cooked ranch food with Shelley and Louis, or cook for yourself in your own cabin. BYOB.
Entertainment: Small library in recreation room, also pool table and table tennis. Outdoor volleyball, badminton, croquet, horseshoe pitching, baseball.
Summary: Small family-run ranch with flexible cooking and meal program. Very low-key, independent atmosphere. Nearby: Sunlight Basin mountain highway called "Chief Joseph Highway," Beartooth Plateau, Daisy and Lulu mining area, Yellowstone National Park, Buffalo Bill Historical Center and nightly rodeos in Cody.

Lazy L & B Ranch
Dubois, Wyoming

The Lazy L & B Ranch sits in the valley of the Wind River. Its uniqueness is its diversity of terrain. The lodge and cabins are shaded by lush green cottonwoods and the contrasting red clay cliffs of the adjoining Wind River Indian Reservation. Many of the cabins and parts of the main lodge and corrals are the original 1890 sheep and cattle ranch buildings. Riding terrain takes you through rolling prairie, badland country, alpine meadows, and mountain forests, where wildflowers are abundant. The Lazy L & B now lies within one of the most multifaceted pieces of animal habitat in Wyoming. Guests enjoy unspoiled riding and hiking through National Forest, Indian reservation country, and 50,000 acres of elk refuge. In 1993, a new chapter began for the Lazy L & B. Ironically, the brand will stay the same for the new owners, Lee and Bob Naylon. Each has over twenty years experience in backcountry horse packing, hiking, and the ski industry. Their energy and knowledge are assets as they continue the longstanding Lazy L & B tradition.

Address: 1072 East Fork Road, Drawer K, Dubois, Wyoming 82513
Telephone: (800) 453-9488, (307) 455-2839
Airport: Jackson Hole or Riverton; private planes may land on 5,000-foot lighted and paved airstrip in Dubois
Location: 70 miles east of Jackson, 22 miles northeast of Dubois
Memberships: Dude Ranchers' Association
Medical: Doctor in Dubois, hospital in Lander
Guest Capacity: 35
Accommodations: A new addition to the lodge provides two cozy fireplaces, a library, and game tables where guests enjoy entertainment of cowboy songs and poetry. Twelve comfortable log cabins are arranged around a central courtyard and at the riverside. All have private baths or showers and electric heat. Some porches have views of the distant Absaroka and Wind River mountain ranges. Some have wood-burning stoves or fireplaces.
Rates: • $$. American Plan. Children's, large family, and group rates available. Minimal charge for nannies/baby-sitters.
Credit Cards: None. Personal checks, money orders, or cash accepted.
Season: End of May through the end of September
Activities: Most guests come here to ride. Riding groups consist of no more than seven; 2½-hour rides in the morning and afternoon. Wednesday and Thursday are all-day rides. Although most guests wish to ride daily, other activities include hiking, mountain biking, a lapidary shop, and game room for the kids. Anglers enjoy fishing in the ranch's stocked ponds, the East Fork, or the neighboring Wiggins and Bear Creek areas. Swimming in the solar-heated pool and picnic lunches on the deck. Ask about the mountain overnight campsite.
Children's Programs: Children 5 years and older have a supervised wrangler program. Game room and petting farm. Children are supervised while riding, otherwise they are the responsibility of their parents or nanny. Children eat with the wranglers and join the wranglers for activities during adult dinner.
Dining: Good, hearty ranch cooking, family-style meals with freshly baked breads and desserts. On request, special diets provided. Children eat dinner with wranglers while parents enjoy a BYOB happy hour. Lunches and steak fry by the pool.
Entertainment: Sing-alongs, campfires, cowboy poetry, riflery, horseshoes, and Ping-Pong. Float trips can be arranged. Dubois offers square dancing, museum, and the National Big Horn Sheep Center.
Summary: Wonderful family-oriented riding ranch with great hosts! Surrounded by national forest, Indian reservation, and 50,000-acre Elk Refuge. Advanced riders ask about weekly horse drive. September, adults only. Nearby: Grand Teton and Yellowstone national parks.

See color photos, page 288

Lost Creek Ranch
Moose, Wyoming

Lost Creek Ranch is magnificent. Breathtaking views of the mighty Tetons, superb cuisine, and hospitality second to none make Lost Creek what it is today—a world-class showplace! Located on the eastern slope of the Jackson Hole valley at 7,000 feet, the ranch is situated on a rise with commanding views of the entire Teton mountain range and the valley. This privately owned ranch is bordered by Grand Teton National Park and Bridger Teton National Forest. The beautiful lodge and cabins are furnished with the highest quality decor featuring custom-made furniture and original artwork. The cabin amenities, superb service, and tremendous outdoor opportunities make Lost Creek ideal for families, individuals, and corporate groups who appreciate excellence. Ride horses, float the Snake River, hike, enjoy a Dutch oven cookout on Shadow Mountain, or relax on the expansive lodge deck and watch the sun set behind the Tetons. You can do it all at Lost Creek Ranch.

Address: P.O. Box 95 K, Moose, Wyoming 83012
Telephone: (307) 733-3435; fax: (307) 733-1954
Airport: Jackson via Denver or Salt Lake City
Location: 20 miles north of Jackson
Awards: Mobil 4 Star, America's Finest Restaurants, Grand Master Chefs of America, Super Star Hotel Award
Medical: First-aid office at ranch; St. John's Hospital in Jackson, 20 miles
Conference: 100. Five rooms: smallest accommodates 20; largest, 100.
Guest Capacity: 40-74
Accommodations: Guests stay in luxury two-bedroom/two-bath (with tub and shower) cabins providing queen and single beds in all bedrooms. All cabins have refrigerators with ice makers, coffee and hot chocolate, and electric heat. The living room cabins have queen sleeper sofas, full kitchenettes, and free-standing fireplaces. Beds are turned down each evening, and the "mint fairy" always leaves a surprise. Twice daily maid service. Courtesy laundry service.
Rates: $$$$-$$$$$. Full American Plan including service charge. One-week minimum stay, Sunday to Sunday. Off-season nightly, corporate, and group rates.
Credit Cards: None. Personal checks accepted.
Season: Late May through early October
Activities: Full riding program with personal instruction, heated swimming pool, tennis court, Snake River scenic float trips, cookouts, wagon rides, overnight campouts, guided hiking. Many guests enjoy the Yellowstone and Grand Teton National Park tours. Optional wilderness pack trips, guided fishing, and golf nearby (extra).
Children's Programs: Children under 6 do not ride. Game room, video programs, overnight campout, wagon rides. Baby-sitting available during dinner. Many families bring nannies.
Dining: Outstanding cuisine with two entrées served nightly. Wine list is available. Optional dinner hour for children. Special diets served by prior arrangement.
Entertainment: Weekly cookouts, campfire sing-alongs, Indian dances, video programs, western swing dance, weekly gymkhana, weekly rodeo in Jackson, and impromptu programs.
Summary: World-class ranch resort with outstanding service and a panoramic view of the Tetons. Excellent for personal vacations and corporate retreats. Language interpreters available. Nearby: historic western town of Jackson (art galleries, shopping, western events such as shootouts, theater groups, stagecoach rides, and white-water rafting), Yellowstone and Grand Teton national parks, National Elk Refuge.

See color photos, pages 286-287

Lozier's Box R Ranch
Cora, Wyoming

Since the turn-of-the-century when the ranch was first homesteaded, the Lozier family has operated this backcountry working cattle ranch. As in days gone by, the Box R maintains the traditions of the Old West. Sublette County, where the ranch is located, is famous for cattle ranching and its beauty. I know this firsthand because I cowboyed on a neighboring ranch in the late 1970s. Today, Irv Lozier, along with his wife, Robin, and son, Levi, oversee 300 head of cattle and 60 horses and mules. Horseback riding is the main thing. If you would like to spend a week or more with an old time ranching family, give Irv, Robin, or Levi a call.

Address: Box 100-K, Cora, Wyoming 82925
Telephone: (307) 367-4868 (inquiries), (800) 822-8466 (reservations); fax: (307) 367-4757
Airport: Jackson Hole, pick-up available
Location: 10 miles north of Pinedale via State Highway 352, 60 miles southeast of Jackson
Memberships: Dude Ranchers' Association; Wyoming Outfitters Association
Medical: Jackson Hospital, 60 miles
Guest Capacity: 16 adults, 20 family/group
Accommodations: Four log cabins and two three-room lodges. All have private baths and twin and queen-size beds. Rooms range from single cabins to family suites for up to five. Social and recreational rooms adjoin several of the lodge rooms. Ranch generates its own power.
Rates: • $$-$$$. American Plan, Sunday to Sunday. Ask about the ranch float, pack trip, and cattle drive packages. Adults-only weeks.
Credit Cards: Visa, MasterCard, American Express, Discover (5% surcharge). Cash or personal checks preferred.
Season: End of May to mid-September
Activities: Fine working ranch horses and riding mules. You are assigned your own personal horse, and depending on your ability, you may help with early morning wrangling of the horse "Cavy," doctoring the ranch cattle, and locating, salting, and working cattle on the open range. Competent adult riders may ride on their own (talk to Irv about this before you arrive). Authentic cattle drives and roundups in the spring or fall. Adult guests in September can join the casual agenda of fall cattle roundups off the high mountain pastures, serene and peaceful beauty of fall color rides, and excellent trout fishing on the ranch's streams, 11 trout ponds, and several large nearby lakes and rivers. Swimming in seven-mile-long Willow Lake.
Children's Programs: No program per se. Children under 8 are not encouraged. Older children may ride separately or with adults. Swing set, trampoline, pool table, darts, and fishing with parental supervision.
Dining: Family-style meals specializing in wholesome cuisine with ranch beef, fresh salads, homemade breads, pastries, and soups. Drinks, fresh fruit, and cookies are available throughout the day, with evening hors d'oeuvres and social hour in BYOB bar.
Entertainment: Horseshoes, rope "Oscar" the steer, spacious social room, library, and wet bar. Recreation room with pool table, darts, games, and TV/VCR for educational/informational/meeting purposes. Swing set and trampoline. You are on your own after dinner.
Summary: The Lozier's Box R Ranch is a true working cattle ranch in the heart of Wyoming's cattle ranching country, run today by third- and fourth-generation family. Great for active, outdoor folks, both adults and older children, wanting to enjoy the peace and tranquillity of this remote mountain ranch. Ask about cattle drives, pack trips, and float trip packages. Brochures in German and French available. Nearby: Jackson Hole and Yellowstone and Teton national parks.

See color photos, page 289

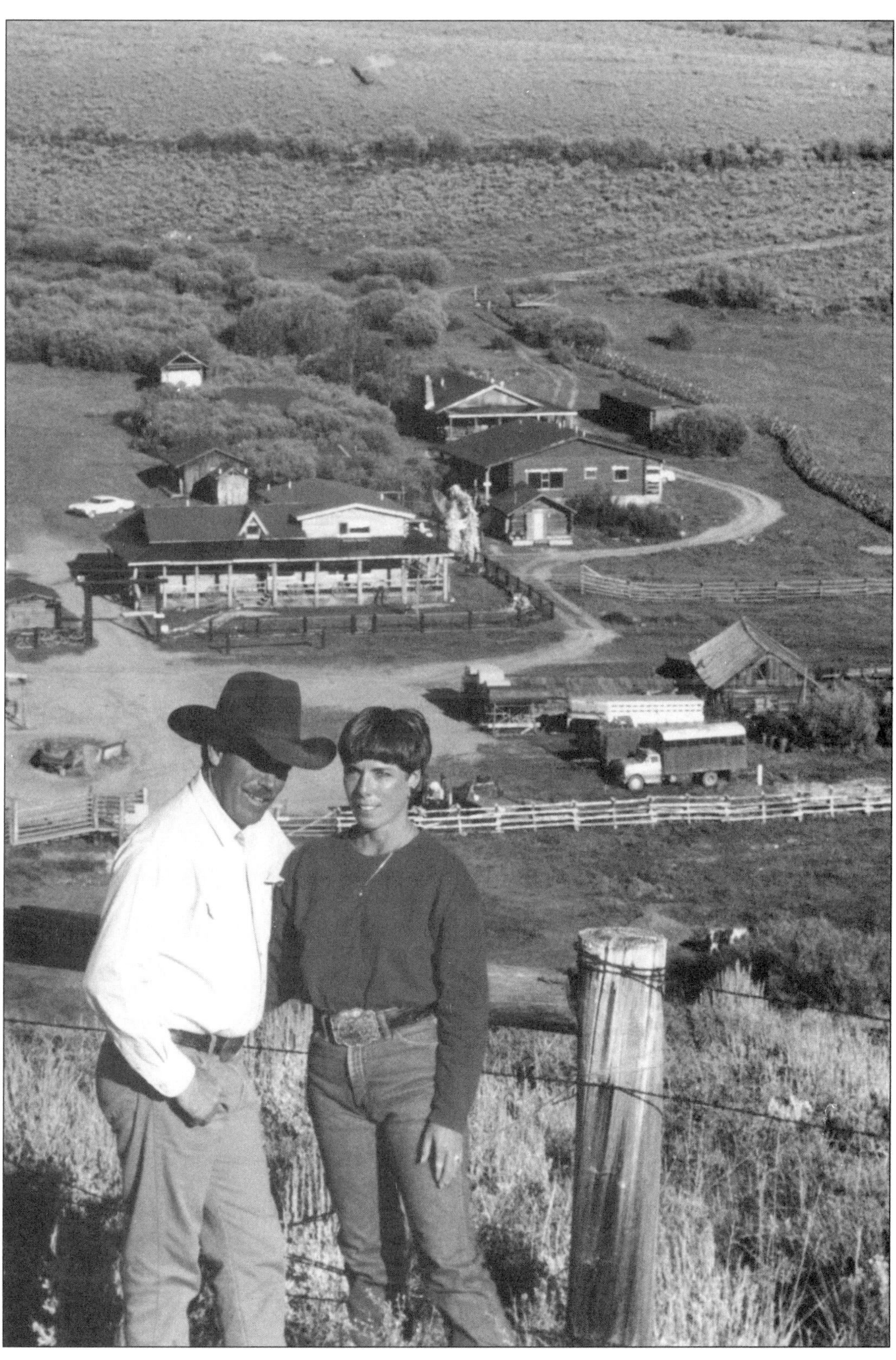

Kedesh Ranch
Shell, Wyoming

Imagine Indians riding across a wind-swept landscape with pastel colors and red rock formations shaped with time, the breeze and the warmth of the hot summer's sun, cottonwood trees along Shell Creek, water fights, fishing, the Big Horn Canyon (third largest on the United States), dinosaur digs, and natural geological formations. Welcome to Kedesh Guest Ranch and the Shell Valley. Kedesh in Hebrew means "sanctuary," and in a way that is exactly what the Lander family (Chuck, Gail, Dana, and Bill) offer. Now don't misunderstand. This is not a hideaway protected by rocky cliffs. It is hidden by cottonwood trees and located right off the road that joins Sheridan and Cody, Wyoming. The Kedesh Ranch concept is simple. Provide a friendly, low-key, family-oriented environment for guests, both young and young at heart, to ride, fish, hike, explore geological formations and dinosaur digs, or just take a walk and talk. Chuck is a geologist by training and spent many years in oil and gas exploration. His knowledge of the area and the geological formations is tremendous. Gail's roots are in Montana, and she has a great love and understanding of the Native American culture. One guest wrote, "It's awesome country. You can't describe it. It's a spiritual place as well."

Address: 1940 Highway 14, Dept. K, Shell, Wyoming 82441
Telephone: (800) 845-3320, (307) 765-2791
Airport: Worland, 50 miles; Cody, 70 miles; Sheridan, 75 miles
Location: 75 miles west of Sheridan, and 20 miles east of Greybull off Highway 14
Memberships: Dude Ranchers' Association, Wyoming Dude Ranchers Association
Medical: Big Horn Clinic, 20 miles; Coe Medical Center, 70 miles
Conference: 24
Guest Capacity: 24
Accommodations: The six green-roofed cabins are arranged in a circle. One fourplex cabin has four undivided rooms and one long deck on the front facing the horse pasture. The back common porch with dividing bamboo screens overlooks Shell Creek. Each has two queen-size beds and private baths. The five other duplex cabins with common screened-in porches have queen-size beds and private baths. All are carpeted. Daily maid service.
Rates: • $$. American Plan. Children's, group, and off-season rates. Three-night minimum stay. Saturday to Saturday and Wednesday to Wednesday stays preferred.
Credit Cards: Visa, MasterCard accepted with handling fee. Personal checks preferred. Traveler's checks and cash accepted.
Season: June to mid-October
Activities: Each day a little something different is planned. Arrival is followed by an evening ride and a game called "sticks." Usually riding in the morning or evening each day. Riding is tailored to avoid the heat of the day. Dana oversees the horseback program. Majority of guests have never ridden. Great fishing in Shell Creek, fossil and arrowhead hunting. Each week is usually filled with many optional off-ranch outings: Big Horn Mountain, Indian petroglyghs, Shell Falls, Medicine Wheel, Cody, dinosaur digs, and Little Big Horn "Custer" Battlefield.
Children's Programs: Weekly dudeo. Kids 5 and up may trail ride. Families interact together.
Dining: You will never be hungry at the ranch. Home-style cooked meals become the main event, served family-style. BYOB with discretion.
Entertainment: Something usually planned each evening. Ranger slide shows, trips to Cody Rodeo, and Buffalo Bill historical center. Evening rides, arrowhead demonstrations. Ask about the hayride.
Summary: Located on Shell Creek in the heart of the magnificent Shell Canyon with incredible geological formations. A low-key very laid-back atmosphere for families, couples, and singles. Many off-ranch activities offered.

See color photos, page 285

Moose Head Ranch
Moose, Wyoming

The Mettlers' Moose Head Ranch is flanked by the spectacular and majestic Teton range. In Jackson Hole at an elevation of 6,870 feet, Moose Head is one of the few privately owned ranches left entirely within the boundaries of Grand Teton National Park. Commanding a sweeping vista of the 13,000-foot peaks of the Teton range, this ranch offers a wonderful western vacation experience. Eleo Mettler spends her winters in Florida, where she recharges her batteries before returning to the ranch to entertain guests from around the world all summer long. Moose Head was actually homesteaded back in 1923. As a boy, John Mettler fell in love with Jackson Hole and vowed someday to put down roots there. In 1967, he and his wife, Eleo, bought Moose Head and have been running it ever since with their daughters, Ellen and Louise, and Louise's husband, Kit Davenport. "We were dudes ourselves so many years that we think we know what people want," says Eleo. The ranch offers plenty of activities and takes no more than forty guests at one time. Some guests enjoy it also because it serves as headquarters for things to see and do in the beautiful Jackson Hole area.

Address: P.O. Box 214 K, Moose, Wyoming 83012
Telephone: (307) 733-3141 (summer), (904) 877-1431 (winter); call for fax number.
Airport: Jackson
Location: 26 miles north of Jackson
Memberships: Dude Ranchers' Association
Medical: St. John's Hospital in Jackson, 26 miles
Guest Capacity: 40
Accommodations: Log cabins are scattered among the aspen, cottonwoods, spruce, and pines. Each of the 14 cabins offers privacy and comfort for singles and families (seven with adjoining living rooms). All have private baths with shower and tub, electric heating, and porches. Coffee and tea may be enjoyed in your cabin before breakfast. Daily maid service. Ice is brought to your cabin each day.
Rates: $$$. American Plan. Rates for children under 6. Five-night minimum stay, arrivals any day.
Credit Cards: None
Season: Mid-June to late August
Activities: Supervised horseback rides go out twice daily with guests divided into small family groups of 5 to 6. Weekly all-day rides. Families usually ride together on more than 14 different trails. Most are scenic rides. Occasionally, there is some cantering. Don't come here to do a lot of fast riding, but do if you want to see lots of wildlife (elk, buffalo, mule deer, antelope, moose, coyotes, etc.). There is fly-fishing (catch and release) on the property in a series of several excellent well-stocked trout ponds with cutthroat trout up to 28 inches. Many fish off the property on the Snake River and other streams. Fishing flies, limited equipment, and instruction available. Tennis and golf can be arranged at local clubs, as can scenic and white water float trips on the Snake River. (A must!)
Children's Programs: No set children's program per se. Limited baby-sitting available. No organized activities.
Dining: The Mettlers feel that good food is just as important as good riding. Outstanding chefs serve breakfast to order, buffet lunches, and single-entrée dinners that the whole family will enjoy. Sunday night cookout. BYOB.
Entertainment: Informal, predinner cocktails each evening where most guests gather and visit. After dinner, as John Mettler says, "most do their own thing." Others enjoy volleyball, Ping-Pong, baseball, and fly-fishing.
Summary: Small family guest ranch looking out to the Tetons. Small groups on rides, and you will almost always see wildlife. Wonderful food. Excellent for family reunions. Superb fly-fishing casting ponds and instruction. Scenic and white water float trips can be arranged. Hiking in the Tetons. Within Grand Teton National Park. Nearby: Yellowstone National Park, Jackson, Teton Village, and Jackson rodeo.

Paradise Guest Ranch
Buffalo, Wyoming

Paradise Guest Ranch offers the traditional dude ranch activities with lots of riding and fishing. Along with this, as Jim says, "We keep an ear to the ground as to what modern-day guests need and expect." In the 1980s the ranch underwent extensive renovation. It lives up to its name "Paradise" for good reason, as it offers the rustic flavor of the Old West along with many modern conveniences. Dude ranches reflect the personality of the owners and hosts. Jim and Leah Anderson love what they do, and it shows. Once the prized hunting ground for the Sioux, Crow, and Cheyenne Indians, the ranch rests in a mountain valley next to the French and Three Rivers creeks, surrounded by tall forests of evergreens. The peace and tranquillity are only occasionally interrupted by the calls of wildlife or the exuberant sounds of families having fun. It is little wonder that the ranch brand is "FUN."

Address: P.O. Box 790 K, Buffalo, Wyoming 82834
Telephone: (307) 684-7876; call for fax number
Airport: Sheridan, Casper
Location: 46 miles south of Sheridan off Hunter Creek Road, 110 miles north of Casper, 176 miles south of Billings
Memberships: Dude Ranchers' Association, Wyoming Dude Ranchers' Association
Medical: Johnson County Memorial Hospital in Buffalo, 16 miles
Conference: 50; 2,400-square-foot meeting space off-season only
Guest Capacity: 70
Accommodations: Eighteen luxury one-, two-, and three-bedroom log homes, each with living room, kitchenette, fireplace, central heat, and deck overlooking pine-covered mountains, Fan Rock, and French Creek. Each day your hot chocolate, tea, and coffee basket will be filled. Nightly turn-down service. Laundry facilities in most cabins.
Rates: • $$-$$$. American Plan. Children's and pack trip rates. One-week minimum stay, Sunday to Sunday.
Credit Cards: None. Personal checks accepted.
Season: Late May to October
Activities: Riding is the main activity. One wrangler to a maximum of seven guests. Nine to twelve separate rides each day. Guests can choose walking, trotting or loping rides. Beginners can learn all three if they wish and are able. Adults and children may ride together or separately. Also offered are bag lunch rides or Jim's special cooked-on-the-trail lunch rides. His mules pack all the grub, and the wranglers do all the cookin'. Ask about rides to Seven Bros. and Sherd lakes and the cattle ranch country ride through spectacular Cougar, Red, and Sales canyons. Rides with and without children. Instruction available on one of the 110 horses. Serious fishermen should bring their own equipment for fishing in stream, pond, lakes, and reservoir. Heated outdoor swimming pool and indoor whirlpool spa.
Children's Programs: Kiddie wrangler/activities counselor for kids 12 and under. Weekly overnight campout. Kids' rodeo in arena with gymkhana events. Children under 6 will be completely looked after if parents desire. These children can be led around the ranch on ponies by parents. Kids and parents may interact together as much or as little as they like.
Dining: All you can eat, three meals a day, family-style. Real mule-drawn chuck wagon dinner and cookouts, home-baked breads. Wine available. Stocked saloon.
Entertainment: Square dancing, talent night, historical talks, sing-alongs, and recreation center. Thursday is parents' night off as kids are camping out. French Creek Saloon with liquor license.
Summary: Jim and Leah's Paradise Ranch is one of the very top guest ranches in the business. Traditional dude ranch values with first-rate accommodations. Excellent for small corporate/business groups off-season. Trips to "Hole in the Wall" country, home of some of the West's early outlaws. Horse and mule colts bred and trained. Guided historical trips, general store. Video available.

See color photos, pages 290-291

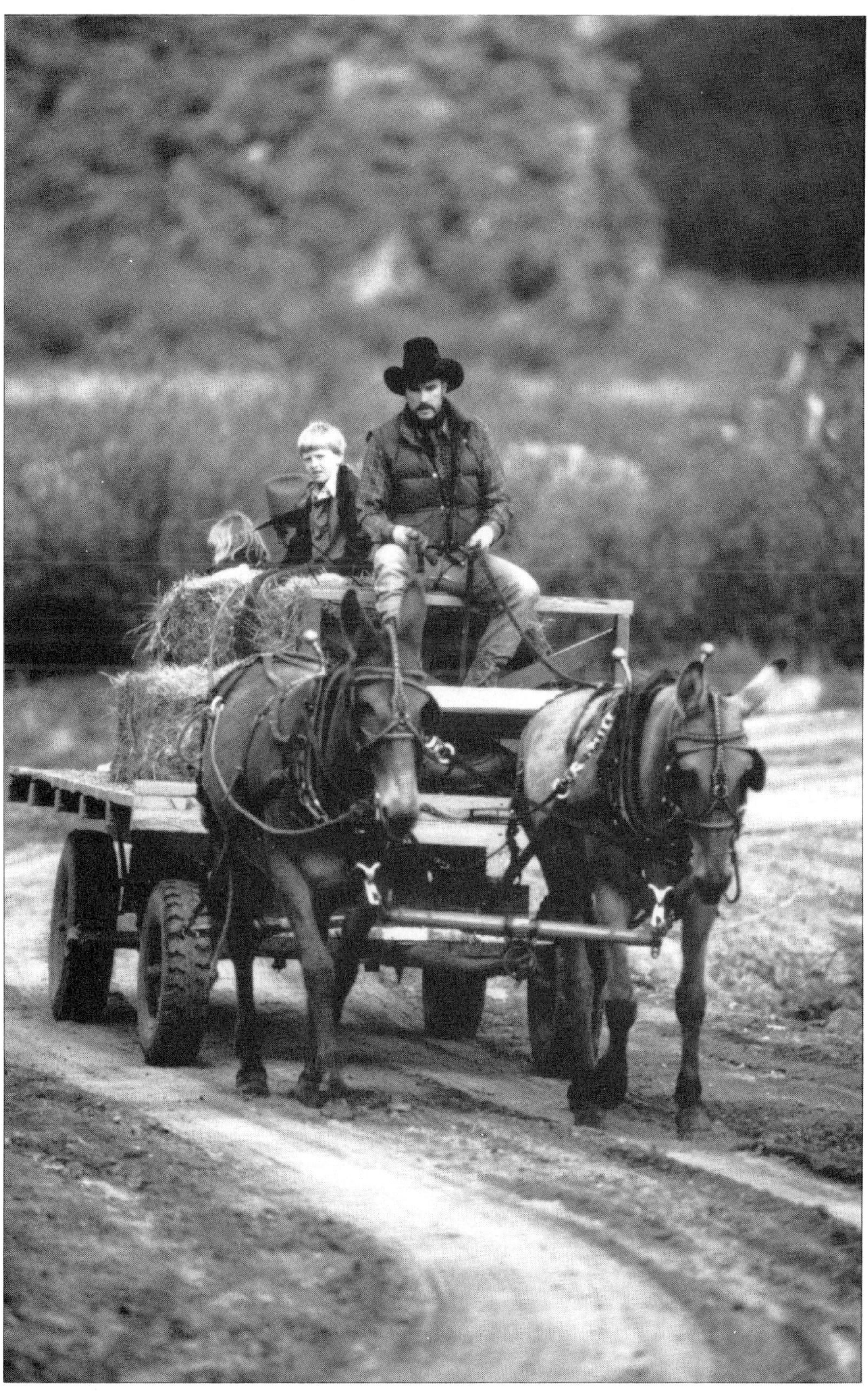

Rafter Y Ranch
Banner, Wyoming

Not far from the Montana border, in north central Wyoming, is the Goodwins' Rafter Y Ranch. Surrounded by pioneer history, this 1,000-acre family-run dude/cattle ranch is nestled in the rolling foothills of the Big Horn Mountains. The Rafter Y leans more toward families and one big family atmosphere. The young college staff exude friendliness and quickly make everyone feel like part of the Goodwin family. Early risers may help wrangle the horses in the morning. You will also see lots of wild game on the ranch property. The Goodwins have a strict no hunting policy. As Ralph says, "The wildlife we have here are almost part of our family." There is nothing fancy about the Rafter Y. It's been around for a long time and exudes lots of western character. With good food and a lovely setting, perhaps most of all this is a great ranch for families to gather and have fun together. Because of its size, the Goodwins can be very flexible with their program and accommodate the needs and wishes of their guests.

Address: 323 Wagon Box Road, Drawer K, Banner, Wyoming 82832
Telephone: (307) 683-2221 (summer), (904) 437-6934 (December-March); call for fax number
Location: 23 miles south of Sheridan off Highway 87, 17 miles north of Buffalo, close to Interstate 90
Memberships: Dude Ranchers' Association, Wyoming Dude Ranchers' Association
Medical: Sheridan Memorial Hospital, 23 miles
Guest Capacity: 17
Accommodations: Three old-fashioned green-roofed log cabins sleep a total of seventeen (2 two-bedroom and 1 three-bedroom). Behind the cabins are huge cottonwood and willow trees and Little Piney Creek. Each has full bath, living room, fireplace, and screened sleeping porch. Housekeeping each morning, nightly turn-down service with a surprise treat. Ice is delivered to cabins each afternoon. For the adventuresome, there is also a sheepherder's wagon; kids and teenagers love this. Laundry facilities.
Rates: • $-$$. American Plan, minimum of four days. Seven-day group and family reunion rates available. Nanny rates, too.
Credit Cards: None. Cash, personal checks, or traveler's checks accepted.
Season: Late June through August
Activities: Riding is the main activity every day except Sunday. Most guests ride each morning with a wrangler. Weekly breakfast and lunch rides. Afternoons are usually filled with other nonriding activities: napping, reading, or visiting local historical sites are favorites. Good selection of ranch horses. As the Goodwins say, "Our horses are all colors, sizes, and speeds." Guests may help with ranch chores, play tennis (excellent tennis court with informal guest/staff matches), swim in the stream-fed swimming hole, fish, hike, or play golf nearby. Photographers should bring lots of film.
Children's Programs: No separate activities program. Families usually interact together. Children are the responsibility of their parents. Bring a nanny if you wish.
Dining: The Goodwins are very proud of their food. Buffet-style, one sitting; second helpings always available. Hilary's famous Rafter Y Sunday brunch. Weekly barbecues at Lake De Smet. Special diets arranged. BYOB.
Entertainment: Informal cocktails and hors d'oeuvres before dinner. Spontaneous softball, volleyball, soccer, and horseshoe games. Local rodeos.
Summary: Wonderful small family owned and operated dude/cattle ranch offering a flexible schedule and individual attention. High percentage of return guests. Great for families and couples, not recommended for singles. Sunday afternoon Big Horn polo matches held at the nearby equestrian center.

Rimrock Ranch
Cody, Wyoming

The Rimrock Ranch is named after the rock formations surrounding the property. It is just 26 miles from Yellowstone National Park's east entrance and at the edge of the Shoshone National Forest. Your hosts, Glenn and Alice Fales, are natives of Wyoming and have been receiving guests since the late 1950s. Alice grew up on a ranch, and Glenn has spent most of his life as a cowboy. They are superb dude ranchers, and most of all, tremendous human beings. This family-owned and operated ranch is one mile from the North Fork of the Shoshone River and near Buffalo Bill Lake—both of which offer superb fishing. The ranch kitchen will prepare the 2- to 3-pound trout that guests catch. Rimrock has a fine string of about 100 horses. The ranch's 5- to 10-day pack trips are famous. The log ranch house is a gathering spot at the end of the day and exudes rustic warmth and hospitality. Many like to just stretch out here and enjoy its history while reading a favorite book. Glenn and Alice are modest people and won't tell you they have hosted some of the world's VIPs.

Address: 2728 North Fork Road, Dept. K, Cody, Wyoming 82414
Telephone: (307) 587-3970; fax: (307) 527-4633
Airport: Cody, Wyoming, or Billings, Montana
Location: 26 miles west of Cody
Memberships: Dude Ranchers' Association, Wyoming Outfitters Association
Medical: Cody Hospital, 26 miles
Guest Capacity: 32
Accommodations: Comfortable, simple, and homey, each of the nine log cabins (two of which can accommodate up to 8 people) is furnished with western decor. Some have stone fireplaces. All have private baths with hot and cold running water. Each has a porch; all but one have carpeting. Heated with gas. Laundry facilities.
Rates: • \$-\$\$. American Plan. Pack trip rates available. Ask about sliding scale rates for more than one person. One-week minimum stay, Sunday to Sunday.
Credit Cards: None. Personal checks accepted.
Season: Last week in May through September
Activities: All-day and half-day trail rides. Glenn says, "Guests should learn how to ride at three gaits—walk, trot, and canter." Plenty of loping for those riders who can handle it. Ask about the Table Mountain Ride, breakfast ride to Green Creek, and the wine and cheese ride to Lost Creek. Guests get their own horse for the week. Six to eight guests per ride with a wrangler. Separate from ranch activities are horse pack trips into Yellowstone Park and Teton and Shoshone national forests. Ask about trips to South Fork of the Shoshone and Yellowstone River. Fishing, swimming, and weekly river rafting in the North Fork of the Shoshone River.
Children's Programs: No special programs. Children's fishing pond. Children's rides. Babysitting available. Very young children not advised.
Dining: On or off the trail, healthy and hearty ranch cooking. Alice's famous prime rib is a specialty. Special diets can be arranged. BYOB.
Entertainment: Glenn and Alice host an "introduction party" every Sunday evening. Cookouts, sing-alongs, and singing cowboys several times a week. Shuffleboard, table tennis, cards, and billiards in the recreation room with lots of memorabilia. Cody nightly rodeo and square dancing.
Summary: Glenn and Alice exemplify the true meaning and "down-to-earth" spirit of dude ranching. Excellent wilderness pack trips and famous white mule string. Because Yellowstone National Park is so close, Alice takes guests on a guided tour through the park. Nearby: Buffalo Bill Historical Center, July Fourth Cody Stampede.

See color photos, page 293

Red Rock Ranch
Kelly, Wyoming

Nestled in a secluded valley high (7,200 feet) on the eastern slope of Jackson Hole's spectacular mountain country is Red Rock Ranch, named for the Indian red cliffs and rock formations one sees driving up from the little one-horse town of Kelly, some 15 miles from the ranch gates. This operating old-time cattle ranch, homesteaded in 1890, offers some of the best guest ranching in the business. Since 1972 it has been owned by the MacKenzie family. With a first-rate string of horses, wranglers will take you through spectacular country. Fly-fishermen will enjoy the stocked ranch pond and Crystal Creek, a 2½-mile fly-fishing, catch and release stream, which runs through the ranch. RRR is one of the best!

Address: P.O. Box 38 K, Kelly, Wyoming 83011
Telephone: (307) 733-6288; fax: (307) 733-6287
Airport: Jackson
Location: 26 miles northeast of Jackson
Memberships: Dude Ranchers' Association, Wyoming Dude Ranchers' Association
Medical: St. John's Hospital, Jackson, 26 miles
Conference: 30, early June and September
Guest Capacity: 30
Accommodations: There are nine authentic log cabins named after such famous Native American tribes . . . Apache, Navajo, Sioux, and Cheyenne. These cabins were built in the early 1950s and are one- and two-bedrooms with private baths for each bedroom. All have twin or queen-size beds, adjoining living rooms, electric heat, wood stoves, small refrigerators, and carpeting. They are tastefully decorated in western style. Each cabin has a small porch with a chair or bench. A comfortable lodge, dining room, and adult pool hall/bar are available to guests. An activities room for square dancing and western swing is a new addition. There is also a children's recreation room. Laundry facilities are available.
Rates: $$. American Plan, includes all activities except pack trips, river trips, and pick-up at airport. Off-season rates.
Credit Cards: None. Personal checks or cash accepted.
Season: June through early October
Activities: Here you can enjoy some of the most beautiful riding in the country. Morning, afternoon, and all-day rides are offered. You may ride in smaller groups if you wish. Monday morning orientation rides in the arena acquaint guests with their horse for the week. Ask about the White Canyon and Grizzly Lake rides and four- to five-day pack trips into the Gros Ventre Wilderness. There is swimming in a heated pool, an eight-person hot tub, hiking, and plenty of relaxing. Scenic river trips can be arranged down the Snake River—a must!
Children's Programs: Wranglers take kids on day rides. One night a week they take an overnight pack trip. The age limit for riding is 6 years and older. There is a children's recreation room and a weekly gymkhana. Nannies are encouraged for young children.
Dining: Generally, just down-home, darn good ranch cooking, served family-style or buffet-style. Weekly cookouts for breakfast and on Sunday evening; special diets catered to with advance notice. Children eat evening meal before adults (teens optional). BYOB.
Entertainment: Hors d'oeuvres and drinks (BYOB) before dinner. Sing-alongs, weekly rodeo in Jackson, pickle ball (mini-tennis) court, dancing in the Dance Hall.
Summary: A fun, family-oriented guest ranch with lots of camaraderie and Old West spirit. Unspoiled wilderness, plenty of horseback riding. Return guests rarely leave the ranch once they arrive. Laid-back, relaxing atmosphere. Working cattle ranch, pack trips, cattle roundup in spring and fall, horse-drawn surrey rides. Women's fitness week.

See color photos, page 292

R Lazy S Ranch
Teton Village, Wyoming

Beautiful scenery, a friendly staff, wonderful food, and western hospitality make the R Lazy S one of the great guest ranches. Since 1947, the McConaughy family has operated this wonderful ranch, almost at the foot of the majestic Tetons, bordering Grand Teton National Park. In 1975, Howard and Cara Stirn purchased the McConaughys' interest. Since then, both the Stirns and the McConaughys have been hosts to families from all over. While it is close to Jackson and the world-class ski resort at Teton Village, the ranch still maintains its privacy and solitude. Being so close and yet so far gives guests many options for activities and excursions. If you plan to try to do everything, better stay three to four weeks. By the end of one week, you will have only begun. Regardless of how long you stay, you will enjoy the friendly spirit and the magnificent mountain scenery.

Address: Box 308 K, Teton Village, Wyoming 83025
Telephone: (307) 733-2655
Airport: Jackson
Location: 13 miles northwest of the town of Jackson, 1 mile north of Teton Village
Memberships: Dude Ranchers' Association
Medical: St. John's Hospital, 13 miles
Guest Capacity: 45
Accommodations: There are 12 beautifully modernized one-, two-, and three-bedroom log cabins, all with electric blankets and fabulous views, scattered beautifully around the ranch property among the aspen trees. All have one or two bathrooms, depending on size; some have living rooms; all have electric heaters or wood-burning stoves and lovely hanging baskets with colorful flowers. There is one teen dorm (boys or girls) with bathroom that sleeps 4 in bunk beds. The main lodge, with its cathedral ceilings, is a favorite gathering place at day's end. Laundry facilities available.
Rates: $$-$$$. American Plan. Minimum one-week stay, Sunday to Sunday.
Credit Cards: None. Personal checks accepted.
Season: Mid-June through September, adults-only month of September
Activities: The nearby Snake River (a mile from ranch buildings) and neighboring Teton Mountain trails offer many activities. The ranch offers a full riding program. Half-day and all-day rides with picnic lunches. No riding on Sundays. Pack trips and riding instruction available. An extensive fly-fishing program is available. Claire and Bob's daughter and son-in-law are partners in Westbank Anglers, a first-rate guide and fly-fishing shop three miles from the ranch. Fishing on the Snake, South Fork, Green, and North Fork rivers and streams, lakes, and stocked ranch pond. Weekly fishing clinic. Hiking, swimming in ranch swimming hole, or tubing. River rafting, tennis, and golf can be arranged nearby. Water-skiing or scenic boat rides once a week on Jackson Lake.
Children's Programs: The ranch is unable to accommodate children under 6 years of age. Kiddie wranglers with programs for kids and teenagers. Children eat together in own dining room. Gymkhanas.
Dining: The lovely dining room looks out to the meadows and the Tetons beyond. Family- and buffet-style food. Ranch hosts Sunday welcome happy hour. Weekly cookouts. BYOB.
Entertainment: Kids' marshmallow roasts, hayrides to cookouts and around the ranch. Jackson Rodeo, volleyball, softball, and horseshoes. Evening western swing. Nature walk and fishing clinic.
Summary: Wonderful family ranch. Spectacular setting looking to the Tetons. Adults only in September for peak fly-fishing season. R Lazy S is great for single parents and their children. Ask the ranch about their R Lazy S cookbook. Nearby: shopping, rodeo, and melodrama in town of Jackson, Teton Village with its mountain tram, Yellowstone National Park.

Savery Creek Thoroughbred Ranch
Savery, Wyoming

Savery Creek Thoroughbred Ranch is the home of Joyce Saer. It borders her family's historic old dude ranch—the Boyer YL Ranch, which has been turned out to pasture. Savery Creek offers unique riding opportunities for more advanced riders. Joyce is a soft-spoken woman who has four grown children—a physician, a veterinarian, a navy flier, and a married daughter. She has spent much of her life in Europe, particularly in Spain, and is an outstanding horsewoman. Guests stay with Joyce in her ranch house. The ranch is in one of the last unspoiled, untouristy areas in Wyoming, where cattle and sheep still graze. The name "Wyoming," an Indian word meaning "mountains and valleys alternating," could have originated in the Savery Valley. Savery Creek Thoroughbred Ranch is for experienced English and western riders wishing to savor the Old West in total privacy and low-key, unregimented, western comfort, with lots of warmth and hospitality.

Address: Box 24 K, Savery, Wyoming 82332
Telephone: (307) 383-7840; call for fax number
Airport: Steamboat Springs, Colorado; paved landing field at Dixon, 11 miles
Location: 70 miles south of Rawlins; 60 miles north of Craig, Colorado; 280 miles from Denver
Medical: Steamboat Hospital, 2 hours; clinic at Baggs, 20 miles
Guest Capacity: No more than 6
Accommodations: The house is beside Savery Creek in cottonwood trees facing the beautiful Savery Valley. There are three guest bedrooms upstairs, attractively furnished with antiques. One is spacious, overlooking the creek, with fireplace, king-size four-poster bed, sitting area, and private bath and entry. The other two bedrooms have queen-size beds and share a bathroom. For the adventurous, there are two covered wagons.
Rates: • $$. American Plan. Rates on request. Three-day minimum stay.
Credit Cards: Personal checks and traveler's checks accepted.
Season: May to October; winter months by special arrangement
Activities: This is a riding ranch with one to three horses per guest. The horses are exceptional, of competition and show quality. It is possible to ride in three directions without seeing another person. Savery Creek is best suited for intermediate and advanced riders and caters to expert riders especially. Western and English saddles, jumping, and jumping lessons available. Ask Joyce about her award-winning granddaughter whom she has trained and who competes regularly. Fly-fishing on Savery Creek, the Little Snake, or on Hog Park Reservoir. Tennis, swimming in Savery Creek, hiking, badminton, and seasonal hunting.
Children's Programs: No program. Best for young people who can ride.
Dining: Superb meals, specializing in leg of lamb, sherry chicken, green salads, fresh fruit, homegrown vegetables, cookouts. Chardonnays and cabernets served.
Entertainment: Cowboys practice once a week at Dixon Arena; evening conversation and bridge; large selection of books, classical music, and newspapers and magazines including the *New Yorker* and the *Wall Street Journal*.
Summary: Small intimate ranch offering unlimited riding opportunities catering to experienced riders (both English and western) and a very limited number of guests. Experts in their fields (both professional and creative) find Savery Creek particularly enjoyable. Superb cuisine, Red Desert riding trip, individualized service. Spanish and some French spoken. Nearby: Savery Museum, Encampment Museum, old mining towns, Steamboat Springs, Overland Trail, wildflowers, fossils and wildlife, Medicine Bow National Forest.

See color photos, page 294

Seven D Ranch
Cody, Wyoming

The Seven D Ranch is a cozy haven in the midst of a magnificent wilderness. It was bought in the late 1950s by Dewey and Lee Dominick, a surgeon and his wife. Today, the family tradition continues under their son, David, who has a background in environmental law and is a past president of the Denver Audubon Society. The ranch is in the remote and beautiful Sunlight Basin deep within Shoshone National Forest. It is surrounded by the Absaroka Mountains and has vast pastures where the horses are turned out each night to play and graze and where you will find a small herd of registered Black Angus cattle. The Seven D appeals to all ages. For those who wish to relax, the ranch offers the peace of a mountain hideaway. Those with more energy may want to take a leisurely morning or afternoon ride, cast for trout, or hike into the Absaroka Wilderness. And those with more get-up-and-go may enjoy a full day of riding, fishing, or a wilderness pack trip into Yellowstone Park. Most of all, there is a wonderful atmosphere of camaraderie, laughter, and energetic participation. If you have ever wondered where Marlboro Country is, many of the photographs were taken right here at the Seven D.

Address: P.O. Box 100 K, Cody, Wyoming 82414
Telephone: (307) 587-3997 (summer), (307) 587-9885 (winter)
Airport: Cody
Location: 50 miles northwest of Cody via Chief Joseph Scenic Highway (Hwy 296) and Sunlight Basin Road, a beautiful 1½-hour drive
Memberships: Dude Ranchers' Association
Medical: Cody Hospital, 50 miles
Conference: 28
Guest Capacity: 28
Accommodations: Twelve rustically comfortable cabins are spaced apart in a beautiful aspen grove and have names like Trapper, Aspen, Buffalo, Waldorf, and the Fireplace. Cabins vary from one to four bedrooms each, with private baths and wood stoves. Fire starter and wood provided. Guests enjoy these stoves during delightfully cool summer evenings. Daily maid service. Laundry facilities available.
Rates: • $$-$$$. American Plan. Children's off-season rates. Minimum one-week stay, Sunday to Sunday. Pack trip and hunting rates available.
Credit Cards: None. Personal checks or cash accepted.
Season: Early June through September, fall hunting
Activities: Seventy excellent riding horses. Rides every day except Sunday. Your choice of long, short, half-day, or all-day rides. Riders are accompanied by experienced wranglers on beautiful and varied trails. Five to eight riders go out per ride. Ask about the Big Skyline ride with views into Montana. Instruction available. Two- to ten-day horse pack trips by advance arrangement into the North Absaroka Wilderness and Yellowstone Park for groups of 6 or fewer. This has been a trip of a lifetime for many. Fishing on and off the property, four-wheel-drive trips, trap shooting (guns provided), hiking (ask about David's bird walks), and fall hunting trips may be arranged. Volleyball, soccer, and baseball. Float trips available in Cody.
Children's Programs: Counselors for children age 6 to age 15. Pony rides for children under age 5. The ranch encourages you to bring your own nanny for your young children.
Dining: Excellent ranch food, topped only by the beautiful old ranch dining room. Naturally raised, low-fat ranch-raised beef. Special diets catered to with advance notice. BYOB.
Entertainment: Books at the main lodge. Recreation room with piano, table tennis, billiards, square dancing with live caller. Gymkhanas, horseshoes. Some occasionally go to the rodeos in Cody.
Summary: The Seven D is one of the great old guest ranches. The Dominick family exudes warmth and plenty of western hospitality. Lots of family reunions here. A good number stay a week at the ranch, then go on a Seven D pack trip. Excellent wilderness pack trips. September is adults-only month. Birding, photography workshops.

Spear-O-Wigwam Ranch
Sheridan, Wyoming

As you peer through the log-framed entrance supporting the oversized cast iron ranch brand, it may seem that you are on a dirt runway and about to take off into the wild blue yonder. Fear not. It is only the dirt road leading straight to the ranch. As your car rumbles over the cattle guard, be prepared. You are about to take off on a tremendous ranch vacation. Spear-O-Wigwam was established in the early 1920s by the Willis Spear family, who entertained many Eastern friends. An early guest was Ernest Hemingway who, in 1928, completed *A Farewell to Arms* at the ranch. Hemingway was overheard saying one day, "There are two places I love, Africa and Wyoming." The ranch is in the Big Horn National Forest. At 8,300 feet, the air is clear, mountain water pure, summer days cool, and the scenery spectacular.

Address: Box 1081 K, Sheridan, Wyoming 82801
Telephone: (307) 674-4496 (summer); (307) 672-0002 (winter). No telephone at the ranch, only two-way radio.
Airport: Sheridan via Denver
Location: 30 miles southwest of Sheridan
Medical: Sheridan Memorial Hospital, 30 miles
Memberships: Dude Ranchers' Association, Wyoming Dude Ranchers' Association
Conference: 32
Guest Capacity: 32
Accommodations: Seven old-fashioned beautiful log cabins, one to four bedrooms each, all with private baths, heat, and western decor. Cabins are known by such names as Hemingway, Porcupine, Chipmunk, and Bears Den. The main lodge has a huge fireplace, library, bar, and dining room. Laundry facilities available. Daily maid service with nightly turn-down service. No lights out here—the ranch generates its own electricity, and the generator works around the clock.
Rates: \$-\$\$. American Plan. Children's, group, and off-season rates available. Three-day minimum stay, arrival any day.
Credit Cards: None. Personal checks accepted.
Season: Mid-June to mid-September
Activities: Informal program. Riding and relaxing are the two main activities. Riding every day—your choice of half-day or all-day rides. Guests put together their own riding groups and select their own rides. Because of the mountain terrain and high altitude, there is little opportunity for fast rides. The emphasis here is on the scenery and wildlife. No riding Friday afternoons. Pack trips (extra) to remote Beaver Lake, with its own permanent tent camp. Trout fishing in streams or lakes, kiddie pond, excellent hiking and nature photography, weekly picnic rides, breakfast cookouts, and evening barbecues. Swimming and boating on nearby park reservoir.
Children's Programs: No separate program. Families are encouraged to participate as families. Baby-sitters can be arranged for small children. Some families bring their own baby-sitters. Cribs available. Varied riding program for young kids. Call for details.
Dining: Meals served family-style at one long table seating 32. Excellent western cuisine featuring prime rib, fried chicken, steaks, home-baked breads, and desserts. BYOB.
Entertainment: BYOB. Happy hour each evening. Rodeos in Sheridan and Buffalo, weekly polo in Big Horn, 20 miles away. Recreation room with pool table, table tennis, and cards; occasional songfest. No television. Jim may yodel or sing a few songs.
Summary: Informal, relaxed atmosphere. As Barbara says, "We just sort of let things happen, and you don't have to do anything if you don't want to." The ranch has a magnificent setting. Riding and relaxing are the two main activities. Many couples and families return year after year. Abundant wildlife and wildflowers of the Big Horn Mountains. Pets are allowed, but arrangements must be made in advance.

See color photos, page 295

Squaw Creek Ranch
Cody, Wyoming

The ranch is an old homestead that has changed hands a few times since it was originally established. In 1986, a wonderful family bought the beautiful ranch with the express purpose of sharing this spectacular area with guests and providing them with "the Wyoming Experience." After the purchase, construction of a new lodge and cabins was begun and finished in 1990. With resident managers, Squaw Creek Ranch hosts families, couples, singles, and business retreats.

Address: 4059 Crandall Road, Dept. K, Cody, Wyoming 82414
Telephone: (307) 587-6178, (800) 532-7281; fax: (307) 587-5249
Airport: Cody, Wyoming, or Billings, Montana (free airport pick-up)
Location: 60 miles northwest of Cody off Wyoming Highway 296; 120 miles southwest of Billings, Montana; 23 miles from the northeast entrance of Yellowstone National Park
Memberships: Dude Ranchers' Association, Wyoming Outfitters Association, Cody Country Outfitters Association
Medical: West Park Hospital, 60 miles
Conference: 40
Guest Capacity: 30
Accommodations: Guests stay in one-, two- and four-bedroom cabins. All have double beds, private bathrooms, electric heat, small writing desks, and balloon curtains. With the exception of one of the original homestead cabins, all were built between 1987 and 1990. The cabins are all named for colorful individuals and Indian tribes that played a part in the area's history. The main lodge offers a sitting area/dining room around the native stone fireplace, a small library and game room, and extra shower rooms. There are also tepees for adults or children with a sense of adventure.
Rates: • $$. American Plan. Children's rates, conference/group rates, and off-season rates available. Three-night minimum stay in summer, no minimum stay in winter.
Credit Cards: Mastercard/Visa
Season: Year-round
Activities: Horseback riding is the main activity and is offered Monday through Saturday. No riding on Sundays. Because of the terrain, trail rides are at a walk; there are miles of trails for riding and hiking. Morning, afternoon, and all-day rides. Ask about Crandall Trail, Squaw Creek, and Clark's Fork rides. Guests are assigned their own horses, which you may brush and saddle if you wish. Multiday pack trips can be arranged with prior notice. Numerous streams and high mountain lakes for fishermen; bring your own gear. Par course fitness trail on ranch. Yellowstone National Park tours, a day in Cody to visit the Buffalo Bill Historical Center, Old Trail Town, and the cody Night Rodeo. Rafting trips on the Yellowstone or Shoshone rivers. Winter offers cross-country skiing on groomed and backcountry trails. Access to the Cooke City, Montana, and the Beartooth snowmobile areas. Call for details.
Children's Programs: Children are always welcome at Squaw Creek Ranch. There is no special program. Nannies are welcome for the cost of their meals only. Age limit for riding is 6 years old, 8 years old for pack trips.
Dining: Hearty, home-cooked meals served family-style or buffet-style depending on the number of guests. Special diets are catered to. BYOB with discretion.
Entertainment: Informal program. Relaxing around a campfire, roasting marshmallows with an occasional impromptu sing-along or mountain man tall tales. Spontaneous games of volleyball, horseshoes, or roping "Homer." The Koinonia Room has a small library, Ping-Pong, and assorted games.
Summary: Small, family-oriented, year-round guest ranch with a warm, friendly atmosphere. It is a mile off-road. There are only three ways into the ranch: over Chief Joseph Scenic Highway, over Beartooth Scenic Byway, or through Yellowstone National Park—all magnificent!

Terry Bison Ranch
Cheyenne, Wyoming

Terry Bison Ranch is 30,000 acres of rolling grasslands, canyons, hills, and 2,000 head of buffalo. After several years of planning and extensive building, this historic ranch opened its doors to the public in 1993. Just off Interstate 25 and only seven miles south of Cheyenne, the ranch offers an interpretive historical perspective on the buffalo, more correctly referred to as bison, and the role they played in the development of the West. Unlike many dude ranches, guests here may come for the day, stay for the night in one of the new log cabins, or park their RV in the recreational vehicle park. The Thiel family bought the ranch in 1992 with the sole purpose of opening it up to the public. As Dan Thiel says, "There are not many ranches that have a herd of 2,000 buffalo. We want people who come to see both the new and old west and leave with a better understanding about the life our forefathers lived. Most of all, we want families and children to have fun." Terry Bison Ranch is, indeed, where the buffalo roam.

Address: 51 I-25 Service Road East, Dept. K, Cheyenne, Wyoming 82007
Telephone: (307) 634-5347, (307) 634-4171; call for fax number
Airport: Cheyenne Municipal Airport
Location: 7 miles south of Cheyenne on Interstate 25
Memberships: American Bison Association, Commercial Good Sam, Family Motor Coach Association
Medical: First-aid-trained staff; Cheyenne Memorial Hospital in Cheyenne, 10 miles
Conference: 450
Guest Capacity: 150
Accommodations: The ranch offers accommodations for just about every type of traveler and for every type of budget. There are three charming one-room guest cabins overlooking the historic ranch area, with private baths and kitchenettes. A large, 17-room, two-story bunkhouse, built around the turn-of-the-century and remodeled for guests to occupy, has one full bed per room and centralized men's and women's bathrooms. There are also 100 RV spaces with full hookups, showers, and laundry facilities. This site is in conjunction with the "recreational village," which you can see from the road.
Rates: • $-$$. Everything is à la carte. Daily, group, and winter season rates available. Call for details.
Credit Cards: Visa, MasterCard
Season: Year-round
Activities: The ranch is divided into two areas: the historic ranch complex, which is secluded, and the new recreational village, which is just off Interstate 25. The main activities here are guided horse-drawn wagon and motor vehicle tours of the buffalo herd. Horseback rides go out on an hourly basis beginning at 10:00 a.m. and ending at 4:00 p.m. Recreation Center is equipped with hot tub, pool tables, and video games. Volleyball and horseshoes.
Children's Programs: Kids are the responsibility of parents. No baby-sitting available. Lots of animals in the corrals to learn about. Recreation Center.
Dining: Restaurant and café open all day long, to ranch guests and the public. Chuck wagon dinner with fixed menu of beef or buffalo and western fare served buffet-style with entertainment is featured on weekends.
Entertainment: Occasional weekly entertainment, dance hall with music. The Terry Bison Trailblazers entertain audiences at the Chuckwagon Dinner. Occasional barn dance allows guests to kick up their heels Wyoming-style in the historic area of the ranch.
Summary: Buffalo ranch divided into two areas—the old and the new. An eye-opening look at Old West history and the buffalo. Guests may stay in cabins, recreational village, or RV campsite. Ideal for family reunions or conferences. Located right off Interstate 25. Wonderful for weddings, dances, and private parties. This century-old ranch is brand new and ready to go!

T-Cross Ranch
Dubois, Wyoming

The T-Cross Ranch is an authentic, old-time dude ranch that has been in operation since 1920. It is nestled in a picturesque, isolated valley surrounded by the spectacular Shoshone National Forest. Homesteaded in the 1800s by a fugitive from the Johnson County cattle wars, T-Cross is steeped in western history and atmosphere. The main lodge and cabins were handcrafted out of the ranch's own lodgepole pines and are heated by wood stoves. Guests experience the feeling of having stepped back in time to the Old West. Your hosts are Ken and Garey Neal, second-generation dude ranchers, who are well known for their warm hospitality. Old-time dude ranching just doesn't get any better! The T-Cross is very, very special!!

Address: P.O. Box 638 K, Dubois, Wyoming 82513
Telephone: (307) 455-2206 (summer), (307) 733-2225 (winter); fax (307) 455-2720 (summer only)
Airport: Jackson or Riverton, Wyoming. Surfaced airstrip 3 miles west of Dubois for private jets and planes. Pick-up service available (extra).
Location: 15 miles north of Dubois off Highway 26/287, 85 miles east of Jackson Airport
Memberships: Dude Ranchers' Association, Wyoming Dude Ranchers Association, Nature Conservancy
Medical: Dubois Clinic, 15 miles
Conference: 24 (June and September)
Guest Capacity: 24
Accommodations: A wonderful blend of rugged atmosphere and modern amenities. Seven cozy log cabins tucked in the pines have down quilts, wood stoves or fireplaces, hot showers, and individual porches. The main lodge is filled with western charm.
Rates: • $$. American Plan. Off-season, group, and nanny rates available. Sunday to Sunday arrival in July and August.
Credit Cards: None. Personal checks and cash accepted.
Season: Early June to late October
Activities: Activities are informally organized. The main activities are riding, hiking, fishing, and relaxing. Guests are assigned a horse for the duration of their stay. Morning and afternoon rides go out daily except Sunday. All-day rides go out at least twice a week with a pack mule carrying lunch and fishing gear. Ask about rides to Five Pockets, Rams Horn Basin, Deacon Lake, and Twilight Falls. Depending on ability, walk, trot, and loping rides. Fly-fishermen enjoy Horse Creek, which runs through the ranch. Another favorite is the Wiggins Fork of the Wind River (a 20-minute drive). There are also high mountain lakes, hiking and climbing opportunities, bird-watching, wildflowers, picnicking, wading in the river, or relaxing on the porch and soaking in the hot tub at the end of the day.
Children's Programs: Children under 6 are the responsibility of parents or nannies. Kids 6 and older ride, hike, and tube float with a kiddie wrangler. Ask about overnight tepee campouts. Friday morning gymkhanas.
Dining: Wholesome ranch cooking. Cook will prepare your freshly caught fish. Breakfast, lunch, and dinner cookouts. Happy hour each evening in the lodge. BYOB.
Entertainment: Usually on your own in the evening. Weekly square dancing, sing-along campfires, croquet, volleyball and softball.
Summary: The Neals are great hosts who love what they do, and they do it so well. The relaxed, unstructured vacation atmosphere of the 1930s is still found at this remote ranch and is enjoyed by the young and the young-hearted. T-Cross is warm and personable. Ideal for family reunions and small groups. Those who come don't want to leave, and that's just the way it is!

See color photos, page 296

Trail Creek Ranch
Wilson, Wyoming

Trail Creek Ranch is very special to me. It is the ranch where my parents took my sister and me as young children. It is here that a seed was planted which blossomed into my love for this incredible way of life. I am proud to say that Trail Creek Ranch is responsible for this guidebook. Back in the 1940s, a young Olympic skier named Elizabeth Woolsey bought a rundown ranch at the foot of Teton Pass, ten miles from Jackson. With her tenacity and tremendous spirit, Betty transformed the ranch into a gold mine of charm. It is one of the prettiest family-oriented ranches in the country and offers sincere western hospitality. To the east, the property consists of a lush green hay meadow; the rest is timbered with many bridle trails and crystal clear streams, bordered by national forest. Trail Creek is a working ranch, raising hay that supports a fine string of horses and pack mules. Daily riding and pack trips are the main activities. Betty has touched many lives over the years. Together with her exceptional staff, Trail Creek Ranch continues to greet guests, make new friends, and offer the very best in the West.

Address: P.O. Box 10 K, Wilson, Wyoming 83014
Telephone: (307) 733-2610
Airport: Jackson via Salt Lake City or Denver
Location: 2 miles west of Wilson, 10 miles west of Jackson
Memberships: Dude Ranchers' Association
Medical: St. John's Hospital, Jackson
Guest Capacity: 25 (summer); 10-12 (winter)
Accommodations: The Main Lodge, with the living room, library, dining rooms, and sun deck, is the heartbeat of Trail Creek. Two family cabins and cabins made up of several bedrooms with private baths comfortably house the guests. They all overlook the hay meadow and beyond to the Sleeping Indian, a beautiful mountain in the Gros Ventre range. There are also several rooms in the Main Lodge and separate boys' and girls' bunkhouses for teenagers.
Rates: $$. American Plan. Everything included except pack trips. Some guests stay 10 days to two weeks.
Credit Cards: None. Personal checks accepted.
Season: Mid-June to mid-September (summer); February and March (winter). One-week minimum stay.
Activities: In summer, riding is the main activity. All rides, fast, medium, and slow, go out in groups of 5 to 6 twice a day. There are also all-day luncheon rides to Ski Lake and Grand Teton Park (more experienced riders). Pack trips are special at Trail Creek, with families or groups going out for 2- to 7-day trips into the high country (arranged in advance.) Fishing in the Snake River, nearby lakes, and ranch pond. Canoeing, hiking, swimming in heated pool. River rafting with local outfitter. In winter, Betty takes no more than 10 to 12 guests, who enjoy cross-country skiing on the ranch and nearby downhill skiing, both in the backcountry and at the Jackson Hole Ski Resort and Grand Targhee Ski Resort.
Children's Programs: No formal program, but kids have the times of their lives. Kids may ride together if they wish. Parents with young children are encouraged to bring their own baby-sitter or nanny. The ranch has no baby-sitting program.
Dining: A ranch garden supplies lettuce, asparagus, and herbs for family meals of roast beef, pork chops, baked ham, roast chicken, fish, soups, and salads. BYOB. Informal cocktail hour before dinner daily.
Entertainment: Many go to the Stagecoach Bar in Wilson for country-western dancing or into Jackson. Jackson rodeo twice a week.
Summary: One of the all-time great guest ranches. Lovely setting and great people. French spoken. Nearby: the Tetons, Yellowstone National Park, Jackson, National Elk Refuge. Be sure to buy a copy of Betty's *Off the Beaten Track*.

See color photo, page 297

V-Bar Guest Ranch
Laramie, Wyoming

Owned by former broadcasting executive Duane Harm, V-Bar Guest Ranch is located in the wide-open Centennial Valley near the Snowy Range Mountains west of Laramie. The V-Bar is a showplace of western charm and rustic elegance with meadows, streams, and even a railroad. It is truly a Shangri-la serving lots of comfort, western ambience, and some of the finest horseback riding anywhere. Susan Harm has brought this historic stagecoach stop alive with her designer touches. Together, they have created a rustically elegant retreat with superb dining, great western riding, and fishing.

Address: 2091 State Highway 130, Drawer K, Laramie, Wyoming 82070
Telephone: (307) 745-7036, (800) 788-4630; fax: (307) 745-7433
Airport: Brees Field, Laramie, Wyoming (ranch offers free pick-up service to and from the airport)
Location: 20 miles west of Laramie off Highway 130
Memberships: Dude Ranchers' Association
Medical: Ivinson Memorial Hospital, 20 miles east of Laramie
Conference: 35
Guest Capacity: 35
Accommodations: All accommodations in the lodge and cabins reflect quality and comfort that characterizes the V-Bar Guest Ranch. Rooms and lodge filled with antiques and artifacts. Six lodge rooms and three cabins.
Rates: • $$$. American Plan. Children's and group rates. Train ride and skeet shooting extra. Arrivals Saturday to Saturday. One-week minimum stay. Three-day stays possible if available. Off-season bed and breakfast rates.
Credit Cards: None. Personal checks and cash accepted.
Season: Mid-May through September; bed and breakfast the rest of the year
Activities: Most come here to ride, have a combination of western experiences, and fish this great two-mile trout stream. This is truly a riding ranch, coupled with good taste and lots of charm. Variety of riding opportunities including meadow, open range, and mountain trails. Morning, afternoon, and all-day rides, with all levels of abilities catered to. Guests are invited to watch the horse roundup every morning. Many enjoy unsaddling their horses at the end of the day. Ask about team-drawn haywagon lessons. Trap shooting, archery, and hiking. Bring your own fly-fishing gear. Be sure to ask about the Wyoming excursion train that stops right on the ranch and goes into the Snowy Range Mountains.
Children's Programs: No programs for children under 6. Nannies stay free. Older children have a better time here. Kids over 6 may ride together or with adults.
Dining: Family-style dining with an elegant gourmet touch. Steaks to salmon, roast beef to prime rib, lunches and dinners served on "The Island." Full liquor license and saloon. Wine available with dinner.
Entertainment: Something is planned every evening. Country-western singing and dancing in the ranch's Hickok Old West Saloon. Laramie rodeo once a week. Evening hayrides.
Summary: Historic western ranch, best described as rustically elegant, with lots of warmth and charm! One of the finest western horseback opportunities in the country. The Little Laramie River runs through the ranch. Historic train stops at the ranch. Spring and fall cattle drives. Nearby: Territorial Prison Theme Park.

See color photos, pages 298-299

Triangle X Ranch
Moose, Wyoming

Known for its beauty, hospitality, and caring spirit, Triangle X has just about everything one could ask for, including a million-dollar view. Just outside Moose, Triangle X has panoramic views of the awesome Teton Range and Snake River valley. The ranch was established in 1926 by John Turner, Sr., as a cattle and hunting ranch. The Turner family runs a first-rate operation. Their repeat business (some guests have been returning for over 40 years) proves it. Among the ranch's unique features are its location, the river rafting program, and its well-supervised Little Wrangler riding program for kids 5 through 12. This program makes the Triangle X a perfect family stay.

Address: Star Route Box 120K, Moose, Wyoming 83012
Telephone: (307) 733-2183; fax: (307) 733-8685
Airport: Jackson Hole Airport
Location: 25 miles north of Jackson
Memberships: Dude Ranchers' Association, Wyoming Outfitters Association
Medical: St. John's Hospital in Jackson, 25 miles
Conference: 50, off-season only
Guest Capacity: 75
Accommodations: Guests stay in one-, two-, or three-bedroom log cabins with private baths, warm wool blankets, and covered porches. Cabins are very clean (with polished wood floors), comfortable, and ranch cozy. Laundry facilities available. Small ranch gift shop with hats, shirts, nature books, Indian jewelry, and river rafting reception area.
Rates: • \$-\$\$. American Plan, one-week minimum stay. Off-season and pack trip rates available.
Credit Cards: None. Personal checks or traveler's checks.
Season: May to November; January to April
Activities: Triangle X is predominantly a riding ranch. Riders enjoy a variety of trails to the tops of timbered mountains, through wildflower meadows, over sagebrush, and along the Snake River, always with the magnificent Teton Mountain Range as a backdrop. Breakfast rides and weekly Dutch oven suppers. Scenic, medium, and faster rides. Weekly nature ride by Forest Service personnel. Hiking and Triangle X Snake River rafting program. Trout fishing on the famous Snake River for either the expert or the beginner. In-house fishing guides who are well-versed on fly- or spin-fishing. Triangle X offers the ultimate wilderness experience in the form of four-day to two-week pack trips into the Teton Wilderness and southern Yellowstone areas. Here, the finest of scenery, wildlife, relaxing, and fishing can be experienced. In addition, fall hunting trips for elk, moose, and deer are conducted. In winter, cross-country skiing across the vast parklands and snowmobiling on adjacent National Forest lands.
Children's Programs: Kiddie wrangler with riding lessons, nearby swimming, rafting, and museum trips. Children under 5 do not ride. Parents ride with kids, but kids do not ride with parents. Parents do interact with children throughout the day.
Dining: Meals are hearty and delicious, served family-style in a wonderful dining room with commanding views overlooking the Tetons. Cookouts include Sunday ranch cookout, Wednesday evening ride cookout, and Friday morning breakfast ride. Children dine separately at all meals. Parents can eat with kids, but kids do not eat with parents. BYOB in cabins only.
Entertainment: Monday evening social. Campfires with old-fashioned sing-alongs, western guitar music, square dancing, rodeos in Jackson, weekly slide shows of local history. Forest Service nature talks.
Summary: Triangle X and the Turner family are old-time greats in the dude ranch business. Besides its location, million-dollar views of the Tetons, and Old West atmosphere, Triangle X is known for its riding, river rafting, and superb 4-day to 2-week pack trips. Winter snowmobiling. Nearby: Grand Teton and Yellowstone national parks.

Black Cat Guest Ranch
Hinton, Alberta, Canada

The Black Cat Guest Ranch is located on the eastern slopes of the Canadian Rocky Mountains and Jasper National Park. Jerry and Mary Bond and their daughter and son-in-law, Amber and Perry Hayward, have been hosting guests since 1970. People come from around the world to stay in the huge rustic, two-story, sixteen-room, cedar-sided lodge; each room looks out to the spectacular Rockies. The lodge is the center of attraction, next to the surrounding wilderness area, and features many comforts. Among them are a large living room with picture windows, fireplace, piano, comfortable chairs, and well-stocked library, all in a warm, homelike atmosphere. Outside lies a breathtaking wilderness in which an abundance of wildlife can be seen. The Black Cat Ranch is the perfect place for adults and older children to relax and escape from the hectic pace of everyday life to the seclusion of a mountain wilderness ranch.

Address: Box 6267 K, Hinton, Alberta, Canada T7V 1X6
Telephone: (403) 865-3084; fax: (403) 865-1924
Airport: Edmonton International, 3 hours; Hinton-Jasper airstrip for private airplanes
Location: 350 miles west of Edmonton, 5 hours northwest of Calgary, 15 miles northwest of Hinton off Highway 40 North
Medical: Hinton Hospital, 20 minutes
Memberships: Alberta Guest Ranch Association
Conference: 30, September through May only
Guest Capacity: 40
Accommodations: The lodge is modern but rustic looking. Each guest room is carpeted and has a fully equipped bath. All the rooms open to a balcony overlooking the front range of the Rockies. Motel-like rooms with a western twist.
Rates: • $. American Plan. Children's, senior citizens', and special rates available.
Credit Cards: Visa, MasterCard. Personal checks accepted.
Season: Year-round. Open Thanksgiving, New Year's, and Easter.
Activities: In summer, half-day and all-day guided trail rides. Ask about Solomon Mountain, Summit, Shangri-La, and High Valley. Due to the terrain, mostly walking and trotting. Superb, marked hiking trails, swimming, canoeing and fishing on Jarvis Lake (15 miles) or down the Athabasca River (five miles), cookouts. In winter, hiking and riding trails become terrific cross-country ski trails, which are machine-groomed single track. Night skiing and excellent double track trails at Athabasca Nordic Center nearby. Guests find New Year's a memorable experience. Both winter and summer, enjoy the outdoor hot tub.
Children's Programs: The ranch is oriented to adults and children 10 and older. No baby-sitting or children's program.
Dining: Home-cooked, family-style meals with fresh bread and desserts daily. Outdoor weekly barbecues. Vegetarian and special diets on request. BYOB.
Entertainment: Lounge with dart board and other games. In the fall the ranch features "murder mystery weekends."
Summary: Magnificent setting in Alberta's pristine wilderness. Complete home-style family comfort in the wilderness, three miles off the main road. The only sounds you may hear are the horse bells. Best for active people who love the wilderness. Spring and fall art workshops—watercolor, photography, creative writing. Caving in Cadomin Caves. Elderhostel programs for seniors. Spectacular drive to Columbia Ice Field and Jasper National Park.

Brewster's Kananaskis Guest Ranch
Banff, Alberta, Canada

The Kananaskis Guest Ranch is the Brewster family's original homestead. Established in 1923 by Missy Brewster, it is owned and operated by fifth-generation Brewsters. The ranch is an hour west of Calgary in spectacular Kananaskis country right on the edge of the Bow River and at the end of Banff's mountain corridor. This area has been known to produce gusts of wind that bring cool summer breezes and drifts of winter snow. *River of No Return* and *Little Big Man* were both filmed in this area. The modern lodge and several of the cabins overlook the Bow River.

Address: P.O. box 964, Dept. K, Banff, Alberta, Canada T0L 0C0
Telephone: (403) 673-3737; fax: (403) 762-3953
Airport: Calgary International, 60 miles
Location: 28 miles east of Banff, 45 minutes west of Calgary off the Trans-Canada Highway
Memberships: Alberta Guest Ranch Association, Alberta Hotel Association
Medical: Canmore Hospital, 15 minutes
Conference: 60; Lyster seminar building; Brewster Donut Tent especially for barbecues accommodating up to 1,000
Guest Capacity: 70
Accommodations: Thirty cabins and chalet accommodations. One- or two-bedroom units feature cedar interiors with antique dressers and nightstands, wall-to-wall carpeting, double and single beds, full shower and bath. Some cabins are original Brewster family dwellings. The main lodge houses the X Bar X cocktail lounge and a fully licensed dining room.
Rates: • $. American Plan. Includes one hour of horseback riding a day; bed and breakfast and children's rates available. Barbecue rates and seminar packages. No minimum stay.
Credit Cards: Visa, MasterCard, American Express. Traveler's checks accepted.
Season: May through mid-October
Activities: Hourly, half-day, and all-day rides. A favorite is riding to the ridge on Yamnuska Mountain. Ask about the ride and rafting packages from the ranch. Overnight pack trips to the historic Brewster Company ranch in the Devil's Head Mountain area. Riding is also available at the family's Lake Louise Stables (in Banff National Park) where you can ride to the spectacular Lake Agnes or Plain of Six Glacier. Hiking trips to Shadow Lake Lodge. Four golf courses within 30 minutes of the ranch; ranch will assist with golf arrangements where possible. Ranch will advise guests on local courses. Indoor heated whirlpool. Heli-hiking and touring and white water rafting trips down the Bow River. For groups of 100 or more the ranch will organize on-site rodeos with many local cowboys.
Children's Programs: No children's programs. Parents must supervise children.
Dining: Open to the public. Conference and group menus include British Columbia salmon steak fries, barbecued baron of beef, and lobster, served in the scenic dining room overlooking the Bow River. Enjoy prime rib and charcoal-broiled steaks. Wine and liquor are served.
Entertainment: The lounge just off the dining room features a pool table, country music, piano, and television. Hardwood floors, small bar, and stone fireplace make for a cozy atmosphere.
Summary: Brewster's Kananaskis Guest Ranch is a division of Brewster's Rocky Mountain Adventures based in Banff. The ranch offers guests freedom to do whatever they want. There are no schedules. Your time is your own. Many stop over here on their way to Banff and Calgary. This family-run company offers a host of activities and tours in the Kananaskis, Banff, and Lake Louise areas. If you are planning a trip from the ranch to Banff and Jasper, these are the people to talk to. Groups and corporations should ask the Brewsters about their famous Donut Tent for barbecues. Also ask about their daughter Cori's country-western single.

Homeplace Guest Ranch
Priddis, Alberta, Canada

The Homeplace Ranch is a year-round, low-key guest ranch in the Canadian Rocky Mountain foothills, 30 miles southwest of Calgary. The ranch is bordered by several beautiful ranches and the Kananaskis Forest Reserve. Mac Makenny, his wife, Jayne, and their young daughter, Jessi, offer guests a way of life for which southern Alberta is known. Every week a small number of people share the traditions, heritage, recreation, and natural beauty that constitute this unique lifestyle. There is abundant seasonal wildlife (deer, elk, moose, beaver, and grouse and other wild birds) and native flowers and trees. Camera buffs and artists ought to bring their gear. At Homeplace, the staff-guest ratio is high. Mac welcomes you to his home and makes every effort to see that you are well looked after. If you are from another country, he may raise your flag to welcome you.

Address: Site 2, Box 6, RR1, Dept. K, Priddis, Alberta, Canada T0L 1W0
Telephone: (403) 931-3245; fax: (403) 931-3245
Airport: Calgary
Location: 30 miles west of Calgary off Route 22, 50 miles east of Banff off Route 22
Memberships: Dude Ranchers' Association, Alberta Guest Ranch Association, Alberta Outfitters Association
Medical: Foothills Hospital in Calgary, 30 miles
Conference: 12, winter only; Alberta barbecue for 150
Guest Capacity: 12
Accommodations: Guests are comfortable staying in the lodge in eight small private rooms. All rooms are finished in cedar. Guest bedrooms are on both levels of the two-story lodge. All have private baths; some with twin futon beds, others with four-poster beds. Some of the rooms step out to balconies or decks. There is a hot tub outside on the back lower deck of the lodge. There is also a one-bedroom, 1912 log cabin about 200 yards away with a bathroom, no shower. Great for couples and honeymooners.
Rates: • $-$$. Full American Plan. Rates vary depending on the season. Ask about the three-, four-, and seven-day packages, particularly the Rocky Mountain Ranch Rodeo Holiday. Three-day minimum.
Credit Cards: None
Season: Year-round
Activities: In summer, full riding program. Excellent horses from gentle to spirited polo ponies. Wonderful all-day and half-day rides through neighboring ranches and along ridgetops with wonderful vistas. Ask about the Hog-Back, Kananaskis, and Fish Creek Run rides. Occasionally each week Mac will take a few of his guests down to the neighboring Harvey Ranch to check on their 200 head of cattle—no cattle driving, just watching and listening. Pack trips, riding instruction available (many come from Calgary for daily instruction in the off-season), fishing, and hiking. Eighteen- and nine-hole golf and tennis nearby. In winter, cross-country skiing, sleigh rides, downhill skiing at Banff, 45 minutes away.
Children's Programs: No planned program. Children over 7 may ride. Mac usually takes the kids aside and asks them about their riding desires, and he sure does hear some exciting stuff. As Mac says, "Kids tell it like it is!"
Dining: Food is a key ingredient to a successful ranch. There is lots of homemade everything here, from applesauce muffins to fresh blackberry pie and big beef barbecues. Special food prepared on request. Beer is always in the refrigerator. BYOL.
Entertainment: Nothing formal is planned. Occasional hay wagon rides, dances, and exhibition polo in Calgary.
Summary: Very small guest ranch run by the Makenny family. Warm hospitality. Great for people who like horses. The whole program is built around the horse and the heritage of Alberta as it relates to horses. Serious horse lovers, be sure to ask Mac about Spruce Meadows. Close and yet so far from Calgary. Branding weekends end of May, Calgary Stampede early July. Polo three times a week, June to September. Nature from the saddle workshops.

TL Bar Ranch
Trochu, Alberta, Canada

The TL Bar Ranch is located along the Red Deer River in the beautiful Valley of the Dinosaurs. This working cattle and quarter horse ranch is owned and operated by Tom and Willie Lynch. Horseback riding is the main activity, with miles of scenic trails to explore. Fishermen will enjoy fishing the Red Deer River at the back door of the ranch. For rock and archaeology lovers, the Tyrrell Museum of Palaeontology is just 45 miles away. Guests live and, if they wish, work right along with the Lynches and experience firsthand what a working cattle and horse ranch is all about. Guests become one of the family here, and all ages are welcome to share and enjoy this way of life. One couple from Germany wrote, "The last seven days at the TL Bar Ranch were the highlight of our impressive trip across British Columbia and Alberta. We find it hard now to leave this treasure of peace and hospitality."

Address: Box 217 K, Trochu, Alberta, Canada TOM 2C0
Telephone: (403) 442-2207
Airport: Calgary International
Location: 100 miles northeast of Calgary, 10 miles east of Trochu on Highway 585
Medical: Trochu Hospital, 10 miles
Memberships: Alberta Country Vacations Association
Guest Capacity: 10
Accommodations: Guests stay with the Lynch family in their log ranch home, which accommodates two with shared bath, two with private bath. There is a large living room with a stone fireplace. For those who wish, there is satellite television. A cottage nearby sleeps four to six with private bath and full cooking facilities. Some guests prefer to do all their own cooking. No daily maid service. If you stay longer than a week, Willie will do your laundry.
Rates: $ Canadian. American Plan. Off-season weekend rates available. No minimum stay.
Credit Cards: None. Cash and traveler's checks accepted.
Season: May through October, including Canadian Thanksgiving
Activities: Each evening Willie discusses with you what you would like to do the following day. Except for meals, you set your own schedule. Depending on the season, you may, if you wish, help with ranch work. Riding must be kept to a slower pace because of the rough terrain. Riding arena on ranch for those who wish to try their hand at gymkhana events. Hiking, swimming, canoeing on Red Deer River—very quiet and relaxing with lots of deer, beaver, geese, ducks; picnic lunch provided; nine-hole golf nearby. Fishing for gold eye, perch, and pickerel. Bring your own fishing gear.
Children's Programs: No special programs, but kids are welcome. Willie will watch your very young children if you are out riding or canoeing.
Dining: Nothing fancy, just good, old-fashioned ranch cooking. BYOB.
Entertainment: Do your own thing. Television, pool table, cookouts, rodeos in surrounding towns. Nearby Buffalo Jump, Prairie Steam locomotive tours, the Guzoo (ask Willie about this), the town of Rowley.
Summary: Very low-key, small family ranch with wonderful Canadian hosts. Mostly just riding, relaxing, and visiting with friendly people. Do your own thing, and help with ranch work if you wish. Rustic campground for tents, trailers, and motor homes. Nearby: Tyrrell Museum of Palaeontology.

See color photos, page 301

Rafter Six Ranch Resort
Seebe, Alberta, Canada

At the threshold to the Rockies lies the Rafter Six Ranch Resort. Whether you stay for a day or a week, the ranch offers boundless activities and down-home western hospitality for singles, families, couples, and bus tours. Because of its natural beauty and western atmosphere, Rafter Six has become a location for movies and commercials. Step back in time. Here the hustle and bustle are behind you, and fresh mountain air, pine-scented forests, and sparkling river waters are abundant. In 1976, with a lot of hard work, this old ranch was rebuilt and turned into one of Canada's finest. Here you will savor magnificent scenery and experience for yourself pure country living. The Stoney Indian Reservation is to the east, and Bow Valley Park is to the west. On this historical site, over 100 years ago, the Rafter Six horse brand was used by Colonel Walker of the Northwest Mounted Police. Some of the log buildings are modern but maintain the rustic charm of days gone by. Everyone becomes a part of the living history at the Rafter Six Ranch.

Address: P.O. Box K, Seebe, Alberta, Canada T0L 1X0
Telephone: (403) 673-3622; fax: (403) 673-3961
Airport: Calgary
Location: 45 miles west of Calgary off Trans-Canada Highway
Memberships: Alberta Guest Ranch Association
Awards: AAA 2 Diamond, Gold Award Alberta Hotel Association, Canadian Association's Three Star Award
Medical: Hospital in Canmore
Conference: 40
Guest Capacity: 60
Accommodations: The three-story log lodge has guest rooms, some with balconies, on the second and third floors. Each room has a hand-painted mural, as do many of the doors, each created by Stan, his father, and brother. The lodge is the hub for activities, with its dining room, coffee shop, cocktail lounge, sitting, game, and Jaccuzi rooms, and gift shop. Five historic cabins each have shower units, double and twin beds, and carpeting. One of these is a honeymoon cabin with a bed of native logs.
Rates: • \$-\$\$. American Plan. Ranch packages and children's rates available. Open to public. Hourly rides available.
Credit Cards: Visa, MasterCard, American Express, Enroute
Season: May through October, including Canadian Thanksgiving
Activities: One-, two-, and four-hour trail rides, all-day rides, hay and carriage rides, breakfast and supper rides and overnight pack trips, heated outdoor pool, indoor whirlpool, and hiking. Eighteen-hole golf, fishing nearby. River rafting and voyageur canoes. Heli-hiking and touring.
Children's Programs: Play area. Baby-sitting available. Petting zoo with pig, goat, sheep, ducks, geese, chickens, and donkeys.
Dining: Award-winning dining room with much of Stan's artwork. Rafter Six specializes in steaks, ribs, and buffalo. Guests can select from a varied menu. Mad Trappers Dining Room and Bearspaw Lounge, Saturday night hoedowns.
Entertainment: Western entertainment (shoot-outs, Indian dancing, ranch display rodeos, guest fun time rodeo), Calgary Stampede in July, pow-wows at Indian reservation, Buffalo Indian Days in Banff in August.
Summary: Some of the best scenery in the world is in Kananaskis country. The ranch is very western with all-log construction. Appeals to a wide variety of people—families, couples, singles, and bus tours. Many movies have been shot at the ranch and in the surrounding areas. Outdoor chapel overlooking Kananaskis River. Cowley's Passing of the Legends (an Indian legends museum). Stan and Gloria have extensive knowledge of and background in Indian history and culture, plus a great museum. Book shop on the ranch. French and German spoken.

See color photos, page 300

Big Bar Guest Ranch
Clinton, British Columbia, Canada

Nestled in the valley that lies between the Marble Mountains and Big Bar Mountain is Big Bar Guest Ranch, which opened in 1989. It is situated on 104 acres of rolling pastureland and jack pine forests. The ranch was originally homesteaded in 1936 as part of the OK Cattle Ranch. Brian Gunn, a retired international engineering consultant, prides himself in a professional, small, low-key operation. In Brian's words, "Big Bar Guest Ranch offers an antidote to fast-paced city life. It's a chance to breathe pure, clean air, drink natural spring water, and watch eagles, hawks, and Canadian geese circulating over the untouched terrain with the sounds of coyotes yipping in the clear night air. It has the power to restore a sense of perspective to even the most harried city visitor."

Address: P.O. Box 27K, Clinton, B.C., Canada V0K 1K0
Telephone: (604) 459-2333; fax: (604) 459-2333 (call before sending)
Airport: Vancouver International Airport
Location: Approximately 270 miles car from Vancouver, 6 hours by car, 30 miles northwest of Clinton off Highway 97
Memberships: British Columbia Guest Rancher's Association
Medical: Ashcroft Hospital, 1½ hours
Conference: 14
Guest Capacity: 30
Accommodations: Twelve guest rooms in the new two-story main lodge, all with private baths. Six rooms have bunk lofts for children. Two rustic log cabins with kitchens, full baths, wood-burning stoves, and covered porches overlooking Big Bar Creek. The original homestead lodge has a cozy fireside lounge and billiard room. Just outside is the hot tub overlooking distant Mount Bowman and the Marble Mountains. Pets are welcome.
Rates: • $-$$. American Plan. Horseback riding and other activities are on a pay-as-you-use basis. All-inclusive packages are available and include the "City Slicker" Overnight Packtrip and Honeymoon/Romance package. No minimum stay.
Credit Cards: Visa, MasterCard
Season: Year-round
Activities: Summer: Two-hour morning, afternoon, and evening rides. All-day rides, "City Slicker" Overnight Pack Trips from May to September (6-guest minimum, 10-guest maximum). Hayrides, canoeing, fishing, hiking. Pan for gold on the Fraser River. Outdoor riding arena for instruction and gymkhanas. Winter: Christmas is a special time at the ranch. Winter horseback riding, sleigh rides, cross-country skiing, skating on the handmade outdoor ice rink, jingle bells, Christmas carols, eggnog, and shortbread cookies. All-inclusive package rates available.
Children's Programs: All children, regardless of age, may ride. In many instances they can be led or can share a saddle with parent or wrangler. Lessons are available. Video games room, board games, campfires. Baby-sitters can be arranged. Children are the responsibility of their parents.
Dining: Ranch country kitchen, family-style dining, licensed dining room with a selection of Australian, Californian, and European wines. Children eat with the adults. You won't forget Mary's famous biscuits, jelly rolls, rhubarb pies, chocolate chip cookies, and the rest of her delicious fare. Special dietary requests can be accommodated.
Entertainment: Learn to rope, stargaze with eight-inch tracking telescope, relax in the hot tub, occasional live bands, campfires, volleyball, or baseball games. Visiting the marmot holes and beaver dams, evening slide shows, sing-alongs at the campfire.
Summary: Small family-operated guest ranch offers a glimpse of cowboy history and charm of days gone by, as well as the modern luxury and comforts of living in the 20th century. Friendly staff and hosts. Summer and winter horseback riding. Beautiful countryside and historic Harrison House.

Bull River Ranch
Cranbrook, British Columbia, Canada

Bull River Ranch is owned by Joseph and Margit Eitzenberger, a German couple who moved to British Columbia in the late 1970s. This is a small working ranch with cows, chickens, horses, and cattle. Margit oversees all ranch operations and works from sunrise to sunset tending to all the ranch chores. The ranch has a Bavarian flavor and is located in a beautiful valley in the shadows of British Columbia's Canadian Rocky Mountains. Catering largely to Europeans, Margit's ranch offers guests from Canada, the United States, and abroad tremendous charm and beauty. Rather than offering a structured program, she allows everyone to do completely as they wish, using the ranch and the cabins as a hub for many outdoor recreational activities. You may rent one of the cabins for a day, a week, a month, or all summer. It gets very warm in the summer, but it is a beautiful spot and allows you the freedom to cook when you wish and enjoy ranch life with a European touch.

Address: Box 133 K, Cranbrook, British Columbia, Canada V1C 4H7
Telephone: (604) 429-3760 (ranch), (604) 426-7474 (leave message)
Airport: Kimberly
Location: 38 miles southeast of Cranbrook. Call for directions.
Memberships: AAA
Medical: Cranbrook Hospital, 38 miles
Guest Capacity: 25
Accommodations: There are seven attractive log guest cabins nicely spaced apart. Each has its own kitchen, fireplace, common area, bunk beds, and a bedroom with twin beds. Each cabin has Bavarian accents, full bathroom, and covered porches. All bedding and dishes are provided.
Rates: • $. Horseback riding extra.
Credit Cards: None. Personal checks or cash.
Season: May to November
Activities: You are on your own to do what you wish. Informal guided horseback riding on an hourly basis. Mostly walking trail rides. Lots of hiking, canoeing on the ranch's little lakes and on the Bull River, fishing (bring your own gear). Bring your cameras.
Children's Programs: No program. Children welcome. Wonderful environment for parents and children.
Dining: You are on your own for all your meals. Cooking facilities provided in each cabin. In true European tradition, coffee and cake are served in the saloon at 5:00 p.m. each afternoon.
Entertainment: The Bavarian "saloon" is a gathering spot for guests and friends.
Summary: Small, working ranch—lots of animals. Run by German family with Bavarian spirit. Beautiful setting. Cook for yourself in one of the log cabins. If you want to be independent and do your own thing, give Margit a call. Side trips to Kimberly, Fort Steele, Banff, and Waterton Park.

Chilcotin Holidays Guest Ranch
Whistler, British Columbia, Canada

Kevan Bracewell comes from one of Canada's pioneer ranching families. He is a man who grew up in British Columbia's wilderness and knows it well. Sylvia Waterer knows B.C.'s wilderness from her years of researching the best that B.C. has to offer in outdoor adventure. Together, they run their wilderness adventure business taking guests into some of Canada's most pristine back-country. The ranch is a staging area for mountain horseback riding, pack trips, big game viewing, fishing, educational tours, winter snowmobiling, and skiing. Licensed to guide within a 2,000-square-mile territory, this area is prime habitat for California bighorn sheep, mountain goats, and grizzly bear. The ranch offers novice riders the opportunity to become competent mountain riders. As skill levels increase, riders venture farther from the ranch to the magnificent alpine meadows. Unique to Kevan's operation are the mountain cayuse horses. Born and raised in the Cariboo-Chilcotins, they are surefooted mountain climbers and are accustomed to wildlife. Kevan and Sylvia combine guest ranching with exciting adventure wilderness experiences.

Address: P.O. Box 152 K, Whistler, British Columbia, Canada V0N 1B0
Telephone: (604) 238-2274; fax: (604) 238-2274
Airport: Vancouver International
Location: 4½ hours drive north of Vancouver International Airport off B.C. Highway 40, 2-hour drive from Whistler Resort
Memberships: British Columbia Guest Rancher's Association, Freshwater Fishing Resort and Outfitter's Association
Medical: Squamish Hospital, 1- to 1½-hour drive. Emergency helicopter available.
Conference: 20
Guest Capacity: 20
Accommodations: Located on a 40-acre parcel surrounded by wilderness, the two-story ranch house sleeps 20. There are nine private rooms with twin, queen, bunk bed, and shared baths. Daily maid service with all linens and towels provided. Off-ranch accommodations include three main base camps accessible by horse, float planes, or helicopters. All camps have radio telephones.
Rates: • $$-$$$. American Plan. Call for package rates and schedules for adventure programs. Special group and family rates.
Credit Cards: MasterCard. Traveler's checks and cash accepted.
Season: Year-round, including holidays and special Christmas events
Activities: The guest ranch stay prepares the novice rider for the Pioneer Trip, conducted out of a base camp in the alpine meadows. The Explorer Trip, which progresses through three alpine base camps, is usually done after a Pioneer Trip, as is the Wildlife Viewing Trip. The Mountain Challenge Trip is the most advanced and is taken after guests have become good mountain riders. Includes camping out in small alpine basins with the wildlife. Horseback trips vary in length from day to week-long trips. All are graduated and progress in skill levels from one to the next. All activities are customized to individual guests or groups.
Children's Programs: Instructional riding. Children included with parents in all riding. Baby-sitting available.
Dining: Healthy country cooking served family-style. Native Indian cooking with salmon on an open fire with pine nuts. Wait until you taste the Indian ice cream and wild potatoes.
Entertainment: Horse sports, horse logging and training. Target practice and fossil exploring.
Summary: Chilcotin Holidays Guest Ranch offers a tremendous variety of adventure experiences. The guest ranch is the staging ground for novice to advanced riders to begin the journey to become competent mountain riders. Groups are small, and riders are matched according to their abilities, interests, and composition. Tremendous scenery and wildlife. Great for singles, couples, families, and groups. Bring a group of six and you stay free.

Cariboo Rose Guest Ranch
Clinton, British Columbia, Canada

Cariboo Rose is a small adult-oriented ranch where you will enjoy the life-style of a bygone era—unspoiled wilderness, scenic lakes, hearty home-cooked meals, and of course, old-fashioned western hospitality. The ranch is surrounded by the wilderness of the Marble Mountains and the gentle lake and meadow country for which the Southern Cariboo is famous. Following a day in the saddle, most guests take in the breathtaking mountain view with a cool drink on the porch or a leisurely soak in the hot tub. The day's events and cool mountain air serve to guarantee an evening of restful sleep and pleasant dreams. Host Karl Krammer was born in Austria, the son of a blacksmith and farrier, and studied mechanical engineering before moving to British Columbia. After a long search he found this lovely ranch and bought it in 1987. Karl and his wife, Teresa, have kept the ranch small, taking only eight guests at a time. At the Cariboo Rose you can enjoy peace and tranquillity. Listen to hoofbeats on a mountain path, saddle leather creaking, or the sound of horse bells. Most of all, leave civilization behind and pause for a week or more to recharge. The main focus here is quality horseback riding. As Karl says, "Our repeat customers are those who love the outdoors, wilderness, and good horses."

Address: P.O. Box 160 K, Clinton, B.C., Canada V0K 1K0
Telephone: (604) 459-2255
Airport: Vancouver. Charter and helicopter flights available to ranch.
Train: B.C. Rail from North Vancouver to Clinton
Location: 4 hours northwest of Vancouver by car, 1 hour by air; 15 miles northwest of Clinton
Memberships: British Columbia Guest Ranchers Association, Cariboo Tourist Association
Medical: Ashcroft Hospital, 40 miles
Guest Capacity: 8
Accommodations: Guests stay in the privacy of their own small cabins, fully equipped with bathroom and showers, queen- or twin-size beds and comforters. A few steps away, the log ranch house provides the opportunity to socialize in the loft-style game room or relax in front of a cozy fire. Ranch generates its own power. Solar-powered hair dryers recommended—ask Teresa!
Rates: • $$. American Plan. No minimum stay, but five days recommended.
Credit Cards: Visa, MasterCard, American Express
Season: April through October, including Canadian Thanksgiving and Easter
Activities: The ranch caters to those with a serious interest in riding and horsemanship. Half-day and all-day rides with lunch camps on the trail. Rides are tailored to be as easy or as challenging as required. Ask Karl about Wild Horse Pass, Strawberry Lake, and Coyote Lake. No riding on Fridays. Trout fishing on Big Bar Lake. Bring your own equipment. Hiking, sauna, and whirlpool hot tub. Riding clinics are offered in April and June. The covered indoor and outdoor open riding arenas are available for informal riding instruction throughout the season.
Children's Programs: This is an adult-oriented ranch.
Dining: Hearty, family-style meals including roast beef with Yorkshire pudding, baked chicken and fettucine Alfredo, lasagna, homemade desserts, and cowboy coffee, all served in the dining room with a beautiful Marble Mountain view. BYOB.
Entertainment: Loft-style game room with pool table, board games, and dart board. No planned evening entertainment.
Summary: Very private, very small, very personal with a warm "at home" feeling. The main thing here is quality horseback riding in small groups. Rides go into the unspoiled wilderness of the Marble Mountains. Well-trained horses, western riding clinics geared for the beginner, local rodeos in May and August. Fluent German spoken.

Elkin Creek Guest Ranch
North Vancouver, British Columbia, Canada

Located in British Columbia's Chilcotin country is Elkin Creek Guest Ranch, hosted by Paul and Barbara. The Nemaiah Valley is a corridor of natural beauty with the coast range mountains and distant Mt. Tatlow rising over 10,000 feet. Unique to Elkin Creek is its proximity to Vedan Lake, almost a stone's throw from the main lodge. Right in front of the ranch itself are hay fields with generously wooded sloping terrain behind. In operation since 1987, this 640-acre ranch offers a host of riding and lake activities for families, couples, and single people. Elkin Creek is, without question, one of British Columbia's finest new ranches combining western hospitality with incredible natural beauty. Unlike many, the ranch brochure will give you a wonderful eye-opening feel for this scenic part of British Columbia and the ranch setting.

Address: 4462 Marion Rd., Dept. K, North Vancouver, B.C., Canada V7N 2W6 (office); General Delivery, Drawer K, Nemaiah Valley, B.C., Canada V0L 1X0 (ranch). Please direct all inquiries to office.
Telephone: (604) 984-4666 (office); fax: (604) 984-4686 (office); (604) H497533 (ranch radio telephone); ask B.C. operator for radio operator in Prince George. Ask Prince George operator for Alexis Creek Channel 604-H497533. Direct all inquiries to office.
Airport: Williams Lake and 4,300-foot-long dirt airstrip at ranch (call for details)
Location: 48 miles south of Alexis Creek, 120 miles southwest of Williams Lake, B.C.
Memberships: British Columbia Guest Ranch Association, Cariboo Tourist Association
Medical: Medical clinic at Alexis Creek, 48 miles; Cariboo Memorial Hospital at Williams Lake, 120 miles
Conference: 40
Guest Capacity: 35
Accommodations: Seven traditionally built log cabins, each consisting of two double bedrooms, two separate bathrooms, a comfortably appointed living room, and separate storage rooms. Twin, queen-size, and king-size beds. Individually controlled electric heat in all cabins.The main lodge houses the dining room, lounge, and western-style bar.
Rates: • $$-$$$. American Plan. Gold panning and overnight pack trips extra. Children's rates available. No minimum stay.
Credit Cards: Visa, MasterCard, American Express. No personal checks.
Season: May to mid-November
Activities: Unlimited horseback riding with picnic lunches on the trail. Beginner, intermediate, and advanced trails with hourly, half-day, and all-day rides to Kartif Mountain and the scenic six-hour round-trip Koni Fire Lookout rides. Small group pack trips, wagon rides. Lake activities include fishing (limited gear available), motorboating, sailing, windsurfing, canoeing, and swimming. Hiking, indoor game room, sauna, and seasonal ranch activities.
Children's Programs: None. Children are the responsibility of parents. Small children not recommended.
Dining: Good, hearty ranch meals served family-style. Special diets on request. Barbecues and cookouts. Full bar.
Entertainment: Game room with regulation-size pool table, Ping-Pong table, shuffleboard, fooseball table, darts, and assorted board games.
Summary: Small, working cattle ranch in scenic valley near a lake. A variety of riding and lake activities. German hosts. Not recommended for young children. Wide variety of riding opportunities and lake activities. Guest participation encouraged with cattle work, April branding, fall cattle roundup, range riding. Photo-safaris and wildlife observation of mountain goats, deer, moose, and beaver.

The Hills Health and Guest Ranch
100 Mile House, British Columbia, Canada

In 1984, Pat and Juanita Corbett created the Hills Health and Guest Ranch. The Hills offers a combination of comfort, independence, and a range of horseback activities. Summer and winter guests may choose to take part in aerobics, stretch and flex classes, aqua fit, and no-bounce aerobics. The ranch also offers full personal care, from facial treatments to massage, herbal wraps, waxing, clay packs, manicures, and pedicures. If that's not enough, you can go for a hayride pulled by two huge draft horses and then dine on gourmet cuisine prepared by a Swiss chef. At The Hills you may ride, hike, take a variety of fitness classes, or do absolutely nothing. You decide.

Address: C-26, 108 Ranch 100 Mile House, Dept. K, B.C., Canada V0K 2E0
Telephone: (604) 791-5225; fax: (604) 791-6384
Airport: Williams Lake via Vancouver International
Location: 8 miles north of 100 Mile House off Highway 97, 295 miles north of Vancouver
Memberships: British Columbia Guest Ranchers Association, Cross-Country Division of the Canadian West Ski Areas Association
Medical: 100 Mile House, 8 miles
Conference: 200; 4,300-square-foot meeting space
Guest Capacity: 114
Accommodations: The Hills is perched on one of the Cariboo hilltops. As you drive up the hill, you first encounter the two-story log-sided main lodge. Around the bend on either side of the ridge are 20 A-frame, two-level modern cabins, with kitchens and two decks. These comfortable chalets are on either side of a road, with the "sunrise" cabins on the left and the "sunset" cabins on the right. Each cabin looks out over virgin Cariboo country. Also, a new ten-room lodge. You may rent a chalet and cook your own meals or take part in the full American plan. Laundry service.
Rates: • $-$$. American Plan. Many packages available, including spa package. Children's and group rates.
Credit Cards: Visa, MasterCard
Season: Year-round
Activities: Horseback riding and hiking are the main activities in the summer. Half-day horseback riding with cowboy breakfast served at Willy's Wigwam. One- to two-hour and all-day "mountain top" rides with lunch. Indoor 20-by-40-foot heated pool, two Jacuzzis, and two saunas open to public members as well as guests. Fitness programs include aerobics studio, weight room, hydrogym, weights, tanning salon, massage and beauty salon, and exercise rooms. Superb Swiss fitness, nutritional, and kinesiology counselors. Fishing at nearby lakes for rainbow, eastern brook, and lake trout. Guided hiking. PGA par-72 golf course and 5 tennis courts nearby. Winter: See Cross-Country Skiing Ranches.
Children's Programs: Supervised program. Kiddie wrangler. Children under 6 ride with parents. In winter, kids' ski school. Baby-sitting available.
Dining: The Hills' fine restaurant, Trail's End, is open to the public and is overseen by a superb Swiss chef. He offers a range of dishes from delicate culinary delights to low-calorie spa cuisine and ranch-style meals, depending on the package. Fully licensed bar. Mostly European wines served.
Entertainment: Fitness workshops, horse-drawn hayrides, television in each chalet, sing-alongs in "Willy's Wigwam" (a tepee in the woods), some of Canada's best live country music in dining room three nights with wonderful local singer Bob Dalrymple.
Summary: An affordable family guest ranch as well as a health and fitness ranch spa. Wonderful musical entertainment. Numerous lakes, historic gold mining, Cariboo Trail, Williams Lake Stampede July Fourth, Anaheim Lake Stampede in early July. French, German, and Italian spoken.

Flying U Ranch
70 Mile House, British Columbia, Canada

The Flying U Ranch, the oldest guest ranch in Canada, is on the north shore of beautiful 15-mile Greenlake and covers 40,000 acres. The ranch was established by rodeo personality Jack Boyd. As early as 1924, two western movies were made here, directed by A. D. "Cowboy" Kean. Guests have come from around the world and most states and provinces of the United States and Canada. The ranch is owned and operated by the Fremlin Seniors, four sons and their wives, who moved to British Columbia from California and Nevada in 1980. This talented family includes a university professor, artist, lawyer, house builder, and musician. Early Indians and fur trappers frequented these parts. Just ask the Fremlins; they'll be glad to tell you about it. The Flying U has preserved the spirit of the early West. Here it is rustic, and you may still ride on your own.

Address: Box 69 K, N. Greenlake, 70 Mile House, B.C., Canada V0K 2K0
Telephone: (604) 456-7717; fax: (604) 456-7455
Airport: Vancouver International; 3,000-foot grass airstrip on ranch. Land and sea charter flights available to ranch.
Train: B.C. rail from North Vancouver to Flying U Station, 5 miles away. This is very popular.
Location: 20 miles south of 100 Mile House, 5 hours northeast of Vancouver by car
Memberships: Texas Longhorn Association, Wilderness Tourism Counsel, B.C. Cattleman's Association
Medical: 100 Mile House Hospital, 20 miles
Conference: 65
Guest Capacity: 65
Accommodations: Guests stay in 23 "chinker" log cabins (sleeping two to eight), arranged in a "U" shape around the main lodge. Each of these rustic cabins is heated with a wood stove and features hand-hewn log furniture and a sitting porch. Separate men's and women's shower house with shower and bathroom amenities and 15-person sauna. Covered porches with rocking chairs.
Rates: • $-$$. American Plan. Children's, group, and weekly rates. Two-day minimum; three-day minimum on holiday weekends.
Credit Cards: Visa, MasterCard, American Express
Season: April to November
Activities: Upon arrival, each guest is assigned a horse according to his or her ability. Guests are given a trail map and are free to ride alone or with other guests. The Flying U has 120 horses and thousands of acres. Riders may saddle up after breakfast each day, including Sunday. Fishing, swimming, and canoeing on Greenlake. Hiking.
Children's Programs: No formal children's programs. Children participate with parents. Babysitting available.
Dining: The Flying U has an authentic western saloon separate from the main lodge. Cocktails are served to the sounds of the circa 1880 nickelodeon. Mealtime at the lodge is announced with the clanging of the old ranch bell. Family and friends eat together ranch-style. Weekly outdoor lunch and dinner barbecues. Beer and a selection of wine available with meals.
Entertainment: Movies, horse-drawn hayrides, barbecues, and bonfires are topped off with an old western whoop-de-doo square dance Wednesday and Saturday nights, when Pete tunes up the eight-piece Flying U Band.
Summary: Canada's oldest guest ranch, on beautiful Greenlake, hosted by a terrific family and their Flying U Band. The big thing here is that guests may horseback ride on their own without supervision. One of the few ride-on-your-own ranches left in North America. One hundred Texas longhorns on ranch, small Flying U Western Historical Museum, general store. Authentic western saloon. A little Japanese, German, French, and Spanish spoken.

See color photos, page 302

Springhouse Trails Ranch
Williams Lake, British Columbia, Canada

Springhouse Trails Ranch is the home of Werner and Suzi Moessner, two very kind and friendly people who moved to British Columbia from Stuttgart in 1978. Werner grew up on a farm. As a young man, he started a construction firm, which is still run by his son and daughter. In the late 1970s, the Moessners flew to British Columbia, rented an RV, and began looking at ranches. They found Springhouse Trails, and Werner spent two years rebuilding the ranch. In 1980 they took their first guests. Today, the ranch is run with the help of the Moessner's daughter, Eve, and her husband, Herbert. At 3,000 feet, the property overlooks a small lake, grass-covered rolling hills, and open meadows. They grow many of their own vegetables and serve fresh eggs from their 30 plus chickens. At Springhouse Trails they pretty much let you do as you please. Many of the guests are Europeans who enjoy the fact that the Moessners are bilingual. In fact, they like it so much, they stay for three to six weeks at a time. In traditional German fashion, the property and accommodations are immaculate, the food hearty, and yes, there is beer available.

Address: Box 2 K, Springhouse Trails R.R. 1, Williams Lake, B.C., Canada V2G 2P1
Telephone: (604) 392-4780; fax: (604) 392-4780
Airport: Williams Lake Airport via Vancouver International; private planes to Springhouse airport
Location: 11 miles southwest of Williams Lake on Dog Creek Road, 6 hours northeast of Vancouver by car
Memberships: British Columbia Guest Ranchers Association
Medical: Williams Lake Hospital
Guest Capacity: 30
Accommodations: Guests stay in four log cabins with full kitchens and two large, one-story, new complexes. One is a dorm building that has a common hallway with ten rooms and two end units with full kitchen facilities for those making extended visits. The second building has individual units with separate entrances. Also available are 12 RV hookups, with shower and laundry facilities.
Rates: • $-$$. American Plan. European Plan, RV, tenting, children's rates, and five-day packages available. No minimum stay.
Credit Cards: Visa, MasterCard, American Express
Season: May to September
Activities: Informal program. Ride, hike, walk, canoe, or just relax as you wish. Most guests ride with other guests or alone. Guided riding is available. Werner and Herbert assign horses according to a rider's ability, with hour rides and all-day picnic rides available.
Children's Programs: No children's programs, but kids are welcome. If a 2-year-old can ride, Werner will put him on a horse.
Dining: The ranch has a large, separate, fully licensed restaurant with views and a fireplace in the center. Hearty ranch food, including favorites such as German schnitzel and barbecues twice a week. Wine (mostly Canadian) and liquor are served. Special coffees (Spanish, Swiss, Irish, Monte Cristo, and Rudesheimer iced coffee).
Entertainment: Nothing formal. Guests usually make their own.
Summary: Bilingual German hosts with many European guests. Many guests stay up to three weeks and longer. RV hookups. Ride on your own. Nearby: Indian arts and crafts, Indian rodeos, Williams Lake Stampede Rodeo.

Sundance Guest Ranch
Ashcroft, British Columbia, Canada

In British Columbia's high semiarid desert country with sun-drenched sagebrush, the Sundance Ranch looks out to Cornwall and the Glossy Mountains high above the Thompson River. The ranch ran cattle in the late 1800s and began taking dudes in the 1940s. In 1978, Stan Rowe, one of Canada's leading business equipment salesmen, bought Sundance and fulfilled a boyhood dream. Stan and his family had been guests at the ranch since the early 1960s. When it was offered for sale, the Rowes didn't take much time to decide they wanted it. Stan and his wife, Vicki, and their grown children have made their operation one of Canada's most successful. Sundance runs 100 horses over 20,000 acres. Most guests come to ride. Stan and his crew run a first-rate riding program. No one gets on a horse without cowboy boots (which can be rented at the ranch office). When you have proven that you can really ride, ask about the Sioux Lookout ride. Sundance is for those who like to ride and enjoy the high desert country. Summers are warm.

Address: Box 489 K, Ashcroft, B.C., Canada V0K 1A0
Telephone: (604) 453-2422/2554; fax: (604) 453-9356
Airport: Kamloops (one-hour drive)
Location: 200 miles or 4-hour drive north of Vancouver, 55 miles west of Kamloops along the Trans-Canada Highway
Medical: Ashcroft Hospital, 6 miles
Memberships: British Columbia Guest Ranchers Association
Awards: 1987 British Columbia Resort Operator of the Year
Conference: 60
Guest Capacity: 70
Accommodations: Twenty-eight simply decorated rooms connected by the sprawling L-shaped extension of the ranch house with covered walkways. Some rooms open to the parking area and riding arena, others to pastures overlooking a herd of buffalo and the hills beyond. All rooms are carpeted, have private bath/shower, and air-conditioning; one deluxe suite, with king-size bed and wood stove. Lawns are trimmed, and flowers abound in the summer.
Rates: • $-$$. Full American Plan. Children's rates available. Two-day weekend and three-day minimum stays on holiday weekends.
Credit Cards: Visa, MasterCard
Season: March through October. New Year's Eve program, open Thanksgiving and Easter.
Activities: Summer riding season March through October. Gentle trail horses to frisky mounts; two rides per day, two to three hours each. Sioux Lookout ride. Ask the ranch about "Topping Off" in March, lots of riding excitement. Hiking, tennis, swimming in 45-foot outdoor heated pool, volleyball, and horseshoe pitching. Float trips and golf available nearby.
Children's Programs: Children eat lunch and dinner together before adults. Children under 8 do not go on trail rides but may be led around in arena by parents or guardian. Children's lounge and game room. Wide-screen video movies. Baby-sitting available.
Dining: Candlelight dinners. Varied menus. Will cater to special requests. Barbecues, cookouts, and buffalo hip roasts on patio. The five-sided dining room has a lovely view and is licensed for beer and wine service. BYOB bar lounge for adults.
Entertainment: Game room for adults with pool tables, card tables, and darts. Gymkhanas with ribbons for first, second, and third places, nearby rodeos. Country-rock dance Saturday nights.
Summary: Family owned and operated. Especially popular with families. Many young couples and singles visit Sundance as well. Riding is the main activity. "Topping Off" in March. Cowboy boot rentals available. Some French and German spoken. Nearby: herd of buffalo, town of Ashcroft, Ashcroft Museum.

Three Bars Ranch
Cranbrook, British Columbia, Canada

When it comes to the superstars in the deluxe guest ranching business, the Three Bars Cattle and Guest Ranch is right at the top. This magnificent ranch couples old guest and cattle ranch tradition with all the deluxe, modern-day comforts you would expect from a world-class luxury resort hideaway. The Old West charm has been carefully crafted with log architecture. The old guest ranch hospitality has been preserved under the direction of Jeff and April Beckley, a young couple who grew up in the cattle and guest ranch business. When they say the welcome mat is out and the coffee pot is always on, they mean it! From ranch espresso coffee to an honest ranch handshake—they have it all.

Address: S.S. 3, Site 19-62 K, Cranbrook, British Columbia, Canada V1C 6H3
Telephone: (604) 426-5230; fax: (604) 426-8240
Airport: International airports in Calgary, Edmonton, and Vancouver link regular scheduled flights to Cranbrook Airport
Location: 6 miles north of Cranbrook off Highway 93/95 in southeastern British Columbia
Memberships: Dude Ranchers' Association
Medical: Cranbrook Regional Hospital, 9 miles
Conference: 45
Guest Capacity: 45
Accommodations: Ten hand-hewn log duplex cabins provide 20 units. Three of the duplexes are adjoining for families. Units each have one queen-size and two double beds, private full baths, handmade furniture, custom-built doors and windows, hardwood floors adorned with Navajo pattern rugs, private porches, and gardens all set within a landscaped yard and adjoined with wooden boardwalks. The ranch's 5,000-square-foot log lodge hosts the dining room, fireplace lounge, library, and turn-of-the-century bar, complete with pool table and conference room.
Rate: • $$. Full American Plan. Children's and group rates. Four-night minimum stay. No minimum stay in winter.
Credit Cards: Visa
Season: Mid-April to mid-October riding program; mid-December to mid-March skiing program
Activities: For all of its class and comfort, Three Bars is a commercial ranch. Guests are invited to join in on the cattle drives or ride with the cowboys to check on the ranch's herd of cattle when work is being done. This does not happen every day. Most guests prefer to trail ride and perhaps take in a riding lesson in the ranch's riding arena. Breakfast rides and barbecue cookouts. Guided hikes into the mountains and guided fly-fishing are also available. Weekly river float trips. The tennis court, indoor heated swimming pool, outdoor Jacuzzi, horseshoe pit, children's play area, and petting zoo are gathering places for friends and families.
Children's Programs: Three Bars is home to kids ages 2 to 13. Children's riding program and a special dining time for the children. Kids are only looked after when they are horseback riding and at dinner. Kids under 6 do not ride.
Dining: Superb and exciting! From three-course dinners with wines from around the world to riverside cookouts.
Entertainment: Informal and spontaneous. Evenings usually are spent trading anecdotes on the day's riding activities in the old-time saloon while shooting a game of pool, or relaxing around the fireplace. Line dancing and staff guest volleyball.
Summary: Jeff's and April's Three Bars Guest Ranch is without question, world-class—definitely a top gun! Deluxe western accommodations coupled with full guest and cattle ranch activities. Video available on request.

See color photos, page 303

Top of the World Guest Ranch
Steele, British Columbia, Canada

Top of the World is just that—on top of the world. It sits in a valley; the farther up you go, the more rugged it gets. Most guests cannot believe the splendor, the wide open country, and the beauty of this 45,000-acre cattle/guest ranch. Lloyd and Rowena Jones, whose family has been in ranching for four generations, have a wealth of knowledge about horses, cattle, and area history. Trail rides follow the old stagecoach route from historic Fort Steele to Golden, past the remnants of corrals that once trapped wild horses, to falls that cascade from the Canadian Rockies, and through meadows. You may help with spring branding or fencing, salting, and moving cattle to summer pastures. At the end of the day, you can sit on your cabin porch with a cool drink watching the sun set behind the Purcell Mountains. The last rays remind you that you are, indeed, on Top of the World.

Address: Box 29 K, Fort Steele, B.C., Canada V0B 1N0
Telephone: (604) 426-6306; call for fax number
Airport: Cranbrook, via Calgary or Vancouver
Location: 16 miles north of Cranbrook off Highway 93/95, 135 miles south of Banff, 200 miles southeast of Calgary, 180 miles north of Spokane
Memberships: British Columbia Guest Ranchers Association
Medical: Cranbrook Hospital, 16 miles
Conference: 45, October through March
Guest Capacity: 35
Accommodations: Six log cabins are in a semicircle around the two-story log lodge. Each summer the Joneses plant lots of flowers and mow an acre of grass—plenty of room for children to play. Each cabin has carpeting, twin and queen beds, woodstove and electric heat, private bath with tub and shower, and a covered porch. Four rooms on the second floor of the lodge have private baths. All accommodations are comfortably furnished. Main lodge has a large deck where guests relax and watch hummingbirds.
Rates: • $-$$. Full American Plan. Winter, children's, large family, and group rates. July and August, 5- and 7-day stays only. Sunday arrivals.
Credit Cards: Visa
Season: April through September; open most holidays
Activities: Riding is the main activity here, but everyone will find lots to do. Summer riding program for all levels. Better riders may help with cattle. Morning, afternoon, long, and some moonlight rides. Usually no more than seven per ride. Weekly breakfast rides. Yearly cattle drives. Three lakes on property; Loon Lake is the favorite for rowboats or canoes. Lots of hiking, volleyball, and horseshoes. Swim in Lake Wasa, 5 miles away. Have an ice cream cone on the way home at the country store. Eighteen-hole golf at area courses. In winter, cross-country skiing and downhill skiing nearby.
Children's Programs: Children are the responsibility of parents. Baby-sitting available with advance notice. Children under 6 ride in arena only. Children's program with petting farm. Enclosed playground.
Dining: "We are not gourmet, we are simple ranch," says Rowena. Top of the World grows its own vegetables and serves ranch beef, fresh eggs, fruit, and well-balanced meals. Buffet lunches. Dinners are more formal, topped off with fresh berry pies. Weekly cookouts. Wine and beer available.
Entertainment: Depends on the guests' interests. Pony chuck wagon races in nearby towns, occasional rodeos, piano in lodge, occasional sing-alongs. Recreation room with pool table, Ping-Pong, and darts. Ask about the Wild Horse Theatre Players at Fort Steele and helicopter tours.
Summary: One of the great guest ranching families in North America. Western hospitality and spirit reign supreme here. The Jones have lived ranching all their lives. Best known for hospitality and horses. Some cattle work and lots of wildlife. Guests come from Europe, the United States, and Canada. Ask about nearby historic Fort Steele—a must!!

See color photos, page 304

Tyax Mountain Lake Resort
Gold Bridge, British Columbia, Canada

Tyax Mountain Lake Resort, a luxury hideaway, is in the breathtaking wilderness of the Chilcotin Mountains. This rustically handsome lodge, one of the largest log structures in North America, is made from hand-hewn spruce logs, with ceilings soaring to 30 feet. Summers here are hot and sunny, and winters afford some of the best downhill helicopter skiing and mountain snowmobiling in the world. Owner/ operator Gus Abel, who has German roots, runs a first-class operation. (Gus has a Master Oceangoing Degree —he used to pilot supertankers.) He has brought many European amenities to Tyax. You can hot tub under the stars, sleep under eider down, and wake to views of the lake and mountains with the smell of fresh-baked bread from Dutch ovens. Tyax offers a vacation to remember.

Address: Tyaughton Lake Road, Dept. K, Gold Bridge, B.C., Canada V0K 1P0
Telephone: (604) 238-2221; fax: (604) 238-2528
Airport: Vancouver International; charter float plane or ski plane service to Tyax Lake
Location: 5 hours by car north of Vancouver, north of Highway 99 to Duffey Lake Road
Memberships: British Columbia Motel and Resort Association, Federation of B.C. Wilderness
Medical: Lillooet Hospital, 60 miles
Conference: 80; 2 conference rooms, 1,120 square feet and 651 square feet; spring, fall, and winter
Guest Capacity: 100
Accommodations: Twenty-nine comfortable suites feature balconies with views of the lake and pine-studded mountains. Five modern log chalets with fireplace, kitchen, and 3, 4, and 6 bedrooms. All rooms are furnished in pine. The lodge has a large sun deck, lounge and western bar, conference room, and lower level fitness center. Laundry service available.
Rates: • $$-$$$$. Seasonal rates available, group discounts. Meals and activities extra. Almost everything is à la carte.
Credit Cards: Visa, MasterCard, American Express
Season: Year-round, including Thanksgiving, Christmas, and Easter
Activities: Summer activities include horseback riding, with hourly, daily, and overnight pack trips. Lake and stream fishing for Dolly Varden, kokanee, Eastern brook, cutthroat, and rainbow trout. Fly-fishing in remote lakes. Well-stocked fishing tackle/gift shop. Rental rods available. Helicopter hiking. Fly out with a float plane for fishing for trophy rainbow trout. Gold panning and mountain biking. Rental bikes available. Tennis court, sailing, sailboarding, canoeing, lake swimming, whirlpool, and sauna. Winter: cross-country skiing on well-groomed trails, helicopter skiing, snowmobiling, ice skating, ice fishing, sleigh rides. Rent skis, skates, snowshoes, and snowmobiles at Tyax.
Children's Programs: Parents are responsible for their kids. Disney movies, ponies, paddle-boats, and kids' bikes. Baby-sitting on request.
Dining: Restaurant with wonderful home-cooked meals overlooking Lake Tyaughton. Full menu. Weather permitting, steak and salmon barbecues lakeside with singing cowboy. Tyax specialties: leg of lamb, T-bone steaks, barbecued chicken. Children's menu. Extensive wine list and full liquor license.
Entertainment: No formal evening program. Billiard and table tennis room, dance area with live music, campfires.
Summary: A wilderness resort for families and couples who enjoy the great outdoors and appreciate an unstructured environment. Here you may do exactly as you please. Tyax attracts a large number of guests from Europe, the United States, and Canada. Mountain lake retreat. The Tyax float plane will take you to wilderness areas for summer and winter sports. Eight RV sites available. French and German spoken. Nearby: Bralorme ghost town, pioneer mines.

Wells Gray Ranch
Clearwater, British Columbia, Canada

Despite the rapid growth of its urban centers, much of western Canada is still wild and untamed. At the entrance to Wells Gray Park, British Columbia's third-largest provincial park, is Wells Gray Ranch. Known for its mountain ranges, deep blue lakes, and waterfalls, this magnificent region of British Columbia links the romantic western past with mountain scenery and wildlife. Wells Gray Ranch is along a private corridor that reaches into the park. It is managed by Mike and Regina Mueller, both with extensive travel and marketing backgrounds. These two Austrians have a zest for life, people, and the outdoors. Built in 1980, the ranch has that western town flavor. It offers guests from the United States, Canada, and abroad (many come from Switzerland, Germany, and England) a base camp for all kinds of outdoor adventures. As Mike says, "You can do just about anything here provided you respect nature and appreciate wonderful scenery. We are not a fancy resort, rather a variety of accommodations surrounded by incredible beauty."

Address: P.O. Box 1764 K, R.R. 1, Clearwater, British Columbia, V0E 1N0, Canada
Telephone: (604) 674-2792, (604) 674-2774; fax: (604) 674-2197
Airport: Kamloops via Calgary or Vancouver. Private airstrip on ranch. Ask about private air service from Vancouver.
Location: 2-hour drive north of Kamloops, 6-hour drive northeast of Vancouver
Memberships: British Columbia Guest Ranch Association
Medical: Helmcken Memorial Hospital, 18 miles
Conference: 30
Guest Capacity: 40 in log cabins and ranch house, 34 in bunkhouse, 50 in campground
Accommodations: Ten rooms in two duplex-triplex log cabins arranged in a quarter circle. Rooms are nicely furnished with private showers and kitchenettes and covered front porches. The farm house, just a few minutes away by car, overlooks the valley. It is ideal for families, with kitchen, dining/living area, three bedrooms, two baths, and a porch. There are seven camping cabins with shower house and a separate campground with seven RV sites.
Rates: • \$-\$\$. Various rates and packages available, including American Plan. Call for details. No minimum stay.
Credit Cards: Visa, MasterCard
Season: May through mid-October, mid-December to mid-April
Activities: Summer: There are 70 horses (many raised on the ranch). Wilderness trail rides go out in the morning and afternoon for 2½ to 3 hours. All-day rides on request. Ask about Table Mountain, Hemp Creek Canyon Land, and White Horse Bluff rides. Ask about the multi-day pack trips. Other popular activities include canoeing, hiking, mountain biking, white water rafting, fishing, and boating on Clearwater and Azure lakes. For some, sightseeing is the main thing. Winter: With 60 huskies, the main emphasis is dog sledding. Also cross-country skiing on 30-kilometer Wells Gray Loppet Trail. Snowmobiling and snowshoe hikes into the park. Ask about the helicopter mountain chalet trips.
Children's Programs: No program. Children are welcome. Children under 6 ride with parents.
Dining: Meal package includes breakfast, packed lunch, and dinner. Hearty country food served buffet-style. Soft drinks and alcoholic beverages are served in the dining room. You may cook in your cabin if you wish.
Entertainment: The Black Horse Saloon is the evening gathering spot to tell stories or listen to music. Park visitors' program offers talks and slide show. Table tennis, darts, horseshoes.
Summary: In the heart of British Columbia's magnificent wilderness. A base camp ranch/retreat with something for everyone who loves the outdoors and adventure. Terrific Austrian hosts. Large, international clientele. Fluent French and German spoken.

Fly-Fishing Ranches

Introduction

This fly-fishing section was designed for the novice as well as the expert angler. If you have never had a fly-rod in your hands, do not worry about it. Fifty percent of the people who visit these lodges are people just like you. For one reason or another, they have dreamed about fly-fishing but have never taken the time to try it. The other 50 percent may be intermediate-to-expert anglers. Regardless of your level of skill or aptitude, you will have a fun and exciting time. Those of you who are experts will be challenged. Those of you who don't know the difference between one fly and another will have the time of your life. Remember this, the ranches and lodges listed here are doing what they do for two reasons—they love people, and they love to fish. They are running their operations for you and will do everything possible (within reason, of course) to ensure that your time with them is both pleasurable and exhilarating.

Fly-fishing is booming. If you doubt my words, look at some of the major outdoor wear/sporting goods companies and mail order catalogs. You will see complete sections, sometimes entire catalogs, devoted to water and fish and all the exciting equipment that goes with them. Fly-fishing, like golf, is a very exacting sport, and to become an expert takes a tremendous amount of skill, patience, and dedication. Those unfamiliar with the sport might wonder why anyone would put on a pair of waders that come up to your Adam's apple and stand in the middle of a cold, whirling stream, casting a long, colored line back and forth. But millions of people around the world have found that once they try it, they are likely to get hooked. Besides the marvelous array of equipment and the thrill of hooking and landing a trophy-size fish or even a small one, fly-fishing offers men, women, and children a chance to get out into nature and away from the pressures of daily living.

Realizing the demand for quality fly-fishing retreats where people can receive guidance and instruction, not to mention camaraderie, I have included some of the top fly-fishing lodges in the United States. While many of the ranches in this guide offer fly-fishing and are located on or near superb trout waters, this section is devoted to those that offer top instruction and guide service.

In selecting a facility, you must first decide where in North America you would like to go. Read the descriptions and write or call for a brochure. Some of the brochures are very modest, so do not judge the facility solely on this basis. As with all ranches in this guide, remember that each is unique and represents the personality of the host. Ask for references and find out if the level of instruction is sufficient to help you achieve your expectations. Every property in this section will show you a wonderful fishing experience.

Even though it is an exacting sport, the basics of fly-fishing are not difficult to master. A tremendous amount of information is available in books and videos. I highly recommend that you contact a fly-fishing school before embarking on a fly-fishing vacation. Most of the leading instructors of this sport would agree that if you can master, or at least become familiar with, the techniques of fly casting before you leave, your overall experience will be much more enjoyable and fulfilling. The easiest way to find out about these schools is to contact your local fly-fishing store/outfitter.

Before buying any equipment, check with the lodge to see what you will need to bring. Many have their own shops and can take care of most of your needs. Don't be afraid to ask questions. The more you learn about this sport, the more fun you will have. Now go out and tie one on.

Author's Note: You will notice that some of the ranches and lodges have under "Awards" the phrase "Orvis-Endorsed Lodge." Each of these properties has been endorsed by the world-renowned Orvis Company. This retail/mail order company is dedicated to enriching lives and providing not only top merchandise but also first-rate service. Toward this end, Orvis has developed this Orvis-Endorsed Lodge program as a special service to its customers. These fly-fishing lodges and ranches are monitored by Orvis personnel and must maintain high standards. Thus, Orvis can recommend each and every one with confidence. We are delighted to include this Orvis endorsement and feel that it complements and enriches our goal of providing you with the very best fly-fishing opportunities.

Crystal Creek Lodge
Dillingham, Alaska

You have probably dreamed about Alaska—and with good reason. It is big, fresh, wild, free, and filled with adventure. This is a land of mountains, tundra, glaciers, and lakes, where the scenery is overwhelming and the wildlife untamed. Located amid all of this is Crystal Creek Lodge. Terry Eberle created this premier Alaskan fishing retreat to complement a life of adventure. He offers men and women alike an Alaskan adventure/fishing experience second to none. At Crystal Creek, you will be treated like a king and get to see and fish as much of Alaska as you could possibly want in a week. If you are one of those who likes to really rough it or doesn't like to fly, this probably is not the place for you. The lodge offers all upscale amenities, and fly-out service each day with your guide is a major part of this exhilarating Alaskan experience.

Address: P.O. Box 3049 K, Dillingham, Alaska 99576 (summer); 3819 E, Drawer K, LaSalle, Phoenix, Arizona 88504 (information and reservations)
Telephone: (800) 525-3153, (602) 437-8780
Location: Bristol Bay area, southwest Alaska; 320 miles southwest of Anchorage, 15 miles northwest of Dillingham
Memberships: Federation of Fly-Fishermen
Awards: Orvis-Endorsed Lodge
Medical: Kannaknek Hospital in Dillingham, 20-minute helicopter flight
Conference: 20
Guest Capacity: 20
Accommodations: The 9,800-square-foot main lodge is the center of operation. There are thirteen double-occupancy rooms on two levels (1-7 lower, 8-13 upper); room 3 is the most spacious. Each is modern with full amenities including queen-size beds, full bathrooms (tub and shower combination) with plenty of hot water, even though the lodge is powered by its own generator, and individual temperature controls. Because during the summer months it is light almost 20 hours a day, there are "blackout" shades in each room. Daily maid and laundry service is provided. The lodge also has changing and boot-drying rooms.
Rates: • $$$$$. Full American Plan. Saturday to Saturday with six days fishing and seven nights lodging. Includes everything except round-trip airfare to Dillingham, fishing licenses, flies/lures, and liquor (drinks during happy hour and wine with dinner included).
Credit Cards: Visa, MasterCard
Season: Mid-June to mid-September
Activities: The lodge is located right on Lake Nunavaugaluk, which is in the center of southwest Alaska's Bristol Bay area, known for its large salmon runs and trophy class fishing. There are five planes and two helicopters to take you and your guide to remote fishing areas. Here you will fish for king, chum, sockeye, pink, and silver salmon, rainbow and lake trout, arctic char, arctic grayling, Dolly Varden, and northern pike. Fully equipped tackle shop in lodge. Call for more details.
Children's Programs: Children are welcome. Not recommended for children under 10.
Dining: Breakfast is cooked to order. After breakfast the chef will ask you for dinner preference from three different entrées that change daily. Streamside sack lunches (you give your lunch order the night before), and occasionally your guide will prepare fresh-caught salmon. Happy hour at 5:00 p.m. (complimentary open bar) with hors d'oeuvres. Wine served with dinner.
Entertainment: After a full day of fishing and flying, most guests are delightfully worn out.
Summary: Crystal Creek Lodge offers excellent personal service, comfort, and superb daily fly-in/fly-out fishing in seven aircraft. You will see an abundance of wildlife. Ask about the bear sanctuary and the scenic helicopter flights to Wood-Tikchik State Park. If you desire, your legal limit of freshly caught salmon will be cleaned, vacuum-packed, and frozen for your trip home. (Author's Note: You should definitely like to fly and enjoy fishing. Avid photographers should bring plenty of film.)

See color photos, page 177

Arcularius Ranch
Mammoth Lakes, California

Arcularius Ranch is one of the premier catch and release, wet and dry fly-fishing ranches in California. Since 1919, the Arcularius family has run this 1,000-acre cattle ranch and has been concerned stewards of their property. In the main lodge, numerous photo albums pay tribute to guests who have come to enjoy this fishing haven, including such notables as the late Herbert Hoover. The ranch is near Mammoth Mountain and fifty-three miles northeast of Bishop (famous for its annual Mule Days). It maintains almost five miles of private stream on the Owens River, one of the richest fly-fishing streams in the country, where record 5-pound to 7-pound rainbow and German brown trout have been landed. Astounding as it may sound, some 50,000 fish inhabit this five-mile stretch of water, all of them wild trout, not hatchery transplants. John Arcularius limits the number of fishermen and has a strict catch and release policy! One guest commented, "It's a great place, and the fishing is the icing on the cake." The fly-fishing here is challenging. Most of the guests who come have been doing so for years. They know the waters and have learned how to catch the fish.

Address: Route 1, Box 230 K, Mammoth Lakes, California 93546
Telephone: (619) 648-7807 (summer); (805) 238-3830 (winter)
Airport: June Mammoth Airport; Reno International, 150 miles
Location: 14 miles due northeast of Mammoth Lakes off Highway 395, 53 miles northeast of Bishop, 150 miles south of Reno
Medical: Mammoth Lakes Hospital, 14 miles
Guest Capacity: 75
Accommodations: Fifteen one- to six-bedroom housekeeping cabins, with knotty pine interiors and very clean kitchens, equipped with everything you need. All cabins (except the Bob Steel Cabin) have bathrooms with showers, heaters, and electricity; some have porches. No daily maid service, but sheets will be changed on request. In the main lodge there is a tackle shop, small country grocery store, common living room for all guests, a pool table, and selection of fly-fishing videos.
Rates: $. Weekly rates. Check with ranch for rates.
Credit Cards: None. Personal checks accepted.
Season: Late April to November
Activities: Catch and release fly-fishing only on Hot Creek. Fishing also on Crowley Lake and lakes of the eastern Sierras. Most of the guests fish morning, noon, and into the twilight hours. Guides are available if arranged in advance. Bring your own equipment. Recommended flies—Adams Fly, Elk Hair Cadis, Gold Ribs, Hairs Ear, Pheasant Tail Nymph, Maribu Streamer. If you don't fish, you can relax or hike into the nearby Sierras.
Children's Programs: None, kids are the responsibility of parents. Children fish or run wild and have the times of their lives.
Dining: You are on your own in the cooking department. Cabins have cooking facilities and all kitchen utensils. Groceries should be purchased before you arrive. Many nice restaurants are just fourteen miles away.
Entertainment: Tell your big fish stories in the main lodge. Fishing videos.
Summary: Very peaceful, low-key, ranch next to the pines with high desert scenery. John reports 85% repeat customers each summer. One guest has returned every year since 1923. Recommended for experienced anglers. Catch and release only; John is very strict and conservation minded. Nearby: Bodie ghost town (40 miles), Devil's Post Pile (25 miles), Mammoth Resort (14 miles), and Mono Lake (20 miles).

Elk Creek Lodge
Meeker, Colorado

In describing their vacation at Elk Creek Lodge, one couple wrote, "It was a fishing vacation dreams are made of." And so it is. Since 1930 the Wheeler family has owned over 20,000 acres in northwestern Colorado. In previous years, the family ran an extensive cattle operation. In 1989, Bill Wheeler, with the support of his Kansas-based family, began work on a longtime family dream. Elk Creek Lodge opened its doors to the world in early 1990. What makes the Wheelers' fishing operation unique is the fact that guests have access to so much private land and fishing water. Elk Creek runs right past the lodge with over 100 log-dammed pools. Guests also fish on six private miles of the White River, on Trapper Lake (the second largest natural lake in Colorado), as well as on a variety of streams, rivers, and high mountain lakes. For those with real adventure in their blood, Elk Creek offers fly-out fishing (1½ hours to first cast) to Utah's Green River, known for its great dry fly-fishing and thousands of trout per mile. Bill, together with manager Steve Herter and a great staff, will give you the fishing vacation of a lifetime.

Address: P.O. Box 130K, Meeker, Colorado 81641
Telephone: (303) 878-5454 (lodge summer), (303) 878-5232 (winter reservations), (303) 878-4565 (answering service); fax: (303) 878-5311
Airport: Steamboat Springs, Aspen, and Grand Junction
Location: 2 hours north on Aspen on Highway 13, 180 miles west of Denver, 250 miles east of Salt Lake City
Memberships: Trout Unlimited, Rocky Mountain Elk Foundation, Nature Conservancy, Ducks Unlimited
Awards: Orvis-Endorsed Lodge
Medical: Meeker Hospital, 20 miles
Conference: 25. Excellent for corporate retreat. Sleeping accommodations in various ranch quarters.
Guest Capacity: 16
Accommodations: There are eight suites in three buildings. Each has its own private bath, living area, and common porch. All have twin beds, electric blankets, and flannel sheets. Some have lofts.
Rates: • $$$$$. Full inclusive package rates. Preferred package is five days, six nights with one day of fly-out fishing. Nonfishing spouse, group (over 12), and corporate rates.
Credit Cards: None. Personal checks and cash accepted.
Season: July to mid-October; hunting, September to mid-November
Activities: All anglers, expert and beginner, will have a unique fishing experience. However, if you are an expert who likes to make sure everyone knows you are tops to the detriment of beginners, this is not the place for you. Wide variety of fishing. Professional and friendly guides. Fully stocked tackle shop. Horseback riding from Trappers Lake 35 minutes by car. Ask about High Lake fishing on horseback. Hiking, mountain biking, nature photography, and trap shooting. Elk hunters, ask Steve about his fall hunting program.
Children's Activities: Children under 15 are not recommended. Best for children who really wish to learn or are already enthusiastic about fly-fishing.
Dining: Elk Creek takes great pride in its unique gourmet cuisine. Guests eat together at one large table. All meals are served individually. Hosted dinners with extensive wine list. All liquor complimentary. Variety of shore/fishing lunches. Weekly guides, hosted outdoor barbecue.
Entertainment: Fishing movies, casting demonstrations, fly-casting "golf" course, horseshoes.
Summary: Exciting fly-fishing lodge with a tremendous variety of fly-fishing on private waters. Fly-out fishing to Utah's Green River, a premier western tail water. Excellent for both beginners and experts. Group fishing schools.

Elktrout Lodge
Kremmling, Colorado

Elktrout Lodge is one of America's premier fly-fishing retreats. At 7,375 feet, this fly-fisherman's haven was founded by a group of businessmen who were also anglers dedicated to providing unsurpassed trout fishing. The property sits on a rise overlooking hay meadows and includes five miles of private Gold Medal water on the Colorado River. These waters are full of large brown and rainbow trout. In addition, guests fish on the Blue River, Troublesome Creek, and several connecting large ponds, holding large numbers of brook and rainbow trout. One can also fish the ranch ponds for 18- to 24-inch rainbows and browns. Guests who hook these become members of the highly coveted Elktrout "21" Club. Beginners are welcome; Elktrout offers an extensive instructional program. Professional guides are selected for their friendliness, teaching ability, and fly-fishing know-how. Besides the superb fly-fishing, Elktrout provides cozy accommodations and delicious meals. Ask about the excellent private fall hunting program.

Address: P.O. Box 614 K, Kremmling, Colorado 80459
Telephone: (303) 724-3343; fax: (303) 724-9063
Airport: Denver; private planes and small jets at Kremmling Municipal Airport, 5,500-foot paved runway
Location: 110 miles northwest of Denver, 50 miles south of Steamboat Springs off Highway 40, 70 miles east of Vail
Memberships: Trout Unlimited
Awards: Orvis-Endorsed Lodge, *Hideaway Report*
Medical: Kremmling Hospital, 2 miles
Guest Capacity: 22
Accommodations: Eight-bedroom, hand-hewn log lodge. All rooms have private baths. Lodge looks up the Colorado Valley and over hay meadows and distant neighbors. The owners' "Executive Cabin," a lovely two-bedroom log home, is available when the owners are not in residence. Ask about the nifty cabin with loft and porch called Rainbow. All beds have electric blankets. In the two-story living room of the main lodge are a tremendous fireplace and a wet bar, where guests relax and share fishing stories. Tasteful antique western furnishings.
Rates: • $$$$$. American Plan (guides included). Special rates for nonfishing spouses.
Credit Cards: Visa, MasterCard. Personal checks accepted.
Season: Late May to mid-October
Activities: Fly-fishing is the main activity. Elktrout has some of the finest private trout fishing in the western United States. All fishing is on private water exclusive to the lodge's guests: five miles of Colorado River, three miles of Blue River, a Gold Medal stream, ponds, and small streams. All fishing must be done with provided fishing guides. Tackle shop on premises. Equipment rental available. For nonfishing spouses/guests, the management will make arrangements for horseback riding, hiking, tennis, golf, shopping, or sight-seeing, but guests must provide their own transportation.
Children's Programs: None. Only recommended for children who do enjoy or want to learn how to fly-fish.
Dining: Bountiful meals. Huge breakfasts. Lunch is usually eaten on the river. Elegant evening dining with crystal and china, illuminated with antique oil lamps and candles. Four-course dinners, with complimentary California cabernet and chardonnay. Once a week, there is a marvelous authentic barbecue dinner right on the Blue River with entertainment. Fruit, cookies, and beverages always available. BYOB.
Entertainment: Fly-tying and fishing videos. Most guests prefer to fish, and fish, and fish. Rodeo in September.
Summary: World-class fly-fishing with expert guides. Great for adults (couples and singles) who enjoy lots of fly-fishing. Fly-fishing schools for seasoned and novice anglers. Excellent for small groups and corporate retreats. Nearby: Rocky Mountain National Park, town of Kremmling.

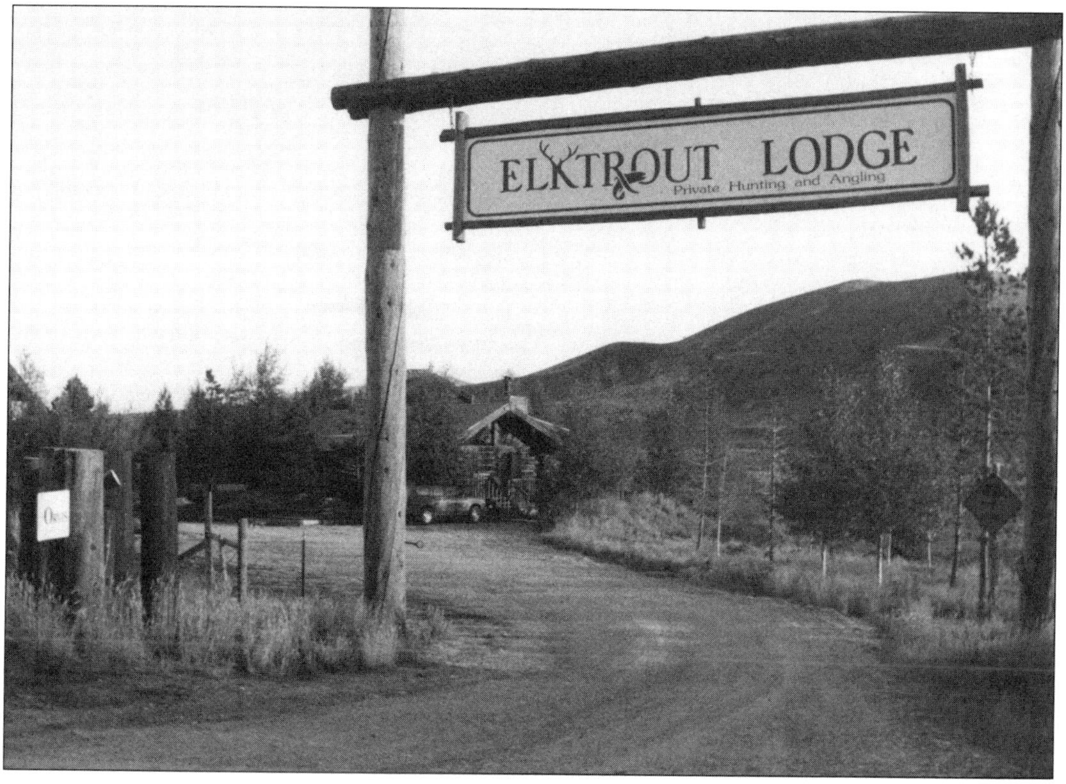
ELKTROUT LODGE
Private Hunting and Angling

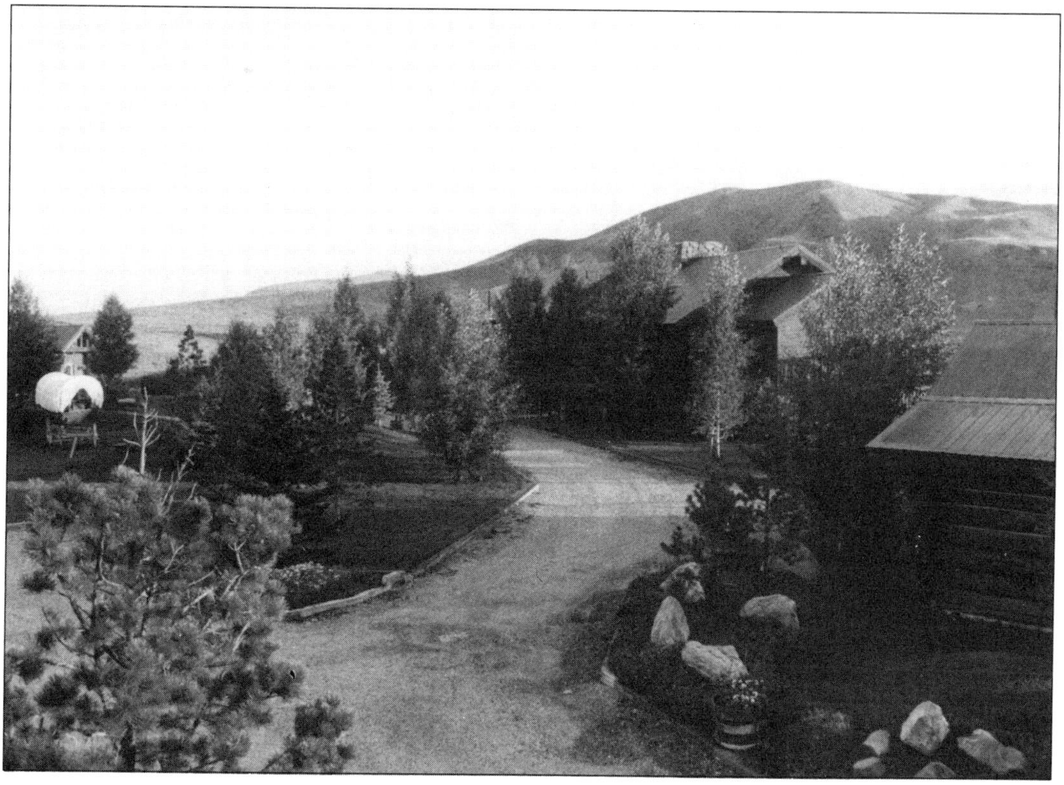

Fryingpan River Ranch
Meredith, Colorado

The Fryingpan River Ranch is a small, family ranch located on the upper waters of the renowned Fryingpan River looking over Nast Lake and down the Fryingpan Valley. The ranch offers guided and unguided fishing on the Fryingpan and Roaring Fork rivers, as well as many of the high lakes surrounding the ranch. After fishing the Gold Medal catch and release waters of the Fryingpan below Ruedi Dam or floating the Roaring Fork, many guests find the wild trout and challenging waters of the upper Fryingpan a welcome diversion. Nast Lake, less than 100 yards from the lodge, is full of brook and rainbow trout and will add to the confidence of beginners and experts alike. Fryingpan River Ranch is perfect for families in which some members are avid fishermen and others prefer guest ranch activities.

Address: 32042 Fryingpan Road, Drawer K, Meredith, Colorado 81642
Telephone: (303) 927-3570; fax: (303) 927-9943 (call first)
Airport: Aspen or Denver
Location: 31 miles up the Fryingpan River from Basalt, Colorado; 1 hour from Aspen
Memberships: Dude Ranchers' Association, Colorado Dude and Guest Ranch Association
Awards: Orvis-Endorsed Lodge
Medical: Aspen or Glenwood Springs, 50 miles
Conference: 36
Guest Capacity: 36
Accommodations: Guests stay in six cabins and two lodge suites. Each cabin has its own special charm. Some offer views of Nast Lake, while others overlook the Fryingpan River. Two are secluded in the pines away from the main activity of the lodge and conference center. Most rooms and cabins were redecorated in 1987-88. Pine and antique furnishings reflect the heritage of the ranch, accented with art collected by Jim and Paula. Each cabin or suite has its own private bath and excellent beds. The hot tub overlooking Nast Lake is available year-round. No smoking in any of the buildings.
Rates: • $$$-$$$$. American Plan. Rates available with and without guide service. Rates vary depending on the season. Three-day minimum stay.
Credit Cards: Visa, MasterCard. Personal checks and traveler's checks accepted.
Season: Year-round
Activities: Fishing guests who select a vacation with guides will fish a variety of waters—the Gold Medal catch-and-release fishing below Ruedi Dam, floats or walk-wade fishing on the Roaring Fork, and a variety of private waters on both of these rivers. Above the ranch are eight miles of pristine, seldom-fished, never-stocked water where wild fish and wild country combine for an unforgettable experience. Nast Lake sits less than a hundred yards from the lodge and is full of brook and rainbow trout. Fishing is also available in the high lakes and streams that surround the ranch. For the not-so-serious angler, the ranch offers a full horse program including instruction, half- and full-day rides, and a breakfast ride once a week. Overnight pack trips are available (extra). Guided hiking, as well as mountain bikes, trap and rifle shooting, along with archery, river rafting, and four-wheel-drive trips are available. Some swim in Nast Lake. The hot tub at the end of the day soothes casting arms as well as tired riders.
Children's Programs: No children's programs.
Dining: Superb, hearty, and healthy varied ranch menus include beef, lamb, pork, chicken, and trout. Early fishing breakfasts. BYOB.
Entertainment: Well-stocked library, VCR with a selection of fishing videos, and a cozy log lodge.
Summary: A great fly-fishing vacation for the whole family! Excellent for those who love to fish morning, noon, and night, and for those members of the family who would rather ride, hike, paint the wildflowers, or just relax. Great hosts—Paula is a fabulous wildlife artist. Nearby: the town of Aspen, 75 minutes away.

See color photos, pages 204-205

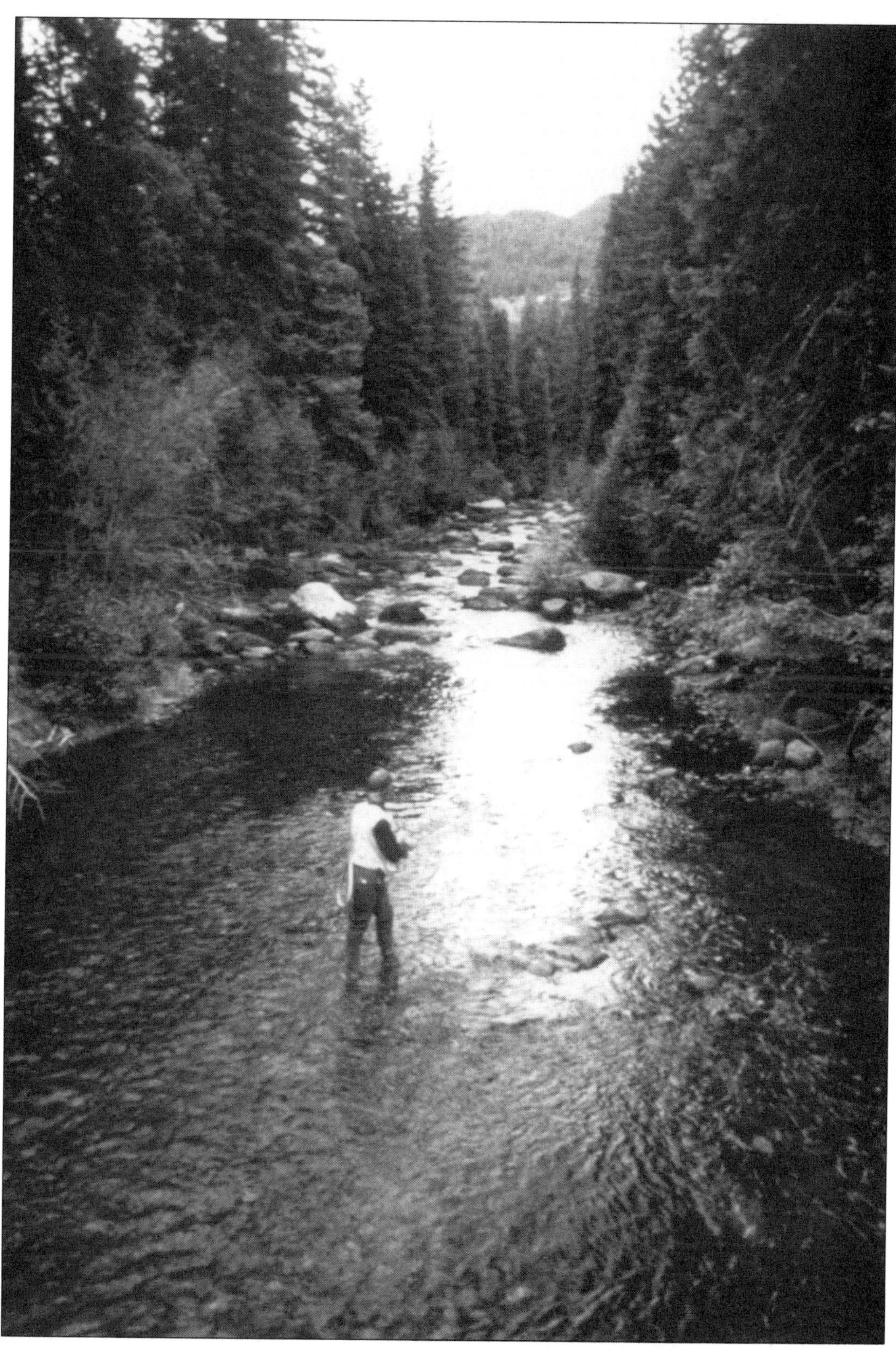

Three Rivers Ranch
Ashton, Idaho

Three Rivers Ranch is one of the top catch-and-release fishing lodges in North America. You can expect a first-class fishing program. Hostess and owner, Lonnie Allen, her family, and her wonderful fishing guides, combine Idaho hospitality and fishing savvy. The ranch is licensed to guide on some of the most famous fishing rivers in the West, including the Madison, Henry's Fork, and the South Fork of the Snake River. Three Rivers is about an hour's drive northeast of Idaho Falls. You'll see the Idaho side of the sawtoothed Grand Tetons towering in the distance as you drive to the ranch from Jackson.

Address: P.O. Box 856 K, Warm River, Ashton, Idaho 83420
Telephone: (208) 652-3750; fax: (208) 652-3788
Airport: Idaho Falls
Location: 52 miles northeast of Idaho Falls, 9 miles from Ashton off Highway 20 onto Highway 47
Memberships: Outfitters and Guides of Idaho, Nature Conservancy, Trout Unlimited
Awards: Orvis-Endorsed Lodge
Medical: Ashton Hospital, 9 miles
Conference: 22
Guest Capacity: 22
Accommodations: Guests stay in six rustic cabins (three have recently been rebuilt) under tall shade trees along Robinson Creek and in five rooms at Three Rivers Ranch, House overlooking Warm River, a separate facility within walking distance accommodating up to ten, which is excellent for corporate, business, or family groups. All cabins have porches, western antiques, carpets, and electric heat. All cabins and rooms have private baths and showers.
Rates: • $$$$$. American Plan. Day trips and weekly packages available. Saturday to Friday.
Credit Cards: American Express
Season: Late May to mid-October
Activities: Fishing days can be arranged to satisfy the desire of each angler. Most guests split their time wading and floating. Fishing options are limitless. The ranch is licensed on an honor roll of rivers in both Idaho and Montana. Programs are designed for beginners, intermediates, and advanced fishermen. All flies are hand-tied by guides at the ranch. Individual instruction is given as needed. All Three Rivers guides are pros, and there are never more than two guests to each guide. Nonfishing spouses enjoy guided tours of the area, shopping (Jackson and West Yellowstone), or just plain old relaxing. Hiking, trail rides, pack trips, and overnight fishing float trips on the South Fork of the Snake River are available but extra.
Children's Programs: Children over age 14 only. Best for kids who want to learn or are already hooked on fishing.
Dining: Except for most lunches, which are eaten riverside with fishing guides, meals are served either in the handsome lodge filled with antiques and memorabilia or at the ranch house. The evening meal is a special part of the day. Each evening Lonnie hosts a happy hour. Prime rib with Idaho potatoes and Cornish game hen are just two of the wonderful dishes. Rum cakes and apple pie are dessert specialties. All guests enjoy the weekly old-time steak barbecue—a time to tell your fishing tale of the week on a wonderful deck overlooking Robinson Creek.
Entertainment: Guests either visit after dinner, sipping on a little brandy while swapping fish stories, or retire after a long day.
Summary: The spirit here is one of family togetherness. Superb fly-fishing and excellent guides, several of whom have been here over 15 years. Tackle shop on property. Nearby: Yellowstone Park, Mesa Falls, tours in the Targhee National Forest, the town of Jackson, Railroad Ranch, and Harriman State Park.

Falcon, Inc.
Bangor, Maine

Spencer Lake Lodge, Hardscrabble Lodge, and Drop Camps are all part of Falcon, Inc.—a new wilderness lodging company based in Bangor and specializing in remote wilderness retreat fishing and hunting. Set in Maine's western mountains and North Country, the Falcon properties are surrounded by thousands of acres of privately managed woodlands with majestic views and quiet natural isolation. The Falcon program can be experienced three ways, ranging from total rugged luxury to roughing it at Drop Camps. Whichever you choose, you will be enveloped in spectacular Maine backcountry in the heart of excellent fishing and hunting. Falcon's premier property is Spencer Lake Lodge, an expansive six-bedroom log lodge with cathedral ceilings, a granite fireplace, and a host of VIP activities all included in the fare. The second property is Hardscrabble, a smaller, more intimate lodge offering excellent fishing and hunting without a lot of extras. This is a happy medium for sportsmen who want quality guided fishing and hunting in beautiful surroundings. For those who like to commune with nature and don't need luxuries, at least for a few days, Falcon's Drop Camps take advantage of the full wilderness experience.

Address: P.O. Box 1899 K, Bangor, Maine 04402-1899
Telephone: (207) 990-4534; (800) 825-8234
Airport: Bangor International, 120 miles
Location: Spencer Lake, 120 miles west of Bangor; Hardscrabble Lodge, 130 miles northwest of Bangor
Memberships: Maine Professional Guide Association, Main Sporting Camp Association
Medical: Jackman, 14 air miles
Conference: 12 (Spencer Lake Lodge)
Guest Capacity: 26 (both lodges)
Accommodations: Luxurious Spencer Lake Lodge offers six private, soundproof rooms with baths, 122 feet of deck overlooking Spencer Lake, private patio doors opening onto a deck, and a fully stocked fly-tying bench. Hardscrabble Lodge, on a point that affords a beautiful panoramic view of upper Spencer Lake, is a rustic lodge that can accommodate 14 guests in its 5 comfortable private cabins. At the Drop Camps, which are selected for the quality of fishing and hunting, you must bring your own food, clothing, sleeping gear, fishing, and hunting equipment. Falcon supplies the rest, including canoes and boats.
Rates: • \$-\$\$\$\$\$ Call for packages. Corporate/group and children's rates available. Minimum stay policy. Licenses extra.
Credit Cards: Visa, MasterCard, American Express
Season: Year-round
Activities: General fishing begins early April and runs through September. True Maine wilderness fishing for brook trout, lake trout, and landlocked salmon, much of it on cold water lakes and ponds, accessible by four-wheel drive or floatplane. Hunting season normally begins early September. Superb trophy white-tailed deer hunting in both locations. All Falcon locations are in prime bear country. Maine is one of the premier bear hunting states in the country. Winter activities are cross-country skiing, snowshoeing, ice fishing. Snowmobile weekend packages available.
Children's Programs: None. Not advised for young children. Children should be old enough to fish. Children 12 and older may stay at Spencer Lake Lodge.
Dining: Ranges from gourmet to cook-your-own trout, depending on which property you choose. Fine wines and preferred beverages provided.
Entertainment: Most just relax and enjoy each other's company.
Summary: Executive retreat, luxury lodge, Drop Camp tents. Superb fishing and hunting. Prior to arrival, each lodge guest is contacted about preferences concerning culinary, fine wine, beverage, and other needs. Maine is alive with bear and moose. Video available on request.

Big Hole River Outfitters
Wise River, Montana

Craig Fellin may not tell you this, but his operation is considered one of the finest in North America. Craig is modest in his demeanor, soft spoken, and very low-key. He is, in fact, a giant in his knowledge and fly-fishing expertise. What makes his operation unique is the size, the personal attention, superb guides, and proximity to diverse unpressured fishery waters in southwestern Montana. In 1983, Craig set about to find a wilderness setting that would offer discriminating guests a superb fishing vacation as well as an enriching experience savoring the beauty and splendor of the American West. And that's exactly what he did. In addition to being near some of Montana's great trout fishing waters, his lodge is in the heart of Montana's ranch country and close to one of the most historic Indian battlefields. Craig's philosophy is simple: "Take only ten guests and give them one of the greatest fishing experiences of their life." And that's exactly what he does! Big Hole River Outfitters offers great fishing, genuine western camaraderie, hearty laughter, and fun for all. Fellin's outfit is first-class.

Address: P.O. Box 156 K, Wise River, Montana 59762
Telephone: (406) 832-3252; call for fax number
Airport: Butte via Salt Lake City
Location: 50 miles southwest of Butte
Memberships: Montana Trout Foundation, Trout Unlimited, Fishing Outfitters of Montana
Medical: St. James Hospital, Butte
Guest Capacity: 10
Accommodations: Guests stay in a large cedar cabin with two bedrooms, a duplex cabin, or a two-bedroom log cabin along the Wise River. All have electric heat and private bathrooms with shower and bathtubs. Two of the cabins have wood stoves, kitchens, living rooms, and screened open porches.
Rates: • $$$$-$$$$$. American Plan. Six-night and five-day packages only. Saturday to Friday.
Credit Cards: None. Personal checks accepted.
Season: Early-June to mid-October
Activities: The fly-fishing program is tailored to guests' level of experience. Beginners and advanced fishermen are welcome. Personal and patient instruction for beginners is one of Craig's specialties. Each group will be challenged. One guide to a maximum of two guests. Guided float or wading trips on the Big Hole, Beaverhead, and Wise rivers. Excellent fly-fishermen should ask Craig about Poindexter Slough, a classic spring creek. Be sure to ask Craig about his private water trophy trout fishery. Horseback trips to a mountain lake can be arranged by a local outfitter. No rental equipment available; however, Craig has a very well stocked fly shop with Winston rods. On those days you do not care to fish, your fishing guide will take you on a wonderful sightseeing trip.
Children's Programs: Young children not advised. Craig encourages teens who want to learn about fly-fishing. Ask Craig about his special father/son and father/daughter weeks.
Dining: Country family-style meals. Lunches are served streamside with cloth napkins and tablecloths. Happy hour before dinner. Fine dining by candlelight with soft music in the new lodge. California wines served.
Entertainment: After a relaxing dinner, most people are so pleasantly tired that they are ready to drift off to sleep. Some, though, enjoy fishing in the evening within steps of the main lodge.
Summary: Top fly-fishing with personalized, caring hospitality and service. Only 10 guests. Craig has been featured on the Today Show, ESPN's "Fishing the World," and in *Condé Nast Traveler.* Nearby: Dillon Rodeo, hot springs, Big Hole Monument Battlefield, historic wilderness mining mill.

Eagle Nest Lodge
Hardin, Montana

In 1981, Alan Kelly opened a new chapter in his life and began Eagle Nest Lodge, with excellent trout fishing during the summer months and gamebird hunting in the fall. Alan was a U.S. Fish and Wildlife Service biologist who was responsible for the fishery supplying one of the nation's richest trout streams, the Big Horn River. With his thorough knowledge of fish, the Big Horn River, and his love for this part of the country, Alan and his wife, Wanda, built Eagle Nest Lodge. Today, Eagle Nest is run by Nick and Francine Forrester, who share with their guests superb food, lots of personal attention, and world-class fishing. Nick and Francine take only 16 guests at a time. The Big Horn River is clear and cold year-round, yet never freezes. Fly hatches are almost continuous and at times unbelievably abundant. Nick also offers terrific fall hunting for upland birds, including pheasant, partridge, and sharptail grouse. Montana's grandeur, vastness, and diversity provide a backdrop for unforgettable experiences. Eagle Nest Lodge is for magnificent fly-fishing and upland bird hunting. Nick and Francine love what they do, and it has earned them a great reputation and many loyal guests. Smokers, be forewarned: there is a strictly enforced no smoking policy in the main lodge.

Address: P.O. Box 470 K, Hardin, Montana 59034
Telephone: (406) 665-3799; fax: (406) 665-3762
Airport: Logan International Airport, Billings, 50 miles
Location: 3 miles south of Hardin, 50 miles east of Billings off Interstate 90
Memberships: Trout Unlimited, American Museum of Fly-Fishermen
Awards: *Hideaway Report*, Orvis-Endorsed Lodge
Medical: Hardin Hospital, 3 miles
Conference: 12
Guest Capacity: 16
Accommodations: The two-story, log Eagle Nest Lodge was built in 1985. It is set back from the river and features large bedrooms with two single beds and private baths. There is a trophy-studded dining room with an outside screened porch and old-fashioned swing. Rocking chairs are provided.
Rates: • $$$$$. American Plan. Weekly all-inclusive packages and day trips available. No minimum stay. Three-day, two-night stays recommended.
Credit Cards: None. Personal checks accepted.
Season: Mid-April to mid-November
Activities: The main activity here is fly-fishing in the summer and bird hunting in the fall. Most fishing takes place on the Big Horn River. All fishing guests are guided in drift boats with stream wading. There is fishing year-round here, but the best months are May through November. Nick will tell you exactly what you need to bring and what he can supply. At Eagle Nest, there is an Orvis fly shop. Nick makes it clear there are only five things to do: fish in the summer, hunt in the fall, eat like a king, sleep like a baby, and enjoy the peace of Mother Nature.
Children's Programs: Children 13 and older are welcome, but make sure they really like fly-fishing.
Dining: Excellent, first-rate, gourmet, four-course meals featuring European and Continental menus with wild game delicacies, garden vegetables, fresh-baked bread, and scrumptious desserts. There are many guests who would come back just for the food. BYOB.
Entertainment: Fly-fishing and shooting instruction.
Summary: Eagle Nest Lodge is for discriminating sports-minded people only. Excellent fly-fishing and fall bird hunting. Nick suggests that guests learn how to fly cast and/or shoot before arrival so that they will enjoy optimum fishing and/or hunting. Most come and enjoy superb food, service, fly-fishing and/or bird hunting. No smoking in main lodge. Nearby: Custer Battlefield.

Diamond J Ranch
Ennis, Montana

If you are looking for a fly-fishing experience that combines excellent fishing with a wonderful guest ranch program, the Diamond J may just be the answer. So many times, anglers will have a member of the family who does not fish. Many families have forgone summer vacations together just for this reason. More often than not, husbands have gone off fishing, leaving their families behind. The Diamond J Ranch is the perfect solution. If you are a diehard angler, the ranch is situated in the center of some of the best Blue Ribbon streams in Montana. If other members of your family wish to horseback ride, play tennis, hike, or just relax, they can do it. Everyone can be happy at the Diamond J. This marvelous ranch is run by Peter and Jinny Combs, along with their son, Tim.

Address: P.O. Box 577 K, Ennis, Montana 59729
Telephone: (406) 682-4867; fax: (406) 682-4106
Airport: Bozeman
Location: 14 miles east of Ennis off Highway 287, 60 miles south of Bozeman
Memberships: Dude Ranchers' Association
Awards: Orvis-Endorsed Fly-Fishing and Wing Shooting Lodge
Medical: Ennis Hospital, 14 miles
Conference: 36 (June, September, October, and November)
Guest Capacity: 36
Accommodations: There are ten cozy log cabins, each with hardwood floors, a rock fireplace, matching furniture, and beds. Each has a full bath with separate shower stalls and a cast iron tub. Cabins have their own writing desks and porches.
Rates: • $$-$$$$$. American Plan. Call ranch for specifics.
Credit Cards: Visa, MasterCard
Season: June through November
Activities: The ranch is in the Madison River valley and very close to its crown jewel, the Madison River. Many take side trips to fish the Beaverhead, Big Hole, Missouri, Jefferson, Gallatin, and Yellowstone Park waters (Firehole and Gibbon). The ranch has its own little stream they call Jack Creek and a two-acre lake. Most fishing takes place from June through November with wet flies and salmon fly hatches in June. Dry fly-fishing July and August and streamer fishing for spawning browns in September. Available trips include wading, floating, belly tubes on Ennis, Quake, and Hebgen lakes and on mountain lakes, rivers, and springs. Ask about the two-day overnight comfort camping float trips. Full guide service available. Usually one guide per two guests. Full tackle shop in Ennis. All trips are tailored individually to each guest. Nonfishing members of the family will enjoy full horseback riding, tennis, swimming, hot tub spa, scenic float trips, and hiking. Do as much or as little as you wish. For you bird hunters, be sure to talk with the ranch about their superb wing shooting program. Wild birds include chukar, Hungarian partridge, pheasant, mountain grouse, ducks, and geese.
Children's Programs: No set program. Kiddie wrangler with instruction. Kids usually ride together. Baby-sitting available.
Dining: Sack and barbecue lunches on shore for all those who fish. Anglers on overnight float trips get to experience the tent "chalet." Back at the ranch, family-style hearty dining in three (they prefer no smoking) dining rooms. BYOB happy hour.
Entertainment: Campfires, sing-alongs, and a great library. The Combses subscribe to the best-seller list.
Summary: An excellent fly-fishing ranch for the entire family. Those who love to fish are in excellent hands. And for those who do not stay awake at night dreaming about fly-fishing, the ranch has a host of nonfishing activities. Superb upland bird and waterfowl hunting on 30,000-acre ranch. Nearby: Yellowstone National Park, historic Virginia and Nevada cities, Museum of the Rockies in Bozeman.

See color photos, page 239

BUD LIGHT
BUD LIGHT

GUEST RANCH
ENNIS, MT.

Parade Rest Ranch
West Yellowstone, Montana

Parade Rest Ranch is in the heart of some of North America's best fly-fishing. With Grayling Creek literally at the back door and Blue Ribbon trout streams surrounding it, Parade Rest is a parade of outdoor activities, natural beauty, and, for those more inclined, lots of rest. Here there is no timetable or regimented activity list. Your time is your own, and you may do as much or as little as you wish. Walt and Shirley Butcher have been in the guest ranching business since the late 1970s. They are in their late sixties and extend true western hospitality in all respects. Life at "PR" is informal. The dress code is whatever is comfortable, and, for the most part, that means an old pair of jeans. Mornings and evenings are cool, with midday temperatures in the mid- to high 80s. Parade Rest is a small dude/fly-fishing ranch run the old-fashioned way.

Address: 7979 Grayling Creek Road, Drawer K, West Yellowstone, Montana 59758
Telephone: (406) 646-7217, 1-(800) 758-5934 (summer); (602) 983-2653 (winter)
Airport: West Yellowstone, or Gallatin Field at Bozeman; also, commuter flights from Salt Lake City to West Yellowstone
Location: 8 miles northwest of Yellowstone, 90 miles south of Bozeman off Highway 191
Medical: Yellowstone Medical Clinic
Conference: 60
Guest Capacity: 60
Accommodations: Fifteen turn-of-the-century log cabins with one to four bedrooms each. They radiate western warmth and are cheerfully furnished. All are named after famous fishing rivers nearby. Ask Shirley about the Homestead cabin and her favorite Grayling single. All have porches, wood-burning stoves, full baths, and comfortable beds; the newest, three-story cabin is Aspen North. Several are along Grayling Creek. Nightly turn-down service. The Gallatin Lodge is a happy gathering spot for reading, visiting, playing games, and listening to music.
Rates: • $-$$$. Full American Plan. Children's, corporate, off-season, and fly-fishing guide rates available.
Credit Cards: Visa, MasterCard, American Express
Season: Mid-May through September
Activities: Very few areas in the country offer such a diversity of fine fishing. Through the ranch flow one and a half miles of Grayling Creek, an excellent fly-fishing stream. Within minutes are the Madison, Gallatin, Firehole, and Gibbon. Full guide service is available. Just let Shirley know what you would like to do and she will arrange it for you. Also, ask her about the 3-day fly-fishing schools. Parade Rest is well known by all the local guides. Horseback riding is geared to your desires. Rides are accompanied by a wrangler and vary from an hour to all day. White water and scenic raft trips. Ask Shirley about the wilderness float trip. Ten-person hot tub outside Gallatin Lodge overlooking Grayling Creek.
Children's Programs: No special programs. Children are welcome. Kids will not have enough time in the day to do everything they would like. Children are the responsibility of parents.
Dining: Even if you are late from your fishing excursion, dinner will be waiting for you and your guide. The warm and friendly atmosphere is matched by great, hearty ranch cooking. Packed lunches are available to those wishing to ride, fish, raft, or explore all day. All meals are served all-you-can-eat, buffet-style in a central dining room. BYOB.
Entertainment: Nothing special. Many of the diehard fishermen eat dinner, then go back out for more fishing. Cookouts on Monday and Friday nights. western entertainment. Volleyball, basketball, and horseshoes.
Summary: Great fishing, hearty food, a relaxed atmosphere. Sincere western ranch hospitality.

The Lodge at Chama
Chama, New Mexico

The unspoiled, picturesque San Juan Mountains of northern New Mexico are home to the 32,000-acre Lodge at Chama ranch. The ranch has been in one family since 1950, and today it maintains the highest standards of excellence in fishing, special hunting, and lodging amenities. Both lake and stream fly-fishing are the highlights of guest activities from June to October. Rainbow, brown, brook, and cutthroat trout thrive in this pristine environment of isolated, high-country lakes and miles of crystal-clear streams. Heavy-bodied fish from 16 inches to 25 inches will test your fishing skills. Your fishing guide will put you where the fish are, share some of his Chama fishing secrets, and help to give you the fishing experience of a lifetime. Hunters, be sure to talk with General Manager Frank Simms about the world-class fall and winter hunting/lodging program.

Address: Box 127K, Chama, New Mexico 87520
Telephone: (505) 756-2133; fax: (505) 756-2519
Airport: Albuquerque International, private jets to Pagosa Springs. Call regarding ranch airstrip.
Location: 100 miles north of Santa Fe, 90 miles west of Taos
Awards: *Hideaway Report:* 1986 Fishing/Hunting Lodge of the Year; *Hideaway Report:* 1990 Best Sporting Retreat
Medical: Hospital in Española; emergency helicopter service available
Conference: 24 in board meeting room
Guest Capacity: 24
Accommodations: The handsome, 13,500-square-foot lodge offers panoramic views of the beautiful Chama Valley and snow-capped Colorado peaks from its twelve rooms. The huge living room is dominated by a 20-foot-wide rock fireplace, original western art and sculpture, and fish and wildlife mounts. There are ten luxurious rooms with private baths, sitting/desk areas, lofty ceilings, large closets, and upscale amenities. Two spacious junior suites, named Roadrunner and Bear, have fireplaces, vanity baths, televisions, and lounging areas.
Rates: • $$$-$$$$$. Full American Plan. Special fly-fishing and hunting packages available on request. No minimum stay.
Credit Cards: None
Season: May to October for fishing; mid-September to January for hunting; conferences and viewing of wildlife (elk, buffalo, mule deer, bear) year-round.
Activities: Private lake and stream fishing. Some waters reserved for catch and release only. Fishing equipment available; however, most people bring their own gear. Self-guided nature trail from lodge. Hiking, picnics, wildlife tours, photography trips. Guided ranch trail rides. Non-fishing spouses enjoy off-ranch activities including narrow gauge train rides, shopping tours to Taos or Santa Fe, and white-water rafting. After a full day of outdoor activities, you may relax in a ten-person, indoor, hydrotherapy whirlpool or enjoy a sauna. Superb fall elk and mule deer hunting on limited basis.
Children's Programs: Minimum age of 12 unless by special arrangement.
Dining: Trail lunches and fishermen's special shore lunches. Excellent varied cuisine for all three daily meals. Ranch specialties include steaks, chops, buffalo, trout, and fowl as well as New Mexican specialties made with wonderful chilies grown in New Mexico. Home-baked bread, rolls, desserts, and pastries. Complimentary bar, wine separate.
Entertainment: Wide-screen television offers network programs, VCR movies, and fishing and wildlife videos.
Summary: Tremendous personal service. Excellent fishing and corporate retreat. You will come as guests and leave as friends. Elk and deer are frequent sundown visitors to the Lodge grounds. Spectacular sunsets, wildlife viewing. One of the world's largest private elk herds, ranch buffalo herd.

See color photos, pages 254-255

Vermejo Park Ranch
Raton, New Mexico

In northeastern New Mexico is a 600,000-acre paradise called Vermejo Park Ranch. Since the turn of the century, this privately owned retreat has played host to professional, corporate, and creative individuals who have sought refuge from the stresses and strains of city life. Vermejo Park is, without question, one of the world's unique wilderness sanctuaries, offering those who come abundant wildlife and beauty as far as the eye can see. Because of its size, Vermejo offers anglers tremendous lake fishing in addition to 25 miles of mountain streams. Experts, intermediates, and beginners will enjoy the diversity and many fishing challenges. German brown, brook, rainbow, and the rare Rio Grande cutthroat are all here. Each summer the ranch hosts a fly-fishing clinic with internationally known instructors. Those who come, anglers, naturalists, hikers, photographers, hunters, historians, families, and corporate groups, will experience the best of the best. Vermejo Park Ranch has a tradition of excellence.

Address: P.O. Drawer E, Dept. K, Raton, New Mexico 87740
Telephone: (505) 445-3097, 445-5028; fax: (505) 445-3474
Airport: Private aircraft and small jets to Crews Field, Raton, New Mexico; commercial flights to Albuquerque, New Mexico, or Denver (call for details)
Location: 45 miles west of Raton on Highway 555, 265 miles northeast of Albuquerque, 270 miles south of Denver
Medical: Miner's Colfax Medical Center; 40 miles, emergency helicopter service
Conference: 60
Guest Capacity: 75
Accommodations: Seven newly remodeled turn-of-the-century guest homes with 3 to 12 bedrooms. All are carpeted, with twin beds, amenity basket, and oversized cotton towels. A newly constructed main log lodge houses a complete tackle shop, great room, dining room, and lounge and upstairs conference facilities. The self-sufficient, rustic, full-service, 6-room Costilla Lodge at 10,000 feet is 28 miles away and is available for groups of 12 people.
Rates: $$$$-$$$$$. American Plan. Fishing guides and vehicles extra. All-inclusive hunting packages and group rates available. Children age 12 and under, 50% off.
Credit Cards: None. Personal checks accepted.
Season: Summer, June through August; October to December, elk and deer hunting; mid-April to mid-May, turkey hunting
Activities: At check-in, the front desk will brief you on all the activities available. Full range of fly- and spinning-reel fishing. Lakes are stocked continually throughout the year. You can expect to catch 1-lb. to 5-lb. fish. All but a few lakes are accessible by car. The high lakes at 12,000 feet can only be reached by four-wheel drive, on horseback, or on foot. Trolling boats on many of the lakes. The tackle shop has over 200 flies. Limited fly and spinning rods. Favorite flies: Royal Wulff, Damsel Nymph, Woolly Bugger, and the ranch's own Wonder Fly. Horseback riding, skeet shooting, and sporting clays (guns and ammunition provided) are also available.
Children's Programs: No formal children's programs. Children are the responsibility of their parents. Ask about the NRA program at Whittington Center for children ages 13-17.
Dining: You will dine in a spacious area complete with fireplace, elk antler chandeliers, and Southwest-style furnishings. Dinner menu changes daily from western to southwestern favorites to gourmet meals. Picnic lunches available. Full bar.
Summary: Executive world-class fishing and hunting retreat. Excellent for those who love fishing or just want to get away from it all, enjoying the serenity of 600,000 acres of private land with 21 lakes and 25 miles of fishing streams with an abundant amount of wildlife. Very low-key and instructional.

Morrison's Rogue River Lodge
Merlin, Oregon

Morrison's Lodge was built in the mid-1940s on the banks of the Rogue River, now a federally designated wild and scenic river. The lodge is 16 miles downriver from Grants Pass, amid groves of evergreen and oak. Morrison's is owned and operated by B.A. and Elaine Hanten and is well known for its blend of country style and gourmet cuisine with traditional family-style service. The big fishing season on this stretch of the Rogue is in the fall, with the best steelhead fishing September through November and salmon fishing in September. The lodge has maintained a fine reputation for fishing and retains some of the best licensed guides in the area. Morrison's uses traditional dory fishing boats for guided fishing, all equipment provided. For the bank or wading fisherman, the Rogue has easy access for fly-fishing (nonguided). Bank and wade fishermen must provide their own equipment. During the fishing season the lodge will make jet boat runs to spot fly-fishermen in prime fly casting waters each morning and evening. Though Morrison's traditionally has been an anglers' lodge, today it is equally popular with families, outdoorsmen, and romantics, especially in the summer. A major attraction is white water rafting, with one- to four-day trips available.

Address: 8500 Galice Road, Dept. K, Merlin, Oregon 97532
Telephone: (800) 826-1963, (503) 476-3825; fax: (503) 476-4953
Airport: Medford Commercial Airport, 1 hour; private planes, Josephine County Airport, 8 miles
Location: 46 miles northwest of Medford, 16 miles northwest of Grants Pass off I-5
Memberships: Oregon Guides and Packers
Awards: Orvis-Endorsed Lodge
Medical: Two hospitals in Grants Pass, 16 miles
Conference: 32
Guest Capacity: 32
Accommodations: Nine red-trimmed cottages and four rooms inside the lodge. All cottages, with comfortable furnishings, are on the second story with carports underneath. All feature a deck looking over a well-kept lawn, pines, and the Rogue River. All have private bath, wall-to-wall carpeting, air-conditioning, fireplaces, and television; four are equipped with full kitchenettes for summer housekeeping. The newly remodeled rooms in the lodge feature country decor and private baths. All accommodations receive daily maid service.
Rates: • $-$$$. Modified American Plan or Housekeeping Plan in summer. American Plan in fall. Rates vary depending on the season. Special fishing packages available.
Credit Cards: Visa, MasterCard, American Express
Season: May to mid-November
Activities: Fall steelhead and salmon fishing. Summer white water rafting trips. One-day scenic float trips; two- to four-day trips through the wild and scenic section of the Rogue; two-day, three-day, and combination white water trips to rustic lodges; and four-day camping trips available. Heated swimming pool, hot tub, two tennis courts, putting green, and walking trails. Nearby jet boating and golf.
Children's Programs: No special programs. Children are the responsibility of their parents.
Dining: Four-course menu nightly, family style in the dining room or on the spacious redwood deck overlooking the river, weather permitting. Entrées may include grilled leg of lamb, roast duck with plum sauce, or salmon with a green chile butter sauce. Beer, wine, and liquor served.
Entertainment: In-circuit movie is shown nightly.
Summary: Family owned and operated. Very homey atmosphere. Lots of return guests. Wide range of clientele—the young and the young-at-heart. Women particularly enjoy fishing here. Excellent fall steelhead fishing from dory boats. Summer white water rafting. As for the cuisine, Elaine says, "Don't come here to lose weight," but Weight Watchers dinners are served for those who are weight-conscious. Video of white water rafting trips available. Nearby: Shakespeare Festival in Ashland, Crater Lake National Park.

Crescent H Ranch
Wilson, Wyoming

Crescent H Ranch was built in the late 1920s. Today, this 1,500-acre property is a world-class fly-fishing and horseback riding guest ranch, surrounded by the breathtaking magnificence of the Jackson Hole valley. In 1963, Don Albrecht bought the old ranch as a summer retreat. In 1973, the Crescent H resumed receiving guests. With the guidance of Vern Bressler, an experienced fish biologist and fly-fisherman, the ranch developed its international reputation. The Crescent H is run by Albrecht's son, Scott. "We specialize in personal service coupled with traditional western hospitality," says Scott. "People who stay in elegant, metropolitan hotels will be comfortable here, but we offer a swing on the porch instead of a television in the room." Here you will experience magnificent rustic elegance, mouth-watering cuisine, and an excellent fly-fishing and horseback riding.

Address: Box 347 K, Wilson, Wyoming 83014
Telephone: (307) 733-3674; fax: (307) 733-8475
Airport: Jackson Hole
Location: 5 miles west of Jackson on Fall Creek Road
Memberships: Trout Unlimited, Jackson Chamber of Commerce
Awards: Original Orvis-Endorsed Lodge in North America
Medical: St. John's Hospital, Jackson Hole
Conference: 50
Guest Capacity: 40
Accommodations: There are about 30 log buildings on the ranch, all in harmony with the surroundings. There are ten darkly stained, charming log cabins in a large semicircle above the main lodge, each set on a gentle slope with views. Cabins have one, two, or three bedrooms, all decorated in a hunter green motif. Each has a shower, marble-topped bedside tables, carpeting, brass beds, and baskets of fresh fruit for new arrivals. The handsome log main lodge reflects the elegant rustic spirit here, with 30-foot ceilings, two stone fireplaces, wagon wheel lamps, original western art, and bronze sculptures.
Rates: • $$$-$$$$. American Plan. Children's, group, corporate, and fly-fishing packages and schools available. Seven-night minimum stay July and August, Saturday to Saturday.
Credit Cards: None. Personal checks accepted.
Season: Early June through September
Activities: The fly-fishing program is under the direction of Ed Ingold. Experienced guides will show you the tremendous variety of fishing opportunities in the Jackson Hole area. The ranch owns more than seven miles of private spring creeks, with native cutthroat up to 22 inches. These challenge even the experienced fisherman. Float the Snake River through Grand Teton National Park or fish for large browns and rainbows in the Green River. Ranch guests also fish the nearby South Fork (in Idaho) and the Firehole and Yellowstone rivers in Yellowstone National Park. Horseback riding; half-day and all-day rides with riding instruction if desired. Rides go out seven days a week with no more than 8 riders per guide. Children under age 5 are led around the ranch. Weekly breakfast cookout rides. Two tennis courts, swimming in free-form, oval, heated pool, hiking, guided nature walks, float trips, and 18-hole golf nearby.
Children's Programs: Daily and evening children's program with early dinner hour.
Dining: Elegant cuisine! Specialty game, fresh fish, two nightly entrées, and mouth-watering desserts. Fine wine and liquor served (included). A weekly Grand Barbecue overlooking the Snake River with cowboy music.
Entertainment: Scott or Ed host cocktail hour each evening. Nature and fly-fishing videos. Jackson weekly rodeo. Cowboy poetry.
Summary: Premier fly-fishing and guest ranch with private fishing guides, Liar's Den fly shop, superb cuisine, rustic elegance. Be sure to ask Scott about Wiute at the ranch. Orvis fly-fishing schools and equipment. Nearby: Jackson, Teton Village, and Yellowstone and Grand Teton national parks.

See color photos, pages 278-279

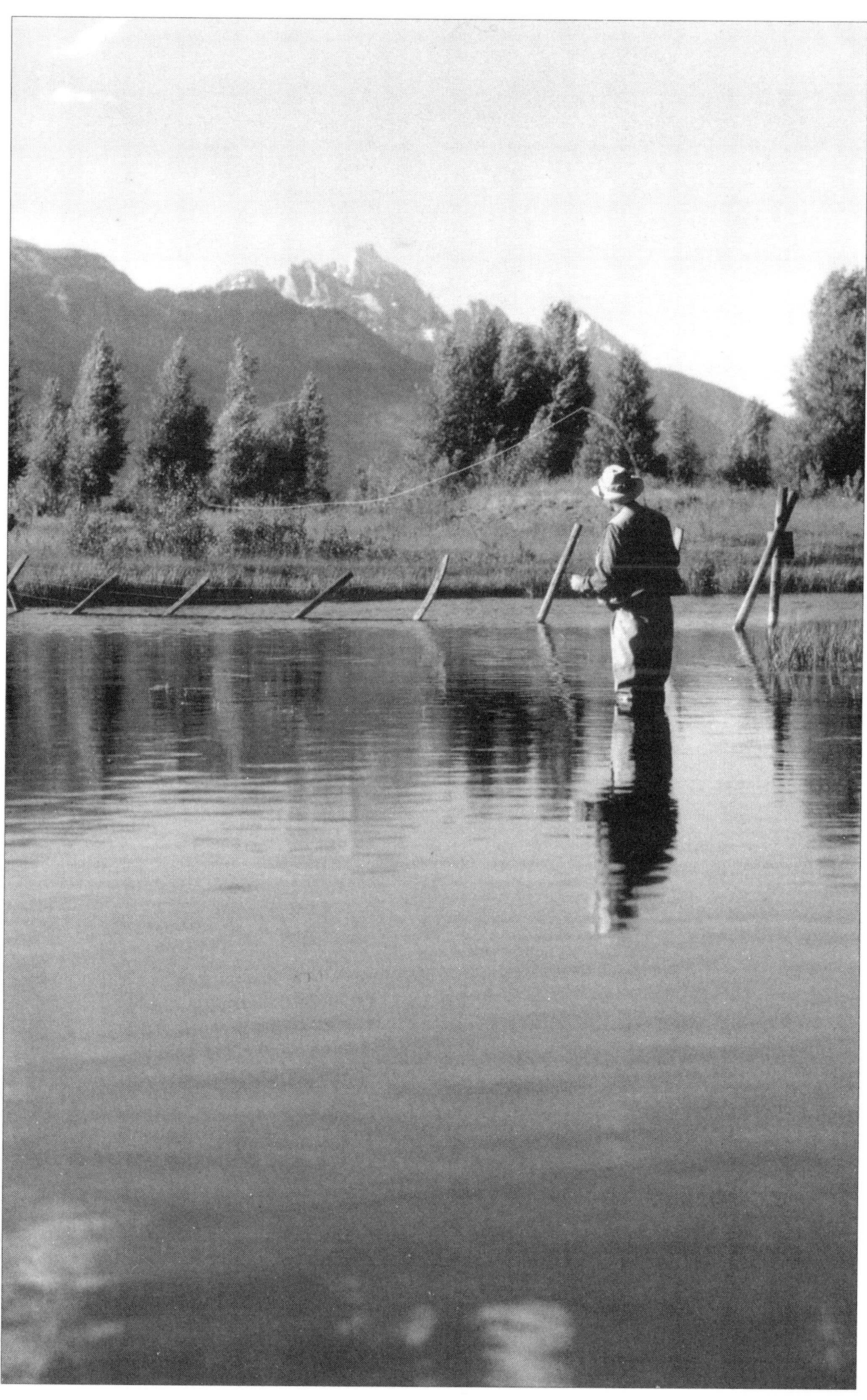

Cross-Country Skiing Ranches

Introduction

Unlike Scandinavians, for whom cross-country skiing is a way of life, most North Americans have discovered the sport only in the last two decades. Many of us used to think of nordic or "skinny skiing," as it is sometimes called, not as recreation but largely as an occupational necessity. It was one of those things done by mountain climbers, snowbound villagers, and *National Geographic* crews working on stories in the Antarctic.

Now, cross-country skiing is taking winter by storm. Wellness experts give it their stamp of approval as the top sport for low-impact cardiovascular exercise. But it is more than a great workout, combining natural splendor, camaraderie, and winter magic. Cross-country skiing offers families a delightful complement or alternative to downhill skiing.

Skinny skiing is friendly and fun. It is so suited for the whole family that almost half the adults out on the trails have children under 18. The best way to start off is with a skiing professional on machine-groomed trails, learning not just how to travel across the flats but also the whole gamut of descent techniques (more kinds of turns than in downhill skiing). When you can stay on the tracks, try "skating," graduate to back country touring, telemark on lift-served slopes, enjoy hut-to-hut trips.

As cross-country journalist, guide, and consultant Jonathan Wiesel of Nordic Group International explains, "Machine-set tracks guide skis forward so your ankles don't have the chance to splay out to the side. This transforms walking on skis into gliding, helping you out-think your feet. Groomed trails open the grace and beauty of winter, not just to super-athletes but to anyone at any pace, giving you the thrill of speed with confident control. Best of all, cross-country consumes enough calories that two hours on skis justifies a second dessert."

Equipment has evolved at a dizzying pace. There are track and skating skis, wider boards for breaking your own trail, and metal-edged gear for telemarking. The latest innovation is the "micro ski," which is three-fourths the length of the older models. They look like toys, but turning and learning is a breeze on packed snow and falls are reduced by 50 percent.

In this guide, I have included facilities that offer excellent service. Each ranch has its own character, programs, and beauty. I suggest asking the following of your prospective host:

- How many kilometers of machine-groomed track does the ranch have? Are there skating lanes as well?
- What kids' programs and facilities are available—day-care or baby-sitting, special narrow track setting, snow play area, ski equipment, special trails?
- What kinds of equipment are available—track, touring, telemarking, micro skis? Do they have modern boot-binding "systems"?
- Is instruction included in the package? Guide service?
- What other recreation is available on-site? Is there a downhill ski area nearby?

Winter ranches are famous for hospitality, diverse entertainment and culinary excellence. Regardless of whether you are a single person, couple, or family, you can use cross-country skiing as an excuse to visit. Then you can snowshoe, ice skate, take a sleigh ride, sit in the Jacuzzi enjoying splendid mountain views, or relax in front of the fire with a glass of mulled wine. And on a clear day, you can ski forever!

The Aspen Lodge Ranch Resort
Estes Park, Colorado

High in the beautiful Rocky Mountains just outside Estes Park is a resort ranch that offers outstanding scenery and wonderful skiing opportunities. Aspen Lodge provides a unique environment for the winter enthusiast. Away from the hustle and bustle of the big ski resorts, this small, uncrowded resort is a masterpiece of amenities. The newly constructed lodge, over 30,000 square feet, is the largest log structure in Colorado. It features 36 guest rooms, massive moss rock fireplaces, exquisite meeting rooms, and a lobby that will take your breath away. There are also comfortably appointed cabins that are cozy, warm, and spaciously designed, making them perfect for couples and families. Featuring 15 kilometers of cross-country trails, with many acres of untracked trails in Rocky Mountain National Park, Aspen Lodge at Estes Park is suited for both beginner and expert. Their complete rental center and available instruction can help the beginner quickly advance to high comfort levels in days.

Address: 6120 Highway 7-K, Estes Park, Colorado 80517
Telephone: (303) 586-8133, (800) 332-MTNS (6867); fax: (303) 586-8133, ext. 403
Airport: Denver
Location: 65 miles northwest of Denver off Highway 25, 7 miles south of Estes Park
Memberships: Colorado Dude and Guest Ranch Association, Cross-Country Ski Area Association
Awards: Mobil 3 Star, AAA 3 Diamond
Medical: Full hospital, 7 miles
Conference: 150, with excellent conference facilities; seven meeting rooms, some with fireplaces, all with windows and porches with superb views to Longs Peak
Guest Capacity: 150
Accommodations: The lodge features several hospitality suites and can accommodate up to 150 guests. Choose from 36 beautiful lodge rooms or 20 multiroom cabins with porches. Each is designed with comfort in mind. No matter which accommodations you choose, their rustic yet elegant motif ensures a pleasurable stay.
Rates: • $-$$. À la carte. Special group and holiday packages. Snowmobiles, sleigh rides, and horseback riding extra. Plan based on double occupancy. Rentals extra; special Christmas package available.
Credit Cards: Visa, MasterCard, American Express, Diners Club, Discover
Season: Year-round
Activities: Cross-country skiing with rentals and instruction available. The ranch caters primarily to backcountry skiing. If you are looking for tracked trails, this is not the ranch for you. Intermediate and expert skiers will enjoy guided tours to Wild Basin of Rocky Mountain National Park. There are no set tracks or skating trails. Romantic sleigh rides both day and evening, snowmobile tours, ice skating, tobogganing, racquetball, sauna, hot tub, weight and exercise room in sports center.
Children's Programs: On request. Baby-sitting available.
Dining: The Dining Lodge looks out to Long's Peak. It offers meals ranging from traditional western to gourmet continental, served in the award-winning casual dining room without the restriction of rigid meal times. Count on a varied menu, prepared with imagination and dedicated to your satisfaction. Children's menu available. Breakfast buffets ensure that everyone has plenty to eat before hitting the trails.
Entertainment: No regularly scheduled entertainment. Special Christmas and Easter programs. Children enjoy sleigh rides.
Summary: Winter ranch resort with magnificent 30,000-square-foot lodge. Ideal for conferences, groups, and family retreats. Handicapped facilities and access.

See color photo, page 197

C Lazy U Ranch
Granby, Colorado

On 2,000 acres in the heart of the Colorado high country, the C Lazy U Ranch offers an outstanding winter vacation program and a fully supervised children's program all season long. Knicker Knickerland, a unique winter playground for children (adults may enter if accompanied by a child), provides for hours of outdoor fun. Cross-country skiing at the ranch is a never-to-be-forgotten experience. Of note, too, is the wonderful Christmas and New Year's celebration each year. If you can make a reservation, you and your family will have the old-fashioned Christmas you have always dreamed about. The holiday spirit comes alive when Santa arrives in his red horse-drawn sleigh. Then everyone enjoys a magnificent turkey dinner. No matter when you go, you will find a warm and caring staff and miles of skiing trails. Ski touring is the specialty and can be enjoyed by all members of the family. All tours are gauged to the level of the individual. Both beginner and advanced skiers will find challenging terrain. For the adventurous, there are usually miles of untracked powder in the backcountry areas. Full instruction and guide service are included. Over 25 kilometers of machine-groomed trails meander through the property.

Address: P.O. Box 379 K, Granby, Colorado 80446
Telephone: (303) 887-3344; fax: (303) 887-3917
Airport: Denver
Train: Granby
Location: 6 miles northwest of Granby, off Highway 125; 90 miles west of Denver
Memberships: Cross-Country Ski Association
Awards: Mobil 5 Star, AAA 5 Diamond
Medical: Granby Medical Clinic, 6 miles
Conference: 65
Guest Capacity: 40-90
Accommodations: Eighteen fully insulated, comfortable units. Suites vary from one- to three-room family units with baths and carpeting. Some have fireplaces and Jacuzzi bathtubs. Daily fresh fruit; fireplace restocked every day. Hair dryers, nightly turn-down, bathrobes, and coffee makers with everything you need.
Rates: • $$$-$$$$. American Plan. Everything but the bar tab and trap shooting is included. Substantial children's discount January to March.
Credit Cards: None. Personal checks accepted.
Season: Mid-December through March
Winter Activities: Fifteen kilometers of groomed trails for ski skating; 25 kilometers of groomed trails for ski tracking. Ice skating, sledding, inner tubing, horse-drawn sleigh rides, and trap shooting. Full indoor luxurious health spa with whirlpool and sauna. New championship racquetball court. Downhill skiing nearby at Silver Creek and Winter Park, transportation provided. All ski equipment, skates, and racquetball provided. Fully equipped exercise room with fitness machines in the patio house sports center.
Children's Programs: Premier full children's program all winter long.
Dining: Excellent cuisine, including homemade corn chowder or beef barley soup, rack of lamb, chicken Jerusalem, orange roughy, ice cream pie. Full service bar. Extensive wine list.
Entertainment: Christmas and New Year's programs. Game room, country-western singing, ice skating party with bonfire and schnapps, weekly night cross-country skiing along a torch-lit trail to the awaiting bonfire and goodies.
Summary: World-class, year-round destination ranch. Excellent Christmas program. Superb children's program morning, noon, and night. Parents and kids love it. Best for families and couples. Full winter activities. Spanish, French, and German spoken.

See color photos, page 200

The Home Ranch
Clark, Colorado

The Home Ranch is one of the premier ranch cross-country skiing havens in North America. Host-owner Ken Jones and his wife, Cile, along with a very competent and friendly staff, combine the best of two worlds—rustic elegance and winter adventure. Here, guests from around the world gather to enjoy what the Home Ranch has to offer. In the beautiful Elk River valley near the small town of Clark, not far from Steamboat Springs, this ranch provides a gracious combination of western warmth and lively outdoor activity. The ski trails that radiate from the property give skiers varied terrain, rolling valleys, and glistening forests. If that is not enough, a short drive to Steamboat will put you on downhill slopes that will challenge even the most advanced skier.

Address: P.O. Box 822 K, Clark, Colorado 80428
Telephone: (800) 223-7094, (303) 879-1780; fax: (303) 879-1795
Airport: Steamboat Springs and Hayden
Location: 18 miles north of Steamboat Springs
Memberships: Dude Ranchers' Association, Colorado Cross-Country Ski Association, Relais and Chateaux, Colorado Dude and Guest Ranch Association
Awards: Mobil 4 Star
Medical: Routt Memorial Hospital
Conference: 30
Guest Capacity: 40
Accommodations: Guests stay in seven secluded cabins and six beautiful lodge rooms furnished with antiques, Indian rugs, original artwork, down comforters, and robes. Each cabin has its own wood stove and a private enclosed outdoor whirlpool. Large families may elect to stay in the 2,500-square-foot, hand-hewn, spacious, and beautifully trimmed log cabin.
Rates: • \$\$\$-\$\$\$\$. American Plan.
Credit Cards: Visa, MasterCard, American Express
Season: Late December to early April
Activities: This ranch offers more than 50 kilometers of tracked trails throughout the valley, 20 kilometers of which are groomed for telemark practice. The instructor-guides are qualified to teach all levels of cross-country skiing. One of the more popular excursions is lunch at the lamasery. Guests ski or take the sleigh about 1 mile up to the mountain cabin, have a lunch of gourmet western fare, and return to the main lodge. Heated outdoor swimming, snowshoeing, and sauna. Equipment is available for both adults and children. Downhill skiing and hot air balloon rides at Steamboat.
Children's Programs: Arts and crafts. During the winter there usually are not many children here. Children under 3 not allowed.
Dining: Excellent meals with many Home Ranch specialties, such as breast of duck, fresh fish, filet mignon, European dishes, praline cheesecake. BYO wine and liquor (ranch will pick up with advance notice).
Entertainment: Well-stocked library, grand piano, recreation hall, Home Ranch band "The Rocking V Wranglers" perform once a week. Ask Ken about his "meanwhile back at the ranch album."
Summary: One of the prettiest ranches in North America. Great for people who like to ski hard and eat well and for those who don't like to ski—that's O.K. too. Famous ski town of Steamboat Springs nearby. French spoken.

See color photo, page 203

Fryingpan River Ranch
Meredith, Colorado

Looking for a winter getaway in the Colorado Rockies with thousands of acres of untracked snow, beautiful white-studded pine trees, and old-fashioned mountain hospitality? Welcome to the Fryingpan River Ranch. Located about one hour and fifteen minutes from Aspen, the ranch is a haven for singles, couples, and families who wish to experience peace and solitude, coupled with all the trappings that go with romantic winter splendor. What makes this ranch unique is that it is on the 10th Mountain Hut and Trail System, a 300-mile backcountry network of trails linking the wilderness surrounding Aspen, Vail, and Leadville. This trail system was fashioned after the European Haute Route system and is maintained by volunteers of the 10 Mountain Trail Association. They call this hut-to-hut skiing, and for many, the ranch is a one- or two-night stopover. Others prefer to make the Fryingpan River Ranch their home base and venture out each day exploring remote valleys and tree-lined mountains. Skiers and nonskiers alike will enjoy the warmth and kind hospitality that Jim and his staff share with those who visit them.

Address: 32042 Fryingpan Road, Drawer K, Meredith, Colorado 81642
Telephone: (303) 927-3570; fax: (303) 927-9943 (call first)
Airport: Aspen or Denver
Location: 31 miles up the Fryingpan River from Basalt, Colorado; 1¼ hours from Aspen
Memberships: Dude Ranchers' Association, Cross-Country Ski Association, Colorado Dude and Guest Ranch Association
Awards: Orvis-Endorsed Lodge
Medical: Aspen or Glenwood Springs, 50 miles
Conference: 25
Guest Capacity: 25
Accommodations: Four cabins and two two-bedroom lodge guest rooms, each with private baths and decorated in a cozy country motif. The spirit of winter and Christmas comes alive in the main lodge. A fire is always burning.
Rates: • $$-$$$. American Plan. No minimum stay. Snowmobiles extra.
Credit Cards: Visa, MasterCard. Personal checks and traveler's checks accepted.
Season: Year-round
Activities: There are a variety of winter activities. Expert cross-country skiers will find unlimited skiing opportunities. The ranch will arrange for guides. Instruction is available for both beginner and intermediate skiers. Many like snowshoeing on the historic Colorado Midland Railroad grade. Ice skating and snowmobiling. Equipment and snowmobiles can be arranged with advance notice. Diehard anglers, be sure to talk with Jim about his winter fly-fishing program.
Children's Programs: Children are welcome, but there are no organized children's programs.
Dining: The ranch is getting quite a reputation for its cuisine. All meals have a western flair and are prepared in a healthful way. Lunch is served in the lodge or on the trail. Ask about lunch al fresco at Sellers Meadow. Dinner may be wild turkey, beef, or lamb accompanied by wild rice and homemade bread. Often elk or venison is served. Wine available. Open to the public. BYOB.
Entertainment: Most of the guests are pretty well worn out at the end of a full day of skiing and a wonderful dinner. Some, though, will read by the fire (there is a good selection of books), watch a movie from the video library, or gaze at the heavens from the outdoor hot tub.
Summary: Historic guest ranch located on the 10th Mountain Hut and Trail System. Great for those who enjoy backcountry skiing and for those who simply want to get away from it all in the middle of winter. Ask about the Christmas week and Jim's winter fly-fishing program. German spoken. (Author's note: While exhilarating and beautiful, backcountry skiing is not for everyone. You should be in reasonably good physical shape and enjoy the challenges of knee-deep untracked powder.)

See color photos, pages 204-205

Latigo Ranch
Kremmling, Colorado

Cross-country skiers who keep returning to Latigo Ranch are drawn by the relaxed atmosphere, spectacular scenery, superb cuisine, and warm hospitality of the owners. Latigo is tucked on the side of Kasdorf Mountain in a corner of Arapaho and Routt national forests. With a 100-mile panorama of the Continental Divide and a quarter of a million acres of national forest bordering it, Latigo Ranch offers the recreational skier a variety of scenery and skiing. Latigo machine grooms and packs 35 kilometers of track and skating lanes through meadows and pine and aspen forests. The trails are ideal for the beginner as well as the advanced skier. There is also unlimited backcountry and telemark skiing for the more adventurous. Since the ranch lies at 9,000 feet on top of Colorado's Gore Range, snow conditions are ideal. Most of the winter, several feet of dry powder make it just perfect for all kinds of winter activities. Hosts Kathie Yost and Lisa George have both been schoolteachers (music and English). Randy George has a degree in engineering and an M.B.A. Jim Yost has a Ph.D in anthropology and has taught anthropology and linguistics at the University of Colorado. A stay at Latigo is not only a recreational heaven but also a stimulating intellectual experience. Above all, Latigo offers a low-key and relaxing ambience. People leave here feeling like they have been with family at their private winter retreat.

Address: Box 237, Drawer K, Kremmling, Colorado 80459
Telephone: (800) 227-9655, (303) 724-9008; fax: (303) 724-9009 (call before sending)
Airport: Steamboat Springs in Hayden, Stapleton International in Denver
Train: Amtrak to Granby
Location: 16 miles northwest of Kremmling, 55 miles southeast of Steamboat Springs, 130 miles west of Denver. Ranch will send detailed map.
Memberships: Colorado Cross-Country Ski Association, Dude Ranchers' Association
Medical: Kremmling Memorial Hospital, 16 miles
Conference: 35 if staying overnight
Guest Capacity: 35
Accommodations: Three log duplex cabins, three bedrooms on each side with sitting room, electric heat, and wood-burning stove. A four-plex consists of four single bedrooms with two queen beds and two with double beds.
Rates: • $-$$. American Plan. Group rates available.
Credit Cards: Visa, MasterCard, American Express
Season: Mid-December to early April. Open Christmas.
Activities: The main activity is cross-country skiing, and you can do as much as you wish. Daily lessons are provided for beginner and advanced skiers on both cross-country and telemark technique. Be sure to ask Randy or Jim about their packed telemark slope and moonlight fondue ski tours. Tubing and sledding are also enjoyed by many. Bring your own ski gear, or rentals are available enroute to Latigo.
Children's Programs: No special program. Children's lessons available. Baby-sitting by prior arrangement. Talk to Kathy about the options for your children.
Dining: Full breakfast. You order what you want. Hot lunch (sack lunch by arrangement), family-style dinner. Can cater to special diets. BYOB.
Entertainment: VHS player available, pool table, Ping-Pong and foosball. Guests enjoy lively discussions.
Summary: The Latigo winter experience is best for those who appreciate the majesty of the mountains and value the solitude and serenity of this remote location. After an invigorating day of exercise, skiers can soothe tired muscles in the whirlpool, unwind with a game of pool, or relax with a book in front of a fireplace. Ask about Jim's movie on Ecuador, *Nomads of the Rain Forest*. Spanish spoken.

See color photos, page 208

Peaceful Valley Lodge and Ranch Resort
Lyons, Colorado

The Boehm family arrived in the valley in 1953 and began building toward their dream of a ski lodge for winter recreation and a ranch for promoting the beauty of the Rockies in the summer. While the ranch hosts many families during the winter months, many conference groups come here as well. Guests can choose from a variety of winter activities, including snow coach tours, cross-country skiing, horse-drawn sleigh rides, a trip to nearby Rocky Mountain National Park or nearby downhill skiing, or just relaxing in front of the fire or enjoying the indoor sauna and whirlpool. Advanced cross-country skiers may be shuttled into the depths of the Roosevelt National forest, where unbroken powder skiing is at its best. Winter in the Rockies is not complete without experiencing a traditional horse-drawn sleigh ride. The Boehms' horse-drawn sleigh rides are wonderful. For the family or a larger group, there is a sleigh drawn by a team of Belgians. The combined Western hospitality and European charm of the Boehm family and the commitment of both owners and staff to personal attention assure guests of a most memorable winter vacation.

Address: Star Route, Box 2811 K, Lyons, Colorado 80540
Telephone: (303) 747-2881, (800) 95-LODGE (955-6343 for reservations only); fax: (303) 747-2167
Airport: Stapleton International in Denver
Train: Denver, shuttle service available
Location: 60 miles northwest of Denver on Highway 72
Memberships: Cross-Country Ski Areas Association, Dude Ranchers' Association, Colorado Cross-Country Ski Association, Colorado Dude and Guest Ranch Association
Awards: AAA 3 Diamond, Mobil 3 Star
Medical: Longmont Community Hospital
Conference: 80; full conference facilities. Extensive conference brochure available on request.
Guest Capacity: Winter, 80
Accommodations: Accommodations at the lodge include cozy lodge rooms, modern chalet rooms, and comfortable cabins with fireplaces, some with hot tubs. Deluxe rooms with Jacuzzi tubs. Coin-operated laundry machines.
Rates: • $$-$$$. Includes lodging and three meals. Children's, conference, and bed and breakfast rates available. No minimum stay.
Credit Cards: Visa, MasterCard, American Express, Diners Club, Discover
Season: Early December through April. Lodge open year-round. Open all holidays.
Activities: Cross-country skiers are on their own. There are no groomed trails; however, there are miles of cross-country wilderness skiing opportunities. Most guests who come enjoy being on their own. Beginners and intermediate skiers will find the trails from Peaceful Valley to the national forest excellent for cross-country skiing. Downhill skiing and cross-country lessons at nearby Eldora, 24 miles away, with groomed cross-country ski trails. Shuttle is available. Full indoor pool and spa facilities.
Children's Programs: Children are welcome, but there is no children's program available in winter.
Dining: Large, home-cooked, family-style meals are served in the dining rooms with a great view of the mountains. Beer, wine and liquor available. Ask about the wonderful fondue dinner at New Year's Eve.
Entertainment: Game room, shuffleboard, swimming pool, sauna, whirlpool, and ski movies. Christmas is especially festive at Peaceful Valley.
Summary: Excellent winter ranch resort for conference groups, families, and couples. Festive holiday package available. Backcountry cross-country skiing for independent skiers who don't need instructor and/or guides. The Boehms blend western culture, European charm, and southern hospitality. Winter video available.

See color photos, pages 214-215

Vista Verde Guest and Ski Touring Ranch
Steamboat Springs, Colorado

With blue Colorado sky overhead and four feet of powdery snow on the ground, this secluded ranch looks like Vista Blanca and captivated new owners John and Suzanne Munn. Following their purchase in 1991, they have continued to develop Vista Verde into a top-notch Nordic center. There are over 30 kilometers of groomed trails with double tracks and skating lanes, unlimited telemark and backcountry opportunities in the surrounding national forest, professional instruction, complimentary guided ski tours, and first-class rental equipment. The characteristics of the summer guest ranch carry over with a limited number of guests, handsomely furnished cozy log cabins, fine dining, and a wide variety of activities, in addition to cross-country skiing. It's both a working ranch where you can help feed the animals and a relaxing ranch, whether soaking in the indoor and outdoor hot tubs or simply reading by the fire. Holidays are traditional and special with horse-drawn sleighs and caroling. Winter at Vista Verde is a happy, heartwarming time and brings exhilarating outdoor winter fun. If great food, winter romance, and lots of outdoor winter fun is what you are looking for, better give Vista Verde a call.

Address: P.O. Box 465K, Steamboat Springs, Colorado 80477
Telephone: (800) 526-7433, (303) 879-3858; fax: (303) 879-1413
Airport: Special winter service to Yampa Valley Regional Airport (American, Northwest, United) or direct service from Denver into Steamboat Springs (Continental Express)
Train: Amtrak to Granby, Colorado
Location: 25 miles north of Steamboat Springs
Memberships: Cross-Country Ski Areas of America, Professional Ski Instructors of America, Colorado Dude and Guest Ranch Association, Dude Ranchers' Association
Medical: Steamboat Springs Hospital
Conference: 25, September through May; meeting brochure available
Guest Capacity: 35
Accommodations: Authentic log cabins are nestled among the aspens and pines overlooking the snow-covered meadows and forest. Newly furnished, they include cast-iron wood stoves, full baths, down comforters, antiques and artwork. New lodge rooms offer splendid views.
Rate: $$-$$$. American Plan. Children's, post-holiday, and package rates available. Ski rental, snowmobiling, dog-sledding, and ice-climbing extra. Minimum stays (call for details).
Credit Cards: None. Personal checks or traveler's checks accepted.
Season: Christmas to mid-March
Activities: Ski instructors meet each morning at breakfast to organize activities with guests. Many like to go off and ski on their own. A good number enjoy being guided. Variety of on- and off-ranch skiing, snowshoeing, sleigh rides, horseback riding, ski-in lunches at the old homestead cabin, moonlight skiing, dog-sledding, ice-climbing, and off-ranch snowmobiling. Spa building with indoor and outdoor hot tubs, sauna, exercise equipment. Masseur available. Daily transportation provided to the nearby Steamboat Ski Area for downhill diehards.
Children's Programs: Other than at the holidays there are few children—they are in school. Fun in the snow activities at the sledding hill, snow cave, and igloo, feeding the animals, and indoor games in the Hole-in-the-Wall hangout.
Dining: Dining is a major part of Vista Verde's winter experience. Candlelight dinners overlooking the snow-laden meadows, pack lunches for backcountry skiers, and hearty, scrumptious winter breakfasts. Special diets catered to. Beer and wine available.
Entertainment: Occasional light folk music, fireside chats with local personalities, occasional dancing. Moon and lantern evening skiing. Holiday program.
Summary: A real romantic winter getaway. Candlelight dining, great food, and lots of snow. Perfect for honeymoons and couples who savor warmth, good news, and lots of outdoor winter activities.

See color photos, page 222

Skyline Guest Ranch
Telluride, Colorado

Do you yearn for a classic ski lodge, where you can sit around the potbelly stove, sip hot cider, and eat freshly made cookies after a fabulous day of skiing? You will find that experience at Skyline Guest Ranch. The beauty of the mountains and the warmth of the Farny family will set you aglow. Skyline Guest Ranch is just 3 miles from the Telluride Ski Resort, where you will find incredible terrain for alpine and Nordic skiing. The resort has 10 lifts, one of which is used for Nordic access to the mountaintop, where they have groomed and set 30 kilometers of trails. If one wishes to ski at the ranch, there are 5 kilometers of set track and marked trails for the backcountry skier. A guide may be hired for skiing back to the ranch on fresh, untracked powder from the ski area. Skyline is noted for its spectacular setting: you can see three 14,000-foot peaks from the front porch. Skyline feels secluded enough, yet it is only eight miles from the wonderful historic mining ski town of Telluride, 15 minutes away.

Address: Box 67 K, Telluride, Colorado 81435
Telephone: (303) 728-3757; fax: (303) 728-6728
Airport: Telluride
Location: 8 miles from Telluride
Memberships: Dude Ranchers' Association, Colorado Dude and Guest Ranch Association
Medical: Telluride Medical Center, 8 miles
Conference: 35
Guest Capacity: 35
Accommodations: Each of the ten lodge rooms has its own comfortable log bed with down comforter and sheepskin bed pad, its own thermostat control, and a private bath. Attached to the lodge is a log addition with two apartments equipped with kitchenettes. There are four housekeeping cabins, each with a kitchen for those who wish to have their home away from home. They can accommodate from two to six skiers. Suntan lotion and lip gloss provided. No smoking in any buildings.
Rates: • \$-\$\$. European Plan. Breakfast included.
Credit Cards: Visa, MasterCard, American Express
Season: Early December to early April. Open Christmas.
Activities: Alpine and Nordic skiing, machine-groomed single-track trails (6 km). Cross-country equipment available, and instruction is available with advance notice. Snowmobiling up to old mining ghost town can be arranged (extra). Snowshoeing (BYO). Small retail store. Wonderful outdoor hot tub and sauna available.
Children's Programs: None, but children are welcome. Excellent ski program at Telluride ski area for kids. Cribs and high-chairs available.
Dining: The kitchen cooks a hearty skier's breakfast with a special each morning. You are on your own for lunch; however, there are wonderful après ski delicacies and hot cider. Dinners are prepared nightly for guests and served family-style.
Entertainment: Cozy evening fires at the ranch and local entertainment in Telluride. Be sure to see Mountain Splendor, a multi-image slide show.
Summary: Small and friendly classic ski lodge/ranch with excellent food and hospitality close to the famous ski town of Telluride. Skyline is a marvelous base camp for a host of winter fun in and around Telluride. Incredible setting surrounded by 14,000-foot mountain peaks and lots of sunshine and mountain joy. Great for both cross-country and downhill skiing.

See color photos, pages 220-221

Wapiti Meadow Ranch
Cascade, Idaho

Wapiti Meadow Ranch is a remote wilderness getaway owned and operated by Diana Haynes, a former Virginian who combine her loves of cooking, entertaining, and antiques, and her partner Barry Bryant, a native of Idaho with all the essential outdoor skills. Together they share their adult-oriented backcountry paradise with those who wish to really get away from it all, enjoy good food, a pristine winter wonderland, and stimulating conversations. Wapiti (Indian for elk), offers more than just a cross-country skiing experience. Perhaps most of all, it provides the wilderness launching pad for numerous winter and summer activities. Here you may do it all—and many do from sunrise to sunset. Or you can do nothing—but rest, recharge, and savor romantic winter solitude, 60 miles from the nearest town, deep in the mountains.

Address: H.C. 72 K, Cascade, Idaho 83611
Telephone: (208) 382-4336 year-round (radio phone), (208) 382-3217 (for reservations or to leave messages November-May)
Airport: Boise, Idaho
Location: 60 air miles east of McCall, Idaho, in the heart of the Salmon River Mountains.
Memberships: Dude Ranchers' Association, Cross-Country Ski Areas Association, Idaho Outfitters and Guides Association, Idaho Conservation League, Idaho Guest and Dude Ranch Association
Medical: McCall Memorial Hospital, 60 miles; Life Flight from Boise
Conference: 15
Guest Capacity: 15
Accommodations: Three two-bedroom cabins, one one-bedroom cabin, each with living room, bath, and kitchen (for coffee and snacks). All have wood stoves, baseboard heat, and views from the windows of foraging elk. Three comfortable lodge rooms share a bath. Twin, double, and queen rooms available.
Rates: $-$$. Group rates available. Three-, four-, and seven-night packages include four-by-four or ski plane transportation from Boise or Cascade/McCall area.
Credit Cards: None. Cash or personal checks accepted.
Season: Year-round
Activities: Skiing from your door through meadows and timbered flats surrounded by 8,000-foot peaks and ridges, bordering beautiful Johnson Creek, a Salmon River system tributary, on set track, groomed trail, and powder. With 20 kilometers of set track, 70 kilometers of tilled and groomed trails, and unlimited backcountry powder, there are endless opportunities for beginner and advanced cross-country skiers to experience the sounds of wilderness in winter. Snowshoe mountain climbing (equipment provided) where "skis don't want to go." Wildlife viewing at ranch and "safaris" to elk and deer wintering ranges. Ski rentals available in Boise and McCall (extra). Lessons available by prior arrangement (extra). Summer activities in season (see Guest and Resort Ranches).
Children's Programs: None, atmosphere more suited to adults. No child care available.
Dining: "Hearty gourmet" cuisine. Diana uses all of her fine china and silver at every meal to compliment the antique-filled lodge dining room. Trailside barbecue lunches or homemade soup/sandwich/salad midday dining at the lodge.
Entertainment: Watching the elk and horses mingle in the meadows, enjoying the antics of the ranch dogs in the snow, hot tub stargazing, fireside visiting and relaxing. The extensive and varied ranch library, which is dispersed among the cabins and the lodge, is at every guest's fingertips. Board games and jigsaw puzzles abound.
Summary: A really remote, small, intimate wilderness retreat for those who appreciate nature's beauty. Stimulating conversations, fine food, and winter country charm and romance. Their delightful, 23-page brochure tells it all!

See color photos, page 237

Lone Mountain Ranch
Big Sky, Montana

Lone Mountain Ranch is a wonderful destination for vacationing Nordic skiers. Early each week, the Schaaps host wine and cheese party to welcome guests. Lone Mountain Ranch offers a variety of skiing opportunities right from each cabin's doorstep. The double-wide, machine-tilled, and tracked trail system winds 75 kilometers through meadows, across ridges, and up deep Rocky Mountain valleys. In addition, miles of ungroomed trails lead guests to spots where they can ski and carve telemark turns in untracked powder. Every effort has been made to design a trail system to please every level of skier. Many of the guests participate in optional all-day guided ski trips into the backcountry of Yellowstone or the Spanish Peaks surrounding the ranch. All trips are led by guides who are knowledgeable about skiing, the winter environment, and the area's natural history. One of the more popular trips leads skiers to the interior of Yellowstone by snow coach. Guests then disembark for backcountry skiing through the geyser basins, viewing wintering elk and grazing buffalo. The ranch recommends that all beginners take lessons from the ranch's professionally certified instructors to help develop the skills needed to enjoy this lifetime.

Address: P.O. Box 160069 K, Big Sky, Montana 59716
Telephone: (406) 995-4644; fax: (406) 995-4670
Airport: Bozeman
Location: 40 miles south of Bozeman
Memberships: Cross-Country Ski Area Association, Professional Ski Instructors of America (PSIA), Dude Ranchers' Association
Awards: 1991 *Snow Country* Magazine Award
Medical: Bozeman Deaconess Hospital
Conference: 50
Guest Capacity: 60
Accommodations: Twenty-three fully insulated one- and two-bedroom cabins with comfortable beds, electric heat, modern bathrooms with tub/shower, and rock fireplace or Franklin stove.
Rates: • $$-$$$. American Plan. Children's rates.
Credit Cards: Visa, MasterCard, Discover
Season: Early December to early April
Activities: Seventy-five kilometers of tilled and tracked cross-country trails through meadows, across ridges, and up valleys. Miles of ungroomed trails. Retail and rental cross-country shop. Lessons, naturalist guide, and trips to Yellowstone backcountry. Outdoor whirlpool. Nightly sleigh rides open to the public.
Children's Programs: Best for children old enough to ski. Toddlers not advised. Full children's program in summer.
Dining: Tremendous log dining room open to the public. The food has received rave reviews. Guests enjoy an old-fashioned sleigh ride to dinner and the famous on-the-snow trail buffet lunch. Everyone's favorite is the North Fork cabin dinner. A 20-minute sleigh ride up to this beautiful cabin is just the beginning. The cabin is lit by kerosene lanterns, and food is cooked on a magnificent 100-year-old wood cookstove. Guests enjoy a prime rib dinner and musical entertainment before their ride back to the ranch. The weekly trail buffet lunch is presented on a huge snow bar, with fare ranging from salmon pâté and other appetizers to roast beef or turkey, boiled shrimp, cheese, fresh fruits and vegetables, homemade breads, and a huge variety of desserts, hot beverages, and beer and wine. Guests ski to a scenic spot on the trail system to enjoy this feast.
Entertainment: Throughout the winter there are many evening programs, including naturalist presentations on grizzly bears and the greater Yellowstone ecosystem. Weekly musical programs.
Summary: World-class cross-country skiing with dependable snow and meticulously groomed trails. Sleigh rides and dining room open to the public. Winter guided fly-fishing trips. Big Sky Ski Resort for downhill skiing. Winter video available. Convenient airline connections.

See color photos, page 246

Woodside Ranch
Mauston, Wisconsin

Woodside Ranch is a year-round operation. The winter season runs from December to mid-March. During this time, Woodside takes only weekend guests, except during the Christmas and Easter holidays, when the ranch is open during the week. Woodside is run by Lucille Nichols and her nephews, Ray and Rick Feldmann. Unlike other ski areas in southern Wisconsin, guests here can ski from their cabins. There are five main loop trails and several advanced trails with names like Half Way Hut and Prairie View Run. Beginners will enjoy loops one and two and Coyote Run. There are two warming huts on the trail system, both with fireplaces, great for having a picnic lunch. For backcountry skiing, there are more than 700 acres of mixed hardwood and pine forests.

Address: Highway 82, Box K, Mauston, Wisconsin 53948
Telephone: (608) 847-4275, (800) 626-4275
Airport: Madison, Wisconsin; small private airport in Mauston-New Lisbon, 11 miles
Train: Wisconsin Dells, 20 miles away; Greyhound bus to Mauston, 4 miles
Location: 5 miles each of Mauston, 20 miles northwest of Wisconsin Dells, 220 miles north of Chicago, 200 miles south of Minneapolis on Interstate 90/94
Memberships: Wisconsin Innkeepers Association
Medical: Hess Memorial Hospital, 6 miles
Conference: 60
Guest Capacity: 125
Accommodations: Twenty one-, two-, and three-bedroom log cabins and white-sided cottages behind the main lodge, with names like Abe Lincoln, Fireside, Last Frontier, and Old 99. All have fireplaces and thermostatically controlled heat, double beds, and bunk beds. The main lodge has 14 rooms that sleep two to four people with private baths.
Rates: $-$$. American Plan. Rates vary depending on the plan you choose. Children's rates available. Three-day, two-night weekend stays available. Pet owners should ask about pet rates.
Credit Cards: Visa, MasterCard
Season: December to March for skiing, weekends only.
Activities: There are more than 12 miles of marked ski trails, all machine groomed for single set track. There are also 5 miles of sleigh ride trails. A 1,000-foot downhill slope with a rope tow is available for beginner skiers and telemarkers. Night skiing is offered. Free downhill and cross-country ski instruction. Experts and beginners will find the cross-country terrain challenging. All skiing facilities are open to the public. Downhill and cross-country equipment can be rented at Woodside. Horse-drawn sleigh rides, horseback riding, ice skating, and tubing. Large steam sauna. Ask about the new sport called snow runners.
Children's Programs: Pony rides in ring for children of all ages. Supervised kinder school. Christmas week games for kids.
Dining: Meals are served family-style at long tables. Filling ranch breakfasts, homemade soups and chili, ski lunch buffet, roast beef and roast chicken. Occasionally buffalo is served. Full bar.
Entertainment: Trading Post lounge with hot buttered rum, hot cider, and hot chocolate. The Round Up Room, which is part of the ranch Trading Post, has arcade games, table tennis, ski movies, and Saturday night barn dance with social, line, and square dancing.
Summary: Family-owned and operated ranch for families featuring log cabins with fireplaces. Weekend and holiday cross-country skiing only, beginner downhill skiing, ski-in/ski-out access to cabins, night skiing. Horseback riding, sleigh rides, the Trading Post souvenir shop. Antiques and shopping in small towns of New Lisbon, Adams Friendship, Mauston.

Brooks Lake Lodge
Dubois, Wyoming

History, romance, magnificence: Brooks Lake Lodge captures the spirit and tradition of the Old West. It is a winter Shangri-la high in the Wyoming Rockies. Owned and managed by the Carlsberg and Rigsby families, the lodge is located about 63 miles northeast of Jackson, famous for Les Grand Tetons named by early French explorers. Driving either from the small towns of Dubois or Jackson, Brooks Lake staff will meet you at the trailhead just off Togwotee Pass Highway. Warm smiles and hot cider are just the beginning. From this point, guests are shuttled by snowcoach or snowmobile five miles to the lodge. Some prefer to cross-country ski in. Whatever you decide to do, you are in for the time of your life. Whether you are sitting by one of the blazing fires in the midst of a snowstorm or exploring the magical mountain splendor on a crisp blue sky day, the Brooks Lake Lodge experience is a winter vacation you will never forget. Never!

Address: 458 Brooks Lake Road, Drawer K, Dubois, Wyoming 82513
Telephone: (307) 455-2121; fax: (307) 455-2121 (call first)
Airport: Jackson, 60 miles
Location: 60 miles northeast of Jackson off Highway 287/26, 23 miles west of Dubois off Highway 287/26
Memberships: Dude Ranchers' Association, Wyoming Dude Rancher's Association, Association of Historic Hotels of the Rocky Mountain West
Medical: Jackson, 60 miles
Conference: 26 (overnight); 250 day only
Guest Capacity: 26
Accommodations: Six comfortable lodge rooms with a distinctive motif and exquisite handcrafted lodgepole furnishings. There are also six cabins nestled in the spruce behind the lodge which offer wood-burning stoves, electric heat, and private baths with bathrobes. Several have wonderful old clawfoot bathtubs. The massive log lodge is furnished with wicker, antiques, and handcrafted works by Wyoming artists. No telephones or televisions. There is a separate spa cabin.
Rates: • $$$. American Plan. Snowmobiles and dog-sledding and liquor extra. No minimum stay.
Credit Cards: Visa, MasterCard, American Express
Season: Late December to mid-April. Open for lodging Wednesday through Sunday.
Activities: The lodge is situated in the midst of the awesome Pinnacle formation of the Absaroka Mountains, Brooks Mountain to the west, and the Continental Divide to the north. You may cross-country ski, snowmobile (all guided trips), snowshoe, or with prior arrangement, take a thrilling dog-sled ride. Guests usually use the lodge as a base camp for myriad outdoor adventures. Overnight trips into Yellowstone National Park by snowmobile are available, too. Ask about Sublette Meadow, Bear Cub Pass, Austin Peak, and bighorn sheep.
Children's Programs: None. Kids do have fun. Younger children should be accompanied by a nanny if parents wish to be active outdoors.
Dining: Hearty winter fare. Delicious homemade soups and freshly baked breads. Lots of pasta. Lunches open to the public. Liquor and wine served.
Entertainment: The Diamond G Saloon is a gathering place before and after dinner. At 6:00 p.m. hors d'oeuvres are served. A game of pool, darts, or a video. Evening poetry readings (guests recite their favorite poems, too) and occasional local entertainment.
Summary: Old West beauty, warmth, and mountain splendor. The Brooks Lake Lodge winter experience is magical. Superb accommodations, great food, and terrific hospitality. You will cherish your time here for the rest of your life! Lodging open Wednesday through Sunday. Lunches open to the public. Five-mile trip in winter to lodge on skis, snowmobiles, or snowcat.

See color photos, pages 272-273

Darwin Ranch
Jackson, Wyoming

The skiing at the Darwin Ranch is as varied and challenging as you and your guide want to make it. The emphasis is on getting into the country, enjoying the game, the mountain vistas, the untracked powder, and the company of friends. If you have never skied before, your guide will help you learn along the way. Bacon Ridge, a 10,000-foot mountain immediately to the east of the ranch, lies just outside the wilderness area, permitting snowcat-assisted ascents for practicing those telemark turns. The real luxury of being snowbound is having life on your own terms. The Darwin Ranch is spacious, comfortable, and civilized—and yours to live in as you see fit. The entire ranch is available to groups of six or more who are willing to stay for at least a week. The atmosphere is more like an extended house party than a public ski lodge. They mean it when they say, "We want you to make this oasis in the wilderness your home for a week." So bring your family or a group of friends you would enjoy being snowed-in with, and prepare to slow down and enjoy a unique winter experience high in the Wyoming Rockies.

Address: P.O. Box 511 K, Jackson, Wyoming 83001
Telephone: (307) 733-5588
Airport: Jackson Hole, Wyoming
Location: 30 miles east of Jackson Hole, in the Gros Ventre Range. Talk with Loring about helicopter service to the ranch.
Memberships: Dude Ranchers' Association, Wyoming Dude Rancher's Association
Medical: St. John's Hospital, Jackson Hole, 30 miles
Guest Capacity: 12 (minimum party of 6)
Accommodations: The main lodge was built as a private log home by a diplomatic couple who had endured several winters in Russia during the Second World War. There is a large sitting room with a stone fireplace, an informal bar, a piano, a dining room, and kitchen. There are lots of books and games and a stereo with tape deck. Spacious sleeping accommodations with private bath are available in the loft apartment. The rest are in two other cabins not far from the front door. A rustic sauna is located in its own building near the river a short distance away.
Rates: $$. American Plan.
Credit Cards: None. Cash or personal checks accepted.
Season: Mid-December through early April
Activities: The focus is backcountry skiing and wilderness experiences. Groomed trails are limited. Rental equipment in town. Guide service and instruction are available. Some people enjoy snowshoeing as well. Snowmobile trips are an option. Many people enjoy the outings to two snowed-in elk feeding grounds, both about 15 miles away. Ask Loring about the snowmobile program. The sauna is always available.
Children's Programs: None. The ranch provides a wonderful experience for families. Older children will have a better time.
Dining: If you wish to discuss menus and food preferences before you arrive, the chef will be happy to go over plans with you on the phone. The ranch provids excellent food, both summer and winter, but during the ski season it makes a special effort to turn meals into major events. Repertoire is pretty eclectic, from spicy Thai cuisine to gourmet French. BYOB.
Entertainment: Nothing scheduled on a regular basis, but it's your ranch while you are there, so you can be as creative as you like.
Summary: A house party in the winter wilderness for your own family or friends. Guides and instruction for cross-country skiing. Gourmet food, lots of game, spectacular scenery, and total privacy. Fluent French, Mandarin, Taiwanese and some German spoken.

See color photos, page 281

The Hills Health and Guest Ranch
100-Mile House, British Columbia, Canada

Pat and Juanita Corbett had a vision of creating one of the most extensive cross-country ski complexes in North America. Today, their facility, perched on a hill, is nearly in the center of a maze of trails that wind in all directions. The Hills is part of a communitywide 200-kilometer trail system. The complex has hosted such major Canadian events as the Cariboo Marathon (western Canada's largest, with more than 1,000 skiers), the Canadian Junior Championship, the B.C. Cup Race, the Kahlua Treasure Hunt on skis, the Timex, and the Skiathlon. At the Hills, you can ski hut-to-hut and among other lodge facilities. Pat and Juanita have opened membership at the Hills to the community. With a membership, families can use the indoor pool, two whirlpools, dressing rooms, and saunas. They keep busy at the Hills; they like what they do, and it shows. Their staff is extremely friendly and helpful. Juanita's Kentucky warmth and charm are contagious.

Address: C-26, R.R. 108, Dept. K, 100-Mile House, B.C., Canada V0K 2E0
Telephone: (604) 791-5225; fax: (604) 791-6384
Airport: Williams Lake, British Columbia
Train: 100-Mile House
Location: 8 miles north of 100-Mile House off Highway 97, 50 miles south of Williams Lake, 290 miles north of Vancouver
Memberships: Canada West Ski Areas Association, British Columbia Guest Ranch Association
Medical: 100-Mile House Hospital, 8 miles
Conference: 200; 4,300-square-foot meeting space
Guest Capacity: 114
Accommodations: Twenty chalets (sunrise or sunset views) line the ridge, with a road up the middle. Each has a full kitchen, small living/dining area, color television, upstairs and downstairs bedrooms, porch, and daily maid service. New ten-room lodge.
Rates: • $-$$. European/American packages available. Children's and group rates available.
Credit Cards: Visa, MasterCard
Season: December through March (open Christmas)
Activities: Full cross-country ski program, 200 kilometers of machine-groomed and double-tracked trails, 20 kilometers of skating trails, ski shop with rentals/sales and ski school, sleigh rides, full spa facilities. Winter spa facilities include exercise room, aerobics studio, power walking, weights, massage, facials, pedicures, nutritionist, and personal training.
Children's Programs: Swimming classes (all ages). Baby-sitting available.
Dining: Fully licensed dining room. Superb Swiss chef prepares wonderful meals in the Trails End Dining Room. Weight Watchers spa meals available.
Entertainment: The weekend dinner music is one of the most delightful features of the Corbetts' operation. Several very talented professional musicians are part of the musical family. European wine served.
Summary: Full cross-country ski program with double-tracked trails with full ski shop and instruction. Professional musical entertainment, spa facilities. German, French, and Italian spoken.

Tyax Mountain Lake Resort
Gold Bridge, British Columbia, Canada

At Tyax Resort, winter is a time of reflection and contemplation. The forest, lake, and mountains are covered with snow, often up to four feet deep. On clear nights, you might hear the lonely cry of a timber wolf as you sit in the outside Jacuzzi. During the day you can get away from it all, snowshoe in knee-deep powder, and enjoy crystal clear skies and a virgin timbered winter wonderland. At day's end, return to the luxurious log lodge and warm your feet by the open fireplace. The rooms are warm and spacious, and most overlook Lake Tyaughton. Around the resort, you will find 20 miles of set track and groomed cross-country ski trails. If you want to go farther, there are unlimited miles of trails, some of which will take you above the tree line to virgin alpine meadows. Tyax has guides for mountain touring, as well as for heli-skiing. Snowmobiling to mountain cabins is offered. Cross-country and telemark skis are available for rental at the lodge. Because of its remoteness, there are no lifts. A helicopter will fly you to 8,000-foot mountaintops. You can rent ice skates, snowshoes, toboggans, and snowmobiles. At Tyax you can take a sleigh ride or just relax.

Address: Tyaughton Lake Road, Dept. K. Gold Bridge, B.C., Canada V0K 1P0
Telephone: (604) 238-2221; fax: (604) 238-2528
Airport: Vancouver; direct charter ski plane flights available
Train: British Columbia Rail from Vancouver to Lillooet
Location: About 5 hours north of Vancouver
Memberships: British Columbia Motel and Resort Association
Medical: Lillooet Hospital, 60 miles
Conference: 60
Guest Capacity: 100
Accommodations: Tyax is one of the largest log lodges in western North America and overlooks beautiful Tyaughton Lake. There are 29 rooms on three floors. Each has pine furnishings, twin or queen-size beds, down comforters, and balconies. The lodge also features a winter bar and giant native rock fireplace with built-in Dutch ovens. Outside, a spacious sun deck with whirlpool overlooks the lake. There are also five luxurious lakefront log chalets with full kitchens and fireplaces.
Rates: • $$-$$$$. American Plan. Modified American and European plans available. Special chalet rates. Everything here is à la carte.
Credit Cards: Visa, MasterCard, American Express
Season: January through late April; also Thanksgiving, Christmas, and Easter
Activities: Cross-country ski trails are groomed with single track set. Full instruction available. Guests enjoy lake ice skating and often play hockey and broomball. Two big thrills are heli-skiing and mountain snowmobiling. Bring your own downhill equipment for heli-skiing. There is also ice fishing, tobogganing, snowshoeing, snowmobiling, and horse-drawn sleigh rides. Fitness center with massage and aerobics. Cross-country and ice skating equipment can be rented at store on property.
Children's Programs: No special program. Babysitters available. Nannies encouraged. Tobogganing and ice skating are favorites.
Dining: The restaurant seats 100 guests and has a 30-foot ceiling and a stone fireplace. Looking out the large windows, you see the lake, forest, and mountains. Specialties include rack of lamb, T-bone steak, barbecued salmon, and cheesecake. Extensive wine list, specializing in Australian wines.
Entertainment: Special hot rum drinks in western bar, dance floor with live music, billiard and table tennis room.
Summary: Wonderful "à la carte" wilderness resort, helicopter skiing, snowmobiling, sleigh rides, massage. Convenience store with souvenirs, clothes, and snacks. French and German spoken. Video available on request.

Ranches, Listed Alphabetically

Special Ranch Features

Accessible Only by Boat, Horseback, Helicopter, Plane, or Train
Kachemak Bay Wilderness Lodge, Alaska
Bar Ten Ranch, Arizona
Phantom Ranch, Arizona
Muir Trail Ranch, California
Tall Timber, Colorado
Allison Ranch, Idaho
Shepp Ranch, Idaho
Falcon, Inc., Maine
Klicks' K Bar L Ranch, Montana
Minam Lodge, Oregon
Chilcotin Holidays Guest Ranch, British Columbia, Canada

Adults-Oriented Ranch (some are adults-only, some have adults-only weeks/months)
Grapevine Canyon Ranch, Arizona
Scott Valley Ranch, Arkansas
Coffee Creek Ranch, California
Highland Ranch, California
Howard Creek Ranch, California
7 W Ranch, Colorado
C Lazy U Ranch, Colorado
Colorado Trails Ranch, Colorado
Coulter Lake Ranch, Colorado
Don K Ranch, Colorado
Elk Creek Lodge, Colorado
Forbes Trinchera Ranch, Colorado
Lake Mancos Ranch, Colorado
Lost Valley Ranch, Colorado
Skyline Ranch, Colorado
Waunita Hot Springs Ranch, Colorado
Wilderness Trails Ranch, Colorado
Double JJ Ranch, Michigan
Mountain Sky Guest Ranch, Montanta
Triple Creek Ranch, Montana
The Lodge at Chama, New Mexico
Pinegrove Resort Ranch, New York
Snowbird Mountain Lodge, North Carolina
Garrett Creek Ranch, Texas
Firefly Ranch, Vermont
Woodside Ranch, Wisconsin
Breteche Creek Ranch Retreat, Wyoming
Flying A Ranch, Wyoming
Lazy L & B Ranch, Wyoming
Lozier's Box R Ranch, Wyoming
R Lazy S, Wyoming
Savery Creek Thoroughbred Ranch, Wyoming
Seven D Ranch, Wyoming
T-Cross Ranch, Wyoming
Black Cat Guest Ranch, Alberta, Canada
Cariboo Rose Guest Ranch, British Columbia, Canada

Airstrip (on or near ranch)
Grand Canyon Bar Ten Ranch, Arizona
Kay El Bar Ranch, Arizona
Rancho de los Caballeros, Arizona
Wickenburg Inn, Tennis and Guest Ranch, Arizona
Coffee Creek Ranch, California
Drakesbad Guest Ranch, California
Hunewill Circle H Ranch, California
Spanish Springs Ranch, California
Trinity Mountain Meadow Ranch, California
Elktrout Lodge, Colorado
Everett Ranch, Colorado
4UR Ranch, Colorado
Outdoor Resorts River Ranch, Florida
Allison Ranch, Idaho
Diamond D Ranch, Idaho
Shepp Ranch, Idaho
Falcon, Inc., Maine
Double JJ Ranch, Michigan
Diamond J Ranch, Montana
Hargrave Guest Ranch, Montana
Lazy K Bar Ranch, Montana
Nez Perce Ranch, Montana
Nine Quarter Circle Ranch, Montana
Cottonwood Ranch, Nevada
Western Hills Guest Ranch, Oklahoma
Flying M Ranch, Oregon
Minam Lodge, Oregon
Morrison's Rogue River Lodge, Oregon
Western Dakota Ranch Vacations, South Dakota
Y.O. Ranch, Texas
Hidden Valley Guest Ranch, Washington
Woodside Ranch, Wisconsin
CM Ranch, Wyoming
Darwin Ranch, Wyoming
Flying A Ranch, Wyoming
Lazy L & B Ranch, Wyoming
T-Cross Ranch, Wyoming
Cariboo Rose Guest Ranch, British Columbia, Canada

Elkin Creek Ranch, British Columbia, Canada
Flying U Ranch, British Columbia, Canada
Springhouse Trails Ranch, British Columbia, Canada
Tyax Mountain Lake Resort, British Columbia, Canada

Bring Your Own Horse
The Muleshoe Ranch, Arizona
Price Canyon Ranch, Arizona
White Stallion Ranch, Arizona
Highland Ranch, California
Spanish Springs Ranch, California
Trinity Mountain Meadow Ranch, California
Aspen Canyon Ranch, Colorado
Fryingpan River Ranch, Colorado
McNamara Ranch, Colorado
Rawah Ranch, Colorado
Bar H Bar Ranch, Idaho
Idaho Rocky Mountain Ranch, Idaho
Indian Creek Ranch, Idaho
Double JJ Ranch, Michigan
El Rancho Stevens, Michigan
Bear Mountain Guest Ranch, New Mexico
Cottonwood Ranch, Nevada
Ridin-Hy Ranch, New York
Logging Camp Ranch, North Dakota
Flying M Ranch, Oregon
Flying W Ranch, Pennsylvania
Blue Bell Lodge & Resort, South Dakota
Nemo Guest Ranch, South Dakota
Western Dakota Ranch Vacations, South Dakota
Firefly Ranch, Vermont
Flying L Ranch, Washington
Hidden Valley Guest Ranch, Washington
Woodside Ranch, Wisconsin
Breteche Creek Ranch Retreat, Wyoming
Brooks Lake Lodge, Wyoming
Heart Six Ranch, Wyoming
V-Bar Guest Ranch, Wyoming
Big Bar Guest Ranch, British Columbia, Canada

Buffalo Ranch
Terry Bison Ranch, Wyoming

Cattle Roundups, Cattle Drives
Grapevine Canyon Ranch, Arizona
Hunewill Circle H Ranch, California
Spanish Springs Ranch, California
Coulter Lake Ranch, Colorado
Elk Mountain Ranch, Colorado
Everett Ranch, Colorado
Lost Valley Ranch, Colorado
Vista Verde Guest and Ski Touring Ranch, Colorado
Wilderness Trails Ranch, Colorado
Bar H Bar Ranch, Idaho
Circle Bar Guest Ranch, Montana
Hargrave Guest Ranch, Montana
Schively Ranch, Montana
Sweetgrass Ranch, Montana
Pinegrove Resort Ranch, New York
Cottonwood Ranch, Nevada
Soldier Meadows Ranch, Nevada
Spur Cross Ranch, Nevada
Logging Camp Ranch, North Dakota
Ponderosa Cattle Company and Guest Ranch, Oregon
Western Dakota Ranch Vacations, South Dakota
Y.O. Ranch, Texas
Rockin' R Ranch, Utah
Breteche Creek Ranch Retreat, Wyoming
Brush Creek Ranch, Wyoming
Cheyenne River Ranch, Wyoming
David Ranch, Wyoming
High Island Ranch, Wyoming
Lozier's Box R Ranch, Wyoming
Red Rock Ranch, Wyoming
Elkin Creek Ranch, British Columbia, Canada
Three Bars Ranch, British Columbia, Canada
Top of the World Guest Ranch, British Columbia, Canada

Cross-Country
The Aspen Lodge Ranch Resort, Colorado
C Lazy U Ranch, Colorado
Fryingpan River Ranch, Colorado
The Home Ranch, Colorado
Latigo Ranch, Colorado
Peaceful Valley Lodge and Guest Ranch, Colorado
Skyline Guest Ranch, Colorado
Vista Verde Guest and Ski Touring Ranch, Colorado
Lone Mountain Ranch, Montana
Woodside Ranch, Wisconsin
Brooks Lake Lodge, Wyoming
Darwin Ranch, Wyoming
The Hills Health and Guest Ranch, British Columbia, Canada
Tyax Mountain Lake Resort, British Columbia, Canada

English Riding
Price Canyon Ranch, Arizona
Spanish Springs Ranch, California
C Lazy U Ranch, Colorado
Colorado Trails Ranch, Colorado
The Home Ranch, Colorado
Triple Creek Ranch, Montana
Timberlock, New York
Firefly Ranch, Vermont
Bitterroot Ranch, Wyoming
Savery Creek Thoroughbred Ranch, Wyoming

V-Bar Guest Ranch, Wyoming
Homeplace Guest Ranch, Alberta, Canada

Executive Conference

Grapevine Canyon Ranch, Arizona
Rancho de la Osa, Arizona
Rancho de los Caballeros, Arizona
Tanque Verde Ranch, Arizona
White Stallion Ranch, Arizona
Wickenburg Inn Tennis and Guest Ranch, Arizona
Alisal Guest Ranch, California
Coffee Creek Ranch, California
Highland Ranch, California
Spanish Springs Ranch, California
Aspen Canyon Ranch, Colorado
The Aspen Lodge Ranch Resort, Colorado
C Lazy U Ranch, Colorado
Colorado Trails Ranch, Colorado
Coulter Lake Guest Ranch, Colorado
Deer Valley Ranch, Colorado
Don K Ranch, Colorado
4UR Ranch, Colorado
Forbes Trinchera Ranch, Colorado
Fryingpan River Ranch, Colorado
The Home Ranch, Colorado
Lazy H Ranch, Colorado
Lost Valley Ranch, Colorado
Peaceful Valley Lodge and Guest Ranch, Colorado
Rawah Ranch, Colorado
Sylvan Dale Ranch, Colorado
Tall Timber, Colorado
Vista Verde Guest and Ski Touring Ranch, Colorado
Wind River Ranch, Colorado
Wit's End Guest Ranch and Resort, Colorado
Outdoor River Resort, Florida
Double JJ Ranch, Michigan
Diamond J Ranch, Montana
Flathead Lake Lodge, Montana
Lone Mountain Ranch, Montana
Lost Fork Ranch, Montana
Mountain Sky Guest Ranch, Montana
Nine Quarter Circle Ranch, Montana
Triple Creek Ranch, Montana
West Fork Meadows Ranch, Montana
The Bishop's Lodge, New Mexico
The Lodge at Chama, New Mexico
Vermejo Park Ranch, New Mexico
Hidden Valley Mountainside Resort, New York
Pinegrove Resort Ranch, New York
Roaring Brook Ranch and Tennis Resort, New York
Rocking Horse Ranch, New York
Cataloochee Ranch, North Carolina
Western Hills Guest Ranch, Oklahoma
Flying M Ranch, Oregon
Rock Springs Guest Ranch, Oregon
Dixie Dude Ranch, Texas
Flying L Guest Ranch, Texas
Garrett Creek Ranch, Texas
Lazy Hills Guest Ranch, Texas
Prude Ranch, Texas
Y.O. Ranch, Texas
Reid Ranch, Utah
Rockin' R Ranch, Utah
Flying L Ranch, Washington
Hidden Valley Ranch, Washington
Brooks Lake Lodge, Wyoming
Cody's Ranch Resort, Wyoming
Crescent H Ranch, Wyoming
H F Bar Ranch, Wyoming
Lost Creek Ranch, Wyoming
Paradise Ranch, Wyoming
Terry Bison Ranch, Wyoming
V-Bar Guest Ranch, Wyoming
Black Cat Guest Ranch, Alberta, Canada
Rafter Six Ranch, Alberta, Canada
The Hills Health and Guest Ranch, British Columbia, Canada
Sundance Guest Ranch, British Columbia, Canada
Three Bars Ranch, British Columbia, Canada
Tyax Mountain Lake Resort, British Columbia, Canada

Fly-Fishing

Crystal Creek Lodge, Alaska
Arcularius Ranch, California
Elk Creek Lodge, Colorado
Elktrout Lodge, Colorado
Fryingpan River Ranch, Colorado
Three Rivers Ranch, Idaho
Falcon, Inc., Maine
Big Hole River Outfitters, Montana
Diamond J Ranch, Montana
Eagle Nest Lodge, Montana
Lone Mountain Ranch, Montana
Parade Rest Ranch, Montana
The Lodge at Chama, New Mexico
Vermejo Park Ranch, New Mexico
Morrison's Rogue River Lodge, Oregon
Crescent H Ranch, Wyoming

Foreign Language

Circle Z Ranch, Arizona-Spanish
Rancho de la Osa, Arizona-Spanish
Tanque Verde Ranch, Arizona-Spanish, French, German, Japanese
White Stallion Ranch, Arizona-Spanish, German
Alisal Guest Ranch, California-Spanish, French, German, Italian
Circle Bar B Ranch, California-Spanish
Coffee Creek Ranch, California-Spanish, Dutch, German
Highland Ranch, California-French, Italian

Howard Creek Ranch, California-Italian, Dutch, German
Rankin Ranch, California-Spanish
Spanish Springs Ranch, California-Spanish
C Lazy U Ranch, Colorado-Spanish, French, German
Forbes Trinchera Ranch, Colorado-Spanish
Fryingpan River Ranch, Colorado-German
The Home Ranch, Colorado-French
Latigo Ranch, Colorado-Spanish
Peaceful Valley Lodge and Guest Ranch, Colorado-German
Rawah Ranch, Colorado-Norwegian
Skyline Guest Ranch, Colorado-French, German
Sylvan Dale Ranch, Colorado-Spanish
Wilderness Trails Ranch, Colorado-Spanish, French
Idaho Rocky Mountain Ranch, Idaho-Spanish
Turkey Creek Ranch, Missouri-French
Circle Bar Guest Ranch, Montana-French
Diamond J Ranch, Montana-Spanish
Flathead Lake Lodge, Montana-Interpreters available
Hargrave Guest Ranch, Montana-German
Lone Mountain Ranch, Montana-Multi-lingual
Pine Butte Guest Ranch, Montana-German
West Fork Meadows Ranch, Montana-German
The Bishop's Lodge, New Mexico-Spanish, French, German
Vermejo Park Ranch, New Mexico-Spanish, German
Pinegrove Resort Ranch, New York-Spanish, Portuguese
Rocking Horse Ranch, New York-Spanish, German
Allen Ranch, Oklahoma-Spanish
Baker's Bar M Ranch, Oregon-Spanish
Ponderosa Cattle Company and Guest Ranch, Oregon-French, German, Russian
Dixie Dude Ranch, Texas-Spanish
Lazy Hills Guest Ranch, Texas-Spanish
Prude Ranch, Texas-Spanish
Y.O. Ranch, Texas-Spanish
Reid Ranch, Utah-Spanish
Firefly Ranch, Vermont-German
Bitterroot Ranch, Wyoming-French
Breteche Creek Ranch Retreat, Wyoming-French
Brooks Lake Lodge, Wyoming
Brush Creek Ranch, Wyoming-German
Darwin Ranch, Wyoming-German, Mandarin, Taiwanese, French
Heart Six Ranch, Wyoming-French, German
Lost Creek Ranch, Wyoming-Interpreters Available
Savery Creek Thoroughbred Ranch, Wyoming-Spanish, French
Trail Creek Ranch, Wyoming-French
Homeplace Guest Ranch, Alberta, Canada-German
Rafter Six Ranch, Alberta, Canada-French, German, Japanese
Cariboo Rose Guest Ranch, British Columbia, Canada-German
Elkin Creek Ranch, British Columbia, Canada-German
Flying U Ranch, British Columbia, Canada-German, French, Spanish
The Hills Health and Guest Ranch, British Columbia, Canada-German, French, Dutch, Italian
Springhouse Trails Ranch, British Columbia, Canada-German
Sundance Guest Ranch, British Columbia, Canada-German, French
Tyax Mountain Lake Resort, British Columbia, Canada-French, German
Wells Gray Ranch, British Columbia, Canada-French, German

Handicapped/Wheelchair Accessible
Rancho de los Caballeros, Arizona
Tanque Verde Ranch, Arizona
Coffee Creek Ranch, California
Wind River Ranch, Colorado
Blue Spruce Lodge and Guest Ranch, Montana
Vermejo Park Ranch, New Mexico
Roaring Brook Ranch and Tennis Resort, New York
Terry Bison Ranch, Wyoming

Horse Drives
Sylvan Dale Ranch, Arizona
Spanish Springs Ranch, California
Diamond J Ranch, Montana
Cottonwood Ranch, Nevada
Rock Springs Guest Ranch, Oregon

Hot Springs
Drakesbad Guest Ranch, California
Muir Trail Ranch, California
Deer Valley Ranch, Colorado
4UR Ranch, Colorado
Waunita Hot Springs Ranch, Colorado
Idaho Rocky Mountain Ranch, Idaho
Klicks' K Bar L Ranch, Montana
Soldier Meadows Ranch, Nevada
Baker's Bar M Ranch, Oregon

Large Outdoor Business/Group Barbecues
Rancho de los Caballeros, Arizona
Tanque Verde Ranch, Arizona
Sylvan Dale Ranch, Colorado
Outdoor Resorts River Ranch, Florida
Double JJ Ranch, Michigan
Ponderosa Ranch, Nevada
Roaring Brook Ranch, New York
Rocking Horse Ranch, New York
Allen Ranch, Oklahoma

Flying M Ranch, Oregon
Rock Springs Guest Ranch, Oregon
Flying L Guest Ranch, Texas
Garrett Creek Ranch, Texas
Prude Ranch, Texas
Texas Lil's Diamond A Ranch, Texas
Y.O. Ranch, Texas
Brooks Lake Lodge, Wyoming
Terry Bison Ranch, Wyoming

Large Tours
Scott Valley Resort and Guest Ranch, Arkansas
Spanish Springs Ranch, California
Outdoor Resorts River Ranch, Florida
Double JJ Ranch, Michigan
Ponderosa Ranch, Nevada
Pinegrove Resort Ranch, New York
Roaring Brook Ranch, New York
Allen Ranch, Oklahoma
Western Hills Guest Ranch, Oklahoma
Nemo Guest Ranch, South Dakota
Flying L Guest Ranch, Texas
Prude Ranch, Texas
Texas Lil's Diamond A Ranch, Texas
Y.O. Ranch, Texas
Rockin' R Ranch, Utah
Woodside Ranch, Wisconsin
Terry Bison Ranch, Wyoming
Big Bar Guest Ranch, British Columbia, Canada

Pets Allowed
Price Canyon Ranch, Arizona
Howard Creek Ranch, California
Spanish Springs Ranch, California
Avalanche Ranch, Colorado
Lane Guest Ranch, Colorado
Sweetwater Ranch, Colorado
Outdoor Resorts River Ranch, Florida
Indian Creek Ranch, Idaho
Flying M Ranch, Oregon
Hunter Peak Ranch, Wyoming
Spear-O-Wigwam Ranch, Wyoming
Flying U Ranch, British Columbia, Canada
Wells Gray Ranch, British Columbia, Canada

Ranch Inn Bed and Breakfasts
Howard Creek Ranch, California
Avalanche Ranch, Colorado
McNamara Ranch, Colorado
Sylvan Dale Ranch, Colorado
Idaho Rocky Mountain Ranch, Idaho
Laughing Water Ranch, Montana (Winter Only)
Bear Mountain Guest Ranch, New Mexico
Nemo Guest Ranch, South Dakota
Western Dakota Ranch Vacations, South Dakota
Lazy Hills Guest Ranch, Texas
Pack Creek Ranch, Utah
Firefly Ranch, Vermont
Flying L Ranch, Washington
Cheyenne River Ranch, Wyoming
Savery Creek Thoroughbred Ranch, Wyoming

Ranch Resort
Rancho de los Caballeros, Arizona
Tanque Verde Ranch, Arizona
Wickenburg Inn Tennis and Guest Ranch, Arizona
Alisal Guest Ranch, California
Aspen Lodge Ranch Resort, Colorado
C Lazy U Ranch, Colorado
Colorado Trails Ranch, Colorado
Lane Guest Ranch, Colorado
Lost Valley Ranch, Colorado
Peaceful Valley Lodge and Guest Ranch, Colorado
Tall Timber, Colorado
Wit's End Guest Ranch and Resort, Colorado
Outdoor Resorts River Ranch, Florida
Double JJ Ranch, Michigan
El Rancho Stevens, Michigan
Turkey Creek Ranch, Missouri
Flathead Lake Lodge, Montana
Mountain Sky Guest Ranch, Montana
The Bishop's Lodge, New Mexico
Hidden Valley Resort, New York
Pinegrove Resort Ranch, New York
Ridin-Hy Ranch Resort, New York
Roaring Brook Ranch and Tennis Resort, New York
Rocking Horse Ranch, New York
Western Hills Guest Ranch, Oklahoma
Rock Springs Guest Ranch, Oregon
Blue Bell Lodge & Resort, South Dakota
Flying L Guest Ranch, Texas
Lost Creek Ranch, Wyoming
Three Bars Ranch, British Columbia, Canada
Tyax Mountain Lake Resort, British Columbia, Canada

Ride on Your Own without Wrangler (generally for experienced riders only, at ranch's discretion)
Soldier Meadows Ranch, Nevada
Logging Camp Ranch, North Dakota
Flying M Ranch, Oregon
Western Dakota Ranch Vacations, South Dakota
Hidden Valley Guest Ranch, Washington
Cheyenne River Ranch, Wyoming
Darwin Ranch, Wyoming
Eaton Ranch, Wyoming
HF Bar Ranch, Wyoming
Lozier's Box R Ranch, Wyoming
Big Bar Guest Ranch, British Columbia, Canada
Flying U Ranch, British Columbia, Canada

The Hills Health and Guest Ranch, British Columbia, Canada
Springhouse Trails Ranch, British Columbia, Canada

RVs
Price Canyon Ranch, Arizona
Everett Ranch, Colorado
Outdoor Resorts River Ranch, Florida
Bear Mountain Guest Ranch, New Mexico
Pisgah View, North Carolina
Allen Ranch, Oklahoma
Western Hills Guest Ranch, Oklahoma
Flying M Ranch, Oregon
Flying W Ranch, Pennsylvania
Western Dakota Ranch Vacations, South Dakota
Prude Ranch, Texas
Y.O. Ranch, Texas
TL Bar Ranch, Alberta, Canada
The Hills Health and Guest Ranch, British Columbia, Canada
Springhouse Trails Ranch, British Columbia, Canada
Tyax Mountain Lake Resort, British Columbia, Canada

Travel Industry Awards
Kachemak Bay Wilderness Lodge, Alaska
Lazy K Bar Guest Ranch, Arizona
Rancho de los Caballeros, Arizona
Tanque Verde Ranch, Arizona
White Stallion Ranch, Arizona
Wickenburg Inn Tennis and Guest Ranch, Arizona
Alisal Guest Ranch, California
Howard Creek Ranch, California
Aspen Lodge Ranch Resort, Colorado
C Lazy U Ranch, Colorado
Colorado Trails Ranch, Colorado
Deer Valley Ranch, Colorado
Elk Mountain Ranch, Colorado
Elktrout Lodge, Colorado
The Home Ranch, Colorado
Latigo Ranch, Colorado
Lost Valley Ranch, Colorado
Peaceful Valley Lodge and Guest Ranch, Colorado
Tall Timber, Colorado
Vista Verde Guest and Ski Touring Ranch, Colorado
Waunita Hot Springs Ranch, Colorado
Wilderness Trails Ranch, Colorado
Wind River Ranch, Colorado
Turkey Creek Ranch, Missouri
Eagle Nest Lodge and Outfitters, Montana
Flathead Lake Lodge, Montana
Mountain Sky Guest Ranch, Montana
Triple Creek Ranch, Montana
The Bishop's Lodge, New Mexico
Roaring Brook Ranch and Tennis Resort, New York
Rocking Horse Ranch, New York
Cataloochee Ranch, North Carolina
Snowbird Mountain Lodge, North Carolina
Rock Springs Guest Ranch, Oregon
Flying L Guest Ranch, Texas
Hidden Valley Guest Ranch, Washington
Absaroka Ranch, Wyoming
Castle Rock Lodges Guest Ranch, Wyoming
Cody's Ranch Resort, Wyoming
Lost Creek Ranch, Wyoming
Rafter Six Ranch Resort, Alberta, Canada
Flying U Ranch, British Columbia, Canada
Sundance Guest Ranch, British Columbia, Canada

Working Cattle
Northland Ranch Resort, Alaska
Grand Canyon Bar Ten Ranch, Arizona
Grapevine Canyon Ranch, Arizona
Price Canyon Ranch, Arizona
Rancho de los Caballeros, Arizona
Sprucedale Ranch, Arizona
Hunewill Circle H Ranch, California
Quarter Circle U Rankin Ranch, California
Spanish Springs Ranch, California
Aspen Canyon Ranch, Colorado
Everett Ranch, Colorado
Lost Valley Ranch, Colorado
Whistling Acres Guest Ranch, Colorado
Sylvan Dale Ranch, Colorado
Wilderness Trails Ranch, Colorado
Bar H Bar Ranch, Idaho
C-B Ranch, Montana
Circle Bar Guest Ranch, Montana
G Bar M Ranch, Montana
Hargrave Guest Ranch, Montana
Lazy K Bar Ranch, Montana
Schively Ranch, Montana
63 Ranch, Montana
Sweet Grass Ranch, Montana
Cottonwood Ranch, Nevada
Soldier Meadows Ranch, Nevada
Spur Cross Ranch, Nevada
Ponderosa Cattle Company and Guest Ranch, Oregon
Western Dakota Ranch Vacations, South Dakota
Prude Ranch, Texas
Y.O. Ranch, Texas
Rockin' R Ranch, Utah
Breteche Creek Ranch Retreat, Wyoming
Brush Creek Ranch, Wyoming
Cheyenne River Ranch, Wyoming
David Ranch, Wyoming
High Island Ranch, Wyoming
Lozier's Box R Ranch, Wyoming
Rafter Y Ranch, Wyoming

Red Rock Ranch, Wyoming
TL Bar Ranch, Alberta, Canada
Bull River Ranch, British Columbia, Canada
Elkin Creek Ranch, British Columbia, Canada
Flying U Ranch, British Columbia, Canada
Three Bars Ranch, British Columbia, Canada
Top of the World, British Columbia, Canada
Wells Gray Ranch, British Columbia, Canada

Workshops

Kachemak Bay Wilderness Lodge, Alaska-Photography
Tanque Verde Ranch, Arizona-Naturalist
White Stallion Ranch, Arizona-Elderhostel
Hunewill Circle H Ranch, California-Watercolor
Spanish Springs Ranch, California-Cowboy Camp
"Trinity" Mountain Meadow Ranch, California-Photography
Bar Lazy J, Colorado-Fishing School
Elktrout Lodge, Colorado-Fishing
4UR Ranch, Colorado-Fishing
Latigo Ranch, Colorado-Photography
Peaceful Valley Lodge and Guest Ranch, Colorado-Naturalists, Crafts
San Juan Guest Ranch, Colorado-Photography
Sylvan Dale Ranch, Colorado-Family, Nature
Diamond D Ranch, Idaho-Crafts
Double JJ Ranch, Michigan-Corporate Management
Boulder River Ranch, Montana-Fishing, Art
Circle Bar Guest Ranch, Montana-Art
Flathead Lake Lodge, Montana-Photography, Art
Hargrave Guest Ranch, Montana-Women
Lakeview Guest Ranch, Montana-Outfitting/Horsemanship
Lone Mountain Ranch, Montana-Fly-fishing, Photography
Lost Fork Ranch, Montana-Fly-fishing
Mountain Sky Ranch, Montana-Horse, Fly-fishing
Pine Butte Guest Ranch, Montana-Nature Photography, Bears, Birds, Mammal Tracking
63 Ranch, Montana-Photography
Bear Mountain Guest Ranch, New Mexico-Birding, Pottery, Archaeology
Vermejo Park Ranch, New Mexico-Fly-fishing
Timberlock, New York-Canoe
Snowbird Mountain Lodge, North Carolina-Wildflowers, Dulcimer
Cataloochee Ranch, North Carolina-Photography, Nature
Western Hills Guest Ranch, Oklahoma-Horse Care/Riding
Rock Springs Guest Ranch, Oregon-Photography
Pack Creek Ranch, Utah-Elderhostel
Reid Ranch, Utah-Reading, Computers
Flying L Ranch, Washington-Wildflower, Artist, Hiking, Natural History
Breteche Creek Ranch Retreat, Wyoming-Fly-fishing, Astronomy, Photography
Brooks Lake Lodge, Wyoming-Photography
Castle Rock Lodges Guest Ranch, Wyoming-Multiworkshops
Crescent H Ranch, Wyoming-Fly-fishing School June and September
High Island Ranch, Wyoming-Basket Weaving
Lozier's Box R Ranch, Wyoming-Horsemanship
Red Rock Ranch, Wyoming-Women's Week
Seven D Ranch, Wyoming-Birding, Photography
V-Bar Guest Ranch, Wyoming-Team Driving Clinic
Black Cat Guest Ranch, Alberta, Canada-Art, Photography, Writing
Homeplace Guest Ranch, Alberta, Canada-Nature on Horseback
Cariboo Rose Guest Ranch, British Columbia, Canada-Riding Clinics Safari
Chilcotin Holidays Guest Ranch, British Columbia, Canada-Horse Packing, Horse Logging, Guided Outfitters School

Appendix

Associations

Colorado Dude and Guest Ranch Association
P.O. Box 300K
Tabernash, CO 80478
(303) 887-3128

The Dude Ranchers' Association
P.O. Box 471K
LaPorte, CO 80535
(303) 223-8440

Alberta Guest Ranch Association
Box 6267 K
Hinton, Alberta Canada T7V 1X6

British Columbia Guest Ranch Association
P.O. Box 4501 K
Williams Lake, British Columbia Canada V2G 2V8
1 (800) 663-6000 (Tourism British Columbia)

Bureaus of Tourism

Alabama
(800) ALABAMA (252-2262)
(Nationwide, AK and HI)

Alaska
(907) 465-2010
(907) 586-8399 FAX

Arizona
(602) 542-8687
(800) 842-8257

Arkansas
(501) 682-7777
(800) 643-8383

California
(916) 322-2881
(800) 862-2543 (ext. A1003)

Colorado
(303) 592-5510
(800) 433-2656

Connecticut
(203) 566-3948
(800) 282-6863

Delaware
(302) 739-4271
(800) 441-8846

District of Columbia
(202) 789-7000

Florida
(904) 487-1462

Georgia
(404) 656-3590
(800) VISIT-GA

Hawaii
(808) 923-1811

Idaho
(208) 334-2470
(800) 635-7820

Illinois
(312) 917-4732
(800) 223-0121 (nationwide)
(312) 280-5740 (Chicago only)

Indiana
(317) 232-8860
(800) 2-WANDER

Iowa
(515) 242-4705
(800) 345-IOWA

Kansas
(913) 296-2009
(800) 252-6727

Kentucky
(800) 225-TRIP (225-8747)
(800) 255-PARK

Louisiana
(504) 342-8100 (in state)
(800) 334-8626 (out of state)
(504) 342-3207 FAX

Maine
(207) 289-2423
(800) 533-9595 (out of state)

Maryland
(301) 333-6611
(800) 543-1036 (all U.S.)
(800) 282-6632 (Baltimore City)

Massachusetts
(617) 727-3201

Michigan
(517) 373-0670
(800) 5432-YES

Minnesota
(612) 296-5029 (Twin Cities)
(800) 657-3700

Mississippi
(601) 359-3297
(800) 647-2290

Missouri
(314) 751-4133
(800) 877-1234

Montana
(406) 444-2654
(800) 541-1447

Nebraska
(402) 471-3796
(800) 228-4307 (out of state)

Nevada
(702) 687-4322
(800) 237-0774

New Hampshire
(603) 271-2666 or
(603) 271-2343

New Jersey
(609) 292-2470
(800) JERSEY-7

New Mexico
(800) 545-2040 (out of state)

New York
(518) 474-4116 (in state)
(800) 225-5697 (continental U.S.)

North Carolina
(919) 733-4171
(800) VISIT-NC

North Dakota
(701) 224-2525 (local Bismark)
(800) 437-2077 (out of state)
(800) 435-5663

Ohio
(800) BUCKEYE

Oklahoma
(405) 521-2409 (in state)
(800) 652-6552 (out of state)

Oregon
(503) 373-1270
(800) 547-7842 (out of state)

Pennsylvania
(717) 787-5453
(800) VISIT-PA (847-4872)

Rhode Island
(401) 277-2601
(800) 556-2484 (Maine, Virginia, North Ohio)

South Carolina
(803) 734-0122

South Dakota
(605) 773-3301
(800) 843-1930 (out of state)

Tennessee
(615) 741-2158

Texas
(512) 462-9191
(800) 8888-TEX (all U.S.)

Utah
(801) 538-1030

Vermont
(802) 828-3236

Virginia
(804) 786-4484 (questions)
(800) VISITVA (answering service and general information)

Washington
(206) 586-2088/2102 (travel counseling)
(800) 544-1800 (all U.S. and Canada)

West Virginia
(304) 348-2286

Wisconsin
(608) 266-2161

Wyoming
(307) 777-7777
(800) 225-5996
Alberta, Canada

(800) 661-8888 (outside Alberta)
(403) 427-4321 (local)

British Columbia, Canada
(604) 387-1642/660-2861
(800) 663-6000

Western Museums

Gene Autry Western Heritage Museum
4700 Western Heritage Way
Zoo Drive Los Angeles, CA 90027
(213) 667-2000

Buffalo Bill Historical Center
P.O. Box 1000 Cody, WY 82414
(307) 587-4771

Buffalo Bill Museum
P.O. Box 1000 Cody, WY 82414
(307) 587-4771

Amon Carter Museum
P.O. Box 2365
Fort Worth, TX 76113
(817) 738-1933

Cowboy Artists of America Museum Foundation
1550 Bandera Highway
Box 1716
Kerrville, TX 78028
(210) 896-2553

Cowboy Hall of Fame and Western Heritage Center
Campus of N.M. Junior College
5317 Lovington Highway
Hobbs, NM 88240
(505) 392-4510, Ext. 371

Eiteljorg Museum
500 West Washington St.
Indianapolis, IN 46204
(317) 636-WEST (9378)

Gilcrease Museum
1400 Gilcrease Museum Road
Tulsa, OK 74127
(918) 596-2700

Joslyn Art Museum
2200 Dodge Street
Omaha, NE 68102
(402) 342-3300

Montana Historical Society
225 N. Roberts
Helena, MT 59620
(406) 444-2694

Museum of Fine Arts
107 W. Palace
Santa Fe, NM 87503
(505) 827-4455

Museum of Indian Arts and Culture
710 Camino Lejo
Santa Fe, NM 87503
(505) 827-8941

Museum of International Folk Art
706 Camino Lejo
Santa Fe, NM 87503
(505) 827-8350

Museum of Western Art
1727 Tremont Place
Denver, CO 80202
(303) 296-1880

National Cowboy Hall of Fame
1700 N.E. 63rd Street
Oklahoma City, OK 73111
(405) 478-2250

The R.W. Norton Art Gallery
4747 Creswell Avenue
Shreveport, LA 71106
(318) 865-4201

Palace of the Governors
On the Plaza, W. Palace
Santa Fe, NM 87504
(505) 827-6483

Phoenix Art Museum
1625 N. Central Avenue
Phoenix, AZ 85004-1625
(602) 257-1222

Plains Indian Museum
P.O. Box 1000
Cody, WY 82414
(307) 587-4771

Pro Rodeo Hall of Fame and Museum of the American Cowboy
101 Pro Rodeo Drive
Colorado Springs, CO 80919-2396
(719) 593-8847 / 593-8840

Frederic Remington Art Museum
303 Washington St.
Ogdensburg, NY 13669
(315) 393-2425

Sid Richardson Collection of Western Art
309 Main Street
Fort Worth, TX 76102
(817) 332-6554

The Rockwell Museum
111 Cedar St.
Corning, NY 14830
(607) 937-5386

C.M. Russell Museum
400 13th Street North
Great Falls, MT 59401
(406) 727-8787

Stark Museum
P.O. Box 1897
Orange, TX 77630
(409) 883-6661

Whitney Gallery of Western Art
P.O. Box 1000
Cody, WY 82414
(307) 587-4771

Wildlife of American Western Art
110 N. Center Street
P.O. Box 2984
Jackson, WY 83001
(307) 733-5771

Cody Firearms Museum
P.O. Box 1000
Cody, WY 82414
(307) 587-4771

Woolaroc Museum
Route 3, Box 1647
Bartlesville, OK 74003
(918) 336-0307

Wagon Trains

In addition to a ranch vacation, you may want to consider a wagon train adventure. The wagon train operators listed below offer wonderful trips that take you back to the time when pioneers crossed the plains. In most instances, you will travel by covered wagon, experiencing the bumps and splendor of days gone by. You will dine on delicious fresh chuck wagon food and enjoy some modern conveniences including showers and rest rooms. (This varies considerably so check with the outfitter.) Sleep under the stars, listen to the distant howls of coyotes, smell pungent sage, and, most of all, relive history. Each of these outfitters will happily send you information and references.

National Trail Ride and Wagon Train Association
Art Howell
P.O. Box 8625 K
Gadsden, AL 35902
(205) 442-8493

Bar T Five Outfitters
Bill and Joyce Thomas
P.O. Box 3415 K
Jackson, WY 83001 (307) 733-5386

Flint Hills Overland Wagon Train Trips
Ervin E. Grant
Box 1076 K
El Dorado, KS 67042
(316) 321-6300

Fort Seward Wagon Trains, Inc.
Phylis Klein Knecht
Box 244 K
Jamestown, ND 58402
(701) 252-6844

Honeymoon Trail Co.
Mel Heaton
Honeymoon Trail Co., Dept. K Moccasin, AZ 86022
(602) 643-7292

Oregon Trail Wagon Train
Gordon and Patty Howard
Route 2, Box 502 K
Bayard, NE 69334
(308) 586-1850

Peterson's Wagons West
Everett and Pat Peterson
Box 1156 K
Afton, Wyoming 83110
(800) 447-4711

Wagons Ho Inc.
Ruth and Frank Hefner
P.O. Box 60098 K
Phoenix, AZ 85082
(602) 230-1801; (602) 977-7724

Western Dakota Ranch Vacations
HCR1, Box 9, Dept. K
Wall, South Dakota 57709
(605) 279-2198
(10 person minimum)

Ranch Camps

One of the most exciting experiences for any young person is to spend the summer, or at least part of the summer, at a ranch camp. Since the first edition was published, I have been asked about ranch camps. Many parents are looking for summer camps for their children. Today, ranch camps provide a healthy, happy, summer environment that will, without a doubt, broaden each child's experiences. These camps provide opportunities for youngsters to be in the outdoors, exposing boys and girls to refreshing challenges, both educationally and developmentally. It would be impossible to list all the ranch camps throughout North America. Remembering the old adage "less is more" I have chosen to list below just a few camps. Each has a fine reputation and has been in the ranch camp industry for many years. As with all the other ranch properties in this guide, I recommend that you contact the camp and talk with them directly. Ask for references. Each of the camps listed below would be delighted to provide you with all the information that you will need to help you select the best ranch camp for your child.

Brush Ranch Camp
P.O. Box 5759K
Santa Fe, New Mexico 87502
(505) 757-8821

Cheley Colorado Camps
P.O. Box 6525K
Denver, Colorado 80206
(303) 377-3616 (winter)
(303) 586-4244 (summer)

Jameson Ranch Camp
Box K
Glenville, California 93226
(805) 536-8888

Teton Valley Ranch Camp
Jackson Hole
Box 8K
Kelly, Wyoming 83011
(307) 733-2958

Top 20 PRCA Rodeos

Professional Rodeo Cowboys Association
101 Prorodeo Drive
Colorado Springs, Colorado
PRCA Media Dept.
(719) 593-8840

Women's Professional Rodeo Association
Route 5, Box 698
Blanchard, Oklahoma 73010
(405) 485-2277

Date	City	Event
Mid-January	Denver, CO	National Western Stock Show and Rodeo
Late January	Fort Worth, TX	Southwestern Exposition and Stock Show Rodeo
Early February	El Paso, TX	Southwestern International Rodeo
Early February	San Antonio, TX	San Antonio Livestock Exposition Rodeo
Mid-February	Houston, TX	Houston Livestock Show and Rodeo
Late February	Tucson, AZ	La Fiesta de los Vaqueros
Mid-March	Pocatello, ID	Dodge National Circuit Finals Rodeo
Mid-May	Cloverdale,B.C.,Canada	Cloverdale Rodeo
Early June	Reno, NV	Reno Rodeo
Early July	Calgary, Alberta, Canada	Calgary Stampede
Early July	Greeley, CO	Greeley Independence Stampede
Late July	Cheyenne, WY	Cheyenne Frontier Days
Mid-July	Salinas, CA	California Rodeo
Early August	Dodge City, KS	Dodge City Days Rodeo
Mid-August	Colorado Springs, CO	Pikes Peak or Bust Rodeo
Mid-September	Albuquerque, NM	New Mexico State Fair Rodeo
Mid-September	Pendleton, OR	Pendleton Round-up Rodeo
Late September	San Francisco, CA	Grand National (Cow Palace) Rodeo
Late September - Early October	Oklahoma City, OK	State Fair Championship Rodeo
Early December	Las Vegas, NV	National Finals Rodeo

Annual Western Events in the United States and Alberta and British Columbia, Canada

The following is a selection of annual western events. These events and dates are subject to change. Telephone the appropriate office of tourism listed to verify dates.

Date	City	Event
ALABAMA		
Late January	Town Creek	National Field Trials
Late February	Birmingham	Harper and Morgan Rodeo
Early March	Gadsden	Alabama Wagon Train
	Opp	Opp Jaycee Rattlesnake Rodeo
Late March	Montgomery	Southeastern Livestock Exposition Rodeo and Livestock Week
Mid- to Late April	Bridgeport	Indian Day
	Clayton	Little Britches Rodeo
Late April	Decatur	Annual Racking Horse Spring Celebration
Late June	Clayton	Stetson Hoedown Rodeo
Late July	Selma	Selma Jaycee's Annual Southeast Championship Rodeo
Early August	Gadsden	Boys Club Annual Rodeo
Mid- to Late August	Gadsden	Cherokees of Northeast Alabama Indian Powwow Festival
Mid-September	Huntsville	Ole Time Fiddling and Bluegrass Convention
Late September	Winfield	Mule Days
	Decatur	Racking Horse World Celebration
Late September-Early October	Mobile	Greater Gulf State Fair and PRCA Rodeo
Early October	Montgomery	South Alabama State Fair
	Birmingham	Alabama State Fair
	Athens	Annual Tennessee Valley Old Time Fiddlers Convention
Early November	Montgomery	Southern Championship Charity Horse Show
Late November	Atmore	Annual Porch Band and Creek Indians' Thanksgiving Day Powwow
ALASKA		
February	Anchorage	Anchorage Fur Rendezvous
Early April	Juneau	Annual Alaska Folk Festival
Late May	Delta Junction	Buffalo Wallow Statewide Square Dance Festival
Mid-August	Palmer	Alaska State Fair Rode' and Parade
	Kodiak	Alaska State Fair and Rodeo
	Fairbanks	Tanana Valley State Fair
	Haines	Southeast Alaska State Fair
Early July	Delta Junction	Buffalo Barbecue
	Skagway	Soapy Smith's Wake
ARIZONA		
January	Phoenix	Arizona National Livestock Show and Old Timers Rodeo

Mid-January	Tucson	Turquoise Pro Rodeo Circuit Finals
Late January to Early February	Scottsdale	Parada del Sol Parade and Rodeo
February	Phoenix	A-Z National Horse Show
	Tucson	Tucson Winter Classic Horse Show and Grand Prix World Cup
	Tucson	Jumping Horse Fiesta Horse Show
	Goodyear	Estrella Rodeo
Mid-February	Yuma	Yuma Jaycees Silver Spur Rodeo
	Scottsdale	All Arabian Horse Show and Sale
	Wickenburg	Gold Rush Days and Rodeo
Late February	Tucson	La Fiesta de los Vaqueros Rodeo
Early March	Phoenix	World Championship Jaycees' Rodeo of Rodeos
Mid-April	Globe/Miami	Copper Dust Stampede Rodeo
May	Payson	Old Time rodeo Cowboys Reunion
Late May	Tombstone	Wyatt Earp Days
June	Payson	Annual Junior rodeo
	Alpine	Annual Rodeo, Parade, and Barbecue
June-August	Flagstaff	Hopi and Navajo Craftsman Exhibitions
Early June	Sonora	Quarter Horse Show
Mid-June to Early July	Flagstaff	Festival of Native American Arts
Early July	Springerville	Round Valley Rodeo and Parade
	Prescott	Frontier Days and World's Oldest Rodeo
	Window Rock	Fourth of July Celebration PRCA Rodeo & Pow Wow
Late July	Snowflake	Pioneer Days Celebration
August	Williams	Cowpunchers' Reunion rodeo
Late August	Payson	World's Oldest Continuous PRCA Rodeo and Parade
September	Tucson	Old Pueblo Horse Show
	Window Rock	Navajo Nation Fair
	Payson	State Championship Old Time Fiddlers Contest
Early September	Tombstone	Wild West Days
	Taylor	Sweet Corn Festival
	Window Rock	Annual Navajo Nation Fair and Rodeo
Late September	Sonora	PRCA Rodeo, Santa Cruz County
	Willcox	Rex Allen Days
Early October	Scottsdale	Wrangler Jeans Rodeo and Showdown
Mid-October	Tombstone	Helldorado Days
Early November	Sells	Sells All-Indian Rodeo
Late October-Early November	Phoenix	Cowboy Artists of America Exhibition
November	Phoenix	Native American Arts Show
Early December	Mesa	Fiesta del Sol Rodeo

ARKANSAS

Mid-April	Cabot	Old West Daze
Early May	Booneville	Booneville Riding Club Spring Rodeo
Late May-Early June	Fort Smith	Annual Old Fort Days Rodeo
	Shirley	Annual Homecoming and Rodeo

Early June	Calico Rock	IRA Championship Rodeo
	Huntsville	Hawgfest Pig Race, Rodeo, Music
	Newport	Riverboat Days and State Catfish Cooking Contest (Rodeo)
Mid-June	Mountain View	Western Music Weekend
	Booneville	Riding Club Rodeo
	Calico Rock	Annual IRA Championship rodeo
	Dardanelle	Annual PRCA Rodeo
	Siloam Springs	Annual Rodeo and Parade
Early July	Springdale	Annual Rodeo of the Ozarks
	Caraway	Annual Community Picnic and Rodeo
Early August	Mena	Polk County Rodeo
	Crossett	Annual Rodeo Roundup Day
	Crossett	Annual PRCA Rodeo
	Crossett	Annual Miss Rodeo Arkansas Pageant
Late August	Foreman	Little River County Fair and Rodeo
Late August-Early September	Clinton	Arkansas Championship Chuck Wagon Races
	Malvern	Hot Spring County Fair and Rodeo
Mid-September	Fort Smith	Arkansas/Oklahoma State Fair
	Harrison	Northwest Arkansas District Fair and PRCA Rodeo
	Mountain View	Arkansas Old Time Fiddlers Association State Championship Competition
	DeQueen	Annual Sevier County Fair and Rodeo
	Jonesboro	Annual Northeast Arkansas District Fair Rodeo
	Marshall	Annual Searcy County Fair and Rodeo
Late September	Pine Bluff	Annual Southeast Arkansas Livestock Show and Rodeo
Late September-Early October	Texarkana	Annual Four States Fair and Rodeo
Early October	Little Rock	Arkansas State Fair and Livestock Show
	Marshall	Falling Water Trail Ride
	Pea Ridge	International Mule Jump

CALIFORNIA

Late January	Red Bluff	Red Bluff Bull Sale
Mid-February	Kernville	Whiskey Flat Days
Late February	Palm Springs	Mounted Police Rodeo and Parade
Mid-April	Bakersfield	Kern County Horse Show Classic on the Green
Late April	Red Bluff	Roundup Rodeo and Parade
	Auburn	Wild West Stampede (PRCA)
	Clovis	Clovis Rodeo
May	Marysville	Marysville Stampede
Mid-May	Redding	Redding Rodeo Week (PRCA)
	King City	Salinas Valley Fair
	Cottonwood	Cottonwood Rodeo
	Angels Camp	Calaveras County Fair, Frog Jumping Jubilee and Rodeo
Late May	Bishop	Mule Days Celebration
	Yucca	Valley Grubstake Days and PRCA Rodeo
Late May to Early June	Santa Maria	Annual Elks Rodeo and Parade

June	Anderson	Shasta District Fair/Rodeo
	Quincy	California State High School rodeo Championships
Early June	Livermore	World's Fastest Rodeo
	McKinleyville	Pony Express Days
Mid-June	Middletown	Middletown Days
Late June	Diamond Springs	Hangtown Annual Pioneer Days Celebration
Early July	Folsom	Folsom Championship PRCA Rodeo
	Lakeport	Lake County Rodeo
July	Santa Barbara	Horse and Flower Show (PRCA)
	Fortuna	Fortuna rodeo, "Oldest, Longest, Most Westerly"
	Orick	Orick Rodeo
Mid-July	Merced	Merced County Fair
	Plymouth	Amador County Fair
Late July	Susanville	Doyle Days Rodeo
	Ruth	Ruth Rodeo
Late July to Early August	Paso Robles	California Mid-State Fair
Early August	Santa Barbara	Old Spanish Days
	Grass Valley	Nevada County Fair
	Quincy	Plumas County Fair
Mid-August	Susanville	Lassen County Fair
	Truckee	Truckee Rodeo (PRCA)
Mid-August to Early September	Sacramento	California State Fair
Late August	Lancaster	Antelope Valley Fair, Alfalfa Festival and Rodeo
September	Coulterville	Annual Gunfighters Rendezvous
Early September	Barstow	Calico Days Stampede Rodeo
Late September	Ridgecrest	Western Heritage Mining Days
Early October	Calico	Calico Days
Mid-October	Paso Robles	Pioneer Days
	Kernville	Kernville Stampede
	City of Industry	Industry Hills Annual Charity Pro Rodeo
	Palms	Pioneer Days Celebration and PRCA Rodeo
Late October	San Francisco	Grand National Rodeo and Horseshow and Livestock Exposition
November	Brawley	Cattle Call and Rodeo
Early November	Death Valley	Annual Death Valley Encampment
Mid-December	Clovis	Lex Connelly Memorial Rodeo
Late December	Red Bluff	New Year's Eve Pro Rodeo and Celebration

COLORADO

Early January	Denver	National Western Stock Show and Rodeo
Mid-January	Steamboat Springs	Cowboy Downhill
May to September	Durango	Durango Pro Rodeo
	Colorado Springs	Little Britches Rodeo
	Ute	Mountain Rodeo
Late June	Grand Junction	Colorado Stampede
	Glenwood Springs	Roaring Fork Rodeo
	Greeley	Independent Stampede Greeley Rodeo
Late June to Late August	Snowmass	Snowmass Stables Rodeo

July	Canon City	Royal Gorge Rodeo
	Loveland	Jaycees' Rodeo
	Estes Park	Arabian Horse Show
Early July	Greeley	Biggest Fourth of July Rodeo
	Steamboat Springs	Cowboys' Roundup Rodeo
Mid-July	Estes Park	Rooftop Rodeo
Late July	Boulder	Powwow Rodeo and Horse Show
	Monte Vista	Ski-Hi Stampede, Ski-Hi Park
	Fairplay	Burro Days
	Gunnison	Cattlemen's Days, Rodeo and Celebration
Early August	Colorado Springs	Pikes Peak or Bust Rodeo
	Evergreen	Mountain Rendezvous
	Leadville	International Pack Burro Race Championships
	Aspen	Aspen Rodeo
	Evergreen	Rodeo Weekend
Mid-August	Loveland	Larimer County Fair and Rodeo
Late August	Pueblo	Colorado State Fair, Livestock Show and Rodeo
	Glenwood Springs	Garfield County Fair and Rodeo

DISTRICT OF COLUMBIA

October	Largo, MD (D.C.)	Washington International Horse Show

FLORIDA

Mid-January	Davies	5-Star Pro Rodeo Davies Series Rodeo (PRCA)
Early February	Homestead	Homestead Championship Rodeo
	Fort Pierce	Cattleman's Day Parade and Shrine
	West Palm Beach	Winter Equestrian Festival
Early February to Mid-February	Tampa	Florida State Fair PRCA Rodeo
	Kissimmee	Annual Edition Silver Spurs Rodeo
	Hollywood	Seminole Tribal Fair and Rodeo
Late February	Homestead	Frontier Days Rodeo
Mid-March	Tampa	Winter Equestrian Festival
Early April	Tampa	Volvo Federation Equestrian International World Cup Finals
Late June	Kissimmee	82nd Edition Silver Spurs Rodeo
Late September	Tallahassee	Native American Heritage Festival
	Titusville	North Brevard Area Rodeo
Early October	Pensacola	St. Anne's Autumn Round-up
Mid-October	Orlando	Pioneer Days
Late November	Ocula	Thanksgiving Arabian Show
	Davies	Sunshine State Pro Rodeo Championship

IDAHO

Mid-January	Boise	National Snaffle Bit Futurity
Late January	Sun Valley	Sun Valley Winter Carnival
Mid-March	Pocatello	Dodge National Circuit Finals Rodeo
Late April	Lewiston	Lewiston Rodeo: Dogwood Festival
Mid-June	Weiser	National Old Time Fiddlers' Contest
Early July	Salmon	Salmon River Days Rodeo
Mid-July	Nampa	Snake River Stampede

	Driggs	Fourth Annual High Country Cowboy Festival
August	Caldwell	Caldwell Night Rodeo
	Fort Hall/Blackfoot	Shoshone-Bannock Indian Festival Rodeo
Late August	Blackfoot	Eastern Idaho Fair
	Ketchum	Ketchum Wagon Days Celebration
Early September	Lewiston	Lewiston Roundup
ILLINOIS		
Mid-January	Peona	"World's Largest Rodeo"
INDIANA		
October	Lafayette	Feast of the Hunter's Moon
IOWA		
Late May	Fort Madison	Trading Post Days and Buckskinners Rendezvous
Late May-Early June	Cherokee	Cherokee Rodeo
Early June	Fort Dodge	Frontier Days
Mid-June	Albia	Iowas High School Rodeo Finals
Late June	Edgewood	Edgewood Rodeo Days
Early July	Bloomfield	Fort Bloomfield IRCA Rodeo
	Lake City	Top Rail Saddle Club Rodeo and Western Days
Mid-July	Woodbine	Rodeo Days
Late July	Lenox	Lenox rodeo
Early August	Carson	Carson Rodeo
	Sidney	Iowa Championship Rodeo
	Toledo	Double "D" Rodeo
Early September	Fort Madison	Tri-State Rodeo Festival
KANSAS		
Early May	Hays	Annual Spring Rodeo, FHSU
Early June	Fort Scott	Good Ol' Days Celebration
	Dodge City	Longhorn Steer Drive
	Garden City	Beef Empire Days
Late July	Wichita	Mid-America Inter-Tribal Indian Powwow
Early August	Dodge City	Dodge City Days (PRCA Rodeo)
Mid-August	Abilene	Central Kansas Free Fair and Wild Bill Hickok Rodeo
Early September	Topeka	Railroad Days
	Medicine Lodge	Indian Summer Days
Early October	Medicine Lodge	Indian Peace Treaty Pageant (Every 3 years starting 1991)
KENTUCKY		
Early and Mid-February	Bowling Green	Kyana Quarter Horse Show
Mid-February	Bowling Green	Championship Rodeo
Early March	Bowling Green	Kyana Quarter Horse Show
	Bowling Green	Spring Festival Horse Show
Late March	Florence	Turfway Festival & Jim Beam Stakes

	Benton	Tater Day Rodeo and National Championship Horse and Mule Pulls
	Winchester	Point-to-Point Races
Early April	Lexington	Ha'Penny Horse Trials
Mid-April	Lexington	Spring Horse Affair
	Henderson	Tri-Fest Firemen's Rodeo
Late April	Lexington	Rolex Kentucky International 3-Day Event
	Lexington	High-Hope Steeplechase
Early May	Louisville	The Kentucky Derby
	Lexington	Kentucky Spring Premier Saddlebred Show
Mid-May	Lexington	Kentucky Spring Hunter/Jumper Show
	Florence	Mason-Dixon Steeplechase
Late May	Lexington	Kentucky Dressage Association
	Carter County	Grayson Memory Days Jaycees Horse Show
	Prospect	Hard Scuffle Steeplechase
	Bowling Green	Bluegrass Paint Horse Show
	Georgetown	Rotary Horse Show
Early June	Lexington	The Egyptian Event
	Bowling Green	Appaloosa Horse Show
	Hartford	AQHA Horse Show
Mid-June	Bowling Green	Saddlebred Horse Show
	Olive Hill	Carter County Horse Show
Early July	Lexington	Lexington Junior League Horse Show
Mid-July	Lexington	Paint Horse National Show
	Grayson County	Official Kentucky State Championship Old Time Fiddlers Contest
	Hartford	World Championship Rodeo
Early August	Lexington	Greater Eastern Appaloosa Regional Show
	Lexington	Wild Horse & Burro Adoption & Exposition
Mid-August	Lexington	Bluegrass Festival Hunter/Jumper Show
	Louisville	Kentucky State Fair, Horse Show and Rodeo
	Harrodsburg	Pioneer Days Festival & Old Time Fiddler's Contest
Late August	Lexington	Kentucky Hunter/Jumper Association Horse Show
	Lexington	Lexington Grand Prix
Late August-Early September	Lexington	Yamaha All-Arabian Combined Classic

LOUISIANA

Mid-January	Lake Charles	Calcasieu Parish Livestock Show
Late January	Lake Charles	Southwest District Livestock Show and Rodeo
Late February	Covington	Dixie Trail Riders
Late March	Lake Charles	Silver Spur Riders Club
Late April	Lake Charles	Silver Spur Riders Club
Late May	Lake Charles	Silver Spur Riders Club
Late July	Lake Charles	Silver Spur Riders Club
Late August	Lake Charles	Silver Spur Riders Club
Late August-Early September	Lake Charles	McNeese Classic Livestock Show and Louisiana Classic Agricultural Expo
Mid-September	Lake Charles	Tennessee Walking and Racking Horse Show
Late September	Lake Charles	Silver Spur Riders Club

October	Angola	Angola Prison Rodeo
Mid-October	Raceland	LaFourche Parish Agriculture Fair and Livestock Show
	Loranger	Old Farmers' Day
Late October	Lake Charles	Silver Spur Riders Club
Late November	Lake Charles	Silver Spur Riders Club
MAINE		
January	Kingfield	White White World
MARYLAND		
Early June	Pinefield	Piscataway Indian Festival and Powwow
Early July	McHenry	Annual American Indian Inter-Tribal Cultural Organization Powwow
Early August	Cordova	Old St. Joseph Jousting Tournament and Horse Show
Late September	Timonium	Eastern National Livestock Show
MICHIGAN		
Mid-February	Traverse City	VASA Cross-Country Ski Race
Late May	Shakopee	Eagle Creek Rendezvous
MINNESOTA		
Late February	Kenyon	Horse and Cutter Day
Early March	New Ulm	Horse and Mule Parade
Late April	St. Paul	Minnesota Horse Exposition
Early May	Crookston	Great Northern Horse Extravaganza
Mid-May	Bagley	Minnesota High School Rodeo
	Lake Benton	Saddle Horse Days
Late May	New London	Little Britches Rodeo
Early June	Granite Falls	Western Fest Rodeo
	Buffalo	Buffalo Rodeo
Mid-July	Isanti	Rodeo Jubilee Days
	Hawley	Hawley Rodeo
Mid-August	Hutchinson	McLeod County Rodeo
Mid-October	Crookston	Midwest International Horse Show
MISSISSIPPI		
Early February	Jackson	Jackson Dixie National Livestock Show and Rodeo and Western Festival
Mid-July	Natchez	Choctaw Rodeo
Late July-Early August	Phil	Neshoba County Fair
MISSOURI		
Late June	Kansas City	Kansas City Rodeo
Early September	Independence	Santa-Cali Gun Days
Mid-September	Sikeston	PRCA Rodeo
Early November	Kansas City	American Royal Livestock, Horse Show and Rodeo

MONTANA

Early February	Billings	Northern Rodeo Association Finals
	Seeley Lake	OSCR 50K Nordic Ski Race
	Helena	Race to the Sky Sled Dog Race
Mid-February	Anaconda/Butte	Big Sky Winternational Sports Festival
Mid-March	Great Falls	C.M. Russell Auction of Original Western Art
	Missoula	Montana State Expo
Early April	Whitefish	Whitefish North American Cross-Country Ski Championships
Early May	Missoula	Western Heritage Days
Mid-May	Conrad	Whoop-up Trail Days
	St. Ignatius	Buffalo Feast and Pow Wow
	Miles City	Miles City Bucking Horse Sale
Late May	Virginia City	Spring Horseback Poker run
June	Hardin	Custer's Last Stand Re-enactment
Early June	Forsyth	Forsyth Horse Show and Rodeo
Mid-June	Bozeman	College National Finals Rodeo
	Lewistown	Snowy Mountain Regional Fiddlers Contest
Late June	Virginia City	Buffalo Runners Shootin' Matches
	Stevensville	Western Days
	Hamilton	Hamilton Old Timers Rodeo
Early July	Red Lodge	Home of Champions Rodeo
	Butte	Butte Vigilante Rodeo
	Roundup	Musselshell Valley July 4th Celebration and Rodeo
Mid-July	Browning	North American Indian Days
	Wolf Point	Wolf Point Wild Horse Stampede
Late July	Lewistown	Central Montana Horse Show Fair and Rodeo
	Helena	Last Chance Stampede and Fair
	Libby	Libby Logger Days
	Deer Lodge	Grant-Kohrs Ranch Annual Celebration
	Red Lodge	Red Lodge Mountain Man Rendezvous
Early August	Missoula	United Peoples Pow Wow and Emcampment
	Glendive	Dawson County Fair and Rodeo
Mid-August	Big Timber	Montana Cowboy Poetry Gathering
	Crow	Agency Crow Fair
	Billings	Montana Fair
	Plentywood	Sheridan County Fair and Rodeo
Late August	Roundup	Roundup Cattle Drive
	Plains	Sanders County Fair and Rodeo
	White Sulpher Springs	Labor Day Rodeo and Parade
Early September	Reedpoint	Running of the Sheep-Sheep Drive
Mid-September	Great Falls	Annual Old Timers Rodeo
Late September	Libby	Nordicfest
October	Billings	Northern International Livestock Exposition and Rodeo
Early October	Boise	Bison Roundup (National Bison Range)
November	West Yellowstone	Cross-Country Fall Camp

NEBRASKA

Mid-June	Hastings	Cottonwood Prairie Festival

	North Platte	Celebration and Buffalo Bill Rodeo
July	Burwell	Nebraska's Big Rodeo
Early July	Crawford	Crawford Rodeo
	Chadron	Fur Trade Days and Buckskin Rendezvous
Late July	Winnebago	Indian Pow Wow
Mid-August	Ogallala	Ogallala Roundup Rodeo
Late August	Sidney	Cheyenne County Fair
	Gordon	Sheridan County Fair and Rodeo
September	Bayard	Chimney Rock Pioneer Days
Mid-September	Ogallala	Indian Summer Rendezvous
Late September	Omaha River	City Roundup and World Championship Rodeo

NEVADA

Every other weekend except during August	Mesquite	Peppermill Year-Round Roping Competition
Early January	Elko	Cowboy Poetry Gathering
	Reno	Biggest Little Cutting Horse in the World Competition
Mid-January	Reno	Miller Team Roping Horse Competition
Early March	Ely	Bristlecone Chariot Races
Mid-March	Reno	National Reining Cowhorse Association Hackamore Futurity
	Reno	Romagnola Cattle Show/Sale
	Reno	Beefmasters Cattle Show/Sale
Late April	Reno	Miller Team Roping Horse Competition
	Reno	Angus Cattle Show/Sale
Early May	Reno	Angus Cattle Show/Sale
Mid-May	Reno	Nevada Junior Livestock State Show
	Reno	Comstock Arabian Horse Show
Late May	Reno	Silver State Morgan Horse Show
May to June	Las Vegas	Helldorado Rodeo
June	Wells	Wells Bustin' and Dustin' PRCA Rodeo
Early June	Reno	Pacific Coast Cutting Horse Association Competition
	Reno	Reno Rodeo (PRCA)
	Carson City	Annual Kit Carson Rendezvous and Wagon Train Days
	Ely	White Pine Rodeo
Mid-June	Reno	Reno Rodeo Carson City Historic Pony Express Ride
Late June	Reno	Reno Grand Prix Jumping Classic Horse Show Competition
July	Fallon	All Indian Stampede and Pioneer Days
Early July	Fallon	Nevada International Invitational Rodeo
Mid-July	Reno	Comstock Arabian Horse Show
Early August	Reno	Peruvian Paso Horse Show
Late August	Reno	Paint-O-Rama Western States Horse Show
	Reno	Pacific Coast Quarter Horse Spectacular Horse Show
	Ely	White Pine Country Days Fair and Pony Express Horse Races

September	Virginia City	Virginia City Camel Races and 1880 Grand Ball
	Winnemucca	Nevada's Oldest Rodeo & Western Art Round-up Show and Sale
	Winnemucca	Winnemucca Parade and Rodeo
	Sparks	Western States Indian Rodeo Regional Finals
Mid-September	Reno	National Reining Cowhorse Association Snaffle Bit Futurity Competition
	Ely	White Pine Silver Stampede
	Carson City	Open Horse Show
Late September	Reno	National Team Penning Finals Horse Competition
	Ely	Whitepine High School Rodeo
Early October	Reno	Western Open Cutting Horse Competition
Late October	Carson City	Nevada Day Celebration
Early November	Reno	North American Indian Championship Rodeo
Mid-November	Reno	National Old Timers Finals Rodeo
December	Las Vegas	National PRCA Finals Rodeo
Early December	Las Vegas	NFR Bucking Horse and Bull Sale

NEW JERSEY

Late May-Late September (Every Saturday)	Woodstown	Woodstown Weekly Rodeo (PRCA)
Late May-Late September	Netcong	Wild West City—Replica of Dodge City

NEW MEXICO

Early January	Red River	Red River Winterfest
Late February	Chama	High Country Winter Carnival
	Angel Fire	Angel Fire Winter Carnival Festival Weekend
Late March	El Paso/Shakespeare	New Mexico Renegade Ride
Mid-April	Truth or Consequences	Ralph Edwards Fiesta and Rodeo
Mid-May	Deming	Fiddlers' Contest
Late May	Silver City	Endurance Horse Ride
	Cloudcroft	Mayfair Hayrides and Rodeo
Early June	Clovis	Pioneer Days Celebration and PRCA Rodeo
	Fort Sumner	Old Fort Days
	Mescalero	Apache Indian Maidens' Puberty Rites and Rodeo
	Las Vegas	Rails and Trails Days
	Farmington	Sheriff Posse Rodeo
Mid-June	Cloudcroft	Western Roundup
	Dulce	All-Indian Rodeo
	Taos	San Antonio Corn Dance
	Gallup	Lions Club Western Jubilee Week and Rodeo
Late June	Taos	Rodeo de Taos
	Tucumcari	Piñata Festival and Lions Club Rodeo
Late June-Early July	Clayton	Rabbit Ear Roundup Rodeo
Early July	Cimarron	Cimarron Rodeo
	Eunice	Eunice Fourth of July Celebration and Junior Rodeo
	Santa Fe	Rodeo de Santa Fe

	Taos	Taos Pueblo Powwow
Mid-July	Carlsbad	Western Days and AJRA Rodeo
	Dulce	Little Beaver Roundup Rodeo
	Galisteo	Galisteo Rodeo
Late July	Taos	Fiesta de Santiago y Santa Ana
August	Lovington	Lea County Fair and PRCA Rodeo
	Gallup	Inter-Tribal Indian Ceremonial and Rodeo
Early August	Los Alamos	Los Alamos County Fair and Rodeo
Mid-August	Capitan	Lincoln County Fair
	Santa Fe	Indian Market
	Albuquerque	Bernalillo County 4-H Fair and Rodeo
September	Albuquerque	New Mexico State Fair and Rodeo
	Santa Fe	Fiesta de Santa Fe
Early September	Socorro	Socorro County Fair and Rodeo
	Ruidoso Downs	All American Futurity
	Clayton	Hayden Rodeo
Late September	Lovington	Days of Old West Ranch Rodeo
	Las Cruces	Southern New Mexico State Fair and Rodeo
	Roswell	Eastern New Mexico State Fair and Rodeo
	Deming	Southwestern New Mexico State Fair
	Taos	The Old Taos Trade Fair
	Taos	San Geronimo Day Trade Fair
Mid-October	Carlsbad	Alfalfa Fest (Mule Races, Largest Parade, and Hayride)
Late October	Truth or Consequences	Old-Time Fiddlers Contest
Mid-November	Hobbs	Llano Estacado Party and Cowboy Hall of Fame and Western Heritage Center Introduction Banquet
Late November	Albuquerque	Indian National Finals Rodeo
Late December	Taos	The Matachines Dances at Taos Pueblo

NEW YORK

July through September	Lake Luzerne	Adirondack Championship Rodeo
Early August	Attica	Attica Rodeo
Mid-September	Lake Ontario	Trout and Salmon Derby, Niagara River
For Dates Contact: American Horse Show Association 598 Madison Avenue New York, NY 10022 (212) 736-6314	New York City	New York State National Horse Show at Madison Square Gardens
	Syracuse	New York State Fair International Horse Show
	Lake Placid	I Love New York Horse Show

NORTH CAROLINA

Mid-January	Raleigh	Midwinter Quarter Horse Show
Early February	Raleigh	Southern National Draft Horse Pull
Late March	Raleigh	North Carolina Quarter Horse Association Spring Show Championship Rodeo
	Pinehurst	Kiwanis Charity Horse Show

	Raleigh	Great Smokies Pro Rodeo
	Oak Ridge	Oak Ridge Easter Horse Show & Fiddlers Convention
	Fayetteville	Annual Shrine Club Rodeo
Early April	Blowing Rock	Annual Opening Day Trout Fishing Derby
	Southern Pines	Moore County Annual Pleasure Horse Drive Show
	Pembroke	Spring Racking Horse Show
	Pinehurst	Harness Horse Racing Matinee
	Raleigh	Appaloosa Horse Show
Mid-April	Raleigh	Easter Bunny Quarter Horse Circuit
	Tryon	Tryon Thermal Belt Chamber of Commerce Annual Horse Show
Late April	Asheville	Carolina Mountains Arabian Show
Early May	Statesville	Tarheel Classic Horse Show
	Asheville	Southern Horse Fair
Mid-May	Burnsville	Annual Jaycees Championship Rodeo
	Monroe	Mid-Atlantic Championship rodeo
	Raleigh	NC All Arabian Horse Show
	Southern Pines	Sandhills Combined Driving Event
Late May	Union Grove	Old Time Fiddlers' and Bluegrass Festival
	Raleigh	Southern States Morgan Horse Show
	Tryon	Tryon Horse Show
Early June	Raleigh	Capitol Dressage Classic
	Wilmington	Sudan Horse Patrol Coastal Plains Horse Show
Mid-June	Love Valley	Junior Showdown
	Raleigh	Appaloosa Horse Show
Late June	Love Valley	Frontier Week Rodeo
	Andrews	Annual Wagon Train
	Raleigh	NC Hunter Jumper Association Show
	Pembroke	Racking Horse Show
Early July	Hayesville	Clay County Rodeo
	Sparta	Annual Lions Club Horse Show
Mid-July	Love Valley	Junior Showdown
	Raleigh	NC State 4-H Horse Show
	Waynesville	Waynesville Lions Club Horse Show
Late July	Waynesville	Trail Riders Horse Show
	Raleigh	NC All Amateur Arabian Horse Show
	Raleigh	Raleigh Summer Hunter Jumper Show
	Asheville	Carolina Mountains Summer All Arabian Horse Show
	Blowing Rock	Blowing Rock Charity Horse Show
	Tryon	Tryon Thermal Belt Chamber of Commerce Annual Horse Show
Early August	Robbins	Annual Farmer's Day & Wagon Train
	Waynesville	Fraternal Order of Police Horse Show
Early September	Mocksville	Lake Myers Rodeo
Mid-September	Monroe	Mid-Atlantic Championship rodeo
	Raleigh	NC State Championship Charity Horse Show
Late September	Asheville	Carolina Mountains Fall All Arabian Horse Show
Early November	Pinehurst	Fall Horse Carriage Drive
Late November	Raleigh	Eastern Quarter Horse of NC-Show & Futurity

NORTH DAKOTA

Early March	Valley City	North Dakota Winter Show and Rodeo
Mid-April	Grand Forks	Native American Days
Late May	Medora	Dakota Cowboy Poetry Gathering
Early June	Bottineau	Old Time Fiddlers Contest
	Trugby	North Dakota State Championship Horse Show
Mid-June	Williston	Fort Union Trading Post Rendezvous
Late June	Jamestown	Fort Seward Wagon Train
	Mandan	Frontier Army Days
Early July	Dickinson	Rough Rider Days
Early August	Sentinel Butte	Champions Ride Rodeo, Home on the Range for Boys
Mid-August	West Fargo	Pioneer Days
September	Bismarck	United Tribes International Pow-Wow

OHIO

Mid-January	Dayton	World's Toughest Rodeo
October	Columbus	All-American Quarter Horse Congress

OKLAHOMA

Mid-January	Oklahoma City	International Finals Rodeo
Late January	Tulsa	Longhorn World Championship Rodeo
February-May	Oklahoma City	Parimutuel Thoroughbred Horse Racing
February-December	Sallisaw	Parimutuel Mixed Breed Horse Racing
Early February	Guthrie	Bullmania
Late February	Guthrie	Timed Event Championship of the World
Mid-March	Oklahoma City	4-H and FFA Junior Livestock Ranch Rodeo
Late March	Tulsa	Oklahoma Quarter Horse Spring Show
Early April	Guthrie	Lazy E Reining Classic
	Fairview	Farm and Ranch Day
Mid-April	Guthrie	Lazy E Spring Barrel Racing Futurity, 89er Day Celebration and Rodeo
	Oklahoma City	Centennial Horse Show
Late April	Waurika	Rattlesnake Hunt
	Mangum	Rattlesnake Hunt
May-July	Oklahoma City	Parimutuel Quarter Horse Racing
Early May	Guthrie	Ben Johnson Pro Celebrity Rodeo
	Guymon	Pioneer Day Celebration and Rodeo
Late May	Guthrie	Oklahoma Cattlemen's Range Roundup
	Boise City	Santa Fe Trail Daze
June-September	Bixby	Moonlight Horseback Rides
Early June	Claremore	Will Rogers Stampede Rodeo
Mid-June	Pawhuska	Ben Johnson Memorial Steer Roping Contest
Early July	Oklahoma City	Hunter-Jumper Horse Show
Mid-July	Pawhuska	International Roundup Club Cavalcade
	Tulsa	Palomino World Show, National Pinto Horse Show
Late July	Shawnee	National High School Finals Rodeo
Early August	Tulsa	American Junior Quarter Horse World Finals
Mid-August	Vinita	Will Rogers Rodeo

Late August	Oklahoma City	National American Miniature Horse Show
	McAlester	Oklahoma State Prison Rodeo
September-December	Oklahoma City	Parimutuel Thoroughbred Horse Racing
Early September	Guthrie	Women's National Finals Rodeo
Mid-September	Oklahoma City	Rodeo and Horse Show of the State Fair of Oklahoma
Late September	Tulsa	Rodeo and Horse Show of the Tulsa State Fair
	Chelsea	Bushyhead's World's Richest Calf Roping
Early October	Oklahoma City	Grand National and World Championship Morgan Horse Show
Mid-October	Guthrie	National Finals Ranch Rodeo
	Oklahoma City	Festival of the Horse
Late October	Guthrie	PRCA Prairie Circuit Finals Rodeo
Early November	Claremore	Will Rogers Days
	Oklahoma City	World Championship Quarter Horse Show
	Guthrie	U.S. Team Roping Championship
Late November	Guthrie	National Finals Steer Roping
December	Bixby	Holiday Rides
Early December	Oklahoma City	World Championship Barrel Racing Futurity
Mid-December	Oklahoma City	Sunbelt Cutting Futurity Horse Show
Late December	Tulsa	Holiday Circuit Quarter Horse Show

OREGON

Mid-January	Portland	"World's Toughest Rodeo"
	Salem	Oregon Stallion Showcase
Late January	Portland	AG Show
Mid-May	Tygh Valley	Tygh Valley Rodeo
	Rogue Valley	Rogue Valley Roundup
Early July	St. Paul	St. Paul Rodeo
	Molalla	Molalla Buckeroo
Mid-July	Prineville	Crooked River Roundup
	Philomath	Frolic and Rodeo Festival
Late July	Joseph	Chief Joseph Days Rodeo
Early August	Madras	Jefferson County Fair and Rodeo
Late August	Grant County	Grant County Fair and Rodeo
	Salem	Oregon State Fair and Rodeo
Mid-September	Pendleton	Pendleton Roundup
Mid-October	Klamath Falls	Klamath Basin Horse Show
Late October	Madras	Cutting Horse Show

PENNSYLVANIA

Late May	Devon	Devon Horse Show and County Fair
Early June	New Castle	Pennsylvania Appaloosa Association Horse Show
Mid-June	Meridian	Butler Rodeo
	New Castle	Arabian Horse Show
	New Castle	Tri-State Reining Association Horse Show
Late June	Shartlesville	Professional Rodeo
	Kellettville	Trail Ride
	Ridgeway	Independence Day Festival

Mid-July	Benton	Frontier Days and Rodeo
Late July	Mercer	Jefferson Township Fair
	Driftwood	Tom Mix Roundup
	Kellettville	Allegheny Mountain Championship Rodeo
	New Castle	Quarter Horse Association Horse Show
	New Castle	Lawrence County Charity Horse Show
Mid-August	No. Washington	North Washington Rodeo
	New Castle	Quarter Horse Association Horse Show
Late August	Shartlesville	Professional Rodeo
Early September	Coatesville	Buffalo Bill Days & Western Horse Show
Mid-October	Harrisburg	Pennsylvania National Horse Show
Late October	Harrisburg	Pennsylvania 4-H Horse Show
	Uniontown	Old-Time Fiddlers State Championship

SOUTH CAROLINA

Late March	Aiken	Steeplechase and Hunt Meet
	Santee	Elloree Trials
Early May	Inman	IPRA World Championship Rodeo
Early August	Blacksburg	Ed Brown Rodeo
Late September	Inman	IPRA World Championship Rodeo
Early November	Camden	Colonial Cup International Steeplechase

SOUTH DAKOTA

Late January	Rapid City	Black Hills Stock Show and Rodeo
Early June	Lake City	Fort Sisseton Historical Festival
Early July	Belle Fourche	Black Hills Roundup
Late July	Mitchell	Corn Palace Stampede Rodeo
Early August	Deadwood	"Days of '76"
Early October	Custer State Park	Buffalo Roundup Days

TENNESSEE

Late April	Paris	World's Biggest Fish Fry Rodeo
Mid-May	Nashville	Iroquois Steeplechase
Early June	Wartrace	Strolling Jim Memorial Horse Show Heyday
Late June	Smithville	Old Time Fiddlers' Jamboree and Crafts Festival
Late July	Clarksville	Walking Horse Show
Early August	Murfreesboro	International Grand Championship Walking Horse Show
Late August	Gray	Appalachian Fair, Shelbyville, Tennessee Walking Horse National Celebration
Late September	Memphis	Midsouth Fair and Exposition, Rodeo

TEXAS

Mid-January to Early February	Bandera	Bandera County Junior Livestock Show
	Fort Worth	Southwestern Exposition Stock Show and Rodeo
Early February	El Paso	Southwestern Livestock Show and Rodeo
	San Antonio	Annual Livestock Show and Rodeo
Mid-February to Early March	Houston	Houston International Livestock Show and Rodeo
Late February to Early March	Brownsville	Charro Days

Spring Weekends	Kerrville	Longhorn Trail Drive
March	Lubbock	ABC Rodeo
Mid-March	San Angelo	Stock Show and Rodeo
	Shamrock	St. Patrick's Day Celebration
Late March	Palestine	Dogwood Trials Festival and Rodeo
April-September	Mesquite	Mesquite Rodeo (Every Friday and Saturday)
Early April	Woodville	Dogwood Festival: Western Weekend Rodeo
Mid-April	San Antonio	Fiesta San Antonio
Mid-May to Mid-September	Amarillo	Cowboy Morning
May	Dallas	Western Days PRCA Pro Rodeo
Early May	Del Rio	PRCA Rodeo and Bull Riding
Mid-May	Laredo	Frontier Days
Late May	Bandera	Funtier Days and Parade
Early June	Fort Worth	Chisholm Trail Roundup
Late June	Stamford	Texas Cowboy Reunion
	Pecos	West of Pecos Rodeo (PRCA Approved)
Mid-July	Pampa	Top O' Texas Rodeo Denison Western Days
Early August	Dalhart	XIT Rodeo and Reunion
Mid-September	Fort Worth	Pioneer Days Celebration
Late September	Dallas	State Fair Texas Rodeo and Livestock Show
Early October	Gonzalez	Come and Take it Celebration
	Waco	Heart O' Texas Fair and Rodeo
Early December	Forth Worth	World Championship National Cutting Horse Futurity
Late December	Fort Worth	Texas Pro Rodeo Circuit Finals Rodeo
	Odessa	Sand Hills Hereford and Quarter Horse Show and Rodeo

UTAH

Mid-January	Snow Basin	Utah Winter Games
	Ogden	Winter-Hof Festival
January	Moab	Annual Winter Festival
Early June	Roosevelt	Rough Rider Days
June	Ogden	National Old Time Fiddle Contest
Mid-June	Helper	Butch Cassidy Days
	Coalville	Annual Coalville Fishing Derby and Balloon Rally
Mid-June	Moab	Canyonlands PRCA Rodeo/Butch Cassidy Days
Late June	Vernal	Amateur Rodeo
	Ft. Duchesne	Celebration "Ute Indian Powwow"
	Price	Black Diamond Stampede PRCA Rodeo
Early July	Oakley	Oakley Rodeo
Mid-July	Salt Lake City	"Days of '47" Celebration and Rodeo
	Vernal	Dinosaur Roundup Rodeo
	Nephi	Annual Ute Stampede
Late July	Ogden	Pioneer Days Rodeo and Celebration
	Logan	Festival of the American West
	Wellington	Wellington Rodeo
Early August	Morgon	Morgon County Rodeo and Fair

	Kaysville	Davis County Fair and Livestock Show
	Trichfield	Sevier County Fair Garden City Annual
	Bear Lake	Raspberry Days
	Castle Dale	Emery County Fair
	Logan	Cache County Fair and Rodeo
	Price	Carbon County Fair and International Day
	Spanish Fork	Utah County Fair
	Heber City	Wasatch County Fair and Rodeo
Mid-August	Minersville	Beaver County Fair
	Tooele	Tooele County Fair
	Monticello	San Juan County Fair and Junior Livestock Show
	Hurricane	Washington County Fair
	Duchesne	Duchesne County Fair and Rodeo
	Park City	Park City Ride 'n' Tie
	Park City	North American Supreme Championship Sheep Dog Trials
	Orderville	Kane County Fair
	Coalville	Summit County Fair
	Ogden	Weber County Fair
	Junction	Piute County Fair
	Loa	Wayne County Fair
	Randolph	Rich County Roundup Days
Late August	Tremonton	Box Elder County Fair and Rodeo
	Manti	Sanpete County Fair
Early September	Cedar City	Iron County Fair
	Moab	Annual La Sal Mountain Horse and Rider Endurance Race
	Parowan	Iron County Fair
	Park City	Lewis Field Rodeo Challenge
	Hooper	Tomato Days and Rodeo
	Cedar City	Southwest Livestock Show
	Salt Lake City	Utah State Fair
	Brigham	Peach Days
Mid-September	St. George	Dixie Roundup
Early November	St. George	Southern Utah Endurance Ride
Mid-November	Moab	Western Poetry Writers Party and Reading Celebration
	Ogden	PRCA Rodeo
Late November	Moab	Mountainman Rendezvous
	Santa Clara	Thanksgiving Day Rodeo
Mid-December	Salt Lake City	Crossroads of the West Gun Show

VERMONT

Late May	Manchester	Annual Bennington County Horse Show
Early to Mid-July	Killington	Killington Mountain Horse Show July
Mid-July	Killington	Vermont Summer Classic-Equestrian Summer Showcase
Late July	Waitsfield	Valley Class-Equestrian Summer Showcase
Late July to Early August	Waitsfield	Sugarbush Horse Show
Early August	Waitsfield	Mad River Festival-Equestrian Summer Showcase

	Bellows Falls	Annual Vermont State Championship Old Time Fiddlers' Contest
Mid-August	Stowe	Midsummer Festival-Green Mountain Equestrian Finale
Late August	Stowe	Midsummer Festival-Green Mountain Equestrian Finale
Late September	Bridport	Krawczyk Horse Farm Open Barn and Sale
WASHINGTON		
Early June	Roy	Roy Pioneer Rodeo
	Bickleton	Alder Creek Picnic and Rodeo
Mid-June	Bremerton	Little Britches Rodeo
	Colville	Fort Colville Days and Rodeo (PRCA)
Late June	Sedro Woolley	Logger Rodeo
	Darrington	Darrington Timber Bowl Rodeo
Early July	Oakville	Oakville Rodeo
Mid-July	Cheney	Cheney Rodeo (PRCA)
Late July	Deer Park	Deer Park WRA Rodeo
Mid-August	Omak	Stampede and Suicide Race (PRCA)
Late August	Bremerton	Kitsap County Fair
Late August-Early September	Walla Walla	Southeastern Washington Fair & Frontier Days
	Ellensburg	Ellensburg Big 4 PRCA Rodeo Early
September	Puyallup	Western Washington Fair and Rodeo
Mid-September	Othello	Othello PRCA Rodeo
Late September	Ridgefield	Northwest Cutting Horse Association Annual Futurity Festival
WISCONSIN		
Early January	Milwaukee	"World's Toughest Rodeo"
Late February	Cable	American Birkebeiner (cross-country ski event)
May to September	Black River Falls	Indian Powwows
Early May	Statewide	Fishing Season Opener
June	Fond du Lac	Walleye Weekend Festival on Lake Winnebago
	Milwaukee	Wonago World Championship Rodeo
July	Manawa	PCRA Rodeo Madison All-American Rodeo of Rodeos (PRCA)
	Spooner	Heart of the North Rodeo (PRCA)
	Lake Michigan	Fishing Contest and Festivals Shore
	Eagle	Summer of the Farm
Early September	Sauk City-Prairie du Sac	State Cow Chip Throwing Contest
	Praire du Chien	Villa Louis Carriage Classic
WYOMING		
Early January	Ft. Washakie	Eastern Shoshone PowWow
	Lander	Wyoming State Winter Fair
Mid-January	Torrington	Shriners' Invitational Cutter Races
February	Riverton	Wild West Winter Carnival
Early February	Gillette	Coors PRCA Rodeo
Mid-February	Casper	WRA Rodeo
Early March	Casper	WRA Rodeo

Late March	Cheyenne	LCCC Golden Eagle Rodeo
Early May	Rock Springs	All Girl Rodeo
Mid-May	Rock Springs	Flaming Gorge Fishing Derby
	Rock Springs	Sweetwater Frontier Days
Late May	Shoshoni	Old Timer's Fiddlers' Contest
	Jackson	Old West Days
	Jackson	Jackson Hole Shoot Out
	Dubois	Annual Pack Horse Race
	Douglas	All Girl Roping
	Riverton	Wyoming Indian High School Powwow
	Ethete	Yellowcalf Memorial Powwow
	Ft. Washakie	Shoshone Relay Association Horse Races
All Summer	Cody	Cody Nite Rodeo
June	Saratoga	Saratoga Cutting Horse Contest
Early June	Hulett	Hulett Rodeo
	Casper	Pack Horse Races
	Casper	Cowboy State Games
	Greybull	Days of '49
	Gillette	Cowboy State Games
	E. Wilkins	St. ParkPack Horse Races
	Douglas	All Girl Roping
	Gillette	Old Timer's Rodeo
	Gillette	WCHA Cutting Horse Show
	Greybull	Days of '49
	Evanston	Bear River Spring Classic Horse Show
	Douglas	Wyoming Paint Horse Show
	Sheridan	Big Horn Mountain Horse Show
Mid-June	Cody	Frontier Festival BBHC
	Encampment	Woodchoppers' Jamboree
	Gillette	High Energy Quarter Horse Show
	Grand Targhee	Annual High Country Cowboy Festival
	Ten Sleep	Wyoming Junior Rodeo
Late June	Cody	Plains Indian Powwow
	Lander	Wind River Indian Reservation Summer Rodeo and Pow-wow Days, Fort Washakie
	Lovell	Mustang Days Celebration
	Douglas	Jackalope Days and High School Rodeo Finals
	Cody	Powwow at Buffalo Bill Historical Center
	Pinedale	Western Heritage Festival
	Ft. Washakie	Eastern Shoshone Powwow and Rodeo
	Cody	Annual Plains Indian Powwow
	Pinedale	Roundup Rodeo
Early July	Afton	Parade and Night Rodeo
	Green River	Flaming Gorge Days
	Cody	Cody Stampede Days
	Ten Sleep	Ten Sleep Rodeo
	Laramie	Laramie Jubilee Days
	Lander	Pioneer Days and July Fourth Parade
	Guernsey	Old Timer's Rodeo
	Jackson	Fourth of July Celebration
	Big Piney	Chuck Wagon Days
	Pinedale	Chuck Wagon Days
	Buffalo	Wild West Show

	Medicine Bow	Medicine Bow Days
	Jackson	Mountain Man Rendezvous
Mid-July	Jackson	Cowboy Poetry Gathering
	Sheridan	Sheridan WYO Rodeo Sundance Memorial Youth Rodeo
	Wright	Wright Roundup and Rodeo
	Lusk	Legend of Rawhide/Vigilante Day
	Pinedale	Green River Rendezvous
Late July	Riverton	Riverton Rendezvous
	Jackson	Teton County Fiddle Contest
	Jackson	Teton County Fair
	Cheyenne	Cheyenne Frontier Days
	Gillette	Old Timer's Rodeo
	Rock Springs	Red Desert Rodeo
August	Wheatland	Platte County Fair and Rodeo
Early August	Casper	Central Wyoming Fair
	Lusk	Niobrara County Fair, Rodeo and Dance
Mid-August	Riverton	Fremont Fair and Rodeo
	Buffalo/Sheridan	Bozeman Trail Days
	Sheridan	Eric Mygard Memorial Woodchopper's Rodeo
	Dubois	Wind River Rendezvous
	Douglas	National Old Timer's Rodeo
Late August	Douglas	Wyoming State Fair/Mixed Team Roping
	Jackson	Old Timer's Rodeo
	Jackson	Trout Unlimited National Convention
	Buffalo	Johnson County Fair and Rodeo and Klondike Rush
Early September	Evanston	Little Britches Rodeo
	Evanston	Cowboy Days Rodeo
	Cheyenne	Cowboy All Weather 1000
	Meeteetse	Labor Day Rodeo
Late October	Casper	PRCA Pro Rodeo
	Gillette	Snaffle Bit Futurity
Late November	Gillette	NRCA Rodeo
Late December	Ft. Washakie	Eastern Shoshone Powwow
	Casper	Cowboy Shootout

ALBERTA

Late March	Edmonton	Northlands Super Rodeo (PRCA)
Mid-April	Lethbridge	Whoop-Up Quarter Horse Circuit
	Trochu	FCA Indoor Rodeo
Late April	Red Deer	Silver Buckle Rodeo
	Grande Prairie	Whispering Pines Rodeo
Late May	Red Deer	Westerner Spring Quarter Horse Show
Early June	Calgary	The National Horse Show, Spruce Meadows
Late June	Ponoka	Ponoka Annual Stampede
Early July	Calgary	The Invitational Horse Show, Spruce Meadows
	Calgary	Calgary Exhibition and Stampede
Mid-July	Red Deer	Westerner Days
	Edmonton	Edmonton's Klondike Days
Late July	Medicine Hat	Exhibition and Stampede
	Lethbridge	Whoop-Up Days

Early September	Calgary	The Masters Horse Show, Spruce Meadows
Mid-November	Edmonton	Canadian Finals Rodeo (PRCA)

BRITISH COLUMBIA

Mid-January	100 Mile House	Ski-A-Thon, Hills Health and Guest Ranch
Early February	Lac La Hache	Lac La Hache Winter Carnival
Late February	100 Mile House	Kahlua Boo Treasure Hunt on Skis
	Wells	Heritage Ski Festival
April	Kamloops	Kamloops Professional Indoor Rodeo
May	Clinton	Clinton Rodeo
	100 Mile House	Little Britches Rodeo
	Metchosin	Luxton Rodeo
	Lillooet Lake	Lillooet Lake Rodeo
	Keremeos	Elks Rodeo
	Kelowna	Black Mountain Rodeo
	Falkland	Falkland Stampede
	Princeton	Princeton Rodeo
	Ashcroft	Ashcroft Rodeo
Late May	Cloverdale	Cloverdale Rodeo
June	Riske Creek	Riske Creek Rodeo
	Prince George	Prince George Rodeo
	Doe River	Doe River Rodeo
	Smithers	Smithers Kinsmen Rodeo
Early June	Horsefly	Horsefly Rodeo
	Hudson's Hope	Hudson's Hope Rodeo
Late June	Williams Lake	Williams Lake Stampede Rodeo
July	Anaheim Lake	Anaheim Lake Stampede
	Clinton	Clinton Old Timers' Rodeo
	Summerland	Stra Rodeo
Early July	Bella Coola	Bella Coola Annual Rodeo/Dance
Mid-July	Quesnel	Annual Bill Barker Days Festival
Late July	Bridge Lake	Bridge Lake Stampede
August	Port St. John	North Peace Rodeo and Fair
	Dawson Creek	Dawson Creek Rodeo
Early August	100 Mile House	Great Cariboo Ride
Mid-August	Riske Creek	Riske Creek Rodeo
Late August	Riske Creek	Jack Palmentier Frontier Days
September	Merritt	Merritt Rodeo

WE WANT TO HEAR FROM YOU

Guidebooks are like children, constantly growing and changing. One of the joys of writing this guide has been receiving many letters from our readers. Your thoughts and ideas are important to us.

The best travel guides are great largely because of the contents and suggestions their authors receive from readers, so tell us about your favorite ranch and your not-so-favorite ranch. Tell us about new ranches that you have discovered.

We would also enjoy knowing what additional information you would like to see in future editions. We hope that you will continue to share your comments with us. You may write to us at:

Kilgore's Ranch Vacations
P.O. Box 1919
Tahoe City, California 96145
Ranch Country, U.S.A.

Thank you.

Other Books from John Muir Publications

Travel Books by Rick Steves
Asia Through the Back Door, 4th ed., 400 pp. $16.95
Europe 101: History and Art for the Traveler, 4th ed., 372 pp. $15.95
Europe Through the Back Door, 12th ed., 434 pp. $17.95
Europe Through the Back Door Phrase Book: French, 112 pp. $4.95
Europe Through the Back Door Phrase Book: German, 112 pp. $4.95
Europe Through the Back Door Phrase Book: Italian, 112 pp. $4.95
Europe Through the Back Door Phrase Book: Spanish & Portuguese, 288 pp. $4.95
Mona Winks: Self-Guided Tours of Europe's Top Museums, 2nd ed., 456 pp. $16.95
See the 2 to 22 Days series to follow for other Rick Steves titles.

A Natural Destination Series
Belize: A Natural Destination, 2nd ed., 304 pp. $16.95
Costa Rica: A Natural Destination, 3rd ed., 320 pp. $16.95 (available 8/94)
Guatemala: A Natural Destination, 336 pp. $16.95

Undiscovered Islands Series
Undiscovered Islands of the Caribbean, 3rd ed., 264 pp. $14.95
Undiscovered Islands of the Mediterranean, 2nd ed., 256 pp. $13.95
Undiscovered Islands of the U.S. and Canadian West Coast, 288 pp. $12.95

For Birding Enthusiasts
The Birder's Guide to Bed and Breakfasts, U.S. and Canada, 288 pp. $15.95
The Visitor's Guide to the Birds of the Central National Parks: U.S. and Canada, 400 pp. $15.95 (available 8/94)
The Visitor's Guide to the Birds of the Eastern National Parks: U.S. and Canada, 400 pp. $15.95
The Visitor's Guide to the Birds of the Rocky Mountain National Parks, U.S. and Canada, 432 pp. $15.95

Unique Travel Series
Each is 112 pages and $10.95 paper.
Unique Arizona (available 9/94)
Unique California (available 9/94)
Unique Colorado
Unique Florida
Unique New England
Unique New Mexico
Unique Texas

2 to 22 Days Series
Each title offers 22 flexible daily itineraries useful for planning vacations of any length. Included are "must see" attractions as well as hidden "jewels."
2 to 22 Days in the American Southwest, 1994 ed., 192 pp. $10.95
2 to 22 Days in Asia, 1994 ed., 176 pp. $10.95
2 to 22 Days in Australia, 1994 ed., 192 pp. $10.95
2 to 22 Days in California, 1994 ed., 192 pp. $10.95
2 to 22 Days in Eastern Canada, 1994 ed., 192 pp. $12.95
2 to 22 Days in Europe, 1994 ed., 304 pp. $14.95
2 to 22 Days in Florida, 1994 ed., 192 pp. $10.95
2 to 22 Days in France, 1994 ed., 192 pp. $10.95
2 to 22 Days in Germany, Austria, and Switzerland, 1994 ed., 240 pp. $12.95
2 to 22 Days in Great Britain, 1994 ed., 208 pp. $10.95
2 to 22 Days Around the Great Lakes, 1994 ed., 192 pp. $10.95
2 to 22 Days in Hawaii, 1994 ed., 192 pp. $10.95
2 to 22 Days in Italy, 1994 ed., 208 pp. $10.95
2 to 22 Days in New England, 1994 ed., 192 pp. $10.95
2 to 22 Days in New Zealand, 1994 ed., 192 pp. $10.95
2 to 22 Days in Norway, Sweden, and Denmark, 1994 ed., 192 pp. $10.95
2 to 22 Days in the Pacific Northwest, 1994 ed., 192 pp. $10.95
2 to 22 Days in the Rockies, 1994 ed., 192 pp. $10.95
2 to 22 Days in Spain and Portugal, 1994 ed., 208 pp. $10.95
2 to 22 Days in Texas, 1994 ed., 192 pp. $10.95
2 to 22 Days in Thailand, 1994 ed., 192 pp. $10.95
22 Days (or More) Around the World, 1994 ed., 264 pp. $13.95

Other Terrific Travel Titles
The 100 Best Small Art Towns in America, 256 pp. $12.95 (available 8/94)
Elderhostels: The Students' Choice, 2nd ed., 304 pp. $15.95
Environmental Vacations: Volunteer Projects to Save the Planet, 2nd ed., 248 pp. $16.95
A Foreign Visitor's Guide to America, 224 pp. $12.95
Great Cities of Eastern Europe, 256 pp. $16.95
Indian America: A Traveler's Companion, 3rd ed., 432 pp. $18.95
Interior Furnishings Southwest, 256 pp. $19.95
Opera! The Guide to Western Europe's Great Houses, 296 pp. $18.95
Paintbrushes and Pistols: How the Taos Artists Sold the West, 288 pp. $17.95
The People's Guide to Mexico, 9th ed., 608 pp. $18.95
Ranch Vacations: The Complete Guide to Guest and Resort, Fly-Fishing, and Cross-Country Skiing Ranches, 3rd ed., 512 pp. $19.95
The Shopper's Guide to Art and Crafts in the Hawaiian Islands, 272 pp. $13.95
The Shopper's Guide to Mexico, 224 pp. $9.95
Understanding Europeans, 272 pp. $14.95
A Viewer's Guide to Art: A Glossary of Gods, People, and Creatures, 144 pp. $10.95
Watch It Made in the U.S.A.: A Visitor's Guide to the Companies that Make Your Favorite Products, 272 pp. $16.95 (available 7/94)

Parenting Titles
Being a Father: Family, Work, and Self, 176 pp. $12.95
Preconception: A Woman's Guide to Preparing for Pregnancy and Parenthood, 232 pp. $14.95
Schooling at Home: Parents, Kids, and Learning, 264 pp., $14.95
Teens: A Fresh Look, 240 pp. $14.95

Automotive Titles
The Greaseless Guide to Car Care Confidence, 224 pp. $14.95
How to Keep Your Datsun/Nissan Alive, 544 pp. $21.95
How to Keep Your Subaru Alive, 480 pp. $21.95
How to Keep Your Toyota Pickup Alive, 392 pp. $21.95
How to Keep Your VW Alive, 15th ed., 464 pp. $21.95

TITLES FOR YOUNG READERS AGES 8 AND UP

American Origins Series
Each is 48 pages and $12.95 hardcover.
Tracing Our Chinese Roots
Tracing Our German Roots
Tracing Our Irish Roots
Tracing Our Italian Roots
Tracing Our Japanese Roots
Tracing Our Jewish Roots
Tracing Our Polish Roots

Bizarre & Beautiful Series
Each is 48 pages and $14.95 hardcover.
Bizarre & Beautiful Ears
Bizarre & Beautiful Eyes
Bizarre & Beautiful Feelers
Bizarre & Beautiful Noses
Bizarre & Beautiful Tongues

Environmental Titles
Habitats: Where the Wild Things Live, 48 pp. $9.95
The Indian Way: Learning to Communicate with Mother Earth, 114 pp. $9.95
Rads, Ergs, and Cheeseburgers: The Kids' Guide to Energy and the Environment, 108 pp. $13.95
The Kids' Environment Book: What's Awry and Why, 192 pp. $13.95

Extremely Weird Series
Each is 48 pages and $9.95 paper. $12.95 hardcover editions available 8/94.
Extremely Weird Bats
Extremely Weird Birds
Extremely Weird Endangered Species
Extremely Weird Fishes
Extremely Weird Frogs
Extremely Weird Insects
Extremely Weird Mammals
Extremely Weird Micro Monsters
Extremely Weird Primates
Extremely Weird Reptiles
Extremely Weird Sea Creatures
Extremely Weird Snakes
Extremely Weird Spiders

Kidding Around Travel Series
All are 64 pages and $9.95 paper, except for *Kidding Around Spain* and *Kidding Around the National Parks of the Southwest*, which are 108 pages and $12.95 paper.
Kidding Around Atlanta
Kidding Around Boston, 2nd ed.
Kidding Around Chicago, 2nd ed.
Kidding Around the Hawaiian Islands
Kidding Around London
Kidding Around Los Angeles
Kidding Around the National Parks of the Southwest
Kidding Around New York City, 2nd ed.
Kidding Around Paris
Kidding Around Philadelphia
Kidding Around San Diego
Kidding Around San Francisco
Kidding Around Santa Fe
Kidding Around Seattle
Kidding Around Spain
Kidding Around Washington, D.C.

Kids Explore Series
Written by kids for kids, all are $9.95 paper.
Kids Explore America's African American Heritage, 128 pp.
Kids Explore the Gifts of Children with Special Needs, 128 pp.
Kids Explore America's Hispanic Heritage, 112 pp.
Kids Explore America's Japanese American Heritage, 144 pp.

Masters of Motion Series
Each is 48 pages and $9.95 paper.
How to Drive an Indy Race Car
How to Fly a 747
How to Fly the Space Shuttle

Rainbow Warrior Artists Series
Each is 48 pages and $14.95 hardcover.
Native Artists of Africa
Native Artists of Europe (available 8/94)
Native Artists of North America

Rough and Ready Series
Each is 48 pages and $12.95 hardcover.
Rough and Ready Cowboys
Rough and Ready Homesteaders
Rough and Ready Loggers (available 7/94)
Rough and Ready Outlaws and Lawmen (available 6/94)
Rough and Ready Prospectors
Rough and Ready Railroaders

X-ray Vision Series
Each is 48 pages and $9.95 paper.
Looking Inside the Brain
Looking Inside Cartoon Animation
Looking Inside Caves and Caverns
Looking Inside Sports Aerodynamics
Looking Inside Sunken Treasure
Looking Inside Telescopes and the Night Sky

Ordering Information
Please check your local bookstore for our books, or call **1-800-888-7504** to order direct. All orders are shipped via UPS; see chart below to calculate your shipping charge for U.S. destinations. **No post office boxes please; we must have a street address to ensure delivery**. If the book you request is not available, we will hold your check until we can ship it. Foreign orders will be shipped surface rate unless otherwise requested; please enclose $3 for the first item and $1 for each additional item.

For U.S. Orders Totaling	Add
Up to $15.00	$4.25
$15.01 to $45.00	$5.25
$45.01 to $75.00	$6.25
$75.01 or more	$7.25

Methods of Payment
Check, money order, American Express, MasterCard, or Visa. We cannot be responsible for cash sent through the mail. For credit card orders, include your card number, expiration date, and your signature, or call **1-800-888-7504**. American Express card orders can only be shipped to billing address of cardholder. Sorry, no C.O.D.'s. Residents of sunny New Mexico, add 6.125% tax to total.

Address all orders and inquiries to:
John Muir Publications
P.O. Box 613
Santa Fe, NM 87504
(505) 982-4078
(800) 888-7504